upholstering
for
everyone

upholstering
for
everyone

PAGE PARKER
J. G. FORNIA
ALICE FORNIA
with Ben Adams

Drawings by G. P. Parker
Photographs by J. R. Walsh and G. P. Parker

RESTON PUBLISHING COMPANY, INC.
Reston, Virginia
A Prentice-Hall Company

Library of Congress Cataloging in Publication Data

Parker, Page, 1913–
  Upholstering for everyone.

  Includes index.
  1. Upholstery. I. Fornia, Alice, joint author.
  II. Title.
  TT198.P344   684.1'2   76-3665
  ISBN 0-87909-857-0

© 1976 by
Reston Publishing Company, Inc.
A Prentice-Hall Company
Reston, Virginia 22090

10 9 8 7 6 5 4 3 2 1

Printed in the United States of America.

contents

preface

Do-it-yourself upholstering is basically easy whether you build a new article from the raw frame or redo an old one, and it need not be expensive. It is the purest type of custom upholstery—you build what you want, the way you want it, with the materials you want.

The frame, the foundation of all chairs and sofas (which are only extra-wide chairs), is of simple construction (Chapter 4), and there are almost countless designs and styles. Throughout upholstering the seat, legs, arms, wings, and back are considered distinct units. They are not dependent upon one another for shape and size, but generally are built in proportion to each other. For instance, a chair or sofa having high, thin, delicate-looking legs may seem top-heavy and unstable if its seat, arms, and back are thickly upholstered.

Within limits set by pleasing proportions, there is wide room for personal likes and treatment. Straight or curved arms go well with a back that is flat or barrel-shaped, square or rounded, high or low. A back with or without springs can be either heavily or lightly upholstered. Its style of finishing, like that of the arms, may be plain, buttoned, channeled (fluted, piped), or tufted. The cover can be dark or light, plain, striped, or figured. Representative types and designs of chairs, stools, and sofas, and various styles of finishing them are shown in Chapter 1.

Mistakes? It is best, of course, to correct a mistake by doing that work over again. But when much additional work has been done before a mistake is recognized, it can often be "covered" later on— perhaps by using extra cotton padding with the cover, perhaps by altering the cover. Should the mistake be in cutting or installing a cover, disguise it by "balancing"—by duplicating on the left arm, for example, an error made on the right. Cleverly covered or balanced mistakes often seem a part of the planned style of finishing, and so go unnoticed or sometimes admired. If a mistake does not weaken the upholstery, does not show, and cannot be readily felt, do not worry about it.

Does upholstery call for much strength? Some strength is necessary—enough to drive a tack, tie a knot. But for setting springs or working a cover smooth and tight, strength alone cannot do the job properly.

On first learning the number of materials commonly used in all but the simplest articles, even do-it-yourself upholstery seems expensive. Add tools to materials, and it seems quite expensive. But the cost of tools is easily reduced by building some of them yourself and by substituting cheaper items (Chapter 2). Cut the cost of materials (Chapter 3) by purchasing the exact amount needed, when possible, and in large rather than small quantities. "Exact amount" is vague; some materials can be figured quite closely in advance by inexperienced upholsterers; for others only a rough guess can be made. However, most experienced upholstery shop operators can estimate quite accurately the amounts of needed materials and basic supplies (such as tacks, twine, etc.).

Upholstering within a limited budget often can be done satisfactorily by salvaging materials from a well-made chair or sofa. However, this should be attempted only with a fairly good understanding of the qualities and purposes of the various materials. Often a frame can be repaired or restyled quite inexpensively (Chapters 25 and 26), and in any event, a good used frame is better than a poor new one.

Cheap upholstery materials usually are false economy, although for some purposes less expensive items are better. Inferior materials generally are weak and difficult to handle and build hard or lumpy surfaces. Omitting materials and work-steps lowers quality and often makes the work harder and even more costly for inexperienced upholsterers.

The cover usually is the most expensive part of upholstery. But this is one case when a cheaper material may be a far better buy than the most expensive; a cover should be selected on the basis of what is wanted of it, not on price alone. Fortunately, there are attractive and serviceable textiles, plastics, and leathers to meet every budget.

Large articles usually are easier to upholster than small ones. A cover usually tends to lie smooth on a large article. As a rule the larger a surface is, the less noticeable mistakes are. However, mistakes on small articles often are less expensive to correct.

Regardless of the upholstering to be done, Chapter 5, Basic Operations, should be studied carefully in advance.

And now to work. It is for you, the upholsterer, to decide on the kind of chair, sofa, or other upholstered article you want, what you want it to look like, how comfortable you want it to be. Keep these goals in mind while working, build and shape each unit with your goals in mind, and you probably will produce durable, attractive, and genuinely comfortable articles that will compare favorably with top quality custom upholstery.

PAGE PARKER
J. G. FORNIA
ALICE FORNIA

acknowledgments

The authors wish to give special thanks to the following for their generous assistance through furnishing technical information and illustrations (affiliations listed reflect positions held at the time such assistance was provided):

Jack J. Morrill, Upholstery Supplies, Van Waters & Rogers, Brisbane, California.

J. B. "Pat" Bagnall, General Rubber Products, Pirelli Limited, London, England.

Trip Umphred, Umphred Furniture, San Leandro, California.

Robert B. Logan, Western Furniture Manufacturing, Los Angeles, California.

Earl D. Wareham, Rolfe C. Spinning, Inc., Birmingham, Michigan.

William K. Gardner, Gardner-Clark Spring Company, Los Angeles, California.

illustration
credits

Figs. 1:03; *a* 1:41; 1:60—*Courtesy of Ben Adams, Santa Cruz, California.*

Figs. 1:04; 1:05; 1:06; 1:24; 1:25; 1:26; 1:32; 1:33; *a* 1:38; 1:39; 1:40; *b* 1:41; *b* 1:42; 1:43; 1:44; 1:47; *c* 1:48; *c* 1:50; *h* 1:51; 1:54; 1:55; 1:56; 1:57; 1:61; 1:62; 1:63; 1:66—*Courtesy of Umphred Furniture, San Leandro, California.*

Figs. *c, d* 3:20B; 3:20C; *d* 3:21C—*Courtesy of Gardner-Clark Spring Company, Los Angeles, California.*

Figs. *a, b, c* 3:21C; 3:21D; 3:21E; 3:21G; *a, b* 3:21H; 3:21J; 3:21M; 3:21N; 3:21O; 3:21Q; and Tables 3:21L; 3:21O—*Courtesy of Kay Manufacturing Co., Brooklyn, New York.*

Fig. 3:21P—*Courtesy of Rolfe C. Spinning, Inc., Birmingham, Michigan.*

Figs. 3:22B; 3:22D; 3:22E; 3:22H; 3:22I; 3:22J; 3:22K—*Courtesy of Pirelli Limited, London, England.*

easy,
pinpoint
reference

Throughout *Upholstering for Everyone,* all paragraphs and illustrations are marked, and reference to them made, by section numbers, such as "Sec. 5:11D[*1*]." Digits left of the colon specify the chapter, digits on the right specify the "section" or part of a chapter; a subsection or further division (when there is more than one paragraph) is specified by a capital letter following the section number; this is sometimes followed by an italic number within brackets in order to pinpoint or isolate a particular part of a sub-section. Thus, "Sec. 5:-11D[*1*]" refers to Chapter 5, 11th section, D sub-section, item #1 in it. Illustrations and tables of data are marked and referred to in the same way, except "Fig." or "Table" replaces "Sec." as in "Fig. 5:11F"; when an illustration or table has more than one part, each usually is identified by an italic lower-case letter following "Fig." or "Table," such as "Fig. *b* 5:11F."

1

representative articles

Sec. 1:00A / Articles shown in this chapter were selected to cover a wide range of upholstery from antiques to ultra modern. Of course, many designs and styles are not included; but most can be done by copying various parts of these articles—arms from one, seat from another, and so on. Because of the differences in similar articles and the various ways in which a frame usually can be upholstered, it is advisable to read all pertinent parts of this book instead of just the listed materials and work-steps.

Sec. 1:00B COMMENTS / As a guide to the upholstering actually done and that which could have been done there is with each representative article a general description of its type or use, the upholstery involved, suggestions and comments such as "a wider version of," "loose cushion, plain spring edge seat," "simplest work, upholster with compact stuffing," "pillow should be about three inches higher," "not recommended as a first project," and "best results, use modern upholstery," and basic dimensions of the item.

1

Sec. 1:00C Frames / Most chair, love seat, and larger frames can have spring seats built with either traditional coil springs (Secs. 3:15–3:18) or with modern zigzag springs or rubber webbing (Secs. 3:21, 3:22), provided the frames are modified to suit the springs to be used. However, some frames, such as that for Fig. 1:60, are engineered for a particular kind of spring, and while another could possibly be used, the overall effect might spoil the proportions of the various parts. For best results inexperienced upholsterers should describe or show the frame to a professional upholsterer to find out what kind of springs should be used or frame changes needed for a different kind of spring.

Sec. 1:00D Materials / With most articles are listed (as in Sec. 1:32) the two types of upholstery materials needed other than basic supplies such as tacks, twine, etc.: traditional and modern (Sec. 3:00C). Traditionals are listed first, immediately followed by the traditional work-steps (Sec. 1:00E); then modern materials and their work-steps are listed. Except for traditional coil springs, the amounts needed contain a small allowance for waste, and therefore should be treated as guides, not definite yards and pounds. Regarding cover goods, usually the most costly item, for best results build an article in muslin, then measure and plot the yardage needed to prevent waste yet have enough (Chapter 11). For the same reason, do not cut without first measuring the amount, length, or width needed; this is particularly important in the cases of zigzag springs and rubber webbing. Usually it is best to obtain all supplies and materials from a professional upholsterer or an established upholstery shop; if possible show a picture of the article, or one very much like it, to be upholstered. People not familiar with the problems of upholstering, or who cannot see the article to be upholstered, may recommend wrong grades, amounts, kinds, or sizes of various items.

NOTE: [1] Cover width: *Unless a different width of goods is specified, all listed yardages of cover needed are for 54-inch wide upholstery goods.*   [2] Bias welt cover (*Sec. 11:25*): *Except for small, simply shaped surfaces as in Fig. 1:03, listed cover yardage needed is based on bias welt cover; except in very large articles, such as Fig. 1:66, the basic bias welt allowance is 1 yard of 54-inch width goods, yards of 36-inch goods. If non-bias welt will be used, plot for it with the other cover cuts* (*Sec. 11:24*).

Sec. 1:00E Work-Steps / The work-steps listed with an article are to assist you in upholstering it as it was done by or under the supervision of an experienced upholsterer. Of course, you may wish to upholster your article differently—and most frames can be upholstered various ways, Sec. 1:35. Regardless, work will be easier and probably better if you study an entire chapter, not just the parts listed with each article. Most listed work-steps contain references to other pertinent sections or chapters. Special attention should be given to Chapter 5, Basic Operations.

SEC. 1:00F **APPEARANCE** / With few exceptions the articles in this chapter were photographed shortly after being upholstered. Since nearly all upholstery packs slightly through use, many of the articles, and cushions especially, are a little too puffy.

SEC. 1:01   Multi-purpose small chair, antique design, flat pad open-frame seat, Fig. 1:01. Dimensions of chair: 18″ wide, 20″ deep, 33″ high. TRADITIONAL UPHOLSTERY: *Materials*—Webbing, 3 yds., 3½″ width; burlap,

Fig. 1:01

½ yd., 40″ width; stuffing, ½ lb. loose hair; muslin, ⅔ yd., 36″ width; natural cotton padding, ½ lb.; cover, ⅔ yd., 24″ width; gimp, 2¼ yds.; dust cover, ½ yd., 36″ width. For upholstering with compact stuffing: 2½ sq. ft., medium or firm, ¾″ thick stock, no loose stuffing (seat too small to need understuffing for compact stuffing); build crown (Sec. 5:14) with extra padding when incasing or covering. Antique trim nails optional. *Work-Steps*—Through muslin casing: frame Secs. 4:10–4:12, 4:18; seat 6:02. Cover: seat Sec. 13:09; outside surfaces 18:15, 18:16, 18:18. MODERN UPHOLSTERY: Same as traditional except use rubber webbing (4½ yds., 2½″ width, Standard, Secs. 3:22, 7:33) and compact stuffing. Pad with synthetic cotton for maximum initial softness.

SEC. 1:02   Multi-purpose small chair, perennial design, flat pad solid-base slip-seat, Fig. 1:02. Dimensions of chair: 18″ wide, 20″ deep, 35″ high.

Fig. 1:02

TRADITIONAL UPHOLSTERY: *Materials*—Stuffing, ½ lb. loose hair; muslin, ⅔ yd., 36″ width; natural cotton padding, ½ lb.; cover, ¾ yd., 36″ width; dust cover (optional), ⅔ yd., 36″ width. For upholstering with compact stuffing: 2½ sq. ft., medium or firm, 1″ thick stock, see Sec. 1:01. *Work-Steps*—Through muslin casing: frame Sec. 4:18; seat 6:03. Cover: seat Sec. 13:10; outside surfaces 18:15. MODERN UPHOLSTERY: Same as traditional with compact stuffing. Pad with synthetic cotton for maximum initial softness.

SEC. 1:03   Multi-purpose small chair, antique style, open-frame spring seat, quilted cover, Fig. 1:03. Seat was made somewhat puffy to show quilting (Sec. 3:57) to best advantage. Instead of gimp, the edges of the seat cover were finished with welt (Sec. 13:07). Roll edges on seat if upholstering with loose stuffing only. Dimensions of chair: 18″ wide, 23″ deep, 35″ high. TRADITIONAL UPHOLSTERY: *Materials*—Webbing, 6 yds., 3½″ width; seat springs, 8 No. 1-H; burlap, 1½ yds., 40″ width; stuffing, 5 lbs. loose hair; muslin, ⅔ yd., 36″ width; natural cotton padding, 1 lb.; cover, ⅔ yd. quilted, 36″ width; welt cord 2¾ yds.; dust cover, ⅔ yd., 36″ width. For upholstering with compact stuffing (Sec. 7:20): 3 sq. ft., medium, 2″ to 2½″ thick stock, no loose stuffing; build crown (Sec. 5:14) with extra padding when incasing or covering.   *Work-Steps*—Through muslin casing: frame Secs. 4:11, 4:13, 4:18; seat 7:05, 7:07, 7:08, 7:11–7:14, 7:18, 7:19. Cover: seat Secs.

Fig. 1:03

3:57, 13:02, 13:06, 13:07, 13:11; outside surfaces 18:15. MODERN UPHOLSTERY: Same as traditional except for building seat with zig-zag springs or rubber webbing (Secs. 3:21, 7:32; 3:22, 7:33). 2 yds. zigzags; loose or compact stuffing. 6 yds., 2½″ width, Standard, rubber webbing; upholster with 3 sq. ft., 3″ to 3½″ thick compact stuffing; build crown (Sec. 5:14) with extra layers of padding when incasing or covering. Pad with synthetic cotton for maximum puff-out and initial softness.

SEC. 1:04   Multi-purpose small, modern style chair with spring seat, padded armboards, open-frame pad back, Fig. 1:04. Close set decorative nails are excellent trim. This type article is more likely to be modern than traditional upholstery. Note slope of seat at front. Roll edges on seat, simulated roll edges on inside back if upholstering these with loose stuffing. Dimensions of chair: 25″ wide, 23″ deep, 29½″ high. TRADITIONAL UPHOLSTERY: *Materials*—Webbing, 5 yds., 3½″ width; seat springs, 7 No. 1-H; burlap, 1½ yds., 40″ width; stuffing, 5 lbs. loose hair; muslin, 1 yd., 36″ width; natural cotton padding, 2 lbs.; cover, 1 yd., 54″ width; welt cord, 3 yds.; trim nails as required; dust cover, 1 yd., 36″ width. For upholstering with compact stuffing: for seat, 4 sq. ft., medium or firm, 2″ to 2½″ thick stock; for armboard and inside back, 2½ sq. ft., firm, 1″ thick stock; no loose stuffing; build crown (Sec. 5:14) with extra padding when incasing or covering. *Work-Steps*—Through muslin casing: frame Secs. 4:11, 4:13, 4:14, 4:18; seat 7:05, 7:07, 7:08, 7:11–7:14, 7:18, 7:19; armboards 8:07, 8:20; inside back 10:02, 10:06, 10:10, 10:18, 10:20, 10:22–10:24. Cover: seat Secs.

Fig. 1:04

13:02, 13:06, 13:11; armboards 14:02; inside back 16:01; outside surfaces 18:14, 18:15. MODERN UPHOLSTERY: Armboards, same as traditional upholstery. Inside back, same as traditional; rubber webbing not practical unless left over from seat upholstery. Seat upholstery same as traditional except for building with zigzag springs or rubber webbing (Secs. 3:21, 7:32; 3:22, 7:33). 2 yds. zigzags; upholster with loose or compact stuffing. 5 yds., 2½″ width, Standard, rubber webbing; upholster with 4 sq. ft., medium or firm, 2½″ to 3″ thick compact stuffing. Pad with synthetic cotton for maximum initial softness.

SEC. 1:05   Multi-purpose small, modern-style chair with loose-cushion solid-base slipseat and knife-edge back pillow (no boxing) held in place on a solid- or cane-base by buttons, Fig. 1:05. Seat cushion should have minimum crown (Sec. 5:14). Make paper pattern for back pillow; it should fill back "cavity" without excessive overlap. Twines holding pillow buttons may be run through buttons on the outside back, essentially as in Sec. 18:01D, for special effect. Traditional work with modern materials is the practical upholstery for this article. Dimensions of chair: 23¼″ wide, 21¼″ deep, 28½″ high. *Materials*—For slipseat: compact stuffing, 3 sq. ft., firm, 1″ thick; muslin, 1 yd., 36″ width; natural cotton padding, 1 lb. Cover: 1½ yds., 54″ width; welt cord, 6 yds.; buttons, 8 or 16; dust cover (optional), 1 yd., 36″ width. Seat cushion, back pillow: filling, 1″ thick, firm, foam rubber or polyfoam (Secs. 3:41, 3:43); wrap each filler with three layers of synthetic cotton padding, approximately 6 lbs. total. *Work-Steps*—Through muslin casing: frame Secs. 4:11, 4:12, 4:18; seat 6:03; Cover: seat Sec. 13:10; seat cushion 17:04–17:08, 17:14, 17:15; back pillow 17:17 (no boxing), 17:18; outside covers 18:01, 18:15.

Fig. 1:05

SEC. 1:06   Multi-purpose small, semi-formal, modern-antique style chair with
loose-cushion solid-base saddle-shaped slipseat and open-frame pad
back, Fig. 1:06. Buttoned seat cushion should be firm, with minimum
crown (Sec. 5:14); make paper pattern for it, as it should fit snug
against but not bulge around the posts. Back buttons chiefly decorative. Close set decorative nails are excellent trim on inside and outside
exposed-wood backs; areas should be gimped first. Traditional work
with modern materials is the practical upholstery for this article.

Fig. 1:06

Dimensions of chair: 25″ wide, 20″ deep, 32″ high. *Materials*—Webbing, 3 yds., 3½″ width jute or 2½″ width, Standard, rubber webbing;
burlap, ½ yd., 40″ width; compact stuffing, 6 sq. ft., firm, 1″ thick
stock (includes cushion filling); natural cotton padding, 2 lbs.; cover,
1½ yds., 54″ width; welt cord, 4 yds.; buttons for cushion, back, 12;

gimp, 4½ yds.; trim nails as required; dust cover (optional), 1 yd., 36″ width. For cushion: foam rubber or polyfoam stuffing, included above, to fit, wrap with two layers of synthetic cotton padding (approximately 4 lbs.). *Work-Steps*—Through muslin casing: frame Secs. 4:11, 4:12, 4:18; seat 6:03; inside back 10:02, 10:09, 10:33. Cover: seat Sec. 13:10; inside back 16:01; cushion 17:04–17:08, 17:14, 17:18, 18:01D; outside surfaces 18:01, 18:14–18:16, 18:18.

SEC. 1:07   Multi-purpose small, antique-style, spring seat chair, open-frame pad back, Fig. 1:07. Bridle-built hard edge seat and inside back. Seat can be bridle spring edge (Sec. 7:23), but may be uncomfortable (Sec. 7:01A[3]); 9 ft. spring edge-wire needed. Due to the size, shape and thinness of frame, burlapping the outside back is neither necessary nor advisable. Dimensions of chair: 18″ wide, 23″ deep, 24″ high.

Fig. 1:07

TRADITIONAL UPHOLSTERY: *Materials*—Webbing, 6 yds., 3½″ width; seat springs, 9 No. 1-H; burlap, 2 yds., 40″ width; stuffing, 7 lbs. loose hair; muslin, 1½ yds., 36″ width; natural cotton padding, 1½ lbs.; cover, 1½ yds., 54″ width; gimp, 7 yds.; dust cover, ⅔ yd., 36″ width. For upholstering with compact stuffing: 3 sq. ft., medium, 1″ thick stock for seat, 3 sq. ft., medium, 1″ to 1½″ thick stock for inside back, only 3 lbs. loose stuffing (for understuffing seat, Sec. 7:26; understuffing back not necessary), 1 yd. more muslin; build seat fairly thin. *Work-Steps*—Through muslin casing: frame Secs. 4:11, 4:13, 4:18; seat 7:05, 7:07, 7:08, 7:11–7:14, 7:18, 7:21, 7:22, 7:26; inside back 10:01, 10:09. Cover: seat Sec. 13:11, inside back 16:01; outside surfaces 18:14–

18:16. MODERN UPHOLSTERY: Same as traditional except for building seat with zigzag springs or rubber webbing (Secs. 3:21, 7:32; 3:22, 7:33) and back with rubber webbing (Sec. 10:33). 2 yds. zigzags; upholster with loose or compact stuffing. 4 yds., 2½″ width, Standard, rubber webbing for seat and 2 yds., preferably 1⅛″ width, for back; upholster with same compact stuffing as for traditional work, except use 2″ thick stock for seat. Pad with synthetic cotton for maximum initial softness.

SEC. 1:08

Corner or bustle chair, antique style, spring seat, solid-base back-arms, Fig. 1:08. Double-welt (Sec. 11:08) used instead of gimp. Roll edges on seat, back-arms if upholstering with loose stuffing only. Compact stuffing highly recommended for back-arms. Dimensions of chair: 30″ wide, 24″ deep, 26″ high. TRADITIONAL UPHOLSTERY: *Materials—* Webbing, 6 yds., 3½″ width; seat springs, 8 No. 2-M; burlap, 1 yd., 40″ width; stuffing, 8 lbs. loose hair for seat, 3 lbs. for back-arms; muslin, 1½ yds., 36″ width; natural cotton padding, 3 lbs.; double welt cord, 5 yds.; cover, 2½ yds., 54″ width. For upholstering with compact stuffing: 5 sq. ft., medium, 1″ to 1½″ thick stock for seat, 4 sq. ft., medium, 2½″ to 3″ thick stock for back-arms; only 4 lbs. loose stuffing (for understuffing seat, Sec. 7:20; no understuffing for back-arms), 1 yd. more muslin. *Work-Steps—*Through muslin casing: frame Secs. 4:11, 4:13, 4:18; seat 7:05, 7:07, 7:08, 7:11–7:14, 7:18, 7:19; back-arms are really armrest pads, 8:06, but are treated as scroll or rounded armtops, 8:12. Cover: seat Sec. 13:11; back-arms 14:01, 14:08; outside surfaces 18:15, 18:17. MODERN UPHOLSTERY: Same as traditional

Fig. 1:08

with compact stuffing except for building seat with rubber webbing (Secs. 3:22, 7:33, set diagonally). 6 yds., 2½″ width, Standard, rubber webbing, 4 sq. ft., medium, 3″ thick compact stuffing. Pad with synthetic cotton for maximum initial softness.

SEC. 1:09

Three styles of upholstering a multi-purpose small, modern-type, spring seat chair with open-frame pad back, Fig. 1:09. Seat upholstery through muslin casing is the same for all three chairs. *a* and *c* have boxed seat covers, *b* a pull-over; on small chairs subject to much use, seat boxing welt can soil or wear badly in relatively short time; seat covers could be bordered (Fig. *b* 1:29). *a* and *b* back upholstery is the same except for buttons; channeling makes the back in *c* appreciably larger. Roll edges on seat, simulated roll edges on backs *a* and *b*, if upholstering with loose stuffing only. Dimensions of chairs: 18″ wide, 17″ deep, 32″ high.

Fig. *a* 1:09—TRADITIONAL UPHOLSTERY: *Materials*—Webbing, 3 yds., 3½″ width; seat springs, 5 No. 1-H; burlap, 1 yd., 40″ width; stuffing, 3 lbs. loose hair; muslin, 1 yd., 36″ width; natural cotton padding, 1 lb.; cover, 1⅛ yds., 36″ width; welt cord, 5 yds.; buttons for back, 3; dust cover, 1 yd., 36″ width. For upholstering with compact stuffing: 4½ sq. ft., medium, 1″ to 1½″ thick stock, only 1½ lb. loose hair (for understuffing seat, Sec. 7:20; back does not require understuffing), ½ yd. more muslin. *Work-Steps*—Through muslin casing: frame Secs. 4:10, 4:11, 4:13, 4:18; seat 7:05, 7:07, 7:08, 7:11–7:14, 7:18, 7:19; inside back 10:02, 10:10, 10:18, 10:22–10:24. Cover: seat Sec. 13:14; inside back 16:03, 16:06; outside surfaces 18:01, 18:14, 18:15. MODERN UPHOLSTERY: Same as traditional except for building seats with zig-zag springs or rubber webbing (Secs. 3:21, 7:32; 3:22, 7:33). 1½ yds. zigzags; upholster with loose or compact stuffing. 3 yds., 2½″ width, Standard, rubber webbing; upholster with 3 sq. ft., firm, 1½″ to 2″ thick compact stuffing for seat, no loose stuffing; rubber webbing impractical for back unless have leftover from seat. Pad with synthetic cotton for maximum initial softness.

Fig. *b* 1:09—Student built. TRADITIONAL UPHOLSTERY: *Materials*—Same as for *a* except only 3 yds. welt cord. *Work-Steps*—Same as *a* except seat cover, Sec. 13:12. MODERN UPHOLSTERY: Same as traditional and *a*.

Fig. *c* 1:09—Student built. TRADITIONAL UPHOLSTERY: *Materials*—Same as *a* except no buttons needed. *Work-Steps*—Through muslin casing: frame, seat same as *a*; inside back Secs. 10:09, 10:10, 20:05–20:07. Cover: seat Sec. 13:14; inside back 20:08, 20:09; outside surfaces 18:14, 18:15. MODERN UPHOLSTERY: Same as traditional except for springing seat, *a*.

a

b

Fig. 1:09   *c*

SEC. 1:10   Multi-purpose small, modern type, spring seat chair with keyhole solid-base pad back, Fig. 1:10. Pull-over seat cover; could be boxed (Fig. *a* 1:09), or bordered (Fig. *b* 1:29). Roll edges on seat, simulated roll

Fig. 1:10

edges on inside back, if upholstering with loose stuffing only. Dimensions of chair: 18″ wide, 17″ deep, 32″ high. TRADITIONAL UPHOLSTERY: *Materials*—Same as Fig. *a* 1:09 except for compact stuffing: 2½ sq. ft., medium, 1″ to 1½″ thick for seat, 2 sq. ft., medium, ½″ to 1″ thick for inside back. *Work-Steps*—Through muslin casing: frame, seat same as Fig. *a* 1:09; inside back Sec. 10:27. Cover: seat Sec. 13:12; inside back 16:04; outside surfaces 18:14, 18:15. MODERN UPHOLSTERY: Same as traditional except for springing seat, Fig. *a* 1:09.

SEC. 1:11

Deep buttoned or tufted small chair, antique type, sag seat (Sec. 6:05), open-frame pad back, Fig. 1:11. This style of upholstery was popular and practical for antique side and bedroom chairs; usually quite comfortable. This type chair may have a French back (Sec. 10:05). Tufting (Chapter 21) must be planned carefully for appearance and to build smoothly shaped surfaces; tufting, especially a French back, should not be a first project. Decorative nails and buttons on front of chair are optional. Roll edges on seat, inside back if upholstering them with loose stuffing only. Dimensions of chair: 18″ wide, 23″ deep, 34″ high. TRADITIONAL UPHOLSTERY: *Materials*—Webbing, 3 yds., 3½″ width; burlap, ½ yd., 40″ width; stuffing, 5 lbs. loose hair; muslin, 1½ yds., 36″ width; natural cotton padding, 2 lbs.; cover, 1½ yds., 54″ width; gimp, ⅔ yd.; buttons, 33; trim nails as needed; dust cover, 1 yd., 36″ width. For upholstering with compact stuffing: 6 sq. ft., medium, 1½″ to 2″ thick stock, no loose stuffing. *Work-Steps*—Through muslin casing: frame Secs. 4:11, 4:12, 4:18; seat 6:05, Chap. 21; inside back

Fig. 1:11

10:02, 10:09, 10:10, 10:18, Chap. 21. Cover: seat, inside back Secs.
21:09, 21:10; outside surfaces 18:01, 18:14–18:16. MODERN UPHOL-
STERY: Same as traditional with compact stuffing. Pad with synthetic
cotton for maximum initial softness.

SEC. 1:12

Multi-purpose small chair, flat pad solid-base slipseat, curved open-
frame pad back, Fig. 1:12. Install vertical inside back webbing
cautiously. Dust cover usually omitted. Dimensions of chair: 20″ wide,
24″ deep, 35″ high. TRADITIONAL UPHOLSTERY: *Materials*—Webbing,
2 yds., 3½″ width; burlap, ⅔ yd., 40″ width; stuffing, 1½ lbs. loose hair;

Fig. 1:12

muslin, 1½ yds., 36" width; natural cotton padding, 2 lbs.; cover, 1½ yds., 54" width; gimp, 4 yds. For upholstering seat, inside back with compact stuffing (7 sq. ft., medium or firm, 1" thick stock) see Sec. 1:01. *Work-Steps*—Through muslin casing: frame Secs. 4:10–4:12, 4:18; seat 6:03; inside back 10:02, 10:06–10:10, 10:18, 10:22, 10:23, 10:24E. Cover: seat Sec. 13:10; inside back 16:01; outside surfaces 18:11, 18:14–18:16. Modern Upholstery: Same as traditional with compact stuffing; rubber webbing impractical for such a thin back. Pad with synthetic cotton for maximum initial softness.

SEC. 1:13   Multi-purpose small chair, perennial style, spring seat, open-frame pad back, Fig. 1:13. Boxed seat cover, see comments on small seat covers Sec. 1:09. Roll edges on seat, simulated roll edges on inside back if upholstering them with loose stuffing only. Dimensions of chair: 20" wide, 18" deep, 38" high. Traditional Upholstery: *Materials*—Webbing, 9 yds., 3½" width; seat springs, 5 No. 1-H; burlap, 2 yds., 40" width; stuffing, 4 lbs. loose hair; muslin, 1½ yds., 36" width; natural cotton padding, 2 lbs.; cover, 1⅔ yds., 54" width; welt cord, 7 yds.; dust cover, ⅔ yd., 36" width. For upholstering with compact stuffing: 5½ sq. ft., medium, 1½" thick stock, only 1½ lbs. loose stuffing (for under-stuffing, Sec. 7:20), 1½ yds. more muslin. *Work-Steps*—Through muslin casing, same as Fig. *a* 1:09. Cover: seat Sec. 13:14; inside back 16:07; outside surfaces 18:11, 18:14, 18:15. Modern Upholstery: Same as traditional except for building seat with zigzag springs or

Fig. 1:13

rubber webbing (Secs. 3:21, 7:32; 3:22, 7:33), and inside back with rubber webbing (Sec. 10:33). 2 yds. zigzags for seat; upholster with loose or compact stuffing. 5 yds., 2½″ width, Standard, rubber webbing for seat; 6 yds., preferably 1⅛″ width for back; upholster seat with 3 sq. ft., medium to firm, 2″ to 2½″ thick compact stuffing, back with 3 sq. ft., 1½″ thick stock. Build extra crown (Sec. 5:14) with padding. Pad with synthetic cotton for maximum initial softness.

SEC. 1:14   Multi-purpose small chair, modern type, spring seat, open-frame pad back, single-piece boxed cover for seat and inside back, Fig. 1:14.

Fig. 1:14

Joined seat, inside back upholstery is difficult to do smoothly; tends to wrinkle, possibly split at junction of seat and back. Roll edges on seat, inside back if upholstering them with loose stuffing only. Dimensions of chair: 17″ wide, 21″ deep, 20″ high. TRADITIONAL UPHOLSTERY: *Materials*—Webbing, 9 yds., 3½″ width; seat springs, 5 No. 1-H; burlap, 2 yds., 40″ width; stuffing, 4 lbs. loose hair; muslin, 1½ yds., 36″ width; natural cotton padding, 2 lbs.; cover, 1¾ yds., 54″ width; buttons, 9; welt cord, 4 yds.; dust cover, ⅔ yd., 36″ width. For upholstering with compact stuffing: 5 sq. ft., medium, 1″ or 1½″ thick stock, only 1 lb. loose stuffing (for understuffing, Sec. 7:20), 1½ yds. more muslin. *Work-Steps*—Through muslin casing: frame Secs. 4:10, 4:11, 4:13, 4:18; seat 7:05, 7:07, 7:08, 7:11–7:14, 7:17–7:19; inside back 10:02, 10:10, 10:18, 10:20, 10:22–10:24. Cover: seat Sec. 13:15; back 16:10; outside surfaces 18:01, 18:14, 18:15. MODERN UPHOLSTERY: See Sec. 1:13.

4 yds. zigzag springs for seat. 8 yds. rubber webbing for seat, 8 yds. for inside back.

SEC. 1:15   Multi-purpose small wing chair, modern type, sag seat, open-frame pad back, student built, Fig. 1:15. Buttons, made of short lengths of colored yards, soften formality of cover, hold seat, inside back covers in place and eliminate need of conventional crown (Sec. 5:14). Not enough sag in seat to require hold-down webbing (Sec. 6:05F). Boxed arm-wing covers. Seat, inside back could be upholstered with compact stuffing (6½ sq. ft., medium, 1″ to 1½″ thick, no loose stuffing) but gain in comfort would be small. Roll edge on front of seat, simulated roll edge at top of inside back if upholstering them with loose stuffing.

Fig. 1:15

Dimensions of chair: 23″ wide, 20″ deep, 35″ high. TRADITIONAL UPHOLSTERY: *Materials*—Webbing, 9 yds., 3½″ width; burlap, 1½ yds., 40″ width; stuffing, 3 lbs. loose hair; muslin, 2 yds., 36″ width; natural cotton padding, 3 lbs.; cover, 2⅓ yds., 54″ width; welt cord, 7 yds.; buttons, 10; dust cover, ¾ yd., 36″ width. *Work-Steps*—Through muslin casing: frame Secs. 4:11, 4:12, 4:18; seat 6:05; arms 8:14, 8:15, 8:21, 8:22; wings 9:09–9:13; inside back 10:01, 10:10, 10:18, 10:22–10:24. Cover: seat Sec. 13:11; arms 14:07–14:09; wings 15:04; inside back 16:07; outside surfaces 18:01, 18:11–18:15. MODERN UPHOLSTERY: Pad with synthetic cotton for maximum initial softness.

SEC. 1:16   Occasional chair, modern type, spring seat and inside back, Fig. 1:16. Panel covers for sides of seat, back; note how cover design extends into panels. Pull-over or bordered covers (Fig. *a, b* 1:29) could be used,

Fig. 1:16

but panels are easier, more practical for this type chair. Roll edges on seat, inside back if upholstering them with loose stuffing only. Dimensions of chair: 24″ wide, 24″ deep, 30″ high. Traditional Upholstery: *Materials*—Webbing, 9 yds., 3½″ width; seat springs, 9 No. 1-H; back springs, 9 6-inch; burlap, 2 yds., 40″ width; stuffing, 7 lbs. loose hair; muslin, 2 yds., 36″ width; natural cotton padding, 2 lbs.; cover, 2 yds., 54″ width; welt cord, 6 yds.; dust cover, ¾ yd., 36″ width. For upholstering with compact stuffing: 8¾ sq. ft., medium, 1″ to 1½″ thick stock, only 2 lbs. loose stuffing (for understuffing, Sec. 7:20), 2 yds. more muslin. *Work-Steps*—Through muslin casing: frame Secs. 4:11–4:13, 4:18; seat 7:05, 7:07, 7:08, 7:11–7:14, 6:04, 7:18, 7:19; inside back 10:03, 10:11, 10:13, 10:15, 10:18, 10:20–10:24. Cover: seat Sec. 13:13; inside back 16:07; outside surfaces 18:02, 18:14, 18:15. Modern Upholstery: Same as traditional except for building seat and back with zigzag springs or rubber webbing (Secs. 3:21, 7:32, 10:31; 3:22, 7:33, 10:33). 2½ yds. zigzags for seat, 2½ yds. for back; upholster with loose or compact stuffing. 6 yds., 2½″ width, Standard, rubber webbing for seat, 6 yds., preferably 1⅛″ width, for back; upholster with 8¾ sq. ft., medium 2″ to 2½″ thick compact stuffing; build additional crown (Sec. 5:14) with padding. Pad with synthetic cotton for maximum puffiness and initial softness.

SEC. 1:17   Small occasional chair, modern type, pad open-frame seat and inside back, single-piece boxed cover for seat and back, set-back front rail, Fig. 1:17. Regarding single-piece seat-back cover see Sec. 1:14. Roll edges on sides of seat, inside back if upholstering them with loose

Fig. 1:17

stuffing only. Set-back front rail requires special treatment (Sec. 6:04). Dimensions of chair: 24″ wide, 24″ deep, 30″ high. TRADITIONAL UPHOLSTERY: *Materials*—Webbing, 18 yds., 3½″ width; burlap, 2 yds., 40″ width; stuffing, 3½ lbs. loose hair; muslin, 2 yds., 36″ width; natural cotton padding, 2 lbs.; cover, 1¾ yds., 54″ width; welt cord, 6 yds.; dust cover, ¾ yd., 36″ width. For upholstering with compact stuffing: 9¾ sq. ft., medium, 1″ to 1½″ thick stock; only 2 lbs. loose stuffing (for understuffing, Sec. 5:13), 1½ yds. more muslin. *Work-Steps*—Through muslin casing: frame Secs. 4:11, 4:12, 4:18; seat 6:04; inside back 10:01, 10:10, 10:18–10:24. Cover: seat Sec. 13:15; inside back 16:10; outside surfaces 18:14, 18:15. MODERN UPHOLSTERY: Same as traditional except for building seat and inside back with rubber webbing (Secs. 3:22, 7:33, 10:33); 9 yds., 2½″ width, Standard, rubber webbing for seat; 10 yds., preferably 1⅛″ width for back; same amount of compact stuffing as for traditional, but 2″ to 2½″ thick stock, no loose stuffing; build additional crown (Sec. 5:14) with padding. Pad with synthetic cotton for maximum softness; be careful not to make article too puffy, which can destroy square shape between inner and side surfaces.

SEC. 1:18   Occasional chair, perennial style, spring seat and inside back, student built, Fig. 1:18. Banded seat cover would look better if it did not arch along sides. Paneled back cover; could have been bordered. Bridle-built spring-edge seat. Roll edges on sides of inside back if upholstering it with loose stuffing only. Dimensions of chair: 24″ wide, 29″ deep, 30″ high. TRADITIONAL UPHOLSTERY: *Materials*—Webbing, 16 yds., 3½″ width; seat springs, 16 No. 3-H or 4-S; seat spring edge-wire, 10 ft.; back springs, 12 6- or 8-inch; burlap, 4 yds., 40″ width; stuffing, 8 lbs. loose hair; muslin, 2 yds., 36″ width; natural cotton padding, 3 lbs.; cover, 2¾ yds., 54″ width; welt cord, 5 yds.; fringe, 3½ yds.; dust cover, ¾ yd., 36″ width. For upholstering with compact stuffing (over-stuffing, Secs. 7:26, 10:22): 4 sq. ft., medium, 1″ to 1½″ thick stock, only 3 lbs. loose stuffing, 2 yds. more muslin. *Work-Steps*—Through muslin casing: frame Secs. 4:11, 4:13, 4:15, 4:18; seat 7:05, 7:07, 7:08, 7:11–7:16, 7:18, 7:23, 7:28; inside back 10:03, 10:11, 10:13, 10:15, 10:18–10:24. Cover: seat Sec. 13:17; inside back 16:07; outside surfaces 18:02, 18:06, 18:14, 18:15. MODERN UPHOLSTERY: Same as traditional except for building seat and inside back with zigzag springs (Secs. 3:21, 7:32, 10:31), or inside back with rubber webbing (Secs. 3:22, 10:33). 3 yds. zigzags for seat, 11 edge springs; 2 yds. zigzags for back; upholster with loose or compact stuffing. 5 yds., 1⅛″ width, Standard, rubber webbing for inside back; upholster with 5 sq. ft., medium, 2″ to 2½″ thick compact stuffing; no loose stuffing for back; build additional crown (Sec. 5:14) with padding. Pad with synthetic cotton for maximum initial softness.

Fig. 1:18

SEC. 1:19   Large occasional chair, modern style, spring seat, open-frame pad back, Fig. 1:19. Build seat, inside back fairly soft (but not weak) so that buttons can pull in cover. Pull-over cover on front, back, sides of

Fig. 1:19

seat; piece extra goods on both sides if necessary; blind-stitch (Sec. 13:04) side covers to front, back seat covers near legs. Roll edges on seat, inside back if upholstering them with loose stuffing only. Dimensions of chair: 29″ wide, 28″ deep, 26″ high. Traditional Upholstery: *Materials*—Webbing, 10 yds., 3½″ width; seat springs, 9 No. 3-H; burlap, 1½ yds., 40″ width; stuffing, 6 lbs. loose hair; muslin, 2 yds., 36″ width; natural cotton padding, 2 lbs.; cover 1¾ yds., 54″ width; welt cord, 2½ yds.; buttons, 14; dust cover, 1 yd., 36″ width. For upholstering with compact stuffing: 9 sq. ft., medium, 1½″ thick stock, only 3 lbs. loose stuffing (for understuffing seat, Sec. 7:20; understuffing back not necessary), 1 yd. more muslin. *Work-Steps*—Through muslin casing: frame Secs. 4:11–4:13, 4:18; seat 7:05, 7:07, 7:08, 7:11–7:14, 7:18, 7:19; inside back 10:01, 10:09, 10:10, 10:18, 10:22–10:24. Cover: seat Secs. 13:12, 13:04; inside back 16:03, 16:06; outside surfaces 18:01, 18:14, 18:15. Modern Upholstery: Same as traditional except for building seat with zigzag springs or rubber webbing (Secs. 3:21, 7:32; 3:22, 7:33), back with rubber webbing (Sec. 10:33). 4 yds. zigzags for seat; upholster with loose or compact stuffing. 10 yds., 2½″ width, Standard, rubber webbing for seat and back (back too small to need back-type webbing); 6 sq. ft., medium to firm, 3½″ to 4″ thick compact stuffing for seat, 3 sq. ft., medium, 1½″ thick for back; build additional crown with cotton padding. Pad seat, inside back with synthetic cotton for maximum puff and initial softness.

SEC. 1:20   Occasional chairs, modern type, spring seat, open-frame pad inside arms and back, Fig. 1:20. Welt cover cut on bias to prevent hit-or-miss matching of stripes in covers and welt. Although flange skirt in *b* seems to increase bulk of chair, *a*, at the same time *b* may seem slightly smaller than *a*, possibly an optical illusion caused by the stripes. Roll edge on seat front, simulated roll edges on inside arms and back if upholstering them with loose stuffing only. Dimensions of chairs: 27″ wide, 24″ deep, 28″ high.

Fig. *a* 1:20—TRADITIONAL UPHOLSTERY: *Materials*—Webbing, 12 yds., 3½″ width; seat springs, 9 No. 1-H; burlap, 3 yds., 40″ width; stuffing, 6 lbs. loose hair; muslin, 3 yds., 36″ width; natural cotton padding, 4 lbs.; cover, 3¾ yds., 54″ width (bias welt); welt cord, 6 yds.; dust cover, ⅔ yd., 36″ width. For upholstering with compact stuffing: 12 sq. ft., medium, 1½″ thick stock, only 3½ lbs. loose stuffing (1½ lbs. for understuffing seat, Sec. 7:20; 1 lb. for arms; 1 lb. for inside back, Sec. 5:13), 3 yds. more muslin. *Work-Steps*—Through muslin casing: frame Secs. 4:11–4:13, 4:18; seat 7:05, 7:07, 7:08, 7:11–7:14, 7:18, 7:19; inside arms 8:03, 8:09–8:12, 8:14, 8:15, 8:21, 8:22; inside back 10:02, 10:10, 10:18, 10:22–10:24. Cover: seat Sec. 13:16; inside arms 14:04, 14:05; inside back 16:05, 16:06; outside surfaces 18:13–18:15. MOD-

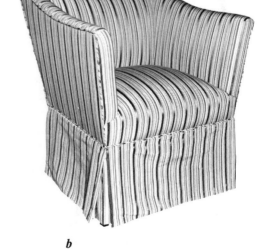

a   *b*

Fig. 1:20

ern Upholstery: Same as traditional except for building seat with zigzag springs or rubber webbing (Secs. 3:21, 7:32; 3:22, 7:33), inside arms and back with rubber webbing (Secs. 8:09, 10:33). 4 yds. zigzags for seat; upholster with loose or compact stuffing. 8 yds., 2½″ width, Standard, rubber webbing for seat, 18 yds., 1⅛″ width for inside arms and back; upholster with 4½ sq. ft., medium to firm, 2″ to 2½″ thick compact stuffing for seat, 7½ sq. ft. 1½″ thick stock for inside arms, back; build crown (Sec. 5:14) with padding. Pad with synthetic cotton for maximum initial softness.

Fig. *b* 1:20—Same as *a* except that for flange skirt (Secs. 18:04–18:06) 1 yd. more cover; 1 yd. skirt lining, 54″ wide; 3 yds. more welt cord are needed.

SEC. 1:21

Occasional armchair, spring seat remodeled from sag seat, open-frame pad back, student built, Fig. 1:21. Remodeling consisted only of changing from sag seat upholstery (Sec. 1:22) to spring; seat could have been conventional pad instead of spring construction. Pull-over seat cover; could have been bordered or boxed (Fig. *b, d* 1:29). Roll edges on seat if upholstering it with loose stuffing only. Dimensions of chair: 26″ wide, 27″ deep, 32″ high. Traditional Upholstery: *Materials*—Webbing, 8 yds., 3½″ width; seat springs, 9 No. 1-H; burlap, 2 yds., 40″ width; stuffing, 4 lbs. loose hair; muslin, 1½ yds., 36″ width; natural cotton padding, 2 lbs.; cover, 1½ yds., 54″ width; welt cord,

Fig. 1:21

2 yds.; dust cover, ¾ yd., 36″ width. For upholstering with compact stuffing: 9¾ sq. ft., medium, 1″ to 1½″ thick stock; only 1½ lbs. loose stuffing (for understuffing seat, Sec. 7:20), 1½ yds. more muslin. *Work-Steps*—Through muslin casing: frame Secs. 4:11–4:13, 4:18; seat 7:05, 7:07, 7:08, 7:11–7:14, 7:18, 7:19; inside back 10:02, 10:10, 10:18, 10:22–10:24. Cover: seat Sec. 13:11; inside back 16:03; outside surfaces 18:14, 18:15. MODERN UPHOLSTERY: Same as traditional except for building seat with zigzag springs or rubber webbing (Secs. 3:21, 7:32; 3:22, 7:33), inside back with rubber webbing (Sec. 10:33). 4 yds. zigzags for seat; upholster with loose or compact stuffing. 8 yds., 2½″ width, Standard, rubber webbing for seat; 5 yds., preferably 1⅞″ width, for inside back; upholster with 5 sq. ft., medium to firm, 2″ thick compact stuffing for top of seat, 4¾ sq. ft., medium, 1″ to 1½″ thick stock for sides of seat and inside back; no loose stuffing; build crown (Sec. 5:14) with padding. Pad with synthetic cotton for maximum initial softness.

SEC. 1:22   Occasional armchair, perennial style, sag seat, open-frame pad arms and inside back, student built, Fig. 1:22. Single-piece arm covers finish on bottom of arm rails. Instead of sag, seat could have been conventional pad, or spring upholstery (Sec. 1:21), but front rail would have had to be made flat top and bottom instead of scooped. Roll edges on seat, simulated roll edges on arms, inside back if upholstering them with loose stuffing only. Dimensions of chair: 28″ wide, 24″ deep, 29″ high. TRADITIONAL UPHOLSTERY: *Materials*—Webbing, 8 yds., 3½″

Fig. 1:22

width; burlap, 2 yds., 40" width; stuffing, 5 lbs. loose hair; muslin, 2 yds., 36" width; natural cotton padding, 4 lbs.; cover, 2 yds., 54" width; welt cord, 2 yds.; buttons, 5; dust cover, ¾ yd., 36" width. For upholstering with compact stuffing: 9½ sq. ft., medium, 1" to 1½" thick stock; only 1 lb. loose stuffing (for understuffing seat, Sec. 7:20; inside back, Secs. 6:04G, H, 10:21), 2 yds. more muslin. *Work-Steps*— Through muslin casing: frame Secs. 4:11, 4:12, 4:18; seat 6:05; arms 8:09–8:11, 8:14–8:17; inside back 10:02, 10:10, 10:18, 10:22–10:24. Cover: seat Sec. 13:11; arms 14:05; inside back 16:03, 16:06; outside surfaces 18:01, 18:14, 18:15. MODERN UPHOLSTERY: Traditional sag seats not suitable for modern springing. Pad with synthetic cotton for maximum initial softness.

SEC. 1:23   Horizontal channeled side chair, seat and back solid-base pad upholstery, Fig. 1:23. As upholstered, with only padding and cover, article is impractical; channels soon pack flat, hard. For more durable, comfortable upholstery build with 4 lbs. loose hair stuffing, 4 yds. 36" wide muslin and 2 lbs. natural cotton padding; or with 9½ sq. ft.,

Fig. 1:23

medium, 1½" thick compact stuffing, 4 yds. muslin and 2 lbs. cotton padding, Sec. 20:13. Dimensions of chair: 27" wide, 22" deep, 32" high. TRADITIONAL UPHOLSTERY AS BUILT: *Materials*—Natural cotton padding, 5 lbs.; cover, 2 yds., 54" width; gimp, 4 yds.; trim nails, optional, as required. *Work-Steps*—Frame Secs. 4:11, 4:18; channeling 20:11, 20:13; outside surfaces 18:16, 18:18. MODERN UPHOLSTERY: Same as traditional with compact stuffing. Pad with synthetic cotton for maximum initial softness, resilience.

SEC. 1:24   Multi-purpose modern side chair, loose cushion seat upholstery, solid-base slipframe back, Fig. 1:24. These articles usually quite comfortable. Traditional, specialty, rubber, or decorative webbing (Secs.

Fig. 1:24

3:11, 3:13, 3:22, 3:23) may be used for seat cushion support, which is often installed ½″ to 1″ below top of seat frame. Slipframe back usually is built as a cushion with a solid base. Except for the kinds of webbing available there is no difference between traditional and modern upholstery of this type article. Dimensions of chair: 24″ wide, 24″ deep, 29″ high. *Materials*—Webbing, approximately 3 yds., depending on kind used; seat, back cushion fillings and paddings according to sizes of cushions (Secs. 3:61, 7:34B); natural cotton padding, 1½ lbs.; cover, 1 yd., 54″ width. Pad with synthetic cotton for maximum initial softness. *Work-Steps*—Frame Secs. 4:11, 4:18; seat 7:34, Chap. 17; back 10:37.

SEC. 1:25   General purpose modern armchair, attached cushion solid-base slip-seat, padded armboards, solid-base slipframe back, Fig. 1:25. This type chair usually quite comfortable. Slipframe back built as a cushion with a solid base; can also be built as an attached cushion similar to seat. Wrap-around arm upholstery finishes on bottom of armboard. Seat slipframe usually padded with two or three layers of cotton. No difference between traditional and modern upholstery of this type article except for using synthetic instead of natural cotton padding in the modern upholstery for maximum initial softness. Dimensions of chair: 24″ wide, 30″ deep, 28″ high. *Materials*—Seat, back cushion fillings and paddings according to sizes of cushions (Secs. 3:61, 7:34B); natural

Fig. 1:25

cotton padding, 2 lbs.; cover, 1½ yds., 54″ width; welt cord, 2 yds.; dust cover, optional, ¾ yd., 36″ width. For maximum softness and resilience, upholster arms with 2 sq. ft., medium, 1″ thick compact stuffing. *Work-Steps*—Frame Secs. 4:11, 4:18; seat 6:03, 22:07; armboards 8:07, 14:02; back 10:37; dust cover 18:15.

SEC. 1:26   Open-frame highback modern armchair, attached cushion solid-base slipseat, padded armboards, loose cushion back, Fig. 1:26. Note that the lower back cushion is about ⅙ taller than the upper one; build them

Fig. 1:26

separately, but before filling sew the boxings of the top and bottom casings together, midway between top and bottom covers of casings, to points about 2 inches from the sides. Support for back cushions may be traditional, specialty, rubber, or decorative webbing (Secs. 3:11, 3:13, 3:22, 3:23). Except for the kinds of webbing available, and use of synthetic instead of natural cotton padding for greater initial softness, there is no difference between traditional and modern upholstery of this type article. Dimensions of chair: 26″ wide, 30″ deep, 40″ high. *Materials* —Webbing, approximately 6 yds., depending on kind used; seat, back cushion fillings and paddings according to sizes of cushions (Secs. 3:61, 7:34B); natural cotton padding, 2 lbs.; cover, 3 yds., 54″ width; welt cord, 9 yds.; dust cover, optional, ⅔ yd., 36″ width. *Work-Steps*—For seat, arms, dust cover same as Sec. 1:25; back cushions, Chapter 17.

SEC. 1:27   Antique style tilt-back armchair, loose cushion seat and back upholstery, padded armrests, Fig. 1:27. Seat and back cushions usually rest on horizontal wooden rods, and must be firm and thick enough, generally about 4 inches, to keep rods from being felt; because of rod imprints on cushion casings, such cushions are for practical purposes non-reversible. Top of back cushion is often shaped for headrest. But-

Fig. 1:27

tons eliminate need of crown (Sec. 5:14) and maintain shape of cushions; buttons on both surfaces of cushions. Completely upholster armrests, finishing cover on bottom, then fasten to frame. Traditional and modern upholstery the same for this type chair except for using synthetic instead of natural cotton padding for maximum initial softness. Dimensions of chair: 26″ wide, 32″ deep, 38″ high. *Materials*— Stuffing, 12 lbs. loose hair, or, preferably, slabs of firm rubberized hair the planned size, shape, and thickness of seat and back cushions (Sec. 3:61); hair-proof ticking, 3 yds., 36″ width for loose stuffing, or muslin for rubberized hair; natural cotton padding, 5 lbs.; cover, 3 yds., 54″ width; buttons, as required. *NOTE:* Instead of loose or rubberized hair cushion stuffings, 4″ thick polyfoam of proper size and wrapped with two or three layers of synthetic cotton is often used; however, these cushions may not have the overall firmness that many people want in this type chair. *Work-Steps*—Frame Secs. 4:11, 4:18; armrests 8:06, 8:13C–D, 14:01; cushions 17:13 (boxed ticking optional), 17:14, 17:16, 17:18; outside surfaces 18:01 (fasten both buttons with same twine, tie ends of twine together and bury knot).

SEC. 1:28   French back armchairs, perennial designs, spring seats, padded armrests, pad inside backs, Fig. 1:28. French backs (Sec. 10:05) are not recommended for inexperienced upholsterers. French back chairs are somewhat delicate and should be treated carefully. Bridle hard-edge spring seat, bridle inside back if upholstering with loose stuffing only. Dimensions of chairs: 27″ wide, 22″ deep, 26″ high. Traditional Upholstery: *Materials*—Webbing, 6 yds., 3½″ width; seat springs, 9 No. 1-H; burlap, 2 yds., 40″ width; stuffing, 3½ lbs. loose hair; muslin, 1½ yds., 36″ width; natural cotton padding, 1½ lbs.; cover, 1½ yds., 54″ width; double welt cord for *a*, 7 yds.; gimp for *b* and *c*, 7 yds.; dust cover, ¾ yd., 36″ width. For upholstering with compact stuffing: 9 sq. ft., medium, 1″ to 1½″ thick stock (1″ stock, or trim thicker stock to 1″, for armrests); only 1 lb. loose stuffing (for understuffing seat, Sec. 7:26; understuffing back not necessary), 1 yd. more muslin. *Work-Steps*— Through muslin casing: frame Secs. 4:11, 4:13, 4:18; seat 7:05, 7:07, 7:08, 7:11–7:14, 7:18, 7:21, 7:22, 7:26; arms 8:06; inside back 10:02, 10:05, 10:09, 10:20. Cover: seat Sec. 13:11, arms 14:01; inside back 16:01; outside surfaces 18:15, 18:16 for gimp, 18:17 for double welt. Modern Upholstery: Same as traditional except for building seat with zigzag springs or rubber webbing (Secs. 3:21, 7:32; 3:22, 7:33). 3 yds. zigzags for seat; upholster with loose or compact stuffing. 6 yds., 2½″ width, Standard, rubber webbing for seat; upholster with 4½ sq. ft., medium to firm, 2″ thick compact stuffing, no loose stuffing; build crown (Sec. 5:14) with cotton padding. Pad with synthetic cotton for maximum initial softness.

a

b

c

Fig. 1:28

Fig. *a* 1:28—Floral-stripe cover pattern popular for French back chairs. Modern touch with double or French welt (Sec. 11:08) instead of gimp.

Fig. *b* 1:28—For needlepoint cover, the best way to determine size and shape of cover pieces is to build seat and arms in muslin, then add 2 inches to each greatest measured width and length (Chapter 11); to estimate size and shape of inside back, add 4 inches to greatest measured width and length or height; for outside back add 2 inches to greatest measurements of raw frame between walls of rabbets. Size and shape of seat and armrests may be estimated safely only by experienced upholsterers.

Fig. *c* 1:28—Broad texture stripes give a modern touch to a French back.

SEC. 1:29

Bedroom chairs, perennial types, spring seat, open-frame pad back, covered armboard, Fig. 1:29. Except for arms, all are upholstered essentially the same way through muslin casing. Aside from shape and cover, differences in appearance are due chiefly to seat coverings. Roll edges on seats if upholstering them with loose stuffing only.

Fig. *a* 1:29—Pull-over seat cover, flange skirt; heavy or coarse goods often do not make a neat skirt. Dimensions of chair: 19″ wide, 20″ deep, 32″ high. TRADITIONAL UPHOLSTERY: *Materials*—Webbing,

Fig. a, b 1:29   *a*   *b*

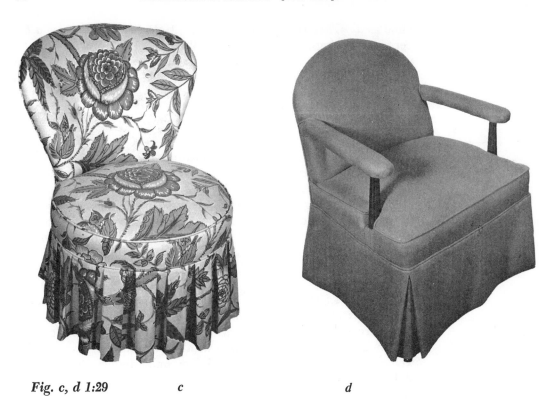

Fig. c, d 1:29   c   d

8 yds., 3½″ width; seat springs, 5 No. 1-H; burlap, 1½ yds., 40″ width; stuffing, 5 lbs. loose hair; muslin, 1½ yds., 36″ width; natural cotton padding, 2 lbs.; cover, 2½ yds., 54″ width, with skirt, 1½ yds. without; skirt lining, 1 yd., 54″ width; welt cord, 4 yds.; dust cover, ⅔ yd., 36″ width. For upholstering with compact stuffing: 6 sq. ft., medium, 1″ to 1½″ thick stock; only 2½ lbs. loose stuffing (1½ lbs. for understuffing seat, Sec. 7:20; 1 lb. for back, Sec. 5:13), 1½ yds. more muslin. *Work-Steps*—Through muslin casing: frame Secs. 4:11–4:13; 4:18; seat 7:05, 7:07, 7:08, 7:11–7:14, 7:18, 7:19; inside back 10:02, 10:10, 10:18, 10:22–10:24. Cover: seat Sec. 13:11; inside back 16:05, 16:06; outside surfaces 18:03, 18:14, 18:15. MODERN UPHOLSTERY: Same as traditional except for building seat with zigzag springs or rubber webbing (Secs. 3:21, 7:32; 3:22, 7:33), inside back with rubber webbing (Sec. 10:33). 6 yds. zigzags for seat; upholster with loose or compact stuffing. 12 yds., 2½″ width, Standard, rubber webbing for seat; 4 yds., preferably 1⅛″ width, for inside back; upholster with 3 sq. ft., medium to firm, 2″ thick compact stuffing for seat, 3 sq. ft. 1″ to 1½″ thick for back; no loose stuffing; build crown (Sec. 5:14) with cotton padding. Pad with synthetic cotton for maximum initial softness.

Fig. *b* 1:29—Bordered seat cover, box-pleated skirt. Dimensions same as *a*. TRADITIONAL UPHOLSTERY: *Materials*—Same as for *a* except: seat springs, 5 No. 2-H; cover, 4½ yds., 36″ width with skirt, 2½ yds. without; skirt lining, 2 yds., 36″ width; welt cord, 6 yds.; same compact stuffing, extra muslin as in *a*, but only 3 lbs. loose stuffing (2 lbs. for understuffing seat, 1 lb. for inside back). *Work-Steps*—Through muslin casing, same as in *a*. Cover: seat Sec. 13:13; inside back 16:05, 16:06; outside surfaces 18:07, 18:14, 18:15. MODERN UPHOLSTERY: Same as for *a*.

Fig. *c* 1:29—Boxed seat cover, box-pleated skirt. Buttons to help hold back upholstery in shape. Dimensions of chair: 20″ wide, 24″ deep, 30″ high. TRADITIONAL UPHOLSTERY: *Materials*—Same as *b* except: seat springs, 7 No. 1-H; burlap, 2 yds.; buttons as required; for compact stuffing, same as *a* except only 1 yd. more muslin (understuffing inside back not necessary). *Work-Steps*—Through muslin casing, same as *a*. Cover: seat Sec. 13:14; inside back 16:05, 16:06; outside surfaces 18:01, 18:07, 18:14, 18:15. MODERN UPHOLSTERY: Same as *a*.

Fig. *d* 1:29—Boxed seat cover, flange skirt, covered armboards. Dimensions of chair: 27″ wide, 27″ deep, 28″ high. TRADITIONAL UPHOLSTERY: *Materials*—Same as *a* except: seat springs, 9 No. 1-H; muslin, 2 yds.; cover, 3 yds., 54″ width, with skirt, 2 yds. without; welt cord, 7 yds.; dust cover, ¾ yd. For upholstering with compact stuffing: 10 sq. ft., medium, 1″ to 1½″ thick stock for seat and inside back, 2 sq. ft. ½″ thick for arms; only 2½ lbs. loose stuffing (1½ lbs. for understuffing seat, Sec. 7:20; 1 lb. for inside back, Sec. 5:13), 2 yds. more muslin. *Work-Steps*—Through muslin casing, same as *a* except covered armboards Sec. 8:07. Cover: seat Sec. 13:14; arms 14:02; inside back 16:05, 16:06; outside surfaces 18:04–18:06, 18:14, 18:15. MODERN UPHOLSTERY: Same as *a*.

SEC. 1:30   Small armchair, perennial style, spring seat, open-frame pad arms and back, Fig. 1:30. Note how a dominant figure of the cover pattern is repeated in the inside back, seat, seat border, and inside arms; similar repeats on outside surfaces would have required much more cover for very little gain in appearance. Roll edge on seat if building it with loose stuffing only. Dimensions of chair: 26″ wide, 27″ deep, 33″ high. TRADITIONAL UPHOLSTERY: *Materials*—Webbing, 13 yds., 3½″ width; seat springs, 9 No. 3-M; burlap, 3 yds., 40″ width; stuffing, 6 lbs. loose hair; muslin, 2½ yds., 36″ width; natural cotton padding, 4 lbs.; cover, 4½ yds., 36″ width; welt cord, 7 yds.; dust cover, ¾ yd., 36″ width. For upholstering with compact stuffing: 8 sq. ft., medium, 1½″ thick stock for seat, inside back; 5 sq. ft., ¾″ thick for inside arms; only 3½ lbs. loose stuffing (1½ lbs. for understuffing seat, Sec. 7:20; 1 lb. for arms, 1 lb. for back, Sec. 5:13), 2½ yds. more muslin. *Work-Steps*—Through mus-

Fig. 1:30

lin casing: frame Secs. 4:11–4:15, 4:18; seat 7:05, 7:07, 7:08, 7:11–7:14, 7:18, 7:19; inside arms 8:03, 8:09, 8:12, 8:14, 8:15, 8:21, 8:22; inside back 10:02, 10:10, 10:18, 10:22–10:24. Cover: seat Sec. 13:16; inside arms 14:04, 14:05; inside back 16:05, 16:06; outside surfaces 18:13–18:15. MODERN UPHOLSTERY: Same as traditional except for building seat with zigzag springs or rubber webbing (Secs. 3:21, 7:32; 3:22, 7:33), inside arms and back with rubber webbing (Secs. 8:09A, 10:33). 4 yds., zigzags for seat; upholster with loose or compact stuffing. 8 yds., 2½″ width, Standard, rubber webbing for seat, 14 yds., preferably 1⅛″ width for inside arms and back; upholster with same quantities of compact stuffing as for traditional work, but use 2″ thick stock for seat and inside back, 1″ stock for inside arms; no loose stuffing; build crown (Sec. 5:14) with padding. Pad with synthetic cotton for maximum initial softness.

SEC. 1:31   Small armchairs, perennial designs, spring seats and inside backs, open-frame pad arms, Fig. 1:31. Tight, overall floral pattern of cover in *a* excellent for box-pleat skirt. In *b*, accent welt and a matching pillow prevent what could be a monotonous plain cover.

Fig. *a* 1:31—Bridle spring edge seat, banded seat cover. Scooped arms. Spring back. Dimensions of chair: 29″ wide, 32″ deep, 33″

a

b

Fig. 1:31

high. TRADITIONAL UPHOLSTERY: *Materials*—Webbing, 15 yds., 3½"
width; seat springs, 9 No. 4-M; seat spring edge-wire, 10 ft.; back
springs, 9 6-inch; burlap, 6 yds., 40" width; stuffing, 14 lbs. loose hair;
muslin, 3 yds., 36" width; natural cotton padding, 5 lbs.; cover, 7¾
yds., 36" width, with skirt, 5 yds. without; skirt lining, 2¾ yds.,
36" width; welt cord, 9 yds.; dust cover, 1 yd., 36" width. For upholstering with compact stuffing: 17 sq. ft., medium, 1" thick stock
for seat, inside arms and back; only 6 lbs. loose stuffing (3 lbs. for
bridle building and understuffing seat, Sec. 7:20; 1½ lbs. for understuffing inside arms, 1½ lbs. for back, Sec. 5:13), 3 yds. more muslin.
Work-Steps—Through muslin casing: frame Secs. 4:11–4:15, 4:18; seat
7:05, 7:07, 7:08, 7:11–7:16, 7:18, 7:23, 7:26; inside arms 8:03, 8:09–
8:12, 8:14–8:20; inside back 10:03, 10:11, 10:13, 10:15, 10:18, 10:19,
10:21–10:24. Cover: seat Sec. 13:17; inside arms 14:03–14:05; inside
back 16:05, 16:06; outside surfaces 18:07, 18:13–18:15. MODERN
UPHOLSTERY: Same as traditional except for building seat and inside
back with zigzag springs (Secs. 3:21, 7:32, 10:31), inside back and
arms with rubber webbing (Secs. 3:22, 10:33, 8:09A). 4 yds., zigzag
springs for seat, 5 edge springs; 2½ yds. zigzags for inside back; upholster with loose or compact stuffing. 9 yds., 1⅛" width, Standard,

rubber webbing for inside arms, back; upholster with 5 sq. ft., medium, 1½″ thick compact stuffing for arms, 6 sq. ft., 2″ thick for back; no loose stuffing; build crown (Sec. 5:14) with padding. Pad with synthetic cotton for maximum initial softness.

Fig. *b* 1:31—Loose cushion spring seat with pull-over seat cover. Boxed arm-fronts. Flange skirt. Roll edge on seat, inside back stitched for flat top and square sides (Sec. 10:25) if they are upholstered with loose stuffing only. Dimensions of chair: 23″ wide, 25″ deep, 30″ high. TRADITIONAL UPHOLSTERY: *Materials*—Webbing, 13 yds., 3½″ width; seat springs, 9 No. 1-H; back springs, 9 6-inch; seat spring edge-wire for shaping back, 6 ft.; burlap, 3 yds., 40″ width; stuffing, 11 lbs. loose hair; muslin, 2½ yds., 36″ width; natural cotton padding, 4 lbs. (7 lbs. if having a traditional inner-spring cushion); cover, 4¾ yds., 54″ width, with skirt, 3¾ yds. without; skirt lining, 1 yd., 54″ width; decking, ⅔ yd., 36″ width; welt cord, 12 yds.; dust cover, ¾ yd., 36″ width. Inside back may be built with 18 × 24-inch inner-spring unit (Sec. 10:29) and 3 lbs. less loose stuffing. For upholstering with compact stuffing: 3½ sq. ft., medium, 1″ thick stock for seat, 7½ sq. ft. of 1½″ thick stock for inside back, 5 sq. ft. of ¾″ stock for inside arms; only 5 lbs. loose stuffing (2 lbs. for understuffing seat, Sec. 7:29; 1 lb. for understuffing arms and 2 lbs. for back, Sec. 5:13), 2 yds. more muslin. For seat cushions see Sec. 3:61; for down cushion, 2 lbs. down-filling, 2 yds. down-proof ticking, 36″ width. For back pillow and welt: ½ yd., 36″ width cover goods, 1 lb. down-filling, 1 yd. down-proof ticking. *Work-Steps*—Through muslin casing: frame Secs. 4:11–4:15, 4:18; seat 7:05–7:08, 7:11–7:14, 7:18, 7:19; inside arms 8:03, 8:08–8:12, 8:14, 8:15, 8:21, 8:22; inside back 10:03, 10:11–10:13, 10:15, 10:18, 10:22–10:25. Cover: seat Sec. 13:16; inside arms 14:04, 14:06; inside back 16:05, 16:09; cushion, pillow 17:01–17:15; outside surfaces 18:04–18:06, 18:13–18:15. MODERN UPHOLSTERY: Same as traditional except for building seat and back with zigzag springs or rubber webbing (Secs. 3:21, 7:32, 10:31, 10:32; 3:22, 7:33, 10:33), inside arms with rubber webbing (Sec. 8:09A). 3½ yds. zigzag springs for seat, 3 yds. for back; upholster with loose or compact stuffing, with inner-spring unit if desired. 9 yds., 2½″ width, Standard, rubber webbing for seat, 9 yds., preferably 1⅜″ width for arms and back; upholster with compact stuffing, 11 sq. ft., medium, 2″ thick stock for seat and inside back, 5 sq. ft. of 1½″ stock for arms; build crown (Sec. 5:14) with padding. Pad with synthetic cotton for maximum initial softness.

SEC. 1:32   Lowback loose cushion armchair, modern design, spring edge seat, open-frame pad arms, open-frame pad back with loose cushion upholstery treatment (Sec. 17:21), Fig. 1:32. Flange skirt. Scooped arms with pull-around cover. Dimensions of chair: 32″ wide, 31″ deep, 27″

Fig. 1:32

high. TRADITIONAL UPHOLSTERY: *Materials*—Webbing, 18 yds., 3½″ width; seat springs, 12 No. 2-M; seat spring edge-wire, 10 ft.; burlap, 4 yds., 40″ width; stuffing, 7 lbs. loose hair; muslin, 3 yds., 36″ width; natural cotton padding, 6 lbs. (9 lbs. if having traditional inner-spring seat cushion); cover, 6 yds., 54″ width, with skirt, 5 yds. without; skirt lining, 1 yd., 54″ width; decking for seat, 1 yd., 36″ width; welt cord, 14 yds.; buttons, 7; dust cover, 1 yd., 36″ width. For inside back pillow see Sec. 17:21. For upholstering with compact stuffing: 14 sq. ft., medium, 1″ thick stock for seat and deck, and inside arms; only 3 lbs. loose stuffing, for back, Sec. 5:13. For seat cushion, Secs. 3:61–3:73; for down cushion, 2 lbs. down-filling, 2 yds. down-proof ticking, 36″ width. *Work-Steps*—Through muslin casing: frame Secs. 4:11–4:15, 4:18; seat 7:05–7:08, 7:11, 7:12, 7:14–7:16, 7:18, 7:29; inside arms 8:03, 8:09–8:12, 8:14, 8:15, 8:21; inside back 10:02, 10:10, 10:18, 10:19, 10:21–10:24. Cover: seat Sec. 13:16; inside arms 14:07, 14:08; inside back 16:05, 17:21; seat cushion 17:01–17:15; outside surfaces 18:04–18:06, 18:13–18:15. MODERN UPHOLSTERY: Same as traditional except for building seat and inside back with zigzag springs (Secs. 3:21, 7:32, 10:31), inside back and arms with rubber webbing (Secs. 3:22, 10:33, 8:09A). 3 yds. zigzags for seat, 4 edge springs; 2 yds. zigzags for inside back; upholster with loose or compact stuffing (5 sq. ft., medium, 1″ thick for back). 6 yds., 1⅞″ width, Standard, rubber webbing for inside arms, back; upholster with 5 sq. ft., medium, 1″ thick compact stuffing for inside back, 8 sq. ft., 1½″ to 2″ thick stock for arms; no loose stuffing; build necessary crown (Sec. 5:14) with padding. Pad with synthetic cotton for maximum initial softness.

SEC. 1:33   Modern lowback, T-shaped loose cushion plain spring-edge seat chairs with sloping square-scroll open-frame pad arms, identical ex-

Fig. 1:33   *a*   *b*

cept for inside back and covers, Fig. 1:33. Most chairs can be upholstered in a variety of ways, with minor and/or major differences.
Skirts could be added to these chairs. Dimensions of chairs: 30″ wide,
31″ deep, 29″ high.

Fig. *a* 1:33—Solid back; buttons mainly decorative. Vertical
stripes in cover have slenderizing effect; horizontal stripes could make
low chair seem too squat. Pull-over seat cover with border encompassing chair. Roll edges at arm fronts if upholstering arms with
loose stuffing only. Inside back can be inner-spring unit (Sec. 10:29)
instead of spring edge coil spring upholstery. Spring edge seat.   TRA-
DITIONAL UPHOLSTERY: *Materials*—Webbing, 15 yds., 3½″ width; seat
springs, 12 No. 2-M; seat spring edge-wire, 10 ft.; back springs, 9
6-inch; back spring edge-wire, 6 ft.; burlap, 4 yds., 40″ width; stuffing,
6 lbs. loose hair; muslin, 4 yds., 36″ width; natural cotton padding, 6
lbs. (9 lbs. if having traditional inner-spring cushion); cover, 5½ yds.,
54″ width (bias welt); buttons, 3; decking, 1 yd., 36″ width; welt cord,
20 yds.; dust cover, 1 yd., 36″ width. For building inside back with
inner-spring unit instead of coil springs: 18 × 20″ unit, no back edge-
wire. For upholstering with compact stuffing: 15 sq. ft., medium, 1″
thick stock for seat edge, deck, inside arms; 4 sq. ft., 1½″ thick for
back; only 2 lbs. loose stuffing (1 lb. for understuffing arms, Sec. 5:13,
1 lb. for back), 2½ yds. more muslin. For seat cushion, Secs. 3:61–3:73;
for down cushion, 3 lbs. down-filling, 2½ yds. down-proof ticking, 36″
wide. *Work-Steps*—Through muslin casing: frame Secs. 4:11–4:13,
4:15, 4:18; seat 7:05–7:09, 7:11, 7:12, 7:14–7:16, 7:18, 7:29; inside
arms 8:03, 8:08–8:11, 8:13–8:15, 8:21; inside back, 10:03, 10:11, 10:13,

10:15, 10:16, 10:18–10:25, 10:29. Cover: seat Sec. 13:17; inside arms 14:07, 14:09; inside back 16:05, 16:11; cushion 17:01–17:15; outside surfaces 18:01, 18:13, 18:14, 13:08, 18:15. MODERN UPHOLSTERY: Same as traditional except for building seat, inside back with zigzag springs (Secs. 3:21, 7:32, 10:31, 10:32); inside back, arms with rubber webbing (Secs. 3:22, 10:33, 8:09A). 4 yds. zigzag springs for seat, 7 edge springs, 2 yds. zigzags for inside back; upholster with loose or compact stuffing, or for back add inner-spring unit. 6 yds., 1⅛″ width, Standard, rubber webbing for inside arms, 5 yds. for back; upholster with 4 sq. ft., medium, 1½″ thick compact stuffing for inside arms, 4 sq. ft., 3″ thick for back; build crown (Sec. 5:14) with padding. Pad with synthetic cotton for maximum initial softness.

Fig. *b* 1:33–Loose cushion open-frame pad back. Compact stuffing for loose cushion inside back is practical only to the extent that it simplifies work. Generally not practical, in modern upholstery with conventional thick back cushion, to build inside back with zigzag springs or rubber webbing. TRADITIONAL UPHOLSTERY: *Materials*–Same as *a* except no back springs, back edge-wire, buttons; relatively thin inside back reduces total amount loose stuffing needed to 4 lbs.; due to back cushion, 2 lbs. more natural cotton padding (5 lbs. more if having traditional inner-spring back cushion); 1 yd. more cover; 3 yds. more welt; for back cushion, Secs. 3:61–3:73, for down cushion 1½ lbs. down-filling and 1½ yds. down-proof ticking. *Work-Steps*–Through muslin casing: frame, seat, inside arms same as *a;* inside back Secs. 10:02, 10:10, 10:18–10:20, 10:22–10:24. Cover: seat, inside arms same as *a;* inside back Secs. 16:05, 16:07; seat, back cushions, outside surfaces same as *a* except no buttons 18:01. MODERN UPHOLSTERY: Same as *a* except zigzag springs only for seat, rubber webbing only for inside arms.

SEC. 1:34   General purpose small armchair, loose cushion T-shaped spring seat, open-frame pad arms, loose T-shaped cushion open-frame pad back, Fig. 1:34. Back pillow would look and fit better if boxed on sides, bottom. Flange skirt; quilted cover not usually suitable for box-pleat or gathered skirts. Hard edge spring seat with bordered cover. Boxed arm fronts; roll edges at fronts of arms if upholstering them with loose stuffing only. Dimensions of chair: 24″ wide, 30″ deep, 28″ high. TRADITIONAL UPHOLSTERY: *Materials*–Webbing, 14 yds., 3½″ width; seat springs, 9 No. 1-H; burlap, 3 yds., 40″ width; stuffing, 8 lbs. loose hair; muslin, 3 yds., 36″ width; natural cotton padding, 4 lbs. (7 lbs. if having traditional inner-spring seat cushion); cover, 10½ yds., 36″ width (bias welt), with skirt, 9½ yds. without; skirt lining, 1½ yds., 36″ width; decking, ⅔ yd., 36″ width; welt cord, 14 yds.; dust cover, 1 yd., 36″ width. For upholstering with compact stuffing: 12 sq. ft., medium,

Fig. 1:34

1″ thick stock for seat, inside arms; only 4 lbs. loose stuffing (3 lbs. for inside back; 1 for understuffing inside arms, Sec. 5:13), 1 yd. more muslin; compact stuffing for loose cushion inside back practical only to extent that it simplifies work. For seat cushion, Secs. 3:61–3:73; for down cushion, 2½ lbs. down-filling and 2 yds. down-proof ticking, 36″ width. For back pillow: 2 lbs. down-filling, 2 yds. down-proof ticking. *Work-Steps*—Through muslin casing: frame Secs. 4:11–4:15, 4:18; seat 7:05–7:09, 7:11–7:14, 7:18, 7:24, 7:27; inside arms 8:03, 8:08–8:12, 8:14, 8:15, 8:21, 8:22; inside back 10:02, 10:10, 10:18, 10:22–10:24. Cover: seat Sec. 13:16; inside arms 14:07, 14:09; inside back 16:05, 16:07; cushion, pillow 17:01–17:20; outside surfaces 18:04–18:06, 18:13–18:15. MODERN UPHOLSTERY: Same as traditional except for building seat with zigzag springs or rubber webbing (Secs. 3:21, 7:32; 3:22, 7:33C) inside arms with rubber webbing (Sec. 8:09A). 4 yds. zigzag springs for seat; upholster with loose or compact stuffing. 8 yds., 2½″ width, Standard, rubber webbing for seat; 7 yds., preferably 1⅛″ width for inside arms; upholster seat with 4½ sq. ft., medium, 1″ thick compact stuffing, inside arms with 7½ sq. ft., 1½″ thick stock; build extra crown (Sec. 5:14) with padding. Pad with synthetic cotton for maximum initial softness.

SEC. 1:35   Three small, open-frame pad barrel-back armchairs with spring seats; identical frames, completely different styles of upholstery except for arms, Fig. 1:35. Thinness of scooped armfronts makes pull-around the

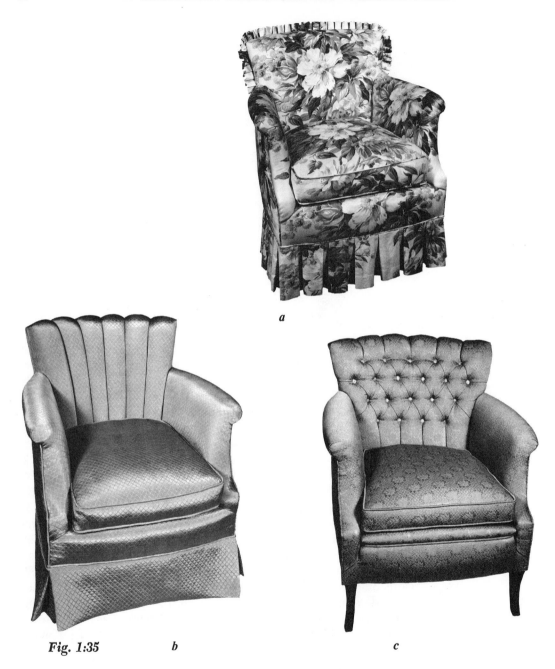

a

Fig. 1:35 *b*   *c*

most practical and durable arm upholstery. Curve of the backs is less than in most regular barrel-back or tub chairs (Figs. 1:36–1:41); it is excellent for channel and tufted upholstery, *b, c*; large plain backs usually are buttoned in order to hold shape and keep the cover from wrinkling, but in small backs, *a*, buttons are optional. Dimensions of chairs: 27″ wide, 28″ deep, 31″ high.

Fig. *a* 1:35—"Bedroomy" effect given by ruching (Sec. 11:22) on outside back. Pull-over seat cover. Box-pleat skirt. Plain hard edge spring seat. Student built. TRADITIONAL UPHOLSTERY: *Materials*—Webbing, 12 yds., 3½″ width; seat springs, 9 No. 1-S; burlap, 4 yds., 40″ width; stuffing, 8 lbs. loose hair; muslin, 3 yds., 36″ width; natural cotton padding, 5 lbs. (8 lbs. if having traditional inner-spring cushion); cover, 10½ yds., 36″ width (bias welt), with skirt, 8 yds. without; skirt lining, 2½ yds., 36″ width; decking, 1 yd., 36″ width; welt cord, 11 yds.; dust cover, 1 yd., 36″ width. For cushion, Secs. 3:61–3:73; for down cushion, 2 lbs. down-filling and 1½ yds. down-proof ticking, 36″ width. For upholstering with compact stuffing: 4½ sq. ft., medium, 1″ thick stock for seat edge and deck, 6 sq. ft. ¾″ stock for inside arms, 4½ sq. ft. 1½″ stock for inside back; only 3 lbs. loose stuffing (2 lbs. for seat, Sec. 7:27; 1 lb. for understuffing arms, Sec. 5:13; back does not need understuffing), 1½ yds. more muslin. *Work-Steps*—Through muslin casing: frame Secs. 4:11–4:15, 4:18; seat 7:05, 7:07, 7:08, 7:11–7:14, 7:18, 7:24, 7:27; inside arms 8:03, 8:09–8:12, 8:14–8:20; inside back 10:02, 10:10, 10:18, 10:22–10:24. Cover: seat Sec. 13:16; inside arms 14:07, 14:08; inside back 16:05, 16:07; cushion 17:01–17:15; outside surfaces 18:07, 18:10, 18:13–18:15. MODERN UPHOLSTERY: Same as traditional except for building seat with zigzag springs (Secs. 3:21, 7:32); seat, inside arms, and back with rubber webbing (Secs. 3:22, 7:33, 8:09A, 10:33). 4 yds. zigzags for seat; upholster with loose or compact stuffing. 8 yds., 2½″ width, Standard, rubber webbing for seat; 6 yds., preferably 1⅛″ width, for inside arms and 4 yds. for back; upholster with same quantities of compact stuffing as for traditional work, but use 1″ stock for inside arms; build extra crown (Sec. 5:14) if necessary with padding. Pad with synthetic cotton for maximum initial softness.

Fig. *b* 1:35—Same as *a* except for channel back instead of plain, no ruching, flange instead of box-pleat skirt. TRADITIONAL UPHOLSTERY: *Materials*—Same as *a* except: cover, 6⅓ yds., 54″ width (bias welt), with skirt, 5⅓ yds. without; skirt lining, 1 yd., 54″ width; for upholstering with compact stuffing, 2″ thick stock for inside back. *Work-Steps*—Through muslin casing: frame, seat, inside arms same as *a;* inside back Secs. 10:02, 10:10, 10:18, 20:03–20:07. Cover: seat, inside arms same as *a;* inside back Secs. 16:05, 20:08, 20:09; cushion 17:01–17:15; outside surfaces 18:04–18:06, 18:13–18:15. MODERN UPHOLSTERY: Same as *a* except for back upholstery above.

Fig. *c* 1:35—Same as *a* except tufted instead of plain inside back, no ruching, no skirt, spring instead of hard edge seat, banded seat cover. TRADITIONAL UPHOLSTERY: *Materials*—Same as *a* except: seat springs, 9 No. 2-S; seat spring edge-wire, 10 ft.; cover, 4½ yds., 54″

width (bias welt); welt cord 9 yds.; buttons, 20; for upholstering with compact stuffing, understuff seat, Sec. 7:29, 2″ stock for inside back. *Work-Steps*—Through muslin casing: frame same as *a;* seat Secs. 7:05, 7:07, 7:08, 7:11–7:16, 7:18, 7:25, 7:29; inside arms same as *a;* inside back 10:02, 10:10, 10:18, 21:03, 21:04, 21:06, 21:07. Cover: seat Sec. 13:17; inside arms 14:06–14:08; inside back 16:05, 21:09; cushion 17:01–17:15; outside surfaces 18:01, 18:13–18:15. Modern Upholstery: Same as *a* except: rubber webbing not advisable for seat; back upholstery as above.

SEC. 1:36

Two side, occasional, or bedroom chairs, very different in appearance but quite similar in upholstery. Solid spring seats, open-frame pad barrel backs with two styles of tufting. Welt and buttons in contrast to cover, *a*, is a modern trim in keeping with an antique design. Note that the ruching in *b* encompasses the outside back top and sides.

Fig. *a* 1:36—Roll edge spring seat with boxed cover; roll edges on seat if upholstering it with loose stuffing only. Extreme right and left bottom parts of inside back may be covered with small pieces to allow use of narrower cover goods. Dimensions of chair: seat diameter 23″, 31″ high. Traditional Upholstery: *Materials*—Webbing, 7 yds., 3½″ width; seat springs, 7 No. 1-H; burlap, 2½ yds., 40″ width; stuffing, 6 lbs. loose hair; muslin, 2 yds., 36″ width; natural cotton padding, 2½ lbs.; cover, 3 yds., 54″ width; buttons, 20; welt cord, 4 yds.; dust cover, ¾ yd., 36″ width. For upholstering with compact stuffing: 6 sq. ft., medium, 1½″ thick stock for seat and inside back; only 1½ lbs. loose stuffing (for understuffing seat, Sec. 7:20; back does not need understuffing), 1 yd. more muslin. *Work-Steps*—Through muslin casing: frame Secs. 4:11–4:13, 4:15, 4:18; seat 7:05, 7:07, 7:08, 7:11–7:14, 7:18, 7:19; inside back 10:02, 10:10, 10:18, 21:03, 21:04, 21:06, 21:07. Cover: seat Sec. 13:14; inside back 21:09; outside surfaces 18:01, 18:14, 18:15. Modern Upholstery: Same as traditional except for building seat with zigzag springs or rubber webbing (Secs. 3:21, 7:32; 3:22, 7:33), inside back with rubber webbing (Sec. 10:33). 3½ yds. zigzags for seat; upholster with loose or compact stuffing. 7 yds., 2½″ width, Standard, rubber webbing for seat, 5 yds., preferably 1⅛″ width webbing, for inside back; upholster with 3 sq. ft., medium, 2″ thick compact stuffing for seat, 3 sq. ft. 1½″ thick for back; build extra crown (Sec. 5:14) if necessary with padding. Pad with synthetic cotton for maximum initial softness.

Fig. *b* 1:36—Bridle hard edge spring seat with bordered cover. Tufting would have been neater had cover been heavier goods than chintz; compare with Fig. *c* 1:35. Dimensions of chair: 28″ wide, 30″ deep, 36″ high. Traditional Upholstery: *Materials*—Webbing, 10 yds., 3½″ width; seat springs, 8 No. 3-M; burlap, 4 yds., 40″ width;

a   *b*

Fig. 1:36

stuffing, 6 lbs. loose hair; muslin, 2 yds., 36″ width; natural cotton
padding, 3 lbs.; cover, 6 yds., 36″ width (bias welt); buttons, 18; welt
cord, 6 yds.; dust cover, 1 yd., 36″ width. For upholstering with compact stuffing: 12 sq. ft., medium, 1½″ thick stock for seat, inside back;
only 2 lbs. loose stuffing (for understuffing seat, Sec. 7:20; understuffing back not necessary), 2 yds. more muslin. *Work-Steps*—Through
muslin casing: frame same as *a;* seat Secs. 7:05, 7:07, 7:08, 7:11–7:14,
7:18, 7:21, 7:22, 7:26; inside back same as *a.* Cover: seat Sec. 13:13;
inside back 21:09; outside surfaces 18:01, 18:10, 18:14, 18:15. Modern Upholstery: Same as *a* except: 4 yds. zigzag springs for seat;
8 yds. rubber webbing for seat, 8 yds. for inside back, 6 sq. ft. 3″ compact stuffing for seat, 6 sq. ft. 1½″ stock for inside back.

SEC. 1:37   Lowback, modern barrel-back or tub chairs with loose cushion spring
hard edge seats, open-frame pad inside arms and backs, Fig. 1:37.
Oddly shaped cushions such as these often are best made with down

b

Fig. 1:37   *a*

filling or modern cushions units; traditional inner-spring units need excessive padding to fill front and back corners, and deleting springs at back corners may be necessary; regular foam rubber, polyfoam units must be rebuilt to shape of seat.

Fig. *a* 1:37—Channel back, plain arms. Bordered seat front only, sides and back regular outside covers. Bordered arm- and back-tops require special cover planning (Sec. 11:15H). Plan channeling (Chapter 20) as first step of upholstering. Dimensions of chair: 28″ wide, 28″ deep, 25″ high. TRADITIONAL UPHOLSTERY: *Materials*—Webbing, 12 yds., 3½″ width; seat springs, 9 No. 1-S; burlap, 4 yds., 40″ width; stuffing, 7 lbs. loose hair; muslin, 3 yds., 36″ width; natural cotton padding, 5 lbs. (8 lbs. if having traditional inner-spring cushion); cover, 4½ yds., 54″ width (bias welt); decking, 1 yd., 36″ width; welt cord, 13 yds.; dust cover, 1 yd., 36″ width. For cushion, Secs. 3:61–3:73; for down cushion, 2 lbs. down-filling and 2 yds. downproof ticking, 36″ width. For upholstering with compact stuffing: 5 sq. ft., medium, 1″ thick stock for seat edge and deck, 6 sq. ft. ¾″ stock for inside arms, 4 sq. ft. 1½″ stock for inside back; only 1 lb. loose stuffing (for basic seat work; understuffing inside back, arms not necessary). *Work-Steps*—Through muslin casing: frame Secs. 4:11–4:13, 4:15, 4:18; seat 7:05, 7:07, 7:08, 7:11–7:14, 7:18, 7:24, 7:27; inside arms 8:03, 8:09, 8:10; 8:14–8:20; inside back 10:02, 10:10, 10:18, 20:03–20:07. Cover: seat Secs. 13:13, 13:16; inside arms 14:07, 14:08; inside back 20:08, 20:09, 14:08; cushion 17:01–17:15; outside surfaces 18:13–18:15. MODERN UPHOLSTERY: Same as traditional except for building seat with zigzag springs or rubber webbing (Secs. 3:21, 7:32; 3:22, 7:33), inside arms and back with rubber webbing (Secs. 8:09A, 10:33). 3½ yds. zigzags for seat; upholster with loose or compact stuffing. 7 yds., 2½″ width, Standard, rubber webbing for seat; 6 yds., preferably 1⅛″ width webbing for inside arms and 3 yds. for back; upholster with compact stuffing, 4 sq. ft., firm, 1″ thick for understuffing seat, same as traditional for regular stuffing of seat, arms and back; build extra crown (Sec. 5:14) if needed with padding. Pad with synthetic cotton for maximum initial softness.

Fig. *b* 1:37—Channeled inside arms and back, may be built as one or as three separate units; plan channels (Chapter 20) as first step in upholstering. Front of seat cover boxed; chair might look better with pull-over seat cover. Dimensions of chair: 27″ wide, 30″ deep, 29″ high. TRADITIONAL UPHOLSTERY: *Materials*—Webbing, 12 yds., 3½″ width; seat springs, 9 No. 1-S; burlap, 4 yds., 40″ width; stuffing, 9 lbs. loose hair; muslin, 5 yds., 36″ width; natural cotton padding, 6 lbs. (9 lbs. if having traditional inner-spring cushion); cover, 6 yds., 54″ width (bias welt); decking, 1 yd., 36″ width; welt cord, 11 yds.; dust cover, 1 yd., 36″ width. For cushion, Secs. 3:61–3:73; for down cushion, 2½ lbs. down-filling and 2 yds. down-proof ticking, 36″ width. For upholstering with compact stuffing: 5 sq. ft., medium, 1″ thick stock for seat edge and deck, 18 sq. ft. 1½″ stock for inside arms and back; only 1 lb. loose stuffing for basic seat work (arms, back do not require understuffing). *Work-Steps*—Through muslin casing: frame, seat same as *a;* inside arms, back Secs. 8:03, 8:09, 8:10, 10:02, 10:10, 10:18, 20:03–20:07. Cover: seat Sec. 13:14, 13:16; inside arms, back 20:08, 20:09; cushion 17:01–17:15; outside surfaces 18:13–18:15. MODERN UPHOLSTERY: Same as *a* except: 4 yds. zigzag springs for seat; 8 yds. rubber webbing for seat, 7 yds. for inside arms and back; 5 sq. ft., firm, 1″ thick compact stuffing for understuffing seat, same as traditional compact stuffing for regular stuffing of seat, arms and back.

SEC. 1:38   Low and high barrel-back armchairs featuring joined inside arm and back upholsteries, Fig. 1:38. Buttons to hold large inside backs in shape are advisable, but usually not essential. Inside arm and back upholsteries must be fairly firm; if the back, especially, is too soft or weak, back and arm covers may split at the seams. Utmost care and precision is essential in all phases of inside arm and back work in order to build a neat, durable article. Chairs of this type can easily be built with separately upholstered inside arms and back—the method recommended for inexperienced upholsterers.

Fig. *a* 1:38—Modern lowback barrel chair with solid spring seat,

a   b

Fig. 1:38

open-frame pad inside arms and back. Solid seat covered with double boxing to resemble cushion seat; main seat cover and upper boxing are essentially the top cover and boxing of a boxed cushion casing (Chapter 17), although a few inches behind the armfronts the boxing may be replaced by cover stretcher goods. This type seat may be bridle built hard edge with coil or zigzag springs, but is simpler to upholster the modern way with rubber webbing and a thick slab of compact stuffing. Dimensions of chair: 25″ wide, 27″ deep, 30″ high. TRADITIONAL UPHOLSTERY: *Materials*—Webbing, 8 yds., 3½″ width; seat springs, 8 No. 2-M; burlap, 2½ yds., 40″ width; stuffing, 6 lbs. loose hair; muslin, 3 yds., 36″ width; natural cotton padding, 3 lbs.; cover, 4½ yds., 54″ width (bias welt); welt cord, 8 yds.; dust cover, 1 yd., 36″ width. For upholstering with compact stuffing: 4 sq. ft., medium, 3″ thick stock for seat, 8½ sq. ft., 1½″ thick for inside arms and back; only 1 lb. loose stuffing (for understuffing seat, Sec. 7:26; not necessary to understuff inside arms, back). *Work-Steps*—Through muslin casing: frame Secs. 4:11–4:13, 4:15, 4:18; seat 7:05, 7:07, 7:08, 7:11–7:14, 7:18, 7:21, 7:22, 7:26; inside arms 8:03, 8:09–8:12, 8:14–8:20; inside back 10:02, 10:10, 10:18, 10:22–10:24. Cover: seat (see above regarding preparation of seat cover) Sec. 13:11; inside arms and back 14:04, 16:07; outside surfaces 18:13, 18:14, 13:06, 18:15. MODERN UPHOLSTERY: Same as traditional except for building seat with zigzag springs or rubber webbing (Secs. 3:21, 7:32; 3:22, 7:33), inside arms and back with rubber webbing (Secs. 8:09A, 10:33). 3 yds. zigzags for seat; upholster with loose or compact stuffing. 6 yds.,

2½″ width, Standard, rubber webbing for seat; 8 yds., preferably 1⅛″ width webbing for inside arms, back; upholster with 4 sq. ft., 3½″ thick compact stuffing for seat, same as for traditional work for arms, back; build extra crown (Sec. 5:14) if needed with padding. Pad with synthetic cotton for maximum initial softness.

Fig. *b* 1:38—Traditional style highback barrel chair with loose cushion spring seat, open-frame pad inside arms and back. Plain hard edge seat; pull-over cover, could be bordered instead. Dimensions of chair: 28″ wide, 32″ deep, 36″ high. TRADITIONAL UPHOLSTERY: *Materials*—Webbing, 14 yds., 3½″ width; seat springs, 9 No. 1-S; burlap, 5 yds., 40″ width; stuffing, 9 lbs. loose hair; muslin, 3 yds., 36″ width; natural cotton padding, 5 lbs. (8 lbs. if having traditional inner-spring cushion); cover, 5½ yds., 54″ width (bias welt); decking, 1 yd., 36″ width; welt cord, 14 yds.; dust cover, 1 yd., 36″ width. For cushion, Secs. 3:61–3:73; for down cushion, 2½ lbs. down-filling and 2 yds. down-proof ticking, 36″ width. For upholstering with compact stuffing: 5 sq. ft., medium, 1″ thick stock for seat edge and deck, 15 sq. ft., 1½″ stock for inside arms and back; only 2 lbs. loose stuffing (for understuffing seat, Sec. 7:27; inside arms, back not understuffed). *Work-Steps*—Through muslin casing: frame same as *a;* seat Secs. 7:05, 7:07, 7:08, 7:11–7:14, 7:18, 7:24, 7:26, 7:27; inside arms, back same as *a.* Cover: seat Sec. 13:16; inside arms, back same as *a* except for post pieces, Sec. 14:06; outside surfaces 18:13–18:15. MODERN UPHOLSTERY: Same as traditional except for building seat with zig-zag springs or rubber webbing (Secs. 3:21, 7:32; 3:22, 7:33), inside arms, back with rubber webbing (Secs. 8:09A, 10:33). 4 yds. zigzags for seat; upholster with loose or compact stuffing. 8 yds., 2½″ width, Standard, rubber webbing for seat; 11 yds., preferably 1⅛″ width webbing for inside arms, back; upholster with 20 sq. ft., medium, 1½″ thick compact stuffing for seat, arms, back; build extra crown (Sec. 5:14) if needed with padding. Pad with synthetic cotton for maximum initial softness.

SEC. 1:39   Lowback, "heavy modern" deep tufted arm-back chairs with T-shaped loose cushion spring edge seats, Fig. 1:38. Deep tufting is difficult but usually well worth the work (Chapter 21); it should not be a first project. Plan tufting as first step in upholstering; it can be done with traditional loose stuffing, but compact stuffing (preferably polyfoam) usually results in faster, easier work and a neater, more durable job. Plain pull-over seat cover. Except for skirt or kick-flounce, *a* and *b* are identical in materials and work-steps. Dimensions of chairs: 33½″ wide, 33″ deep, 29½″ high.

Fig. *a* 1:39—Bordered seat front. TRADITIONAL UPHOLSTERY: *Materials*—Webbing, 12 yds., 3½″ width; seat springs, 5 No. 2-S and

a   b

Fig. 1:39

5 No. 2-H; seat spring edge wire, 11 ft.; burlap, 3½ yds., 40″ width; stuffing, 9 lbs. loose hair; muslin, 3½ yds., 36″ width; natural cotton padding, 4½ lbs. (7½ lbs. if having traditional inner-spring cushion); cover, 6 yds., 54″ width (bias welt); decking, 1 yd., 36″ width; welt cord, 11 yds.; buttons, 10 for tufting, 2 for armfronts; dust cover, 1 yd., 36″ width. For cushions, Secs. 3:61–3:73; for down cushion, 2½ lbs. down-filling and 2½ yds. down-proof ticking, 36″ width. For upholstering with compact stuffing: 5 sq. ft., medium, 1″ thick stock for seat edge and deck; 12 sq. ft., medium, 2″ stock for inside arms and back; only 2 lbs. loose stuffing (for understuffing seat, Sec. 7:29; inside back, arms not understuffed). *Work-Steps*—Through muslin casing: frame Secs. 4:11–4:13, 4:15, 4:18; seat 7:05, 7:07, 7:08, 7:11–7:18, 7:25, 7:29; inside arms and back 8:03, 8:08, 8:09, 10:02, 10:10, 21:01–21:04, 21:06, 21:07. Cover: seat Secs. 13:08, 13:17; inside arms, back 14:08, 21:07, 21:10; cushion 17:01–17:15; outside surfaces 18:01, 18:13–18:15. MODERN UPHOLSTERY: Same as traditional except for building seat with zigzag springs (Secs. 3:21, 7:32), inside arms and back with rubber webbing (Secs. 3:22, 8:09A, 10:33). 4 yds. zigzags for seat, 7 edge springs; upholster with loose or compact stuffing. 9 yds., 1⅞″ width, Standard, rubber webbing for inside arms, back; upholster them with compact stuffing as for traditional work; build extra crown (Sec. 5:14) if needed with padding. Pad with synthetic cotton for maximum initial softness.

Fig. *b* 1:39—Same as *a* except flange skirt for entire seat, no front border. *Materials*—Cover, 7 yds., 54″ width; skirt lining, 1 yd., 54″ width. *Work-Steps*—Flange skirt Secs. 18:04–18:06.

SEC. 1:40   Tufted, lowback, modern style armchairs with loose cushion spring seats, Fig. 1:40; despite differences in appearance, chairs are essentially the same in materials and work. Inside back and arms are an unboxed pillow (Chapter 17) made to fit the chair; the outer pillow casing is denim with 2" or 3" strips of cover along the top and sides or fronts; the bottom of the pillow ends about 1 inch below the seat deck, and a stretcher is added for tacking to the frame (Sec. 17:21).

a   b

Fig. 1:40

The outer strips of pillow casing are machine sewn to the strips of cover for the front and top surfaces of the arms and back; for a smooth fit they must be patterned for the shape of those surfaces (Sec. 11:15H) and usually are pieced at the junctions of the arms and back. Plan and plot tufting points (Secs. 21:03, 21:04); plan placement of arm and back webbing to hold button twines where possible. Note treatment of flange skirt in *a;* a sofa with this same style of upholstery is in Fig. 1:62. A chair frame must be specially built for the "upholster to floor" finish in *b.* Loose cushion seats can be spring built with roll or hard edges, or with rubber webbing and compact stuffing. Seat cover is pull-over with a short border in *a,* with tall and short borders in *b.* Dimensions of chairs: 31½" wide, 30½" deep, 26" high.

Fig. *a* 1:40—TRADITIONAL UPHOLSTERY: *Materials*—Webbing, 12 yds., 3½" width; seat springs, 9 No. 2-M; burlap, 3 yds., 40" width; stuffing, 3 lbs. loose hair; muslin, 2 yds., 36" width; natural cotton padding, 5 lbs. (8 lbs. if having traditional inner-spring cushion); cover, 5½ yds., 54" width (bias welt), with skirt, 4½ yds. without; skirt lining, 1 yd., 54″ width; decking, 1 yd., 36″ width; buttons, 20; welt cord, 12 yds.; dust cover, 1 yd., 36″ width. For seat cushion, Secs. 3:61–3:73; for down cushion, 2½ lbs. down filling and 2½ yds. down-proof ticking, 36″ width. For inside arms-back pillow: 2″ thick slab of polyfoam to size wrapped with two or three layers of synthetic cotton padding. For upholstering with compact stuffing: 5 sq. ft., medium, 1″ thick stock for seat edge and deck; only 2 lbs. loose stuffing (for understuffing seat, Sec. 7:20), 1 yd. more muslin. *Work-Steps*— Through muslin casing: frame Secs. 4:11–4:13, 4:15, 4:18; seat 7:05, 7:07, 7:08, 7:11–7:14, 7:18–7:20 or 7:18, 7:24, 7:27; inside arms, back 8:09, 10:10. Cover: seat Secs. 13:08, 13:16; inside arms, back 14:08, 16:07 with padding on front and top surfaces of arms, back; cushion 17:01–17:15; outside surfaces 18:01 (secure button twines to webbing, Sec. 6:05H, where possible), 18:04–18:06, 18:13–18:15. Modern Upholstery: Same as traditional except for building seat with zigzag springs or rubber webbing (Secs. 3:21, 7:32; 3:22, 7:33). 3½ yds. zig-zags for seat; upholster with loose or compact stuffing. 7 yds., 2½″ width, Standard, rubber webbing for seat; upholster with 5 sq. ft., medium, 1½″ to 2″ thick stock for seat.

Fig. *b* 1:40—Same as *a* except: 4¾ yds. cover; no skirt lining; two borders on seat front, Sec. 13:08.

SEC. 1:41   General purpose, modern slimline armchairs with T-shaped loose cushion spring seats, open-frame pad inside arms and back, Fig. 1:41. Comfort of this type chair is generally due to a firm inside back designed and upholstered to give the sitter excellent support, especially in the lumbar area. Despite differences in appearance, *a* and *b* are quite similar in construction. Spring seats can be built with roll or hard edges, or with rubber webbing and compact stuffing. Inside arm and back covers are buttoned to maintain shape, and prevent need of crown (Sec. 5:14), which could spoil the slimline effect. Plan all button sites (Sec. 21:03) as first step in upholstering.

Fig. *a* 1:41—Scroll arms, scoop fronts. Dimensions of chair: 30″ wide, 32″ deep, 34″ high. Traditional Upholstery: *Materials*— Webbing, 13 yds., 3½″ width; seat springs, 11 No. 3-M; burlap, 3½ yds., 40″ width; stuffing, 6 lbs. loose hair; muslin, 4 yds., 36″ width; natural cotton padding, 5 lbs. (8 lbs. if having traditional inner-spring cushion); cover, 6 yds., 54″ width (bias welt), with skirt, 5 yds. without; skirt lining, 1 yd., 54″ width; decking, 1 yd., 36″ width; buttons, 5 in back, arms optional; welt cord, 12 yds.; dust cover, 1 yd., 36″ width. For cushion, Secs. 3:61–3:73; for down cushion, 3 lbs. down-filling and 2 yds. down-proof ticking, 36″ width. For upholstering with compact stuffing: 12 sq. ft., medium, 1″ thick stock for seat, inside arms and back; only 2 lbs. loose stuffing (for understuffing seat,

a

b

Fig. 1:41

Sec. 7:20 or 7:27; inside arms, back not understuffed).   *Work-Steps—*
Through muslin casing: frame Secs. 4:11–4:13, 4:15, 4:18; seat 7:05,
7:07, 7:08, 7:11–7:14, 7:18–7:20 or 7:18, 7:24, 7:27; inside arms 8:03,
8:08–8:12, 8:14–8:20; inside back 10:02, 10:10, 10:18–10:24, 10:28.
Cover: seat Sec. 13:16; inside arms 14:06–14:08; inside back 16:05,
16:07; cushion 17:01–17:15; outside surfaces 18:01, 18:04–18:06,
18:13–18:15. Modern Upholstery: Same as traditional except for
building seat with zigzag springs or rubber webbing (Secs. 3:21, 7:32;
3:22, 7:33), inside arms and back with rubber webbing (Secs. 8:09A,
10:33). 4 yds. zigzags for seat; upholster with loose or compact stuffing. 9 yds., 2½″ width, Standard, rubber webbing for seat; 8 yds.,
preferably 1⅛″ width, webbing for inside arms and back; upholster
with compact stuffing the same as for traditional work, except use 1½″
to 2″ stock for seat; build extra crown (Sec. 5:14) if needed with
padding. Pad with synthetic cotton for maximum initial softness.

Fig. *b* 1:41—Pleats or tucks in inside arm covers are effective
"trim" (mock tufting, Sec. 12:01) and allow for unnoticeable piecing
of cover if necessary. Dimensions of chair: 30″ wide, 32″ deep, 34″

high. TRADITIONAL UPHOLSTERY: *Materials*—Webbing, 13 yds., 3½″ width; seat springs, 11 No. 2-M; burlap, 3 yds., 40″ width; stuffing, 8 lbs. loose hair; muslin, 3 yds., 36″ width; natural cotton padding, 5 lbs. (8 lbs. if having traditional inner-spring cushion); cover, 6 yds., 54″ width (bias welt); decking, 1 yd., 36″ width; buttons, 13; welt cord, 12 yds.; dust cover, 1 yd., 36″ width. For cushion, Secs. 3:61–3:73; for down cushion, same as *a*. For upholstering with compact stuffing: 6 sq. ft., medium, 1″ thick stock for seat edge and deck; 8 sq. ft., 2″ stock for inside arms and back; only 2 lbs. loose stuffing (for understuffing seat, Sec. 7:20; inside arms, back not understuffed). *Work-Steps*—Through muslin casing: same as *a*. Cover: same as *a* except: no skirt; border on seat front Sec. 13:08; pleats, tucks, mock tufting on inside arm covers Sec. 12:01; no armfront panel or border. MODERN UPHOLSTERY: Same as *a*.

SEC. 1:42   Lowback modern club chairs with loose cushion spring seats, open-frame pad arms, spring inside backs, Fig. 1:42. These chairs are basically quite similar and are about as easy to build with traditional and modern upholsteries. Inside backs are stitched (Sec. 10:25) for flat top and square sides if upholstering with loose stuffing only, but not if built entirely or overstuffed with compact stuffing. Regardless of stuffing, inside back upholstery can be simplified, with no loss of quality, by using an inner-spring unit (Sec. 10:29).

Fig. *a* 1:42—Boxed inside back cover; finishing boxing neatly under outside arm covers is apt to be difficult, treatment in *b* and *c* may be more practical. Boxed modern square arms. Plain spring edge seat, banded cover. Dimensions of chair: 30″ wide, 29″ deep, 31″ high. TRADITIONAL UPHOLSTERY: *Materials*—Webbing, 16 yds., 3½″ width; seat springs, 12 No. 2-S; seat spring edge-wire, 10 ft.; seat edge-wire for shaping lower sides of inside back, 6 ft.; back springs, 6 8-inch and 7 6-inch; burlap, 5 yds., 40″ width; stuffing, 9 lbs. loose hair; muslin, 3 yds., 36″ width; natural cotton padding, 5 lbs. (8 lbs. if having traditional inner-spring cushion); cover, 6 yds., 54″ width (bias welt); decking, 1 yd., 36″ width; welt cord, 17 yds.; dust cover, 1 yd., 36″ width. For cushion, Secs. 3:61–3:73; for down cushion, 2½ lbs. down-filling and 2 yds. down-proof ticking, 36″ width. For upholstering with compact stuffing: 6 sq. ft., medium, 1″ thick stock for seat edge and deck; 6½ sq. ft., ¾″ stock for inside arms; 9½ sq. ft., 2″ thick for inside back; only 5½ lbs. loose stuffing (2 lbs. for understuffing seat, Sec. 7:27; ½ lb. for inside arms, Sec. 5:13; 3 lbs. for back), 2 yds. more muslin. For building inside back with inner-spring unit: 5 × 6 unit plus 2 springs for each side of back; upholster with loose or compact stuffing to fit (Sec. 10:29). *Work-Steps*—Through muslin casing: frame Secs. 4:11–4:16, 4:18; seat 7:05, 7:07, 7:08, 7:11–7:16,

Fig. 1:42   *c*

7:18, 7:25, 7:29; inside arms 8:03, 8:09–8:11, 8:13–8:15, 8:21, 8:22; inside back 10:03, 10:11–10:13, 10:15, 10:18, 10:22–10:25 (10:28, 10:29 optional). Cover: seat Sec. 13:17; inside arms 14:07–14:09; inside back 16:05, 16:10; cushion 17:01–17:15; outside surfaces 18:13–

18:15.   MODERN UPHOLSTERY: Same as traditional except for building seat and inside back with zigzag springs (Secs. 3:21, 7:32, 10:31, 10:32), inside arms and back with rubber webbing (Secs. 3:22, 8:09A, 10:33). 4 yds. zigzags for seat, 5 edge springs; 3 yds. zigzags for back; upholster with loose or compact stuffing, or inner-spring unit for back. 12 yds., 1⅛″ width, Standard, rubber webbing for inside arms, back; upholster arms with same compact stuffing as for traditional work; stuff back with 6 sq. ft., firm, 4″ thick stock; build extra crown (Sec. 5:14) if needed with padding. Pad with synthetic cotton for maximum initial softness.

Fig. *b* 1:42—Boxed inside back cover finishes around inside arms. Combination covered armboard and bordered arm cover. Plain spring edge T-shaped seat with pull-over cover. Note novel buttoning of skirt planned for this article, ties in well with buttons of inside back. Dimensions of chair: 28½″ wide, 31½″ deep, 30½″ high. TRADITIONAL UPHOLSTERY: *Materials*—Webbing, 12 yds., 3½″ width; seat springs, 11 No. 2-M; seat spring edge-wire, 10 ft.; seat edge-wire for shaping lower sides of inside back, 4 ft.; back springs, 13 6-inch; burlap, 3½ yds., 40″ width; stuffing, 9 lbs. loose hair; muslin, 3 yds., 36″ width; natural cotton padding, 5 lbs. (8 lbs. if having traditional inner-spring cushion); cover, 6½ yds., 54″ width (bias welt), with skirt, 5½ yds. without; skirt lining, 1 yd., 54″ width; decking, 1 yd., 36″ width; buttons, 3 for back, 16 for skirt; welt cord, 12 yds.; dust cover, 1 yd., 36″ width. For cushion, Secs. 3:61–3:73; for down cushion, 2½ lbs. down-filling and 2 yds. down-proof ticking, 36″ width. For upholstering with compact stuffing: 6 sq. ft., medium, 1″ thick stock for seat edge and deck; 2 sq. ft., firm, 2″ thick for armtops; 6 sq. ft., medium, ¾″ stock for inside arms; 8 sq. ft., medium, 1″ thick for inside back; only 5 lbs. loose stuffing (2 lbs. for understuffing seat, Sec. 7:29; 3 lbs. for inside back, Sec. 10:21; arms not understuffed); 2½ yds. more muslin.   *Work-Steps*—Through muslin casing: frame, seat same as *a;* inside arms Secs. 8:03, 8:07–8:11, 8:13–8:15, 8:21, 8:22; inside back same as *a.* Cover: seat Sec. 13:17; inside arms 14:02, 14:07, 14:08; inside back, cushion same as *a;* outside surfaces 18:01, 18:04–18:06, 18:13–18:15. MODERN UPHOLSTERY: Same as *a* except 7 edge springs for zigzags on seat.

Fig. *c* 1:42—When covering a spring edge seat with patterned goods, a pull-over cover often looks better than a banded one; however, the banded cover is generally more durable. Boxed inside back cover finishes around inside arms. Dimensions of chair: 30″ wide, 29″ deep, 31″ high. TRADITIONAL UPHOLSTERY: *Materials*—Same as *a* except: cover, 7 yds.; skirt lining, 1 yd., 54″ width; welt cord, 20 yds.   *Work-Steps*—Through muslin casing: same as *a.* Cover: seat, inside arms, back, cushion same as *a;* outside surfaces Secs. 18:04–18:06, 18:13–18:15.   MODERN UPHOLSTERY: Same as *a.*

SEC. 1:43   Small modern club chair with loose cushion spring seat, open-frame pad inside arms and back, loose back pillow, Fig. 1:43. Boxed modern square inside arm, back covers. Roll or hard edge seat with pull-over

Fig. 1:43

cover with machine-sewn mitered corners; may be built with rubber webbing and compact stuffing instead of springs. Dimensions of chair: 29″ wide, 33″ deep, 28½″ high. TRADITIONAL UPHOLSTERY: *Materials* —Webbing, 12 yds., 3½″ width; seat springs, 9 No. 1-M; burlap, 4 yds., 40″ width; stuffing, 5 lbs. loose hair; muslin, 3 yds., 36″ width; natural cotton padding, 5 lbs. (11 lbs. if having traditional inner-spring seat cushion, back pillow); cover, 6 yds., 54″ width (bias welt); decking, 1 yd., 36″ width; welt cord, 20 yds.; dust cover, 1 yd., 36″ width. For cushion, pillow, Secs. 3:61–3:73; for down cushion, 3 lbs. down-filling and 2½ yds. down-proof ticking, 36″ width; for down pillow, 1½ lbs. down-filling and 2 yds. down-proof ticking. For upholstering with compact stuffing: 12 sq. ft., medium, 1″ thick stock for seat, inside arms and back; only 2 lbs. loose stuffing (for understuffing seat, Sec. 7:20 or 7:27; inside arms, back not understuffed); 1 yd. more muslin. *Work-Steps*—Through muslin casing: frame Secs. 4:11–4:13, 4:15, 4:18; seat 7:05, 7:07, 7:08, 7:11–7:14, 7:18–7:20 or 7:18, 7:27; inside arms 8:03, 8:09–8:11, 8:13–8:15, 8:21, 8:22; inside back 10:02, 10:10, 10:18, 10:20–10:24. Cover: seat Sec. 13:16; inside arms 14:07–14:09; inside back 16:05, 16:10; cushion, pillow 17:01–17:20; outside surfaces 18:13–18:15. MODERN UPHOLSTERY: Same as traditional except for building seat with zigzag springs or rubber webbing (Secs. 3:21, 7:32; 3:22, 7:33), inside arms and back with rubber webbing (Secs. 8:09A, 10:33, seldom practical unless buying rubber webbing for seat). 5 yds.

zigzags for seat; upholster with loose or compact stuffing. 10 yds., 2½″ width, Standard, rubber webbing for seat; 7 yds., 1⅛″ width preferably, for inside arms and back; upholster with 6 sq. ft., firm, 1″ thick compact stuffing for understuffing seat, same compact stuffing as in traditional work for completing seat and stuffing arms and back; build extra crown (Sec. 5:14) if needed with padding. Pad with synthetic cotton for maximum initial softness.

SEC. 1:44   Small, barrel back club chairs with T-shaped loose cushion spring edge seat, open-frame pad inside arms and back, loose pillow back, Fig. 1:44. Skirt tends to make *b* appear more massive than *a;* but this is somewhat reduced by the slenderizing effect of thin vertical stripes in *b* cover. Back pillow full at edges but not boxed, needs careful pleating at corners. Scroll arms; scooped fronts with panel-type borders. Seat pull-over cover has machine-sewn mitered corners. Dimensions of chairs: 29″ wide, 33″ deep, 28″ high. Chairs identical except for seat border on *a*, flange skirt on *b*.

Fig. *a* 1:44—Traditional Upholstery: *Materials*—Webbing, 12 yds., 3½″ width; seat springs. 9 No. 2-M; seat spring edge-wire, 10 ft.; burlap, 4½ yds., 40″ width; stuffing, 8 lbs. loose hair; muslin, 4 yds., 36″ width; natural cotton padding, 5 lbs. (11 lbs. if having traditional inner-spring cushion, pillow); cover, 6½ yds., 54″ width (bias welt); decking, 1 yd., 36″ width; buttons, 4; welt cord, 18 yds.; dust cover, 1 yd., 36″ width. For cushion, pillow, Secs. 3:61–3:73; for down cushion,

a

b

Fig. 1:44

3 lbs. down-filling and 3 yds. down-proof ticking, 36″ width; for down pillow, 1½ lbs. down-filling and 2 yds. down-proof ticking. For upholstering with compact stuffing: 19 sq. ft., medium, 1″ thick stock for seat edge and deck, inside arms and back; only 2 lbs. loose stuffing (for understuffing seat, Sec. 7:29; arms, back not understuffed), 1½ yds. more muslin. *Work-Steps*—Through muslin casing: frame Secs. 4:11–4:13, 4:15, 4:18; seat 7:05, 7:08, 7:11–7:16, 7:18, 7:19, 7:28; inside arms 8:03, 8:08–8:12, 8:14–8:20; inside back 10:02, 10:10, 10:18–10:24. Cover: seat Secs. 13:16, 13:08; inside arms 14:07, 14:08; inside back 16:05, 16:07; cushion, pillow 17:01–17:20; outside surfaces 18:01, 18:13–18:15. MODERN UPHOLSTERY: Same as traditional except for building seat with zigzag springs (Secs. 3:21, 7:32), inside arms and back with rubber webbing (Secs. 3:22, 8:09A, 10:33). 5 yds. zigzags for seat, 7 edge springs; upholster with loose or compact stuffing. 7 yds., preferably 1⅛″ width, Standard, rubber webbing for inside arms and back; upholster with 13 sq. ft., medium, 1″ thick compact stuffing; build extra crown (Sec. 5:14) if needed with padding. Pad with synthetic cotton for maximum initial softness.

Fig. *b* 1:44—Traditional and modern upholstery same as *a* except: *Materials*—Cover, 1 yd. more for skirt; skirt lining, 1 yd., 54″ width. *Work-Steps*—Cover: seat omit Sec. 13:08; outside surfaces add 18:04–18:06.

SEC. 1:45   Despite differences in shape and style of upholstery, the lounge or club chairs in Fig. 1:45 are similar in construction. Because of their size they are often easier than smaller articles for inexperienced upholsterers to build neatly; minor flaws in arms, sides of a seat or back, etc., are more noticeable and harder to correct on small than on large surfaces. All these chairs can be built equally well and with about the same amount of work with either traditional or modern upholstery.

Fig. *a* 1:45—Plain spring edge seat; pull-over cover, machine-sewn corner miters; border across front of seat only. Scroll, paneled arms. Roll edges on arm posts and sides of inside back, and on sides of a back stitched for flat shape (Sec. 10:25), if upholstering these surfaces with loose stuffing only. Spring inside back; can be built with innerspring unit (Sec. 10:29). Dimensions of chair: 33″ wide, 33″ deep, 38″ high. TRADITIONAL UPHOLSTERY: *Materials*—Webbing, 16 yds., 3½″ width; seat springs, 12 No. 3-S and 2 No. 1-H; seat spring edge-wire, 10 ft.; seat edge-wire for shaping lower sides of inside back, 6 ft.; back springs, 12 8-inch; burlap, 5 yds., 40″ width; stuffing, 14 lbs. loose hair; muslin, 4 yds., 36″ width; natural cotton padding, 5 lbs. (8 lbs. if having traditional inner-spring cushion); cover, 6 yds., 54″ width (bias welt); decking, 1 yd., 36″ width; welt cord, 12 yds.; dust cover, 1 yd., 36″ width. For cushion, Secs. 3:61–3:73; for down cushion, 3 lbs.

Fig. a 1:45

down-filling and 2 yds. down-proof ticking, 36″ width. For upholstering with compact stuffing: 22 sq. ft., medium, 1″ thick stock for seat edge and deck, inside arms and back; only 8 lbs. loose stuffing (2 lbs. for understuffing seat, Sec. 7:29; 2 lbs. for arms, Sec. 5:13; and 3 for back), 4 yds. more muslin. For building inside back with inner-spring unit: 6 × 6 unit plus 3 springs on each side; upholster with loose or compact stuffing to fit (Sec. 10:29). *Work-Steps*—Through muslin casing: frame Secs. 4:11–4:16, 4:18; seat 7:05–7:09, 7:11–7:18, 7:25, 7:29; inside arms 8:03, 8:08–8:12, 8:14, 8:15, 8:21, 8:22; inside back 10:03, 10:11–10:13, 10:15, 10:18–10:25. Cover: seat Sec. 13:17; inside arms 14:06–14:08; inside back 16:05, 16:11; cushion 17:01–17:15; outside surfaces 18:02, 18:13–18:15. Modern Upholstery: Same as traditional except for building seat, inside back with zigzag springs (Secs. 3:21, 7:33, 10:31, 10:32), inside back and arms with rubber webbing (Secs. 3:22, 10:33, 8:09A not practical unless buying webbing for back). 4 yds. zigzags for seat, 6 edge springs, 4 yds. zigzags for inside back; upholster seat, back with loose or compact stuffing, or build back with inner-spring unit and stuffing. 11 yds., 2½″ width, Standard, rubber webbing for inside back and arms; upholster with compact stuffing, 8 sq. ft., firm, 2″ thick stock for back, 10 sq. ft., 1½″ stock for inside arms; build extra crown (Sec. 5:14) if needed with padding. Pad with synthetic cotton for maximum initial softness.

Fig. *b* 1:45—Machine sew pleats at top corners of inside back when preparing cover. Pull-over inside arm covers. Banded cover on

Fig. b 1:45

spring edge seat. Dimensions of chair: 31″ wide, 40″ deep, 36″ high. Traditional Upholstery: *Materials*—Same as *a* except: 12 lbs. loose stuffing; 14 sq. ft. compact stuffing for inside arms and back.   *Work-Steps*—Same as *a* except no armfront panels Sec. 18:02. Modern Upholstery: Same as *a*.

Fig. *c* 1:45—When cover goods have little stretch (Sec. 3:53C, Chap. 19) stuff surfaces fairly hard in order to hold shape; upholstering with soft or medium compact stuffing is not advisable for inexperienced upholsterers; for best results, pad with synthetic cotton. Panels on armfronts, upper sides of back. Banded, bordered cover on spring edge seat. Dimensions of chair: 31″ wide, 33″ deep, 38″ high.   Traditional Upholstery: *Materials*—Same as *a* except: 6 yds. cover (1 yd. more for bias welt if using fabric); 13 yds. welt cord; no extra springs for inside back inner-spring unit.   *Work-Steps*—Through muslin casing: frame, seat, inside arms same as *a*; inside back Secs. 10:03, 10:11–10:13, 10:18–10:24. Cover: seat, inside arms same as *a*; inside back Secs. 16:05, 16:07; cushion, outside surfaces same as *a*. Modern Upholstery: Same as *a*.

Fig. *d* 1:45—Rounded arms; roll edges on arm posts from inside bottom to outside bottom if upholstering arms with loose stuffing only; single-piece cover for inside and outside arms; wood post panels. Boxed inside back cover. Exposed-wood plain spring edge seat, banded cover gimped at bottom; antique nails optional. Welt only on seat banding, and at top of fringe on outside back. Dimensions

Fig. c 1:45

of chair: 26" wide, 38" deep, 33" high. TRADITIONAL UPHOLSTERY: *Materials*—Same as *a* except: seat springs, 12 No. 2-S and 2 No. 1-H; back springs, 12 6-inch; natural cotton padding, 6 lbs. (9 lbs. if having traditional inner-spring cushion); welt cord, 4 yds.; brush fringe, 9 yds.; gimp, 1½ yds.; down cushion, 2½ lbs. down-filling; compact stuffing, 6 sq. ft. for seat edge and deck, 16 sq. ft. for inside arms and back. *Work-Steps*—Same as *a* except cover: outside surfaces Secs. 18:09, 18:13–18:16, 18:18 optional. MODERN UPHOLSTERY: Same as *a*.

Fig. *e* 1:45—Inner-spring unit for this shape inside back will, if large enough, require tie-down shaping along top and upper sides. Thick scroll arms with boxed, paneled fronts; roll edges on arms only, see Fig. *a* 1:45. Plain spring edge seat, banded, bordered cover. Student built. Dimensions of chair: 36" wide, 30" deep, 32" high. TRADITIONAL UPHOLSTERY: *Materials*—Same as *a* except: seat springs, 12 No. 3-S; back springs, 9 8-inch; welt cord, 14 yds.; down cushion, 2 lbs. down-filling; compact stuffing, 6 sq. ft. for seat edge and deck, 16 sq. ft. for inside arms and back, only 10 lbs. loose stuffing (2 lbs. for understuffing seat, Sec. 7:20; 5 lbs. for understuffing arms, Sec. 5:13; and 3 for back), 3 yds. more muslin; inner-spring unit for inside back upholstery, 6 × 6 plus 1 on each side. *Work-Steps*—Through muslin casing: frame, seat, inside arms same as *a;* inside back Secs. 10:03, 10:11–10:13, 10:15, 10:18, 10:19, 10:21–10:24, 10:29. Cover: seat Sec. 13:17; inside arms 14:06, 14:07, 14:09; inside back 16:05, 16:06; cushion same as *a;* outside surfaces 18:02, 18:13–18:15.

d

e

Fig. d, e 1:45

MODERN UPHOLSTERY: Same as *a* except amounts, qualities of materials. [*1*] 4 yds. zigzag springs for seat, 5 edge springs, 4 yds. zigzags for inside back. [*2*] 11 yds. rubber webbing for inside back and arms; compact stuffing, 8 sq. ft., firm, 2″ thick for inside back, 10 sq. ft. 1½″ stock for inside arms.

SEC. 1:46   Major difference between the lounge or club chairs in Fig. 1:46 is the arms; T-shaped in *a*, square-scroll in *b*; simplest and usually most durable upholstery for both types is with compact stuffing. Plain back pillow in *a* is down-filled; pillow usually is boxed, as in *b*, for inner-spring, foam rubber, or polyfoam unit filling.

Fig. *a* 1:46—Inside back can be either pad or spring upholstery. Roll edges on tops of T-shaped arms if upholstering them with loose stuffing only; recommend building armtops with 3½ sq. ft., medium, 1″ to 2″ thick compact stuffing, no understuffing. Plain spring edge seat, banded cover. Dimensions of chair: 27″ wide, 34″ deep, 31″ high. Traditional Upholstery: *Materials*—Webbing, 16 yds., 3½″ width; seat springs, 12 No. 3-S; seat spring edge-wire, 10 ft.; back springs (optional), 6 6-inch; burlap, 5 yds., 40″ width; stuffing, 10 lbs. loose hair; muslin, 4 yds., 36″ width; natural cotton padding, 6 lbs. (12 lbs. if having traditional inner-spring seat cushion, back pillow); cover, 8¾ yds., 54″ width (bias welt); decking, 1 yd., 36″ width; welt cord, 15 yds.; dust cover, 1 yd., 36″ width. For cushion, pillow, Secs. 3:61–3:73 (traditional inner-spring type not recommended for pillow); for down cushion, pillow: each, 2½ lbs. down-filling and 2 yds. down-proof ticking, 36″ width. For upholstering with compact stuffing: 18

a

b

Fig. 1:46

sq. ft., medium, 1″ thick stock for seat edge and deck, inside arms below armtops, and inside back, only 5½ lbs. loose stuffing (2 lbs. for understuffing seat, Sec. 7:29; ½ lb. for understuffing lower inside arms, Sec. 5:13; 3 lbs. for inside back, Sec. 10:21), 3 yds. more muslin. *Work-Steps*—Through muslin casing: frame Secs. 4:11–4:15, 4:18; seat 7:05–7:08, 7:11–7:18, 7:25, 7:29; inside arms 8:03, 8:09–8:11, 8:13–8:15, 8:21, 8:22; inside back, pad, 10:02, 10:10, 10:18, 10:22–10:24; inside back, spring, 10:03, 10:11, 10:13, 10:15, 10:18, 10:22–10:24. Cover: seat Sec. 13:17; inside arms 14:06, 14:07, 14:10; inside back 16:05, 16:06; cushion, pillow 17:01–17:20; outside surfaces 18:13–18:15.   Modern Upholstery: Same as traditional except for building seat and inside back with zigzag springs (Secs. 3:21, 7:32, 10:31), inside back and lower inside arms with rubber webbing (Secs. 3:22, 8:09A, 10:33; rubber webbing for arms impractical buy unless using it for inside back). 4 yds. zigzags for seat, 6 edge springs, 4 yds. zigzags for inside back; upholster with loose or compact stuffing. 12 yds., preferably 1⅛″ width, Standard, rubber webbing for inside arms and back; upholster with 8 sq. ft., firm, 1″ thick compact stuffing for inside back, 5 sq. ft., medium, 1″ stock for lower inside arms; build extra crown (Sec. 5:14) if needed with padding. Pad armtops with synthetic cotton for maximum initial softness.

Fig. *b* 1:46—Back pillow should have been two or three inches taller for better comfort and appearance. Inside back can be pad or spring upholstery. Roll edges at front of arms from inside bottom to end of scroll at top outside if upholstering them with loose stuffing only; recommend building arms with compact stuffing, no understuffing; regardless of stuffing, there should be fairly sharp breaks between all surfaces of square-scroll. Bordered armfronts. Plain spring edge seat, banded cover. Student built. Dimensions of chair: 31″ wide, 33″ deep, 34″ high. Traditional Upholstery: *Materials*—Same as *a* except: welt cord, 18 yds.; for compact stuffing, 11 sq. ft., medium, 1″ thick stock for inside arms. *Work-Steps*—Through muslin casing: same as *a*. Cover: seat Sec. 13:17; inside arms 14:06–14:08; inside back, cushion, pillow, outside surfaces same as *a*.   Modern Upholstery: Same as *a* except use traditional work compact stuffing, above, for inside arms.

SEC. 1:47   Much of the comfort of a Tuxedo wing chair, Fig. 1:47, is due to the central area of the thick back being pulled in by buttons (Chapter 21); the lower area, not pulled in, offers greater lumbar support. Solid, spring inside back; stitch flat top (Sec. 10:25) if upholstering it with loose stuffing only; back can be built with inner-spring unit mounted on traditional webbing or on zigzag springs (Secs. 10:29, 10:32). Top of inside back cover boxed; boxing sides might save cover goods. Pad

Fig. 1:47

wings; roll edges at top, front if upholstering with loose stuffing only; pull-over inside wing covers. Pad scroll arms; roll edges at front if upholstering them with loose stuffing only; boxed fronts. Roll or hard edge T-shaped loose cushion spring seat; pull-over cover; machine-sewn mitered corners; border. Welted bottom of seat. Dimensions of chair: 33″ wide, 34″ deep, 36½″ high. TRADITIONAL UPHOLSTERY: *Materials*—Webbing, 12 yds., 3½″ width; seat springs, 9 No. 1-M; back springs, 12 8-inch; burlap, 3½ yds., 40″ width; stuffing, 8 lbs. loose hair; muslin, 4 yds., 36″ width; natural cotton padding, 5 lbs. (8 lbs. if having traditional inner-spring cushion); cover, 7 yds., 54″ width (bias welt); decking, 1 yd., 36″ width; buttons, 9; welt cord, 20 yds.; dust cover, 1 yd., 36″ width. For cushion: Secs. 3:61–3:73; for down cushion, 3 lbs. down-filling, 3 yds. down-proof ticking, 36″ width. For upholstering with compact stuffing: 18 sq. ft., medium, 1″ thick stock for seat edge and deck, inside arms and wings; 8 sq. ft., 1½″ thick for inside back; only 6 lbs. loose stuffing (2 lbs. for understuffing seat, Sec. 7:20 or 7:27; 1 lb. for inside arms and wings, Sec. 5:13; 3 lbs. for inside back, Sec. 10:21), 3 yds. more muslin. For upholstering inside back with inner-spring unit: 5 × 6 unit, 4 lbs. loose stuffing, or 15 sq. ft., firm, 1½″ thick compact stuffing and complete as for upholstering with compact stuffing, above. *Work-Steps*—Through muslin casing: frame Secs. 4:11–4:16, 4:18; seat, 7:05–7:09, 7:11–7:14, 7:18–7:20 or 7:18, 7:27; inside arms 8:03, 8:08–8:12, 8:14, 8:15, 8:21, 8:22; inside wings 9:05–9:12; inside back 10:03, 10:11, 10:13, 10:15, 10:18–10:25, 10:28, 10:29. Cover: seat Secs. 13:08, 13:16; inside arms 14:06, 14:09; inside wings 15:01; inside back 16:07, 16:09, 16:11; cushion 17:01–

17:15; outside surfaces 18:01, 18:12–18:14, 13:06, 18:15. MODERN UPHOLSTERY: Same as traditional except for building seat and inside back with zigzag springs or rubber webbing (Secs. 3:21, 7:32, 10:31, 10:32; 3:22, 7:33, 10:33), inside arms and wings with rubber webbing (Secs. 8:09A, 9:06, impractical unless buying rubber webbing for seat and/or inside back). 5 yds. zigzags for seat, 3½ yds. zigzags for inside back; upholster with loose or compact stuffing, or with inner-spring unit for back. 10 yds., 2½″ width, Standard, rubber webbing for seat; 7 yds., preferably 1⅛″ width, for inside arms, wings, back; upholster with compact stuffing, 6 sq. ft., firm, 1½″ thick for seat, same as for traditional work for inside arms and wings, 8 sq. ft., medium, 2½″ to 3″ thick for inside back; build extra crown (Sec. 5:14) if needed with padding. Pad inside arms, wings, back with synthetic cotton for maximum initial softness.

SEC. 1:48   Although traditional in design, the wing chairs in Fig. 1:48 are well suited to modern upholstery, particularly zigzag springs and rubber webbing construction. All items have loose cushion roll or hard edge spring seats, spring backs with plain pull-over covers. Main differences are in arm and wing treatments except *b*, which has a single-piece arm-wing cover. Roll edges on inside arms and wings if upholstering them with loose stuffing only.

Fig. *a* 1:48—Bordered seat cover. Bordered armfronts, made of one stripe of goods. Dimensions of chair: 30″ wide, 34″ deep, 42″ high. TRADITIONAL UPHOLSTERY: *Materials*—Webbing, 13 yds., 3½″ width; seat springs, 9 No. 1-S; back springs, 12 6-inch; burlap, 4 yds., 40″ width; stuffing, 12 lbs. loose hair; muslin, 3 yds., 36″ width; natural cotton padding, 4 lbs. (7 lbs. if having traditional inner-spring cushion); cover, 5½ yds., 54″ width (bias welt); decking, 1 yd., 36″ width; welt cord, 13 yds.; dust cover, 1 yd., 36″ width. For cushion, Secs. 3:61–3:73; for down cushion, 2½ lbs. down-filling, and 2 yds. down-proof ticking, 36″ width. For upholstering with compact stuffing: 20 sq. ft., medium, 1″ thick stock for seat edge and deck, inside arms, wings and back; only 7 lbs. loose stuffing (2 lbs. for understuffing seat, Sec. 7:20 or 7:27; 2 lbs. for understuffing inside arms and wings, Sec. 5:13; 3 lbs. for back, Sec. 10:21), 2½ yds. more muslin. *Work-Steps*—Frame Secs. 4:11–4:15, 4:18; seat 7:05–7:08, 7:11–7:14, 7:18, 7:24, 7:27; inside arms 8:03, 8:08–8:12, 8:14, 8:15, 8:21, 8:22; inside wings 9:05–9:12; inside back 10:03, 10:11, 10:13, 10:15, 10:18, 10:19, 10:21–10:24. Cover: seat Secs. 13:08, 13:16; inside arms 14:07, 14:08; inside wings 15:01; inside back 16:05, 16:06; cushion 17:01–17:15; outside surfaces 18:12–18:15. MODERN UPHOLSTERY: Same as traditional except for building seat and inside back with zigzag springs or rubber webbing (Secs. 3:21, 7:32, 10:31; 3:22, 7:33, 10:33), inside

Fig. a, b 1:48   a   b

arms with rubber webbing (Sec. 8:09A, impractical unless buying rubber webbing for seat and/or back). 5 yds. zigzags for seat, 4 yds. zigzags for back; upholster with loose or compact stuffing. 12 yds., 2½″ width, Standard, rubber webbing for seat; 8 yds., preferably 1⅛″ width, for inside arms and back; upholster with compact stuffing, 6 sq. ft., firm, 1½″ thick for seat; 8 sq. ft., medium, 2″ thick for inside back; same as for traditional work for inside arms, wings; build extra crown (Sec. 5:14) if needed with padding. Pad inside back, arms, wings with synthetic cotton for maximum initial softness.

Fig. *b* 1:48—Single-piece inside arm-wing cover; for best results, starting with the stuffing build these surfaces as a unit; bordered arm-wing covers are the most practical. Pull-over seat cover. Dimensions of chair: 27″ wide, 33″ deep, 35″ high. Traditional Upholstery: *Materials*—Same as *a* except: back springs, 9 6-inch; fringe, 5 yds. *Work-Steps*—Through muslin casing: frame, seat same as *a;* inside arms, wings (upholster simultaneously) Secs. 8:03, 8:08–8:12, 8:14, 8:-15, 8:21, 8:22, 9:05–9:12; inside back same as *a.* Cover: seat Sec. 13:16; inside arms-wings 14:12, 15:03; inside back, cushion same as *a;* outside surfaces 18:09, 18:12–18:15. Modern Upholstery: Same as *a.*

Fig. *c* 1:48—These inside wings often are somewhat softly upholstered (but not weak) as, with their depth and height, this type chair seems designed for comfortable napping; be careful not to destroy shape of inside wings when upholstering. Note two styles of

Fig. c 1:48

covering wings; the more conventional pull-around inside wing cover finishing on the outside surface, and somewhat unusual treatment of finishing the outside wing cover over the inside cover on the top and front surfaces (finish the outside cover into welt, or cover tacking line with gimp before installing decorative nails). Scroll arms, bordered fronts. Plain pull-over seat cover. Bottom of seat, outside arm and back covers are welted. Dimensions of chair: 31″ wide, 31″ deep, 40″ high. TRADITIONAL UPHOLSTERY: *Materials*—Same as *a* except: muslin, 4 yds.; natural cotton padding, 5 lbs. (8 lbs. if having traditional inner-spring cushion); cover, 6 yds.; gimp, trim nails as required. *Work-Steps*—Through muslin casing: same as *a*. Cover: seat Sec. 13:16; inside arms, wings (unless finished as described above), back, cushion same as *a*; outside surfaces 18:12–18:14, 13:06, 18:15. MODERN UPHOLSTERY: Same as *a*.

Fig. *d* 1:48—Scroll arms, plain pull-around cover; pleat, finish cover with button on armfront. Plain, pull-over cover on T-shaped seat; machine sew mitered corners of cover. Dimensions of chair: 30″ wide, 34″ deep, 40″ high. TRADITIONAL UPHOLSTERY: *Materials*—Same as *a*, plus 2 buttons. *Work-Steps*—Same as *a* except: no seat border; no armfront border; button on armfront, Sec. 18:01. MODERN UPHOLSTERY: Same as *a*.

Fig. *e* 1:48—Inside back buttons chiefly for looks. Double-scroll inside arms somewhat unusual; piecing cover at lower front of inside arm, just behind vertical scroll, may save considerable yardage. Plain pull-over cover on T-shaped seat; machine sew mitered corners of cover. Dimensions of chair: 31″ wide, 33″ deep, 39″ high. TRADI-

d

Fig. d, e 1:48   e

tional Upholstery: *Materials*—Webbing, 15 yds., 3½″ width; seat springs, 9 No. 1-H; back springs, 12 6-inch; burlap, 5 yds., 40″ width; stuffing, 13 lbs. loose hair; muslin, 3½ yds., 36″ width; natural cotton padding, 5 lbs. (8 lbs. if having traditional inner-spring cushion); cover, 5 yds., 54″ width (bias welt); decking, 1 yd., 36″ width; welt cord, 13 yds.; buttons, 5; antique nails, gimp, as wanted; dust cover, 1 yd., 36″ width. For cushion, Secs. 3:61–3:73; for down cushion, 3 lbs. down-filling and 2 yds. down-proof ticking, 36″ width. For upholstering with compact stuffing: 21 sq. ft., medium, 1″ thick stock for seat edge and deck, inside arms, wings and back; only 7 lbs. loose stuffing (2 lbs. for understuffing seat, Sec. 7:20 or 7:27; 2 lbs. for understuffing inside arms, Sec. 5:13; 3 lbs. for inside back, Sec. 10:21), 2½ yds. more muslin.   *Work-Steps*—Through muslin casing: same as *a*. Cover: seat Sec. 13:16; inside arms 14:07, 14:09; inside wings, back, cushion same as *a*; outside surfaces 21:03, 18:01, 18:12–18:15, 18:16, 18:18.   Modern Upholstery: Same as *a* except amounts, kinds of materials: zigzag springs for seat, 4 yds.; zigzags for inside back, 3 yds.; rubber webbing for seat, 9 yds., for inside back, arms, and wings, 12 yds.; compact stuffing for seat, 6 sq. ft., 1½″ thick, for inside back, 8 sq. ft., 2″ thick, for inside arms and wings, 9 sq. ft., 1″ thick.

SEC. 1:49   The major difference between wing chairs in Figs. 1:48 and 1:49 is spring edge seats. Seats with spring edges are generally more comfortable than those with roll or hard edges, and most large wing chairs are built primarily for maximum comfort; however, many seat frames are suitable only for a roll, hard, or spring edge (Secs. 3:16B, 5:04B, C, D, 7:00A). For all articles in Fig. 1:49: loose cushion spring edge seats, banded seat cover; roll edges on inside arms and wings if upholstering them with loose stuffing only; spring inside backs. There is little difference in either the amount or difficulty of work between traditional and modern upholstery of these chairs, but *c* is not recommended as a first project.

Fig. *a* 1:49—This upholstery was made extra puffy for a special appearance of softness and comfort; it must not be too weak to hold shape. Scroll armfronts, as shown, are paneled; borders may be easier to use (Secs. 11:05, 11:15G, 18:13F). Dimensions of chair: 32″ wide, 36″ deep, 40″ high. TRADITIONAL UPHOLSTERY: *Materials*—Webbing, 15 yds., 3½″ width; seat springs, 9 No. 3-M; seat spring edge-wire, 10 ft.; back springs, 9 8-inch and 3 6-inch; burlap, 5 yds., 40″ width; stuffing, 15 lbs. loose hair; muslin, 5 yds., 36″ width; natural cotton padding, 5 lbs. (8 lbs. if having traditional inner-spring cushion); cover, 7 yds., 54″ width (bias welt); decking, 1 yd., 36″ width; welt cord, 12 yds.; dust cover, 1 yd., 36″ width. For cushion, Secs. 3:61–3:73; for down cushion, 3 lbs. down-filling and 2 yds. down-proof ticking, 36″ width. For upholstering with compact stuffing: 26 sq. ft., medium, 1″ thick stock for seat edge and deck, inside arms, wings and back; only

Fig. a 1:49

10 lbs. loose hair (2 lbs. for understuffing seat, Sec. 7:29; 4 lbs. for inside arms, 1 for wings, Sec. 5:13; 3 lbs. for back, Sec. 10:21), 5 yds. more muslin. *Work-Steps*—Through muslin casing: frame Secs. 4:11–4:16, 4:18; seat 7:05–7:08, 7:11–7:16, 7:18, 7:25, 7:29; inside arms 8:03, 8:08–8:12, 8:14, 8:15, 8:21, 8:22; inside wings 9:05–9:12; inside back 10:03, 10:11, 10:13, 10:15, 10:18, 10:19, 10:21–10:24. Cover: seat Sec. 13:17; inside arms 14:06, 14:08; inside wings 15:01; inside back 16:05, 16:06; cushion 17:01–17:15; outside surfaces 18:12–18:15. MODERN UPHOLSTERY: Same as traditional except for building seat and inside back with zigzag springs (Secs. 3:21, 7:32, 10:31); inside back, arms, wings with rubber webbing (Secs. 3:22, 8:09A, 9:06, 10:33; rubber webbing for arms, wings impractical unless buying it for back). 4 yds. zigzag springs for seat, 5 edge springs; 4 yds. zigzags for back; upholster with loose or compact stuffing. 12 yds., 1⅛″ width, Standard, rubber webbing for inside back, arms, wings; upholster inside back with 4 sq. ft., medium, 3″ thick compact stuffing, inside arms and wings with 12 sq. ft., medium, 1½″ thick stock; build extra crown (Sec. 5:14) if needed with padding. Pad with synthetic cotton for maximum initial softness.

Fig. *b* 1:49—Wings similar to Fig. *c* 1:48. Modified T-shaped arms, Fig. *a* 1:46. Exposed-wood bottom of seat, arms, back. Dimensions of chair: 26″ wide, 30″ deep, 34″ high. TRADITIONAL UPHOLSTERY: *Materials*—Same as *a* except: [1] gimp, 3¾ yds.; [2] antique nails, as wanted; [3] for upholstering with compact stuffing, seat same as *a;* for armtops, 2½ sq. ft., medium, 1″ to 1½″ thick stock; for inside wings and lower arms, 11 sq. ft., medium, 1″ thick stock; only 6½ lbs. loose stuffing (2 lbs. for understuffing seat, Sec. 7:29; ½ lb. for lower arms, Sec. 5:13; 4 lbs. for inside back, Sec. 10:29), 4 yds. more muslin. *Work-Steps*—Through muslin casing: Frame as *a;* seat Secs. 7:05, 7:07, 7:08, 7:11–7:16, 7:18, 7:25, 7:29; inside arms 8:03, 8:09–8:11, 8:13–8:15, 8:21, 8:22; inside wings 9:05–9:12; inside back same as *a*. Cover: seat Sec. 13:17; inside arms 14:06, 14:07, 14:10; inside wings, back, cushion same as *a;* outside surfaces 18:12–18:17. MODERN UPHOLSTERY: Same as *a* except for inside back built with rubber webbing, upholster with 5½ sq. ft., medium, 2½″ to 3″ thick compact stuffing.

Fig. *c* 1:49—Extensive tufting and covering with leather are not recommended as first projects. When covering with leather or other goods having little stretch (Secs. 3:53C, 3:54, Chapter 19), build surfaces fairly hard in order to hold cover in shape. The first step in upholstering *c* is to plan channeling and tufting (Chapters 20, 21). Bordered armfronts. For matching ottoman, see Fig. *d* 1:51. Dimensions of chair: 31″ wide, 38″ deep, 38″ high. TRADITIONAL UPHOLSTERY: *Materials*—Same as Fig. *a* 1:49 except: [1] seat springs, 12 No. 3-M; [2] back springs, 12 8-inch; [3] cover, same yardage as

b

c

Fig. b, c 1:49

a, or 70 sq. ft. leather; [4] buttons, 18; [5] for upholstering with compact stuffing, only 6 lbs. loose stuffing (2 lbs. for understuffing seat,

2 for inside arms, 2 for inside back), 1½ yds. more muslin. *Work-Steps*—Through muslin casing: Frame, seat, inside arms, wings same as *a;* inside back Secs. 10:03, 10:11, 10:13, 10:15, 10:18, 10:21, 21:03–21:08. Cover: handling leather Secs. 19:00–19:06; seat 13:17; inside arms 14:06–14:08; inside wings 15:01; inside back 21:09; cushion same as *a;* outside surfaces 18:01, 18:12–18:15. MODERN UPHOLSTERY: Same as *a* except for inside back built with rubber webbing, upholster with 6 sq. ft., medium, 2½″ to 3″ thick compact stuffing.

SEC. 1:50   Except for the seat, the frame of many articles of the type in Fig. *a* and *b* 1:50 is made of metal rods, reeds, or strips of bamboo, and is called a "tubular" or "Turkish" frame. Briefly, those parts of the frame are tightly wrapped with doubled strips of wet burlap about 4 inches wide and, when dry, the various upholstery items (burlap, muslin, etc.) are stitched to it; one such item is two layers of burlap or one of canvas completely filling the arm and back cavities as the base, instead of webbing, for the springs. Tubular frames are extremely difficult to upholster or merely re-cover properly, and should not be attempted by inexperienced upholsterers. Also, any article with extensive tufting, as in *c,* is not recommended as a first project. The articles in Fig. 1:50 have conventional frames and are upholstered the usual ways. Upholster inside arms of *a* and *b* as parts of inside backs, with roll edges if upholstering them with loose stuffing only. First step in upholstering is to plan tufting (Chapter 21).

Fig. *a* 1:50—Bordered arm- and back-top covers. Solid, bridle-built spring edge seat, spring edge finishing on armposts. Simplest upholstery is with compact stuffing; be careful not to bridle-build the seat too thick. Banded and bordered seat cover. Dimensions of chair: 28″ wide, 26″ deep, 33″ high. TRADITIONAL UPHOLSTERY: *Materials* —Webbing, 13 yds., 3½″ width; seat springs, 11 No. 3-H; seat spring edge-wire, 5 ft.; back springs, 18 6-inch; burlap, 4 yds., 40″ width; stuffing, 12 lbs. loose hair; muslin, 2½ yds., 36″ width; natural cotton padding, 4 lbs.; cover, 5¾ yds., 54″ width (bias welt); buttons, 24; welt cord, 10 yds.; dust cover, 1 yd., 36″ width. For upholstering with compact stuffing: 13 sq. ft., medium, 2″ thick stock; only 3 lbs. loose stuffing (for understuffing seat, Sec. 7:28), 1 yd. more muslin. *Work-Steps*—Through muslin casing: frame Secs. 4:11–4:15, 4:18; seat 7:01, 7:05, 7:07, 7:08, 7:11–7:16, 7:18, 7:23, 7:29; inside arms and back 8:03, 8:09, 8:10, 10:03, 10:11, 10:13, 10:17, 21:03–21:07. Cover: seat Sec. 13:17; inside arms and back 21:09; outside surfaces 18:01, 18:14, 18:15. MODERN UPHOLSTERY: Same as traditional except for building seat and inside back with zigzag springs (Secs. 3:21, 7:32, 10:31), inside back and arms with rubber webbing (Secs. 3:22, 10:33, 8:09A impractical unless buying rubber webbing for inside back). 4 yds. zigzag springs for seat, 5 edge springs; 3 yds. zigzags for back; upholster

Fig. a 1:50

with loose or compact stuffing. 8 yds., 1⅛″ width, Standard, rubber webbing for inside back and arms; upholster with 9 sq. ft., medium, 2½″ to 3″ thick compact stuffing; build extra crown (Sec. 5:14) if needed with padding. Pad with synthetic cotton for maximum puffiness and initial softness.

Fig. *b* 1:50—Bordered arm- and back-top covers. Solid bridle-built spring edge seat, spring edge finishing on arm posts. Simplest upholstery is with compact stuffing; be careful not to bridle-build seat too thick. Banded seat cover. Flange skirt; pleat in middle of "front" eliminates need of piecing cover or railroading it. Dimensions of chaise longue: 78″ wide (front), 26″ deep, 33″ high. TRADITIONAL UPHOLSTERY: *Materials*—Webbing, 20 yds., 3½″ width; seat springs, 32 No. 3-M or 4-M; seat spring edge-wire, 18 ft.; back springs, 26 6-inch; burlap, 10 yds., 40″ width; stuffing, 22 lbs. loose hair; muslin, 6 yds., 36″ width; natural cotton padding, 10 lbs.; cover, 11½ yds., 54″ width (bias welt) with skirt, 10 yds. without; skirt lining, 1½ yds., 54″ width; buttons, 34; welt cord, 16 yds.; dust cover, 2½ yds., 36″ width. For upholstering with compact stuffing: 32 sq. ft., medium, 1½″ thick stock, only 10 lbs. loose stuffing (for understuffing seat, Sec. 7:28; inside arms, back not understuffed), 3 yds. more muslin. *Work-Steps* —Through muslin casing and cover same as *a* plus skirt, Secs. 18:04– 18:06. MODERN UPHOLSTERY: Same as *a* except amounts: 11 yds.

Fig. b 1:50

zigzag springs for seat, 18 edge springs; 3 yds. zigzags for inside back. 8 yds. rubber webbing for inside back and arms and 12 sq. ft. compact stuffing.

    Fig. *c* 1:50—Styles other than tufting can be used for the contemporary chaise longue in *c*, but it is very practical for barrel backs. Inside back is spring construction for traditional upholstery; can more easily be built with webbing and compact stuffing. Open-frame, pad, scroll inside arms, boxed front cover; for simplest work upholster with compact stuffing. Loose cushion spring seat with roll or hard edge if upholstering it with loose stuffing only; can be upholstered with rubber webbing and compact stuffing. Any filling can be used for the shaped seat cushion, but foam rubber or polyfoam are the most practical. Dimensions of chaise longue: 27″ wide, 78″ deep, 34″ high. TRADITIONAL UPHOLSTERY: *Materials*—Webbing, 20 yds., 3½″ width; seat springs, 26 2-M; back springs, 12 6-inch; burlap, 6 yds., 40″ width; stuffing, 12 lbs. loose hair; muslin, 6 yds., 36″ width; natural cotton padding, 6 lbs. (11 lbs. if having traditional inner-spring cushion); cover, 8 yds., 54″ width (bias welt); decking, 2 yds., 36″ width; buttons, 7; welt cord, 21 yds.; dust cover, 2½ yds., 36″ width.

Fig. c 1:50

For cushion, Secs. 3:61–3:73; for down cushion, 4 lbs. down-filling and 5 yds. down-proof ticking, 36″ width. For upholstering with compact stuffing: 18 sq. ft., medium, 1″ thick stock for seat, inside arms; 9 sq. ft., medium, 1½″ stock for inside back; only 10 lbs. loose stuffing (4 lbs. for understuffing seat, Sec. 7:20 or 7:27; 6 lbs. for inside back Sec. 10:21; arms not understuffed), 4½ yds. more muslin. *Work-Steps* —Through muslin casing: frame Secs. 4:11–4:16, 4:18; seat 7:02, 7:05– 7:08, 7:11–7:14, 7:18, 7:19 or 7:27; inside arms 8:03, 8:08–8:12, 8:14, 8:15, 8:21, 8:22; inside back 10:03, 10:11, 10:13, 10:17, 21:03–21:07. Cover: seat Sec. 13:11; inside arms 14:06–14:09; inside back 21:09; cushion 17:01–17:15; outside surfaces 18:01, 18:13–18:15. MODERN UPHOLSTERY: Same as traditional except for building seat with zigzag springs (from side to side) or rubber webbing (Secs. 3:21, 7:32; 3:22, 7:33), inside back with zigzags or rubber webbing (Secs. 10:31; 10:33), inside arms with rubber webbing (Sec. 8:09A impractical unless buying rubber webbing for seat or back). 9 yds. zigzag springs for seat, 4 yds. for inside back; upholster with loose or compact stuffing. 19 yds., 2½″ width, Standard, rubber webbing for seat; 9 yds., preferably 1⅛″ width webbing for inside back and arms; upholster with compact stuffing, 14 sq. ft., medium, 1½″ thick stock for seat; 9 sq. ft., medium, 2½″ to 3″ thick stock for inside back; 8 sq. ft., 1″ thick for arms; build extra crown (Sec. 5:14) if needed with padding. Pad with synthetic cotton for maximum puffiness and initial softness.

SEC. 1:51   Most stools, ottomans, etc., Fig. 1:51, can be either traditional pad or spring upholstery; for simplest work, upholster with rubber webbing (for open-frame articles) and fairly thick compact stuffing. Ottoman-type articles, *d–g*, often are companion pieces to chairs (Fig. *d* 1:51 and Fig. *c* 1:49); make the top of the chair cushion or solid seat and the top of the ottoman the same height. Chapter 22 deals with stool, ottoman, and bench upholstery.

Fig. *a* 1:51—For a needle-point cover, make seat cover about 2 inches larger than top of frame, boxing (Sec. 11:13C) about 2½ inches wider than the circumference of the seat rail. Roll edge on seat if upholstering it with loose stuffing only. Dimensions of stool: 16″ diameter seat, 18″ high. TRADITIONAL UPHOLSTERY: *Materials*— Webbing, 3 yds.; 3½″ width; seat springs, 4 No. 1-H; burlap, ½ yd., 40″ width; stuffing, 3 lbs. loose hair; muslin, 1 yd., 36″ width; natural cotton padding, 1 lb.; cover, ⅔ yd., 54″ width; welt cord, 2 yds.; dust cover, ½ yd., 36″ width. For upholstering with compact stuffing: 2½ sq. ft., medium, 1½″ thick stock; only 1 lb. loose stuffing (for under-stuffing seat, Sec. 7:20), ½ yd. more muslin. *Work-Steps*—Through muslin casing: frame Secs. 4:11–4:13, 4:18; seat 7:05, 7:07, 7:08, 7:11–7:14, 7:18, 7:19. Cover: seat Sec. 13:14; outside surfaces 18:15. MODERN UPHOLSTERY: Same as traditional except build seat with rubber webbing (Secs. 3:22, 7:33). 3 yds., 2½″ width, Standard, rubber webbing; upholster with 16½″ diameter slab of medium stock thick enough to build seat to wanted height; build extra crown (Sec. 5:14) if needed with padding. Pad with synthetic cotton for maximum initial softness.

Fig. *b* 1:51—Upholstered-to-floor stool with boxed and bordered seat cover; bordered area (below boxing) often is channeled (Chapter 20). Solid base seat; roll edge if upholstering it with loose stuffing only. Dimensions of stool: 15″ diameter seat, 17″ high. TRADITIONAL UPHOLSTERY: *Materials*—Seat springs, 5 No. 1-H; burlap, 2 yds., 40″ width; stuffing, 3 lbs. loose hair; muslin, 1 yd., 36″ width; natural cotton padding, 2 lbs.; cover, 1 yd., 54″ width; welt cord, 3½ yds.; dust cover, ½ yd., 36″ width. For upholstering with compact stuffing: same as *a*. *Work-Steps*—Through muslin casing: frame Sec. 4:18; seat 7:07,

Fig. a, b 1:51   *a*   *b*

7:09, 7:11–7:14, 7:18, 7:19. Cover: seat Secs. 13:14, 13:08; outside surfaces 18:11, 18:15. MODERN UPHOLSTERY: Same as traditional but upholster seat with 15½″ diameter slab of medium stock thick enough to build seat to wanted height; see *a* for crown, padding.

Fig. *c* 1:51—Fireside bench. Roll edge on spring seat if upholstering it with loose stuffing only; pull-over seat cover. Dimensions of bench: 22″ wide, 18″ deep, 17″ high. TRADITIONAL UPHOLSTERY: *Materials*—Webbing, 6 yds., 3½″ width; seat springs, 12 No. 1-H; burlap, 1½ yds., 40″ width; stuffing, 6 lbs. loose hair; muslin, 1½ yds., 36″ width; natural cotton padding, 1½ lbs.; cover, ¾ yd., 54″ width; dust cover; ⅔ yds., 36″ width. For upholstering with compact stuffing: 4½ sq. ft., medium, 1½″ thick stock; only 3 lbs. loose stuffing (for understuffing seat, Sec. 7:20), 1½ yds. more muslin. *Work-Steps*—Through muslin casing: same as *a*. Cover: seat Sec. 13:11; outside surfaces 18:15. MODERN UPHOLSTERY: Same as traditional except for building seat with zigzag springs or rubber webbing (Secs. 3:21, 7:32; 3:22, 7:33). 3 yds. zigzags; upholster with loose or compact stuffing. 6 yds., 2½″ width, Standard, rubber webbing; upholster with slab of medium compact stuffing thick enough to build seat to wanted height and 1″ wider and deeper than top of seat frame; see *a* for crown and padding.

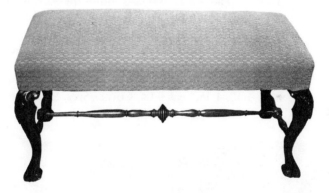

Fig. c 1:51

Fig. *d* 1:51—Tufted ottoman, leather cover, not recommended as a first project. When covering with leather or other goods having little stretch (Secs. 3:53C, 3:54, Chapter 19), build surfaces fairly hard in order to hold cover in shape. Plan tufting (Chapter 21). *d* as built, plain spring edge seat, banded and bordered cover. Spring edges must be exceptionally well tied to prevent undue wobble or tilt of seat. Simpler construction is to build up frame with wood strips to 3 inches less than the wanted finished height of the article, and upholster with rubber webbing and compact stuffing (Modern Upholstery, below), and cover with two borders. Dimensions of ottoman: 22″ wide, 18″ deep, 17″ high. TRADITIONAL UPHOLSTERY: *Materials*—Webbing, 4 yds., 3½″ width; seat springs, 12 No. 3-M; seat spring edge-wire, 8 ft.;

burlap, 1 yd., 40″ width; stuffing, 5 lbs. loose hair; muslin, 1 yd., 36″ width; natural cotton padding, 2 lbs.; cover, 1¾ yds., 54″ width, or 18 sq. ft. leather; buttons, 22; welt cord, 4½ yds.; dust cover, 1 yd., 36″ width. For upholstering with compact stuffing: 3½ sq. ft., medium, 1½ to 2″ thick stock; only 3 lbs. loose stuffing (2 lbs. for understuffing seat, Sec. 7:20; 1 lb. for stuffing banding area), 1 yd. more muslin; bridle-build seat lightly (Sec. 7:23). *Work-Steps*—Through muslin casing: frame Secs. 4:11, 4:12, 4:18; seat 19:00, 7:05, 7:07, 7:08, 7:11–7:16, 7:18, 21:03–21:07, 7:25. Cover: seat Secs. 19:00–19:06, 21:09, 13:17; outside surfaces 18:01, 18:15. Modern Upholstery: Same as traditional except for building seat with zigzag springs (Secs. 3:21, 7:32). 3 yds. zigzags for seat, 14 edge springs; upholster with loose or compact stuffing. For upholstering with rubber webbing (Sec. 3:22), as briefly described above, 6 yds., 2½″ width, Standard, rubber webbing; upholster with 24 × 20-inch slab of medium 2″ to 3″ thick compact stuffing. Install webbing (Sec. 7:33), compact stuffing, tuft (Sec. 21:08); complete as traditional work; crown, padding same as *a*.

Fig. *e* 1:51—Open-lid or box ottoman, solid-base lid; boxed cover for lid, bordered cover for box. Compact stuffing is the most practical, comfortable, durable upholstery; build crown (Sec. 5:14) with padding. Pad with synthetic cotton for maximum puffiness and initial softness. Dimensions of ottoman: 22″ wide, 18″ deep, 18″ high.   *Materials*—3 sq. ft., medium, 2″ thick compact stuffing; muslin, 1 yd., 36″ width; natural cotton padding, 1 lb.; cover, 1⅜ yds., 54″ width; welt cord, 5 yds.; box lining, 1 yd., 54″ width; dust cover (optional), 1 yd., 36″ width. *Work-Steps*—Through muslin casing: frame Secs. 4:11, 4:12, 4:18; seat 6:04. Cover: Secs. 22:09, 18:15.

d   *e*

Fig. d, e 1:51

Fig. *f* 1:51—Attached cushion open-frame ottoman, bordered seat cover. Although this type ottoman (Sec. 22:06) often is built with springs (9 No. 1-H), especially if having a down-filled cushion, simple webbing construction is more practical. Roll edges on tops of rails. Dimensions of ottoman: 22" wide, 18" deep, 17" high. *Materials*— Webbing, 4 yds., 3½" width; burlap, 1 yd., 40" width; stuffing, 1 lb. loose hair; natural cotton padding, 1 lb. (4 lbs. if having traditional inner-spring cushion); cover, 1½ yds., 54" width; welt cord, 7 yds.; dust cover, 1 yd., 36" width. For cushion, Secs. 3:61–3:73; for down cushion, 2 lbs. down-filling and 2 yds. down-proof ticking, 36" width. *Work-Steps*—Frame Secs. 4:11, 4:12, 4:18; seat 22:07; cover 22:07.

Fig. *g* 1:51—Skirts or flounces are somewhat unusual on ottomans. Note additional trim by contrasting-color band near top of skirt, "bow-ties" at corners; simplest work is to hand-stitch band in place around installed skirt, then stitch bows to band. *g* is the same as *f* except: [1] cover, 1 yd. more for flange skirt; [2] skirt lining, 1 yd.,

f

g

Fig. *f, g* 1:51

54" width; [3] trim band, 3¾ yds.; [4] skirt upholstery Secs. 18:04– 18:06.

Fig. *h* 1:51—Double attached cushion, open-frame ottoman, bordered seat cover. Except for size and two cushions, upholstery is essentially the same as *f*. For neatest covering of sides, pin cover strips smoothly in place wrong-side-out, remove carefully and machine sew corner seams and mitered corners for top of base before sewing to bottom covers of cushions. Dimensions of ottoman: 48" wide, 20" deep, 17" high. *Materials*—Webbing, 8 yds., 3½" width; burlap, 1½ yds., 40" width; stuffing, 2 lbs. loose hair; natural cotton padding, 3 lbs. (9

Fig. h 1:51

lbs. if having traditional inner-spring cushions); cover, 3 yds., 54″ width; welt cord, if used, 18 yds.; dust cover, 1½ yds., 36″ width. For each cushion, same as *f*.   *Work-Steps*—Same as *f*.

SEC. 1:52   Contemporary exposed-wood chair and sofa set, Fig. 1:52. Can be either traditional or modern upholstery; either way, work is greatly simplified by upholstering inside arms and back with webbing and compact stuffing. Upholster chair and sofa essentially the same way. For traditional upholstery with loose stuffing only, bridle-build inside arms at front and top, tapering the top slightly as it nears the inside back; if using loose and compact stuffings, use loose stuffing just to build a smooth base for the compact, shape front and top of inside arms with compact stuffing. Plain spring edge loose cushion seat, banded seat cover. Instead of gimp along exposed-wood edges, double-welt (Sec. 11:08) may be an effective trim; for chair 1 yd. more, for sofa 1½ yds. more cover, 54″ width.

Fig. *a* 1:52—Dimensions of chair: 28″ wide, 34″ deep, 28″ high. Traditional Upholstery: *Materials*—Webbing, 12 yds., 3½″ width; seat springs, 9 No. 2-S; seat spring edge-wire, 10 ft.; back springs, 9 6-inch; burlap, 4 yds., 40″ width; stuffing, 10 lbs. loose hair; muslin, 3 yds., 36″ width; natural cotton padding, 4 lbs. (7 lbs. if having traditional inner-spring cushion); cover, 4½ yds., 54″ width (bias welt); decking, 1 yd., 36″ width; welt cord, 10 yds.; gimp or double welt cord, 10 yds.; dust cover, 1 yd., 36″ width. For cushion, Secs. 3:61– 3:73; for down cushion, 2½ lbs. down-filling and 2 yds. down-proof ticking, 36″ width. For upholstering with compact stuffing: 17 sq. ft., medium, 1″ thick stock for seat edge and deck, inside arms and back; only 7 lbs. loose stuffing (2 lbs. for understuffing seat, Sec. 7:29; 3 lbs.

for understuffing arms, Sec. 5:13, and inside back, Sec. 10:21), 2 yds. more muslin. *Work-Steps*—Through muslin casing: frame Secs. 4:11–4:15, 4:18; seat 7:05, 7:07, 7:08, 7:11–7:16, 7:18, 7:25, 7:29; inside arms 8:03, 8:09, 8:10, 8:14, 7:21, 8:15–8:20; inside back 10:03, 10:09, 10:11, 10:13, 10:15, 10:18, 10:22–10:24. Cover: seat Sec. 13:17; inside arms 14:06–14:08, 14:11; inside back 16:05, 16:06; cushion, 17:01–17:-15; outside surfaces 18:13–18:15, 18:06 or 18:18. MODERN UPHOLSTERY: Same as traditional except for building seat and inside back with zigzag springs (Secs. 3:21, 7:32, 10:31), inside back and arms with rubber webbing (Secs. 3:22, 10:33, 8:09A). 4 yds. zigzag springs for

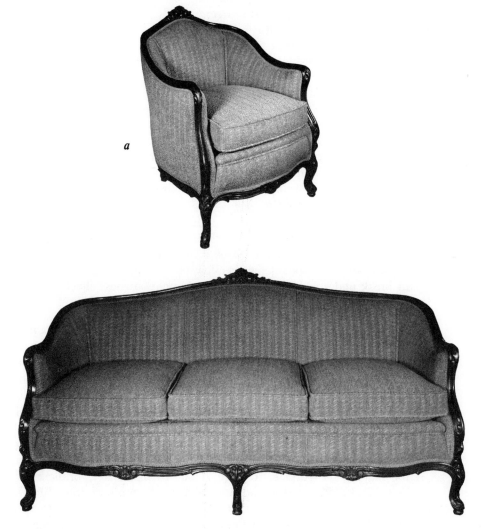

a

Fig. 1:52   *b*

seat, 5 edge springs, 4 yds. zigzags for inside back; upholster with loose or compact stuffing. 14 yds., 1⅛″ width, Standard, rubber webbing for inside arms and back; upholster with 10 sq. ft., medium, 2″ thick compact stuffing for inside back and arms; build extra crown (Sec. 5:14) if needed with padding. Pad with synthetic cotton for maximum initial softness.

Fig. *b* 1:52—Dimensions of sofa: 72″ wide, 34″ deep, 28″ high. TRADITIONAL UPHOLSTERY: *Materials*—Webbing, 34 yds., 3½″ width; seat springs, 27 No. 2-S; seat spring edge-wire, 18 ft.; back springs, 27 6-inch; burlap, 9 yds., 40″ width; stuffing, 20 lbs. loose hair; muslin, 5 yds., 36″ width; natural cotton padding, 9 lbs. (18 lbs. if having traditional inner-spring cushions); cover, 10 yds., 54″ width (bias welt); decking, 2 yds., 36″ width; welt cord, 26 yds.; gimp or double welt cord, 12 yds.; dust cover, 2 yds., 36″ width. For cushions, Secs. 3:61–3:73; for down cushions, 7½ lbs. down-filling and 6 yds. down-proof ticking, 36″ width. For upholstering with compact stuffing: 34 sq. ft., medium, 1″ thick stock for seat edge and deck, inside arms and back; only 15 lbs. loose stuffing (6 lbs. for understuffing seat, Sec. 7:29; 3 lbs. for understuffing arms, Sec. 5:13; and 6 lbs. for inside back, Sec. 10:21), 6 yds. more muslin. *Work-Steps*—Same as *a* plus Chapter 23. MODERN UPHOLSTERY: Same as *a* except amounts: [*1*] 11 yds. zigzag springs for seat, 12 edge springs; [*2*] 12 yds. zigzags for inside back; [*3*] 30 yds. rubber webbing for inside arms and back, and 18 sq. ft. compact stuffing.

SEC. 1:53   Articles in Fig. 1:53 are examples of high-quality exposed-wood upholstered furniture of the 1850s. Many frames of this type were built with some looseness in some joints to allow them to "give" instead of crack or break under sudden stress or strain; such looseness should not be "repaired" by tightening or reinforcing joints. Seats and inside backs of these articles usually were finished plain; backs occasionally were tufted. Reupholstering may be done by either traditional or modern methods; except for understuffing for basic shape, upholstering generally is easier with compact stuffing. Use roll edges on seats when upholstering them with loose stuffing only. Zigzag springs are especially good for this type of solid seat. Rubber webbing is not particularly recommended for this type of seat upholstery, but is very good for inside backs.

Fig. *a* 1:53—When upholstering inside back with loose stuffing only, if there is enough space on the frame, roll edges may be used for shaping the surface; if there is not enough space, bridle-build (Secs. 7:21, 7:22), or stuff and stitch as for a flat-top back (Sec. 10:25). Dimensions of chair: 19½″ wide, 25″ deep, 37½″ high. TRADITIONAL UPHOLSTERY: *Materials*—Webbing, 8 yds., 3½″ width; seat springs, 5 No. 2-M; burlap, 3 yds., 40″ width; stuffing, 10 lbs. loose hair; muslin,

a

Fig. a, b 1:53   *b*

1½ yds., 36″ width; natural cotton padding, 4 lbs.; cover, 1½ yds., 54″ width; gimp, 8 yds.; dust cover, 1 yd., 36″ width. For upholstering with compact stuffing: 4 sq. ft., medium, 1″ thick stock for seat; 4 sq. ft., medium, 1½″ stock for inside back; only 7 lbs. loose stuffing (for understuffing seat, Sec. 7:20), 1 yd. more muslin. *Work-Steps—* Through muslin casing: frame Secs. 4:11, 4:13, 4:18; seat 7:05, 7:07, 7:08, 7:11–7:14, 7:18–7:20; inside back 10:02, 10:09, 10:18, 7:21, 10:23–10:25. Cover: seat Sec. 13:11; inside back 16:07; outside surfaces, 18:14–18:16. MODERN UPHOLSTERY: For zigzag spring seat upholstery (Secs. 3:21, 7:32; 2 yds. zigzags), install zigzags on top of seat frame, cover with burlap. If using compact stuffing from 2″ to 6″ thick, bond it to burlap spring cover and frame; if compact stuffing is less than about 2″ thick, understuff spring surface and complete the traditional way. For rubber webbing inside back (Secs. 3:22, 10:33; 4 yds., 1⅛″ width, Standard, rubber webbing), upholster with same compact stuffing as for traditional work. Pad with synthetic cotton for maximum initial softness.

Fig. *b* 1:53—Essentially same upholstery as *a* except for addition of armrest pads. For best results, build opposite sides of back simultaneously step-by-step. See Chapter 23 for general information on upholstering sofas. Dimensions of sofa: 68″ wide, 33″ deep, 42″ high. TRADITIONAL UPHOLSTERY: *Materials—*Webbing, 28 yds., 3½″ width; seat springs, 18 No. 2-M; burlap, 8 yds., 40″ width; stuffing, 28 lbs. loose hair; muslin, 4 yds., 36″ width; natural cotton padding, 8 lbs.; cover, 8 yds., 54″ width; gimp, 22 yds.; dust cover, 2 yds., 36″ width. For upholstering with compact stuffing: 12 sq. ft., medium, 1″ thick stock for seat; 17 sq. ft., medium, 1½″ thick stock for inside back, armrest pads; only 15 lbs. loose stuffing (for understuffing seat, Sec. 7:20), 2 yds. more muslin. *Work-Steps—*Same as *a* plus armrest pads, Secs. 8:06, 14:01. MODERN UPHOLSTERY: Same as *a* except amounts: [1] 8 yds., zigzag springs for seat; same as traditional amount of thicker compact stuffing; [2] 10 yds. rubber webbing for inside back.

Fig. *c* 1:53—Originally the items in *c* and *d* had the same cover material. In order to avoid the so-called monotony of color often found in antique sets, when these articles were reupholstered a bright floral pattern was chosen for the chair and a somewhat traditional antique "design" for the sofa. Essentially the same upholstery for *c* as for *a*, plus armrest pads. Dimensions of chair: 24″ wide, 30″ deep, 37″ high. TRADITIONAL UPHOLSTERY: *Materials—*Webbing, 9 yds., 3½″ width; seat springs, 7 No. 2-M; burlap, 3 yds., 40″ width; stuffing, 11 lbs. loose hair; muslin, 1 yd., 36″ width; natural cotton padding, 4 lbs.; cover, 2 yds., 54″ width; gimp, 11 yds.; dust cover, 1 yd., 36″ width. For upholstering with compact stuffing: 6 sq. ft., medium, 1″ thick stock for seat; 6 sq. ft., medium, 1½″ thick stock for inside back, armrest pads; only 7 lbs. loose stuffing (for understuffing seat, Sec.

Fig. c 1:53

7:20), 1 yd. more muslin. *Work-Steps*—Same as *a* plus armrest pads, Secs. 8:06, 14:01. Modern Upholstery: Same as *a* except amounts: [*1*] 3 yds. zigzag springs for seat; same as traditional amount, above, of thicker stuffing; [*2*] 4 yds. rubber webbing for inside back; same compact stuffing as for traditional work.

    Fig. *d* 1:53—This is upholstered essentially the same way as *c* except for exposed-wood scroll arms. If upholstering inside arms with loose stuffing only, roll edges going up the inside surfaces and over the armtops should be shaped into smoothly tapering curves and be quite firm in order to hold shape. Armtop understuffing also should be quite firm, usually somewhat firmer than seems necessary, but not as hard as wood; softness of armtops can be developed by the over-stuffing and by padding with synthetic cotton. See Chapter 23 for general information on upholstering sofas. Dimensions of sofa: 75″ wide, 30″ deep, 37″ high. Traditional Upholstery: *Materials*— Webbing, 26 yds., 3½″ width; seat springs, 18 No. 2-M; burlap, 8 yds., 40″ width; stuffing, 28 lbs. loose hair; muslin, 5 yds., 36″ width; natural cotton padding, 10 lbs.; cover, 8 yds., 54″ width; gimp, 22 yds.;

Fig. d 1:53

dust cover, 2⅛ yds., 36″ width. For upholstering with compact stuffing: 29 sq. ft., medium, 1½″ thick for seat, inside arms and back; only 15 lbs. loose stuffing (for understuffing seat, Sec. 7:20), 2½ yds. more muslin. *Work-Steps*—Through muslin casing: frame, seat same as *a;* inside arms Secs. 8:03, 8:09–8:12, 8:15–8:20; inside back same as *a.* Cover: seat Sec. 13:11; inside arms 14:03; inside back, outside surfaces same as *a.*   MODERN UPHOLSTERY: Same as *a* except amounts: [1] 8 yds. zigzag springs for seat; same as traditional amount, above, of thicker stuffing;   [2] 16 yds. rubber webbing for inside back, arms; same compact stuffing as for traditional work.

SEC. 1:54   Modern love seat with exposed-wood armfronts, Fig. 1:54. Inside arms finish into inside back without sharp break. Inside arm and back covers machine sewn together without welt; if blind-stitching (Sec. 13:04), suggest welt in order to hide minor irregularities in work. Double-welt (Sec. 11:08) along exposed-wood front of arms. Unusually wide seat cushion is buttoned to help hold shape and prevent excessive or irreg-

Fig. 1:54

ular crown (Sec. 5:14); foam rubber or polyfoam filling is the most practical. Single-piece pull-over seat cover sustains theme of unbroken inside back and cushion boxing, although segmented cushions and inside backs also are common (Fig. 1:60). This article can be as readily built with either traditional or modern upholstery. Roll edge on spring seat if upholstering it with loose stuffing only. Pad open-frame inside arms; real or simulated roll edges next to exposed-wood portions if upholstering arms with loose stuffing only. Spring inside back. See Chapter 23 for general information on love seats. Dimensions of love seat: 53″ wide, 33″ deep, 33″ high. TRADITIONAL UPHOLSTERY: *Materials*—Webbing, 14 yds., 3½″ width; seat springs, 17 No. 1-M; back springs, 18 6-inch; burlap, 4 yds., 40″ width; stuffing, 16 lbs. loose hair; muslin, 6 yds., 36″ width; natural cotton padding, 5 lbs. (11 lbs. if having traditional inner-spring cushion); cover, 7 yds., 54″ width (bias welt); decking, 2 yds., 36″ width; buttons, 24; welt cord, 21 yds.; dust cover, 2 yds., 36″ width. For cushion, Secs. 3:61–3:73; for down cushion, 5 lbs. down-filling and 5 yds. down-proof ticking, 36″ wide. For upholstering with compact stuffing: 8 sq. ft., medium, 1″ thick stock for seat edge and deck; 16 sq. ft., medium, 2″ thick stock for inside arms and back; only 5 lbs. loose stuffing (for understuffing seat, Sec. 7:20), 2 yds. more muslin.   *Work-Steps*—Through muslin casing: frame Secs. 4:11–4:13, 4:15, 4:18; seat 7:01, 7:05–7:08, 7:11–7:14, 7:18–7:20; inside arms 8:03, 8:09–8:12, 8:14–8:20; inside back 10:03, 10:11, 10:13, 10:15, 10:18, 10:19, 10:21–10:24. Cover: seat Sec. 13:11; inside arms 14:03–14:06, 14:08; inside back 16:07; cushion 17:01–17:15; outside surfaces 18:13–18:15.   MODERN UPHOLSTERY: Same as traditional except for building seat and/or inside back with zigzag springs (Secs. 3:21, 7:32, 10:31) or rubber webbing (Secs. 3:22, 7:33, 10:33), inside arms with rubber webbing (Sec. 8:09A). 9 yds. zigzag springs for seat, 7 yds. for inside back; upholster with loose or compact stuffing. 18 yds., 2½″ width, Standard, rubber webbing for seat; 14 yds., preferably 1⅛″ width rubber webbing for inside back, arms; upholster with compact stuffing same as for traditional work; build extra crown (Sec. 5:14) if needed with padding. Pad with synthetic cotton for maximum initial softness.

SEC. 1:55

The modern sofas in Fig. 1:55 are essentially only wide versions of the general purpose armchair in Fig. 1:25. The major difference between *a* and *b*, Fig. 1:55, is arm upholstery. See Chapter 23 for general information on sofa upholstery. Dimensions of sofas: 86″ wide, 34″ deep, 32″ high.

Fig. *a* 1:55—Wrap-around covered armboard upholstery, slip-frame seat and back upholstery, Sec. 1:25. *Materials*—Seat, back cushion fillings, Sec. 7:34B; seat units approximately 24″ wide, 21½″ deep, 5″ thick; back units approximately 24″ wide, 15″ high, 5″ thick; natural cotton padding, 7 lbs. (25 lbs. if having traditional inner-spring cushion units); cover, 8 yds., 54″ width; dust cover (optional), 2½ yds., 36″ width. For maximum softness and resilience, upholster arms with 2 sq. ft., medium, 1″ thick compact stuffing, pad with synthetic cotton. *Work-Steps*—Same as Sec. 1:25.

Fig. a 1:55

Fig. *b* 1:55—Buttons in back and arm units mainly decorative. Back and arm units are solid-base slipframe upholstery for areas between the bottom of the lower and top of the upper arm and back rails; above that use regular cushion upholstery (Chapter 17, Sec. 17:21) high enough to pull over the top of the rail, *b*, and be fastened

Fig. b 1:55

to the top rail by a flap (Sec. 16:15); for best results, first make paper templates or patterns of the sides of the arm and back units. *Materials*—Seat, arm, back cushion fillings, Sec. 7:34B (but traditional inner-spring cushion work recommended only for seats); seat, back units same as *a;* arm units approximately 21½″ deep, 15″ high, 3″ thick; natural cotton padding, 7 lbs. (16 lbs. if having traditional inner-spring seat cushions); cover, 9 yds., 54″ width; buttons (optional), 10; dust cover (optional), 2½ yds., 36″ width. *Work-Steps*—Frame Secs. 4:11, 4:18; seat 6:03, 22:07; arms, back 10:37, 17:03–17:06, 17:21, 16:15, 18:01, 18:15.

SEC. 1:56   Modern upholstery is the practical way to build the general purpose, 3-place sofa with mock tufting finish (Sec. 21:11) in Fig. 1:56. Boxed covered seat and inside back units are pad, solid-base slipframes (Secs. 6:03, 10:37) upholstered with compact stuffing, then padded, covered, and installed in the sofa frame. For general information on sofa upholstery (Chapter 23). Exposed-wood arms are open-frame pad upholstery. Dimensions of sofa: 78″ wide, 30″ deep, 29″ high. *Materials* —Slipframes are ½″ to ¾″ plywood; usually, to allow for upholstery, they are about ½″ shorter and narrower than the frame area to which they will be attached, depending on the frame, method of attaching, and thickness of cover and padding. Webbing for inside arms, 9 yds., 3½″ width. Burlap for arms, 2 yds., 40″ width. Compact stuffing for seat and back units, 23 sq. ft., 1″ thick medium or soft stock for over-stuffing laminated (Sec. 3:46) onto 3″ to 5″ thick stock (depending on planned height of seat, thickness of inside back, Secs. 6:03, 10:02) for

Fig. 1:56

understuffing; stuffing units usually are 1″ longer and wider than slip-frame. Compact stuffing for inside arms, 7½ sq. ft., medium, 1½″ stock. Padding, preferably synthetic cotton, 12 lbs. Cover, 8 yds., 54″ width. Welt cord, 8 yds. Dust cover, 2¼ yds., 36″ width. *Work-Steps—[1] Frame*, Secs. 4:11, 4:14, 4:18. [2] *Seat, back units*. Prepare mock tufting cover complete with boxing, cover stretchers if needed, and install on slipframe (Sec. 21:11). Install seat unit in frame permanently, finishing seat boxing as a pull-around, bordered cover (Sec. 13:13). [3] *Inside arms*. Completely upholster, finishing cover at top and front into welting (Secs. 8:03, 8:09, 8:10, 8:14, 14:03, 14:07, 14:08). [4] *Back units*. Install outside back cover (Sec. 18:14 except no burlap), with flaps, depending on outside back construction, to conceal fastening to sofa frame (Secs. 16:14, 16:15). [5] *Outside surfaces*. Secs. 18:13, 18:15.

NOTE: Articles in Secs. 1:57–1:61 were selected primarily to show possible placement and treatment of various cover patterns and designs.

SEC. 1:57   Effects of wide and narrow striped covers are shown by the identical loose cushion splitback love seats in Fig. 1:57; *b* cover may be easier to plot economically (Chapter 11) because of smaller pattern repeats. Note alignment of stripes throughout inside back, cushion cover and front boxing, arm fronts, seat cover and flange skirt; the pull-over seat cover is cut and welted at the middle of the front, and the skirt pleated there, to carry the lines of the splitback and seat cushions. Spring edge seat. Roll edges on inside arms and armtops, shaping stitching of the inside back (Sec. 10:25), if upholstering these parts with loose stuffing only. Spring inside back can be upholstered with inner-spring units (Sec. 10:29); boxed cover. Pad, open-frame inside arms, boxed and bordered armfront cover. Article can be built with either traditional or modern upholstery. See Chapter 23 for basic information on love seat upholstery.

a

Fig. 1:57   *b*

Dimensions of love seat: 56″ wide, 35″ deep, 30½″ high. TRADITIONAL UPHOLSTERY: *Materials*—Webbing, 29 yds., 3½″ width; seat springs, 24 No. 2-M; seat spring edge-wire, 14 ft.; back springs, 24 6-inch; edge-wire to shape lower sides of inside back, 6 ft.; burlap, 6 yds., 40″ width; stuffing, 14 lbs. loose hair; muslin, 5 yds., 36″ width; natural cotton padding, 9 lbs. (15 lbs. if having traditional inner-spring cushions); cover, 9 yds., 54″ width (bias welt), with skirt, 8 yds. without skirt; skirt lining, 1 yd., 54″ width; decking, 1½ yds., 36″ width; welt cord, 32 yds.; dust cover, 1⅔ yds., 36″ width. For cushions, Secs. 3:61–3:73; for each down cushion, 3 lbs. down-filling and 3 yds. down-proof ticking, 36″ width. For upholstering with compact stuffing: 16 sq. ft., medium, 1″ thick stock for seat and inside arms; 11 sq. ft., medium, 1½″ stock for inside back; only 9 lbs. loose stuffing (4 lbs. for under-stuffing seat, Sec. 7:29; 1 lb. for understuffing inside arms, Sec. 5:13; 4 lbs. for inside back, Sec. 10:21), 4 yds. more muslin. For upholstering inside back with inner-spring units: 5 × 6 units each with 2 extra springs on one side, upholster with loose or compact stuffing to fit (Sec. 10:29). *Work-Steps*—Through muslin casing: frame Secs. 4:11–4:16, 4:18; seat 7:02, 7:05–7:08, 7:11–7:16, 7:18, 7:25, 7:29; inside arms 8:03, 8:08–8:11, 8:13–8:15; 8:21, 8:22; inside back 10:03, 10:11–10:13, 10:15, 10:18 (10:29), 10:22, 10:25. Cover: seat Sec. 13:17; inside arms 14:06–14:09; inside back 16:10; cushions 17:01–17:15; outside surfaces 18:03–18:06, 18:13 (13:08), 18:14, 18:15. MODERN UPHOLSTERY: Same as traditional except for building seat and inside back with zig-zag springs (Secs. 3:21, 7:32, 10:31, 10:32), inside arms and back with rubber webbing (Secs. 3:22, 8:09A, 10:33). 12 yds. zigzag springs for seat, 12 edge springs, only 6 ft. seat spring edge-wire, 7 yds. zigzags for inside back; upholster with loose or compact stuffing, or upholster inside back with inner-spring units and stuffing. 20 yds., 1⅛″ width, Standard, rubber webbing for inside arms and back; upholster arms with 7 sq. ft., medium, 1½″ thick compact stuffing, back with 11 sq. ft., medium, 3″ stock; build extra crown (Sec. 5:14) if needed with padding. Pad with synthetic cotton for maximum initial softness.

SEC. 1:58   The scenic cover in Fig. 1:58 has two major or dominant "pictures," one used in the left inside back and right seat cushion, the other in the right inside back and left cushion; for sample of goods, Fig. 11:24D. Since the inside back and top of a seat or seat cushion are the most noticeable surfaces, no attempt was made to show a dominant-picture part of the cover on any other front or inside surface. Seat cover and banding were cut and welted at the middle of the front to carry the line of the split back and seat cushions. Spring inside back stitched for flat top and square sides (Sec. 10:25) if it is upholstered with loose stuffing only; back can be upholstered with inner-spring

Fig. 1:58

units (Sec. 10:29); boxed cover. Modern square, pad, open-frame arms, boxed cover. Plain spring edge loose cushion seat, banded cover. See Chapter 23 for general information on love seat upholstery. Dimensions of love seat: 54″ wide, 30″ deep, 32″ high. TRADITIONAL UPHOLSTERY: *Materials*—Webbing, 29 yds., 3½″ width; seat springs, 18 No. 2-S and 6 No. 2-M; seat spring edge-wire, 14 ft.; back springs, 16 6-inch and 16 8-inch; edge-wire to shape lower sides of inside back, 6 ft.; burlap, 6 yds., 40″ width; stuffing, 14 lbs. loose hair; muslin, 5 yds., 36″ width; natural cotton padding, 10 lbs. (16 lbs. if having traditional inner-spring cushions); cover, 7 yds., 54″ width; decking, 1½ yds., 36″ width; welt cord, 30 yds.; dust cover, 1½ yds., 36″ width. For cushions, Secs. 3:61–3:73; for down cushions, each 3 lbs. down-filling and 2½ yds. down-proof ticking, 36″ width. For upholstering with compact stuffing: 16 sq. ft., medium, 1″ thick stock for seat edge and deck, and inside arms; 14 sq. ft., medium, 1½″ to 2″ thick stock for inside back; only 8 lbs. loose stuffing (4 lbs. for understuffing seat, Sec. 7:29; ½ lb. for understuffing inside arms, Sec. 5:13; 3½ lbs. for inside back, Sec. 10:21), 3 yds. more muslin. For upholstering inside back with inner-spring units: 5 × 6 units each with 2 extra springs on one side, upholster with loose or compact stuffing to fit. *Work-Steps*—Through muslin casing: frame, seat same as Sec. 1:57; inside arms Secs. 8:03, 8:09–8:11, 8:13–8:15, 8:21, 8:22; inside back same as Sec. 1:57. Cover: seat

Sec. 13:17; inside arms 14:02, 14:09; inside back, cushions same as Sec. 1:57; outside surfaces 18:13–18:15. Modern Upholstery: Same as Sec. 1:57.

SEC. 1:59

There are two major or more noticeable figures in the cover goods for Fig. 1:59: a light flower with a fairly large dark background and, below it, a "shield." The flower was centered in the inside back sections and the middle seat cushion, the shield in the middle seat cushion boxing and the banding below it. The major figures are off-center in the side seat cushions and seat banding in order to make a more-or-less straight line forward from the figures in the side back sections. Except for the middle back section and the seat cover, upholstery is the same as for Sec. 1:58. Dimensions of sofa: 78″ wide, 35″ deep, 32″ high. Traditional Upholstery: *Materials*—Webbing, 36 yds., 3½″ width; seat springs, 15 No. 2-H and 21 No. 2-S; seat spring edge-wire, 18 ft.; edge-wire to shape lower sides of inside back, 6 ft.; back springs, 13 6-inch and 18 8-inch; burlap, 9 yds., 40″ width; stuffing, 23 lbs. loose hair; muslin, 6 yds., 36″ width; natural cotton padding, 13 lbs. (22 lbs. if having traditional inner-spring cushions); cover 11 yds., 54″ width (bias welt); decking, 2 yds., 36″ width; welt cord, 39 yds.; dust cover, 2½ yds., 36″ width. For cushions, Secs. 3:61–3:73; for each down cushion, 2½ lbs. down-filling and 2 yds. down-proof ticking, 36″ width. For upholstering with compact stuffing: 21 sq. ft., medium, 1″ thick stock for seat edge and deck, and inside arms; 21 sq. ft., medium, 1½″ to 2″ thick stock for inside back; only 12½ lbs. loose stuffing (6

Fig. 1:59

lbs. for understuffing seat, Sec. 7:29; ½ lb. for understuffing inside arms, Sec. 5:13; 6 lbs. for inside back, Sec. 10:21), 4 yds. more muslin. For upholstering inside back with inner-spring units: one 5 × 6 unit, two 6 × 6 units each with 3 extra springs on one side, upholster with loose or compact stuffing to fit (Sec. 10:29). *Work-Steps*—Same as for Sec. 1:58 plus center section of inside back, and border below banding on seat front. Modern Upholstery: Same as Sec. 1:57 except for amounts of items. 15 yds. zigzag springs for seat, 16 edge springs, only 7½ ft. seat spring edge-wire, 11 yds. zigzags for inside back. 26 yds. rubber webbing for inside arms and back, and 21 sq. ft., medium, 3″ thick compact stuffing for back.

SEC. 1:60   The modern sofa in Fig. 1:60 has somewhat unusual treatments of cover and pattern. First, the pull-over seat cover was railroaded (Sec. 11:01) in order to avoid piecing it; the top of the pattern, as indicated by the dominant light flower, is to the left. Second, the dominant figure is centered only in the middle back pillow and seat cushion; it is approximately the same distance from the outer edges of the side pillows and cushions. Actual figure placement in the side pillows and cushions was based on where it would be at the front of the cushions; instead of being made the usual way (top and bottom covers with boxing between, Chapter 17), the top and bottom covers of the cushions go over the sides and are machine sewn, without welt, midway between top and bottom (there being no "boxing" in the true sense of the word). This creates a new dominant figure that carries across the gaps between cushions. Note also how the overall pattern carries across the gaps between back pillows. The frame of this particular sofa

Fig. 1:60

was engineered for upholstering seat and inside back with zigzag springs; either jute or rubber webbing is suitable for pad inside arm upholstery. Compact stuffing is placed directly on burlap spring or webbing cover; there is no understuffing. Dimensions of sofa: 74" wide, 32" deep, 28" high. *Materials*—Webbing, 5 yds., 3½" width, or 8 yds., 1⅛" width, Standard, rubber webbing; burlap, 4½ yds., 40" width; stuffing, 36 sq. ft., medium, 1" thick compact for seat, inside arms and back; muslin, 6 yds., 36" width; natural cotton padding, 8 lbs. (17 lbs. if having traditional inner-spring seat cushions); cover, 12 yds., 54" width; decking, 2 yds., 36" width; dust cover, 2 yds., 36" width. For seat cushions, back pillows, Secs. 3:61–3:73; for each down cushion, 2½ lbs. down-filling and 2 yds. down-proof ticking, 36" width; for each down pillow, 1½ lbs. down-filling and 2 yds. ticking. *Work-Steps*—Frame Secs. 4:11, 4:13, 4:15, 4:18; seat 7:21, 7:32; inside arms 8:03, 8:09–8:11, 8:13, 8:15, 8:21, 8:22; inside back 10:03, 10:31. Cover: seat Sec. 13:11; inside arms 14:06–14:08; inside back 16:07; cushions, pillows 17:01–17:20; outside surfaces 18:13–18:15. For maximum initial softness, pad with synthetic cotton.

SEC. 1:61   Due to careful selection of cover based on widths of back pillows, the dominant figure in Fig. 1:61 repeats well from side to side, back to front, and top to bottom throughout. Loose pillow open-frame pad back, pull-over cover; boxed pillows. Pad, open-frame inside arms, semi square-scroll, small or simulated roll edges at front and on arm-tops if upholstering them with loose stuffing only; boxed cover requires careful preparation and machine sewing. Loose cushion, plain spring edge seat; bordered cover. For general information on sofa upholstery,

Fig. 1:61

Chapter 23. Dimensions of sofa: 95" wide, 34½" deep, 33½" high. TRADITIONAL UPHOLSTERY: *Materials*—Webbing, 40 yds., 3½" width; seat springs, 42 No. 2-M and 2 No. 1-M; seat spring edge-wire, 21 ft.; burlap, 10 yds., 40" width; stuffing, 15 lbs. loose hair; muslin, 6 yds., 36" width; natural cotton padding, 10 lbs. (28 lbs. if having traditional inner-spring cushions, pillows); cover, 13 yds., 54" width (bias welt); decking, 3 yds., 36" width; welt cord, 50 yds.; dust cover, 3 yds., 36" width. For seat cushions, back pillows, Secs. 3:61–3:73; for down cushions, 10 lbs. down-filling and 7½ yds. down-proof ticking, 36" width; for down pillows, 5 lbs. down-filling and 4½ yds. ticking. For upholstering with compact stuffing: 32 sq. ft., medium, 1" thick stock for seat edge and deck, inside arms and back; only 13 lbs. loose stuffing (6 lbs. for understuffing seat, Sec. 7:29; ½ lb. for understuffing inside arms, Sec. 5:13; 6½ lbs. for inside back, Sec. 10:21), 5 yds. more muslin. *Work-Steps*—Through muslin casing: frame Secs. 4:11–4:15, 4:18; seat 7:02, 7:05–7:08, 7:11–7:16, 7:18, 7:25, 7:29; inside arms, back same as Sec. 1:60. Cover: seat Sec. 13:17; inside arms, back, cushions, pillows, outside surfaces same as Sec. 1:60. MODERN UPHOLSTERY: Same as traditional except for building seat and inside back with zigzag springs (Secs. 3:21, 7:32, 10:31), inside back and arms with rubber webbing (Secs. 3:22, 10:33, 8:09A, impractical for arms unless buying rubber webbing for inside back). 16 yds. zigzag springs for seat, 20 edge springs, only 9 ft. spring edge-wire; 12 yds. zigzags for back; upholster with loose or compact stuffing. 26 yds., 1⅛" width, Standard, rubber webbing for inside back and arms; upholster with same compact stuffing as for traditional work; build extra crown (Sec. 5:14) if needed with padding. Pad armtops with synthetic cotton for maximum initial softness.

SEC. 1:62   The tufted sofa in Fig. 1:62 is a wide version of the chair in Fig. 1:40; aside from size, the difference is a plain pull-over instead of bordered seat cover. Piecing of this type of cover goods can be almost invisible; with other goods, the seat cover is usually cut and welted to follow the line from cushion edges to skirt pleat as in Fig. 1:57. For general comments on upholstering this design of sofa see Sec. 1:40; for basic information on upholstering sofas see Chapter 23. Dimensions of sofa: 76" wide, 35" deep, 32" high. TRADITIONAL UPHOLSTERY: *Materials*—Webbing, 36 yds., 3½" width; seat springs, 36 No. 2-M; burlap, 9 yds., 40" width; stuffing, 23 lbs. loose hair; muslin, 6 yds., 36" width; natural cotton padding, 13 lbs. (22 lbs. if having traditional inner-spring cushions); cover, 14 yds., 54" width (bias welt), with skirt, 12 yds. without; skirt lining, 2 yds., 54" width; decking, 2½ yds., 36" width; buttons, 40; welt cord, 40 yds.; dust cover, 2½ yds., 36" width. For cushions, Secs. 3:61–3:73; for down cushions, 7½ lbs.

Fig. 1:62

down-filling and 8 yds. down-proof ticking, 36" width. For upholstering with compact stuffing, 16 sq. ft., medium, 1" thick stock for seat edge and deck; 24 sq. ft., medium 2" thick stock for inside arms-back; only 6½ lbs. loose stuffing (for understuffing seat, Sec. 7:20), 2½ yds. more muslin. *Work-Steps*—Same as Fig. *a* 1:40. MODERN UPHOLSTERY: Same as Fig. *a* 1:40 except amounts: 12 yds. zigzag springs for seat. 25 yds. rubber webbing for seat, 20 yds. for inside arms and back; same compact stuffing as for traditional upholstery, above.

SEC. 1:63

Due to extensive tufting of inside back, the modern 3-place sofa in Fig. 1:63 is not recommended as a first project. However, the covering of the inside and outside arms and the scallop-pleat flange skirt are suitable for other articles. Arm covers are a strip of goods for the front and top over a layer of padding, then a regular padded border, welting, and then major inside and outside arm cover panels; regular inside and outside arm upholstery merely fills the arm cavity. The outside back can be upholstered the same way as the outside arms but seldom is. Make one paper pattern or template to use for all skirt scallops. Spring inside back. Pad open-frame arms. Loose cushion, plain spring edge seat. For tufting, Chapter 21; for basic information on sofa upholstery, Chapter 23. Dimensions of sofa: 81" wide, 37" deep, 30" high. TRADITIONAL UPHOLSTERY: *Materials*—Webbing, 36 yds., 3½" width; seat springs, 36 No. 2-M; seat spring edge-wire, 18 ft.; back springs, 30 6-inch; burlap, 9 yds., 40" width; stuffing, 25 lbs. loose

Fig. 1:63

hair; muslin, 8 yds., 36″ width; natural cotton padding, 10 lbs. (19 lbs. if having traditional inner-spring cushions); cover, 14 yds., 54″ width (bias welt) with skirt, 12 yds. without; skirt lining, 2 yds., 54″ width; decking, 2¼ yds., 36″ width; buttons, 43; welt cord, 36 yds.; dust cover, 2¼ yds., 36″ width. For cushions, Secs. 3:61–3:73; for down cushions, 9 lbs. down-filling and 7½ yds. down-proof ticking, 36″ width. For upholstering with compact stuffing, 26 sq. ft., medium, 1″ thick stock for seat edge and deck, and major parts of inside arms; 16 sq. ft., medium, 2″ stock for inside back; only 6 lbs. loose stuffing (for understuffing seat, Sec. 7:29), 2¼ yds. more muslin. *Work-Steps—*Through muslin casing: frame Secs. 4:11–4:16, 4:18; seat 7:02, 7:05, 7:07–7:16, 7:18, 7:25, 7:29; inside arms 8:03, 8:09, 8:10 (see note above regarding arm upholstery), 8:14, 8:15, 8:21, 8:22; inside back 10:03, 10:11, 10:13, 10:15, 10:18, 21:01–21:04, 21:06–21:08. Cover: seat Sec. 13:17; inside arms 14:02, 13:08, 14:07, 14:08; inside back 21:09; cushions 17:01–17:15; outside surfaces, arms 13:08, 18:13–18:15, 18:03–18:06. MODERN UPHOLSTERY: Same as traditional except for building seat and inside back with zigzag springs (Secs. 3:21, 7:32, 10:31), inside back and arms with rubber webbing (Secs. 3:22, 10:33, 8:09A impractical unless buying rubber webbing for inside back). 12 yds. zigzag springs for seat, 14 edge springs, only 8 ft. spring edge-wire; 10 yds. zigzags for inside back; upholster with loose or compact stuffing. 24 yds., 1⅛″ width, Standard, rubber webbing for inside back and arms; upholster with same compact stuffing as for traditional work; build extra crown (Sec. 5:14) if needed with padding. Pad with synthetic cotton for maximum initial softness.

SEC. 1:64   Unusual lounging comfort was built into the modern sofa in Fig. 1:64 by making spring inside arms. Spring inside arms and back are upholstered essentially the same way except for the tilt of the back; stitch (Sec. 10:25) front of arms and top of arms and back if upholstering them with loose stuffing only. For simpler construction, arms and back can be sprung with inner-spring units (Sec. 10:29), or, in modern upholstery, they can easily be built with rubber webbing and compact stuffing. Boxed, bordered inside arm, back covers. Loose cushion, plain spring edge seat; banded, bordered cover. For general information on sofa upholstery, Chapter 23. Dimensions of sofa: 87″ wide, 35″ deep, 27″ high. Traditional Upholstery: *Materials*—Webbing, 36 yds., 3½″ width; seat springs, 36 No. 3-H or 4-H; seat spring edge-wire, 18 ft.; back springs, 9 6-inch and 27 8-inch; back springs for use in arms, 16 6-inch; burlap, 12 yds., 40″ width; stuffing, 28 lbs. loose hair; muslin, 7 yds., 36″ width; natural cotton padding, 14 lbs. (23 lbs. if having traditional inner-spring cushions); cover, 13½ yds., 54″ width (bias welt); decking, 2½ yds., 36″ width; welt cord, 41 yds.; buttons, 6; dust cover, 2½ yds., 36″ width. For cushions, Secs. 3:61–3:73; for down cushions, 7½ lbs. down-filling and 7½ yds. down-proof ticking, 36″ width. For building inside arms, back with inner-spring units (Sec. 10:29); two 9″ × 30″ units for arms, three 10″ × 20″ units for back. For upholstering with compact stuffing: 27 sq. ft., medium, 1″ thick stock for seat edge and deck, inside arms and back; only 6 lbs. loose stuffing (for understuffing seat, Sec. 7:29), 2½ yds. more muslin. *Work-Steps*—Through muslin casing: frame, seat same as Sec. 1:57; inside arms and back Secs. 8:03, 8:09, 10:03, 10:11, 10:13, 10:15, 10:18, 10:22–10:24, 8:21, 8:22, 10:25, 10:29. Cover: seat Sec. 13:17; inside

Fig. 1:64

arms 14:07–14:09; inside back 16:05, 16:10; cushions 17:01–17:15; outside surfaces 18:01, 18:13–18:15. MODERN UPHOLSTERY: Same as traditional except for building seat, inside arms and back with zigzag springs (Secs. 3:21, 7:32, 10:31, 10:32), inside arms and back with rubber webbing (Secs. 3:22, 10:33). 12 yds. zigzags for seat, 14 edge springs, only 8½ ft. spring edge-wire; 9 yds. zigzags for inside back; upholster with loose or compact stuffing, build inside arms and back with inner-spring units (Sec. 10:32) for softer surfaces. 28 yds., 1⅛″ width, Standard, rubber webbing for inside arms and back; upholster with 14 sq. ft., medium, 3″ thick compact stuffing for inside arms and back; build extra crown (Sec. 5:14) if needed with padding. Pad with synthetic cotton for maximum initial softness.

SEC. 1:65   The modern 2-piece sofa or sectional, as in Fig. 1:65, can be used so many ways that it is an excellent general purpose article. For best results upholster both units together step-by-step throughout. Spring inside back, stitched for flat top and square sides (Sec. 10:25) if upholstering it with loose stuffing only; simplify work by building back with an inner-spring unit (Sec. 10:29), or by overstuffing with compact stuffing, or by upholstering back with rubber webbing and compact stuffing; boxed cover. Pad, open-frame inside arms; roll edges front and top if upholstering with loose stuffing only; for simpler work, upholster with compact stuffing; bordered cover. Loose cushion seat, plain spring edge on front and open side; bordered cover. Dimensions

Fig. 1:65

of each unit: 31″ wide, 33″ deep, 29″ high. TRADITIONAL UPHOL-
STERY: *Materials for each unit—*Webbing, 13 yds., 3½″ width; seat
springs, 12 No. 2-M or 3-M; seat spring edge-wire, 10 ft.; back springs,
12 6-inch; burlap, 4½ yds., 40″ width; stuffing, 11 lbs. loose hair; muslin,
3 yds., 36″ width; natural cotton padding, 6 lbs. (9 lbs. if having traditional inner-spring cushion); cover, 6 yds., 54″ width (bias welt); decking, ⅜ yd., 36″ width; welt cord, 15 yds.; dust cover, 1 yd., 36″ width.
For building inside back with inner-spring unit: 5 × 6 unit; upholster
with loose or compact stuffing to fit (Sec. 10:29). For cushion, Secs.
3:61–3:73; for down cushion, 3 lbs. down-filling and 2½ yds. down-
proof ticking, 36″ width. For upholstering with compact stuffing: 15
sq. ft., medium, 1″ thick stock for seat edge and deck, inside arms and
back; only 4 lbs. loose stuffing (2 lbs. for understuffing seat, Sec. 7:29;
2 lbs. for understuffing inside arm and back, Sec. 10:21), 2 yds. more
muslin. *Work-Steps—*Through muslin casing: frame, seat (front and
open side), inside arm same as Sec. 1:57; inside back Secs. 10:03,
10:11, 10:13, 10:15, 10:18 (10:29), 10:22–10:25. Cover: seat Sec. 13:17;
inside arm 14:06–14:08; inside back 16:05, 16:10; cushion 17:01–17:15;
outside surfaces 18:13–18:15. MODERN UPHOLSTERY: Same as traditional except for building seat (Fig. *d, e* 3:21R) and inside back with
zigzag springs (Secs. 3:21, 7:32, 10:31, 10:32), inside back and arm
with rubber webbing (Secs. 3:22, 10:33, 8:09A impractical unless buying rubber webbing for inside back). 4 yds. zigzag springs for seat,
6 edge springs (for front and open side), only 7 ft. spring edge-wire; 3½
yds. zigzags for inside back; build back with inner-spring unit for extra
softness; upholster with loose or compact stuffing. 12 yds., 1⅛″ width,
Standard, rubber webbing for inside arm and back; upholster inside
arm with 5½ sq. ft., medium, 2″ thick stock, back with 5 sq. ft.,
medium, 3″ thick stock; build extra crown (Sec. 5:14) if needed with
padding. Pad with synthetic cotton for maximum initial softness.

SEC. 1:66   The sectional corner sofa in Fig. 1:66 has two units: a corner-sofa with
left arm finished (with three large back pillows, and a smaller "arm"
pillow facing the left arm), and a one-arm sofa (right arm finished).
Upholstery is not difficult; however, there should be considerable
work-space available, since for best results both units should be upholstered together step-by-step. Loose pillow spring inside back; for
simpler work, build with rubber webbing and compact stuffing; pull-
around cover. Pad, open-frame arms; install arm webbing primarily
horizontally in order to maintain planned shape of arms. Second "arm"
on corner unit is upholstered the same way as the inside back, with
same tilt as in the one-arm sofa. Build corner back pillows after all
others are finished and set in place. Loose cushion, plain spring edge

Fig. 1:66

seats; regular seat construction across front of corner unit, across front and open side of one-arm unit; bordered seat cover. For general information on sofa upholstery, Chapter 23. Dimensions: corner unit 96″ wide, one-arm unit 92″ wide; both units 34″ deep, 28″ high. TRADITIONAL UPHOLSTERY: *Total materials for both units*—Webbing, 72 yds., 3½″ width; seat springs, 96 No. 2-M; seat spring edge-wire, 18 ft. for each unit; burlap, 16 yds., 40″ width; stuffing, 24 lbs. loose hair; muslin, 14 yds., 36″ width; natural cotton padding, 24 lbs. (63 lbs. if having traditional inner-spring cushions, pillows); cover, 27 yds., 54″ width (bias welt); decking, 6 yds., 36″ width; welt cord, 74 yds.; dust cover, 6 yds., 36″ width. For seat cushions, back pillows, Secs. 3:61–3:73; for down cushions, 20 lbs. down-filling and 17 yds. down-proof ticking, 36″ width; for down back pillows, 18 lbs. down-filling and 16 yds. down-proof ticking. For upholstering with compact stuffing: 68 sq. ft., medium, 1″ thick compact stuffing for seats, inside arms and backs; only 17 lbs. loose stuffing (12 lbs. for understuffing seats, Sec. 7:29; 5 lbs. for understuffing inside arms and backs, Secs. 5:13, 10:21), 13 yds. more muslin. *Work-Steps*—Through muslin casing: frame, seat (front of corner unit, front and open side of one-arm unit) same as Sec. 1:57; inside arms (finished) Secs. 8:03, 8:09–8:11, 8:13–8:15, 8:21, 8:22; inside backs (includes back for "arm" pillow of corner unit) 10:03, 10:11, 10:13, 10:15, 10:18, 10:22–10:24. Cover: seat Sec. 13:17; inside arms (finished) 14:07, 14:08; inside backs (includes back for "arm" pillow of corner unit) 16:05, 16:07; cushions, pillows 17:01–17:18; outside surfaces 18:13–18:15. MODERN UPHOLSTERY: Same as traditional except for building seats (Fig. *d, e* 3:21R) and inside backs (including back for "arm" pillow of corner unit) with zigzag springs (Secs. 3:21, 7:32, 10:31), inside backs and arms (finished) with rubber webbing (Secs. 3:22, 10:33, 8:09A impractical unless buying rubber webbing for inside backs). 20 yds. zigzag springs for seat, 31 edge springs, only 10 ft. spring edge-wire for corner unit, 12½ ft. for one-arm unit; 20 yds. zigzags for inside backs; upholster with loose or compact stuffing. 46 yds., 1⅛″ width, Standard, rubber webbing for inside backs and arms; upholster with 36 sq. ft., medium, 1½″ thick compact stuffing for inside arms and backs; build extra crown (Sec. 5:14) if needed with padding. Pad inside arms, armtop with synthetic cotton for maximum initial softness.

2

tools

Basic upholstery tools are: Upholstery trestles, upholsterer's hammer, webbing stretcher, shears, ripping tool, hand needles, regulator, upholstery skewers, mallet, wood rasp, wire-bender, spring-clip pliers, cushion closing equalizer, cushion hand-irons, cushion pliers, sewing machine with cording foot, steel tape measure, white school chalk or tailor's chalk, beeswax, varnished yardstick. Most of the above tools are used regularly in general upholstering. In addition there are tools for use only with certain items; they are treated as part of such items. Tools needed for various work-steps are listed in appropriate chapters or sections. Good quality tools are available through most upholstery shops; poor quality tools are generally unsatisfactory. There are satisfactory, money-saving substitutes for many upholstery tools. Sometimes the most practical "substitute tool" is to take a difficult job, such as machine sewing a leather cushion casing, to an upholstery shop.

**SEC. 2:01
UPHOLSTERY
TRESTLE**

Two upholstery trestles, Fig. 2:01, about 36 inches long and 26 inches high, are needed for most jobs. Set-back legs at one end allow them to be nested, often necessary for small articles. The top of a trestle is a trough about 5 inches wide by ¾-inch deep to keep articles from slipping off. Pad troughs inside and outside with carpeting, heavy plastic, or several thicknesses of burlap to protect surfaces placed on it.

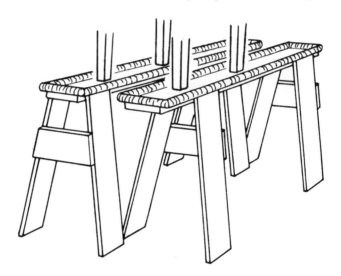

Fig. 2:01

**SEC. 2:02
UPHOL-
STERER'S
HAMMER**

The upholsterer's hammer, Fig. 2:02, is used in most work-steps; there is no good substitute for it. The slightly curved double head, 5 or 6 inches long, has faces about ⅜-inch in diameter. One is magnetized, to hold tacks while setting them. The long, thin head simplifies tacking in hard-to-reach spots. Use the side of a head to knock away sliptacks, smooth covers, pat stuffing and padding into shape. In a well-balanced hammer, distances from the middle of the end of a handle to the center of each face, and to the side of a head at the middle, are equal. A well-balanced hammer makes for faster, more accurate, less tiring work. The closer your hold is to the end of the handle, the more effective the hammer is, and the less strength it takes to drive tacks and nails.

**SEC. 2:03
WEBBING
STRETCHER**

SEC. 2:03A / Webbing generally is used in open-frame surfaces (Sec. 4:12, Figs. 6:02A, 7:05A) as the foundation for other upholstery materials. Webbing usually is stretched during installation. All ordinary types of webbing stretchers and substitutes are used with traditional woven webbing (Sec. 3:11). Do not use prong stretchers (Sec. 2:03B) with rubber or most decorative webbings (Secs. 3:22, 3:23).

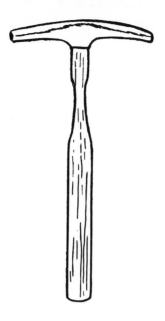

Fig. 2:02

NOTE: Webbing is not used with zigzag springs (Sec. 3:21).

Sec. 2:03B Prong Webbing Stretchers / Prong webbing stretch-
ers, Fig. 2:03B, are wood, about $7 \times 3 \times \frac{3}{4}$ inches, with sharp steel
prongs in one end. Holes made by prongs in traditional jute and
similar woven webbing do not weaken it enough to matter but can
seriously damage rubber and most decorative webbings. The wide-
end stretcher, *a*, can be used with all shapes of frames; pad the plain
end with leather, fairly heavy plastic or rubber matting to prevent
damaging an article being webbed and slippage of the tool in use
(Fig. 5:01E). The small-end stretcher, *b*, is designed for use with
sharply curved frames; pad with rubber crutch tip.

Sec. 2:03C Substitute Webbing Stretchers / Two substitute
webbing stretchers are shown in Fig. 2:03C. [*1*] *Prong type, a:*
Essentially the same as the commercial stretcher (Fig. *a* 2:03B) except
that 1½- or 1¾-inch nails are driven through wood 1 inch from an end,
and filed to sharp, tapering points ½-inch long; pad other end (Sec.
2:03B). Use the same way as the commercial wide-end stretcher except
that the webbing passes down around the end and onto the prongs.
[*2*] *Wrap-around type,* Fig. *b* 2:03C: Suitable for all strip webbings.
Wrap webbing twice around a handy length of about 2×2 inch
wood, brace it against the frame being webbed, and turn or twist the
"stretcher" away from the frame enough to pull webbing sufficiently
tight.

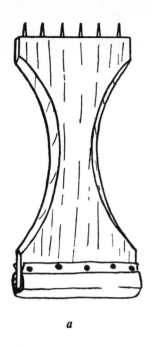

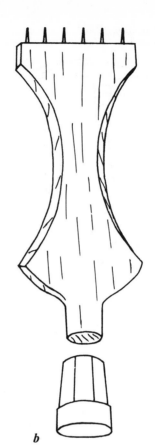

Fig. 2:03B

a

b

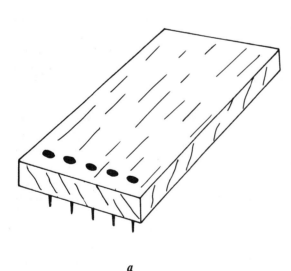

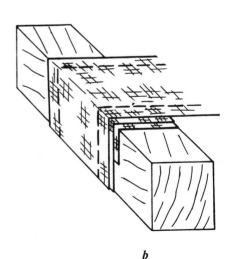

a

Fig. 2:03C

b

Sec. 2:03D Webbing Pliers / Metal webbing pliers, Fig. 2:03D, have scored or grooved jaws to grip webbing, can be used with any type of strip webbing, and sometimes is more convenient than prong stretchers. To use, pull webbing as tight as possible by hand, then grip with pliers close to the frame. Set point of fulcrum against frame, push down the end of the handle to stretch webbing. If a fulcrum must be set against an exposed-wood surface (Sec. 5:01D), put a smooth, strong piece of wood between fulcrum and frame to prevent gouging or denting it. The usual cost of webbing pliers makes them impractical for most non-professional upholsterers.

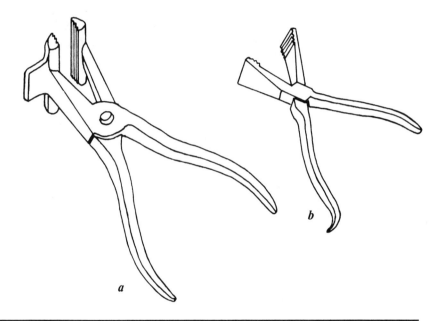

Fig. 2:03D

| SEC. 2:04 SHEARS | Shears or scissors should be heavy enough to cut fairly thick, tightly woven fabrics, heavy plastics, or leather. Select shears the right size for your hand. Keep the blades sharp, especially at the points. Pinking shears have little use in upholstering. |

| SEC. 2:05 RIPPING TOOL | The ripping tool, Fig. 2:05, is for removing tacks and tacked items. Commercial tools, about 9 inches long, may or may not have a notch in the front edge of the beveled blade. An inexpensive wood chisel is a good substitute for the commercial tool, and is preferred by many experienced upholsterers. In use, wedge the front edge of the blade under a tackhead or tacked item. Hold the flat side of the commercial tool, the beveled side of a chisel blade, against the wood to keep from gouging it. Tap the end of the handle smartly with a mallet (Sec. 2:09), or side of an upholsterer's hammer. |

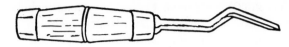

Fig. 2:05

SEC. 2:06 **UPHOLSTERY** **NEEDLES**	The average home upholsterer needs three hand needles—a single-point 7-inch heavy gauge, a 3- or 4-inch light-gauge curved needle, and a double-point 10-inch heavy-gauge straight needle, Fig. 2:06. Large curved needles are for stitching burlap to springs, fastening loose stuffing, and stitching hard and spring edges. Small curved needles are chiefly for blind-stitching. The straight needle is for stitching springs, loose stuffing, and buttons; imperial stitching; stitching roll, hard, and spring edges. [*1*] *Round point needles, b,* are for ordinary stitching of woven materials. [*2*] *Three-point-square needles* have a cutting action; use for stitching leather, imitation leather and plastics, and through felted padding and kapok. [*3*] *Use heavy-gauge needles* with upholstery or mattress twine (Sec. 3:08D). [*4*] *Use light-gauge needles* when hand-stitching twine (Sec. 3:08E), heavy thread, and finely woven textiles such as cretonne and chintz. [*5*] *Sizes*—Curved needles come in lengths of from 1 to 12 inches; straight needles, 6 to 20 inches. [*6*] *Double-pointed needles* are dangerous; store and handle carefully. [*7*] *Keep needle points* sharp, smooth, and gradually tapered to avoid tearing or snagging goods and to make stitching easier. Hone three-point-square needles from time to time so the edges can cut smoothly through leather, plastics, padding, etc.

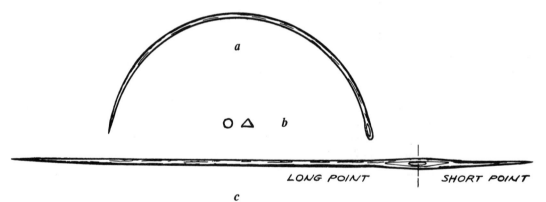

Fig. 2:06

SEC. 2:07 **REGULATOR**	No matter how carefully loose stuffing or padding is installed, small hollows and lumps often show up after they are covered. These are usually corrected by shifting the stuffing or padding with the pointed end of a regulator, Fig. 2:07 (Sec. 5:07). To prevent tearing or snagging a cover, keep regulator point smooth and sharp; most new regu-

Fig. 2:07

lators should be honed to a more gradual point. Use blunt end of regulator to place small wads of padding under a cover, and to work pleats in place. Ordinary ice picks are preferred by many upholsterers to commercial regulators.

NOTE: Do not regulate through leather, plastics, tightly woven or glazed fabrics.

**SEC. 2:08
UPHOLSTERY
SKEWERS**

Upholstery skewers, Fig. 2:08, are for pinning goods in place; they should taper gradually to smooth, sharp points. By moving skewers ahead as work progresses, a dozen usually are enough. Corsage pins may be substituted, but skewers are easier to handle, hold heavy goods better, and last longer.

Fig. 2:08

**SEC. 2:09
MALLET**

A rubber, plastic, or wooden mallet is for use chiefly with the ripping tool (Sec. 2:05).

**SEC. 2:10
WOOD RASP**

To protect various upholstery materials, some edges of wooden frames usually are rounded off (Sec. 5:12) with a 1-inch half-round wood rasp; a sharp knife may be used instead. Hold rasp firmly at both ends; if held loosely it can easily tear skin.

**SEC. 2:11
WIRE-BENDER**

The wire-bender, for shaping some coil springs and spring-edge wire (Secs. 7:07D, 7:16), is a short length of ¼-inch inside diameter pipe.

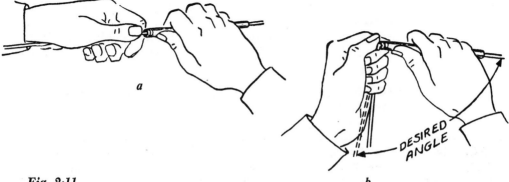

a

DESIRED ANGLE

Fig. 2:11   *b*

Insert spring or edge wire into bender to the planned point of bending, Fig. *a* 2:11. With a fast, snapping action bend spring or wire to an angle slightly sharper than the desired one, *b;* then unbend as necessary. If the initial bending is too slow, it will be rounded instead of relatively sharp. To curve a wire, make a series of small bends an inch or so apart. Instead of conventional wire bending, a spring or edge wire may be locked in a fairly heavy bench vise and bent or hammered to shape.

**SEC. 2:12
SPRING CLIP
PLIERS**

Spring clip pliers, Fig. 2:12, are for crimping or locking the metal clips (Fig. 3:19) used to fasten edge wire to springs in spring edge seats (Figs. 7:15A, *a* 7:16C) and backs. They can be crimped just as tight with ordinary pliers. Or edge wire can be tied to springs (Sec. 7:16C).

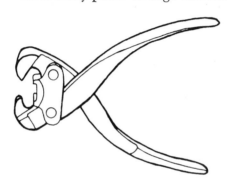

Fig. 2:12

**SEC. 2:13
CUSHION
CLOSING
EQUALIZERS**

Cushion closing equalizers, Fig. 2:13, stretch and hold traditionally made cushion and pillow casing uniformly tight while the opening is hand-stitched shut.   [*1*] *Commercial equalizer, a.* Rachet teeth, *A,* and spring clip, *B,* lock equalizer to a setting. Stick points *C* through corners of cushion cover and boxing, then spread equalizer until edges of cover and boxing are fairly taut.   [*2*] *Substitute equalizer, b,* works well and offers appreciable savings in tool costs. Instead of upholstery skewers (Sec. 2:08), large safety pins may be used at corners, and corsage pins between corners, of cushion cover and boxing. Work on a flat board or tabletop that is at least 2 feet longer than the side of a casing being closed.

NOTE: An equalizer is not needed for zippered boxing or casing (Sec. 17:06).

**SEC. 2:14
CUSHION
HAND-IRONS**

Sec. 2:14A Cushion Hand-Irons / Sheet metal cushion hand-irons, Fig. 2:14A, are for stuffing foam rubber, polyfoam, or spring cushion fillings (Secs. 3:63–3:73) into a casing. [*1*] *Lay irons on a*

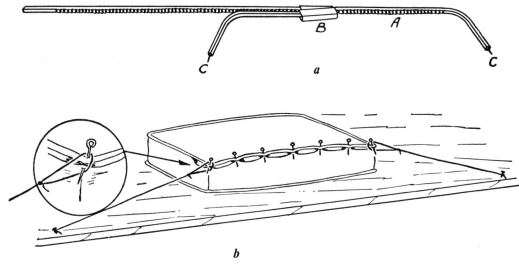

Fig. 2:13

flat surface, hinged sides up, and set to a convenient size for holding the cushion or pillow filling. [2] *Close irons* and squeeze them together, compressing the filling until it is a little narrower than the opening of the casing. Lock irons to size by hooking tabs into holes. [3] *Draw casing* completely over irons, then push filling out toward

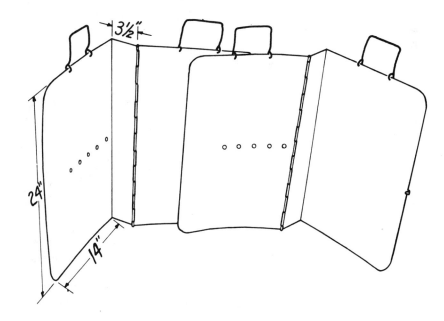

Fig. 2:14A

closed side of casing.   [4] *Upholstery shops* usually have cushion filling machines.

NOTE: Cushions and pillows may be filled without special tools (Sec. 17:13).

SEC. 2:14B SUBSTITUTE IRONS / Inexpensive but serviceable cushion hand-irons can be made with four pieces of very heavy cardboard or posterboard, Fig. 2:14B. The width or height of each back piece, A, is 1 inch less than the height of the cushion boxing. The sides, B, are at least 2 inches narrower than the width of the casing where it is to be closed. Fill cardboard the same way as regular irons (Sec. 2:14A); close them with cushion pliers (Sec. 2:14C).

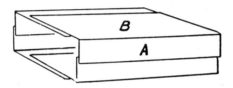

Fig. 2:14B

SEC. 2:14C CUSHION PLIERS / Two cushion pliers, Fig. 2:14C, are needed to hold cardboard cushion irons to a compressed size. Pliers are two pieces of 1-inch wood 3 or 4 inches wide by 3 or 4 feet long, connected by a hinge of woven webbing, heavy burlap, or canvas. The hinge should allow an inside gap of about 3 inches for filling the average upholstery cushion.   [1] *Set pliers in place* back from ends of filled cardboard irons, and tie them shut with several loops of twine.

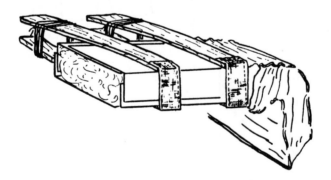

Fig. 2:14C

[2] *Hug or squeeze irons* toward hinges until cushion casing can be drawn in place. When the closed end of a casing is snug against the irons, remove pliers next to the casing; work casing over the irons to the remaining pliers, remove it, and work casing to the end of the irons.   [3] *Pull cardboard irons* out of casing one by one.

| **SEC. 2:15**
SEWING
MACHINE | A sewing machine is not essential for upholstering, but does simplify work. The average home machine is practical only for sewing muslin and most light-weight goods (Sec. 3:53B); it is not recommended for plastics unless it adjusts to five stitches per inch. Good hand sewing is as satisfactory as good machine work, and far better than poor machine work. However, cushion and pillow casings, especially when light-weight goods, are very difficult to hand sew with good results. Aside from welts (Secs. 12:06–12:08) and cushions (Chapter 17), there is little machine sewing in upholstering. A welting, cording, or zipper foot (Fig. 2:15) is almost essential for machine-sewing single welt (Sec. 12:06). For double-welt sewing machine foots see Sec. 12:08, however, all but the most expert sewers should have double-welt made by an experienced upholsterer. |

Fig. 2:15

| **SEC. 2:16**
MISCELLA-
NEOUS TOOLS | Other recommended tools are a steel tape measure; white school or tailor's chalk; small cake of beeswax. Upholstery and stitching twines (Sec. 3:08) are easier to use and will hold in place better if they are first drawn firmly across beeswax. A sharp knife, or razor blade and holder, and a smooth, varnished or lacquered yardstick are handy for many jobs. |

| **SEC. 2:17**
STAPLES | Experienced upholsterers often use staples for work commonly done with No. 8 and smaller tacks (Sec. 3:03). Ordinary semi-heavy-duty staples and spring-drive staple guns may be satisfactory with soft woods; but power stapling is needed for semi-hardwood and harder frames. Stapling is not recommended for inexperienced upholsterers. Unless a job does not require a smooth finished surface, or the upholsterer is skilled enough to by-pass the usual method of installing a casing or cover (Secs. 5:17–5:19), or stapling is done after a casing or cover is tightened, conventional tacking usually is more practical. |

3

materials

Sᴇᴄ. 3:00A / Upholstery materials are grouped by use (Sec. 3:00B), and as traditional or modern (Sec. 3:00C). Salvaging materials should be done cautiously. Few materials are the only "right" one for a job; for best results, use materials that you can handle best. Upholstering methods are given first on the basis of traditional materials, since all upholstering can be done with them, whereas some operations cannot be done as satisfactorily with modern materials. But some jobs can be done better with modern rather than traditional materials. However, most jobs can be done with either traditional or modern and often both are used. Most upholstery shops stock nearly all traditional materials. Some modern materials have too limited a use for regular stocking but may be ordered for you; others will be unavailable (Sec. 3:00C).

Sᴇᴄ. 3:00B Usᴇ / By use, upholstery materials are: glides, Sec. 3:01; wood finishes, Sec. 3:02; tacks, adhesives, Secs. 3:03–3:06; twine, thread, Secs. 3:07–3:09; webbing, Secs. 3:10–3:13; springs, Secs. 3:14–3:23; stuffing, Secs. 3:27–3:47; casing, Sec. 3:48; padding, Sec. 3:49; cover, trims, Secs. 3:50–3:60; cushion, pillow fillings, Secs. 3:61–3:73. Most groups have more than one type of a material. Some materials are in two groups.

SEC. 3:00C TRADITIONAL, MODERN MATERIALS / Materials are classed as traditional or modern depending on their common use by good quality custom upholsterers before about 1945. Most modern or post-1945 materials were developed for factory work. Many of these, such as certain spring-up items (Sec. 3:20), are manufactured for a specific article to be upholstered a specific way, and are not available to general upholsterers; some items are covered in this book for identification and because they may be used when reupholstering. Choosing traditional or modern materials because of the article involved, such as an antique, may not be advisable. For example, the condition of the wood rails in Fig. 4:17 made it better to reupholster this antique with zigzags than with traditional webbing and coil springs. Modern materials are commonly used for reupholstering antiques, and traditionals, such as curled hair, for modern, contour loose cushions.

SEC. 3:00D AMOUNTS / The amounts needed of some materials are based on the rough overall size and shape of an article. Other materials are estimated by measuring a frame. But in most cases the amounts needed depend on how an article is to be upholstered. Before purchasing materials, inexperienced upholsterers should study the articles in Chapter 1, and the work-steps listed. Most upholstery shops will gladly help make estimates; some allow return of certain unused materials. *Covers:* Cover goods can be quite costly. Measure amount needed carefully. Buying too little is risky; more may not be available later. Buying too much usually is money wasted; there seldom is much use for leftover scraps. Except for the simplest surfaces, such as in Figs. 1:01, 1:02: [1] *Build upholstered surfaces* through muslin casing (Chapters 6–10); [2] *Measure surfaces* to be covered (Secs. 11:00–11:23); [3] *Diagram* cover pieces (Sec. 11:24).

SEC. 3:01 **GLIDES,** **CASTERS**	Glides and casters protect the bottom of furniture legs against chipping and splintering. Glides are center- and 3-prong. Use the largest that fits the bottom of a leg with at least ⅛-inch clearance from the sides. Center-prong glides are for very narrow legs. Install glides before upholstering an article, and replace with unscratched glides after all work is done. When glides replace casters a seat is lowered; it may be necessary to build it higher (Sec. 3:16). Traditional casters have

fairly small metal or wooden wheels; they are chiefly for office furniture and antiques. Many modern type casters have a large wheel or ball, and simplify moving furniture on thick, deep-pile carpeting. Modern casters are not used on antique furniture. Most casters are installed in a hole drilled in the bottom of a leg; others, mounted on metal plates, are screwed to the bottom of a leg. When casters are in good condition, replacing them with glides is optional.

SEC. 3:02 WOOD FINISHES	**Sec. 3:02A Wood Finishes** / Apply stain, paint or other finish to legs and exposed-wood parts of frame (Sec. 4:01) just before installing the cover.

Sec. 3:02B Stain / Wood with attractive grain may be worth staining; others usually are painted or given a specialty finish (Sec. 3:02D). Light-color wood may be stained dark to resemble another wood and to emphasize grain or texture; birch is often stained mahogany. Tinted stains (green, yellow, red, etc.) are common; the lighter the natural color of a wood, the more noticeable tinting is. The finer a wood grain, the better it takes stain. Stain penetrates wood and will not chip or scratch off, which is important for the legs of an article. After staining, apply varnish or other protective coating (Sec. 3:02E). Oil-base stains, packaged ready for use, are fairly easy to apply with good results. Spirit- and water-base stains, usually sold as powders, are not difficult to prepare. But they dry much faster than oil stains and need quicker, more skillful application.

Sec. 3:02C Varnish-Stain / Varnish-stain, a stainlike coloring in varnish or other protective material (Sec. 3:02E), is a one-coat finish commonly found on poorer quality furniture. It does not penetrate wood, easily chips or scratches off.

Sec. 3:02D Paint, Specialties / Paint, as well as hiding unattractive or marred wood, offers maximum use of color in conventional and novelty ways. By "conventional" is meant solid, even coating. It can be made a "novelty" by adding trim of another color, tint, or shade . . . by brushing on a thin coat of another paint and wiping most of it off . . . by adding speckle, splatter, or flake effects with regular or metallic paint, etc. In addition to regular and novelty paint finishes there are many specialties, such as "driftwood," "bleach," and "antiquing." There are kits for most of these.

Sec. 3:02E Protective Finishes / Shellac, lacquer, varnish or other coating is given most stained or raw wood surfaces to protect them against soil discoloration. Shellac and lacquer dry quickly; varnish is fairly slow. Most plastic or synthetic coatings dry quickly. After a protective coat, wood often is waxed for extra safeguard against soil and a softer sheen. Before waxing, seal wood with a protective coating; if raw wood is waxed it is quite difficult to apply another finish successfully.

Sec. 3:02F Refinishing / Refinishing wood or changing from one finish to another can be easy or hard. Repainting seldom is a problem. Shellac a stain surface before painting it. Changing from paint to stain or a clear finish may demand much work with paint remover and sandpaper. But when dealing with older-looking furniture, remember that many such items were painted to make them "stylish" at some time, and under paint there may be very attractive wood or grain.

**SEC. 3:03
UPHOLSTERY
TACKS**

Sec. 3:03A Tacks / Tacking is a major part of upholstering. The cut bluesteel upholstery tack, Fig. *a* 3:03A, is best. It is strong, and its sharp, pin-like point sticks with a light tap of a hammer, yet is easy to knock away when sliptacking (Sec. 5:16). The wedge-shaped shaft tends to keep wood from splitting when a tack is fully driven; it also allows easy removal of tacks, even many years later. The small head, in relation to length of shaft, allows tacks to be set close together without their heads overlapping. Other tacks used for upholstering, *b–d,* have nail-like points not suited to sliptacking and have round shafts approximately the same thickness from point to head; they are more difficult to remove than wedge-shaped tacks, *a.* Wire upholstery tacks, *b,* have relatively thin heads that often break off. Trimmer's tacks, *c,* are next best to the wedge-shaped. Carpet tacks, *d,* are generally unsatisfactory for upholstering because of large heads on small tacks and small heads on large tacks. *[1] Upholsterers usually hold tacks in the mouth* and pluck them from between the lips by the magnetized face of a hammer (Sec. 2:02). Buy tacks triple-sterilized in sealed packages, not in bulk. Tacks salvaged from previous work seldom have points sharp enough for efficient work. *[2] Two rules for tacking.* First, have ample supplies of sizes needed (Table 3:03B). Second, always use the *smallest* tack that holds satisfactorily. The smaller a tack, the less it damages wood and other materials, such as the cover.

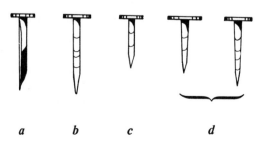

Fig. 3:03A   *a*   *b*   *c*   *d*

SEC. 3:03B   TACK SIZES   /   The tack sizes in Table 3:03B are for top quality wood frames (Sec. 4:03) in good condition. Use tacks one or more sizes larger for soft or spongy wood and wood that is "chewed up" from previous tacks, as the seat rails in Fig. 4:17. Wood as badly tack-damaged as that should be reupholstered by a method that does not require tacking on those surfaces.

TABLE 3:03B
UPHOLSTERY TACK SIZES

SIZE	LENGTH	USE FOR
1	3/16″	Post panel cover.
1½	7/32″	
2	4/16″	Post panel welt. Silk, light damask, similar fabrics; extremely light plastics.
2½	5/16″	Muslin casing. Light-, medium-weight textiles, plastics.
3	6/16″	Medium-weight textiles, plastics.
4*	7/16″	Burlapping. Loose stuffing. Blind-tacking. Cardboarding. Heavy-weight textiles, leather, leather substitutes, plastics. The thicker or heavier the goods being tacked and/or cardboarded, the larger the tack needed.
6*	8/16″	Small prebuilt edging.
8*	9/16″	Webbing.
10	10/16″	Blind-tacking through welt.
12	11/16″	Anchoring back spring twine.
14	12/16″	Large prebuilt edging. Clips for zigzag springs.
16	13/16″	Anchoring seat spring twine.
18	14/16″ }	Foundation work such as webbing, clips for zigzag
20	15/16″ }	springs, anchoring seat spring twine on soft wood.

* Tacks most often used with hardwood in good condition are sizes 4, 6, and 8.

SEC. 3:03C   TRIM NAILS   /   For gimp, trim tacks, and antique nails see Sec. 3:59.

SEC. 3:04 NAILS   In general, upholstery nails are only for installing rubber webbing (Sec. 3:22H), and clips for zigzag springs (Sec. 3:21E). Use the smallest nails that will hold securely.

SEC. 3:05 STAPLES   Instead of tacks, experienced upholsterers often use staples (Sec. 2:17). Fence staples are used to fasten coil springs to wooden webbing or a frame (Sec. 7:09).

SEC. 3:06 **GLUE,** **BONDING** **AGENT**	Gluing is work done with an adhesive, either glue or a bonding agent. Gluing is not common in upholstering, but when it should be done there is no good substitute. Glues and bonding agents sometimes may be used interchangeably. Glue sticks to a substance without becoming part of it. A true bonding agent becomes, chemically, part of the substance to which it is applied. [1] *Gluing* is used most in building frames (Chapter 4). To prevent raveling of a textile, run a light coat of glue along the cut edge. Many natural and synthetic glues, such as polyvinyl acetate or "white" glue, are suitable for upholstering. Get the right adhesive for the items involved; one ideal for wood may be worthless for polyfoam stuffing. Inexperienced workers should avoid instant contact glues. The oldest upholstery glues are hide and fish. Hide glue, the more difficult to work with, dries to maximum strength in a few hours, but takes years to harden to the point of being brittle. It makes strong, relatively flexible joints that usually outlast the rigid, unyielding kind. Hide glue is tedious to prepare and keep in useful condition. It should not be used by inexperienced workers or those wanting fast, shortcut methods. Fish glue is cheaper than hide, easier to prepare and apply, but dries to brittleness much sooner. It often has a strong odor when ready for use, which may recur in warm, humid weather. [2] *Bonding agents* are chiefly for compact stuffings and cushion units (Secs. 3:40–3:44, 3:67–3:70). Many glues will not hold these items; some tend to make stiff, hard joints. The correct bonding agent builds a soft but strong flexible joint.
SEC. 3:07 **TWINE,** **THREAD**	Upholstery twines and threads are tightly twisted natural (linen, cotton, hemp, etc.) and synthetic (rayon, nylon, etc.) fibers; synthetics may be continuous filament. Twine, heavier than thread, is for tying springs and for hand-stitching in general. Thread is for machine- and hand-stitching. In construction, fibers are twisted into cords, cords are counter-twisted into twine or thread. The more cords in a twine or thread, the smoother and stronger it is. Experienced upholsterers generally prefer linen twines and threads. Good quality cotton costs less than linen; cotton is slightly weaker but should not break under normal handling. Hemp and flax are considered the better heavier twines; jute is weaker; synthetics may be available. Bonded nylon thread is popular because of its strength; rayon often is considered too weak. Nylon thread has relatively little stretch and shrinkage, which may cause wrinkles when used with materials having much stretch or shrinkage; however, a stitch adjustment may compensate for this.
SEC. 3:08 **UPHOLSTERING** **TWINES**	Upholstering twines are: seat-spring, back-spring, upholstery or mattress, and hand-stitching. Smaller twines can substitute for larger to some extent but is not recommended. Twines usually are available in

8-ounce balls and large packages. [*1*] *Seat-spring twine,* often called simply spring twine, is for tying seat springs (Secs. 7:14, 7:15). Preferred traditional types are 6-cord hemp and flax; jute is relatively poor for seat springs. Poor quality or 3-cord twine often wears out or breaks in short time, which necessitates extensive seat repair. A 1-pound ball usually will do three large chairs or a sofa. Although more costly and harder than welt- or seaming-cord (Sec. 3:58), spring twine often substitutes for them. Seat-spring twine is fairly stiff and should not substitute for back-spring twine. Modern type seat-spring twine is nylon, rayon, or other continuous filament. [*2*] *Back-spring twine,* similar to but softer and lighter than seat-spring twine, is for tying back or pillow springs (Secs. 10:15–10:17) where strong but very flexible and soft twine is desirable. Double strands of back-spring twine may substitute for seat-spring twine. Upholstery twine may be used for back spring work, but is not recommended. [*3*] *Upholstery or mattress twine* is the most used in upholstering. It is for stitching springs to webbing, anchoring loose stuffing, stitching upholstery edges, tying back and pillow springs, and miscellaneous stitching. [*4*] *Hand-stitching twine* is chiefly for blind-stitching (Sec. 13:04) light- and medium-weight covers. It comes in several colors. Two strands of heavy thread may substitute for hand-stitching twine, but is not recommended; they tend to knot and kink and prevent neat, smooth blind-stitching.

SEC. 3:09 **UPHOLSTERY** **THREADS**	Upholstery threads for machine sewing usually are nylon and cotton; use nylon cautiously (Sec. 3:07). Polyester thread has the best sun resistance. No. 24-4 (size 24, 4 cords) is generally used with medium- and heavy-weight fabrics, plastics, leather substitutes, and other thick or heavy materials. For still heavier or thicker goods, use No. 16-4; for lighter goods, No. 30-4. Nos. 46 or 69 nylon or polyester are preferred for stretchable plastics. Many home machines are not suitable for upholstery (Sec. 2:15).
SEC. 3:10 **WEBBINGS**	Except for a frame, webbing is the foundation for most traditional (Sec. 3:00C) upholstery. Pad upholstery (Sec. 6:00) has a solid base or a webbed open frame. Most coil springs are mounted on webbing. Due to resilience, durability, and easy handling, 3½-inch jute webbing (Sec. 3:11) is used by most custom upholsterers for traditional work except for very thin surfaces such as the slimline type (Figs. 1:25, 1:26, *a* 1:55). There are several substitutes for traditional jute webbing (Secs. 3:12, 3:13). Two modern materials, zigzag springs and rubber webbing (Secs. 3:21, 3:22), combine purposes of webbing and springs and are treated as springs rather than webbing.

| SEC. 3:11 TRADITIONAL STRIP WEBBING | Traditional strip webbing is tightly woven jute, Fig. 3:11. A standard width is 3½ inches, although 2-, 3-, and 4-inch widths often are available; they come in rolls of 72, 100, and 144 yards. A good, serviceable grade of 3½-inch jute webbing for seat application weighs about 18 pounds per 144 yards. Strip webbing also may be cotton and linen, but these usually are too costly except for decorative webbing (Sec. 3:23). Strip webbing is in most traditionally built seats, arms, and backs; the amount needed is based on a frame. Most webbing salvaged from an old article is too inelastic and weak for satisfactory use. Synthetic strip webbing is replacing jute in many custom upholstery shops. |

Fig. 3:11

Polypropylene outdoor webbing is too light for upholstered furniture, but there is a heavy-weight polypropylene upholstery webbing. Rubber webbing (Sec. 3:22) may be used instead of jute webbing in many cases but is not a true substitute for it.

| SEC. 3:12 WOODEN WEBBING | Instead of jute, seats and backs frequently have wooden slat webbing. It lacks the resilience of strip webbing and may be noisy. Slats should be ¾- or 1-inch hardwood, 4 or 5 inches wide. Although often used to cut costs, slats are excellent for those deep frames which, if webbed on the bottom the usual way (Fig. 7:05A), would require extremely large springs (Secs. 3:16E, 7:10). Slat webbing can be set at any height in a cavity.   [1] *In seats*, replacing slat webbing with strip webbing is impractical if it requires use of much larger springs or a different type. [2] *In backs*, slat webbing often is replaced by strip webbing, and perhaps slightly larger springs, usually for a noticeable gain in comfort. |

SEC. 3:13 MISCELLANEOUS WEBBINGS	Metal straps, wires, and sheet webbing, usually consisting of heavy jute cloth or woven polypropylene, are common substitutes for seat and back webbing in factory upholstery. They may have permanently attached coil springs that are tied and otherwise treated the traditional way; modern versions are spring bars and units (Sec. 3:20). All these give good results when used properly, but salvaging for use in a different article is not advisable. If they do not fit together perfectly in all respects, it may take much expert revamping to make them compatible. When reupholstering, if factory substitutes for traditional webbing are in good condition, replacing them may not be practical. Usually it entails much work for small gain in comfort. In most cases greater comfort comes from using more resilient and possibly softer stuffing. But if the substitutes are broken or badly out of shape, they should be replaced.

SEC. 3:14 SPRINGS	Three types of springs are used in upholstering: Coil (Fig. 3:15C), zigzag (Fig. 3:21A), and rubber webbing (Fig. 3:22A). Coil springs can be used for all spring upholstery; but for extremely thin or slimline surfaces (Fig. 1:25), zigzags or rubber webbing are more practical. Zigzags also can be used for all spring jobs; but many experienced upholsterers do not use them for spring-edge seats and backs (Secs. 5:04D, 7:15, 10:16). Rubber webbing, suitable for many spring jobs, is used extensively in slimline and office furniture as well as the so-called Scandinavian. Zigzag springs and rubber webbing are easy to install, but require more careful planning than coil springs.

SEC. 3:15 COIL SPRINGS	Sec. 3:15A Coil Springs / Coil springs are classed by general use, size, firmness, shape, and how end coils are finished. All these factors are needed for ordering them, although not all kinds are regularly manufactured; satisfactory substitutions are easy to make. Sizes and number of coils, and overall shape of a coil spring (Fig. 3:15B), as well as gauge and grade of wire, determine a spring's firmness, efficiency, general quality, and cost. After a few years use, poor quality springs may lose resiliency or temper, resulting in a weak surface with too much go-down; they also tend to get permanent crooks or bends, making them unsuitable for reupholstering. Basic coil springs and uses are: [1] *Upholstery springs,* made from 9- to 11-gauge wire, for seats. [2] *Pillow or back springs,* of finer wire than upholstery springs, for backs and spring arms. [3] *Cushion springs,* of the finest wire generally used for upholstery springs, for cushion fillings; although available individually, they usually are made into inner-spring units (Sec. 3:63) that are used for cushions, pillows, inside backs, and some thick inside arms.

SEC. 3:15B   COIL SPRING SHAPES   /   Coil springs are conical, double helical, and cylindrical, Fig. *a* 3:15B. A conical spring, having only one large or "soft" coil, is harder or firmer than a double-helical, which is harder or firmer than a cylindrical of the same size and temper.

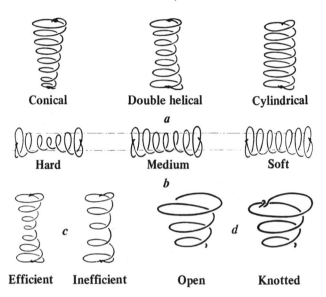

Conical	Double helical	Cylindrical
	a	
Hard	Medium	Soft
	b	
Efficient Inefficient	Open	Knotted

Fig. 3:15B

Upholstery and pillow springs are conical and double-helical; the latter generally is in top quality upholstery. Cushion springs are cylindrical. Double-helical and cylindrical springs can be mounted on all upholstery foundations. Conical springs cannot be mounted satisfactorily on traditional type strip webbing (Sec. 3:11). Double-helical springs the same size and height are rated as Hard, Medium, and Soft, according to the diameter of the middle or waist coil, Fig. *b* 3:15B; the smaller the waist coil, the harder the spring. The fewer the coils, *c,* the weaker and less efficient a spring is. Avoid double-helical springs that taper quickly from large end coils to small waist coils; in use, the hard waist coils pass through the large soft end coils, and the sprung-up surface is initially soft but soon becomes relatively hard and unyielding.

SEC. 3:15C   END COILS   /   End coils are either open or knotted (Fig. *d* 3:15B) and a spring is OBE (Open Both Ends), KOE (Knotted One End), or KBE (Knotted Both Ends). OBE is the least expensive, KBE the most expensive. Knotting end coils strengthens a spring and eliminates a loose wire that could work through upholstery. These good effects are gained for OBE and KOE springs by shaping end coils and tying springs (Secs. 7:07, 7:11). As to end coils for kinds of springs: [1] *Upholstery springs* in the front row of a spring-edge seat (Sec. 7:07C) usually are OBE or KOE to allow for shaping the top coil; KBE springs are satisfactory. The other springs in a seat may be any type.   [2] *Pillow springs* may be any type. Being weaker than upholstery springs, their end coils are easier to shape for a spring-edge back.   [3] *Cushion springs* usually are OBE, incased, and cross-tied (Sec. 3:63).

Sec. 3:15D Substituting, Salvaging / Most shops do not stock all sizes and kinds of coil springs. Stocks usually allow for satisfactory substitutions (Sec. 3:16E). Generally coil springs may be salvaged, or used when reupholstering, unless they are bent or "dead," the type webbing is to be changed, or webbing is to be set at a different level or height. If there are appreciable differences in strength among springs of the same sizes and kinds in a surface, replace all. Cushion springs seldom wear out; casings may. But regardless of condition, most upholsterers discard springs that are more than seven years old.

SEC. 3:16 SPRINGS REQUIRED

Sec. 3:16A Seats / Size and number of coil springs for a seat depend on its planned finished height, height of the front rail above the floor, type seat, compression given springs when tying them, size and shape of the seat. For zigzag springs and rubber webbing see Sec. 3:16I.

Sec. 3:16B Planned Height / At the front, the top of most solid seats (Fig. 1:30) and of the cushion in loose- (Fig. *a* 1:42) and attached-cushion seats (Fig. 1:51) is 16 to 18 inches above the floor. For tall people, 18 inches usually is a comfortable seat height; for short people, 16 inches.

Sec. 3:16C Planned Thickness / Thickness of a seat is its planned height minus height of the bottom of the front rail above the floor. However: [1] *For a coil spring seat webbed on top* of, or inside, a cavity (Sec. 7:03) instead of on the bottom, seat thickness is planned height of seat minus height of webbing above the floor.   [2] *For a pad seat* subtract height of the top of the front rail above the floor from planned height of the top of the seat at the front to find the size roll edge (Sec. 6:04E) and/or thickness of compact stuffing (Sec. 6:04E) to use.

NOTE: Measure all heights above floor after installing glides or casters (Sec. 3:01).

Sec. 3:16D Tied-Down Height of Springs / Installed coil springs are compressed slightly during tying to take out initial slack and make a stronger, more dependable base for stuffing. Knowing the tied-down height, find the free height and from that the size springs (Sec. 3:16E). According to the type seat: [*1*] *Solid seat.* Subtract planned thickness of stuffing from thickness of a seat (Sec. 3:16C) to find tied-down height of coil springs. In most solid seats stuffing is about 2 inches thick. [*2*] *Loose-, attached-cushion seats.* Subtract total thickness of cushion and seat edge and stuffing from planned thickness of a seat to find tied-down height of springs. Most standard seat cushions are about 4½ inches thick; seat edge and stuffing usually total about 1 inch thick.

SEC. 3:16E SEAT COIL SPRING SIZES / Upholstery springs (Sec. 3:15A) are usually compressed about 1 inch when tied. Add 1 inch to tied-down height of a spring to find free height, and from that find spring size in Table 3:16E.

TABLE 3:16E
UPHOLSTERY OR SEAT SPRINGS

FREE HEIGHT	SIZE No.
4 inches	00
5 "	0
6 "	1
7 "	1½
8 "	2
9½ "	3
11½ "	4
13 "	5
14 "	6

SUBSTITUTIONS

[*1*] In spring-edge seats (Sec. 7:07) springs forming the edge are firmer than the others. If a spring the same size as but firmer than the others is not available, use a spring a size higher than the seat requires and tie it down to the same height as the others.

[*2*] If a particular size upholstery spring is not available, use one a size larger and softer, or a size smaller and firmer.

[*3*] No. 4 and larger springs may, due to height, build wobble into a seat.

SEC. 3:16F / Calculation of seat spring sizes (Secs. 3:16A–E) may be clarified by the following:

EXAMPLES OF DESIGNING SEATS FOR HEIGHT

	Coil Spring Seats		Pad Seats
	Loose-, Attached- Cushion	Solid	
Planned height of seat (Sec. 3:16B)	17″	17″	17″
Minus height of front rail (Sec. 3:16C)	−4½″	−10″	−15½″
Overall thickness of seat (Sec. 3:16C)	12½″	7″	1½″
Minus thickness of cushion, edge, stuffing, etc. (Sec. 3:16D)	−5½″	−2″	
Tied-down height of coil springs (Sec. 3:16D)	7″	5″	
Plus initial coil spring compression (Sec. 3:16E)	+1″	+1″	
Free height of springs	8″	6″	
Size of upholstery springs (Table 3:16E)	No. 2	No. 1	

SEC. 3:16G FIRMNESS / Base choice of hard, medium, or soft springs (Sec. 3:15E) on the person the seat is made for and the kind of seat: *[1] Use hard springs* for heavy, soft springs for light-weight people; in case of doubt, use medium or hard. *[2] Thin solid seats* (Fig. 1:03) usually have hard springs; medium and soft springs might let seat top sink into cavity. *[3] Loose- and attached-cushion seats* generally have hard springs in the front row and back corners for comfort and durability. *[4] T-shaped seats* (Fig. c 1:45) usually lack space at the front corners for setting springs on webbing; for spring-edge seats set a No. 1 Hard upholstery spring on seat rails at the corner (Fig. 7:15A); for roll and hard edges, instead of springs, fill corners with a firm stuffing such as kapok (Sec. 3:65).

NOTE: Hard and Soft springs are not always available, and Medium must be substituted. For a Hard spring, substitute Medium one size larger; for a Soft spring, substitute Medium one size smaller.

SEC. 3:16H QUANTITY OF SEAT SPRINGS / The number of coil springs in a seat depends on size and shape of a cavity or base. Subject to generally recommended placements (Sec. 7:07), use as many springs as will fit a space without touching one another.

SEC. 3:16I ZIGZAG SPRINGS, RUBBER WEBBING / Zigzag springs and rubber webbing (Secs. 3:21, 3:22) are usually installed on the top surface of a seat frame. Comfortable seat height is based on height of top of front rail and/or how thick the cushion and/or stuffing must be (Secs. 3:16B, C, D).

SEC. 3:16J FRAMES NOT DESIGNED FOR ZIGZAG SPRINGS, RUBBER WEBBING / When zigzag springs or rubber webbing is used in a frame *not* designed for it, subtract thickness of cushion and/or stuffing from planned height of finished seat to find out how high top of front rail should be. The difference between this and the actual height of the top of the rail must be corrected: [1] *If frame is too high,* cut down legs or use thinner stuffing and/or cushion. Thin cushion or stuffing cautiously; the finished seat may be uncomfortable. [2] *If frame is too low,* build up with wood unless it is only about 1 inch low, in which case use thicker stuffing or cushion.

EXAMPLES OF DESIGNING SEATS FOR HEIGHT
FRAME NOT BUILT FOR ZIGZAG SPRINGS OR RUBBER WEBBING

	LOOSE-, ATTACHED- CUSHION SEAT	SOLID SEAT
Planned height of seat (Sec. 3:16B)	17″	17″
Minus planned thickness of cushion and/or stuffing (Sec. 3:16D)	−5½″	−2″
Required height top of front rail	11½″	15″
Actual height top of front rail	13½″	13½″
Lower seat frame or use thinner stuffing, cushion	−2″	
Raise seat frame or use thicker stuffing, or cushion for a cushion seat		+1½″

SEC. 3:16K FRAMES DESIGNED FOR ZIGZAG SPRINGS, RUBBER WEBBING / With frames built for zigzag springs or rubber webbing it is necessary only to determine how thick stuffing for a solid seat, or combined thickness of stuffing and cushion for a cushion seat, must be to make a comfortable height.

EXAMPLES OF DESIGNING SEATS FOR HEIGHT
FRAME BUILT FOR ZIGZAG SPRINGS OR RUBBER WEBBING

	LOOSE-, ATTACHED- CUSHION SEAT	SOLID SEAT
Planned height of seat (Sec. 3:16B)	17″	17″
Minus height of top of front rail (Sec. 3:16A)	−11½″	−15″
Required thickness of cushion and/or stuffing	5½″	2″

SEC. 3:17 **REQUIRED** **SPRINGS:** BACKS, ARMS	*[1] Backs.* Due to problems of building spring backs, how to figure size and quantity of coil springs needed is in Secs. 10:03, 10:10, 10:11, 10:15. Back or pillow springs (Sec. 3:15A) are sized by free height: 4, 6, 8, 9, and 10 inches; they are not rated in degrees of firmness. *[2] Arms.* Spring armtops (Sec. 8:23) built the traditional way usually have a row of 6-inch back or pillow springs.

SEC. 3:18 **REQUIRED** **SPRINGS:** INNER-SPRING UNIT	Size and quantity of cushion springs (Sec. 3:15A) for an inner-spring unit depend on the size and shape cushion or back pillow and the spring filling used (Chapter 17); and on the size and shape inside back or other upholstered surface and the stuffing to be used. The smaller a cushion spring's diameter, the stronger and more durable it is; smallest diameter is 2½ inches.

SEC. 3:19 **EDGE-WIRE**	Spring edge-wire unites and shapes spring edges in seats and inside backs. Use only the highly tempered steel wire made for this purpose; others may break or bend permanently, requiring extensive seat or back repair. Spring edge-wire is sold in 5- to 12-foot lengths. *[1] Seat* edge-wire (Sec. 7:14) is 9- or 10-gauge; it also is used in some inside backs (Sec. 10:12C). *[2] Back* edge-wire is 12- to 14-gauge. *[3] Metal clips,* Fig. 3:19, fasten edge-wire to springs; twine ties may be used instead (Sec. 7:16C). *[4] Re-use* edge-wire in good condition only if it fits a new spring surface without having to be reshaped.

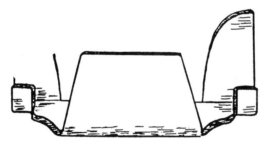

Fig. 3:19

SEC. 3:20 **FACTORY** **SPRINGING,** **SPRING BARS,** **SPRING UNITS**	SEC. 3:20A FACTORY SPRINGING / When reupholstering a seat or back and the design, size, and shape are not to be changed, usually there is no need to replace factory spring bars or units (Sec. 3:00C, 3:20B, C) that are in good condition except for broken ties. But if not in good condition, or changes will be made in a surface, most inexperienced upholsterers should use different springing materials; inexpert repair and modification of bars and units seldom are satisfactory. Replace broken tie twines such as would be used in spring bars (Fig. *a, b* 3:20B) and spring units.

NOTE: Do not confuse "spring unit" with cushion unit, inner-spring unit, marshall unit (Sec. 3:63).

Sec. 3:20B Spring Bars / Spring bars usually are fastened to the top of front and back seat rails, to the front of top and bottom back rails. *Type a* spring bar, Fig. 3:20B, is for seats; the drop bar lowers springs into seat cavity for good spring action without an exceptionally high seat. *Types b, c, d, e* are for backs. Tie top coils of types *a* and *b* as for traditional coil springs (Secs. 7:11–7:15, 10:11–10:15). Border or edge-wire on top coils of types *c, d, e* eliminates most vertical spring tying and simplifies side-to-side tying (Sec. 10:15); it makes a firmer surface than one having free coil springs, type *b*.

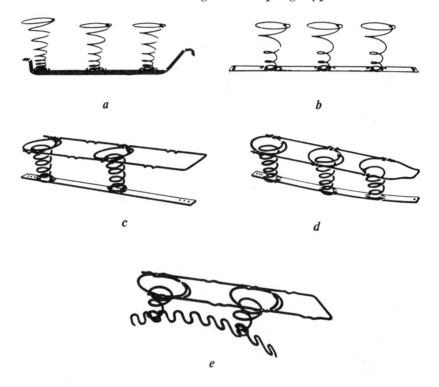

a

b

c

d

e

Fig. 3:20B

Sec. 3:20C Spring Units / Factory spring units are tied down enough in a seat or back cavity to take out initial spring slack and create basic crown (Sec. 5:14), and anchor them in place. *Type a* spring unit, Fig. 3:20C, is for seats. Instead of wire mounts, seat units may have drop or flat bars (Fig. *a, b* 3:20B) and double-helical instead of conical springs. Most seat units are flexibly attached to the front rail and connected by short, strong coil springs to side and back rails to keep the front edge in place and allow maximum spring action else-

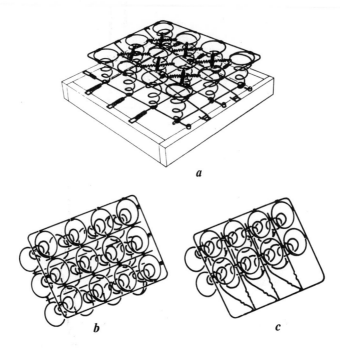

Fig. 3:20C   *b*   *c*

where. The top coils of the best grade seat spring units are "cross-tied" with coil springs. *Types b* and *c*, Fig. 3:20C, for backs, have double-helical springs for maximum softness, edge-wired top coils for durable shape. For extra softness, back spring units are installed on strip webbing (Sec. 3:11) for each vertical and each horizontal row of springs. *Type c* has fewer springs than *b*, but is strengthened (and made harder) by wires from lower border wire to bottom coils.

NOTE: Before modern spring units were developed, a common factory spring-up item was a sheet of heavy canvas or woven fiber on which conical springs were mounted.

SEC. 3:21
ZIGZAG
SPRINGS

SEC. 3:21A ZIGZAG SPRINGS / Zigzag, sinew, sinuous, and arc are some names for the type of modern spring in Fig. 3:21A. It is used in duplication and restoring antiques (Fig. 4:17) as well as in traditional and modern furniture, especially for thin and/or relatively flat surfaces. Zigzags eliminate webbing (Sec. 3:10) and most, sometimes all, spring tying (Secs. 7:11–7:15, 10:11–10:15). If a frame was not built for zigzags, reinforcing it may be necessary. If installed zigzags collapse, which seldom happens and usually is a result of faulty installation, repair generally is more involved than for similar coil spring failure. Most upholstery shops stock zigzags in rolls, 9- and 11-gauges, and will cut lengths to measurement. Zigzags require more advance planning than coil springs but are simpler to install.

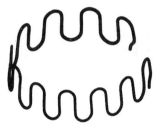

Sec. 3:21B **Basic Installation** / [*1*] *Install zigzag springs* from back to front in seats, Fig. 3:21B; in backs, from bottom rail or liner to top rail (Fig. 10:32B); from side to side in cots, cribs, etc. [*2*] *Space zigzag strands* equidistant from each other and the side rails.

Fig. 3:21B

If this cannot be done, set outside strands close to posts, space others evenly between them. Most seats are wider at the front; strands are closer together at the back. [*3*] *Face adjacent zigzag strands* in opposite directions for connectors (Sec. 3:21C) to work straight across and build a more uniform surface. [*4*] *Ends of strands* usually are held by clips (Sec. 3:21D). [*5*] *Anchor outside strands* to side rails (Sec. 3:21H).

Sec. 3:21C **Spring Action** / Comfort of a zigzag spring surface depends on how freely strands can go down in use. Side movement or strand displacement must be prevented, or hollows may develop and the surface become uncomfortable, lose shape, and fall apart. To prevent this and build uniform surface tension, adjacent strands are connected (Fig. 3:21B). Spring connectors, Fig. 3:21C, give most freedom of movement; wire links and tie twines pull adjacent strands down. Common types of connectors are: [*a*] *Open-hook, close-wound coil.* Use to connect seat springs and anchor outside strands to

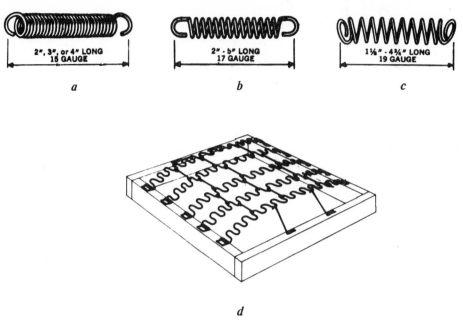

a   *b*   *c*

d

Fig. 3:21C

side rails, metal frames of cots, cribs, etc. (Sec. 3:21H). Builds very firm surface; not for backs. [*b*] *Open-hook, open-wound coil spring.* For seats, backs. Builds smooth, flexible surface not quite as firm as if built with close-wound springs. [*c*] *Open-wound springs,* ends snap easily and permanently into zigzags. More resilient than open-hook types, but less durable. Use only for backs. [*d*] *Wire links,* least independent spring action. For firm surface with relatively little resilience, often wanted in a slimline article with a loose-cushion seat (Sec. 7:00B). *Twine ties* may replace wire links.

Sec. 3:21D Clips, Fasteners / Common clips and other means of fastening ends of zigzag springs to frames are shown in Fig. 3:21D: [*a*] *Flat two-hole clip;* use on front surface of back frame if two nails are satisfactory for permanent fastening. [*b*] *Flat three-hole clip;* use on top surface of seat frame.   [*c*] *Flat clip for one- or two-hole* nailing of lip; may replace clips [*a, b*]. Use one nail for light gauge springs, two for heavy gauge (Sec. 3:21K). [*d*] *Hinge link;* use on rear seat rail to provide a movable pivot permitting higher arc and greater resilience (Sec. 3:21J). Place spring end in clip and hammer lip down before nailing clip to frame. [*e*] *1-inch drop clip;* set spring end 1 inch below top of rail for increased arc, [*d*] above. *NOTE:* When a lower back rail or liner prevents nailing a flat clip on top of a seat

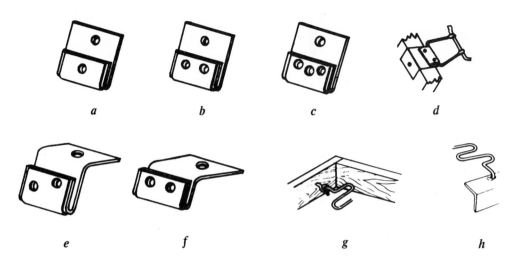

a   *b*   *c*   *d*

e   *f*   *g*   *h*

Fig. 3:21D

rail, a 1-inch drop clip may be nailed to back of seat rail; rail must be exactly 1 inch thick (Sec. 3:21E). [*f*] *½-inch drop clip;* sets spring end ½-inch below top of rail for increased arc, [*d*] above. [*g*] *Screw-eye,* to set spring end a distance other than 1 or ½ inch below top of rail for increased arc, [*d*] above, or when drop clips not available. Use heavy-duty screw-eyes; use eye-bolts if wood will not hold screws. Shape spring ends for anchoring (Sec. 3:21G). [*h*] *For metal frames* shape spring ends (Sec. 3:21G) and hook in holes in frame; not recommended for wood frames (Sec. 3:21F).

SEC. 3:21E INSTALLING CLIPS / For best results nail clips with barbed, cement-coated, solid countersunk-head, ⅞-inch 14-gauge nails for hardwood frames, 1-inch 13-gauge for soft lumber; use nails about ½-inch longer when barbed, cement-coated ones are not available. Set bent end of a flat clip, or of a drop clip used as a flat clip, flush with inside edge of rail, Fig. 3:21E. Clips overhanging edges bend in use and eventually break; if clips are set back from an edge, spring ends rub against rail and squeak. Shape spring ends before installation (Sec. 3:21G). First loosely nail end of clip, then fit spring bar into clip, and nail it. Usually all seat or back clips are nailed loosely first, then one-by-one spring ends are fitted into clips on the back rail of a seat, bottom rail or liner of a back, and the clips nailed down. Then free ends are fitted into clips and nailed down on the other rails.

SEC. 3:21F HOLES IN WOOD FRAMES / Zigzag spring ends sometimes are inserted in holes drilled in wood. This is not recommended. To hold and pivot properly, spring ends must be shaped to the same

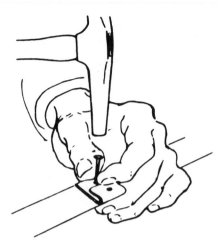

Fig. 3:21E

angles as the holes. Cut ends must be specially coated to keep from enlarging holes.

SEC. 3:21G   SHAPE SPRING ENDS   /   Bend back, Fig. *a* 3:21G, zigzag spring ends to be held by clips to keep them from gouging wood and possibly loosening clips. If an end is to hook in a screw-eye or hole in a metal frame (Fig. *g, h* 3:21D), first bend the outside bar of the spring sharply, at about the middle, toward the point of fastening it; then bend it back to hook securely in metal eye or hole. A tool for shaping ends is shown in Fig. *b* 3:21G; or, clamp spring securely in a bench vise and hammer end to shape. A shop that sells springs usually will cut them and shape the ends.

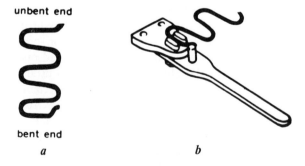

unbent end

bent end

Fig. 3:21G   *a*   *b*

SEC. 3:21H   ANCHORING SIDES   /   Anchor side strands of a zigzag spring surface to side rails (Sec. 3:21C). Use standard connectors (Fig. *a–d* 3:21C) and retainer plates, Fig. *a, b* 3:21H, or tie strands, *c.* [*a*] *Vertical retainer plates,* generally used in cushion seats, let connectors be anchored nearly as high as zigzags should rise above a side rail. This provides mainly horizontal pull on side strands and

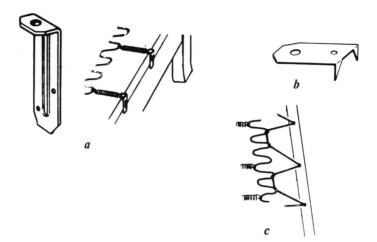

Fig. 3:21H   c

helps build planned arc of a surface (Sec. 3:21K); set top of retainer
to follow arc of spring surface from side to side at that point, usually
somewhat below the outer edge of the spring. Set plate in place, nail
in holes.   [*b*] *Horizontal retainer plates* anchor connectors flush with
top of side rail. They are in most solid seats and may be in cushion
seats (Fig. *d, e* 3:21Q). Set plate with nail holes about midway between edges of rail; hammer pronged corners down tight, then nail.
[*c*] *Tie zigzag springs at sides* with spring twine for seats, back-spring
twine for backs (Sec. 3:08). First set anchor tacks (Sec. 3:03) on side
rails (Sec. 3:21I); near each end set a tack for anchoring twine ends
with an overhand knot (Fig. *b* 7:14B); use two-tack method for all
other anchoring. To side-tie: [*1*] *Securely anchor* an end of a twine,
drive tack in full.   [*2*] *Loop twine around zigzag coil*, Fig. *c* 3:21H,
to pass smoothly to next anchor point.   [*3*] *Loop twine around
anchoring tack* (Fig. *a* 7:14B) next to previous anchoring point. Pull
tight enough to draw outer edge of spring down into planned arc of
spring surface from side to side at that point (Sec. 3:21K); drive tack
in full.   [*4*] *Loop twine around second anchoring tack*, pull tight,
drive tack in full.   [*5*] *Continue anchoring* along the side as in [*2*],
[*3*], [*4*] above. Anchor twine end as in [*1*].

SEC. 3:21I NUMBER, PLACEMENT OF SIDE ANCHORS / Side anchoring makes zigzag springs work as a unit. With too few anchors there
is poor control of shape (Sec. 3:21K), springs are apt to twist, a surface is weak; with too many, a surface is unnecessarily firm and unyielding. Side anchor points usually are directly (Fig. 10:31B) or
indirectly (Fig. 3:21B) in line with connectors to prevent spring twisting. Slope anchoring material from rail to springs uniformly throughout to build a smooth, regular surface. Most surfaces need at least
two anchor points per side.   [*1*] *Seats*. Side anchors are 1 to 2 inches

from ends of side rails, and 4 to 6 inches from other anchor points; actual placement depends on where outside spring loops are (Fig. 3:21B). [2] *Backs.* Springs need maximum individual movement for softness; regardless of size, usually there are only two side anchoring points, evenly spaced, on each side of a back (Fig. 10:31B).

SEC. 3:21J LENGTHS OF ZIGZAG STRANDS / Zigzag strands usually are the same length throughout a surface except in seats with appreciably curved front and/or back rails, in backs with a shaped top rail arching appreciably above the sides, and when rails holding the ends of strands are not parallel. Find length of strands needed by measuring frame, adjusting for unusual arc if any (Sec. 3:21K), and consulting Tables in Sec. 3:21L. Normally, fastening clips are mounted flush with the inside edges of a frame (Sec. 3:21E); measure midway between sides of a seat or back, Fig. 3:21J. For clips mounted other than normally, or when using screw-eyes, measure the same way as for normal installation but between clips or screw-eyes. For spring ends hooking into holes in a frame, measure length from hole to hole.

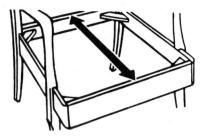

Fig. 3:21J

SEC. 3:21K ARC OF ZIGZAGS / Installed zigzags arc smoothly from end to end, Fig. 3:21K. Installed the regular way, a length of zigzag has normal arc (Sec. 3:21L). [1] *Lower than normal arc.* Reducing arc by using shorter-than-normal length strands makes a harder, flatter, deader (less springy) surface. It may be done for a relatively flat surface, as for an attached-cushion ottoman. For lower than normal arc, deduct length from normal arc lengths. [2] *Normal arc.* Arc that a strand the correct length for a cavity has when installed

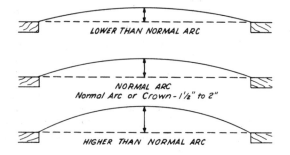

Fig. 3:21K

properly; it usually has the best degree of softness, firmness, and crown (Sec. 5:14) for comfort, durability, and appearance. [3] *Higher than normal arc.* Increasing arc by using longer-than-normal zigzags builds a softer but weaker surface. It is fairly common in pull-over backs (Figs. 1:19, *a* 1:49). For higher than normal arc, add to normal arc lengths; but be cautious, as excessive arc can weaken a zigzag spring surface to the point where it may collapse.

Sec. 3:21L Length, Number of Zigzag Strands Needed / [1] *Length.* Measure frame (Sec. 3:21J). Table 3:21L-I has recommended gauges and lengths of springs for normal arc (Sec. 3:21K); for other arcs see notes below table. Lengths and arcs in the table may be approximations, since other gauges of zigzags often must be used, and frame measurements may not be to exact inches. Also, measurements often must be adjusted to the spring stock when preparing it (Sec. 3:21M). [2] *Number for seats.* As well as the number of strands commonly in a seat, Table 3:21L-II gives normal spacing between clips (Sec. 3:21E), recommended distances from outside anchors to arm posts, and size connectors (Sec. 3:21C). Sometimes recommended spacings must be changed by plus or' minus a half-inch, but seldom more than that. [3] *Number for backs.* Inside backs, subject to less pressure than seats, are meant to be softer and usually have fewer as well as softer strands of zigzags. Generally there is one less strand in the back than in the seat of an article. More strands tend to make a back extra firm, fewer strands may weaken it seriously.

NOTE: Tables 3:21L are for standard or regular Kay-Arc Springs, courtesy of Kay Manufacturing Corp. Data for other brands may be slightly different.

Sec. 3:21M Measuring, Cutting Zigzags / When possible, purchase zigzag springs cut to length and with ends shaped (Sec. 3:21G). [1] *Measuring.* Hold spring stock curving downward, Fig. *a* 3:21M, with the bar at the free end flush with the end of a yardstick, *b*. Roll stock along yardstick to required length; be sure to keep stock flat. Cutpoints at both ends of a strand usually face the same direction, *b*. When rails to which springs are fastened are parallel, only one strand actually is measured; cut others to length by counting the loops along one side. But when springs come from different rolls of stock, or when taking stock from close to the core of a roll, it is better to measure each strand. [2] *Cutting.* There are special tools for cutting zigzag springs, such as the cutter and reel in Fig. *c* 3:21M; or clamp in a vise and cut with a hacksaw.

Sec. 3:21N Stretching Zigzags / Zigzag springs are usually stretched by hand for installation. But for heavy gauge springs, or if

Table 3:21L-I

Seats: Inside Seat dimension	Gauge	Kay-Arc Length	Arc	Backs: Inside back dimension	Gauge	Kay-Arc Length	Arc
12″	11	11¾″	1¼″	16″	12 or 13	16″	1½″
13″	10½	12¾″	1¼″	17″	12 or 13	17″	1⅝″
14″	10	13¾″	1⅜″	18″	12 or 13	18¼″	1¾″
15″	10	14¾″	1½″	19″	12 or 13	19¼″	1⅞″
16″	10	15¾″	1⅝″	20″	12	20¼″	2″
17″	9½	16¾″	1⅝″	21″	12	21¼″	2″
18″	9	17¾″	1¾″	22″	12	22¼″	2″
19″	9	18¾″	1¾″	23″	11, 11½, 12	23½″	2¼″
20″	9	20″	1⅞″	24″	11, 11½, 12	24½″	2¼″
21″	9	21″	1⅞″	25″	11, 11½, 12	25½″	2½″
22″	8½	22″	1⅞″	26″	11-12	26½″	2½″
23″	8½	23″	2″				
24″	8½	24″	2″				
25″	8	24⅞″	2″				
26″	8	25¾″	2″				
27″	8	26¾″	2″				

Table 3:21L-II

Distance Between Arms Along Front Seat Rail	Number of Strands	Center to Center Spacing of Clips	Distance from Center of Outside Clips to Inside of Arm Posts	Size of Connecting Links	Size of Seat Helical or Extension Spring
21″ Chair	5	4¼″	2″	2⅝″	2″
22″ Chair	5	4½″	2″	2⅞″	2½″
23″ Chair	5	4¾″	2″	3⅛″	2½″
24″ Chair	5	5″	2″	3⅜″	3″
25″ Chair	6	4¼″	1⅞″	2⅝″	2″
40″ Sectional	9	4½″	2″	2⅞″	2½″
50″ Love Seat	11	4½″	2½″	2⅞″	2½″
52″ Love Seat	11	4¾″	2¼″	3⅛″	2½″
58″ Sofa	12	5″	1½″	3⅜″	3″
60″ Sofa	13	4¾″	1½″	3⅛″	2½″
62″ Sofa	13	4¾″	2½″	3⅛″	2½″
63″ Sofa	14	4½″	2¼″	2⅞″	2½″
65″ Sofa	14	4¾″	1⅝″	3⅛″	2½″

For lower than Normal Arc (Sec. 3:21K). From lengths in Seats and Backs Table (Table 3:21L–I) *deduct* ¼ inch for each ⅛-inch *less* arc desired. Lengths up to about 15 inches should be shortened only by ¼ inch; greater lengths may be shortened by up to ¾-inch.

For Higher than Normal Arc. To lengths in Seats and Backs Tables above *add* ¼ inch for each additional ⅛-inch, approximate, of arc desired. Upon exceeding ¼-inch additional arc, "pocketing" may occur unless hinge links (Sec. 3:21D) are used; subtract 1 inch from the adjusted length of the strand to allow for the length of the hinge link. When a seat is built with higher than normal arc it may be advisable to increase the pitch (slope down from front to back) in order to maintain seating comfort.

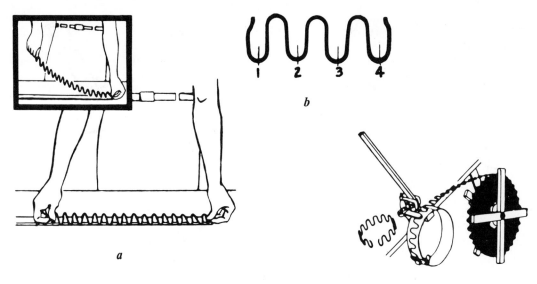

b

a

c

Fig. 3:21M

they are shortened for lower than normal arc (Sec. 3:21L), a spring stretcher may be needed, Fig. 3:21N. Or stretch by tying a spring bar to a stick, then pulling the stick or working it as a lever.

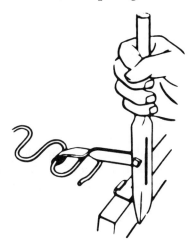

Fig. 3:21N

SEC. 3:21O ZIGZAG SPRING-EDGES / A spring-edge (Sec. 5:04D) seat or back built with zigzags (Secs. 7:32, 10:32) has special edge springs, Fig. *b* 3:21O, to build the front or top of the surface into a relatively flat deck or platform extending to the outer edge of a frame, *a*. Border or edge wire (Sec. 3:19) completes basic spring edge, which is then tied down to desired height. Torsion springs, Fig. *e* 3:21O, may be used to strengthen a spring edge. Edge and torsion springs are

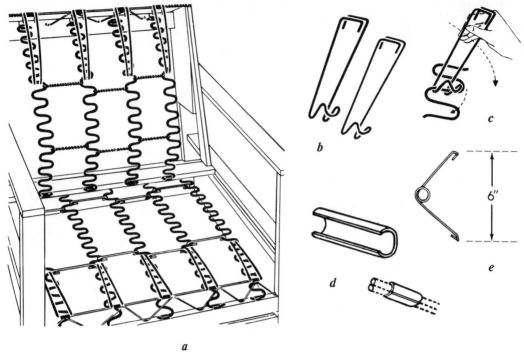

Fig. 3:21O

not always readily available; salvage those in good condition. *Kay-Arc Edge Springs,* Fig. *b* 3:21O, come in several lengths and gauges, Table 3:21O, for use with regular zigzag springs. Each size has two lengths (one-half loop difference) to assure correct positioning of edge wire at the outer edge of a frame. Edge springs are easy to install, *c. C-clips, d,* fasten edge-wire to free ends of installed edge springs, *a.* Small C-clips, for backs, have a maximum closing capacity of two 10-gauge wires or equivalent; large C-clips, for seats, can contain two 8-gauge wires or equivalent. The best clips are lined with paper for a firm, quiet grip. There are special pliers for closing C-clips, but conventional square-nosed pliers do as well; also, edge-wire may be tied to springs (Sec. 7:16C). *Torsion springs,* Fig. *e.* 3:21O, stiffen and

TABLE 3:21O

LENGTH	GAUGE	USE
7″	12 ⎱	Standard
7⅜″	12 ⎰	for seats
6¼″	14 ⎱	Standard
6⅝″	14 ⎰	for backs
5¼″	12 ⎱	Flat deck, low edge seats,
5⅝″	12 ⎰	particularly with foam cushions

strengthen spring edges, especially at corners. The most common size, in 10- and 11-gauge wires, has a freespan of 6 inches, 4¼-inch legs, and a 1¼-inch diameter loop. Fasten ends with C-clips to edge-wire and to a flat clip (Sec. 3:21E) nailed to frame.

Sec. 3:21P   Special Zigzag Edge-Springs   /   Several types of zigzag spring-edge materials, widely used in factory upholstering, may or may not be available to other workers. Border or edge-wire is clipped to the outer free spring bars; the surface is upholstered the usual way for zigzag springing (Secs. 7:32, 10:32). When reupholstering and edge springs are in good condition, keep and use them; they may be salvaged for other articles. Spring edge items in Fig. 3:21P are for specific surfaces and effects: [*a*] *SOF-EDGE*, seats; fasten to frame, clip to zigzag spring; a firm but comfortable edge. [*b*] *CLIP-ON SOF-EDGE*, seats; a length of zigzag clipped to seat strand; the longer it is and the further back it is clipped to the seat strand, the softer the edge is; a clip-on curving down toward the front makes a softer edge than one curving upward. [*c*] *LUXURY-EDGE*, seats; heavy gauge wire with pigtail for fast locking into seat spring. [*d*] *V-ARC*, backs; formed back zigzag spring material for a soft edge at top of back. [*e*] *CLIP-ON BACK SPRING*, backs; fasten to frame, clip to back spring; for soft edge at top of back.

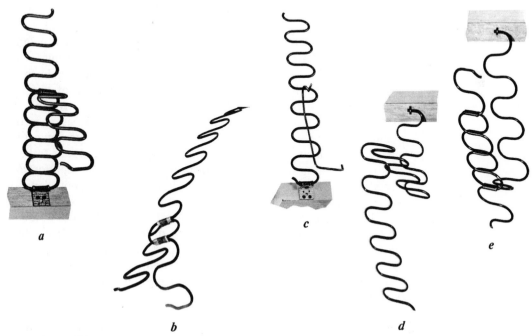

a

b

c

d

e

Fig. 3:21P

SEC. 3:21Q ZIGZAG SPRING SPECIALTIES / Zigzag springs are combined with other materials for factory upholstering which may not be generally available. When reupholstering a surface without changing its design and when such specialties are in good condition, there is no need to discard them; salvaging for use in a different article is not recommended. *Kay Pillo-Arc Bar,* Fig. *a, b* 3:21Q, conical springs usually are 5 inches high, two on zigzag strands under 20 inches long, three on longer strands. They are for backs, generally the Lawson type (Figs. *a* 1:42, *c* 1:42, 1:58, 1:59), and usually are spaced 7½ to 8 inches apart on center. *Kay Arc-Bars, c,* provide the firm, flat contour support often wanted for compact stuffings (Secs. 3:40–3:44) and also serve as frame stretchers (Sec. 3:21R). Arc-Bars usually are nailed on the top of front and back seat rails, Fig. *d, e* 3:21Q, but may be nailed to a drop rail (Sec. 3:21S) at the back for more comfortable seat pitch. Drop rails also are used in the front and back of a seat to allow for a roll or a hard, instead of a spring, edge (Sec. 5:04). Arc-Bars generally are 8 to 10 inches apart on centers. They also are used in studio beds and box springs with vertical side rails.

SEC. 3:21R FRAMES FOR ZIGZAG SPRINGS / Zigzag springs can, unless a frame is built for them, distort rails and cavities. The following features should be in frames suitable for zigzags; strengthen other frames accordingly. [1] *Side rails* set between front and back seat rails, top and bottom back rails; in most backs a reinforced bottom rail or liner is adequate. [2] *Front and back seat rails* 1-inch hardwood; at least 1½ inches thick if not hardwood. Wood thick enough for satisfactory back rails should be adequate for zigzag springs. [3] *One crossbrace or stretcher* (Sec. 4:02) in love seat frame, two in sofas. Stretchers must allow for vertical deflection or go-down of zigzags; this is twice the arc (Sec. 3:21L) plus 1 inch. Fasten stretchers to front and back seat rails, top rail and liner of a back, as near the planned spring surface as the necessary allowance for go-down permits. Attach shaping blocks to stretchers, Fig. 3:21R, and rails to keep rails from twisting or warping from spring pull. [4] *For comfortable seat slope,* the back rail is 1 or 2 inches lower than the front, depending on the depth of a seat; the farther apart the front and back rails are, the greater the slope should be. Most modern furniture frames have adequate seat slope; for more, use drop-rails at the back (Sec. 3:21S), or, if it is big enough, cut away part of the top surface of the back seat rail. Rear legs can be shortened, or exceptionally large casters used on front legs, but these change pitch of a back as well as slope of a seat.

SEC. 3:21S DROP RAIL / A drop rail, Fig. 3:21S, is a strip of

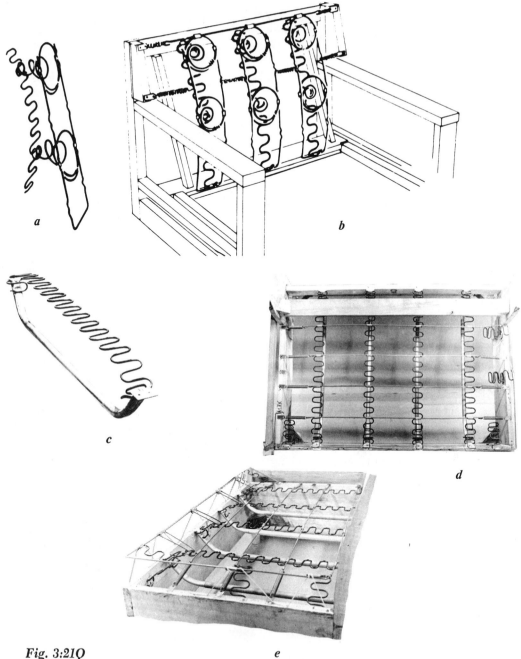

a

b

c

d

Fig. 3:21Q   *e*

straight-grained 1-inch hardwood, screwed and glued to a seat rail, to
lower height at which zigzags are installed.

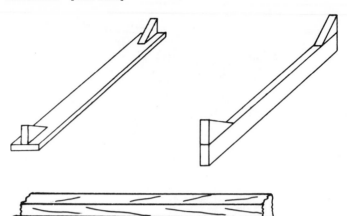

Fig. 3:21R

Fig. 3:21S

SEC. 3:22	**Sec. 3:22A Rubber Webbing** / This modern material (Sec. 3:00C),

SEC. 3:22
RUBBER
WEBBING

Sec. 3:22A Rubber Webbing / This modern material (Sec. 3:00C), fills a frame cavity, Fig. 3:22A, much the same way as traditional strip webbing (Sec. 3:11), but also has spring action, or go-down and rebound. It is excellent for the thin, springy surfaces popular in much slimline furniture, and is often used in period and antique pieces. Generally, rubber webbing is used for cushion-type upholstering (Sec. 17:21), roll edge seats and backs (Secs. 7:33, 10:33), inside arms (Sec. 8:09), and spring armtops (Sec. 8:23I). Rubber webbing is a flat spring, and necessary crown must be built with stuffing (Sec. 5:14). Compact stuffing (Sec. 3:40) should be used for all rubber webbing surfaces. Salvaging rubber webbing is not recommended; whether it is at all practical depends on how it was and is to be installed. If it is to be tacked, stretching previously cut lengths can be difficult; web-

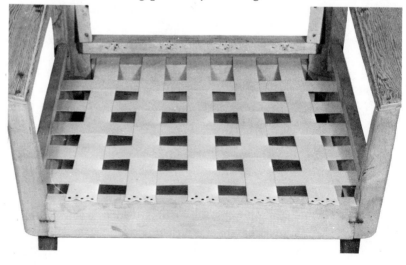

Fig. 3:22A

bing pliers (Sec. 2:03D) may be needed. If clips will be used (Secs. 3:22J, K), the ends of strips must be satisfactory for fastening them. Rubber webbing requires more advance planning than traditional strip webbing and coil springs but is easier to install.

SEC. 3:22B   CONSTRUCTION OF WEBBING   /   Pirelli (patented) bias-cut two-ply rubber webbing is versatile, is easy and economical to use, and has highly effective resilience and control. Most Pirelli webbings are two layers of textile cords bonded together with pliable rubber at opposing angles, Fig. *a* 3:22B. When webbing stretches, the cords turn or pivot toward the direction of stretching, *b,* and twist-compress the rubber bonding. When stretching is lessened or removed, the rubber "untwists" or seeks its original shape, producing resilience or "return action." The more Pirelli webbing is stretched, the firmer and stronger it becomes. The firmness of installed Pirelli depends on the type and width (Sec. 3:22C) and initial stretch (Sec. 3:22D). Each factor affects and is affected by the others, making it a versatile material in that a particular size often can be used satisfactorily for several kinds of jobs, although the proper webbing for a specific surface should be used when available.

NOTE: Do not mix types and widths of webbing in most surfaces, as it tends to make them uneven or lumpy.

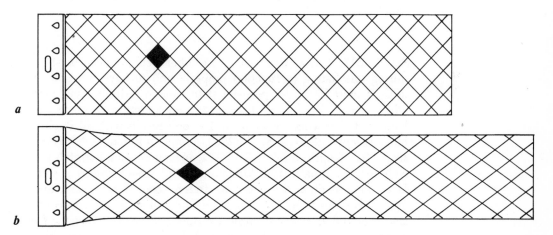

a

b

Fig. 3:22B

SEC. 3:22C   TYPES, WIDTHS OF WEBBING   /   Pirelli strip webbing is commonly available in several types and widths. Each type is rated by maximum stretch, expressed as a percentage of its free or unstretched length. For example, Pirelli Standard has a maximum stretch of approximately 45%; a 10-inch length can stretch about 4½ inches. The narrower a webbing is, the easier it stretches. Common types, widths, and uses are: [1] *Standard*. Approximately 45% maximum stretch; for firmly sprung seats when deep go-down is not wanted, and for large spring-type areas such as beds, sofas, convertible settees, fold-away beds. Use ¾- and 1⅛-inch widths for backs, inside arms, spring arm-tops; 1½-, 2-, 2½-inch widths for seats.   [2] *Super*. Approximately 70% maximum stretch; chiefly for seats; 1¼-, 2-, 2¼-inch widths. Suitable for all seats, but many upholsterers prefer Standard, above, for firm seats when deep go-down is not wanted; Extraflex, below, when extra buoyancy, greater go-down, and more lively rebound or resilience are wanted; or Lite-Tess, below, for small seats.   [3] *Extraflex*. Maximum stretch more than 100%; for extra buoyancy, greater go-down, very lively rebound or resilience; ideal support for cushions. Use 2-inch width for seats; 1½-, 1-inch widths for lighter duties and small seats. [4] *Lite-Tess*. Approximately 50% maximum stretch; chiefly for backs, seats with maximum width or depth of 15 inches or less, and baby cots, cribs. Has only one instead of two plies, stretches easily. This allows for soft yet resilient backs on all styles of furniture, as Lite-Tess can be installed side-to-side, top-to-bottom, and interlaced (Sec. 10:34). Rounded or barrel backs are webbed by varying installation stretch (Sec. 3:22D) and combining widths. For headrests and where a particularly soft effect is wanted, use ¾-inch width. For firmer areas, such as the lumbar region of a person's back, use 1½- or 2-inch wide Lite-Tess.

SEC. 3:22D   INITIAL STRETCH   /   Rubber webbing must be stretched during installation to function properly and to have necessary firmness. It must be under permanent tension in order to stay in place when there is little or no load on it, and to return to place when a load on it is lessened or removed. For best results with all Pirelli webbings except Lite-Tess (Sec. 3:22C), minimum initial stretch is 5% of a strip's free length, for Lite-Tess 10%; maximum initial stretch for any webbing is normally 10%. Minimum initial stretch builds a soft surface; for a medium firm surface, stretch about ½-inch more, and another ½-inch for firm. The more uniformly all strips are stretched, the smoother and more comfortable a surface will be. To figure the free or unstretched lengths of webbing needed: [1] *Measure span,* the distance between points of fastening webbing to a frame, Fig. *a* 3:22D (Secs. 3:22F–J).   [2] *Multiply inches of span* by minimum initial stretch and subtract that amount from span measurement. The result is the stretched length of webbing for a soft surface; subtract ½-inch for a medium, another ½-inch for a firm surface. This is the total stretched length.   [3] *To total stretched length add* allowances for fastening webbing to frame to find the overall free length needed. *EXAMPLE:* If span is 20 inches and initial stretch is 5%, the stretched

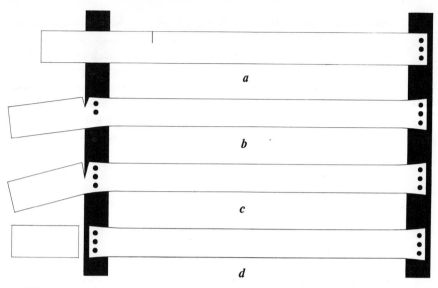

Fig. 3:22D

length for a soft surface is 19 inches (20″ × .05 = 1″; 20″ − 1″ = 19″). Subtract adjustment for medium or firm surface, if necessary, to find total stretched length. Add allowance for fastening ends of strips to find overall free length needed.

SEC. 3:22E   PLACEMENT, SPACING OF RUBBER WEBBING STRIPS   / Plan this carefully; it greatly affects the firmness of a surface, its go-down and return, and durability of upholstery. In general, strips usually are installed (Sec. 3:22F) on top of seat rails, on inner surfaces of back rails. Especially in seats, the more strips there are, the better; but do not use so many that the ends overlap. For best results, the space between strips should not be much more than the width of the webbing. If the stuffing, cushion, or stuffing and cushion will be more than about 4 inches thick, sometimes there are one or even two less strips of webbing than there should be (see [4] below); this is not recommended.

[1] *Seat rails.* Except for very small seats and for round seats, when top surfaces of all seat rails are even, back-to-front webbing, Fig. *a* 3:22E[2], offers adequate distribution of load or weight; however, many custom upholsterers prefer the traditional back-to-front and side-to-side installation (Fig. 3:22A) when possible. In some seats the top of a front rail is below tops of the side and rear rails, and strips must be side-to-side only. This type frame, called *drop rail*, is for a "spring-edge" seat that is built with rubber webbing (Sec. 7:33D). [2] *Seat load.* Maximum impact and regular loads on a seat usually are near the back; set strips closer together there. This is automatic

when back-to-front strips are properly installed in seats that are narrower at the back, Fig. *a* 3:22E[2]. If webbing side-to-side, *b*, set rearmost strip under the planned inner surface of the back or back pillow. Set the second strip no more than half the width of the webbing material from the rearmost strip. In small to medium size seats set the remaining strips two inches or so apart between the second strip and the front rail. In medium size and large seats set side-to-side strips closer together near the middle than at the front, since the middle usually carries the greater load.

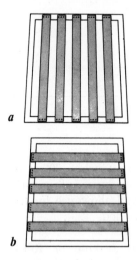

Fig. 3:22E[2]   *b*

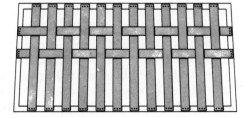

Fig. 3:22E[3]

[3] *Seat interlace.* Interlace side-to-side reinforcing strips in back-to-front seat webbing of club and lounge chairs and other large articles, Fig. 3:22E[3]. Two strips are enough; one just in front of the planned inner surface of a back or back pillow, the other 2 inches nearer the front. For drop rail seats, [1] above, diagonal reinforcing strips are preferred over back-to-front reinforcing strips, frame permitting. In round seats interlace and install strips diagonally. [4] *Inside back webbing.* Strip rubber webbing for inside backs may be primarily vertical or horizontal (Sec. 10:33B). Use horizontal strips to increase back support in lumbar area (Secs. 10:03B[4], 10:33C). Backs usually

have less strips, and spacing between them is greater than in seats since they are subject to far less load. Also, spring-type backs generally are thickly stuffed, or if thinly stuffed have a thick pillow or cushion; a thick stuffing or pillow can distribute the load enough to overcome the effects of wide spaced webbing.

NOTE: Sometimes there are less strips of webbing in a surface than there should be. How detrimental this may be depends on the proper number of strips and width of webbing. The greater the number that should be used, generally the safer it is to omit one or two. Omitting one or even two narrow strips usually is less damaging than omitting one wide strip.

SEC. 3:22F   PREPARE RUBBER WEBBING FOR INSTALLATION   /   Most strip rubber webbing is tacked or stapled to a wood frame (Sec. 3:22H); clips (Sec. 3:22I) generally are used only if webbing and wood frame will be seen when an article is upholstered, as with loose-cushion upholstery (Sec. 17:21). Clips also are made for fastening webbing strips to metal frames (Secs. 3:22J, K). To prepare rubber strip webbing for installation, first find total stretched length (Sec. 3:22D), add fastening allowances, below, and mark webbing for free length of strip or cut-off point; mark with a pencil or chalk line across webbing, or make a notch or cut in an edge. Mark several lengths, from cut-off to cut-off point. Allowances for fastening webbing depend on the frame and method of fastening.   [1] *Wood frame.* Add a total fastening allowance of 1 inch per strip when it will be fastened the usual way with tacks, nails, staples, or standard clips (Secs. 3:22H, I); unusual fastening (Fig. *c, d* 3:22H) requires a longer fastening allowance or different way of measuring span (Sec. 3:22D).   [2] *Metal frame.* Most ways of attaching strip rubber webbing to metal frames require 1 inch of webbing for fastening each end, a total allowance of 2 inches per strip (Sec. 3:22J).

SEC. 3:22G   PREPARE WOOD FRAME   /   Before fastening rubber strip webbing to a wood frame, round off (Sec. 4:12) all edges it will touch (Fig. 3:22H).

SEC. 3:22H   TACK, NAIL RUBBER WEBBING   /   To tack or nail strip rubber webbing to a wood frame you need an upholsterer's hammer (Sec. 2:02), large scissors or knife, #10 upholstery tacks (Sec. 3:03B) or ½-inch flathead or clout nails.   [1] *Space tacks or nails evenly* across width of webbing. For ¾-inch wide webbing, one nail or tack; 1⅛- and 1½-inch webbings, two; 2- and 2¼-inch webbing, three.   [2] *Drive tacks or nails vertically,* Fig. *a* 3:22H. If driven at an angle, *b,* an edge of the head may cut cords of webbing.   [3] *Tack or nail in*

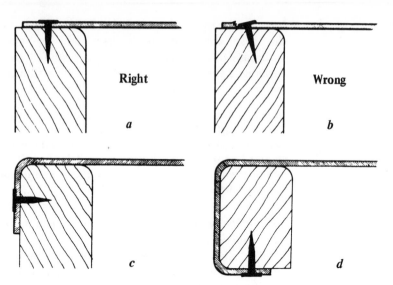

Right *a*

Wrong *b*

c

d

center of rail, *a*.   [4] *If impractical to fasten webbing* to top of seat
rail or front of back rail, or rail is less than 1-inch thick, fasten webbing to the outer side, *c*, at least 1 inch from top or front. If necessary, attach webbing to the bottom, *d*. For either of these unusual
fastenings, adjust span (Sec. 3:22D) or fastening allowance (Sec.
3:22F) accordingly.   [5] *Fasten free end of webbing* to frame (Sec.
3:22G). For working convenience, fasten back-to-front webbing to
rear rail, top-to-bottom strips to bottom rail.   [6] *Stretch webbing*
until cut-off mark (Sec. 3:22F) is ½ inch beyond the planned tacking
point (Fig. 3:22D). Tack or nail, then cut off surplus webbing straight
across cut-off line.

Sec. 3:22I   Clips for Wood Frame   /   If frame and webbing will
be plainly seen in the finished article (Sec. 17:21), strips may be
fastened by patented steel clips set in slots in a frame, Fig. 3:22I. Cut
a continuous slot, or a series of slots each just wide enough for a clip,
a, b. Place slots at the center of a rail, or about ⅛-inch from center
toward the outer edge; they should be ⁹⁄₁₆-inch deep, ⁵⁄₃₂-inch wide,
and slant inward at an angle of from 10 to 15 degrees, *e*, in order to
hook clips firmly in place. Measure and mark webbing strips of the
necessary length (Sec. 3:22F), cut straight across webbing, Fig. *c*.
3:22I, so that ends can butt firmly into clips. Force webbing full way
into a clip, *d*, and close sides of clips firmly in a vise. Press clip down
as far as possible into slot, *e*. Install filled clips in same sequence as
webbing is tacked (Sec. 3:22H).

Sec. 3:22J   Fastening Rubber Webbing to Metal Frames   /   Common ways to fasten strip rubber webbing to metal frames and secure

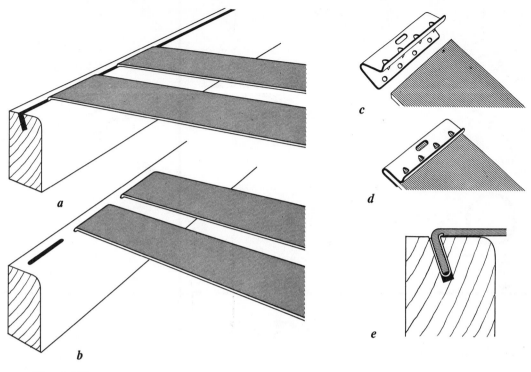

Fig. 3:22I

ends of strips are shown in Fig. 3:22J. Free length of a strip (Sec. 3:22D) depends on how it is fastened to a frame; measure span between crossbars of clips; ending allowance varies with the type clip and how it is used.

  Fig. *a* 3:22J—*Pirelli type A and E wire clips;* for 1½- and 2-inch wide webbings. Use A clips for tubular frames, E clips for tubular and angle iron frames, *c.* Strips can be closer together and to frame with E than with A clips. To install A and E clips, for each prong drill a hole just wide enough for it to fit freely. Holes must be at top dead center, as in "right"; otherwise leverage action may work clip out of frame. Ending allowance: 2 inches when ends of strips are secured with staples and backing plates (Sec. 3:22K).

  Fig. *b* 3:22J—*Pirelli type B wire clip;* for 1½- and 2-inch webbings; use with flat and angle iron metal frames up to ³⁄₁₆-inch thick at point of fastening. To install, drill vertical hole for each prong just large enough for it to be worked into place without being bent or deformed. Ending allowance: see *a* above.

  Fig. *c* 3:22J—*Pirelli type E clip, a* above, with friction endings for tubular and angle iron frames. In a tubular frame, prong holes are 30 degrees from bottom dead center away from the side on which

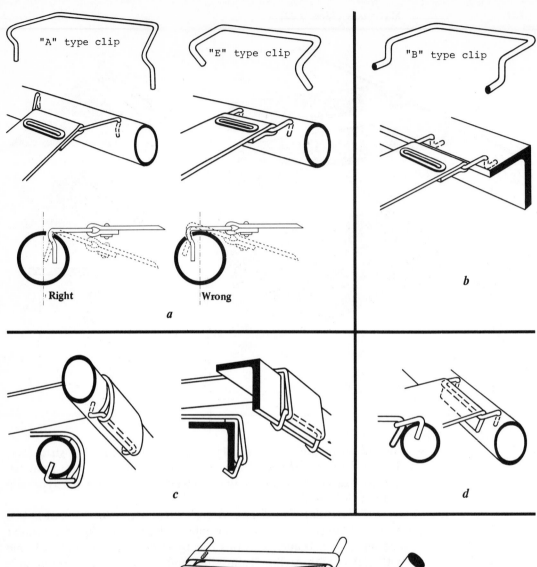

"A" type clip

"E" type clip

"B" type clip

Right

Wrong

a

b

c

d

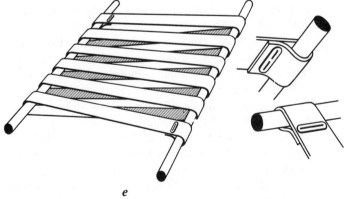

e

Fig. 3:22J

154

webbing presses. Strip ends must be long enough to be held securely by webbing, at least opposite prong holes in tubular frames, at least ½ inch behind edge of an angle iron frame. Initial stretch (Sec. 3:22D) of webbing supplies enough pressure-friction to hold ends firmly at all times. Ending allowance: measure from crossbar of clip to where end of strip will be.

Fig. *d* 3:22J—*Pirelli type E clip, a* above, with steel end clip (Sec. 3:22I); use with tubular frame; brings ends of webbing close to frame and gives very neat appearance. Drill holes for E clip prongs. Secure strip ends in steel clips (Sec. 3:22I). Hook steel clip over crossbar of wire clip. Ending allowance: 1 inch per strip.

Fig. *e* 3:22J—*Continuous wrap-around* strip webbing for exceptionally long or wide tubular frame articles, such as a cot or bench. Gives all "strips" of webbing equal initial stretch (Sec. 3:22D) as, in use, webbing gradually slips around frame to equalize tensions. Staple ends to webbing (Sec. 3:22K[5]). [1] *Span.* Measure each "strip," upper and lower surfaces, from middle of outer surface of one side of a frame to that of the other. [2] *Ending allowance.* Measure from middle of outer surface of frame to ½ inch beyond where staple will be. Set staple far enough from frame for strips of webbing to meet at an angle of not more than 45 degrees.

SEC. 3:22K   STRIP RUBBER WEBBING   /   Secure strip rubber webbing to Pirelli A, E, B wire clips (Sec. 3:22J) with staples and backing plates, Fig. 3:22K. Staples, *a*, are 1-inch wide, for 1½-inch and wider webbing; use two backing plates with a staple. [1] *Punch four holes,*

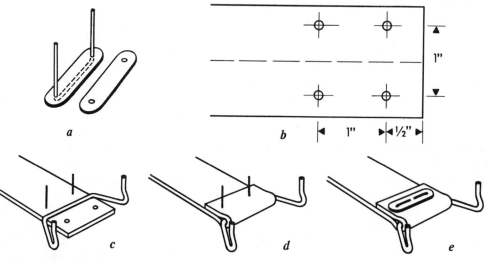

Fig. 3:22K

approximately ³⁄₃₂-inch diameter, at the end of a strip, *b*, equally spaced from the sides of a strip. [2] *Place backing strip on staple, a,* and insert staple through the pair of holes farther from the end of a strip, *c*. [3] *Set wire clip on webbing, c.* By placing clip prong-ends up, the smooth side of a staple will show when clips are installed the usual way (Fig. *a*, *b* 3:22J). [4] *Fit free end of strip* on staple legs, set second backing plate in place, bend staple legs down tight on top of it, *d, e*. [5] *Except that there is no clip,* secure ends of wrap-around strip webbing (Fig. *e* 3:22J) as above. First set free end of webbing in place on frame and staple it. Then install all webbing by wrapping it around frame, pulling it tight enough throughout for initial stretch (Sec. 3:22D). To install second staple, pull the last several wraps of webbing extra tight so that it will be somewhat loose near the end. After stapling, equalize tension of the last several wraps of webbing by snapping them up and down several times.

SEC. 3:22L AMOUNT OF RUBBER WEBBING NEEDED / [1] *Plan placement, spacing* of strips (Sec. 3:22E) to find out how many are needed. Mark frame for placement of each strip, especially when there will be strips of much different lengths. [2] *Determine free lengths* of strips needed (Sec. 3:22D). [3] *Add number of strips* of each length needed to find total length required. If webbing will be tacked or nailed, add 5 inches to total length in order to have enough webbing to hold for stretching the last strip.

**SEC. 3:23
DECORATIVE
WEBBINGS**

Decorative webbings are part of the basic design of an article as in much garden and patio furniture. Most decorative webbings are woven or molded plastics, have about the same stretch as traditional jute webbing (Sec. 3:11), and are factory installed with special metal eyelets, rivets, studs, etc. Molded webbing often can be fastened to a metal frame by clips and staples used for rubber strip webbing (Secs. 3:22J, K). Prevent raveling of ends of woven webbing by taking one or two rows of machine stitching across it about ¼-inch from the end or by gluing or bonding strands together across the end.

**SEC. 3:24
BURLAP**

SEC. 3:24A / Burlap supports upholstery stuffing on most pad open-frame and spring surfaces, is used to build upholstery edges, and helps shape and protect the cover of outside arms, wings, and backs. [1] *Traditional burlap* is fairly tightly woven jute; a good, serviceable grade weighs at least 10 ounces per square yard. [2] *Burlap comes in several widths;* 40-inch is the more generally useful. [3] *Loosely woven or lightweight burlap,* sometimes stiffened by sizing, may stretch excessively or break during or after installation. [4] *Many heavy, tightly woven fabrics* can substitute satisfactorily for burlap; but canvas and similar textiles usually are too stiff for good upholstering work, and often make a scratchy noise against stuffing. [5] *Pieces of burlap* may be sewn together and used for most jobs if sewing is tight and strong. [6] *Burlap dries* and weakens with age; salvaging from an old article is not recommended.

SEC. 3:24B SYNTHETIC BURLAPS / Woven synthetic and continuous filament goods are replacing burlap as a construction material. Woven polypropylene is similar to burlap in toughness, stretch, and flexibility. It is used over springs in seats and backs, but should be covered by a thin layer of felted padding to quiet possible noise. Continuous filament non-woven goods such as spunbonded polypropylene (Dupont Typar) is used as a construction material between wood rails, as in outside arms, wings, backs; it is not recommended over springs.

SEC. 3:25 ROLL EDGES, PREBUILT EDGING	Roll edges or prebuilt edging (the latter commonly called "edging" or "fox edging") are installed (Secs. 5:01–5:06) to shape the edges of a surface that will be upholstered with loose stuffing (Secs. 3:28–3:37). In most cases prebuilt edging is as good as the handmade edge, and due to the time and work it saves is preferred by many top quality upholsterers. Most prebuilt edging consists of a fairly firm jute, paper, rope or cotton core incased by felt or burlap (Fig. 5:06). If a core is not moderately hard, edging soon packs down. Prebuilt edging is made in several sizes, ranging from ¼- to 1½-inches diameter, and is sold by the foot or yard. Prebuilt edging in good condition may be salvaged for reuse. Smooth rope such as sash cord, incased or not, makes a good small edging; 3-ply rope is too rough. Felted cotton or carpet padding rolled into the necessary thickness and firmness, and incased by burlap, is a serviceable edging.
SEC. 3:26 CARDBOARD STRIPPING	Cardboard stripping provides a smooth line of pressure between tacks (Fig. 5:05B), and lets it be set to the edge of a frame. Stripping is used chiefly in building roll edges, installing a cover, and filling gaps in some webbing installations (Fig. 7:05A). Use only the best quality moderately thick, ½-inch wide cardboard stripping, usually available in yard lengths and rolls. Cheap or thin cardboard stripping may break during installation, or bend under the pull of materials it should hold in place. For straight or level cardboarding (Fig. 5:05B), linoleum and thin wood are serviceable substitutes and better than thin or flimsy cardboard. Tacking strips are used instead of cardboard stripping in certain factory blind-stitching operations (Sec. 13:04D).

SEC. 3:27
STUFFING

SEC. 3:27A / Stuffing pads a surface and gives it shape and soft-ness. Loose stuffings, such as curled hair and various fibers (Secs. 3:28–3:37), can be used to upholster all kinds and shapes of surfaces, but compact stuffing often is easier to install. Loose stuffing is commonly used to build basic crown (Sec. 5:14) in compact stuffing surfaces. Compact stuffings, such as polyfoam and rubberized hair (Secs. 3:41–3:44), come in sheets of various thicknesses and degrees of softness; they are highly efficient for building most top quality surfaces. Compact stuffings have certain limitations and for best results in some cases are used with loose stuffing. When selecting a stuffing take into account its resilience, durability, ease of handling, and cleanliness, as well as cost.

NOTE: Stuffing is often called "cushioning" by factory upholsterers; do not confuse "cushioning" with cushion or pillow fillings (Sec. 3:61).

SEC. 3:27B RESILIENCE / Resilient stuffings shape and support a surface by pressing outward against it with a springy action; nonresilient stuffings give shape and support by bulk. Properly installed resilient stuffings of good quality are soft and usually stay so; nonresilient stuffings pack into relatively hard layers, and if poorly installed often have lumps that are uncomfortable and may spoil the looks of an article. Use resilient stuffings for surfaces that should be soft to the touch, such as inside backs, arms, cushions, and some seats. Use nonresilient stuffings for roll edges (Sec. 5:05) and, generally, the understuffing to build crown (Sec. 5:14) for a compact stuffing. Where firmness rather than softness is wanted, nonresilient is better than resilient stuffing.

SEC. 3:27C DURABILITY / Stuffings pack down to some extent. But a durable one retains more resilience for a longer time; as a rule it may be salvaged for reuse.

SEC. 3:27D EASE OF HANDLING / The ease of installing a stuffing often affects the looks and life of an article. The more difficult a stuffing is to work into place, the more apt it is to have hollows, weak spots, lumps. These accumulate dirt and may make a cover wear out prematurely. In general, resilient stuffings are easier to handle than nonresilient, and compact stuffings are easier than loose. Exceptions to these generalities are given with the upholstery jobs involved.

SEC. 3:27E CLEANLINESS / Most new stuffings are clean and dust free. Some old compact stuffings have a brittle skin; rub it off when salvaging them. Loose stuffings that were incased by muslin and padded with cotton, or merely padded with cotton, usually are clean when salvaged from an old article. Brittle stuffings break into dust-like particles, which usually is the dust that comes out of old upholstery.

SEC. 3:27F COSTS / Upholstery costs often can be reduced without much loss of quality by building basic or general shape of a surface with an inferior stuffing and covering it with a layer of the best. In some cases this is actually the best method. A good quality stuffing in good condition may be salvaged from a chair, sofa, footstool, etc.—but not from a mattress. It can be sanitized, but that tends to sharply reduce resilience and make stuffing brittle. Treat salvaged hair stuffing with a demothing compound.

SEC. 3:28 LOOSE STUFFING

Loose stuffings are hairs or fibers not connected to one another except by natural interlocking of materials. In use they are worked into a desired shape, density, and degree of firmness. Loose stuffing generally costs less than compact (Secs. 3:41–3:44) but usually requires more time, work, and skill to build smooth, symmetrical surfaces. Loose stuffings are classed as traditional materials (Sec. 3:00C). Common loose stuffings are horse and cattle hair, moss, palm fiber, cocoa fiber, sisal, tow, excelsior, and tampico (Secs. 3:29–3:37). Except for excelsior, which is not used in top quality upholstery, each loose stuffing has qualities that make it good for some kinds of work and, generally, not good for others.

SEC. 3:29 CURLED HAIR STUFFING

SEC. 3:29A / Curled hair stuffing ranks high in resilience, durability, ease of handling, and cleanliness. It may be used throughout an article, but in some places is not as practical as other stuffings (Sec. 3:29B). Quality of a hair stuffing depends on the type and length of hairs; the longer they are, the stronger and more resilient the stuffing is. Best quality hair stuffing is cattle mane and tail hair. Cheaper grades are mixtures of cattle and horse hair, hog hair or hide scrapings, both of which are short and stiff. Quality decreases as the amount of hog hair or hide scrapings increases. Poorest hair stuffings are mixtures of hog hair and sisal or tampico (Secs. 3:33, 3:36), added to strengthen a mixture and hold hair; these mixtures may usually be legally listed as hair stuffing.

NOTE: A popular compact stuffing is rubberized hair (Sec. 3:44); it also is available in loose form. Rubber coated curled hair has greater resilience than the uncoated; for some work this is not an advantage. Loose rubberized hair usually is not as readily available as either compact rubberized hair or plain loose hair stuffing. Use loose rubberized hair for, and handle it the same way as, plain curled hair stuffing.

SEC. 3:29B RESILIENCE / Fine quality curled hair stuffing often is too resilient for practical purposes. It may be so springy and must be compressed so much to build a reasonably firm surface that an unusually high initial layer is needed (Fig. 8:14D); a less resilient stuffing is easier to handle and can be just about as comfortable. A highly resilient stuffing is not practical for roll edges or for understuffing. Resilience of a loose stuffing usually is increased by picking it (Sec. 3:38). If a stuffing seems too resilient for a job, such as a roll edge, either don't pick it or pick just enough to remove the hardest lumps.

SEC. 3:30 **MOSS** **STUFFING**	Moss is fairly resilient, durable, easy to handle, but not a clean stuffing. It may be used throughout an article, for roll edges and understuffing as well as conventional stuffing. The best quality, XXXX moss, is black or dark brown; the poorest, XX moss, has a greenish color. Often it is better to use the best quality moss than a cheap hair stuffing. Good quality moss may be salvaged for reuse; as a rule additional stuffing will be needed.
SEC. 3:31 **PALM FIBER** **STUFFING**	Palm fiber is coarse and has little resilience. It is durable, fairly easy to handle, and quite clean. New palm fiber is light green in color. In popular-priced upholstery, palm fiber may be the only stuffing. In better articles it is used for understuffing and roll edges. Salvaging palm fiber for understuffing is advisable.
SEC. 3:32 **COCOA FIBER** **STUFFING**	Cocoa fiber is clean and durable but has little resilience. Short, coarse, flat and gritty fibers make cocoa stuffing difficult to handle; it tends to pack into hard layers. Cocoa fiber is light brown in color. It is not used in top quality upholstery except as understuffing where resilience is not wanted, and for roll edges. It can be salvaged for reuse but generally should be discarded.
SEC. 3:33 **SISAL** **STUFFING**	Sisal has very little resilience. It is white, clean, durable, fairly easy to handle, and is available loose and in felted pads. Sisal is not used in top quality upholstery except as an understuffing where resilience is not wanted.
SEC. 3:34 **TOW STUFFING**	Tow is clean, durable, has little resilience, and readily packs into hard layers. Use only for roll edges. Tow may be salvaged for reuse, but this is not practical unless a completed roll edge is to be reused.
SEC. 3:35 **EXCELSIOR** **STUFFING**	Excelsior, also called "wood wool," is too brittle to have much resilience or durability. It readily breaks down and gives off large quantities of dust-like particles.

SEC. 3:36 **TAMPICO** **FIBER** **STUFFING**	Tampico fiber, istle, or pita, is chiefly used in cordage, carpeting, etc. It is not used in upholstery except to strengthen some hair mixture stuffings (Sec. 3:29A).
SEC. 3:37 **COTTON**	Cotton (Sec. 3:49) generally is not considered a stuffing although it is sometimes used to build a small amount of crown. Natural cotton packs down too much, lacks resilience and strength for a good stuffing; synthetic cotton is too expensive.
SEC. 3:38 **PICKING** **STUFFING**	Before use, run a loose stuffing other than cotton through a picking machine or pick by hand to break down hard layers, lumps, and balls, and to remove foreign materials (small sticks, caked dirt, etc.) often found in new stuffings. Salvaged stuffing is picked to fluff it, help restore resilience, and remove tacks and other objects that may have gotten into it. To pick by hand, pull apart or shred a handful of stuffing; the more thoroughly it is picked, the greater its resilience. Stuffing for roll edges and understuffing should not be picked as thoroughly as that intended for more general use.
SEC. 3:39 **AMOUNT OF** **LOOSE** **STUFFING**	The amount of loose stuffing needed depends on its resilience and installation as well as the size and desired shape of a surface. The amounts listed with articles in Chapter 1 are based on actual construction and contain allowances for unskilled handling. Unless radically different shapes are wanted, inexperienced upholsterers should use these amounts rather than make their own estimates, especially if there is no convenient supply of upholstery materials. [1] *About ⅓-pound good hair stuffing* per square foot is enough for a medium soft surface approximately 1-inch thick when compressed by a casing. Increase or decrease the amount to make a surface firmer or softer; but do this cautiously, as a fairly slight decrease of stuffing to soften a surface may make it weak and flimsy. [2] *There is no way to convert* pounds of one type of stuffing into exact pounds needed of another type to build a surface to a given thickness. A fairly safe approximation is that 1 pound of good hair stuffing equals about 1½-pounds of hair-and-fiber, 1¾-pounds moss, 2 pounds palm fiber, cocoa fiber, sisal, or tow.
SEC. 3:40 **COMPACT** **STUFFING**	Compact stuffings come in slabs or sheets. They are cut, or pieces may be bonded together (Sec. 3:46) to make a size and shape wanted. Most compacts cost more than loose stuffings, but save much time and work in building smooth, consistent, symmetrical surfaces. Compact stuffings are classed as modern materials (Sec. 3:00C), but are com-

monly used by the finest craftsmen for reupholstering antiques. Necessary crown (Sec. 5:14) of a compact stuffing surface often is built with loose stuffing understuffing, although sometimes cotton is used instead. Ordinary compact stuffings are polyfoam, foam rubber, and rubberized hair (Secs. 3:41–3:44). Each has qualities that can make it the most practical for a particular type of surface or article that will be used under certain conditions. Rubberized hair is often the understuffing for polyfoam or foam rubber in fairly thick square or square-scroll arms (Fig. *a* 1:46). Thickness of compact stuffing for a surface is approximately the planned thickness of a finished surface as compact stuffings are not appreciably compressed by a casing or cover. For compact stuffing, the thickness of a surface usually is planned or measured outward from the top surface of the understuffing or other base.

SEC. 3:41
POLYFOAM

Polyfoam, Fig. 3:41, is a general name for the plastic or synthetic foam-like materials used for stuffing (Sec. 3:42), quilting (Sec. 3:57), and cushion and pillow fillings (Secs. 3:68, 3:71). Polyfoam started as a substitute for foam rubber, but because of its high resilience, durability, cleanliness, and ease-of-handling, it became accepted as a separate material. Chemical and mechanical differences in polyfoams can affect their reaction to handling and other factors; consult an experienced upholsterer before buying a particular brand of polyfoam.

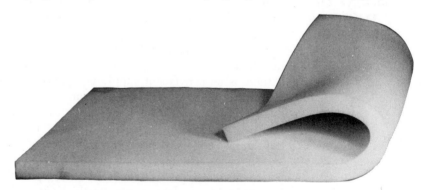

Fig. 3:41

[1] *Thicknesses.* Upholstery shops usually stock polyfoam in ¼- to 4½-inch thicknesses, in sheets up to 54 × 75 inches, and will sell in smaller pieces. Polyfoam can usually be procured up to 3 feet thick on special order. When a particular thickness is not available, thicker stock may be sliced to a wanted thickness, or sheets of thinner stock may be bonded together (Secs. 3:46B, C); the latter is the easier way and tends to make a smoother, more uniformly thick slab.   [2] *Firmness.* Polyfoam is usually marked clearly as firm, medium, or soft. Polyurethane foam varies in density or weight per cubic foot; gen-

erally the heavier weight foam is a better and longer lasting stuffing material. [3] *Use limitations.* Many polyfoams can be used almost anywhere without undue deterioration. But some are sensitive to prolonged exposure to sunlight or excessive heat; use indoors but keep away from heaters, furnace outlets, sunny windows, and similar places. Some polyfoams react poorly to saltwater air and petroleum fumes; do not use them for boat cushions or upholstery. Other polyfoams tend to break down under repeated flexing and are not practical for use on spring surfaces. Many manufacturers specify conditions or uses to avoid for their products. Experienced upholstery supply dealers should know the limitations of the polyfoams they stock. [4] *Salvaging.* Most good quality polyfoam can be salvaged satisfactorily if it is less than about ten years old. There usually is some deterioration, especially along edges. Also, it tends to be permanently compressed, making it thinner, harder, and less resilient.

**SEC. 3:42
USES OF
POLYFOAM**

Polyfoam stuffing is mostly used for (in this order): inside backs, solid seats (Figs. *a* 1:09, 1:19, *b* 1:50), armtops, inside arms, and wings. It seldom is used for outside surfaces other than in rounded arms (Fig. *d* 1:45). Except for large square inside backs and flat-topped arms (Figs. *c* 1:42, *d* 1:46), polyfoam is not particularly suitable for understuffing; usually a loose stuffing (Secs. 3:29–3:33) or rubberized hair (Sec. 3:44) is more practical and costs less.

**SEC. 3:43
FOAM RUBBER**

Foam rubber stuffing ranks high in resilience, durability, ease-of-handling, and cleanliness. Polyfoam stuffing is preferred for most surfaces, but foam rubber is used extensively as a general stuffing and is widely preferred for cushion and pillow fillings (Secs. 3:67, 3:71). [1] *Thicknesses.* Foam rubber is usually available in from ¼- to 4½-inch thicknesses, in sheets up to 27 × 108 inches; most upholstery shops will sell in smaller pieces. For nonavailable thicknesses see Sec. 3:41. [2] *Firmness.* Foam rubber stuffing is graded soft, medium, and hard. Originally there were two types of foam rubber: slab and cored stock. Very little slab stock has been manufactured since the development of polyfoam stuffing. Most modern cored stock has holes about ³⁄₁₆-inch diameter extending inward from both major surfaces, Fig. 3:43, giving it great surface softness and little initial resistance to compression or go-down, without appreciably weakening it. This usually eliminates the need to round off edges (Sec. 3:46D) except when a cover is very thin material. [3] *Foam rubber is adversely affected* by certain conditions (Sec. 3:41[3]). [4] *Foam rubber may be salvaged* (Sec. 3:41[4]); it retains resilience better than and does not become as permanently shaped as polyfoam.

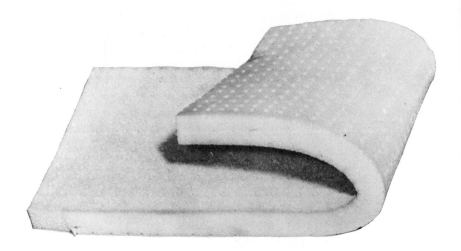

Fig. 3:43

**SEC. 3:44
RUBBERIZED
HAIR**

Rubberized hair stuffing is highly resilient, durable, clean, and relatively easy to handle. It is available as a loose stuffing (Sec. 3:29A) but is more common as compact stuffing, Fig. 3:44. Although suitable for nearly all surfaces, rubberized hair is used more as understuffing (Sec. 5:13) for polyfoam and foam rubber than as the only stuffing for a surface. Often it is easier to install rubberized hair than polyfoam or foam rubber (Sec. 3:47); this, plus cost, can make it a very practical understuffing. [1] *Rubberized hair is not as sensitive* as polyfoam and foam rubber (Sec. 3:41[3]), especially when it is an understuffing. The rubber coating preserves hair curl, does not create it. [2] *Firmness, thicknesses.* Rubberized hair compact stuffing, graded medium and firm, commonly is available in from 1- to 4-inch thicknesses, in sheets up to 24 × 72 inches; most upholstery shops will sell in smaller pieces. For nonavailable thicknesses see Sec. 3:41; if two thicknesses are to be sandwiched together, make the upper thickness a full rather than a sliced one in order to maintain top surface softness. [3] *Surfaces.* One major surface, the "top" of a sheet of rubberized hair, is much softer than the other; install rubberized hair with the top surface up or outward. The "bottom" surface is denser and has more hairs to be held by tacks, stitches, or bonding agent. The bottom surface usually has a coarse netting (Fig. 3:44) to strengthen it against pulling and flexing, help prevent knots or springs cutting into stuffing, and provide a surface that can be held better by tacks and stitches. [4] *Resilience, durability.* Normally rubberized hair packs down very little; it usually can be corrected by rebuilding the planned shape or crown (Sec. 5:14) with good loose stuffing, preferably hair (Sec. 3:29). Rubberized hair generally can be salvaged with complete satisfaction; when salvaging tacked or bonded rubberized hair, take care not to damage or tear it too much for good

Fig. 3:44

use.   [5] *Rubberized hair is "scratchy."* To protect a cover and build
a quiet surface, install felted padding (Sec. 3:49) before covering.

**SEC. 3:45
SELECTING
COMPACT
STUFFING**

Which compact stuffing is best for a surface depends on the surface,
its shape, how thickly it will be stuffed, and on what "best" means. It
can mean greatest softness—soft on top, firm underneath—reasonable
comfort at lowest cost, and so on.   [1] *Overall shape.* Polyfoam and
foam rubber generally are easier to install on highly crowned surfaces.
On a flat surface or one that curves primarily in one direction or
plane, such as the inside-back in Fig. *b* 1:37, rubberized hair is as
easy to install as polyfoam or foam rubber.   [2] *Unitized surface.* To
build a more widely unitized surface (go-down action spread over a
large area instead of being confined to a relatively small part), spring
surfaces may be stuffed with rubberized hair. It may be the understuffing or the only stuffing, depending on the planned thickness of a
surface, [4, 5, 6] below.   [3] *Freedom of movement.* The greater the
freedom of movement in a spring surface, or the less unitized it is,
above, the softer and weaker it is. But spring backs are built primarily
for comfort, not strength, and for greater freedom of movement most
are stuffed with polyfoam or foam rubber. But rubberized hair is
used in spring backs, either as understuffing or as the only stuffing,
depending on shape and planned thickness [1, 4, 5, 6].   [4] *Thickness—up to 1 inch.* When compact stuffing will be less than 1 inch
thick, generally a single layer is used. For upholstery this thin, especially pad on a solid base, medium or firm usually is more comfortable
than soft stuffing. Crown may be built with loose stuffing before installing compact; but in most thin surfaces crown is built when incasing with muslin or covering.   [5] *Thickness—1 to 2 inches.* When
compact stuffing will be from 1 to 2 inches thick, loose stuffing is often
the understuffing for a highly crowned surface, and polyfoam or foam
rubber is the main or overstuffing. Relatively flat surfaces may be
understuffed with compact stuffing, usually rubberized hair because
of its qualities (Sec. 3:44), and its tendency to unitize surfaces, [2]
above, and hold shape better than other compacts. Maximum softness

comes from overstuffing with polyfoam or foam rubber, and padding with polyester (Sec. 3:49). Crown for compact understuffing generally is built with loose stuffing when incasing understuffing with muslin. [6] *Thickness—more than 2 inches.* When a very soft surface more than 2 or 3 inches thick will be built with polyfoam or foam rubber stuffing, some strengthening is needed to keep it from wobbling. For this, understuff with rubberized hair or medium or firm polyfoam or foam rubber. For softness and crown see [5] above.

<table>
<tr><td>

**SEC. 3:46
PREPARING
COMPACT
STUFFING**

</td><td>

SEC. 3:46A / A compact stuffing is often made from thicker or thinner stock (Sec. 3:41[*1*]). Sometimes it must be shaped for a neat, smooth finish at the edges of an upholstered surface.

SEC. 3:46B CUTTING / Cut or slice compact stuffing with a sharp knife, shears, or bandsaw; an electric carving knife is excellent. For thicknesses up to 2 inches, fairly large shears are satisfactory; a knife is good for any thickness. Mark intended cut-line on stuffing. When cutting with a knife or shears, make a series of shallow cuts; the sides of cuts more than about ½-inch deep tend to be lumpy instead of smooth. When cutting with a knife, gently spread stuffing aside just ahead of the blade; but be careful, as heavy pressing or uneven spreading can make a cut jagged instead of smooth. Similarly, when slicing compact stuffing make short slices and check frequently to keep surfaces smooth and flat. If there are holes or depressions in a cut or sliced surface, trim filler patches for a neat, smooth fit and bond in place.

SEC. 3:46C BONDING / Bond compact stuffing with agent (Sec: 3:06) specified by manufacturer; apply as directed. Use a bonding agent that dries odorless. Usually both surfaces of a planned joint or seam are coated lightly with adhesive and let dry until tacky. When bonding together thick pieces or large sheets of compact stuffing, wait until cement odor is nearly gone before joining them. [*1*] *When joining pieces,* Fig. *a* 3:46C, place them on a large-enough flat surface and gently slide together edges to be joined. Hold stuffings well away from a seam in order to get the even overall pressure needed for a uniformly strong seam, and to keep from pressing one stuffing down more than the other, which could make an uneven instead of smooth surface. When stuffings are joined satisfactorily, pat them together gently a few inches from seam. Do not pinch a seam; it can make permanent hard spots. [*2*] *When bonding stuffing to a different material,* align an edge of the stuffing and other material, *b,* and gently lower stuffing into place, keeping the other edges aligned.

</td></tr>
</table>

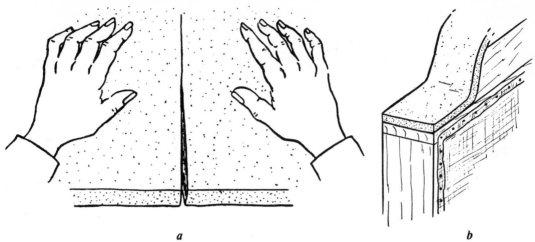

a   *b*

Fig. 3:46C

When stuffing is placed satisfactorily, pat it lightly all over the upper surface. Do not pat hard; it can make permanent depressions and hard spots. [3] *Bonding together or "sandwiching" layers of stuffing* to make a special thickness is essentially the same as in [2] above. But when lowering the upper layer in place, be careful not to stretch or compress it. Either pressure puts stuffings under permanent tension that can weaken them; excessive pressure may make one or both layers warp and twist. [4] *While bonding,* sometimes it is necessary to open a seam or joint and adjust materials, which is why contact or instant cements are not used. Also, it may be necessary to apply more bonding agent after opening a seam; apply cautiously, as too much can weaken instead of strengthen a joint or seam. [5] *Allow ample time for bond to dry* and become permanent. Usually six hours is the minimum time; overnight or a day is better. Most properly bonded joints or seams are stronger than the adjacent materials.

SEC. 3:46D SHAPING EDGES / Compact stuffing often is shaped along edges for neatness and to protect a cover. Shaping ranges from fairly slight rounding of an edge to appreciable taper, Fig. 3:46D. Slight rounding of edges may be necessary when building square-edge surfaces for a one-piece cover (Figs. 1:01, 1:02, 1:03), and for banded, bordered, and boxed surfaces (Secs. 11:04–11:06). Edges of soft poly-foam and foam rubber usually are not rounded, as they pack to shape under pressure of a muslin casing and the cover. But edges of medium or firm polyfoam and foam rubber, and rubberized hair, are rounded to keep dirt and wear lines from developing in a cover. Regardless of the stuffing, when a surface will have a knife edge, or filling is pre-pared for a cushion or pillow to be made in whole or in part without

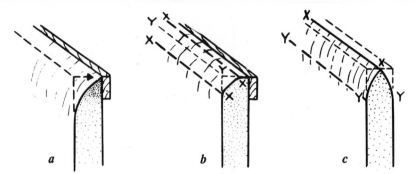

Fig. 3:46D   *a*   *b*   *c*

boxing, shape or taper stuffing. Shape with shears or a sharp knife; many upholsterers grind stuffing to shape with a powered coarse sanding disc.   [*1*] *Knife-edge* (Fig. 10:21C). To shape compact stuffing merely by pressure of a casing or cover tends to pack it into a relatively hard, wide mass along a tapered edge, Fig. *a* 3:46D. To build shape, first fasten stuffing in place (Secs. 5:11D–G) along planned knife-edge. Draw a line on the stuffing to show where taper starts, X-X, Fig. *b* 3:46D; start trimming at the top of the square edge, Y-Y, and work to the wanted shape.   [*2*] *Cushions, pillows* are usually knife-edge on sides that are not boxed (Figs. *b* 1:31, 1:34). Mark such sides of a filling for the tip of the knife-edge, X-X, Fig. *c* 3:46D. Mark top and bottom surfaces for starting the taper, Y-Y, trim filling smoothly to shape.

SEC. 3:47 **INSTALLATION**	Install compact stuffings by bonding, tacking tape, tacking, stitching (Secs. 5:11D–G).

SEC. 3:48 **MUSLIN** **CASING**	Muslin casing compresses and holds stuffing in shape, thus simplifying installation of a cover; protects a cover by limiting outward pressure of stuffing; and gives inexperienced upholsterers valuable practice in handling goods before covering. Many factory articles are not muslin incased; the possible money saved is not worthwhile for the home upholsterer. Muslin also may be used in building cushions. Any good quality, fairly tight-woven unbleached muslin or similar goods is satisfactory. Tightly woven fabrics such as canvas are stiff, inelastic, difficult to handle, and likely to be noisy against loose stuffing or rubberized hair. Thin, loosely-woven fabrics are too stretchy to hold stuffing in shape; bleached muslin, such as bed sheeting, may tear too readily. Accurate estimates of the amount of muslin needed generally can be made only when surfaces are stuffed and ready for incasing. [*1*] *Muslin comes in widths* of 36 to 70 inches. Smaller widths generally are most practical. Pieced-together muslin is satisfactory if seams are tight and strong. Salvaging muslin is not worthwhile; even

if strong enough for reuse, pieces generally are too small for satisfactory handling.   [2] *Continuous filament* (polypropylene, etc.) nonwoven goods are replacing woven muslin in many upholstery factories and custom shops.

<table>
<tr><td>SEC. 3:49
PADDING</td><td>

SEC. 3:49A   FELTED PADDING   /   Upholsterer's felted padding should be spread on all surfaces that are to be incased by a cover. Padding protects a cover by dulling sharp edges of a frame, smoothes minor irregularities in stuffed surfaces, eliminates noise made by most muslin-incased loose stuffings and rubberized hair, and keeps fine hairs and fibers from working through a cover. Padding also is used for minor corrections or improvements in shape of a stuffed surface. In some cases felted padding builds crown (Sec. 5:14). Padding can be estimated in advance with close accuracy for the simplest pad surfaces, outside arms, backs, and wings; measure stuffed and incased surfaces. Felted paddings are natural and synthetic cottons (Secs. 3:49B, C). Salvaging padding from an old article is not practical.   [1] *Except for flat pad seats, some arms, and channeled surfaces*, padding is not a practical stuffing. Natural cotton packs or mats into hard layers; synthetic cotton is too expensive.   [2] *For best results, handle felted padding properly.* Tear or pull it apart; cutting leaves a hard edge. Do not wad padding into small balls or rolls; when filling a small hollow, fold padding over the fingertips or end of a ripping tool, chisel, regulator, or small smooth stick, and work it gently into place. When correcting the shape of a surface, or filling a hollow or soft spot, place the extra padding under the layer that goes next to the cover so that the cover will look and feel smooth. Install padding snugly but without compressing it by hand; a cover compresses it better than hands can. Stitch through padding with a sharp 3-square point needle (Sec. 2:06).

</td></tr>
</table>

SEC. 3:49B   NATURAL COTTON PADDING   /   The best natural padding is felted staple cotton. Due to variations in cotton and its processing, thickness of felting and pounds per roll are not standard. A good thickness is about 1 inch; a roll 27 inches wide containing about 20 yards usually weighs from 15 to 20 pounds. Good quality staple cotton weighs less per yard than cheaper grades. There are several common substitutes for felted staple cotton.   [1] *Felted cotton linters.* Linters, the fibers left after staple cotton is cut from the seed, is weaker, less resilient than staple cotton, and readily mats into hard layers or lumps.   [2] *Wadding.* A thin layer of cotton between two sheets of soft paper, wadding is a poor but easy-to-handle substitute for felted cotton.   [3] *Quilting cotton wadding.* A layer of cotton between a glazed, paper-like film and cheesecloth, made for quilting (Sec. 3:57). It is too costly for general upholstery padding.

SEC. 3:49C   SYNTHETIC COTTON PADDING   /   Polyester fiber is a common name for upholsterer's synthetic cotton padding. Most polyesters are very strong, resilient, durable, and clean. Polyester fiber resembles natural cotton, but usually is a brighter white, much fluffier, and does not have the small lumps nearly always found in natural cotton. Generally, polyester is used only in expensive furniture, and where its exceptional initial softness is most noticeable. For example, polyester is used most in seat cushions, back pillows, solid inside backs; less in inside arms and wings; hardly ever, unless an extremely puffy effect is wanted, in outside surfaces. Its resilience and resistance to matting or packing make polyester unsuitable for some jobs, such as correcting minor depressions or soft spots in stuffed surfaces; natural cotton is better for this work. Polyester padding generally comes in rolls 27 inches wide by about 20 yards long, either felted or "quilted" (sandwiched) between sheets of lightweight muslin.

SEC. 3:50 COVER

SEC. 3:50A   COVER MATERIALS   /   These come in a wide variety of natural and synthetic fabrics, molded plastics, and real and imitation leathers. Choice of solid color, striped, or figured goods is a matter of personal taste. But when selecting a cover, consider its durability, effect on an article, ease of handling, and amount of waste. Fabrics or textiles are woven from natural fibers (cotton, wool, etc.) and from synthetic fibers (rayon, nylon, etc.). Molded or nonwoven plastic or synthetic cover goods, with or without "breather" pores, may or may not have an embossed weave texture or pattern. Here are some general pointers on selecting goods.   [1] *Wear.* Some cover goods are stronger and tend to last longer than others. Wear also is governed by the use given a cover. A favorite chair cover will not last as long as one on a show-piece subject, which receives little, and very careful, use.   [2] *Finish.* Some goods naturally resist, and some are given special finishes to resist, spotting. But they cannot be expected to be proof against all soil and stains, or to eliminate need of proper care. Spots should be removed immediately.   [3] *Synthetics.* Woven and solid or molded plastics or synthetics are not "miracle" goods and do have certain limitations. Before using an unfamiliar synthetic, find out if it requires special handling, care, and cleaning.   [4] *Cleaning.* Vacuum clean covers frequently; soil and dust can cause damage if left to accumulate. Do not wash or use a cleaning agent unless you know it will not damage a material, especially a synthetic.   [5] *Environmental damage.* Unless a cover goods is made for outdoor use, keep it out of direct sunlight; even winter sun can be harmful, especially to delicate colors. Also, goods protected from sunlight often fade or deteriorate some other way due to natural oxidation or various pollutants in the air. Always read manufacturer's warranty of a cover goods and its use limitations.

Sec. 3:50B Amount of Cover / Yardages listed with the articles in Chapter 1 contain allowances for unskilled measuring, planning, cutting, and general waste. Efficient measuring and planning methods, and legitimate ways to reduce cover costs, are in Chapter 11; pay special attention to Sec. 11:24. Salvaging a cover seldom is practical. Most are stretched and trimmed during installation, stretch and fade in use, shrink when cleaned, and are too small to handle satisfactorily. Old covers often are used as cover-stretchers (Secs. 3:55, 11:13B).

| SEC. 3:51 COVER DURABILITY | Regarding durability of a cover: How well will it wear? For how long will you want it? Articles subject to hard usage generally should be covered with goods whose long wear quality is known. Most synthetics are good in this respect. Covers that readily tear or show dirt, are too stretchy, or have loose surface threads seldom last long under hard treatment. Normally, some cover goods retain their new appearance almost indefinitely, others for only a short time. For people who like frequent changes of decor, long-lasting goods such as mohair, synthetics, or leather may be a poor buy. |

SEC. 3:52 EFFECTS OF COVER GOODS

Sec. 3:52A / Consider the overall effect of a cover. Obviously cheap goods usually make expensive furniture look cheap; expensive covers are wasted on obviously cheap furniture. As a rule modern-design goods look better on modern articles, old fashioned types on old fashioned furniture. Coarse textiles, leather, and coarse-textured solid plastics usually show better on massive, sturdy furniture than on light, small pieces where fine, velvety, or silken weaves or textures often are preferable. Brightly colored and plain covers make big articles look bigger. Vertical stripes seem to add height and reduce width; horizontal strips tend to lower and widen an article. The apparent size of furniture is changed least by covering with a moderately sized figure or pattern. Most cover designs are satisfactory on plain, buttoned, or channeled surfaces, but scenic patterns and large, isolated figures often seem lost on channeled surfaces. Covers with wide or vertical stripes, large figures, and scenic or geometrical patterns seldom show to best advantage on tufted or small surfaces.

Sec. 3:52B Covering Techniques / There are many covering techniques that make commonplace furniture distinctive. Outside arm, wing, and back covers may be a different color than, or have the same background but not the dominant figure of, the inside covers. Skirts or flounces appear to lower and perhaps modernize an article, add mass to it, and hide damaged or poorly designed legs. Large or decorative buttons give individuality (Fig. 1:15). Accent color is given articles covered with plain goods by making welts from a different material (Fig. *b* 1:31). A quilted cover adds richness (Fig. 1:34). Ruching dresses the back of a chair (Fig. *a* 1:35). Fringe can soften bulky articles (Fig. *b* 1:48). And one of the oldest tricks of the trade— if it looks all right, put the cover on wrong-side-out (Fig. *d* 1:45).

SEC. 3:53 WORKABILITY AND WEIGHT OF COVER GOODS

SEC. 3:53A / How a cover handles affects the work and, often, appearance of a finished article. Easy-to-handle goods generally fit smoothly, wear well. Hard-to-handle covers often have sags and wrinkles that soil and wear out easily. The "weight" of a material, its weave and texture, pliability and stretch, and the surface on which it is installed, all affect ease-of-handling. The following descriptions of various qualities of cover goods are given chiefly in terms of fabrics, not solid or molded goods. There is as much variety in weight, thickness, stretch, and general handling qualities of solid or molded goods as in natural and synthetic textiles. With a few differences, similar textiles and non-woven goods are handled, and react to handling, much the same way.

SEC. 3:53B WEIGHTS OF GOODS / Classifying upholstery cover goods by "weight" as Light, Medium, and Heavy is arbitrary but practical. Some goods may be in two classes. [1] *Light Weight.* Broadcloth, casement cloth, chintz, cretonne, denim, faille, muslin, moiré, sateen, silk, velourette, and nonwoven goods of similar thickness and body. Usually are easy to install on plain, buttoned, and channeled surfaces but are too weak to hold satisfactorily the pleats made in deep buttoning or tufting. Take special care against ripping, especially glazed fabrics and very thin nonwoven goods. [2] *Medium Weight.* Brocatelle, corduroy, crash, damask, drill, gabardine, linen, monkscloth, rep, sail cloth (canvas), satin, ticking, twill, and nonwoven goods of similar thickness and body. Usually are fairly easy to handle for all surfaces, and hold tufting pleats better than light weight goods, but not as well as the heavy weights. [3] *Heavy Weight.* Brocaded velour, brocaded velvet, chenille, crewel embroideries, frieze (frise), leather, leather substitutes (artificial leather), matelasse, plush, quilted goods, raw silk, tapestry, velour, velvet, wool, and non-woven goods of similar weight and body. Usually are fairly easy to handle on all surfaces and hold pleats made in tufting nicely, but unless special care is taken, particularly when corner-pleating, these goods tend to make lumps. Many heavy weight textiles, nonwoven goods, leather, and leather substitutes are too thick and tough for the average home sewing machine. Very heavy nonwoven goods, leathers, and leather substitutes are often stiff and quite difficult to handle.

NOTE: Most velvets and other pile fabrics should not be in contact with polyfoam or foam rubber, both of which tend to loosen or pull pile threads; some rubber-backed materials tend to stick to polyfoam and foam rubber, which can cause a cushion to become misshapen; for both types of goods incase polyfoam or foam rubber stuffing or filling with muslin, ticking or padding.

[4] *Novelty weaves.* In addition to more or less standard goods, there are "novelty" weaves; they come in all "weights." A light weight novelty usually has the same general qualities as a light weight standard, and so forth.

Sec. 3:53C Stretch / Mechanically, the quality having greatest affect on handling and appearance of a cover is "stretch." In upholstery, stretch means that a cover goods can be pulled or elongated in one or more directions and will seek its original shape when the pull is lessened or removed. Some goods have nearly the same degree of stretch lengthwise and side-to-side, others have much more in one direction than the other; in most cases maximum stretch is on the bias (Sec. 11:25). Some goods have almost no stretch. [1] *Moderate stretch* allows a cover to be worked smoothly into place, to fit itself to a surface, and hold securely in place. A cover that adapts to a surface, around a curve, over edges, etc., is easier to install than one that must be set precisely at every point. A material that tightens and keeps tightening as the surface under it packs down in use looks better than one than loosens, sags, and wrinkles. A good grade of tapestry usually has satisfactory stretch, with side-to-side stretch often a little greater than the lengthwise. Most medium-thick nonwoven materials with a good grade of fabric backing usually have satisfactory stretch, although somewhat greater than that of tapestry and about the same degree in all directions.   [2] *Avoid cover goods* that are weak or too stretchy. They are hard to install neatly, as they lack strength to hold down a surface smoothly between tacking points; cushions covered by them tend to be shapeless instead of relatively square along the edges. Weak or too stretchy covers often look all right when first installed, but soon become loose and develop pull-marks (Fig. 5:19), sags, and wrinkles that wear and show dirt. The looser a weave, the weaker a textile is. Loose novelty weaves and thin solid plastics with a flimsy fabric backing or no backing are often weak or too stretchy. [3] *Cover goods with almost no stretch* are hard to install smoothly because they do not adapt to a surface; instead, the surface must be padded or stuffed to fit, or the cover worked in extremely small segments at a time, for a neat, firm finished surface. The less stretch to a cover the less flexible it usually is, and the harder it is to install without wrinkles, pull-marks, and visible stitches. Cover goods that generally have too little stretch are glazed chintz and similar fabrics, heavy nonwoven goods with or without fabric backing, leather, and leather substitutes. [4] *To test stretch of a textile or a nonwoven goods that has a fabric backing,* pull straight along the warp or the weft (lengthwise or sidewise), not on the bias. Nonwoven goods that do not have a fabric backing or have a knitted backing generally have about equal stretch in all directions.

SEC. 3:53D REPAIR / Repair tack and needle holes in coarse, nubby, most pile, and loosely woven fabrics by pushing threads back in place and lightly rubbing the hole site; velvet, however, is one of the worst fabrics for showing holes. Since holes cannot be repaired in nonwoven goods, leather, leather substitutes, and most hard-surfaced, thin, tightly woven textiles, take extra care to set a cover exactly in place before tacking or stitching it. Unnecessary or unused holes spoil appearance, and weaken a cover.

SEC. 3:53E RAVELING / Raveling is a fault of most loosely woven textiles, although all ravel to some extent. Handle such goods as little as possible (Sec. 11:24).

SEC. 3:54
LEATHER

SEC. 3:54A / Leather comes in a variety of colors. Full top grain leather, the best quality, is sold by the hide, half-hide and, most costly, by square feet cut to size. First- and second-split leathers are cheaper and less pliable grades, taken from a hide after the top-grain is removed; they are sold the same way as top-grain, and in 36-inch wide yardage. The grain on all finished leathers is embossed. Unless each needed cover piece is planned with utmost precision (Chapter 19), there may be considerable waste when cutting from the hide.

SEC. 3:54B FULL TOP GRAIN LEATHER / This usually is available in natural, glazed high gloss and dull finishes. The natural finish has wire cuts and other blemishes that may exist in leather. Glazed high gloss and dull finishes are the result of buffing leather to remove wire cuts and other blemishes. All full top grain leathers are very soft and pliable, and may be used satisfactorily over foam stuffing and down fillings.

SEC. 3:54C LEATHER SUBSTITUTES / These are manufactured and sold in yardage, the same as textiles.

SEC. 3:55
COVER-
STRETCHERS

Cover-stretchers (Sec. 11:09) may be any fairly strong cloth. Scraps of muslin, denim, or pieces of an old cover are commonly used.

SEC. 3:56 **DECKING**	Decking or platform cover is used on loose cushion seats. Although usually not seen, decking should harmonize with the cover; denim and velourette are common deckings. However, interior decorators and custom upholsterers often use cover goods for decking, Fig. 3:56; how practical this is may depend on cost of cover goods. Some upholsterers say that decking is subject to little wear or fading, and that cover goods used for decking may possibly be used to repair or replace a noticeable part of the cover.

Fig. 3:56

SEC. 3:57 **QUILTING**	**SEC. 3:57A QUILTING /** Quilting gives a cover fullness, depth, and greater appearance and feel of luxury. It is most effective on patterned goods (Fig. *a* 1:31). Almost any goods may be quilted (Fig. 1:34); factory-quilted goods usually are available through an upholstery shop. There is generally a wide selection of nonwoven goods with an embossed quilted effect. Quilting is not difficult (Sec. 12:05) if you have an adequate sewing machine. Common quilting materials are quilted cotton wadding, upholsterer's felted cotton padding, and a polyfoam-polyester material.

SEC. 3:57B   WADDING /   When using quilted cotton wadding (Sec. 3:49B), set film side of wadding to wrong side of cover goods.

SEC. 3:57C   PADDING AND MUSLIN /   A layer of upholsterer's cotton on a backing of muslin or cheesecloth makes fuller, richer quilting than cotton wadding. The better the grade of cotton and the thicker it is, the deeper and fuller the quilting. Set cotton to wrong side of cover goods. When quilting glazed chintz or other brittle fabric, and with any cover goods when the free height of a layer of cotton is more than 1 inch, the backing material should be a strong muslin. When tacking a quilted cover, first tack the backing, then the cover goods. This eases strain on the cover, which is very important for weak goods, and keeps quilting from being pulled too flat along the tacked edges.

Sec. 3:57D Polyfoam and Polyester / A quilting material often in luxurious furniture consists of a sheet of polyfoam (Sec. 3:41) bonded to a layer of polyester fiber (Sec. 3:49C). Sold by the yard, this material usually is available with ½-, ¾-, and 1-inch polyfoam. Bond pieces together (Sec. 3:46); make a soft bond, do not get bonding agent on polyester. When bond is thoroughly dry, stroke polyester back and forth gently over seam to mix fibers together. To use in quilting see Sec. 3:57C.

SEC. 3:58 WELT CORD

Welt cord, used for welts (Sec. 11:08) and in some channel covers, is either a solid cord or a core incased by a soft mesh. Welt along the junction of covers gives them a finished, tailored look; compare plain and welted cover junctions (Fig. *a, b* 11:08A). Welts and welt cords are single and double. Single cord may be hard or soft, double welt cord usually is soft. Single cord may be used for single and double-welts; double is only for double-welts, and requires a double-welting foot on a sewing machine. Hard welt cord tends to hold a bend permanently; use where immobile welts go, generally those tacked to a frame, as along the outside back and arm (Fig. *b* 11:24C). Soft welt cord is for cushions, pillows, and wherever welts are subject to much flexing. Single welt cord comes in diameters of ⅛- to 1-inch; those used most are the ⅛- to ⁵⁄₁₆-inch sizes. Double welt cord usually is two soft cores incased by a mesh that shapes each cord separately yet holds them together. Double welt nearly always is tacked to a frame, but soft is preferable to hard since it can easily be curved to follow the shape of a tacking surface. The most common size of double welt cord is ⅛-inch diameter (each cord). Any heavy, strong, pliable, smooth cord, such as jute spring twine (Sec. 3:08) can substitute for single welt cord. It may be salvaged if long enough to use without piecing together and in good condition. French seams (Sec. 12:04) are sometimes used instead of welts.

SEC. 3:59 TRIMS

Sec. 3:59A / Common upholstery trims are gimp, antique and trim nails, fringe, and decorative buttons. All come in many colors and designs, sizes and shapes. Salvaging any except buttons is neither practical nor advisable. [1] *Gimp, double-welt.* Cloth, plastic, or artificial-leather gimp tapes, strips of leather, and double-welt conceal upholstery tacks and edges of a cover on exposed-wood surfaces. Glue gimp and any material used as gimp. If tacked, gimp often develops scallops, and tacks may snag clothing. Find the amount of gimp needed by measuring the appropriate edges of exposed-wood surfaces, and add 1 inch for each ending and sharp corner. [2] *Nails.* Antique or trim nails are primarily on exposed-wood surfaces. Work is often easier and a cover looks better if it is gimped before installing trim nails. Spacing of antique or trim nails is a matter of personal taste. [3] *Fringe.* Fringe often is used instead of welt on some parts of an article (Fig. *b* 1:48). Fringe may be machine sewn to cover panels before installing them, or it may be tacked in place. Find the amount of fringe needed by measuring the appropriate parts of a frame; add a few inches per cut or piece of fringe for handling. Most experienced upholsterers use fringe sparingly; with too much, an article often looks lumpy.

SEC. 3:59B DECORATIVE BUTTONS / Decorative buttons often are used to "break" a plain surface and to cover the ends of pleats in a scroll, Fig. 3:59B. Button forms are plywood, plastic, pressed fiber, and heavy cardboard. They are incased by cover goods, or by harmonizing or contrasting goods. On most surfaces buttons are held by twine. Post-face buttons are tacked or nailed.

Fig. 3:59B

| **SEC. 3:60**
UPHOLSTERY
BUTTONS | Upholstery buttons hold cover in place in barrel backs and tufted surfaces, and may be used for trim or decoration. Cloth-tuft and loop buttons, Fig. *a, b* 3:60, may be used on nearly any surface. Tack buttons, *c,* have upholstery tacks or small nails; install only on solid-base surfaces. Covered buttons, *a, b, c,* are incased and processed by a button machine. Pressed fiber and plastic buttons, *d,* come in loop and |

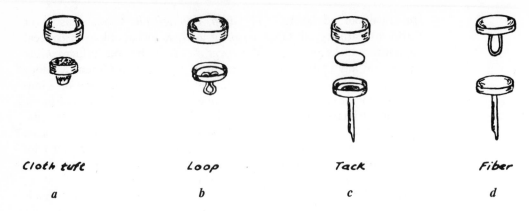

Cloth tuft   Loop   Tack   Fiber

a   b   c   d

Fig. 3:60

tack types, a variety of colors, designs, shapes, and sizes, and are as satisfactory as the other kinds. Use dressmaking buttons if upholstery buttons are not available.

**SEC. 3:61
CUSHION
FILLINGS**

SEC. 3:61A / A cushion or pillow filling and the method of building and padding determine its comfort, life, and looks. Traditional (Sec. 3:00C) fillings are down-feather mixtures, inner-spring unit, hair, and kapok (Secs. 3:62–3:65). Modern fillings are foam rubber, polyfoam, rubberized hair, polyester fiber, and inner-spring units incased by foam rubber, polyfoam, rubberized hair, and polyester fiber (Secs. 3:67–3:73). Traditional padding is felted natural cotton; modern padding is synthetic cotton or polyester fiber (Sec. 3:49): either may be used with any filling, although polyester generally is used for a high degree of initial softness and/or a very puffy appearance.

SEC. 3:61B SIZES OF FILLERS / Regardless of the padding to be used, if any, the size of a cushion or pillow filling is based on the filling and the cover or casing. [1] *Traditional down-filled, spring-down, kapok* cushion or pillow (Secs. 3:62, 3:63, 3:65). Filling should be at least 1 inch wider, longer, and thicker than the casing. [2] *Traditional inner-spring unit to be wrapped with two or three layers of natural cotton padding* (Sec. 3:63). Inner-spring unit should be 1 inch smaller all around (2 inches narrower, 2 inches shorter) than the casing. With T-shaped seats and backs often it is necessary to get too large a unit and cut off springs, or one that's too small for the T-area and add springs. Sometimes instead of adding springs the usual way for maximum width and length, Fig. 3:63B, they are set between springs for a lesser gain of width or length. [3] *Traditional hair fillings, or spring-units incased by hair* (Secs. 3:64, 3:72). Filler should be 1 inch smaller (½ inch narrower, ½ inch shorter) than the casing. [*4*] *Cotton fillings* (Secs. 3:66, 3:70). Size and thickness of the filling depends on the desired thickness and firmness of a cushion or pillow, and density of the cotton (Sec. 17:12). [*5*] *Foam rubber, polyfoam fillings; spring-units incased by foam rubber, polyfoam; spring-unit wrapped with several layers of polyester fiber* (Secs. 3:67, 3:68, 3:71– 3:73). Filling should be at least ½ inch larger (½ inch wider, ½ inch longer) than the casing. [*6*] *All fillings* should be shaped for their casings—straight, curved, T-shaped, etc.

SEC. 3:62 **DOWN** **FILLING**	Down is the light, fluffy filament growing from one quill point on the undercoating of waterfowl. Top quality down fillings are durable, slightly softer than foam rubber and polyfoam, but do not hold shape well. A 100% down filling would be too weak. Down is strengthened by mixing it with, preferably, goose feathers; duck, turkey, and chicken feathers often are used, but they are too brittle for a good, durable mixture. Softness and durability of down-feather blends decrease as the proportion of feathers increases. An 80% down 20% goose feathers mixture is excellent; the minimum good mixture is about 50–50 down and goose feathers. A 100% feather filling generally is unsatisfactory; in fairly short time feather quills usually break and a cushion or pillow becomes flat and lumpy. Salvage down fillings that look and smell clean; as a rule more will be needed. Do not mix kapok or cotton (Secs. 3:65, 3:66) with down or feathers; they will form hard lumps. Incase down fillings in down-proof ticking (Chapter 17). Traditional down-proof ticking is a sized, tightly woven cloth used to keep the down from working into and through a cushion or pillow casing. Modern down-proof ticking often is a nonwoven continuous filament material. The amount of ticking needed depends on the size and shape of a cushion or pillow. In time ticking wears out and loses its protective quality. Do not salvage down-proof ticking.

SEC. 3:63 **INNER-SPRING** **UNITS**	**Sec. 3:63A** / Inner-spring cushions made the traditional way are moderately soft, durable, and inexpensive. Made the modern way, cushions with inner-spring units incased by foam rubber, polyfoam, rubberized hair, or polyester, and padded with polyester (Secs. 3:49C, 3:71D, 3:73) are exceptionally soft and durable and can be quite expensive. A very comfortable, durable modern-type cushion made with traditional materials is the spring-down (Sec. 17:09E), consisting of a special, extra soft inner-spring unit incased by a down-filled ticking pad. **Sec. 3:63B** / An inner-spring cushion unit consists of cushion springs (Sec. 3:18) incased in a compartmentalized ticking, Fig. 3:63B. In

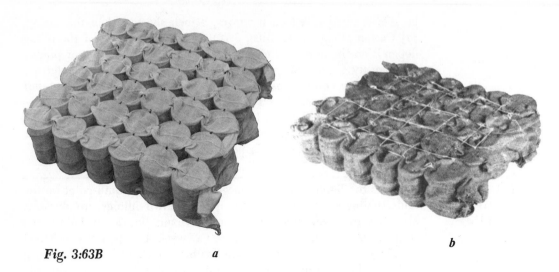

Fig. 3:63B   *a*   *b*

modern units, *a*, usually the ticking is muslin, and springs are held together by hog rings. In older units, *b*, the ticking usually was burlap, although muslin was not uncommon, and springs were stitched together. There is no particular advantage to either type, except that the modern unit sometimes is less expensive. Inner-spring cushion units often are called "marshall" units. They may be made by an upholsterer (Sec. 17:19), and often are used to upholster inside backs (Secs. 10:11, 10:29, 10:30, 10:32, 10:37).

| SEC. 3:64 HAIR | Hair cushions usually are made only for window seats and other places where durability is more important than comfort. Hair (Sec. 3:29) is a good filling; but due to cost, work, and comfort, inner-spring cushions usually are preferred. Hair-proof ticking is needed; as a rule down-proof material is used (Sec. 3:62). |

SEC. 3:64 HAIR

Hair cushions usually are made only for window seats and other places where durability is more important than comfort. Hair (Sec. 3:29) is a good filling; but due to cost, work, and comfort, inner-spring cushions usually are preferred. Hair-proof ticking is needed; as a rule down-proof material is used (Sec. 3:62).

SEC. 3:65 KAPOK

Kapok, an inexpensive but generally impractical cushion or pillow filling, is fairly soft when new, but after fairly little use, breaks into dust. From time to time kapok cushions and pillows should be opened and refilled. Kapok and cotton do not mix. Kapok should be in a muslin inner casing. Discard used kapok.

SEC. 3:66 NATURAL COTTON

Natural cotton (Sec. 3:49) is not a satisfactory cushion or pillow filling; it packs into hard layers and lumps, which no amount of "fluffing up" can correct. Natural cotton is used as padding for traditional inner-spring cushions and pillows and to fill out and shape corners of some cushions when necessary. Synthetic cotton or polyester fiber (Sec. 3:49) is an excellent filling (Sec. 3:70).

SEC. 3:67
FOAM
RUBBER

SEC. 3:67A   FOAM RUBBER UNITS   /   The first modern cushion and pillow filling, foam rubber combines the softness of down-filling with the shape-holding quality of inner-spring units, and is more durable than either. Foam rubber is excellent for reversible cushions or pillows. Foam rubber units have the same general properties and limitations as stuffing (Sec. 3:43). Salvage foam rubber cushion units in good condition unless they are more than about twelve years old.

SEC. 3:67B   SIZE, SHAPE, THICKNESS OF UNITS   /   Foam rubber cushion and pillow units come in a variety of sizes, shapes, and thicknesses, all of which may be reshaped (Sec. 3:46). Most upholstery shops carry various sizes of cored foam rubber cushion stock from which units are cut as needed. Cushion stock usually has front-to-back crown (Sec. 5:14) on the specified upper surface only, Fig. *a* 3:67B; most stock is soft enough for a cushion or pillow casing to form adequate crown on the bottom surface and sides. If a casing is weak or very thin material, it is advisable to build side-to-side crown into a cushion unit by bonding a rectangular band or slab of foam rubber to each side, *b*. The band should be ½-inch stock as long as the side of a unit, and 1 inch less in height than the thickness of the unit at front and back corners. Center band in place and bond to unit, *b*. Then bond together the top, bottom, front, and back corner surfaces of the band and unit, *c*.

SEC. 3:67C   LAMINATED FOAM RUBBER UNITS   /   Instead of prepared foam rubber cushion units or unit stock, many upholsterers prefer to laminate their cushion stock, Fig. 3:67C. The core usually is medium, and the top and bottom layers soft stock (Sec. 3:43), making the unit initially soft but with moderately firm support underneath. Most top and bottom layers are soft enough for a casing to form adequate crown.

SEC. 3:67D   PADDING   /   Foam rubber units often are inserted directly into a casing. But generally it is better to wrap a unit with felted padding (Sec. 3:49), particularly when the cover is velvet or any non-locked pile fabric (Sec. 3:53B[3]).

SEC. 3:68
POLYFOAM

SEC. 3:68A   /   Polyfoam has the same advantages for cushion or pillow filling as it has for a general stuffing (Sec. 3:41). The disadvantage is that it packs down to some extent and does not continue to exert maximum outward pressure against a casing to hold it in shape; this can make polyfoam less than satisfactory for reversible cushions and pillows. Salvaging polyfoam cushion units seldom is practical.

SEC. 3:68B   SIZE, SHAPE, THICKNESS OF UNITS   /   Polyfoam cushion

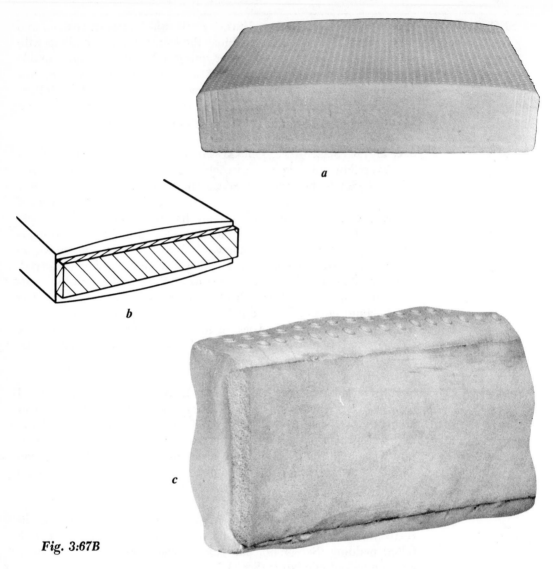

a

b

c

Fig. 3:67B

and pillow units are available in the same varieties as foam rubber units (Sec. 3:67B), but are solid, not cored, and usually not crowned. Normally it is not necessary to build crown (Sec. 5:14) with stuffing or padding or by shaping polyfoam. Unless a casing is weak material or more than about 30 inches wide or long, a polyfoam unit nearly always compresses sufficiently along edges to create adequate crown. Polyfoam units usually are 1 to 2 inches thicker than the sides or boxing of a casing.

SEC. 3:68C LAMINATED POLYFOAM UNITS / These are common,

Fig. 3:67C

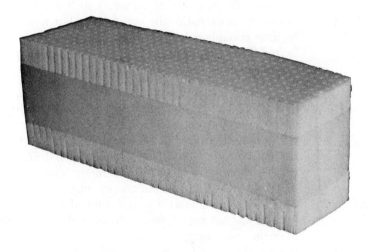

Fig. 3:68C

Fig. 3:68C (Sec. 3:67C) units. Core and layers may be polyfoam, but usually the core is medium density polyfoam and the layers are soft foam rubber. This is noticeably firmer than the all-foam-rubber laminate and less expensive. Some people find an all-rubber laminate too soft for comfort.

SEC. 3:68D PADDING / Polyfoam cushion and pillow units of any type should be padded (Sec. 3:67D).

**SEC. 3:69
RUBBERIZED
HAIR**

SEC. 3:69A / Compact rubberized hair (Sec. 3:44) seldom is a cushion or pillow filling except for small, fairly thin and flat items (not over about 16 inches wide or long and 2 inches thick), or for a fairly thick, large and flat pad such as a window seat or bench cushion. In both cases appearance usually is more important than comfort, and the stiffness of compact rubberized hair stuffing simplifies the building of a smooth flat pad or cushion that will hold shape well.

SEC. 3:69B PREPARATION / For a compact rubberized hair pad or cushion, cut stuffing the shape of the article, but 1 inch thicker, wider, and longer. If necessary, bond two sheets together hard-side-to-hard-side (Sec. 3:46). Wrap one or two layers of felted padding (Sec. 3:49) completely around hair unit, and insert in casing (Secs. 17:07, 17:08). Unless a casing is weak material, as a rule it is not necessary to round off edges of stuffing (Sec. 3:46D). If a cushion or pad will be more than 16 inches wide or long or will be well crowned instead of fairly flat, before padding a unit, build crown on the top and bottom surfaces with loose hair (Sec. 5:14).

SEC. 3:70 **SYNTHETIC** **COTTON**	Occasionally polyester fiber (Sec. 3:49C) is the filling of a back pillow. It makes an exceptionally soft pillow, but is too weak to hold shape well; if enough polyester is used to hold shape well, the pillow will be too firm. A foam rubber, polyfoam, or inner-spring unit incased by polyester usually makes a better cushion or pillow at less cost.

SEC. 3:71
FOAM-SPRING
UNIT

SEC. 3:71A / Foam-spring, a modern cushion or pillow filling, is an inner-spring unit incased by foam rubber or polyfoam. It combines the qualities and limitations of foam rubber and polyfoam with the lively resilience of inner-spring units (Secs. 3:63, 3:67, 3:68), and is durable, easy to handle, and only moderately expensive. Most foam-spring units are prepared for factory upholstering, but are easy to make, Fig. 3:71A, being merely a conventional inner-spring unit (Sec. 3:71B) sandwiched between layers of foam rubber or polyfoam, and the sides filled in with strips of the same material. Top and bottom layers usually are ¾- or 1-inch thick; side strips are as thick as is necessary

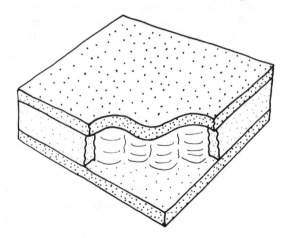

Fig. 3:71A

for a cushion or pillow. Bond sides, top, and bottom layers to each other but not to inner-spring unit. Foam-spring units usually have enough natural crown (Sec. 5:14) that additional stuffing or padding is not needed. Install foam-spring fillings in casings the usual way (Secs. 17:07, 17:08). Salvage foam-spring units in good condition; necessary reshaping can be done by trimming or adding stock (Sec. 3:46).

SEC. 3:71B CONSTRUCTION OF FILLING / The special, extra-soft inner-spring unit of a foam-spring filling should be at least 3 inches narrower and shorter than the planned width and length of the finished filling; this allows for at least 1½ inches of foam along sides, front, and back. The spring unit should be at least ½-inch thinner than the planned thickness of the cushion or pillow at the boxing (Sec. 11:13C), so that the ¾- or 1-inch thick top and bottom layers will fill out the casing fully and firmly, but without excessive pressure on boxing and seams. Strips between top and bottom layers should be 1½ inches less than the height of inner-spring unit in order to pull edges of top and bottom layers closer together and create permanent crown at the middle of the filling.

NOTE: For extra softness and a puffy effect, wrap a layer of polyester fiber around a foam-spring filling before inserting it in a casing.

SEC. 3:72 RUBBERIZED HAIR-SPRING FILLING	Rubberized hair compact stuffing (Sec. 3:44) is often used with an inner-spring unit for a cushion or pillow filling when a fairly firm surface, more than usual go-down, and maximum resilience are wanted. The inner-spring unit is the regular size, thickness, and shape for a particular cushion or pillow. Cut two sheets of ½- or ¾-inch rubberized hair the size and shape of top and bottom surfaces of cushion or pillow casing. Center spring unit between hard surfaces of rubberized hair. Fill space between them with strips of hair (Sec. 3:71) or, as is often done, fairly thick well-packed rolls of cotton. Wrap filling with two layers of felted natural cotton, then insert in casing (Secs. 17:07, 17:08). Wrapping filling with polyester instead of natural cotton makes it soft instead of relatively firm.
SEC. 3:73 POLYESTER-SPRING FILLING	An inner-spring unit incased with polyester fiber is exceptionally soft, has superior go-down and resilience, is durable, and holds shape well. Use the same size inner-spring unit as for a foam-spring filling (Sec. 3:71). One layer of 1½-inch thick quilted polyester loosely wrapped completely around the spring unit, including all sides, is adequate; use two or more wrappings of proportionately thinner quilted polyester. Due to softness of completed filling, no other material or special placement of polyester is needed for crown. The polyester-spring

filling is an expensive, luxury item; use only the finest quality spring unit and polyester fiber available.

SEC. 3:74
DUST COVER

Tacked across bottom of seat cavity after all other work is completed, a dust cover hides webbing or bottom surface of other upholstery materials and edges of the cover and keeps dust and dirt from entering and leaving an article. Traditional dust covers usually are dark, glazed, moderately fine-woven cambric or crinoline, cut 2 or 3 inches larger than the overall bottom of a seat cavity. So-called modern dust covers often are a nonwoven continuous filament goods. It may be cut smaller than a traditional dust cover since edges need not be underturned to prevent raveling. Old dust covers can be vacuum cleaned and reused but generally are discarded.

4

frames

Sec. 4:00A / The frame determines basic shape of an upholstered article. Most frames are wood (Sec. 4:03). Metal rods, bamboo, and reeds were used in so-called Turkish chairs (Sec. 4:00B). Metal frames are popular in certain modern designs (Sec. 4:00C). Upholstery shops are the best source of frames.

Sec. 4:00B / So-called Turkish chairs are commonly considered the most comfortable thickly upholstered furniture. They are readily identified by flexible yet strong arms and back. Due to the difficulty of upholstering or only re-covering them (upholstery materials can be tacked to the seat, but elsewhere must be stitched in place), few have been built since the 1890s. Upholstery should be done only by experts.

Sec. 4:00C / Metal frames are common in modern loose-cushion chairs and chaise longues. These often have an upholstered pad for seat and back, or a seat cushion and separate back pillow, and an open frame with webbing-type support (Sec. 3:10) for the pad or cushions. Rubber webbing (Sec. 3:22) often is used for original or replacement supports; special fittings may be needed.

SEC. 4:00D / Most frames can be upholstered with various styles or finishes—thin, moderate, or thick upholstering—solid or loose cushion seat or back—and a solid back may be finished plain, channeled, or tufted (Fig. 1:35). Some frames are better than others for various styles of upholstery; it depends on seat height, width and depth, thickness of back, and other factors covered in Chapters 6 through 10.

SEC. 4:00E / The comfort of a chair, sofa, or similar article starts with the built-in slope of a seat and tilt or pitch of a back. Seats usually slope down from front to back; if there is too much slope, getting out of it is difficult. If there is no slope or the front is lower than the back, a seat quickly becomes uncomfortable. A back should tilt away from a seat; too much tilt or pitch makes a chair hard to get out of, too little makes it tiring to sit in. Slope and pitch built into frames usually are adequate. Seat slope can be changed slightly by using different sizes of glides or casters (Sec. 3:01) on front and back legs. In fairly large articles slope and pitch can be controlled to great extent by making seat and back upholstery thicker or thinner in certain areas.

SEC. 4:01 FRAME TERMS

[1] *Supporting members* of a frame, Fig. 4:01, are seat-rails and legs; front-, back-, and wing-posts; top-, and wing-rails. [2] *Upholstery pieces* are slats or uprights, underarm strips, and liners, often called *tack rails*. Upholstery pieces shape and hold upholstery materials, but do not support or strengthen a frame. [3] *An open frame* is made by several supporting members; the hollow space is a cavity—seat, arm, wing, back cavity. [4] *A solid base* is a single piece of wood. Many wings and small seats are solid base. [5] *Slipframes.* In some small chairs (Fig. 1:02) an open or a solid base frame is upholstered separately and attached to the article. These are called *slipframes;* the finished surface is a slipseat or a slipback. [6] *Exposed wood, show wood* are parts of a wood frame that are not covered by upholstering (Fig. *a* 1:52).

SEC. 4:02 WIDE FRAMES

To support the frame and upholstery of a love seat or wider article, one or more crossbraces are in seat and back cavities, Fig. 4:02. Double crossbraces in a back allow it to be upholstered in sections (Fig. 1:58).

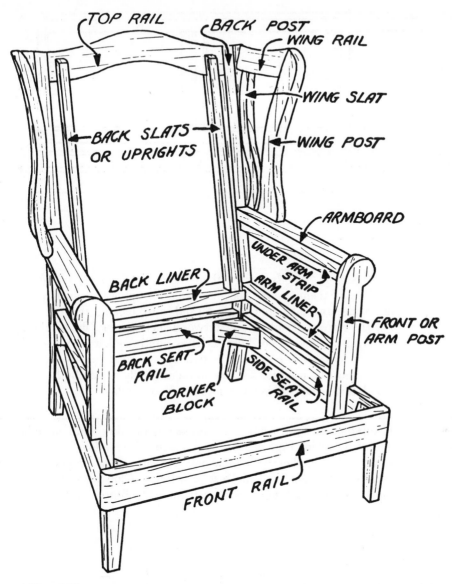

Fig. 4:01

SEC. 4:03 WOODS	Good wood frames are built of 1⅛- to 1½-inch, straight grained semi-hardwood such as alder (the most popular), ash, birch, magnolia, mahogany (chiefly for legs), maple, and oak. These woods are strong enough for upholstery purposes, light enough for easy handling. With normal care and using the smallest tacks for a job (Sec. 3:03), a good quality semi-hardwood frame should last for several complete uphol-

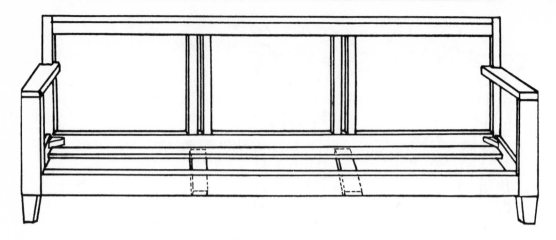

Fig. 4:02

sterings.   [1] *Woods harder* than those listed above, or very hard
varieties of them, are not recommended for upholstering; they tend to
be brittle, and may split when tacked; also, tacking them is difficult.
[2] *Inferior frames* often are softwood such as pine, fir, or philippine
mahogany. They do not hold tacks as tightly as harder woods do, so
larger tacks must be used. Softwoods are relatively weak; thicker
pieces must be used for a frame to be as sturdy as one built of harder
wood; this makes softwood frames heavy and bulky.

SEC. 4:04
FRAME
CONSTRUC-
TION

In top-quality wood frames, all supporting-member joints fit tight, are
double-doweled, Fig. *a* 4:04, and glued. When dowels and frame
surfaces fit together without a gap and are glued properly, a joint
usually is stronger than the rest of a frame. Glue is to bind surfaces
together, not to fill gaps between them.   [1] *Poorly made joints* may

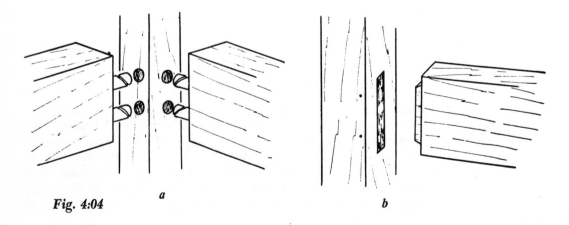

Fig. 4:04   *a*   *b*

loosen or break after relatively little use.   [2] *Screwed and glued joints* are a fair substitute for double-dowel and glue if screws are long enough and threads deep enough to bite strongly into the wood and make a tight joint.   [3] *Tongue-and-groove joints, b,* often are in inferior frames. Since a tongue seldom fills a groove, the surfaces cannot be glued properly. A tongue-and-groove joint usually has two small nails in the grooved member to help hold the tongue in place. [4] *Nailing.* Except for liners and other upholstery pieces (Sec. 4:01), no frame parts should be nailed together. Nails have little resistance to pressures trying to force joints apart. Toe-nailing is not satisfactory.

SEC. 4:05 CORNER-BLOCKS

All frame joints should be corner-blocked, Fig. 4:05, but seldom are except in the seat. Seat corner-blocks help keep a frame rigid and support the legs, and often keep the legs from splitting a frame. Without seat corner-blocks, an entire frame soon may wobble and squeak, which can be corrected only by rebuilding a frame. Corner-blocks should be about 2 inches thick, fill a corner completely, and be properly glued (Sec. 4:04) to all surfaces, Fig. *a* 4:05. A strip of wood set across a corner without filling it, *b,* is only slightly better than no corner-block.

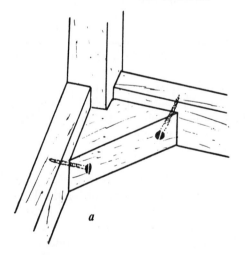
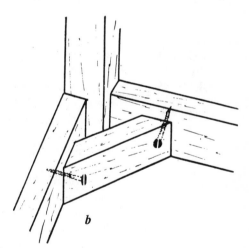

Fig. 4:05

SEC. 4:06 FRAME MODIFICA- TIONS, ASSEMBLY

Except for liners, most wooden frames come assembled (Fig. 4:01) and ready for use. But experienced upholsterers often make modifications, such as adding or improving corner-blocks. Or an upholsterer may reposition various upholstery pieces (Sec. 4:01) to simplify work. On the other hand, most good quality frames are used as delivered. [1] *When buying a frame,* ask an experienced upholsterer if it needs strengthening and if changes should be made for a particular style or method of upholstery.   [2] *Many frames are shipped* with back and arm liners not installed. This is to simplify tying springs of a traditional seat or installing zigzag springs or rubber webbing (Secs. 3:21, 3:22) in a so-called modern seat. Liners often are installed (Sec. 4:15) after a seat is stuffed and incased by muslin.   [3] *Frames for small chairs* (Fig. 3:21B) and even large articles that are to be thinly upholstered often are shipped in kits or units for assembly. Units generally are the back and arms, each containing part of the seat frame, and the front and back seat rails.

SEC. 4:07 **METAL** **FRAMES**	Metal frames were first used chiefly for Turkish chairs (Sec. 4:00B). Metal frames are popular for so-called modern loose-cushion articles (Sec. 4:00C). Repairing broken or bent metal frames should be done only by expert metal workers.
SEC. 4:08 **USED FRAMES**	If buying a used frame, pay special attention to the top and bottom surfaces of the seat frame. A seat-rail that is split or has too many close-set tack holes may not last long. If wood is soft or spongy from previous tacking, extra-large tacks may be needed for upholstering— and they may crack a frame.
SEC. 4:09 **FRAME** **DESIGNS**	**SEC. 4:09A** / Most frames can be grouped in a few basic types, with differences in design made by modifying various parts in fairly simple ways. For example, two chair frames are identical except that the top of the back of one is flat and the other is arched; the upholstered chairs probably will seem quite different in design. Add wings to each back, and two more "designs" are created. Love seats and sofas are merely extra-wide chairs.

SEC. 4:09B / The frame in Fig. 4:09B represents a basic design that can be built and upholstered many ways. The top of the back may be flat, or single- or double-arched, with the latter giving a "heart" effect. The seat may be straight-edge throughout, rounded, or slightly curved. Various arms and shapes of wings can be added. Fig. *a, b* 1:29 have nearly identical frames; Fig. *c* 1:29 is essentially the same, but has a rounded seat and a barrel-type back with flared sides. Fig. *a, c* 1:35 have identical frames; differences in "design" are due entirely to the upholstering.

SEC. 4:09C / Frames in Fig. 4:09C may be upholstered as so-called side, occasional, bedroom, or dining chairs (Figs. 1:16, 1:17, 1:09, 1:19). They are generally regarded as "modern" in relation to the more traditional designs represented by Fig. 4:09B.

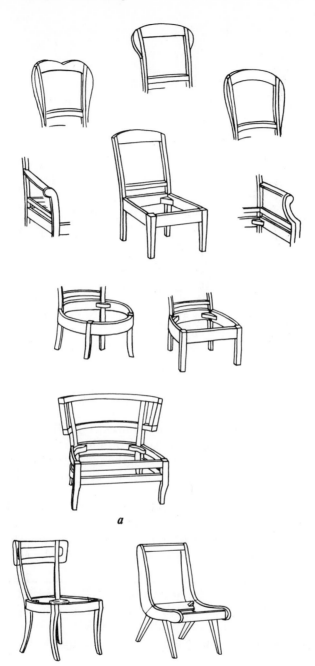

Fig. 4:09B

a

Fig. 4:09C   *b*   *c*

SEC. 4:09D / The general style of chair represented by frames in
Fig. 4:09D is *barrel* or *tub* (Figs. 1:37, *b* 1:38). Any back that curves

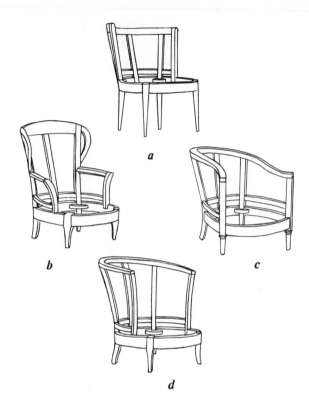

Fig. 4:09D   *d*

between the sides is a barrel back (Figs. 1:09, 1:10, 1:19, *c* 1:29, 1:35). When upholstering a barrel or tub chair, take care not to change shape of an inside back with the upholstery, nor to install it so that it will tear or rip out under normal use.

Sec. 4:09E / Basic frame and modifications in Fig. 4:09E are those common in club, lounge, and other large chairs (Figs. 1:42–1:49). Again, there is almost no limit to the sizes and shapes of seats, backs, wings, and arms, and how they may be combined.

SEC. 4:10 PREPARING FRAMES

Most furniture frames are delivered assembled, although back and arm liners (Sec. 4:01) may not have been installed (Secs. 4:06, 5:15). Before starting to upholster an article, some refinements usually are made on a frame to protect it and the upholstery.

SEC. 4:11 LEGS

Install glides or casters (Sec. 3:01). To avoid pitting glides, use a rubber, wood, or plastic mallet (Sec. 2:09); pad with a piece of cardboard if using a metal hammer. Replace scratched or pitted glides after upholstering an article.

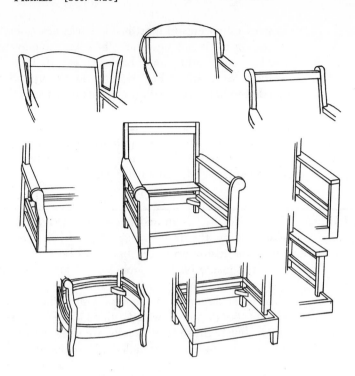

Fig. 4:09E

SEC. 4:12 WEBBING	When strip webbing (Secs. 3:11, 3:22) will go on the top surface of a fairly large pad, sag (Fig. 6:05B), or spring seat, or on the front surface of similar backs, round off the inner edges of a frame to protect the webbing as it flexes over them. Sandpapering just enough to blunt the edge often is enough.

SEC. 4:13 SPRINGS	[1] *Coil springs.* If seat coil springs are to be set down in a cavity (Fig. 7:01A), round off the inner top edge of the front rail, Fig. 4:13, to protect springs and ties. Start about ½ inch from the edge, round off rail enough to remove all sharpness. Use a wood rasp (Sec. 2:10) or

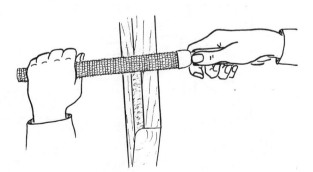

Fig. 4:13

knife. Coil springs in most inside backs are so far from the frame that rounding off is not necessary; however, it may be advisable in some flat-top and spring-edge backs (Figs. 10:15D, 10:16.) [2] *Zigzag springs* (Sec. 3:21). For zigzags do not round off edges; they are needed to help hold spring fasteners in place.

SEC. 4:14 **COVER**	To protect the cover on a pull-around inside arm (Fig. 1:30) that will be upholstered without a roll edge at the front (Sec. 8:08), round off the inner front edge of a front post.

SEC. 4:15
LINERS

Sec. 4:15A / Arm and back liners (Fig. 4:01) may or may not be installed by the framemaker (Sec. 4:06). They usually are needed when the inside arms and back will be fully upholstered, except if a seat and inside back are upholstered together (Fig. 1:16). Most liners are cut to fit properly (Sec. 4:15B) in one part of a cavity; with others, placement depends on the type seat to be built (Sec. 4:15C). Liners should be double-doweled, glued, and corner-blocked (Secs. 4:03, 4:04); but because they usually are subject to relatively little strain or pressure, most liners are nailed, glued, and corner-blocked.

Sec. 4:15B / Arm and back liners support and shape bottoms of inside arms and backs. [*1*] *Set liners parallel* to top surfaces of seat rails throughout, Fig. *a* 4:15B, to build consistent shape around seat. [*2*] *Arm liners usually are flush* with inner surfaces of front and back posts. [*3*] *Do not set* outer surface of a liner projecting beyond outer surfaces of posts, *b;* it will make a lump in the finished outside surface. [*4*] *The inner surface of a back liner* may be flush with that of a back

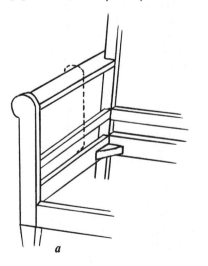
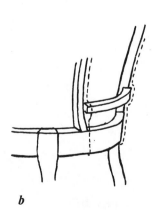

Fig. 4:15B   *a*   *b*

post, *a*, or it may be in front of a post (Fig. 4:16) to build thick spring backs (Fig. 1:42) without thick, heavy back posts.

SEC. 4:15C / Placement of arm and back liners not cut to fit in only one part of a cavity depends on the type seat to be built and, if a spring seat, the planned tied-down height (Sec. 3:15) of springs. [*1*] *In most solid seats* (Figs. 1:13, *c* 1:28), the bottom of a liner is about 1 inch above the rail. [*2*] *In most loose-cushion seats* (Fig. 1:35), the bottom of a liner is at, or slightly below, the level of the top of the tied-down springs at the edges of a cavity. [*3*] *Liners set too high* often leave gaps between the finished seat, arms, and back. [*4*] *Liners set too low* may interfere with springing a seat; for this reason, and to set liners as low as possible, many upholsterers install them after incasing a seat with muslin. [*5*] *Installed liners* may serve as guides for tying springs.

SEC. 4:15D **INSTALLATION** / Arm liners usually are installed first. [*1*] *Mark front, back posts* for placement of bottom of liner, Fig. *a* 4:15D; set two nails just deep enough in posts to hold liners in place during installation. [*2*] *When post is thin enough and not an exposed-wood piece,* drive two or three 3-inch nails through it, an inch or so apart, into the liner. [*3*] *When post cannot be nailed through,* toe-nail a liner, *b*. [*4*] *A reinforcing piece* fitted to the top and outer side of a liner at each end, *c*, is excellent, but not essential; use stock ¼- to ½-inch thick, glue or nail in place.

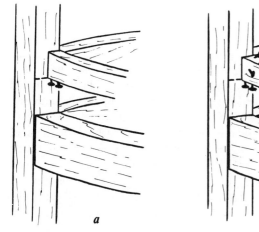
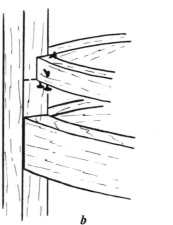

a   *b*   *c*

Fig. 4:15D

SEC. 4:16
THICK BACKS

Thick-back articles (Fig. *a* 1:36) often have complicated arm and back liners made to simplify upholstering a back and eliminate thick, heavy back posts.   [1] *Install back liner,* A, Fig. 4:16, at the proper height (Sec. 4:15C).   [2] *Cut and install arm liner,* B, to fit snug against back liner.   [3] *The upright,* C, keeps back and arm liners from rising, and helps support inner side of armboard, D; upright must fit tight between liner and armboard.   [4] *Brace-block,* E, prevents side movement of arm liner.   [5] *Pieces may be doweled, screwed, or nailed* in place; glue joints and dry under pressure.

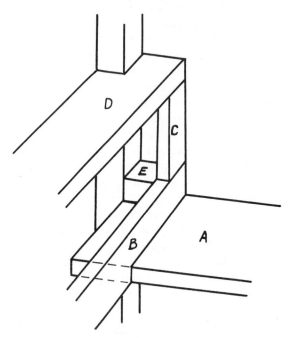

Fig. 4:16

SEC. 4:17 **REINFORCING**	The first step in upholstering an article is to repair any part of a frame that is cracked, loose, or badly tack-damaged. [1] *When wood is badly tack-damaged,* in order to hold upholstery materials securely, extra-large tacks are needed, and they may split a frame. To prevent this, reinforcing rails or strips are installed, as at the back of the seat in Fig. 4:17. [2] *When using zigzag springs* (Sec. 3:21) and frame rails are less than about 1 inch thick, or are thicker but have been badly damaged by tacking, install a reinforcing strip or rail to strengthen the original rail against the more concentrated pressures exerted by zigzag springs.
SEC. 4:18 **FINISHES**	Before installing the cover finish (Sec. 3:02) all exposed-wood parts of a frame (Sec. 4:01). They usually must be sanded smooth; use No. 00 or No. 0 sandpaper. For staining, varnishing, lacquering, or shellacking, sand wood until satiny smooth. Apply finishing compound rapidly

Fig. 4:17

but evenly; when dry stain is overlapped by wet, or when it collects on an edge, that part of a surface usually will be darker than the rest. For painting, sand wood smooth before applying the first coat, but not satiny smooth; some roughness is needed to hold paint. Fine sanding between coats of finish often is easier to do with fine steel wool than sandpaper. Follow the manufacturer's directions for applying a finishing compound or paint, especially a synthetic or plastic-base material. Many products that seem about the same need different methods of application for best results.

5

basic
operations

Except for springs, pad- and spring-upholstered surfaces are the same: foundation, stuffing, casing, padding, cover. [1] *Foundation* is a solid base or an open frame (Sec. 4:01). Stuffing or springs mount directly on a solid base. Open frames are webbed (Sec. 3:10) to complete the foundation if they will be upholstered the traditional way (Sec. 3:00C) with coil springs and stuffing (Secs. 3:15, 3:27); webbing is not used with spring units, zigzag springs, or rubber webbing (Secs. 3:20–3:22). [2] *Stuffing* is installed on a solid base or webbed open frame for pad surfaces, on springs for spring surfaces. [3] *Casing* holds a stuffed surface in shape; although often omitted, incasing with muslin (Sec. 3:48) is an important work-step for inexperienced upholsterers as it gives valuable practice in the handling of a cover. [4] *Padding* (Sec. 3:49) serves many purposes, but is chiefly to protect the *cover*. [5] *Basic operations* are the fundamentals of installing webbing, stuffing, casing, etc. Specialized operations, including springing, are given in chapters on seats, backs, planning a cover, etc. Basic operations are: webbing, Sec. 5:01; burlapping, Sec. 5:02; upholsterer's slipknot, Sec. 5:03; upholstery edges, Secs. 5:04–5:06; regulating, Sec. 5:07; springing, Secs. 5:08–5:10; stuffing, padding, Secs. 5:11–5:13; crown, Sec. 5:14; cutting, Sec. 5:15; sliptacking, Sec. 5:16; pleating, Sec. 5:17; cover, tightening, Sec. 5:18; pullmarks, Sec. 5:19.

SEC. 5:01 WEBBING

SEC. 5:01A / Traditional strip webbing is handled, except for stretching, essentially the same way for all surfaces as for a pad seat. For pad upholstery install webbing on the top surface of a seat, front surface of a back, inside surfaces of arms and wings. Mark edges of a seat cavity for placement of strip webbing (Fig. 6:02A). Use as many strips as will fit without crowding or overlapping; the more webbing there is, the stronger a foundation or base is. Do not cut webbing before installing it. Webbing usually is installed from front to back in a seat, as the back rail, generally straighter than the front, is a better surface for bracing a stretcher; also, the stretcher can't scratch the front rail, which could be quite noticeable in exposed-wood seats (Fig. 1:01). Sometimes back-to-front installation is necessary; for example, some frames have so little space between the lower back rail and seat rail that webbing must be tacked to the outer side of a seat rail. [1] *For spring* seats, backs see Chapters 7 and 10.   [2] *For rubber webbing* see Sec. 3:22.   *Tools:* Upholstery trestles, upholsterer's hammer, webbing stretcher, shears, chalk (Secs. 2:01–2:04, 2:16).   *Materials:* Tacks, webbing (Secs. 3:03, 3:11).

SEC. 5:01B **INSTALLATION** / [1] *Overturn* 1½ inches of webbing, Fig. 5:01B; the top layer absorbs bruises or cuts made by tacking. [2] *Set overturned end* ½ inch or more from the marked limit of upholstery or end of rabbet of an exposed-wood seat, from the

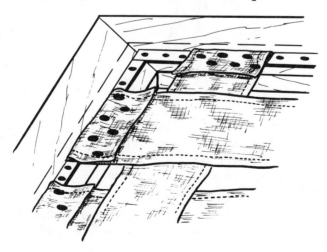

Fig. 5:01B

outer edge of a fully upholstered seat, to leave space for tacking casing and cover. However, there must be enough frame under webbing to hold it securely.   [3] *Permanently tack* overturned end of webbing at six or seven points, evenly spaced and staggered to prevent splitting a frame.

NOTE: When webbing cannot be set back from the marked limit of upholstery or end of rabbet, after installing it tack pieces of cardboard stripping (Sec. 3:26) between strips of webbing, Fig. 5:01B, to fill gaps and build a smooth surface for tacking casing and cover.

SEC. 5:01C   STRETCH, TACK WEBBING   /   Do not stretch webbing too tightly; it may pull out tacks or split a frame. Be sure to allow frame clearance (Sec. 5:01B).   [1] *Brace padded end* of webbing stretcher against the side of a rail, Fig. 5:01C, with the spike end tilted slightly up.   [2] *Pull webbing tight by hand* and force onto spikes; press spike end downward.   [3] *When webbing is stretched tightly enough,* the head of an upholsterer's hammer, dropped freely on the middle of a strip, bounces, or, webbing makes a drummy sound if slapped lightly.   [4] *Hold webbing tightly in place with stretcher,* tack permanently to frame at four or five points evenly spaced and staggered, Fig. 5:01C.

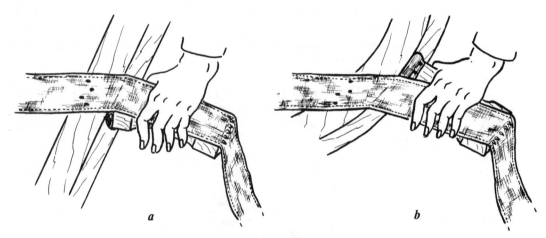

Fig. 5:01C

[5] *Cut webbing* 1½ inches from tacks, overturn end, tack permanently at three or four points.   [6] *Interlace and install side-to-side* webbing (Fig. 6:02A) for a stronger foundation and to prevent sagging of a front-to-back strip that may not be stretched as tightly as the others.

SEC. 5:02
BURLAP

SEC. 5:02A   /   Burlap keeps loose stuffing from working through gaps between webbing of open frame pad surfaces (Sec. 6:02B), between springs and spring ties, and provides a smoother base for compact stuffing. Rubber webbing surfaces are burlapped chiefly to protect compact stuffing (Sec. 5:02C). Cut burlap at least 2 inches wider and longer than a pad surface to be covered; for a spring surface, measure length and width from rail to rail over tied springs. When installing burlap, tighten it just enough to remove initial slack (Secs. 5:02B, C). On a pad surface, burlap stretched tighter, or having less stretch than the webbing, will rip out. *Tools:* Upholsterer's hammer, shears, tape measure, chalk (Secs. 2:02, 2:04, 2:16). *Materials:* Tacks, burlap (Secs. 3:03, 3:19).

Sec. 5:02B   Standard Installation   /   (For rubber webbing, see Sec. 5:02C).   [1] *Center burlap* over surface being covered.   [2] *Start at the middle* of a convenient rail, overturn 1 inch of burlap, and tack permanently, allowing the same clearance as for webbing (Sec. 5:01B).   [3] *Tighten* (Sec. 5:02A) burlap straight toward the middle of the opposite rail, overturn, and tack permanently (Fig. 6:02B).   [4] *Center, tack burlap* on the other two rails.   [5] *Tighten burlap smoothly* throughout surface. Keeping its grain straight, smooth burlap toward the middle of a rail. Work from the middle toward the ends of a rail, overturn, and tack burlap at two or three points an inch or so apart.   [6] *Repeat tightening* and tacking on the opposite rail, then on the others.   [7] *Alternating between rails,* continue tightening and tacking a few points at a time. This method usually removes initial slack evenly and smoothly.   [8] *Cut burlap* to fit around a post or other part of a frame (Sec. 5:15).

Sec. 5:02C   Burlapping for Rubber Webbing   /   A burlap cover reduces friction between rubber webbing and compact stuffing. Install burlap loosely enough to keep from ripping out when pressure on the rubber webbing stretches it.   [1] *Spread a fairly large piece of burlap* over webbed surface, cover with a 1-inch thickness of blanket or padding. Put the surface to normal use, chalkmark burlap carefully where it would be tacked to the rails.   [2] *Remove* blanket or padding. If the person who tested the webbing for go-down weighs less than 150 pounds, set chalkmarks on burlap ½ inch nearer the inner edges of a frame to allow for greater go-down if a heavier person uses the surface.   [3] *Overturn burlap and tack permanently* first at the middle of each rail, then at each corner. Distribute burlap evenly between mid-points and corners, tack at 1-inch intervals.

| SEC. 5:03 SLIPKNOT | The upholsterer's slipknot is used extensively. The "thicker" twine in Fig. 5:03 merely represents the free or working end. Do not pull a slipknot tight until it has been worked into place; then tighten with a quick tug. Pulled tight, it holds permanently. |

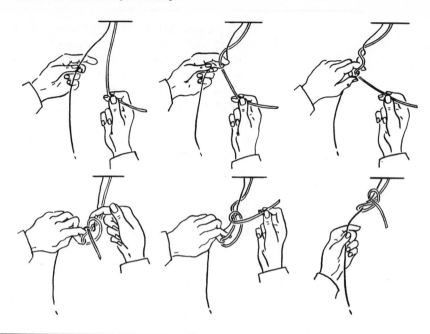

Fig. 5:03

SEC. 5:04
UPHOLSTERY
EDGES

SEC. 5:04A / Upholstery edges act as retaining walls for loose stuffing, build basic shape into a surface, and protect a cover by placing a relatively soft edge under it. Each edge of a loose-stuffing surface that is exposed when upholstering is completed has some sort of built up edge. There are three types: roll edge, hard edge, spring edge. Edges are not as a rule used with compact stuffings; however, corresponding edges of a sheet of stuffing generally are treated to simulate roll edges, or they are simulated with felted padding (Sec. 5:05E). Understuffing for compact stuffing often has roll edges (Sec. 5:13).

SEC. 5:04B ROLL EDGES / Real and simulated roll edges (Sec. 5:05) are for all types of loose-stuffing pad upholstery (seats, arms, backs, wings) and may be used with spring surfaces, such as small seats (Fig. 7:01A). Maximum good height for a roll edge is 1½ inches; higher rolls tend to be weak. If a higher roll is needed, build up the edges of a surface with strips of wood, then install a smaller roll edge; or, for a spring surface, build a hard edge (Sec. 5:04C).

NOTE: Instead of building roll edges, prebuilt edging is commonly used (Sec. 5:06).

SEC. 5:04C HARD EDGE / The hard edge (Sec. 7:01A) is chiefly for spring surfaces when an upholstery edge must rise between 1½ and 3 inches above a rail. For under 1½ inches, roll edges are more practical.

Sec. 5:04D Spring Edge / The spring edge (Sec. 7:01B) is used when the upholstery edge for a spring surface will be more than 3 inches above a rail. Spring edges, especially in seats, commonly go down about 3 inches in use; so unless it is at least 3 inches above a rail, the edge of a surface can be quite uncomfortable. A spring edge allows the edge of a surface to be compressed or go down and resume its original shape without distortion.

SEC. 5:05
ROLL EDGE

Sec. 5:05A / Roll edges are made of burlap strips, loose stuffing, cardboard stripping. [*1*] *Size* of a roll edge depends on planned thickness of a stuffed surface (Sec. 5:04B). If it rises a little more than 1 inch above the top of a frame, the roll edge should be 1 inch high. [*2*] *Use a strip of burlap* 8 inches wider than the planned height of a roll edge, 2 inches longer than its planned length. If a roll follows a curved surface (Fig. *b* 5:05B), add 3 inches to length for pleating burlap along the curve; without pleats (Sec. 5:17) there is not enough burlap for a smooth, nearly vertical roll. [*3*] *Use nonresilient loose stuffing;* a roll edge should be moderately hard and firm, not springy. A well-made roll edge about 1¼ inches in diameter needs about ⅛-pound of hair-and-fiber stuffing per linear foot. [*4*] *Cardboard stripping* holds a roll edge in place. [*5*] *Stitching* increases firmness and durability of shape. *Tools:* Upholsterer's hammer, shears, straight and small curved needles, regulator, tape measure (Secs. 2:02, 2:04, 2:06, 2:07, 2:16). *Materials:* Tacks, upholstery twine, burlap, cardboard stripping, stuffing (Secs. 3:03, 3:08D, 3:24, 3:26, 3:29B).

Sec. 5:05B Building Roll Edge / [*1*] *Tack burlap permanently* only at enough points to hold it in place on a frame, Fig. 5:05B. On a straight surface tack every 2 inches. On a curved surface, *b*, make small pleats or tucks in the burlap every inch, and tack. [*2*] *Set cardboard stripping* on burlap flush with the outer edge of a frame, *c*, or along the planned line of a roll edge on an exposed-wood surface (Fig. *e* 1:48); tack along middle of cardboard at 1-inch intervals. Cardboard holds burlap down tight on a frame, and keeps the bottom of a roll edge firmly and neatly in place along the edge of a frame or planned upholstery area. [*3*] Spread enough loose stuffing (Sec. 5:11B) along burlap and frame to build the planned size and shape roll. Test by drawing the loose burlap flap over stuffing and shaping the roll by hand. [*4*] *Draw burlap flap over stuffing* and down to frame. Shape the roll with a kneading action, working stuffing into it firmly. Tack shaped roll at the back, *c;* catch a small amount of stuffing with each tack to keep it from shifting. Miter the corners, folding under as much of the ends of the burlap strips as necessary. Less re-work usually is needed when corners are finished last. Stitch corners

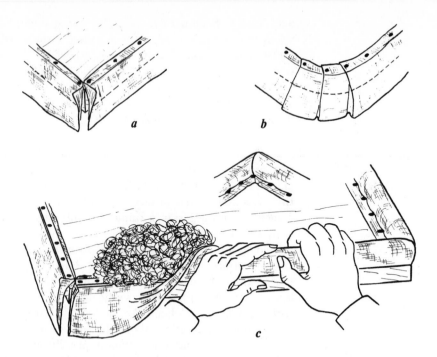

Fig. 5:05B

shut along miter folds with a small curved needle. Roll edges that do not finish into a corner usually butt against part of a frame; this keeps stuffing from working out.

Sec. 5:05C / A roll edge resembles an inverted U. If the lower sides are too close together for its size, it may wobble. Ordinarily a roll is the same height and thickness throughout, and smooth. If lumps and hollows cannot be regulated (Sec. 5:07), open roll and change amount and/or placement of stuffing. Minor flaws usually can be hidden when stuffing a surface or even when covering it; but this should be avoided. A good edge is firm, moderately hard, and retains shape when struck by the side of the hand; if it does not, it's too weak. However, an edge that gives a bruising sensation when struck is too hard; it makes an uncomfortable surface, and may wear through a cover.

Sec. 5:05D STITCHING ROLL EDGES / Stitching a roll edge increases firmness and durability of shape, but generally is not necessary except on large rolls and/or when there will be a fairly sharp break between adjacent surfaces, such as the top and side of a seat (Fig. 1:13). Stitching can be done with a large curved needle, but is easier with a double-pointed straight one.   [1] *Jab needle* through roll at

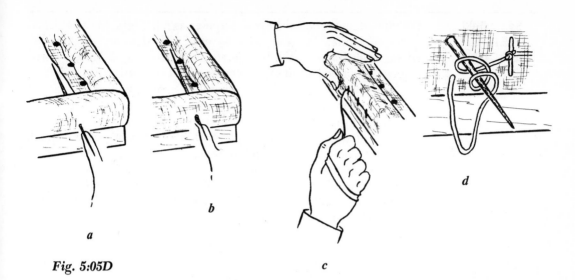

Fig. 5:05D

the front slightly above frame, Fig. *a* 5:05D; pull it clear at the back. [2] *Jab needle through from back* directly above twine about midway between it and the top of a roll, *b*.   [3] *Tie stitch* with upholsterer's slipknot (Sec. 5:03). While tightening knot, shape roll with a squeezing action, Fig. *c* 5:05D. Press back of roll toward the front to take out slack in twine; but press the front toward the back only enough to make it straight and flush vertically with the side of a frame, or perpendicular to the top surface.   [4] *Move needle* 1 inch left of the first completed stitch, repeat steps [1] and [2] above. As needle emerges at the front of a roll, loop twine from the preceding stitch twice around it, *d*. Shape roll as in [3] while pulling slack twine through it and the loops. Lock the stitch by tightening twine with a quick jerk. Continue stitching in this manner.   [5] *Tie off the last stitch* at the end of a twine or roll by looping twine three times around needle as it emerges at the front, and lock as in any other stitch.   [6] *On a curved* roll edge (Fig. *b* 5:05B) set stitches slightly closer together at the back than at the front.   [7] *When turning a corner,* stitch diagonally instead of straight, back and front, in order to keep both front sides of a corner straight and smooth.   [8] *Very large roll edges* may need a second row of stitching (Sec. 7:22C).   [9] *Keep the top* of a roll edge fairly well rounded; a sharp edge can wear through a cover.

SEC. 5:05E   SIMULATED ROLL EDGE /   Small, relatively flat surfaces may need an edge about ¼-inch high. Usually enough stuffing or padding can be pushed in place to simulate such an edge, which a casing or cover can hold in place satisfactorily.

**SEC. 5:06
PREBUILT
EDGING**

Prebuilt edging serves the same purposes as roll edges, but is quicker, easier, and often less expensive to use. *[1] Measure, cut prebuilt edging* to fit frame. Make butt joints at corners, Fig. *a* 5:06; mitered edging cannot be tacked satisfactorily. *[2] On a curve* (Fig. *b* 5:05B) bend edging to shape while installing it; if necessary, make a series of short cuts in the back portion to simplify bending it. *[3] Set edging* (Sec. 5:05B) except that cardboard stripping is not used. *[4] Tack into core of edging* at back, Fig. *b* 5:06. Tack at points close enough together to hold it firmly and prevent any wobble; 1-inch spacing usually is adequate. To simplify work, hammer a tacking site several times before tacking. *Tools:* Upholsterer's hammer, shears, tape measure (Secs. 2:02, 2:04, 2:16). *Materials:* Tacks, prebuilt edging (Secs. 3:03, 3:15).

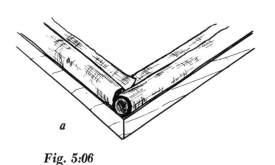

Fig. 5:06   b

**SEC. 5:07
REGULATING**

Loose stuffing is regulated (Sec. 2:07) to break lumps, fill hollows, or shift it after incasing or covering. *[1] Insert point* between threads of a casing or cover. *[2] Hold regulator* with one hand, to serve as a fulcrum, where it enters the goods, Fig. 5:07. *[3] Work regulator* point back and forth and around until necessary changes in density or placement of stuffing are made. *[4] Holes* in muslin casing are unimportant. Small holes in a fabric cover usually are repaired by lightly rubbing or pushing threads back in place. *[5] Felted padding* also is regulated, but less frequently, and usually only to bring it nearer the edge of a surface. Regulate padding carefully; natural cotton tends to pack into hard lumps when pushed or pressed by a regulator. It is better to pull cotton to a desired location.

**SEC. 5:08
COIL SPRINGS,
INNER-SPRING
UNITS**

Coil springs and inner-spring units (Secs. 3:15, 3:63) are stitched to webbing (Sec. 7:08); tacked to a solid base, wooden slat webbing, or rails of a frame (Sec. 7:09); fastened to zigzag springs (Secs. 3:21P, 10:32).

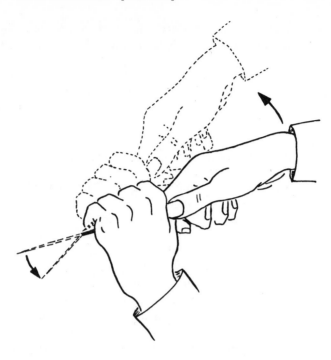

Fig. 5:07

SEC. 5:09 **ZIGZAG SPRING**	Zigzag spring preparation and installation are so interrelated that they are treated jointly in Sec. 3:21.

SEC. 5:10 **RUBBER** **WEBBING**	Rubber webbing preparation and installation are so interrelated that they are treated jointly in Sec. 3:22.

SEC. 5:11 **STUFFING**	**SEC. 5:11A** / Stuffing (Secs. 3:27–3:47) is of major importance in most upholstery. Properly installed good stuffing is resilient, smooth, builds a durable shape, and generally protects a cover.

SEC. 5:11B LOOSE STUFFING / This is "felted" by spreading it thinly a handful at a time. Pull each handful apart to cover as large an area as practical. Overlay the end of each handful with the start of the next to build felted layers held together by interlocking hairs or fibers. Do not leave lumps or holes in spread stuffing; they may show or even be felt through a cover. Well spread resilient stuffing can build up quite high before the necessary amount is placed (Fig. 8:14D).   *Tools:* For solid base pad surface, an upholsterer's hammer (Sec. 2:02); for open frame pad surface, a large straight needle (Sec. 2:06); for a spring surface, a large curved needle. *Materials:* For

solid base pad surface, No. 4 or No. 6 tacks (Sec. 3:03); for open frame pad or a spring surface, upholstery twine (Sec. 3:08D).

SEC. 5:11C INSTALL LOOSE STUFFING / First spread a thin layer of stuffing throughout a surface; anchor it according to the kind of surface, below. As a rule one-quarter or less of the total amount of stuffing, or a layer 1 inch high uncompressed, is ample. Then build surface to desired thickness. [1] *Solid Base.* Plan the site of each anchoring tack; work from the outer edges inward. Do not tack nearer than 1 inch to the limits of upholstery on an exposed-wood surface. Space tacks 3 or 4 inches apart. Tack straight down through stuffing, catching some under the head. Drive tacks tight against base. [2] *Open Frame.* Plan anchoring stitches from the middle of a surface outward, Fig. 5:11C, to prevent making stitches at the middle that are too short and close together, and might cause lumps. Anchor with a simple running stitch, 2 or 3 inches long over the stuffing, ½ inch long under the burlap, in rows 2 or 3 inches apart. Tie the first stitch (Sec. 5:03); do not enclose stuffing in knot. After every three or four stitches give twine a smart tug to draw stitches fairly tight. End the last stitch by tying twine to the nearest stitch with an overhand knot. The method of stitching depends on the type surface, [3], [4] below.

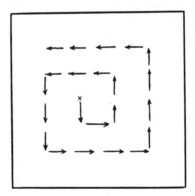

Fig. 5:11C

[3] *Pad Surface.* Jab a double-pointed straight needle straight down through stuffing, burlap, and webbing, and pull clear. Shift it ½ inch to start return stitch. Jab needle back through the materials and pull clear of the stuffing. Then shift the point 2 or 3 inches to start the next stitch. [4] *Spring Surface.* Work a large curved needle fairly straight down through stuffing and burlap, and when possible guide it under the top coil of a spring or a spring tie. Do not stitch under any spring coil except the top one. Guide needle to start the return stitch ½ inch from where it emerged from the burlap under the stuffing. Work it up through the stuffing, pull clear. Shift 2 or 3 inches

to start the next stitch.   [5] *Thickness.* Make the first layer of loose stuffing the same thickness throughout. The next few layers usually are thicker at the middle of a surface and taper to the sides to build crown (Sec. 5:14). The last one or two layers should be the same thickness throughout to assure smooth crown.   [6] *Limitations.* Do not extend stuffing into the actual tacking site of a casing or cover. Tacks driven through stuffing may not hold permanently.

SEC. 5:11D   COMPACT STUFFINGS   /   These are shaped without much difficulty to fit almost any surface (Sec. 3:46). They are installed by bonding, tacking tape, tacking, stitching. Because compact stuffings ordinarily come in flat sheets or slabs there is a problem of crown (Sec. 5:14).   [1] *For very small surfaces,* such as an armrest pad (Fig. 1:05), stuffing usually is trimmed to a shape including crown; if necessary, additional crown is built with felted padding when covering it.   [2] *For small and flat surfaces,* such as the pad seat in Fig. 1:01, when compact stuffing is about ½ inch thick, crown usually is built with a layer or two of felted padding when covering it.   [3] *For most other types of surfaces,* basic shape and crown frequently are built with understuffing (Sec. 5:13).   [4] *Do not extend stuffing* too far (Sec. 5:11C[6]).   [5] *Bond compact* stuffing to a frame and/or burlap webbing- or spring-cover (Sec. 3:46C).

SEC. 5:11E   TAPING COMPACT STUFFING   /   Rubber tacking tape often holds compact stuffings finishing around sharply curved surfaces, Fig. 5:11E. Bond tape (Sec. 3:46C) along edge of stuffing, tack free side of tape to frame; if tape is not wide enough for satisfactory tack-

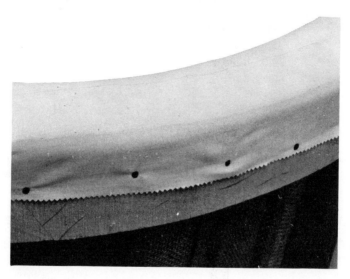

Fig. 5:11E

ing, sew a strip of muslin to it. Tacking tape is neat, but it may be more practical to tack polyfoam or rubberized hair when possible (Sec. 5:11F). A good substitute for tacking tape is a strip of muslin bonded to the stuffing.

SEC. 5:11F   TACKING COMPACT STUFFING / Polyfoam and rubberized hair may be tacked to the edge of a frame; rubberized hair may be tacked away from edges on a solid base. Coring (Sec. 3:43C) makes foam rubber too weak for satisfactory tacking. To tack polyfoam or rubberized hair along an edge, hold it firmly in place, bend upper portion back, Fig. *a* 5:11F, tack close to bottom and outer edge, *b;*

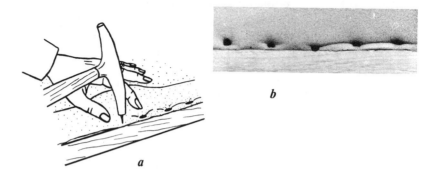

b

Fig. 5:11F   *a*

use No. 4 or No. 6 tacks (Sec. 3:03). Do not stretch or compress stuffing between tacks. Fill tacking hollows in polyfoam with scraps of stuffing or felted padding when incasing with muslin; for rubberized hair, work stuffing back over tacks. To tack rubberized hair throughout to a solid base, for each tack spread a small hole in the stuffing down to ¼ inch from the bottom; tack bottom layer firmly with a fairly large upholstery tack, then close hole in stuffing. Tack at enough points, 3 inches apart, to hold stuffing in place. For best results, bond rubberized hair to base and tack while bonding agent is wet.

SEC. 5:11G   STITCHING RUBBERIZED HAIR COMPACT STUFFING / Stitch rubberized hair stuffing to an open frame or a spring base away from the edges. Stitch the same way as stitching coil springs to webbing (Sec. 7:08), except that the needle is pulled far enough through the stuffing for the twine to enclose ¼ inch of stuffing. For a pad surface, follow the stitching pattern in Fig. 7:05A.

SEC. 5:12
FELTED
PADDING

Felted padding (Sec. 3:49) often is the stuffing for relatively thin, flat surfaces such as the seat in Fig. 1:01 or armtop in Fig. *d* 1:29. When stuffing a solid base surface with more than one layer of felted padding, tack the first layer the same way as loose stuffing (Sec. 5:11C) but at fewer points and spaced farther apart; if using only one layer of padding, tacking is not necessary as friction with base and cover holds padding in place. For open frame surfaces, stitching is not done since padding adheres to burlap.

SEC. 5:13 UNDERSTUFFING

In understuffing for a compact stuffing, basic shape and crown of a surface are built usually with loose stuffing or felted padding and incased with muslin. Fasten compact stuffing to casing and frame the regular way. Understuffing shape must be small enough so that overstuffing will not build the final shape larger or thicker than it should be. Understuffing provides the smoothest crowned base for compact stuffing. Understuffing often is done with a firm compact stuffing that is built or trimmed (Sec. 3:46) to the desired shape and crown.

SEC. 5:14 CROWN; PAD AND SPRING SURFACES

SEC. 5:14A CROWN / To make a casing or cover as tight at the middle as at the edges, a surface is built higher, or crowned, at the middle. Also: [1] *A long or wide* flat surface appears to sag at the middle; crown offsets this, making the surface appear flat or even slightly arched at the middle. A surface that seems to sag or droop at the middle is generally considered unattractive.   [2] *Most stuffings and paddings pack down* after some use; this can be minimized by building crown (Sec. 5:14B).   [3] *Crown prevents a casing or cover* ripping or pulling loose on spring surfaces (Sec. 5:14C).   [4] *Minimum crown* needed is that which is necessary to compress stuffing properly on a pad surface (Sec. 5:14B), or to compensate for go-down in a spring surface.   [5] *Maximum crown* depends on what an upholsterer thinks is attractive.   [6] *All crown* should be smooth, have equal density throughout, and rise gradually from the edges to the middle of a surface.

SEC. 5:14B PAD SURFACES / Most pad surfaces are essentially flat in one or more directions, and a casing or cover tends to compress stuffing or padding more at the edges than the middle, Fig. *a* 5:14B. To equalize compression and firmness of a surface throughout, use more stuffing or padding at and near the middle than at the edges, *b*.

Fig. 5:14B   *a*   *b*

SEC. 5:14C SPRING SURFACES / Unless sufficient allowance is made for go-down in a spring or spring-type surface, its casing and cover will rip out. In Fig. 5:14C, line A represents a casing or cover pulled tight and flat between points where it is fastened over a spring surface. Line B represents how far down line A can go before it is stopped by resistance of springs, maximum stretch of rubber webbing, etc.; a cover or casing represented by line A will, if forced down along line B, rip or pull out. Line C indicates how far a casing or cover must rise above line A so that it can be forced down along line B without ripping or tearing out. The distance from A to C must be at least the same as, but should be slightly more than, the distance from A to B. After springing a surface, measure how far down the middle goes in normal use; this is the minimum distance that casing and cover must crown above the edges of a finished surface; experienced upholsterers usually add at least 1 inch to minimum required crown.   [*1*] *Crown may be built* with springs and stuffing, or with stuffing only.   [*2*] *After incasing a spring surface,* test it again by simulating the pressure or weight that would be put on it in normal use. If a casing rips, tears, or seems likely to, remove it and restuff to build additional crown.   [*3*] *Go-down allowance* sufficient for a casing should be enough for a cover.

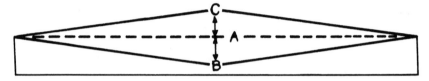

Fig. 5:14C

SEC. 5:15 CUTTING

SEC. 5:15A METHODS / Cut goods to fit around a rail, post, or other part of a frame. Poorly made cuts can be quite costly when working with cover goods. Basic methods of cutting and the common cuts are treated here; cuts made for a special surface or part are given in the pertinent work-steps.   [*1*] *After setting a cover or casing moderately tight* (Sec. 5:18) over a major portion of a surface, push it lightly with the flat of your hand toward the "target" of a cut until you feel it with your fingertips. "Target" is the point to which you will cut, or midway between such points (Secs. 5:15B, C).   [*2*] *Hold goods in place* at the target, draw slack or free goods back over your hand for cutting.   [*3*] *Make the initial cut* shorter than needed; lengthen it or make additional cuts while adjusting and/or tightening the cover or casing.

SEC. 5:15B CORNER CUTTING / To cut goods to finish along two adjacent sides of an object, Fig. 5:15B, the target is the corner made by those sides. The cut need not be made from the corner of the goods, as long as there is enough material on each side of a cut to allow for overturning burlap, underturning (Sec. 5:15E) muslin and cover goods.

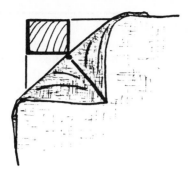

Fig. 5:15B

SEC. 5:15C   CUT TO FIT THREE SIDES, OR AROUND OBJECT   /   To cut goods to finish along three sides or along a rounded object, Fig. 5:15C, the target is the center of the middle side, or innermost point of a rounded surface. Y-cuts allow goods to fit smoothly along opposite sides and snugly against the middle flat surface, and around a curved or rounded object; start a Y-cut about 1 inch from the target.   [1] *For flat surfaces, a,* direct Y-cuts to points that are slightly closer together than the corners.   [2] *For rounded objects, b, c,* Y-cuts end at points in the goods, which, when drawn around the object, will be about midway between the target and the highest and lowest, or thickest, points of an object.   [3] *A series of Y-cuts* may be needed, *c,* to fit goods neatly and tightly around a large round object.

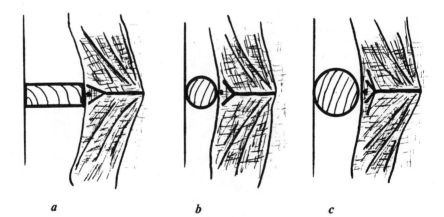

Fig. 5:15C   *a*   *b*   *c*

SEC. 5:15D   ALL CUTS   /   End all cuts made to finish a casing or cover around an object with a very small Y-notch; it need cut only three or four threads. It tends to keep goods from tearing while being tightened around an object. When finishing a casing or cover around an object, underturn all cut edges to make a neater finish and leave a stronger edge against the object.

SEC. 5:16
SLIPTACK,
PINTACK,
STAYTACK,
BASTE

Until all tightening, cutting, and adjustments have been made, slip-tack casings and covers to speed work and reduce tack damage to frame and goods. To sliptack (also called baste, pintack, staytack), tap a tack just hard enough to make it hold; the long sharp points of upholstery tacks (Fig. *a* 3:03A) are ideal for sliptacking. Sliptacks are easily knocked away to free goods for adjustment. When goods have been sliptacked in satisfactory position, drive tacks permanently. Set tacks only as close together as needed to hold a casing or cover straight and even. Smooth, neat covering comes from proper handling of goods, not from tacking at close intervals.

SEC. 5:17
PLEATING

SEC. 5:17A / Pleating can be of utmost importance in upholstering. Well-made pleats, Fig. *a* 5:17A, are flat, neat, regular in size, and hold a surface in shape as securely as the plain portion of a casing or cover. Poorly pleated casing, *b*, may cause lumps and hollows in a cover, and a poorly pleated cover can be an eyesore.   *Tools:* Upholsterer's hammer, shears, regulator, upholstery skewers (Secs. 2:02,

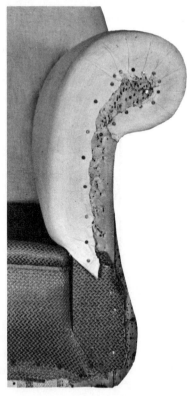

Fig. 5:17A   *a*   *b*

2:04, 2:07, 2:08).   *Materials:* Tacks (Sec. 3:03), additional loose stuffing, felted padding.

SEC. 5:17B   PLANNING PLEATS   /   *[1] Pleat after casing or cover* is worked smooth and tight (Sec. 5:18) and desired shape has been built throughout the rest of a surface.   *[2] Size of pleats.* There is no set size of pleats; it depends on the thickness of the surface being cased or covered and elasticity of the goods. The thicker a surface and more elastic the goods, the larger pleats generally are.   *[3] Number of pleats.* As a rule the fewer the pleats, the better. But there must be enough to build a smooth surface. Making one pleat do the work of two generally results in a lumpy, rough, poorly shaped job.   *[4] Direction of pleating.* The direction toward which they lie is unimportant, but should be consistent; if goods pleat outward at the left front of a seat, they should pleat outward at the right front.   *[5] Adjustment of pleats.* Often shape and/or firmness of a surface must be altered with stuffing or padding in order to make a pleated area as smooth, neat, and firm as other areas.   *[6] The only "tricks"* to good pleating are: I—Estimate accurately the number and sizes of pleats needed, and what each will do toward holding a casing or cover in place. II—Work goods tight and smooth. III—Keep grain of goods as straight as possible throughout.

SEC. 5:17C   GOODS FINISHING ON BOTTOM OF THIN SURFACE   /   Fig. 5:17C: *[1] Remove enough sliptacks* at each side of a corner to permit easy handling of goods.   *[2] Draw goods of Side No. 1* over the lower edge of the frame, tighten in direction shown by arrow, and tack permanently; this tightens casing or cover at and slightly around the top of a stuffed corner.   *[3] Draw excess goods of Side No. 2* over lower edge, tighten as indicated by arrow, tack permanently at the fold of the goods.   *[4] Folds of both pleats,* [2] *and* [3] *above,* should extend to but not beyond the edges of a frame.

SEC. 5:17D   GOODS FINISHING ON SIDES, TOP OF FRAME   /   Fig. 5:17D: *[1] Remove enough sliptacks* at each side of a corner to allow easy handling of goods.   *[2] Tighten goods of Side No. 1* around corner and down from the top of an upholstered surface, as indicated by arrow; this tightens casing or cover at and slightly around the top of a corner. When goods finish on the top surface of a frame, *b,* cut or notch Side No. 1 goods at the corner to "expand" around it; cut carefully (Sec. 5:15).   *[3] Tack goods from Side No. 1 permanently* at a point which allows the folded edge of Side No. 2 goods to finish along the corner. To locate this tacking site, hold goods at an estimated site with the point of a regulator, draw the goods in

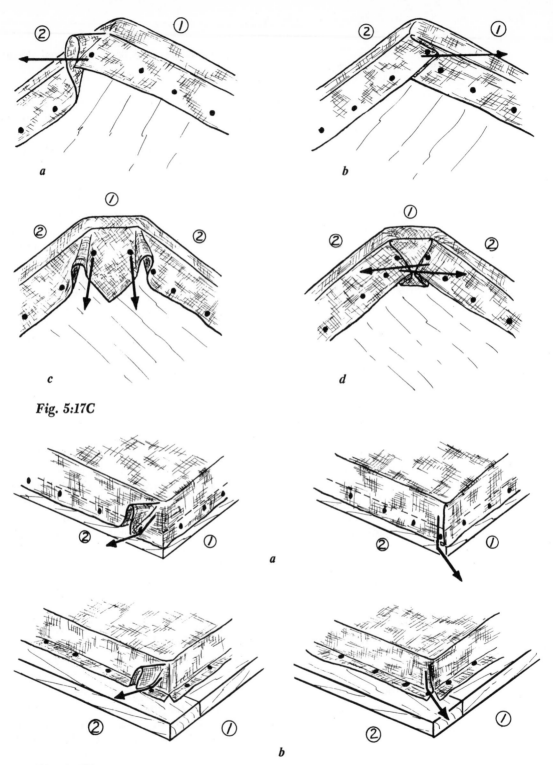

Fig. 5:17C

Fig. 5:17D

place, and shift the tacking site as necessary for a smooth pleat. [4] *Tighten excess goods of Side No. 2* toward Side No. 1 and downward, laying the fold along the edge of a corner, and tack permanently. The fold may extend up to the point of an upholstered corner, but not over into the top surface.

SEC. 5:17E   GOODS FINISHING ON BOTTOM OF THICK SURFACE / Fig. 5:17E: Pleat as in Sec. 5:17D except that some goods may be cut out, Fig. *a* 5:17E, to reduce number of thicknesses in a pleat, usually necessary with fairly heavy goods. Before cutting, fold excess goods of Side No. 2 in place to determine how much to cut out. Do not cut closer than ¾-inch to any part of a corner.

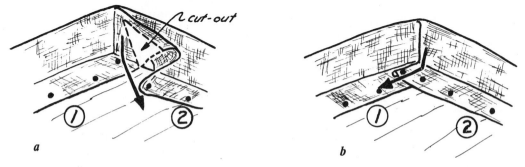

a   *b*

Fig. 5:17E

SEC. 5:17F   SCROLL PLEATING / Scroll pleating (Fig. *a* 5:17A) depends on how a casing or cover is installed before pleating starts. The tighter the goods are worked around a scroll toward the end of it, X, Fig. 5:17F, the smaller and fewer the pleats needed; but be sure to keep the grain of the goods on the top surface of a scroll straight. The key to good scroll pleating is to keep the grain of the goods on the side perpendicular to the break between the side and adjacent surface. In Fig. 5:17F, scroll pleating for an arm front, "side" means the front surface or face of an arm, "top" means the inside arm and outer side of a scroll as well as the actual top surface. In *b*, plain numerals 1, 2, and 3 indicate the first sequence of tacking; single-circled numerals specify the second sequence; double-circled numerals 1 and 2 indicate the first two tacking steps of the third sequence. [1] *Work goods into final position* toward scroll. Work to topmost point at which the grain of the goods on the side is perpendicular to the break between the top and side surfaces of the scroll. Tack permanently here, Point 1. [2] *Keeping grain of goods perpendicular* to the curved break throughout, at three or four points equally spaced along the break between Point 1 and X, *a*, draw goods down over break. Tighten toward approximate center of scroll, sliptack. This fairly

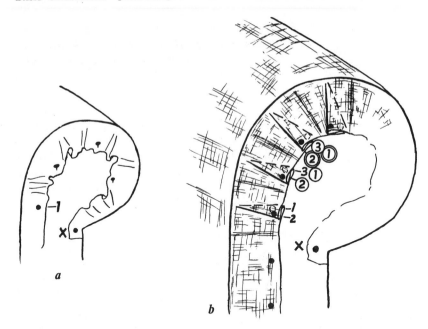

Fig. 5:17F

               a   *b*

evenly distributes the goods to be pleated. [3] *Follow the curving break of a scroll* and keep grain of goods perpendicular to it by changing the direction of grain by pleating over Point 1, *b*. Pleat enough goods so that the fold or crease formed is flat and smooth, and extends near to but not into the curved break. If too little goods is pleated, too many pleats may be needed; if too much is pleated, goods will wrinkle near the break. Sliptack goods drawn over Point 1 at the fold, Point 2, until all pleating is finished. [4] *The third point of tacking* a scroll pleat is a repeat of [1] above, and becomes Point 1 for the second sequence of tacking, or the first point of tacking the succeeding pleat. [5] *Continue pleating in the above manner*, [3], [4], and [1]. Remove sliptacks and retighten goods as necessary. [6] *After finishing all pleats*, tighten goods on the top surface back away from the scroll to take up slack that may have been left in the pleats.

SEC. 5:18
TIGHTENING
CASING,
COVER

Tighten a casing or cover by rubbing it smooth with the flat of the hand or side of an upholsterer's hammer from the middle of a surface toward the point of tacking, Fig. 5:18, while drawing goods firmly toward that point. Rubbing does the actual smoothing and tightening; drawing or pulling goods merely takes up slack caused by the rubbing. [1] *When rubbing*, press goods just enough to move it without shifting the stuffing or padding underneath. [2] *When tightening*, work casing or cover toward the appropriate side of a surface and away

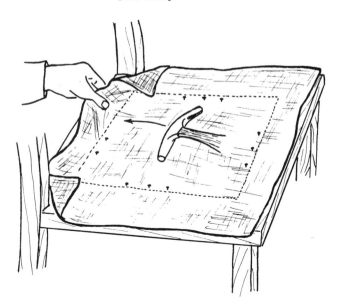

Fig. 5:18

from the previously set tack. For example, if working from the middle of the back of a seat toward the left corner, tighten from the middle toward the back and slanting toward the left corner. [3] *Tighten goods gradually,* sliptacking a few points at a time in alternate directions and on opposite sides of a surface. Trying to tighten it completely in one operation displaces stuffing or padding. [4] *Often it is necessary* to work completely around a surface two or more times, tightening and adjusting little by little, in order to build a smooth, symmetrical shape and to keep the goods straight and free of wrinkles. [5] *A well-tightened cover* cannot readily be pinched up.

| SEC. 5:19 PULLMARKS | Pullmarks, as across the bottom of the seat in Fig. 5:19, usually result from tacking through padding and/or tacking a casing or cover |

Fig. 5:19

directly in front of the point of holding it for tightening or adjusting. [*1*] *Tack about 1 inch* from the point of holding a casing or cover, or approximately midway between the point of holding and the previous tack.   [*2*] *Pullmarks in a casing* often show through a cover, especially if it is lightweight goods and the padding is fairly thin.   [*3*] *When covering with satin or other goods having little stretch, or with goods having too much stretch*, pullmarks may be unavoidable. Sometimes they eventually work out by themselves. Often they may be reduced by cutting, with a sharp pointed blade, three or four threads directly in front of the tack causing the pullmark.

6

building
pad
seats

SEC. 6:00
PAD SEATS

Seats built without springs are pad seats. They are easy to build and comfortable, although generally not as soft or resilient as spring seats. Pad seats and other pad surfaces are essentially the same: a foundation, stuffing, and casing. The foundation is a solid base or an open frame (Sec. 4:01); the latter generally is more comfortable. Most traditional (Sec. 3:00C) open-frame seats have stretched jute webbing; but some, called "sag" seats, are built with loose or sagging webbing (Sec. 6:05). Seats built with rubber webbing (Sec. 3:22) are pad upholstery; but since they are spring-type surfaces, they are treated in Chapter 7.   [1] *Any stuffing and/or padding* can be used for pad upholstery; the better the stuffing, the more comfortable and durable the surface. Based on stuffing, pad upholstery is either traditional or modern. Traditional stuffings are any loose stuffing except rubberized hair, and natural felted cotton padding (Secs. 3:28–3:37, 3:49). Modern stuffings are compacts such as polyfoam, foam rubber, and rubberized hair (Secs. 3:40–3:44).   [2] *Plain* (Figs. 1:01–1:04) *and buttoned*

223

seats (Fig. 1:15) are upholstered alike until covering. But if cloth-tuft or loop buttons (Sec. 3:60) will be used with a solid base, before stuffing drill a small hole for the twines of each button. For channeling and tufting see Chapters 20 and 21.   [*3*] *Many seat frames* may be either pad or spring upholstery. If springs would make a seat too high for comfort (Sec. 3:16B) or looks, it usually is pad upholstered. *Tools:* For solid-base pad upholstery—upholstery trestles, upholsterer's hammer, shears, regulator for loose stuffing, tape measure, chalk (Secs. 2:01, 2:02, 2:04, 2:07, 2:16); also, for open-frame work— webbing stretcher, straight needle (Secs. 2:03, 2:06).   *Materials:* For solid-base work—tacks, stuffing, muslin (Secs. 3:03, 3:28–3:44, 3:48); also, for open-frame work—webbing, upholstery twine, burlap (Secs. 3:10, 3:08D, 3:24).

SEC. 6:01 **TYPES OF** **PAD SEATS**	Types of pad seats are flat pad (Sec. 6:02); those built appreciably above a frame, and simply called pad seats (Sec. 6:04); and sag seats (Sec. 6:05). [*1*] *Pad seats may be built* directly on a chair, or on a separate frame or "slipseat" that later is attached to a chair frame (Sec. 6:03). [*2*] *Articles with fully upholstered arms* seldom have pad seats. This is due more to general practice than to the mechanics of upholstering. [*3*] *Pad seats usually are solid* (Fig. 1:30), not loose cushion (Fig. *b* 1:31). [*4*] *Most seats and backs* are upholstered separately. Some modern-type chairs have a single-piece cover for seat and back (Fig. 1:17), which for the most part are upholstered together. This type article is more difficult to upholster than one having separate seat and back; also, a cover tends to wrinkle at the junction of seat and back. [*5*] *Thickness* of a pad seat is optional, but looks and comfort (Sec. 3:16B) should be considered. A pad seat built too high above a frame often seems, and may be, weak along its edges.

SEC. 6:02 **FLAT PAD** **SEATS**	**SEC. 6:02A** / Flat pad seats (Fig. 1:01) are common on exposed-wood dining, desk, telephone, and other small chairs. Use any stuffing. About ⅜-pound good hair loose stuffing per square foot of seat area usually is ample. Compact stuffing should be ½- to ¾-inch, firm or hard density. Although not recommended, two or three layers of top quality felted padding may be used as stuffing. If a frame is not rabbeted, Fig. 6:02A, mark it with chalk or a nail for the limits of upholstery. If upholstering a solid-base seat, first drill several small breather holes in it; they are particularly important if the cover will be solid plastic, leather, leather substitute or other airtight goods.

SEC. 6:02B   WEB, BURLAP /   Web and burlap (Secs. 5:01, 5:02) an open-frame seat (Figs. 6:02A, B). Cane seats in good conditon usually are burlapped but not webbed. But if cane is badly stretched, has

Fig. 6:02A

Fig. 6:02B

small breaks along the edges, or has large breaks elsewhere, remove it; web cavity. Be careful stretching webbing; the frame may split.

SEC. 6:02C   STUFF / [1] *Loose stuffing* (Sec. 5:11C), incase with muslin (Secs. 6:02D–F). [2] *Compact stuffing* (Secs. 5:11D–G). When upholstering an open frame, first understuff with loose stuffing (Sec. 5:13). Four or five handfuls of loose stuffing usually are enough for a small pad seat; felted padding may be used instead; incase with muslin (Secs. 6:02D–F), but without simulating a roll edge, before installing compact stuffing. Instead of understuffing a surface and bonding compact stuffing to the understuffing's muslin casing, compact stuffing may be bonded to the burlap, and crown may be built with felted padding when installing the cover. Cut compact stuffing the shape of a seat area but to come no closer than ½ inch to the marked limits of upholstery (Secs. 6:02A, 5:11C). Slope or taper of stuffing at the limits of upholstery may be made with a muslin casing. If compact stuffing is much more than ½-inch thick it is advisable to taper bottom edges before installation, Fig. 6:02C.

Fig. 6:02C

SEC. 6:02D MUSLIN CASING / [1] *Measure* greatest width and depth of seat with a steel tape measure pulled tight enough to compress loose stuffing to approximately the planned shape. Add 3 inches to both measurements for general handling. Cut muslin as a rectangle, not the shape of a seat. [2] *Center casing over stuffing*, pull lightly toward the middle of the back, sliptack (Sec. 5:16) ½ inch from the marked limits of upholstery or end of rabbet, Point 1, Fig. 6:02D.

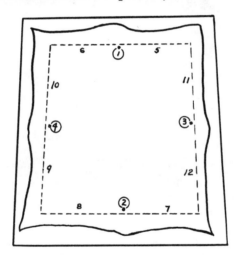

Fig. 6:02D

Textiles can be pulled straight and with least stretch along the warp or weft, not on the bias (Sec. 11:25). Follow a thread from the first sliptack to the front edge of casing, pull casing lightly into place, sliptack at the middle of the front, Point 2. Pulling a casing tight when first setting it tends to dislodge loose stuffing. Draw casing lightly into position from side to side, sliptack at Points 3 and 4. Tighten casing (Sec. 5:18) only when certain that its grain is straight between tacked points. Tighten from the middle of the surface toward Point 1, sliptack; tighten from the middle toward the back midway between Point 1 and a corner, sliptack, Point 5; for large surfaces, set casing at two or three points between Point 1 and a corner. Repeat this operation to the other side of Point 1, then at the front and sides.

NOTE: The first four tacks set casing straight; the others tend to keep it from being pulled crooked while being tightened throughout.

Sec. 6:02E   Tighten, Adjust Casing /   After initial tightening of a casing at wide intervals (Sec. 6:02D), tighten and tack at close enough intervals to make it smooth along the edges and exert equal pressure on the surface throughout. Tighten casing from middle of seat toward the back, retack at Point 1 if necessary, and at a few points about 1 inch apart, working from Point 1 toward the corners, Fig. 6:02E. Continue tightening and sliptacking a few points at a time, working toward corners and alternating between back, front, and sides.

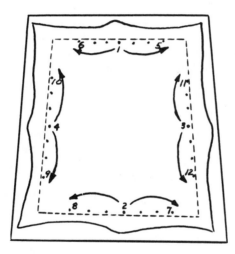

Fig. 6:02E

Avoid pullmarks (Sec. 5:19). While tightening, push loose stuffing back to ½ inch from marked limits of upholstery, or ends of rabbets, in order to simulate a roll edge (Sec. 5:05), and leave space for tacking the cover. While working a casing, rub it lightly every so often with the flat of the hand to locate lumps or hollows in a loose stuffing. Small flaws usually are regulated (Sec. 5:07); for large ones, open casing and rework stuffing.

Sec. 6:02F   Finishing Casing /   When desired shape is built and casing is sufficiently tight, drive tacks permanently, trim off excess goods close to tackheads, Fig. 6:02F. Tacks driven tight against goods and frame hold goods tightly and prevent raveling. The fewer the blows used to drive a tack, the better.

Fig. 6:02F

SEC. 6:03
SLIPSEATS

SEC. 6:03A / Flat, and curved or saddle-shaped slipseats (Sec. (6:03B) are separate frames that fasten on top of or fit into a seat frame, Fig. *a*, *b* 6:03A. Except for finishing the casing and cover, upholster flat solid-base and open-frame slipseats essentially the same way as flat pad seats (Sec. 6:02).   *[1] If using a heavy-weight or thick cover* (Sec. 3:53B) on a slipseat that fits into a cavity, often it is necessary to trim off about ⅛ inch of stock on any two adjacent sides of a slipframe so it can fit into the cavity without bruising, tearing, or wrinkling the cover, or splitting the cavity frame.   *[2] Incase a flat* pad slipseat, Fig. *c* 6:03A, as in Secs. 6:02D–F except that on thin frames it usually finishes on the bottom surface 1 inch from the edges, but if a frame is more than ½-inch thick, casing usually finishes on the

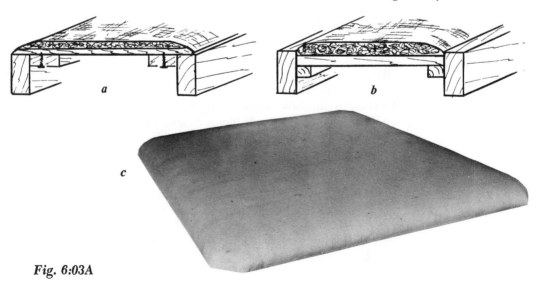

a   *b*

c

Fig. 6:03A

sides; pleat at corners (Sec. 5:17). While tightening casing, push back stuffing or padding that works down the sides of a slipframe. Stuffing should build a fairly firm edge (Sec. 5:05) along the top surface; but on sides it may cause lumps in the finished job and make a slipseat too large to fit smoothly into a cavity.

SEC. 6:03B SADDLE-SHAPED SLIPSEAT / Upholster these essentially the same way as flat slipseats (Sec. 6:03A), but with important differences necessary for shape. [*1*] *Do not interlace* side-to-side webbing strips or tighten with webbing stretcher in a saddle-shaped slipseat, Fig. 6:03B. Run them under and pull snugly against without bending the front-to-back strips; tight side-to-side webbing can destroy the intended shape of a saddle seat. [*2*] *Install and adjust* burlap, casing, and cover primarily between back and front. Tighten to sides only enough to keep goods smooth and taut.

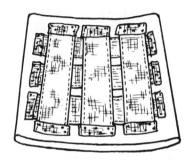

Fig. 6:03B

**SEC. 6:04
LARGE PAD
SEATS**

SEC. 6:04A / These usually are open-frame and upholstered with either loose or compact stuffing. Install roll edges (Sec. 5:05) for loose stuffing. For compact stuffing a surface should first be understuffed (Sec. 5:13). When seat and inside back are upholstered together (Figs. 6:04B, 1:14) the cover is boxed (Sec. 11:06) along the sides; if a casing or cover is pulled over from the top to cover the sides, it is notched at the seat and back junction (Sec. 6:04M) in order to fit smoothly. A pad seat upholstered separately may have a pull-over (Sec. 1:07), boxed (Fig. 1:14), paneled (Fig. 1:17), or bordered (Fig. *b* 1:29) cover. If an exposed-wood seat is not rabbeted, mark it for the limits of upholstery (Sec. 6:02). When seat and back will be upholstered separately, webbing and burlap (Sec. 5:01, 5:02) finish on the top surfaces of the front, back, and side rails.

SEC. 6:04B PAD SEAT, BACK UPHOLSTERED TOGETHER / Fig. 6:04B. For a pad seat and back upholstered together: [*1*] *Install and stretch* side-to-side webbing first. The rearmost strip of seat webbing and lowest strip of back webbing should not be more than 1 inch apart at

Fig. 6:04B

junction of seat and back.   [2] *Install front-to-back webbing* from the top surface of the front seat rail to the inner surface of the top back rail. Interlace webbing the usual way except at seat and back junction, where all strips go under side-to-side webbing. Draw webbing tight enough by hand to hold it snug against without bending side-to-side strips.   [3] *Install burlap* primarily side-to-side; start at the seat and back junction, work toward the front of the seat and top of the back. Tighten burlap only enough to remove initial slack.

SEC. 6:04C SET-BACK FRONT RAIL / Side rails sometimes project ahead of the front seat rail (Fig. *c* 4:09C). To shape the front, stretch webbing between front ends of the side rails (Fig. 6:04B). Pack loose stuffing firmly between webbing and front rail to support seat front upholstery. Burlapping is not necessary; frame and casing seal in stuffing.

SEC. 6:04D SADDLE-SHAPE SEATS / Web and burlap saddle-shape seats (Sec. 6:03B).

SEC. 6:04E ROLL EDGES / Roll edges (Sec. 5:05) for loose stuffing.

[*1*] *Exposed-wood seats.* When the top surface is exposed-wood, the outer sides of roll edges should be ½ inch from marked limits of upholstery, or ends of rabbets, to leave space for casing and cover.   [*2*] *Arms and backs not fully upholstered* (Fig. 1:21). Roll edges are flush with outer sides of all rails. Roll edges butt against arm and back posts unless the front rail is set back from the ends of side rails (Fig. 6:04B), in which case roll edges along the sides generally taper to a finish on the bottom of those rails at the lower front edge of the front rail; no roll edge is needed on the front rail.   [*3*] *Seat finishes against fully upholstered back* (Fig. 1:13). Roll edges on side rails usually butt against back posts. In articles in which seat and back can be upholstered separately or together (Figs. 1:16, 1:17), when the seat is upholstered separately the side roll edges extend back to where the frame starts curving up into the back; no roll edge is on the back rail. [*4*] *Seat and back upholstered together* (Fig. 6:04B). Roll edges along side rails extend from the front rail to the top of the back, depending on the type of top and how the cover will be installed there (Secs. 10:19–10:24).

Sec. 6:04F Loose Stuffing / Fill seat, or seat and inside back when they are upholstered together, with loose stuffing (Secs. 5:11B, C). Build it high and evenly; when compressed by casing, there should be no hollows or weak spots, especially along roll edges.   [*1*] *Unless a seat is stuffed fairly firm,* particularly along built-up edges, it soon packs out of shape and becomes uncomfortable; also, edges may show through and wear out the cover.   [*2*] *Do not let stuffing* hang over the outer sides of roll edges; it may cause lumps in the cover.   [*3*] *When front rail is set back* from the ends of side rails (Fig. 6:04B), be sure to put enough stuffing around and under the front portion to shape it.   [*4*] *When seat finishes against* an inside back that is to be fully upholstered (Fig. 1:13), use enough stuffing there to help close the gap between seat and back.   [*5*] *Depending on size* of seat, much stuffing may be needed to build crown (Sec. 5:14).   [*6*] *The only way to judge* accurately when sufficient stuffing is installed is to incase a surface with muslin (Secs. 6:04I–M); stuffing can be altered while incasing.

Sec. 6:04G Compact Stuffing / [*1*] *Solid-base seats.* Compact stuffings are usually fastened directly to solid-base seats (Secs. 5:11D–F). Before incasing with muslin (Secs. 6:04I–M), build crown (Sec. 5:14) with felted padding for polyfoam, foam rubber, or similar stuffing; with loose stuffing or felted padding for rubberized hair. [*2*] *Open-frame seats.* Web and burlap (Secs. 5:01, 5:02). Compact stuffings may be installed essentially the same way as on a solid base.

But usually it is better to build basic shape and crown with understuffing (Sec. 5:13); incase as in Secs. 6:04I–M.

Sec. 6:04H Prepare, Install Compact Stuffing / Cut and install compact stuffing according to the kind of seat and how it finishes at front and back. [*1*] *Exposed-wood seats.* When a top surface is exposed-wood, cut stuffing the shape of the area to be upholstered, but small enough to clear the marked limits of upholstery, or ends of rabbets, by ½ inch to leave space for casing and cover. [*2*] *Fully upholstered seats.* Stuffing must be wide enough to finish flush with outer top edges of the side rails. [*3*] *Front of seat.* Stuffing usually finishes flush with the outer top edge of a front rail. But if it is set back from the ends of the side rails (Fig. 6:04B), finish stuffing down over the front and on the bottom of the rail just behind the front edge; if stuffing is much more than ½-inch thick, trim bottom surface for the top surface to taper smoothly to the rail when installed, Fig. 6:04H. Tacking tape (Sec. 5:11E) often is needed. [*4*] *Back of seat.* I—When inside back is not fully upholstered, compact stuffing extends to the outer side of the seat rail. II—When back is fully upholstered and finishes against seat, seat stuffing extends to a point about 1 inch short of the back posts, depending on planned thickness of a back (Sec. 10:01). III—When seat and inside back are upholstered together,

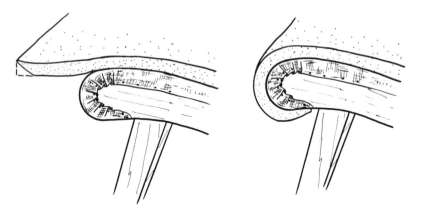

Fig. 6:04H

compact stuffing extends from where it finishes at the front of a seat to the top of a back, depending on the type back (Sec. 10:22). If stuffing is somewhat stiff, hold it in place temporarily at the seat and back junction with a strip of webbing. Sliptack webbing to the outer sides of the frame, drawing it tight enough to hold the stuffing firmly in place without buckling away from the understuffing casing. Remove webbing before incasing with muslin.

Sec. 6:04I Muslin Casing / Measure greatest width and depth of a seat with a steel tape pulled tight enough to compress loose stuffing to approximate desired shape; do not try to compress compact stuffing. Add 3 inches to each measurement for general handling of goods. When the top surface of a seat is exposed-wood, measure between marked limits of upholstery, or end of rabbets.

SEC. 6:04J EXPOSED-WOOD SEATS / For seats with exposed-wood top surface (Fig. 1:01): [*1*] *If seat upholstery is relatively flat,* incase as in Sec. 6:04E. [*2*] *If seat has roll edge, or is upholstered with compact stuffing much more than ½-inch thick,* incase as in Sec. 6:04E except that it goes down over the sides of the roll edge or stuffing to finish within the marked limits of upholstery or ends of rabbets. Pleat at corners (Sec. 5:17). Push back loose stuffing that works over roll edges.

SEC. 6:04K FULLY UPHOLSTERED SEATS; SEATS WITH EXPOSED-WOOD SIDES / Casing usually finishes on the sides of rails about ½ inch from the top. [*1*] *Incase* essentially as in Sec. 6:04E. Cut casing (Sec. 5:15) to finish neat and tight around arm and back posts, Fig. 6:04K. [*2*] *Underturn* cut edges, tighten casing toward post and downward, tack in place with folded edges snug against post to seal in stuffing; pleat corners (Sec. 5:17). [*3*] *If an exposed-wood post* has an upholstery edge (Fig. 13:07C), tack casing to it.

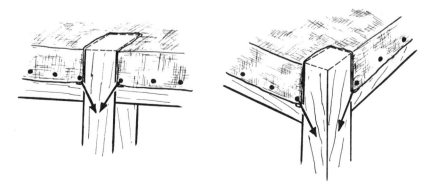

Fig. 6:04K

SEC. 6:04L SEAT FRONT STUFFED / When the entire front surface of a seat is stuffed (Fig. 6:04B), finish casing on bottom of front rail (Fig. 6:04M). Set casing at the back (if seat and back are upholstered separately), front, and sides (Sec. 6:02F); tighten from the middle of the seat toward the front, sliptack at the middle of the bottom of the front rail, Point 1, Fig. 6:04L. Tighten from middle of seat down around the front and toward a side rail, sliptack to outer side of rail just above front rail, Point 2; repeat on other side of seat. These three points of tacking set shape of a seat front. Tighten and tack casing the

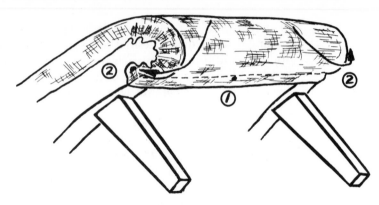

Fig. 6:04L

usual way throughout seat and front. Cut for arm and back posts if any, pleat where necessary (Secs. 5:15, 5:17).

SEC. 6:04M   SEAT AND BACK UPHOLSTERED TOGETHER / Casing extends, Fig. 6:04M, from the point of finishing at the front to the point of finishing at the top of a back (Sec. 10:23). Install casing, tighten (Sec. 5:18) primarily side-to-side. Start at the middle of the junction of seat and back; tighten seat casing forward and toward sides;

Fig. 6:04M

tighten back casing upward and toward sides. Cut or notch casing as necessary along seat and back junction so it can expand to fit smoothly.

**SEC. 6:05
SAG SEATS**

SEC. 6:05A / These are built with a depression and depend on it and the stuffing for comfort. There nearly always is some demand for sag seats in small and medium-size chairs (Figs. 1:15, 1:22). One with too much sag is difficult to get in and out of, and may be uncomfortable due to the height of the front in relation to the middle of a seat. Sag seat stuffing should be at least 1-inch thick; but thicker, up to about 3½ inches maximum, is better. Use loose or compact stuffing (Secs. 3:27–3:44); fairly thick stiff compact stuffing may be difficult to install properly. When covering, use cloth-tuft or loop buttons (Sec. 3:60B) to shape seat; for casing, use twine.

SEC. 6:05B WEBBING / Web (Sec. 5:01) without stretching, Fig. 6:05B. Use strips long enough to build desired sag; as a rule strips are not much longer than they would be if stretched. But until you are experienced in sag upholstery it is advisable to cut strips at least 2 inches longer than you think will be needed. Tack webbing securely enough to hold. Spread a blanket or pad 1 or 2 inches thick over the seat and front rail, and test seat.

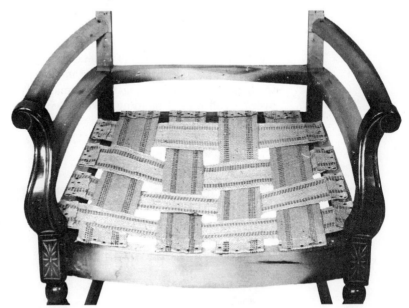

Fig. 6:05B

SEC. 6:05C BURLAPPING / Install burlap (Sec. 5:02). It should lie snug against webbing throughout, but must not be pulled tight or it will tear out or rip when the seat is used. Cut burlap for posts (Secs. 5:15, 6:04K). If arms and back will not be fully upholstered and a roll edge will be installed on the seat (Sec. 6:05D), save time and materials by cutting seat burlap large enough for edges between posts (Sec. 5:05).

SEC. 6:05D STUFFING / If upholstering with loose stuffing, install roll edges; stuff (Secs. 6:04E–H) without building crown. If using compact stuffing, cut it somewhat larger than the top of a seat, set in place and test seat; trim off excess stuffing accordingly.

SEC. 6:05E INCASING / Incase with muslin (Secs. 6:04I–M). After adjusting casing, but before tacking it permanently, install seat shaping twines (Sec. 6:05F) and test for comfort.

SEC. 6:05F SHAPING TWINES / A shaping twine usually is located at the middle of a sag seat to set the point of greatest sag, Fig. *a* 6:05F. Set other twines to build a smooth surface from middle to corners. [*1*] *Mark casing* for locations of shaping twines; when covering, use buttons at same places. [*2*] *Install shaping webbing* (Sec. 5:01), a strip for each row of shaping twines, *b*. To save webbing, twines near corners are often pulled tight and tacked to the bottom of seat rails. [*3*] *At each marked shaping twine location* jab a straight needle straight down through seat and shaping webbing, and pull clear; stitch the other end of the twine the same way, but ½ inch from the first stitch. If stitches are not straight down through seat and webbing, they may dislodge stuffing and spoil the shape of the depression and seat. [*4*] *Starting at the middle of a seat,* pull twines tight to shape it. Tie twines together permanently with a square knot; tie over a small wad of padding to keep twines from cutting the webbing.

Fig. a 6:05F

Fig. b 6:05F

NOTE: *When installing buttons with a cover, stitch both ends of the button twine through the seat together, but through the webbing separately, ½ inch apart.*

7

building
spring
seats

Sec. 7:00A / Basic types of spring seats are solid (Fig. 1:35) and loose-cushion (Fig. *b* 1:31). A version of the latter is the attached-cushion, originally made simply to hold a cushion in place on an ottoman (Fig. *f, h* 1:51, Sec. 7:02). Factory upholstered armchairs often have a type of attached cushion, usually across the front of the seat; when reupholstering, it may be easier to change to a loose-cushion seat. There is no necessary difference in comfort between solid, loose-, and attached-cushion seats. The solid seat is predominantly for small chairs (Figs. 1:03, 1:04, *a* 1:09, 1:30), but often is in larger articles (Figs. 1:19, *a* 1:38, *a, b* 1:50) and ottomans (Fig. *a, d* 1:51). Loose-cushion seats, seldom practical for armless chairs, are in the majority of large chairs, love seats, and other wide articles (Figs. *a* 1:42, *b* 1:46, *c* 1:48, 1:58, 1:61, 1:66), and in most slimline designs (Figs. 1:25, 1:26, *a* 1:55). Choice of solid or loose-cushion seat should be based on which will provide the more comfortable seat height (Sec. 3:16). [*1*] *With the usual allowances* for height of installed springs and average thickness of upholstery cushions (Sec. 17:03A), when the top of the front seat rail is: I—About 14 inches above the floor, a solid seat is usually built. II—Less than about 11 inches above the floor, a seat is usually loose- or attached-cushion. III—Between 11 and 14 inches above the floor, either type seat may be built; few professional frames have front rails in this height range.   [2] *Spring seat upholstery* consists of a foundation, springs, stuffing, casing. The part of a seat on which a cushion rests is the deck or platform. Loose-cushion upholstery is a general method of upholstering, not just seat upholstery (Sec. 7:34).

SEC. 7:00B SPRINGING / The foundation for spring seat upholstery usually is an open frame (Sec. 4:01).   [1] *It is webbed* for coil springs (Secs. 3:10–3:13, 3:15). Zigzag springs and rubber webbing (Secs. 3:21, 3:22) are combination webbing-spring materials. [2] *Traditional coil springs,* generally used in antique and traditional styles, may be used in many modern designs of upholstered furniture.   [3] *Zigzag springs* may be used in many antique and traditional styles, and commonly are used in modern designs, especially the slimline (Fig. 1:41). [4] *Rubber webbing* can be used in some antique and traditional styles of seats but is more common in moderns such as slimline and loose-cushion upholstery (Sec. 7:34). [5] *Regardless* of style or kind of seat, traditional coil spring upholstery is given first, then zigzag spring and rubber webbing construction.

SEC. 7:00C SHAPE, CROWN / Loose stuffing (Secs. 3:27–3:37) can be widely used with coil and zigzag spring. Compact stuffing (Secs. 3:41–3:44) is practical for all springs and rubber webbing. [1] *Loose stuffing* is the more common understuffing to build shape and crown (Secs. 5:11, 5:14) for compact stuffing on coil and zigzag spring seats. Or, shape and crown may be built on top of compact stuffing with loose stuffing or felted padding (Sec. 3:49); natural cotton padding is not recommended due to its tendency to pack. [2] *Crown also may be built* by shaping compact stuffing (Sec. 3:46). [3] *Instead of building crown* for a relatively flat surface, experienced upholsterers often work edges of compact stuffing down with a casing or cover, allowing the middle to crown up; generally this is not practical with rubberized hair.

SEC. 7:00D STYLES / Build plain and buttoned spring seats (Figs. 1:20, 1:19) the same way until installing buttons (Sec. 3:60). For channeling and tufting, see Chapters 20 and 21.

**SEC. 7:01
SOLID SEATS**

SEC. 7:01A / Solid seats are shaped along the front, and sides and back if exposed, by roll, hard, or spring edges (Sec. 5:04), based on the tied-down height of springs (Sec. 3:16). Hard- and spring-edge seats often are bridle-built (Sec. 7:01B). [*1*] *Roll edges* (Secs. 5:05, 5:06) are used chiefly when tied-down springs next to the rails are about 1½ inches above them, Fig. *a* 7:01A; small flat and crowned solid seats (Figs. 1:13, 1:16) often have roll edges. If tied springs next to the rails are more than 2 inches above them, either install a large roll edge, *b*, or build up a seat rail with wood before installing edge, *c;* neither method is recommended for inexperienced upholsterers.

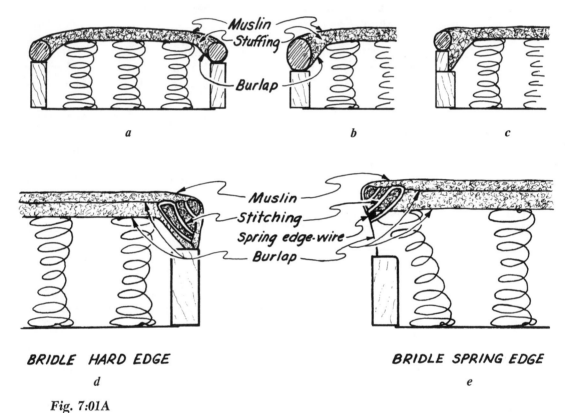

BRIDLE HARD EDGE

d

BRIDLE SPRING EDGE

e

Fig. 7:01A

[*2*] *Hard edges* generally are used when tied-down springs next to the rails are 3 inches or less above them, Figs. *d* 7:01A, *a* 7:02; medium size crowned and flat solid seats (Figs. *b* 1:28, 1:30) usually are hard edge. Being directly attached to rail and springs, a hard edge fills the gap between them better than a roll edge. Hard edges can be used instead of roll edges, but in small seats the extra work seldom is worthwhile. [*3*] *Spring edges* usually are built when tied-down springs next to the rails are 3 or more inches above them, Figs. *e* 7:01A and *b* 7:02; many medium size and most large seats (Figs. 1:32, *a* 1:45, *c* 1:49, 1:66) are spring-edge. In most cases, an

edge is built entirely on springs and freely moves with them as a seat is used. Spring edges are more difficult to build than hard or roll edges, but give more comfort. Spring-edge seats are more easily built with OBE or KOE than KBE springs (Sec. 3:15C). [4] *Zigzag springs* are used in roll and spring-edge solid seats (Sec. 7:32). [5] *Rubber webbing* is used for roll and flexible edge solid seats (Sec. 7:33).

SEC. 7:01B BRIDLE-BUILT / In bridle-built solid seats (Fig. *d, e* 7:01A) a layer of loose stuffing understuffing is installed on the burlap spring cover (Sec. 7:18). A sheet of burlap covers understuffing, and a hard or a spring edge is stitched (Secs. 7:22, 7:23D). Next, over-stuffing, either loose or compact stuffing, is installed. For best quality upholstery, incase overstuffing and completed edge with muslin. Bridle-building, the preferred way to upholster solid seats, provides a firm, smooth base for overstuffing and establishes shape. It is also called *double stuffing*.

SEC. 7:02 LOOSE-CUSHION SEAT DECKS	These usually have plain hard or spring edges, depending on tied-down height of the springs (Sec. 7:00A); they seldom are bridle-built. Some distance back from the edge of a spring area, Fig. 7:02, a strip of burlap is stitched to the burlap spring cover (Sec. 7:18), then drawn over loose stuffing installed for the edge, and the spring edge is stitched (Sec. 7:23D). The slope of the finished edge helps hold a loose cushion in place and lessens the gap between it and the deck. [1] *In loose-cushion seats* the cushion and seat are separate throughout. [2] *In attached-cushion seats* the bottom surface of a cushion casing is sewn to the part of a seat cover that goes on top of the up-

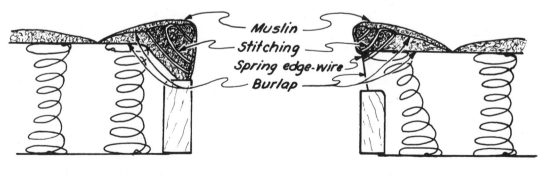

Muslin — Stitching — Spring edge-wire — Burlap

PLAIN HARD EDGE

a

PLAIN SPRING EDGE

b

Fig. 7:02

holstery edge and down over it.   [3] *In factory attached-cushion work* the seat usually is a solid seat with boxing (Sec. 11:06) along the front of the cushion-effect area and for a few inches on the sides; a strip covering the top and front of the seat is sewn to the bottom cover of the cushion area. Seat stuffing, cushion filling, and padding are set on the seat springs and held in place by the seat-cushion cover.

SEC. 7:03 **COIL SPRINGS;** **TRADITIONAL** **UPHOLSTERING**	Calculate size and amount of upholstery springs for a seat (Sec. 3:16). Springs larger than No. 4 can be avoided by using wooden slat webbing (Sec. 3:12A) or in some cases webbing a seat on some place other than the bottom of the rails (Fig. 7:05F). The size spring must be in accord with the planned type of edge (Sec. 7:01A).
SEC. 7:04 **STUFFING**	Loose stuffing is needed for all upholstery edges (Sec. 5:04) except when using prebuilt edging. For best results build edges with non-resilient stuffing, as they should be firm and moderately hard. Solid seats may be completely upholstered with loose stuffing; or under-stuffed with loose stuffing and overstuffed with compact stuffing. Loose- and attached-cushion decks usually are built with loose stuffing.
SEC. 7:05 **WEBBING** **SPRING SEATS**	SEC. 7:05A / Install as much strip webbing in a seat as fits without crowding. For tools, materials, mechanics of webbing (Sec. 5:01). Space strips evenly, Fig. a 7:05A. [1] *The closest that front-to-back* webbing need be to side rails is directly under liners of arms, next to front and back legs of armless articles. [2] *Set front side-to-side strip* close to front legs. When a front rail curves appreciably ahead of the legs (Fig. *a* 1:37), install a side-to-side strip of webbing along the front rail on top of the regular webbing. [3] *Place rearmost side-to-side* strip of webbing at the face or front surface of the back liner. [4] *In most chair seats* back-to-front strips of webbing are closer together at the rear; as a rule as many strips as possible are planned for the rear rail and spread apart proportionately along the front rail after the outer strips are set along the sides of a seat. [5] *If back legs* are too close together for enough back-to-front strips of webbing to fit without overlapping, cut ends of side strips to fit, and tack to rear rail and corner blocks if they are level with the rail; if blocks are too deep in a cavity or appear weak, tack webbing to inner sides of legs close to the bottom of the rear rail. [6] *If seat rails are spongy or weak* from previous tacking, it is advisable to tack webbing to the sides of the rails, Fig. *b* 7:05A; do not overturn ends of the webbing, they could cause lumps in the cover. Fill gaps between webbing strips with pieces of cardboard stripping (Sec. 3:26) to prevent lumps in the cover where it goes around the edge of the rails. [7] *If the bottom*

a

b

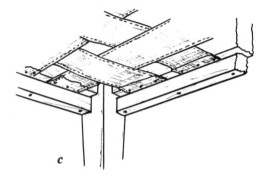

Fig. 7:05A   c

243

of a high-leg article is too visible, fasten strips of wood to the bottom of the rails after webbing a seat, *c*.

SEC. 7:05B DOUBLE RAILS / Some seats (Figs. *a* 4:09C, 1:19) have double rails. Depending on the size springs to be used, web these on the bottom or top of the lower rails, or on the bottom of the upper rails, Fig. 7:05B. Cardboarding between strips of webbing is not necessary.

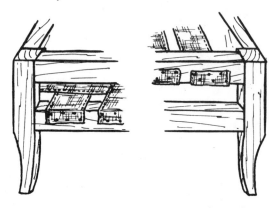

Fig. 7:05B

SEC. 7:06 **ARM ROLL** **EDGES**	Many articles with fully upholstered arms have roll edges along inner sides of front posts starting at the level of the seat rails (Fig. 8:08A). They usually are installed right after webbing the seat.
SEC. 7:07 **SPRINGING** **SEATS**	**SEC. 7:07A /** Arrange seat springs in a neat pattern according to the type of article and edge to be built. [*1*] *Set springs in rows as straight* as possible, Fig. *a–d* 7:07A; the straighter a row, the easier it is to tie springs and build a sturdy seat. [*2*] *Set the small end* of a coil spring on webbing; the large end gives wider support to seat upholstery. But when using KOE springs for a spring edge, set the knotted end down. [*3*] *Corner block.* When necessary, in order to get a good spring pattern, wedge the bottom coil under a corner block; be sure that no other coil touches block. [*4*] *Top coils.* Where possible, keep top coils at least 1½ inches apart, for space to tie springs (Sec. 7:11) and to keep them from rubbing together when a seat is used. [*5*] *Point the free or knotted end* of a top coil toward the center of a seat; the other side of a top coil is stronger and builds a firmer edge for a surface. [*6*] *Bend* down the free end of the top coil of an OBE spring and hook it under the next coil, *e, f*, to keep it from poking through seat upholstery. *Tools:* Wire bender (Sec. 2:11) for OBE springs (Sec. 3:15C); it may be needed for KOE springs.

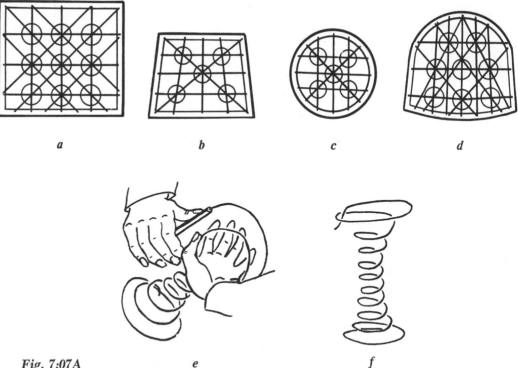

a   b   c   d

Fig. 7:07A   e   f

SEC. 7:07B SPRING PLACEMENT / Placement of seat springs depends on the type of article and edge to be built. [*1*] *Fully upholstered arms/back.* Set top coils of springs about 1 inch from inner sides of arm and/or back liners. [*2*] *Not fully upholstered arms/back.* Set springs for sides and/or back the same as for front of seat. [*3*] *Roll, hard edges.* Set top coils of seat springs about 2 inches from inner side of seat rail. [*4*] *Spring edge.* After shaping springs (Sec. 7:07C) set bottom coils next to but not quite touching the seat rail. For T-shaped seats (Fig. 7:15A), set top coils of the smaller springs used for the corners directly above the outer sides of each corner.

SEC. 7:07C SPRING-EDGE SPRINGS / Shape springs in a spring edge for the completed seat to project about ½ inch beyond the outer side of the rail (Sec. 7:02). To shape a spring, bend the top coil outward and distort it enough, Fig. *a* 7:07C, so that when bent back and "locked" in place it will be directly above the outer edge of the rail, *b*. Unless edge springs are shaped properly and uniformly, the finished seat edge may be irregular instead of straight. Often it is advisable

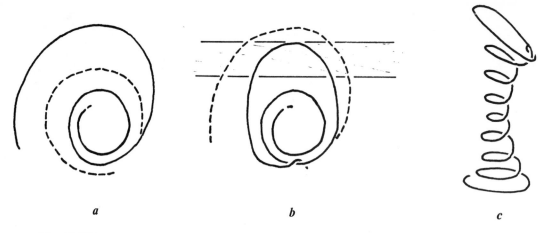

a   *b*   *c*

Fig. 7:07C

to strengthen edge springs by bending them slightly up and toward the back between the second and third coils, *c*. The small springs for the front corners of T-shaped seats do not require shaping.

SEC. 7:08 **ANCHORING** **SPRINGS ON** **WEBBING**	Stitch springs permanently in place on the webbing (Fig. 7:05A). *Tools:* Straight needle (Sec. 2:06). *Materials:* Upholstery twine (Sec. 3:08D). Three stitches per bottom coil, evenly spaced, are enough. [1] *Jab needle up* through webbing close to spring coil, and down on the other side of it. [2] *Tie* first stitch (5:03). [3] *Take next stitch* about a third of the way around the coil, and the last stitch another third of the way. Then take the first stitch on an adjacent spring. [4] *Do not displace* springs while stitching. [5] *Speed work* by taking two stitches on a coil, yank twine tight, then take the third stitch. [6] *Tie only first and last* stitches in a spring surface; if twine is too short, tie another piece to it with an overhand knot and continue stitching. Tying stitches would produce a sawing effect on the twine, as springs move slightly in use. [7] *Tie twine from last stitch* around twine of any other stitch, as in the upper right corner of Fig. *a* 7:05A. *NOTE: Instead of stitching, springs may be fastened to webbing with heavy wire "hog rings"; special pliers are needed. Be careful not to break or tear webbing when hog-ringing.*
SEC. 7:09 **ANCHORING** **SPRINGS ON** **WOOD**	The simplest way to fasten coil springs to a solid base, wooden slat webbing, or frame rails is with fairly heavy common staples; other ways are with strips of webbing, burlap, or canvas. *Tools:* Upholsterer's hammer (Sec. 2:02). *Materials:* ⅞-inch fence staples, or tacks, webbing, burlap, or canvas (Secs. 3:03, 3:11, 3:24, 3:53B); felted

padding (Sec. 3:49).   [*1*] *Hold spring in place* and drive staples over the bottom coil at three or four evenly spaced points, Fig. *a* 7:09.   [*2*] *To "staple" with webbing,* or a double thickness of burlap or canvas, place it over the bottom coil and tack down close to both sides of the wire, *b*.   [*3*] *Prevent spring noise* or rattle against wood by placing a small wad of felted padding between the lowest coils and the base, *c;* this is necessary when springs are fastened with metal staples, advisable when they are held by webbing, burlap, or canvas.

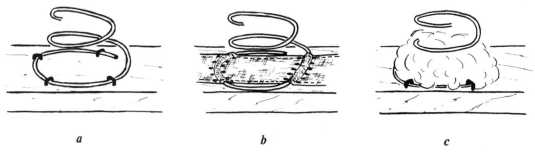

a   b   c

Fig. 7:09

SEC. 7:10 WOOD WEBBING

SEC. 7:10A / Wooden slat webbing (Sec. 3:12) usually is back to front in a seat, and rests on cleats on those rails. Before installing slats, arrange springs, shape and fasten them to slats (Secs. 7:07, 7:09). *Tools:* Saw, chalk, tape measure, hammer, or screwdriver and drill. *Materials:* Nails or screws large enough to hold cleats firmly and keep slats in place; glue (Sec. 3:06); ¾ × 1 inch stock for cleats (Sec. 7:10B). Determine height at which to set cleats, as in Sec. 3:16 except that here: I—Size and tied-down height of springs are known. II—Distance from bottom of seat rails to bottom of springs is to be found; this is the height of the top of the slat webbing above the bottom of the rails.   *EXAMPLE:* Planned height of a loose-cushion seat above the floor is 17 inches; the bottom of the front rail is 3 inches above the floor; No. 2 upholstery springs:

Planned height of seat	17″
Minus height of bottom of front rail	−3″
Overall thickness of seat	14″
Minus thickness of cushion, seat stuffing	−5½″
Tied-down height of springs	8½″
Minus tied-down height of No. 2 springs (Sec. 3:16E)	−7″
Height of top of slat webbing above bottom of seat rails	1½″

SEC. 7:10B INSTALL WOODEN SLAT WEBBING / [*1*] *Mark front and*

back seat rails, Fig. 7:10B, for height of the top of slat webbing.   [2] *Install cleats* on inner surfaces of rails, allowing for thickness of slat webbing. Cleats should extend across the rail from leg to leg or corner-block to corner-block.   [3] *Cut webbing slats to fit snugly* onto cleats, set in place and mark for the position of each spring (Sec. 7:07).   [4] *Remove slats,* anchor springs on them (Sec. 7:09).   [5] *Replace slats* in seat cavity; nail through rails into each end of a slat to hold it in place, or toe-nail slats to rails. Do not nail slats to cleats.

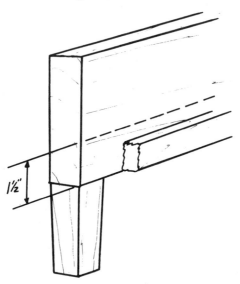

Fig. 7:10B

SEC. 7:11 **PURPOSE OF** **TYING COIL** **SPRINGS**	**Sec. 7:11A** / Tying determines the shape, comfort, durability, and looks of a surface. Inexperienced upholsterers should expect to tie springs three or four times before producing a satisfactory spring-up job. Except in a crowned solid seat (Fig. *b* 1:28), tie all springs in a surface to the same height (Sec. 3:16) above the tops of the seat rails. Eight-way tying of springs (Fig. 7:07A) is the generally accepted best method. However, springs at the corners of a pattern often are tied only six ways or at six points, since they often are not tied in a direction unless there are two or more springs lying in that direction. Four-way tying, fairly common, makes a softer but weaker surface than eight-way tying. Tying more than eight-way is not recommended. [1] *Back-to-front ties* set height of springs and keep them from moving forward or backward. [2] *Cross or side-to-side ties* reinforce height control and, with back-to-front ties, hold springs firmly in position. All springs, and when there is just one in a row (Fig. *c* 7:07A), must be tied back-to-front and crosswise. [3] *Diagonal ties* reinforce the others and provide a finer mesh base for seat upholstery. Tie diago-

nally whenever there are two or more springs in a diagonal row. Diagonal ties need not be as straight as the others. [4] *Whenever tie twines cross* or touch one another between but not within spring coils, tie them the same way as to springs (Fig. 7:14A). This makes a better mesh, stronger support for seat upholstery, and keeps ties from rubbing against one another.

SEC. 7:11B RETURN-TWINE / Return- or "short" twine shapes the top coil of a spring that is next to a rail, Fig. 7:11B, and thus the edge of a seat. Return-twine may be cut and installed separately, but usually is allowed in twines for back-to-front and cross ties. [1] *In small seats,* diagonal ties (Fig. 7:14A) generally serve as return-twine. [2] *In crowned solid seats* (Fig. *b* 1:28) return-twine tilts the top coil (Fig. *a* 7:11B) to help set overall shape. [3] *In flat solid seats and loose-cushion decks to be built with a roll or a hard edge* (Figs. 1:30, *b* 1:31), return-twine, Fig. *b* 7:11B, holds the top coil level. [4]

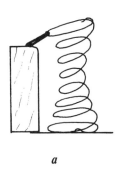 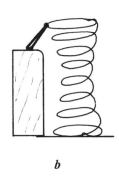 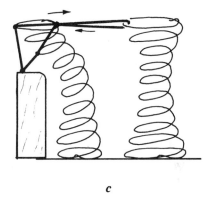

a   b   c

Fig. 7:11B

Return-twine as in [3] *above* is used for the sides and/or back of a seat when arms and/or back will be fully upholstered. [5] *In a spring edge,* return-twine, *c,* sets height of spring, strengthens a front spring by connecting its top coil to that of the spring behind it, and holds the top coil of a front spring level.

SEC. 7:12 LENGTH OF TIE TWINES

Measure length of twine needed by running a tape measure over the free springs between the rails. Add 2 inches per spring in a row for knotting, and a foot or more for easy handling of the twine. For return-twines, add 8 inches for each roll or hard-edge spring twine, 2 feet for each spring-edge spring twine.

SEC. 7:13 **PREPARE** **FRAME**	Round off seat rails (Sec. 4:13).

SEC. 7:14 **TYING SPRINGS** **FOR ROLL,** **HARD EDGES**	**SEC. 7:14A** / Tie springs for roll and for hard edge, Fig. *a, b* 7:14A, and the sides and/or back of a seat when arms and/or back are to be fully upholstered, the same way. For common spring-tying patterns see Fig. 7:07A. The difference between tying spring-edge (Sec. 7:15) and other seats affects only the rows of springs in and directly behind a spring edge. Flat and crowned spring seats are tied the same way except for an occasional difference in height at the middle of a seat and a tilting of top coils along the edges. *Tools:* Upholsterer's hammer, shears (Secs. 2:02, 2:04). *Materials:* Tacks, spring twine (Secs. 3:03, 3:08B).

SEC. 7:14B ANCHORING TWINES / Set two sliptacks (Sec. 5:16) ½-inch apart on the tops of the seat rails at the center of each back-to-front and side-to-side row of springs. Starting at the back, and allowing for return-twine if any is needed there, anchor tie twines, Fig. 7:14B. Loop twine tightly around both tacks, *a,* or tie around one tack with an overhand knot, *b,* and drive tacks permanently; the two-tack anchor is preferred. Anchor all back-to-front ties across the back of a seat, then all cross-ties along a side rail. Diagonal ties can be anchored at this time, but may get in the way.

SEC. 7:14C SPRING HEIGHT / Determine how high springs are to be tied above seat rails (Sec. 3:16).

SEC. 7:14D TYING SPRINGS / Sequences of tying springs from back to front for crowned and flat roll and hard edge seats are in Fig. *a, b* 7:14D. Note that springs are straight up and down regardless of tilt of top coils in a crowned seat, *a;* springs set crookedly may be damaged, and give uneven, irregular support, which tends to make a seat uncomfortable. Tie the middle back-to-front row of springs first to eliminate unwanted crown in the middle of a seat and simplify sloping the other rows to the sides in a crowned seat, or setting them the same height in a flat seat. [1] *Push the middle* spring at the back straight down to the planned tied-down height, *a.* [2] *Loop twine* tightly over a coil, Point 2, which, when the tie is complete, tends to keep the twine fairly straight from its anchorage, Point 1, to the top coil on the other or front side of the spring, Point 3. Draw twine tight against the lower coil, Point 2, *c,* and place a thumb on the looped twine to prevent slippage, *d.* [3] *Press spring toward rail* to loosen

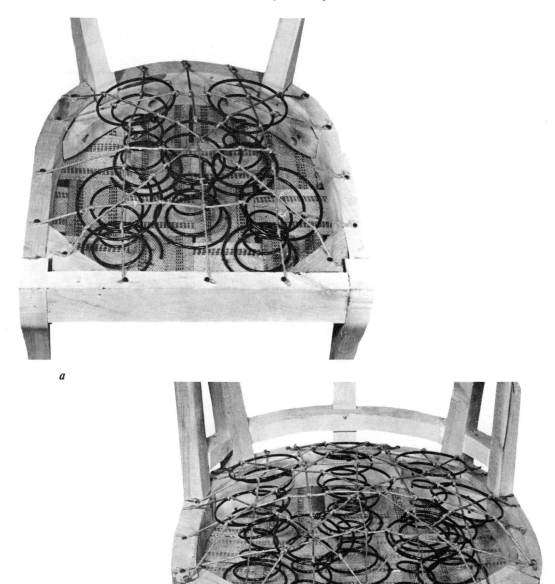

a

b

Fig. 7:14A

twine, complete tie with an overhand knot, *e,* and pull tight; be sure
to hold looped twine firmly against the spring coil until knot is tight.

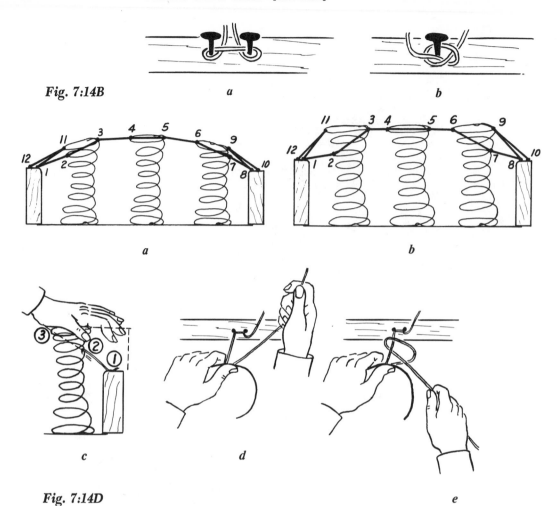

Fig. 7:14B   a   b

a   b

c   d

Fig. 7:14D   e

NOTE: *If the first tie is on too low a coil, the spring will have too little go-down; this results in a hard seat and, often, broken spring ties. If the first tie is on too high a coil, the edge of a seat tends to be weak, and there may be excessive crown. It is better to make the first tie on a coil that is a little too high. When possible in roll and hard edge seats, the coil tied first should be at least 1½ inches above the rail.*

[4] *The second point of tying springs in roll- and hard-edge seats is* on the top coil of the first spring, Point 3, *a, b.* Tie as in [*1*], [*2*], and [*3*] above except that the point of tying is squeezed slightly toward the first knot in order to strengthen the edge of a seat. Enclose the free end of an OBE spring in the knot to strengthen the top coil. [5] *Continue tying from top coil to top coil, a, b,* to the spring at the

front. Tie this the same way as at the back. [6] *Anchor twine at front* by looping it tightly around a sliptack and driving tack permanently. Drive a second tack close to it to eliminate any chance of the twine working loose. [7] *When return-twine will be used,* after anchoring the spring tie secure the twine around another tack (Fig. *a* 7:14B). Anchor a completed return-twine (Sec. 7:11B) the same way as a spring tie twine. [8] *Install* cross ties the same way as the back-to-front. [9] *Diagonal ties.* In large seats install diagonal ties the same way as back-to-front ties except that no return twine is used. In small roll- and hard-edge seats, diagonal ties usually are installed the same way as the back-to-front except that all knots are on top coils (Fig. 7:14A); diagonal ties serve as return-twine to shape the edges of these seats.

Sec. 7:14E Return-Twine / Return-twine in roll and hard edge seats goes from the rail to the outer top coil of a spring (Fig. 7:14D). Tie to top coil, then anchor on rail. In small seats, knot a diagonal tie to the outer side of the top coil, then anchor on rail. [1] *Crowned seat.* Return-twine (Fig. *a* 7:14D) holds the outer side of a top coil down toward the rail. The amount of pull-down depends on the size of a seat. It should be enough to build a smooth, regular curve from one seat rail to the opposite one. [2] *Flat seat.* Return-twine (Fig. *b* 7:14D) holds the top coil of a spring level with top coils throughout a seat.

Sec. 7:14F Testing / When tying is completed, spread a 1-inch thick pad over the seat and try it. It should be reasonably soft, depending on the springs used, and have the same firmness throughout. [1] *Flat seats* should be flat. If springs crown more than about 1½ inches at the middle of a large seat, or 1 inch in a small one, springs should be retied. [2] *Curve of a crowned seat* should be smooth and regular. If the center is too soft or mushy, springs may not have been tied down far enough. Retie or, if that particular amount of crown is wanted, install larger springs. If a crowned seat is unreasonably hard (all spring seats become a little softer from use), retying springs to allow slightly more crown often is better than installing smaller springs. [3] *Along edges* of a seat, springs should be the same height above the rails. When heights vary more than ½ inch, springs should be retied. Often it is necessary to retie only the return-twines.

SEC. 7:15
TYING SPRINGS
FOR SPRING-
EDGES

Sec. 7:15A / Tie loose-cushion spring-edge seats at the sides and/ or back when arms and/or back will be fully upholstered, Fig. *a* 7:15A, as for a roll or a hard-edge flat seat (Secs. 7:14D, E); for solid seats see Sec. 7:15D. The first six points of tying a spring-edge seat,

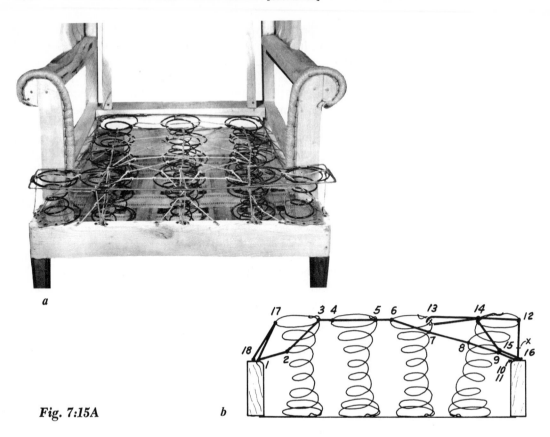

a

Fig. 7:15A   *b*

Fig. *b* 7:15A, are essentially the same as for a roll or a hard-edge seat (Fig. 7:14D). If there were five springs in the row, the fifth would be tied at points corresponding to 4 and 5. Tying a spring edge as in Fig. *b* 7:15A: [1] *Start.* Tying is considered to start on the spring behind the one actually contained in a spring edge. Tie the top coil at the back, Point 6, as it would be tied for a roll or a hard edge flat seat. Tie next, Point 7, at the front on a coil that tends to keep twine fairly straight from Point 6 to an imaginary point, X, about ½ inch above the middle of the rail. Often Point 7 is on the second coil of a spring.   [2] *Height.* Hold the front or spring-edge spring down to its planned height, with the top coil projecting about ½ inch beyond outer edge of rail. Tie on a coil at the back of the spring, Point 8, which tends to keep twine fairly straight from Point 7 to imaginary point X. Point 8 often is on the third or fourth coil. Tie on a coil at the front of the spring, Point 9, which tends to keep twine fairly straight from Point 8 to imaginary point X.   [3] *Anchor twine.* Allowing a ½-inch clearance between rail and nearest spring coil, usually Point 9, anchor spring tie, Point 10, for return-twine.

NOTE: Tying down toward the rail from Point 6 tends to reduce crown at the middle of a seat, and protects and strengthens a spring-edge spring. As tied, this spring should lean over the top of the rail; it is pulled back into position by return-twine (Sec. 7:15B).

SEC. 7:15B   RETURN-TWINE / The sequence of tying return-twine for a spring edge is in Fig. *a* 7:15B. [*1*] *Reanchor twine,* Point 11, so that the pull of the spring tie, Point 10, and the return-twine are not on the same tack. [*2*] *Tie front top coil* of spring-edge spring down to its planned height above the rail, Point 12, to make the top of the spring flat. [*3*] *From Point 12* loop twine over front top coil of adjacent spring, Point 13. Pull free end of looped twine toward front of edge, Point 12, to draw it back until it is directly above the outer edge of the rail. Tie at Point 14, enclosing twine from Points 12 to 13 in knot. Looping twine at Point 13 and tying at Point 14 usually is easier than tying at 13. [*4*] *Tie at Point 15,* next to Point 9 on the spring-edge spring. While tying, pull the back top coil of the spring, Point 14, down flat. [*5*] *Anchor return-twine* on rail, Point 16. [*6*] *For greater protection* against possible wear on a frame, seize tie and return-twines after all tying is complete, Fig. *b* 7:15B.

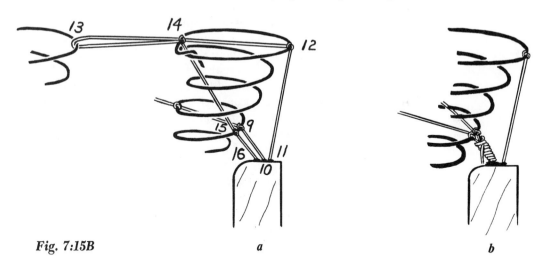

Fig. 7:15B   *a*   *b*

SEC. 7:15C   T-SHAPED SEATS / In T-shaped seats (Fig. 7:15A) tie cross ties and return-twine in front of arms as in the usual spring edge. In armless articles (Fig. 1:18) spring edges encompass a seat from one back post to the other. When arms are not to be fully upholstered, the spring edge usually is only along the front.

SEC. 7:15D   SOLID SEAT SPRING EDGES / Tie spring edges for solid seats are tied the same way as for loose-cushion seats (Secs. 7:15A–D), except that the outer top coils of the spring-edge springs are pulled down, with return-twine, ½-inch below the level of the others, Fig. 7:15D, so that the stuffed edge will not rise appreciably above the rest of a seat.

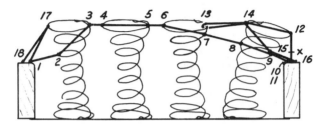

Fig. 7:15D

SEC. 7:15E TESTING / In addition to the usual checking of a spring seat (Sec. 7:14F), make sure that the front of the top coils of spring-edge springs are in line with the outer edge of the rail. If they are not, the finished edge will be uneven or slanting instead of straight and parallel with the outer edge of the rail.

**SEC. 7:16
EDGE-WIRE
FOR SPRING
EDGES**

SEC. 7:16A / Install edge-wire in spring edge seats (Fig. 7:15A) to fill gaps between springs and unitize them, to shape the edge, and generally to strengthen a seat. Where seat edge-wire goes and how it is fastened depend chiefly on how arms will be upholstered. [*1*] *Fully upholstered arms, no arms.* Seat edge-wire encompasses the spring area, Fig. *a, b* 7:16A. Measure accordingly, add 12 inches for overlapping joint. [*2*] *Arms not fully upholstered.* Seat edge-wire usually goes across the front and around to the back of the end springs, *c,* or along inner sides of front posts, *d.* Measure accordingly, add 2 inches for securing each end of edge-wire. Finishing edge-wire on springs, *c,* is the better way, but is not always possible. Do not finish edge-wire on posts when a spring edge is more than 2 inches above the rails.

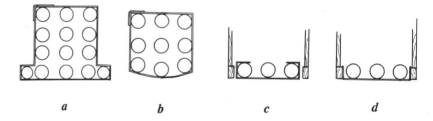

Fig. 7:16A   *a*   *b*   *c*   *d*

Tools: Wire bender (Sec. 2:11); spring clip pliers (Sec. 2:12) if using spring clips. *Materials:* Spring edge-wire, edge-wire clips (Sec. 3:19); upholstery twine (Sec. 3:08) and glue or shellac if tying edge-wire.

SEC. 7:16B SHAPING EDGE-WIRE / Shape edge-wire to fit a spring area, install as snugly as possible without displacing springs. Much depends on how wire ends are fastened. For an overlapping joint, Fig. *a* 7:16B, make the first bend 6 inches from end of wire. For finishing wire on a spring, *b*, or on a post, *c*, bend according to the point of finishing it.

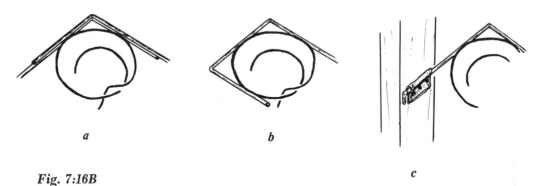

a   *b*

Fig. 7:16B   *c*

SEC. 7:16C FASTENING EDGE-WIRE / Clip or tie edge-wire to springs at all points of contact (Fig. 7:15A). [*1*] *When using clips,* place the long side over the edge-wire, Fig. *a* 7:16C, crimp tabs tightly around wire and spring. [*2*] *To tie edge-wire: b* Start where spring coil and edge-wire meet, loop middle of twine around that

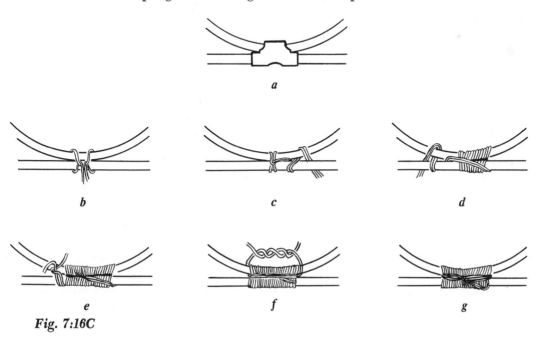

a

b   *c*   *d*

e   *f*   *g*

Fig. 7:16C

point and draw the free end through it. *c* Pull twines tight between spring and edge-wire. *d* Interlace twines around spring and edge-wire seven or eight times, pulling them tight after each interlacing; the tighter the twines are, the better the finished tie will hold and the less chance it will wear out. *e* Pull twines tight across interlacing to the other side of the tie point, and interlace seven or eight times. *f* When the second interlacing is completed and the twines pulled tight, twist one twine around the other, then wrap twines in opposite directions around interlacings. *g* Pull wrap-arounds tight, knot twines together. Strengthen tie by coating it with glue or shellac.

SEC. 7:16D ENDS OF EDGE-WIRE / Secure ends of installed edge-wire last. [*1*] *For an overlapping joint* (Fig. *a* 7:16B), clip the long piece of each end to the spring, then clip wires together at the ends. When tying, tie both wires to each side of a spring; seize the ends (Fig. *b* 7:15B). [*2*] *When edge-wire finishes on a spring* (Fig. *b* 7:16B), clip or tie wire to spring. [*3*] *When edge-wire finishes on a post* (*c*), loop a piece of strip webbing or a double thickness of burlap around the wire, tack it just below the wire to the front edge of the post.

SEC. 7:17 **SPRING SEAT,** **PAD BACK,** **SINGLE-PIECE** **COVER**	Some modern-type articles have a spring seat, pad back, and a single-piece cover (Fig. 1:14). The seats usually have roll edges. After springing, construction follows that of similar pad seat articles (Sec. 6:04) except: [*1*] *Set lowest side-to-side* strip of webbing in back about 1 inch behind the rearmost seat springs. [*2*] *Draw vertical back webbing* between lowest side-to-side strip and springs, and tack to rear seat rail at any convenient place. [*3*] *Stitch* burlap to springs (Sec. 7:18).
SEC. 7:18 **BURLAPPING** **SPRING SEATS**	Cover spring area with burlap to provide a smooth base for stuffing. [*1*] *Measure for burlap,* allowing for roll edges if any (Secs. 5:02A, 5:05A). [*2*] *Install burlap* spring cover, cut and pleat where necessary (Secs. 5:02, 5:15, 5:17). Tack to seat rails only. Fit burlap snug against springs, but not tight enough to compress them. [*3*] *Stitch burlap* to top coils of springs and along edges of a spring area, Fig. *a* 7:18. In seats without edge-wire, stitch along outermost points of top coils forming the edges of a spring area. Stitch shut large pleats. Starting at the corner of a spring area, stitch with a curved needle around a top coil, *b*. [*4*] *Tie first stitch* (Sec. 5:03). For all other stitches, loop twine from a stitch around needle as it emerges from burlap in the next stitch, draw needle through loop and pull twine smartly

Fig. a 7:18

toward the previous stitch. This "locks" a stitch, and if a twine should break, the locked stitches on each side will hold. After locking the last stitch, tie twine around a previous stitch. *Tools:* Upholsterer's hammer, shears, curved needle, tape measure (Secs. 2:02, 2:04, 2:06, 2:16). *Materials:* Tacks, upholstery twine, burlap (Secs. 3:03, 3:08D, 3:24).

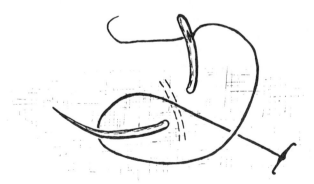

Fig. b 7:18

SEC. 7:19
ROLL EDGE
SPRING SEATS
THROUGH
MUSLIN
CASING

SEC. 7:19A / Roll edges usually are installed only on solid seats (Sec. 7:01A). The finished surface generally is about 2 inches above a burlap spring cover. A roll edge is needed for upholstering with loose stuffing, but not for compact stuffing (Sec. 7:20). *Tools:* Upholsterer's hammer, shears, large curved needle, regulator for loose stuffing (Secs. 2:02, 2:04, 2:06, 2:07). *Materials:* Tacks, upholstery twine, stuffing, muslin (Secs. 3:03, 3:08D, 3:28–3:44, 3:48).

SEC. 7:19B LOOSE STUFFING / After burlapping (Sec. 7:18) install roll edges (Sec. 5:05) on sides of seat that will be exposed when an article is completely upholstered. If arms and/or back are to be fully upholstered, no roll edge is needed between arm and back posts and/or between back posts. [1] *Install loose stuffing* (Secs. 5:11A–C), but instead of stitching the first layer, poke small amounts or wads under burlap spring stitches. [2] *Allow for shape* of a spring surface when stuffing a seat. Even small, flat seats are apt to have some crown at the middle. [3] *Spread stuffing evenly*, but do not neglect to build crown; muslin casing will compress the stuffing, not the springs. [4] *Be sure to place enough stuffing* along built-up edges of a seat; if there is too little, the edges may show through and wear out a cover. [5] *When arms and/or back* are to be fully upholstered, place enough stuffing along seat rails and adjacent burlap to build a firm surface up to the lower edges of arm and/or back liners, or to the top surface of an incased seat if the liners are set too high. This extra stuffing is needed to hold in place the stuffing on the top surface of a seat. The seat is, of course, stuffed out to the liners and down to join the side and back stuffing.

SEC. 7:19C MUSLIN CASING / Measure and install muslin casing as in Secs. 6:02D–F except: [1] *On sides* that will be exposed when upholstering is completed, Fig. *a* 7:19C, tack muslin casing on the sides of the rails about ½ inch from the top, or in the rabbeted area of an exposed-wood seat (Fig. *b* 1:28) when an exposed-wood post has an upholstery edge (Fig. 13:07B), tack muslin to it. [2] *When arms and/or back* will be fully upholstered, tack muslin for these portions of a seat on the top surface of the rails. After setting a casing in place, *a*, work it smooth and tight, cut and pleat as necessary (Secs. 5:15, 5:17). Push back loose stuffing that works over built-up edges; it could cause lumps in a cover. [3] *Before permanently tacking casing*, rub it lightly all over to locate lumps or hollows. Small flaws often can be corrected by regulating (Sec. 5:07). But for large lumps or hollows, open casing and rework stuffing. The seat in muslin, *b*, is essentially the same as it will be in the cover, so before tacking casing perma-

a

Fig. 7:19C   *b*

nently and trimming off excess goods, examine shape and firmness carefully for comfort and appearance.

**SEC. 7:20
COMPLETING
ROLL EDGE
SPRING SEATS:
COMPACT
STUFFING**

For best results when building a roll-edge type seat with compact stuffing (Secs. 3:41–3:46, 5:11D–G), first understuff and incase with muslin (Secs. 5:13, 7:19B, C); built-up edges are not needed. [*1*] *When all sides* of a seat will be exposed (Fig. 7:19C), make stuffing the exact shape of a seat. [*2*] *When arms and/or back will be fully upholstered,* compact stuffing need extend only to the inner sides of the arm and/or back liners. [*3*] *Fasten compact stuffing* to seat surfaces and rails only; do not fasten to posts or liners. Incase stuffed seat with muslin (Sec. 7:19C).

**SEC. 7:21
BUILDING
BRIDLE
HARD-EDGE
SEATS**

SEC. 7:21A / (Sec. 7:01B). [*1*] *In flat bridle seats,* Fig. *a* 7:21A, build understuffing and hard edge about 1 inch above the burlap spring cover at the center of a seat. [*2*] *In crowned bridle seats, b,* the understuffing, usually about 1-inch thick, follows the general contour of a spring area; at the edges, thicker understuffing usually is needed to shape a crowned seat. [*3*] *Regardless of arms and back,* bridle edges should be built completely around a seat, as bridle-building is a method of stuffing an entire seat, not just the edges. *Tools:* Upholsterer's hammer, shears, large curved needle, straight needle, regulator, tape measure, chalk (Secs. 2:02, 2:04, 2:06, 2:07, 2:16). *Materials:* Tacks, upholstery twine, burlap, loose stuffing (Secs. 3:03, 3:08D, 3:24, 3:28–3:38).

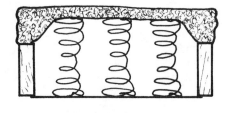

a   *b*

Fig. 7:21A

SEC. 7:21B UNDERSTUFFING / [*1*] *Install enough loose understuffing* (Secs. 5:11, 7:19B) for desired shape and thickness when compressed by a burlap cover. To find the amount of stuffing needed in a hard edge, cover it with burlap and shape temporarily by hand. A soft or flabby hard edge will not hold shape. An edge that is too hard —like wood—builds an uncomfortable seat, and may in time wear out the cover. [*2*] *Cut burlap large enough* to cover a seat down to the tops of the rails without appreciably compressing stuffing. [*3*] *Install burlap moderately tight* (Secs. 5:02, 6:02D, E), tacking it to the tops of the rails, as in Fig. 7:21B. Cut and pleat where necessary (Secs.

Fig. 7:21B

5:15, 5:17). It usually is sliptacked until the middle of a seat is stitched (Sec. 7:21C) and stuffing for the hard edges is adjusted to desired shape and firmness. When a hard edge ends at a post, fold excess burlap in place under stuffing to prevent it from working out.

SEC. 7:21C   STITCH UNDERSTUFFING IN MAIN PART OF SEAT / Stitch understuffing with a straight needle through only both sheets of burlap—spring cover and understuffing cover; do not enclose springs or spring ties. *[1] Start at middle of seat* (Fig. 7:21B) and spiral outward. Tie end of first stitch (Sec. 5:03). *[2] Take stitches* about 3 inches long on top of the understuffing and in rows about 3 inches apart. When stitches are too short or too close together, an understuffed surface tends to be lumpy instead of fairly smooth. Pull stitches tight enough to compress the understuffing to the desired thickness (Sec. 7:21A). *[3] Do not stitch* closer than 3 or 4 inches to the edges of a bridle seat. *[4] Tie off last* stitch to a convenient previous stitch.

SEC. 7:21D   HARD EDGE BEFORE STITCHING / Before stitching, a hard edge usually is about ½ inch above the rest of a bridle-built seat and projects slightly beyond the rails (Fig. 7:21B). Shape and firmness often can be estimated quite accurately by squeezing a hard edge. Regulating (Sec. 5:07) generally is necessary before stitching in order to work stuffing into the outer top portions of a seat front and similar exposed parts. Edges are a most important part of a seat; it may be necessary to stuff and stitch two or more times before building good shape and firmness. Before stitching (Sec. 7:22), tack bottom of burlap understuffing cover permanently to the top surface of the rails (Fig. 7:21B).

**SEC. 7:22
HARD EDGE
STITCHING**

Sec. 7:22A / Two, often three rows of stitching are needed to shape a hard edge, Fig. 7:22A. Only the first row (Sec. 7:22B) is needed along parts of a seat having fully upholstered arms or backs.

Fig. 7:22A

Sec. 7:22B First Row Hard Edge Stitching / The first row of hard edge stitching is essentially the same as in a roll edge (Sec. 5:05H), but done with a large curved needle to force stuffing toward the front of an edge. [1] *Insert needle* about ¼-inch above the rail, Fig. *a* 7:22B, to emerge about 3 inches back from the front edge. To complete stitch, insert needle 1 inch in front of the twine, directing it to emerge at the front 1 inch above start of stitch. Tie (Sec. 5:03) the first stitch. [2] *Space stitches* 1 inch apart. [3] *Squeeze edge* into the approximate desired shape, Fig. *b* 7:22B, while tightening each stitch. [4] *Stitch diagonally* around a corner (Fig. 7:22A) in order to build firm sides.

Sec. 7:22C Second Row Hard Edge Stitching / The second row of hard edge stitching (Fig. 7:22A) shapes the front. Stitch, Fig. 7:22C, with a straight needle. [1] *Insert needle* ½ inch above first-row stitching on the front surface of a hard edge, directing it to emerge ½

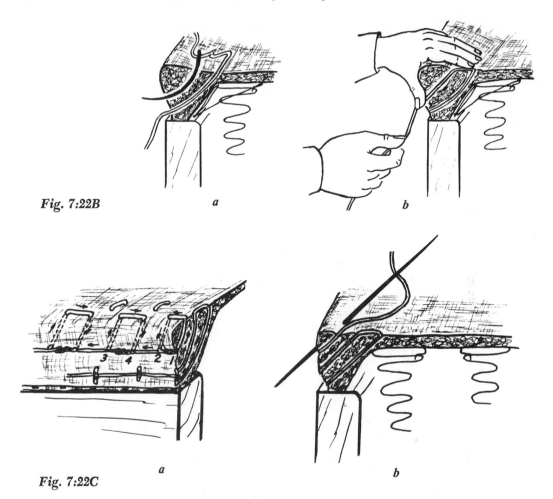

Fig. 7:22B   *a*   *b*

Fig. 7:22C   *a*   *b*

inch in front of first-row stitching on the top surface. Pull needle clear, and complete stitch 1 inch to the left, Point 2, *a*. A cross-section of the stitching is in *b*. [2] *Tie* (Sec. 5:03) completed first stitch. Squeeze edge into shape, *b*, while pulling knot tight. [3] *Start next stitch*, Point 3, *a*, 1½ inches to left of the completion of the first stitch, Point 2. Complete stitch ¾ inch to the right, Point 4. [4] *As needle emerges* at the front at Point 4, loop twine coming from Point 2 twice around it. Draw needle and slack through loops, pull twine tight while shaping edge. [5] *Continue stitching* as in steps [3] and [4]. Stitch diagonally around a corner to build firm sides. After completing the last stitch, tie twine tightly around the preceding stitch with two half-hitches; or, in hard edges only, tack end of twine to a post slightly below the level of the second row of stitching. [6] *On fairly high* hard edges a third row of stitching, done the same way as the second row, may be needed.

NOTE: A finished hard edge must be fairly well rounded (Fig. 7:22A); if too angular or sharp it may wear out the cover.

SEC. 7:22D   CHECK EDGE, COMPLETE SEAT / Lay a yardstick along the finished hard edge. For a smooth, neat seat it must be the same height above the rails throughout. Small lumps along the top of an edge often can be eliminated by tapping them lightly with the side of an upholsterer's hammer. Overstuff and incase bridle hard edge seat with muslin (Sec. 7:26).

**SEC. 7:23
BUILDING
BRIDLE
SPRING EDGE
SEATS**

SEC. 7:23A / Build spring edges, Fig. 7:23A, on all sides of a bridle-built seat having edge-wire (Sec. 7:16A); elsewhere, use bridle hard edges. Except for burlap understuffing cover and a difference in first-row stitching, build a bridle spring edge essentially as a bridle hard edge (Secs. 7:21, 7:22). In addition to tools and materials in Sec. 7:21A: Upholstery skewers (Sec. 2:08).

Fig. 7:23A

SEC. 7:23B   UNDERSTUFFING SPRING EDGE / Understuffing for spring edges extends ½ inch beyond edge-wire, but does not hang down over it. Use enough stuffing to build a small roll above and projecting slightly beyond edge-wire. Usually the cover for a spring-edge seat is stitched to the edge-wire, and completed with banding (Sec. 11:04, Fig. 1:18), or with banding and border (Sec. 11:05, Fig. *a* 1:50). The small roll in a spring-edge allows welt (Sec. 11:08) between seat cover and banding to fit neatly in place.   [1] *When arms and/or back* will be fully upholstered, stuff adjacent parts of a seat the same way as for a bridle hard-edge seat (Sec. 7:21B).   [2] *Burlap understuffing*

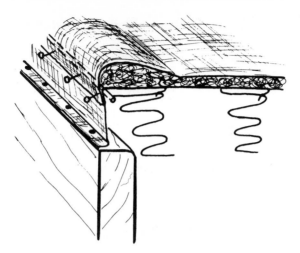

Fig. 7:23B

cover extends 1 inch below the edge-wire. [3] *When arms and/or back* will be fully upholstered, burlap for those parts of a seat extends down to the top of the rails. [4] *While adjusting* burlap understuffing cover along a spring-edge, push up any stuffing that works down over the edge-wire, as it may cause lumps in the cover. [5] *Underturn edges of burlap, pin in place* along edge-wire with upholstery skewers, Fig. 7:23B, entering skewer under edge-wire and slanting it up into the burlap spring cover.

SEC. 7:23C SPRING-EDGE STITCHING / First-row stitching in a bridle spring-edge is the same as in a bridle hard-edge except, Fig. 7:23C, that each stitch starts under the edge-wire and returns over it. This holds the burlap cover firmly to the edge-wire. Second-row stitching is the same as in Sec. 7:22C, but is not done along arm and back

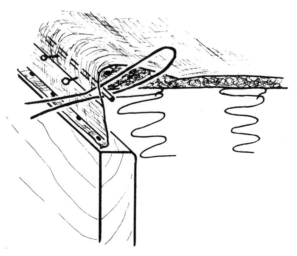

Fig. 7:23C

portions of a bridle spring-edge seat when those members are to be fully upholstered (Fig. 7:23A).

**SEC. 7:24
BUILDING
PLAIN
HARD-EDGE
SEATS**

SEC. 7:24A   /   Most loose-cushion seats have fully upholstered arms and backs; the hard-edge is only along the front, Fig. 7:24A. Use enough loose stuffing to build an edge from the top of the seat rail to 1 inch above the middle of the deck.   *Tools:* Upholsterer's hammer, shears, large curved needle, straight needle, regulator, upholstery skewers, tape measure, chalk (Secs. 2:02, 2:04, 2:06, 2:07, 2:08, 2:16). *Materials:* Tacks, upholstery twine, burlap, loose stuffing (Secs. 3:03, 3:08D, 3:24, 3:28–3:38).

Fig. 7:24A

SEC. 7:24B   PREPARE HARD-EDGE BURLAP CASING   /   Inner limits of plain hard edges are usually at least 4 inches behind the outer edges of the front rail, or just behind the front posts of a T-shaped seat, and follow the contour of the front rail, Fig. 7:24B.   [1] *Chalk mark* hard edge inner limits on burlap spring cover.   [2] *To measure width* of burlap for the hard-edge casing, form the desired shape of the edge with a tape measure from the marked inner limits to the front of the seat rail.   [3] *Measure length* of burlap edge casing straight across the widest part of a seat front; for T-shaped seats, *b*, measure length across the widest part and down to the side rails, shaping at the sides with a tape measure the same way as when measuring width. Add 6 inches to measured width and length for general handling.

Fig. 7:24B   *a*   *b*

SEC. 7:24C INSTALL BURLAP HARD-EDGE / [*1*] *Center* burlap hard-edge casing on the deck just behind marked inner limits of the edge. [*2*] *Overturn* 1 inch of burlap, draw it forward until fold is ½ inch in front of the marked inner limits. [*3*] *Pull casing* fairly taut from side to side, tack to the top surface of the side rails and pin in place along the marked inner limits of the edge, Fig. 7:24C. [*4*] *Sew burlap casing* along marked inner limits from side to side of the spring area; sew with a 1-inch running stitch; enclose a top coil or a spring tie whenever possible. Tie first stitch with a slipknot. [*5*] *Pull all stitches tight*, tie twine from the last stitch around the preceding one. Edge casing must be stitched smooth and tight, or it may break or lose shape in relatively short time.

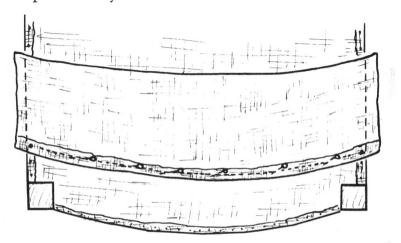

Fig. 7:24C

SEC. 7:24D BUILD HARD EDGE / Install enough loose stuffing (Sec. 5:11) without tacking or stitching it, to build hard edge 1 inch above the middle of a deck. The front of the edge should be in line with the front of the rail, or project slightly beyond it. Except for the difference in height of a plain hard-edge above the deck, and that the deck is not understuffed, build the plain hard-edge the same way as a bridle hard-edge (Secs. 7:21–7:22). [*1*] *In armless hard-edge loose-cushion* seats build a separate edge along each side to the back posts the same way as along the front; miter ends of the burlap casings together at the corners, stitch the joints shut. [*2*] *If arms and/or back* will not be fully upholstered, build separate hard edges between posts.

| SEC. 7:25 BUILDING PLAIN SPRING-EDGE SEATS | Construction of a plain spring edge, Fig. 7:25, is a combination of (Secs. 7:23, 7:24) bridle spring and plain hard edges. [*1*] *Mark inner limits* of spring edge (Sec. 7:24B). Burlap edge-casing extends from inner limits to spring edge-wire; add 8 inches to allow for general handling of the goods. [*2*] *Install edge casing* (Sec. 7:24C) along |

Fig. 7:25

marked inner limits.   [*3*] *Stuff, shape, stitch* edge (Sec. 7:23). When an edge is excessively deep, Fig. 7:25, take the first row of stitches well toward the front.   [*4*] *The finished* plain spring edge should rise smoothly from its inner limits to, at the front, 1 inch above deck. [*5*] *At the end of a plain spring edge* that is not attached to a post, fold casing in under the stuffing and stitch shut with a whip-stitch completely through edge.   [*6*] *Most loose-cushion spring-edge seats* have fully upholstered arms and backs, and have a stuffed edge only along the front.   [*7*] *For armless articles,* and if arms and/or back will not be fully upholstered, see Sec. 7:24D.

**SEC. 7:26
BRIDLE
HARD-EDGE
SEAT
THROUGH
MUSLIN
CASING**

SEC. 7:26A /   A muslin incased bridle hard-edge seat usually has been built up with either loose or compact stuffing about 1 inch above understuffing burlap cover.   *Tools:* Upholsterer's hammer, shears, tape measure; large curved needle, regulator if using loose stuffing (Secs. 2:02, 2:04, 2:16; 2:06, 2:07).   *Materials:* Tacks, stuffing, muslin; upholstery twine if using loose stuffing (Secs. 3:03, 3:28–3:47, 3:48; 3:08D).

SEC. 7:26B LOOSE STUFFING /   [*1*] *Install loose stuffing* (Secs. 5:11A–C) on understuffing cover; poke small wads beneath understuffing stitches to hold it in place.   [*2*] *Stuff to build* desired shape and thickness. Whether a seat is to be flat or crowned, be sure to build enough crown at the middle, as muslin compresses only the stuffing, not the springs and understuffing.   [3] *On sides of seat that will be exposed* when upholstery is completed, stuff up to but not over the crest of a hard edge; stuff the front and other exposed sides of hard edges only enough to smooth out irregularities due to edge-stitching.   [4] *When arms and/or back* will be fully upholstered, pack enough stuffing along those parts of a seat to fill any gaps between it and arm and/or back liners, and to keep seat from wobbling.

SEC. 7:26C   MUSLIN CASING   /   [1] *On armless articles and similarly exposed sides of bridle hard-edge seats,* muslin casing usually finishes near tops of rails (Fig. *b* 7:19C) to allow for a pull-over (Fig. 1:19), boxed (Fig. *c* 1:29), or bordered (Fig. *b* 1:36) cover.   [2] *When only a pull-over or a boxed cover* will be used, muslin casing may finish on bottom of rail, Fig. 7:26C, to eliminate a break or indentation between top and bottom of a seat; however, padding installed with a cover usually produces the same smooth-front effect.   [3] *Measure, install muslin casing* according to where it will finish on a frame (Sec. 6:02D). When an exposed-wood post has an upholstery edge (Fig. 13:07B), tack casing on it.   [4] *On sides of seat* that will be exposed when upholstering is completed, push back stuffing that works over the crest of a hard edge, as it may cause lumps in the cover; also, tack casing to outer sides of posts starting at least 1 inch below the crest of a hard edge, Fig. 7:26C, to leave space for finishing seat and arm and/or back covers neatly and snugly around and against post.

SEC. 7:26D   COMPACT STUFFING   /   For preparatory work and basic mechanics of installing compact stuffing (Sec. 5:11D). For installing muslin casing for the crown stuffing (Sec. 5:13); for full seat muslin casing (Sec. 7:26C).   [1] *Compact stuffing extends* to crests of hard edges on parts of a seat that will be exposed when upholstering is completed.   [2] *When arms and/or back will be fully upholstered,* compact stuffing extends to the inner sides of the liners.   [3] *Fasten compact stuffing* only to stuffed parts of a seat.   [4] *For a smoother finish* along the crest of a hard edge on parts of a seat that will be exposed when upholstering is completed, taper the bottom surface of compact stuffing (Sec. 6:02C).

**SEC. 7:27
PLAIN HARD
EDGE SEAT
THROUGH
MUSLIN
CASING**

SEC. 7:27A   /   Loose-cushion seat deck casing (Fig. 7:26C) consists of two pieces of muslin sewn together and stitched to the deck at the inner limits of a built-up edge. This maintains established shape of seat. Use enough loose stuffing to fill gaps at arm and/or back liners, when they will be fully upholstered, and to build smooth surfaces for deck and edge; usually a layer of loose stuffing ½ inch thick, when

Fig. 7:26C

compressed by a casing, is enough. Compact stuffing can be used (Sec. 7:27E); but many upholsterers feel that the extra work of installing it and its cost are not warranted for loose-cushion seats. *Tools:* Upholsterer's hammer, shears, curved needle, regulator, upholstery skewers, sewing machine, tape measure (Secs. 2:02, 2:04, 2:06, 2:07, 2:08, 2:15, 2:16). *Materials:* Tacks, upholstery twine, upholstery thread, loose stuffing, muslin (Secs. 3:03, 3:08D, 3:09, 3:28–3:38, 3:48).

SEC. 7:27B ARMS, BACKS TO BE FULLY UPHOLSTERED / Deck casing extends from the inner limits of a plain hard edge to the top of the rear seat rail, and from the top of one side rail to that of the other. Edge casing extends from the inner limits of the edge to the point of finishing on a frame (Sec. 7:26B), and across the widest part of a seat from side rail to side rail. Add 3 inches to each measurement for general handling. *[1] Sew deck and edge casings* together with a ½-inch flat seam (Sec. 12:02). *[2] Center sewn casing* on deck with seam stitching just behind the inner limits of the built-up edge. *[3] Pin casing in place* midway between sides, tighten to sides, sliptack to tops of seat rails. Complete pinning casing in place along inner limits of the edge (Fig. 7:24C). *[4] Stitch casing,* just in front of the seam sewing, to burlap spring cover; use a 1-inch running stitch and enclose a spring tie or top coil whenever possible. Stitch from side to side of the spring area only; do not stitch between springs and rails.

Sec. 7:27C Stuff Deck, Hard Edge / *[1] Install only enough loose stuffing* on a deck to build a smooth surface; poke small wads of stuffing under spring stitching to hold it in place. *[2] Pack* enough loose stuffing along seat edges next to arm and back liners, Fig. 7:27C, and down to the rails to close gaps between seat and liners, and prevent seat wobble. Stuffing near liners may be stitched, but as a rule it is held satisfactorily by liners and by interlocking with deck stuffing. *[3] While carefully drawing deck casing* back over a seat, press stuffing lightly but firmly toward the stitched seam; casings tend to force stuffing away from seams and create hollows. *[4]*

Fig. 7:27C

Smooth deck casing into position, cut to fit around the back posts (Sec. 5:15). *[5] Install casing* (Sec. 6:02D), but tighten only toward back and sides. Regulate stuffing (Sec. 5:07) where necessary. Deck casing tacked across the back of a seat looks the same as that tacked along the sides (Fig. *b* 7:29A). *[6] Stuff, incase hard edge* (Sec. 7:26). Cut muslin casing to fit around front posts; behind them, tack casing to tops of seat rails.

Sec. 7:27D Armless Articles, Arms and/or Back Not to Be Fully Upholstered / *[1] Measure deck casing* the shape of, but 1 inch

wider than, that part of a seat, Fig. *a* 7:27D, between inner limits of
the built-up edges. [2] *Measure edge casing* (Sec. 7:27B) long
enough to reach across front of seat to points of finishing on side rails,
and from back posts, *a*, to points of finishing on front seat rail. [3]
Add 3 inches to length of deck casing, and to both length and width
of edge casings, for general handling. [4] *Sew edge casings* (Sec.
7:27B), Fig. *a* 7:27D, to deck casing. [5] *Install deck casing* (Sec.
7:27B) along inner limits of the front built-up edge. [6] *Stuff deck
area* between inner limits of built-up edges (Sec. 7:27C); tighten and
tack deck casing to rear seat rail only. [7] *Stitch deck casing* along
inner limits of the side built-up edges. [8] *Stuff, incase* hard-edge
parts (Sec. 7:26); cut casing to fit around posts. [9] *At corners*, miter
ends of edge casings, stitch them together, *b*.

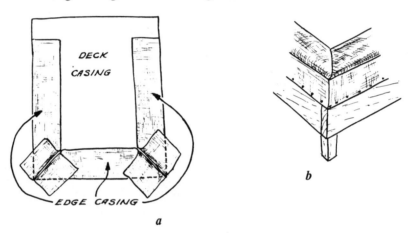

Fig. 7:27D

a

b

SEC. 7:27E   COMPACT STUFFING   /   This simplifies building a smooth
flat deck in a loose-cushion seat. Use any compact stuffing (Secs.
3:41–3:44); but because of the tapering (Sec. 3:46) usually needed
to build smooth surfaces along the inner limits of built-up edges
(Fig. 7:26C), polyfoam or foam rubber may be easier to use than
rubberized hair. Use stuffing ½- to 1-inch thick; thinner stuffing may
not cover springs and ties satisfactorily; thicker stuffing may make a
finished seat too puffy, especially along edges. Incase compact
stuffing the same way as loose stuffing (Secs. 7:27C, D). Differences
in construction between hard-edge seats built with loose and with
compact overstuffing are in installation of the stuffing; understuffing
(Sec. 5:11F) is required for compact stuffing. [1] *Understuff* entire
seat (Sec. 5:13), and incase with muslin the same as for loose stuffing
(Secs. 7:27A–D), except for built-up edge and top surface of deck
area. On these parts use just enough loose stuffing to fill hollows between edge stitches, springs and spring ties, and build a thin smooth

crowned foundation for compact stuffing.   [2] *Prepare, install* muslin casing for compact stuffing the same (Sec. 7:27B–D) as for loose stuffing.   [3] *Prepare compact stuffing* (Secs. 3:45, 3:46) the size and shape of deck area. Stuffing extends from the inner limits of the built-up edges to arm and/or back liners, depending on whether or not arms and/or back will be fully upholstered. For a smooth surface along the inner limits of built-up edges, taper underside of compact stuffing to the edge starting from a point ½-inch back; this is highly important if using ½-inch and thicker stock. Bond compact stuffing to understuffing casing, [1] above. When the bond is secure, complete installation of deck casing the usual way.   [4] *Stuff, incase hard edge* (Sec. 7:26), except that compact stuffing may extend from the inner limits of an edge down over the crest at the front to the top of a seat rail, or from the inner limits only to the crest of an edge; the first method makes a puffier seat front. Also, taper compact stuffing along the inner limits of a hard edge when it will finish there. Bond hard-edge compact stuffing to understuffing casing. At corners, cut stuffing, miter and bond it to build a smooth surface.   [5] *When using rubberized hair compact stuffing*, instead of understuffing and incasing as in [1] above, some upholsterers spread enough loose stuffing to fill hollows, then stitch rubberized hair to burlap hard-edge and deck covers; this is done after the muslin casing is stitched in place, [2] above.

SEC. 7:28 **BRIDLE** **SPRING-EDGE** **SEAT** **THROUGH** **MUSLIN** **CASING**	This has a single piece casing for the top of a seat (Sec. 7:26). Either loose or compact stuffing (Secs. 3:28–3:44) may be used. [1] *When arms and/or back will be fully upholstered,* stuff and incase these parts of a seat with muslin the same way as for corresponding parts of a bridle hard edge seat (Sec. 7:26). [2] *When arms and/or back will not be fully upholstered,* stuff and incase these parts of a seat the same way as for a bridle hard edge at the front of a seat. [3] *In armless articles and at the front of a bridle spring-edge seat,* stuff top of seat the same as a bridle hard-edge seat, but finish casing below the crest of a spring edge and complete the edge as in Sec. 7:29B.
SEC. 7:29 **PLAIN** **SPRING-EDGE** **SEAT** **THROUGH** **MUSLIN** **CASING**	**SEC. 7:29A** / The difference between plain spring-edge, Fig. 7:29A, and plain hard-edge seat construction through muslin casing is in the edge casing. The same general work for plain hard-edge seats (Sec. 7:27A) applies to plain spring-edge seats. Both plain and bridle spring-edge seats usually have banding (Sec. 7:29C). Measure, cut seat casings (Secs. 7:27B, C) except that edge casing extends from the inner limits to 1 inch below the spring edge-wire on all parts of a stuffed spring edge; prepare, stuff, install deck casing.

a

b

Fig. 7:29A

SEC. 7:29B   STUFF, INCASE SPRING EDGE   /   [*1*] *Install enough loose stuffing* along top of spring edge, Fig. 7:29B, to build a smooth surface even with crest of edge. Stuffing should be approximately the same thickness throughout to maintain established shape of seat.   [*2*] *While drawing casing over stuffing*, press stuffing lightly but firmly toward the seam to keep casing from dislodging stuffing and creating a hollow along seam.   [*3*] *Pin casing in place* on the outer side of the spring

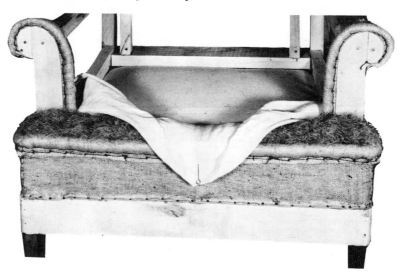

Fig. 7:29B

edge just above edge-wire (Fig. 7:29A), working from middle toward ends of an edge.   [4] *Cut casing* to fit around a post, but do not tack to post.   [5] *Work casing smooth and tight* (Sec. 5:18) throughout edge, repinning as often as necessary. Push back loose stuffing that works over the crest of an edge; it could make lumps in the cover. [6] *When casing is completely adjusted,* stitch in place along top of edge-wire throughout an edge. Use a 1-inch running stitch, pull stitches tight: I—In T-shaped seats, stitch in front and as far around posts as possible. II—In full-arm seats, stitch back between posts and seat. III—If spring edge is attached to posts, underturn muslin casing and draw it down between edges and posts; tack to posts at least 1 inch below crest of edge. Space is needed here for finishing seat and arm covers around and against the post (Fig. 7:26C).

SEC. 7:29C BANDING / Plain and bridle spring-edge seats usually have banding (Sec. 11:04, Fig. 7:29A) to hold and shape loose stuffing between spring edge and seat rail. It usually extends from the top of the edge-wire to ½ inch below top of rail, and along all edge-wire where muslin casing is stitched. Add 3 inches to both measured width and length of goods for general handling. To install banding, underturn 1 inch of goods at top of strip, center folded edge just above edge-wire. Pin fold in place along top of wire, tightening banding from the middle toward the "ends" of a spring edge.   [1] *When edge-wire is not attached* to front posts, the "ends" of a spring edge are just behind the posts; tack ends of the fold to the top of the side seat rails.   [2] *When edge-wire is attached to front posts,* the "ends" are at the inner front corners of the posts; tack ends of the fold to fronts of posts.   [3] *Using an overcast stitch,* Fig. 7:29C, sew the double thickness of banding just

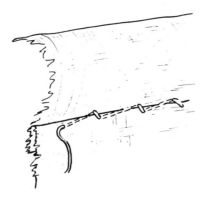

Fig. 7:29C

below the folded edge to the spring edge along top of wire. Sew completely along a spring edge, and down to seat rails at the ends when edge-wire is not attached to front posts.

SEC. 7:29D   STUFF BANDING   /   Install enough loose stuffing on the burlap spring cover below the edge-wire to build a smooth surface crowning slightly beyond the seat rails; stitch stuffing to burlap (Secs. 5:11A–C). Draw banding carefully over stuffing and, working it smooth and tight, tack along rails ½ inch below top edges (Fig. *a* 7:29A). While incasing stuffing, press it lightly but firmly toward the edge-wire to keep casing from dislodging it and leaving a hollow across a spring edge.   [1] *When spring edge is not attached to front posts,* pull ends of banding strip around behind posts and tack (Fig. *b* 7:29A) to top of seat rails.   [2] *When spring edge is attached to front posts,* tack ends of banding strip to front surfaces of posts.

SEC. 7:29E   ARMLESS ARTICLES   /   Spring edge extends around a seat from back post to back post. Prepare muslin casing and stuff deck area (Sec. 7:27C). Incase along exposed sides (Secs. 7:29C, D).

SEC. 7:29F   ARMS AND/OR BACK NOT TO BE FULLY UPHOLSTERED   / Build those parts of a spring-edge seat as hard edges (Sec. 7:27C).

SEC. 7:29G   COMPACT STUFFING   /   With a few differences due to the types of edges, use compact stuffing for loose-cushion spring edge seats the same way (Sec. 7:27D) as hard edge seats.   [1] *Understuff entire seat, incase with muslin* the same as when upholstering with loose stuffing except for deck, spring edge, and banding area. For these parts use just enough loose stuffing to fill hollows between springs, spring ties, and edge stitches, and build a thin smooth crowned foundation for compact stuffing.   [2] *Prepare, install* muslin casing for compact stuffing the same way (Secs. 7:29A–C) as loose stuffing.

[*3*] *Prepare* (Sec. 7:27E[3]) compact stuffing.   [*4*] *Stuff, incase spring-edge* (Sec. 7:29B) except that compact stuffing may extend from inner limits of an edge down over the front of a crest to just above the edge-wire, or from the inner limits only to the crest of a spring edge; the first way makes a puffier spring edge. Also, taper compact stuffing along the inner limits of an edge, and along the crest of an edge when it finishes there. Bond spring-edge compact stuffing to understuffing casing. At corners, cut stuffing, miter and bond it to make a smooth surface.   [*5*] *Install banding* (Sec. 7:29C). Taper compact stuffing for banding area to a smooth fit against edge-wire, bond to understuffing casing.   [*6*] *For special installation* of rubberized hair compact stuffing see Sec. 7:27E[5].   [*7*] *To build a less puffy or perhaps more limber surface,* many upholsterers use compact stuffing for deck and built-up edge, but loose stuffing for banding area; there is no need to understuff banding area.

FACTORY AND MODERN SPRINGING

SEC. 7:30 **SPRING** **MATERIALS**	Factory and modern spring materials are coil springs on bars and in unit assemblies, zigzag springs, and rubber webbing (Secs. 3:20–3:22). Most spring bar and unit assemblies are not available new to nonfactory upholsterers (Sec. 3:00C); some may be salvaged satisfactorily, or used when reupholstering an article (Sec. 7:31). Zigzag springs are usually available, but some accessories or special fittings may not be (Sec. 7:32). Rubber webbing is generally available; special clips and other fittings are desirable, but most work can be done satisfactorily without them (Sec. 7:33).
SEC. 7:31 **SPRING BARS,** **UNITS**	**SEC. 7:31A** / Most of these (Sec. 3:20) are made for specific frames and methods of upholstering. Some can be modified to fit other frames, and some frames can be modified to fit bars or units satisfactorily; but this should be attempted only by experienced upholsterers. When reupholstering, it may be more practical to keep than to replace coil spring bars or units if they are in good condition throughout. But if any coils and/or ties of a spring bar (Fig. 3:20B), or if more than two or three coil springs and/or any tie wires of a spring unit (Fig. 3:20C), are broken or appreciably deformed, the complete spring installation should be replaced with traditional springing (Secs. 7:01–7:29). [*1*] *Spring bars with free top coils* (*Fig. a, b* 3:20B) usually are twine tied the traditional way. Replace badly worn or broken ties. [*2*] *Wired spring bars* (Fig. c, d, e 3:20B) may be twine tied or wired side to side, top, and bottom. If twine or wires are damaged, re-tie springs in the same pattern. [*3*] *Spring units* (Fig. 3:20C) usually are twine tied or wired to a frame at one or more points along each edge to establish

initial compression (Sec. 3:16E) and hold them in place. Replace with twine any damaged ties or wires.

SEC. 7:31B UPHOLSTERING POINTERS / Except that they eliminate webbing and are usually installed on top of seat rails, coil spring bar and unit seats are upholstered approximately the same way (Secs. 7:01– 7:29) as those built with traditional coil springs. [*1*] *Spring bars with free top coils* are upholstered exactly the same way as traditional coil springs. [*2*] *Spring bars with wired top coils* are for backs (Sec. 10:31), not seats. [*3*] *Spring units* (Fig. *a* 3:20C) should be tied to seat rails at three or four points equally spaced along each edge. Anchor each tie (Fig. *b* 7:14B) permanently ½ inch from inner edge of rail. At each tie point, press spring unit down for desired initial spring compression (Sec. 3:16E), and tie to that height with a slipknot (Sec. 5:03). Then upholster as if using traditional springs.

**SEC. 7:32
ZIGZAG
SPRINGS**

SEC. 7:32A / These (Sec. 3:21) are chiefly in solid and loose-cushion roll and spring-edge seats (Secs. 7:00A, 5:04). Hard-edge construction is rare, as it requires edge springs (Figs. *b* 3:21O, *a–c* 3:21P), and the effect of a hard edge may be had by building a larger roll edge or building up seat rails before installing a roll edge; edge springs for zigzags are not always available to nonfactory upholsterers. Zigzag springs in good condition may be salvaged. Place them on edge on a flat surface; they should contract into a smooth, regular, circular shape, and each strip from a surface should form the same shape. If there are flat portions, or strips are irregular in shape, replace them. All edge springs from a surface should be the same size and shape and have the same resistance to go-down.

SEC. 7:32B REUPHOLSTERING ZIGZAGS / When reupholstering a zigzag spring seat, if springs are in good condition it may be more practical to keep than replace them. If a strip appears flat, or is depressed, replace it. If more than one strip is not in good condition, replace all. [*1*] *Replace broken connectors* (Sec. 3:21C) with the same item. If spring or wire connectors are not available, tie (Sec. 7:32C) complete surface with twine. [*2*] *Replace broken anchoring clips* (Sec. 3:21D) with the same basic design or shape clip when possible. [*3*] *Replace broken retainer* plates and connectors for anchoring zigzag springs to a frame (Sec. 3:21H). If replacements are not available, tie springs along sides (Sec. 7:32C).

SEC. 7:32C PREPARATION OF ZIGZAGS / For measuring, arc and crown, length and number of strips needed, and preparation and installation of zigzags, see Secs. 3:21J–Q. For connecting strips of springs and anchoring them along sides with twine (Sec. 3:08D) instead of manufactured fittings: I—Tie strips together at adjacent loops (Fig. *e* 3:21C); make ties just long enough to keep twine taut without pulling a spring strip out of line. II—Tack (Sec. 7:14B) ties anchoring side strips of springs to rails (Fig. 3:21B); note that anchoring ties are looped freely around springs, not tied to them.

SEC. 7:32D ROLL-EDGE SEAT / After springing with zigzags (Sec. 7:32C), install burlap spring cover (Sec. 7:18), Fig. *a* 7:32D. Then build roll edge or install prebuilt edging, *c* (Secs. 5:05, 5:06). If building a solid seat with loose stuffing, proceed as in Sec. 7:19; if using compact stuffing, see Sec. 7:20; however, many upholsterers simply fasten a slab of compact stuffing on the burlapped zigzags and omit roll edges. If building a loose-cushion seat, proceed as for building a plain hard-edge seat (Sec. 7:24).

SEC. 7:32E SPRING-EDGE SEAT / After springing with zigzags (Sec. 7:32C), install edge springs (Sec. 3:21O, Fig. *a* 3:21O). Then fasten edge-wire (Sec. 7:16) to springs (Fig. *b* 3:21O), and tie down with upholstery twine (Sec. 3:08D) to hold edge to desired height (Sec. 3:16E). Anchor (Sec. 7:14B) twine to seat rail ½ inch from inner edge. Tie twine in place at each point on edge-wire with a simple overhand knot to keep it from shifting and wearing. Complete loose-cushion seat the same way as a plain spring edge seat (Sec. 7:25).

SEC. 7:32F SPECIALITIES / Zigzag spring specialities (Sec. 3:21P) often are not available new to nonfactory upholsterers. Since most of them are made for specific frames and method of upholstering, salvaging seldom is satisfactory (Sec. 7:31A). But when reupholstering and these specialities are in good condition (Sec. 7:32B), it may be more practical to keep than replace them.

**SEC. 7:33
RUBBER
WEBBING**

SEC. 7:33A / Rubber webbing (Sec. 3:22) is used chiefly in solid and loose-cushion roll edge seats (Secs. 7:00A, 5:04, 7:33C). Hard and spring-edge constructions are not used, as there are no springs to support the top of a stitched edge. However, *flexible* edge construction is fairly common (Sec. 7:33D). Rubber webbing in good condition may be salvaged. But this is not advisable unless it was fastened to conventional clips and can be used without changing their positions, or the required lengths are so short that the old ends, especially if tacked or stapled (Sec. 3:22K), can be cut off. When reupholstering, if rubber webbing is in good condition, keeping it may be more practical than replacing it; but if more than one strip is damaged, replace all to be sure of building a uniform surface.

SEC. 7:33B PREPARATION / For placement, attaching, amount of

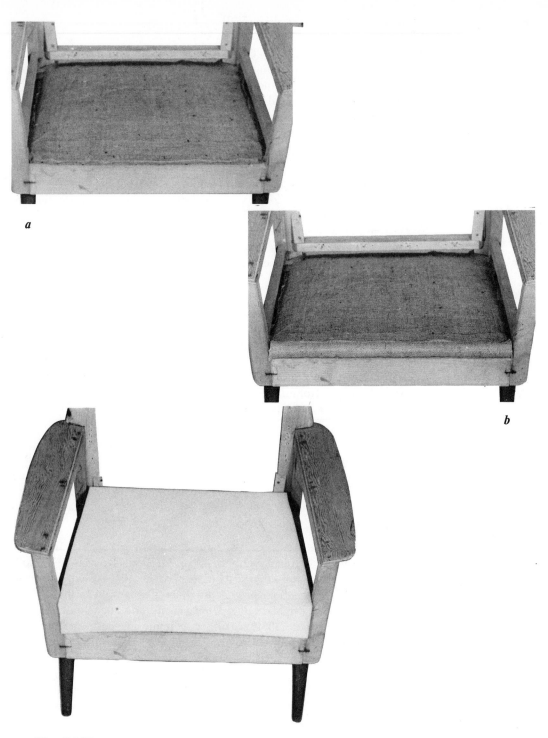

a

b

c

Fig. 7:32D

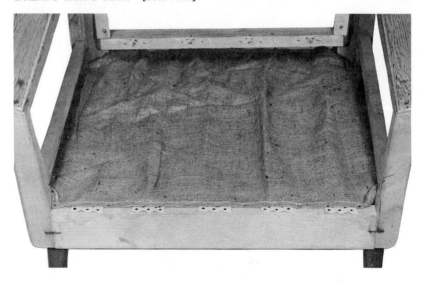

Fig. 7:33B

rubber webbing needed, etc., see Secs. 3:22E–L. Upholstering rubber webbing seats with loose stuffing is impractical; it cannot be packed hard enough to hold shape without making a surface too hard for comfort. After webbing a seat, install a burlap "spring" cover (Sec. 5:02) slack enough to allow for go-down of the flat-spring surface, Fig. 7:33B; burlapping is not essential, but sharply reduces frictional wear between webbing and stuffing. Prepare a sheet of stuffing of the wanted thickness (Sec. 3:16) the same shape as, but 1 inch wider and longer than, the top surface of a seat. Fasten it (Secs. 5:11D–G) to the edge of the seat area (Fig. *b* 7:32D) where there would be built-up edges with loose stuffing upholstery (Sec. 7:19). The elasticity of most compact stuffings and the effect of cutting it oversize and compressing it to fit usually provide ample allowance for go-down without damaging the stuffing. Build crown (Sec. 5:14) on stuffing, incase with muslin. Build crown with several layers of felted padding (Sec. 3:49) diminishing in width and length until desired shape is reached; then cover by a large layer to make a smooth surface, then incase with muslin; or, build crown with a layer of compact stuffing sculptured to build desired shape, and incase with muslin; this is the more complicated method.

Sec. 7:33C   Roll Edge Loose-Cushion Seats   /   These (Figs. *d* 1:29, *a* 1:36, *b* 1:42) are not difficult to build but require extremely careful work throughout; each work-step goes over all preceding work, Fig. 7:33C, and prevents easy corrections or changes.   [*1*] *Install rubber webbing* (Secs. 3:22E–L), Fig. *a* 7:33C.   [*2*] *Install burlap spring cover* (Sec. 7:33B); tack it close to ends of rubber webbing, Fig. *b* 7:33C.   [*3*] *Install compact stuffing, c,* preferably with tacking tape (Secs. 7:33A, 5:11E). Tack edge of tape close to edge of burlap; the edge of the stuffing should be about midway between the inner edge

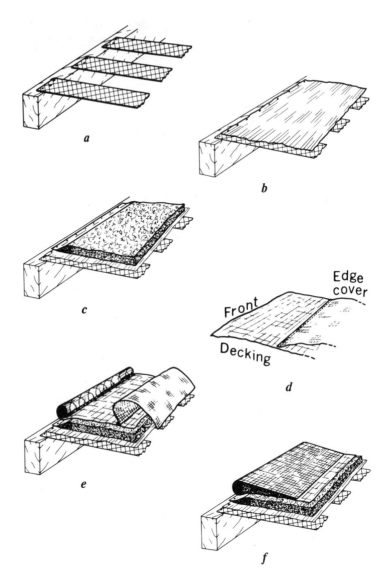

Fig. 7:33C

of the rail and the point of tacking the tape.   [4] *Prepare decking and edge cover, d.* Cut decking at least 2 inches wider and longer than large enough to be tacked on the top surface of all seat rails. Cut a strip of cover for the front of the top surface of the seat (corresponding to the "seat cover" strip in Fig. 13:16E), long enough to finish on the bottom of the front rail for a pull-over cover, or where it is to finish on the front of the rail for a bordered cover. Sew the cover strip to the decking about 5 inches from the planned front edge of the decking; be sure the top of the edge cover points to the seam, and that cover and decking are sewn together smoothly. [5] *Install decking and roll edge*, Fig. *e* 7:33C. Sliptack decking in place, build crown (Secs. 5:14, 7:33B) and test by covering with a few thicknesses of blanket or an upholstery cushion and sitting on it, before driving tacks permanently; if decking pulls loose or tears, increase the amount of crown. To install decking, tack the front at any convenient place on the rail between the outer edge of the tacking tape and that of the rail. After decking is tacked permanently and trimmed across the front, install roll edge or prebuilt edging (Sec. 3:25); it should be flush with the outer side of the rail. [6] *Stuff edge and cover it*, Fig. *f* 7:33C. For loose stuffing, pack enough between the built-up edge and the cover-decking seam to build a smooth, slanting surface; pad with a layer of felted cotton (Sec. 3:49) large enough to extend over the built-up edge to where the edge cover will be tacked (Secs. 13:11, 13:13); work edge cover in place and install. If upholstering with compact stuffing, trim a wedge to fit the space between the built-up edge and the cover-decking seam and build a satisfactory slant to the top of the edge; complete with padding, cover as for loose stuffing. However, instead of padding with cotton, some upholsterers prefer a ½″ thick layer of polyfoam or foam rubber as an easier, faster method. [7] *Be careful not to displace padding* on and behind the roll edge while working edge cover into place. Depending on size of the built-up edge and placement of cardboard stripping, if any, it may be necessary to pack additional padding in that area in order to build a firm but not hard support for the edge cover. *NOTE:* Size of a built-up edge depends on the amount of crown built into the deck, [5] above, and the crown of the bottom of the seat cushion. Unless planning a very fat cushion, an edge built up about 1 inch above the top of the deck crown usually is adequate; for a very flat cushion, a lower built-up edge.

SEC. 7:33D FLEXIBLE EDGE / This edge, Fig. 7:33D, for a loose-cushion seat is easy to build, comfortable, and need not be unattractive. [1] *Rubber webbing is installed* side-to-side and the front seat rail "drops" to allow go-down for the front strip of webbing. In Fig. 7:33D, instead of the front seat rail being cut to shape, ends are built up with blocks; this is common practice and if done properly is satisfactory. [2] *Set front strip of webbing* close to, even flush with, the outer surface of the front rail. [3] *Instead of the usual installation stretch* of 5% to 10% (Sec. 3:22D), stretch the front strip 12½%, or 1¼ inches for each 10 inches free length. This stiffens the seat front slightly, making it more comfortable in use, helping keep a loose cushion in place, and protecting the front cover by decreasing the amount of the go-down. [4] *Use compact stuffing* ½- to 1½-inches thick. As a rule it is fastened (Secs. 5:11D–G) to the front of the rear seat rail, passes over rubber webbing and down front of front rail to

Fig. 7:33D

finish on the bottom. Burlapping (Sec. 7:33B) is advisable, although it can be tacked only to side and rear rails. Bond stuffing to burlap, fasten to rails, then build desired crown, [5].   [5] *Crown* (Sec. 5:14) usually is built on the top surface and along the seat front (Sec. 7:33B). Top surface crown usually ranges from 1½ to 2 inches for the sake of appearance and to allow for go-down at the front without tearing out the cover.   [6] *Muslin casing* finishes on rear rail, bottom of front rail, and at the sides the same way as for a hard-edge seat (Fig. 7:26C). Casing should be tight enough to hold stuffing in shape, but not tight enough to depress rubber webbing more than ¼ inch at most.   [7] *Install cover* essentially the same way as casing and, at the sides, the same way as a plain pull-over cover (Sec. 13:11) for a roll or a hard-edge seat.   [8] *For best appearance* build the seat cushion (Chapter 17) especially to fit front of seat. If it is a reversible cushion, build both top and bottom surfaces with enough crown to fit along the front with some but not excessive gapping (Fig. *b* 1:48).

SEC. 7:34 LOOSE-CUSHION SEAT UPHOLSTERY	**SEC. 7:34A** / Loose-cushion upholstery—also called basic modern, Scandinavian, modern office, fraternity or rooming house, utility, etc. —is simple, efficient, and need not be uncomfortable. Seat upholstery is usually a base and a loose cushion. The base may be an essential part of a frame, but often (Figs. 1:25, *a* 1:55) is a slip-seat (Sec. 6:03). For comfort, the base is usually open frame (Sec. 4:01), but sometimes it is a solid frame and even the bottom of a cushion (Fig. 1:24, Sec. 7:34I). Most spring-type materials used to fill an open frame in factory upholstery are not available new to other upholsterers (Sec. 3:00C); but rubber webbing (Sec. 3:22) usually is.

SEC. 7:34B COMFORT / Comfort of a loose-cushion upholstered seat depends on the cushion and the resilience of the base. Whether a cushion should be fairly flat or well crowned (Sec. 5:14) depends on the exposed edges of a seat (Sec. 7:34D). Any cushion filling (Secs. 3:61–3:73) may be used; foam rubber and polyfoam are the most common. Cushions usually are boxed (Sec. 11:06); and, measured at the edges, seldom are less than 2 or more than 4 inches thick. Cushion thickness should be based on what is needed to build seat to a comfortable height (Sec. 3:16); however, loose-cushion upholstered seats are often one or two inches lower than traditional comfortable height. The cushion also serves as stuffing for a seat (Sec. 3:27). To function satisfactorily as "stuffing," the thinner a cushion is, the firmer it must be; if it is too soft, individual strips of webbing may be felt through it. Actually, much of the comfort of loose-cushion upholstery is due to seat and back being somewhat firm, thus giving more body support than a soft and pillowy surface can.

SEC. 7:34C SEAT TYPE ADVANTAGES / Because the spring area span usually is larger when the foundation is part of a frame than when it is a slipseat, as a rule the former is a more resilient and comfortable seat. But slipseats (Sec. 6:03) generally are easier for inexperienced upholsterers to build. The exposed surface of either type may be covered or left as exposed-wood. This decision is usually based on the wood's attractiveness; but cushion flatness should be considered.

SEC. 7:34D RUBBER WEBBING / In loose-cushion seat upholstery, rubber webbing usually finishes on the top surface of the seat rails or slipseat frame, Fig. *a* 7:34D; but frames also are built, or modified, for webbing to finish on drop bars, *d*. How the front of a seat (and sides and back if they will be exposed when an article is finished) is treated should, for appearance, be based on the cushion. When it is relatively

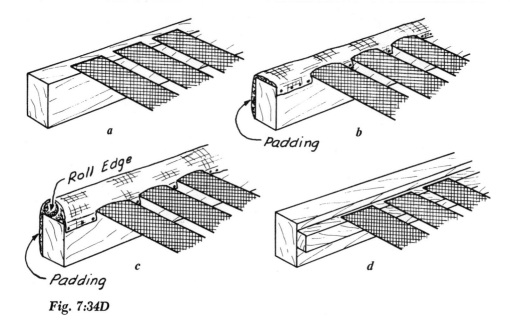

Fig. 7:34D

flat (Fig. 1:24) the rails or frame may be left uncovered, Fig *a* 7:34D, or they may be thinly covered, *b*. But if a cushion will have appreciable crown (Fig. 1:25) it may be desirable to install a built-up edge along the top, *c*, to reduce the gap between seat base and cushion. For planning and installing rubber webbing see Sec. 3:22.

Sec. 7:34E Rail, Frame Upholstery / When a rail or frame will be thinly upholstered (Fig. *b* 7:34D) or have a built-up edge (*c*), as a rule a plain pull-over final cover is installed essentially as in Sec. 13:11. At strips of webbing, cut (Sec. 5:15) cover at each side at a slight angle so as to leave a tab of goods going in under the webbing; underturn cover between cuts and tuck under padding. Pleat (Sec. 5:17), or cut and miter, cover at corners. If using thick or heavy fabric cover goods, it may be advisable to blind-stitch (Sec. 13:04) covers along corner.

Sec. 7:34F Built-Up Edges / A built-up edge (Fig. *c* 7:34D) may be a roll edge or prebuilt edging (Secs. 5:05, 5:06). Make outer side of built-up edge flush with outer surface of rail or slip-frame in order to build a smooth vertical shape. Fill space between top of built-up edge and inner top edge of rail or frame with stuffing to build a smooth shape slanting down to the inner edge; there should be just enough crown to keep a cover smooth and free of wrinkles. Use any stuffing (Secs. 3:27–3:44); a good loose stuffing is generally the easiest to handle. Install cover (Sec. 7:34E).

Sec. 7:34G   Drop Rails / Drop rails (Fig. *d* 7:34D) are generally used when an upholsterer wants a fairly thick cushion with relatively high crown, but does not want to cover the rail or frame. As a rule, the top of a drop rail is not more than about ¾ inch below the top of a seat rail or frame. Use any good hardwood for a drop rail. It should be at least 1½ inches thick and the same height, or more if a frame permits.

Sec. 7:34H   Solid-Base Upholstery / Solid-base loose-cushion seat upholstery (Fig. 1:24) need not be uncomfortable. The seat unit is a boxed (Sec. 11:06) cushion mounted on a solid wooden base, Fig. 7:34H. It is usually 1-inch hardwood or ¾-inch plywood, cut ½-inch narrower and shorter than the space the unit is to fill.   *[1] Drill several ½-inch diameter* or larger breather holes through the base 4 inches from the edges and a few near the middle.   *[2] Use any firm cushion filling* (Sec. 7:34B). Make cushion the usual way (Chapter 17) except that there is no bottom cover and the boxing should be at least 2 inches longer (top to bottom of a cushion) than usual to allow for tacking to bottom of the base.   *[3] When assembling a unit,* first center and securely fasten filling to solid base. Next pad top and sides of filling. Tear off padding that hangs below the bottom edges of the base, as it may interfere with neat installation of the cushion casing; while working a boxing in place enough padding is usually drawn over the edges of a base to protect the cover.   *[4] To install casing,* turn it inside out and center wrong side of top cover on padded filling; with a sort of rolling motion work boxing down over sides. Finish casing on bottom of solid base the same way as a slipseat cover (Sec. 13:10).   *[5] Install welting* (Sec. 11:08) along bottom if desired.

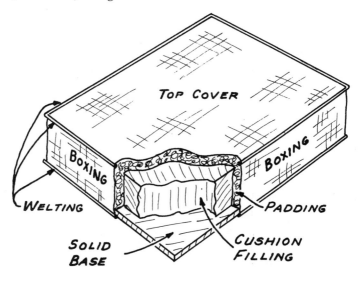

Fig. 7:34H

8

building
arms

SEC. 8:00 Basic types of upholstered arms are the armrest pad (Fig. *b* 1:28), covered armboard (Fig. *d* 1:29), and the so-called fully upholstered arm, most of which actually are fully upholstered (Figs. 1:30–1:49). The last group also contains arms not fully upholstered (Figs. 1:22, *a* 1:52); and arms that are continuations of inside backs (Fig. 1:37), and of wings (Figs. 1:15, *b* 1:48). Most fully upholstered arms have four upholstered parts, Fig. 8:00.   [1] *Arm face or front.* It may be upholstered and covered as an extension of the inside arm (Fig. 1:30); or, upholstered for and covered by a panel (Fig. *c, d, e* 1:45); or, built for a border (Fig. *b* 1:46) or a boxing (Fig. *a* 1:42).   [2] *Outside arm.* This usually is very simple upholstery, done when installing outside covers (Chapter 18). Outside arm upholstery and cover may be continuations of an inside arm, as for a rounded arm (Fig. *d* 1:45).   [3] *Armtop.* Except for T-shaped arms (Fig. *a* 1:46), an armtop is a direct continuation of an inside arm and is treated as such.   [4] *Inside arm.* This generally includes the armtop, even of T-shaped arms. An inside arm may or may not include part or all of an arm face.   [5] *Most arms* are pad upholstery.   [6] *Spring arms* usually have springs only in the armtop; they are soft and durable unless consistently sat on but are fairly difficult to build (Sec. 8:23). The comfort of a spring arm may easily be matched by a pad arm built with compact stuffing.   [7] *In many arms a cover* may be installed more than one way. But often, unless arms are upholstered for a particular type of cover installation, another type must be used or the arms must be rebuilt.   [8] *It is especially important* for inexperienced upholsterers to incase arms with muslin.   [9] *For best results* build arms together phase by phase— webbing, burlap, stuffing, muslin casing—and each phase step by step.

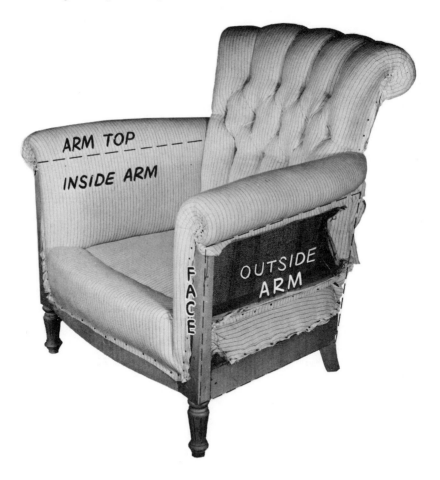

Fig. 8:00

SEC. 8:01
FRAME PARTS

For names of arm frame parts see Fig. 4:01. Most arm frames are not strong enough for use as seats. Arms built for sitting are specially braced and usually are much wider than normal.

SEC. 8:02
ARM TYPES

Basic types of fully upholstered arms are shown in Fig. 8:02. There are numerous combinations of arm parts; scroll arms, for example, may

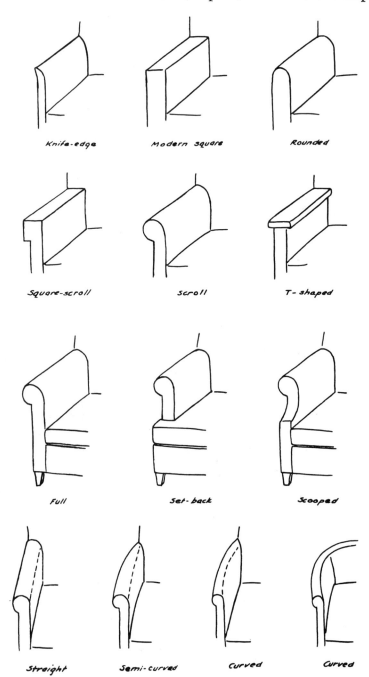

Fig. 8:02

be full, set-back, or scooped. Except for T-shaped arms, all types are built much the same way. Chief differences are due to desired thickness of an arm, width at front, and how it is to finish at the back.

SEC. 8:03 **ARM** **THICKNESS**	Thickness of an arm should be based on its size in relation to the rest of an article, and on desired width of a seat. Arms too thick for their length often seem puffy, swollen. Arms too small for a large, thick back tend to make a finished article seem top-heavy. There are no rules covering ideal thickness of arms. For best results, build seat, arms, and inside back in muslin, then study the article carefully. Rebuild if proportions are not pleasing. Thickness of inside arms determines width of a seat, the average being at least 20 inches wide between front posts. When planning arm thickness, consider the build of the person who will use a chair most often.
SEC. 8:04 **STYLES OF** **INSIDE ARMS**	Inside arms may be plain, buttoned, channeled, or tufted (deep-buttoned). Plain and button arms are upholstered alike until buttons are to be installed, usually with the cover. For channeling, a style of finishing common in barrel chair arms (Fig. *b* 1:37), see Chapter 20. For tufting, a style seldom used for arms, see Chapter 21.
SEC. 8:05 **STUFFINGS**	**SEC. 8:05A** / Padded armrests, covered armboards, all types of armtops usually receive more abuse than any other part of an article. How well they last and keep shape depends on the stuffing. Stuffing must be firm yet resilient to hold shape and keep a cover smooth and tight; also, it should be comfortably soft. The better a stuffing is, the easier it is to build these features into an arm, and the more durable it usually will be. However, installation of stuffing is as important as quality; poor stuffing well-installed usually is better than poorly handled good stuffing.

SEC. 8:05B LOOSE STUFFING / Loose stuffing (Secs. 3:28–3:38) is suitable for all arm upholstery except spring arms built with rubber webbing (Sec. 8:23G). For roll edges and understuffing (Secs. 5:05, 5:11D, 5:13), a hair and fiber mixture is better than all hair and costs less. For regular overstuffing use the best quality hair available.

SEC. 8:05C COMPACT STUFFING / [1] *Rubberized* hair (Sec. 3:44) is a good, easy-to-handle stuffing for padded armrests, covered armboards, square-scroll, and T-shaped armtops. Its stiffness may make it difficult for inexperienced upholsterers to install on knife-edge, scroll, rounded, and curved arms but is well worth the effort. [2] *Polyfoam, foam rubber,* and similar stuffings (Secs. 3:41–3:43) are excellent and easy to handle for padded armrests, covered armboards, and all fully upholstered arms and others treated as such. These stuffings are particularly suited to upholstering arms in which fairly sharp instead of rounded breaks are wanted between top, front, and sides (Fig. *a* 1:42).

SEC. 8:05D   FELTED PADDING   /   Felted natural cotton padding (Sec. 3:37) generally is not satisfactory for stuffing arms; it is, however, commonly used for a few types of arms, and for one type is preferred by many experienced upholsterers. Felted synthetic cotton padding (Sec. 3:49) builds a softer surface than natural cotton and supports a cover better. How to stuff arms with felted cotton is detailed in this chapter, although it usually is done when installing the cover.   [*1*] *Felted padding* may be the stuffing when a hard, flat armtop is wanted, as in club chairs similar to Fig. *a* 1:42, and when only an arm front is to be covered by a boxing (Fig. *b* 1:31). In most cases a thin sheet of compact stuffing is as easy to install and gives better results. [*2*] *Square-scroll and modern square arms* (Figs. *b* 1:46, 1:58) may be stuffed satisfactorily with felted natural cotton, but a thin layer of either loose or compact stuffing is generally better.   [*3*] *The lower portion of T-shaped arms* (Fig. *a* 1:46) generally is stuffed with felted natural cotton.   [*4*] *The lower portion of bordered inside arms* (Figs. *b* 1:42, 1:63) may be built with either loose or compact stuffing, but often is stuffed with natural cotton when an extremely thin and flat surface is wanted.

SEC. 8:06
ARMRESTS

SEC. 8:06A   /   Frames designed for armrest pads usually have rabbeted edges for tacking upholstery materials, Fig. 8:06A. The smallness of the average armrest pad makes it difficult to build two or more exactly alike. Size and limited work space require extra care throughout, especially when tacking. Loose stuffing is traditional;

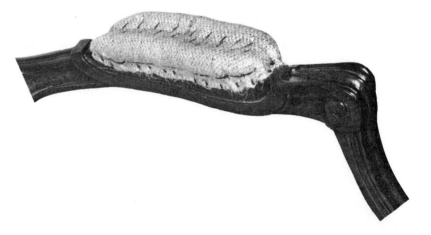

Fig. 8:06A

compact stuffing is in greater use. *Tools:* Upholsterer's hammer, shears, tape measure; large curved needle, regulator for loose stuffing (Secs. 2:02, 2:04, 2:16; 2:06, 2:07). *Materials:* Tacks, stuffing, muslin; upholstery twine, burlap for loose stuffing (Secs. 3:03, 3:28–3:44, 3:48; 3:08, 3:24).

SEC. 8:06B LOOSE STUFFING / Install loose stuffing on armboard (Secs. 5:11B, C). Build armrest pad to desired size and shape. Since they are small, irregularities in size and shape are more noticeable than in larger articles. Minor irregularities often may be corrected satisfactorily when overstuffing (Sec. 8:06D). But when irregularities are large, or a pad is too big or too small for good appearance, the practical solution is to do it over. [1] *Measure* burlap large enough to cover stuffing, with moderate compression, down to armboard; add 3 inches to length and width for general handling. [2] *Install* burlap (Sec. 6:02D); tack close to the top edge of the armboard in the rabbeted area. Tack at a slant, Fig. 8:06B, to prevent splitting wood. Push back stuffing that works down below the burlap; it could cause lumps in the cover. [3] *After tacking* at enough points to hold stuffed pad fairly well, overturn burlap and complete tacking (Fig. 8:06A).

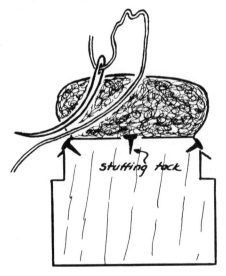

Fig. 8:06B

Pleat (Sec. 5:17) where necessary; make several small pleats instead of a few large ones. [4] *Regulate* stuffing (Sec. 5:07) into top edges of pad if necessary. [5] *Before stitching*, a pad should be moderately hard and firm. Unstitched sides usually project slightly beyond rabbet, Fig. 8:06B. Trim off excess burlap close to tacks. [6] *Stitch* (Sec. 7:22B) and shape armrest pad, Fig. 8:06B. A finished stitched pad should have a smooth, regular shape (Fig. 8:06A). [7] *Install,* without stitching, enough loose overstuffing on top of pad to build a smooth crowned (Sec. 5:14) surface of the desired shape.

Sec. 8:06C Muslin Casing / Incase armrest pad with muslin (Sec. 6:02D). Tack muslin close to edges of burlap to leave space for tacking cover on rabbet. Push back loose stuffing that works down over top edges of a burlap pad. Pleat muslin casing to fit smooth and tight. Trim off excess muslin close to tacks, Fig. 8:06C. Very small armrest pads may be stuffed and incased with muslin only, instead of with burlap and muslin; work as in Sec. 8:06B, except that muslin replaces burlap. When covering, instead of overstuffing use enough extra felted cotton padding to build a smooth crowned pad of the desired shape.

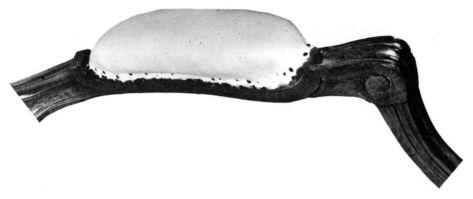

Fig. 8:06C

Sec. 8:06D Compact Stuffing / Upholstering armrest pads with compact stuffing is fast and greatly simplifies building two or more alike. Compact stuffing cannot be regulated into shape, so take special care in preparing it.   [1] *Prepare* stuffing (Sec. 3:46) the desired shape of an armrest pad, but ½ inch longer, wider, and thicker than planned finished size. When compressed by a casing or cover, stuffing exerts enough outward pressure to hold them smooth and tight; it also keeps the pad from being flabby.   [2] *Fasten* shaped stuffing securely to top of armboard (Secs. 5:11D, E).   [3] *Build crown* now with loose stuffing or felted padding (Sec. 8:06C); or, while covering, with felted padding.   [4] *For best results*, stuffing, preferably with crowning material, should be incased with muslin (Sec. 8:06C).

SEC. 8:07 **COVERED** **ARMBOARDS**	**Sec. 8:07A** / Covered armboard upholstery may be only felted padding (Sec. 3:49) and cover (Figs. *d* 1:29, 1:63), or it may be a stuffed surface incased with muslin, then padded and covered (Fig. *b*

1:42). Upholstering with felted padding only is not recommended when a surface will be more than ½ inch thick under a cover. Use loose or compact stuffing (Sec. 3:27) for covered armboard upholstery. When an armboard will be stuffed only with felted padding, it usually is done when covering it (Secs. 8:07B, 14:02). If cloth or loop buttons (Sec. 3:60) will be used, drill small holes in armboard for twines of buttons. *Tools, Materials* (Sec. 8:06A).

SEC. 8:07B FELTED PADDING / When covered armboard upholstery is only felted padding and cover, work is usually done when covering the rest of an article. Use either natural or synthetic felted cotton; the latter builds a softer, more durable surface. Three layers of padding may be used. With more, a surface is apt to be too weak to hold shape satisfactorily, and stuffing should be used instead. [*1*] *There should be at least two layers* of padding; one to stuff armboard, the other to build crown (Sec. 5:14). Put stuffing layer completely over top of armboard; depending on where cover will finish, padding extends down front end and sides to bottom edges of armboard (Fig. *d* 1:29), or only to the upper edges of the front and sides of armboard (Fig. *a* 1:37); but when the front of an arm is a continuation of the top of an armboard (Fig. 1:63), padding extends down front of post. The crown layer of padding is the same shape as the top of an armboard, but 1 inch narrower and shorter. For a thicker build-up of padding, prepare a third layer, the same shape and size as the top of an armboard, and the front of the post if building as in Fig. 1:63. [*2*] *For thin or medium build-up,* center the stuffing layer of padding on armboard. Smooth it in place to where it will finish, and tear it off even with those edges; enough padding works over them to pad them sufficiently when installing cover. Then center the crown layer on top of the stuffing padding; feather edges of crown padding into the other to avoid a line of lumps in the cover. [*3*] *For thick build-up,* center the third layer of padding, [*1*] above, in place on top of armboard, and down front of post if building as in Fig. 1:63, before installing the stuffing layer.

SEC. 8:07C LOOSE STUFFING / Covered armboards upholstered with loose stuffing may have a stitched pad, Fig. *a* 8:07C, or a roll edge, *b*, extending along front and sides of the top of the board. If stuffing will be more than 1-inch thick and up to 2 inches wide, a stitched pad may be easier than a roll edge; but if large enough pre-built edging (Sec. 5:06) is available, and if there is enough space to tack it along top of armboard, using it is easier than stitching a pad. If stuffing will be about ¾-inch thick or less, or if armboard is more than 2½ inches wide at its narrowest, or if it is extensively curved, uphol-stering with a roll edge or prebuilt edging generally is the more prac-

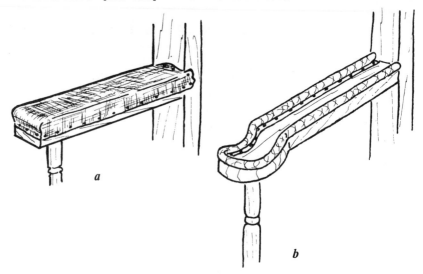

Fig. 8:07C

a

b

tical method. [1] *Stitched pad.* Build stitched pads for covered armboards the same as for armrests (Secs. 8:06B, C), except that at the back tack muslin casing to front and sides of back post, Fig. *a* 8:07C. [2] *Roll edges, prebuilt edging* (Secs. 5:05, 5:06). Install built-up edges on top of armboard along outer edges from one side of the rear of an arm to the other, *b.* Stuff armtop (Secs. 5:11A–C). Be sure to use enough stuffing along built-up edges; otherwise, they may show through and wear out the cover. Incase with muslin (Sec. 8:06C), but at rear of arm tack it to front and sides of back post, *a;* along armboard, tack muslin slightly below top edges.

Sec. 8:07D Compact Stuffing / Upholster covered armboards with compact stuffing the same way as armrest pads (Sec. 8:06D) except that stuffing fits tight against front of back posts.

**SEC. 8:08
BUILT-UP
EDGES FOR
FULLY UP-
HOLSTERED
ARMS**

Sec. 8:08A / For roll edges and prebuilt edging, see Secs. 5:04–5:06. Prebuilt edging generally simplifies upholstering and, especially for inexperienced workers, tends to be more uniform than roll edges. Built-up edges on inner sides of front posts commonly extend down to the level of the seat rails (Fig. 7:15A) and are installed before building a seat. However, an edge may extend only to the top of a seat or deck, Figs. 8:08A, *e* 1:45. Use built-up edges only when building a loose-stuffing arm surface out more than ½ inch from the inner side of a front post. However: [1] *Knife-edge, small scroll, small rounded arms* seldom have built-up edges. [2] *Large scroll* and *rounded arms* usually need built-up edges. In rounded arms (Fig. *d* 1:45) the edge extends down the outer side of a front post to bottom of seat rail; a similar edge on the rear arm post goes from the back post to bottom

Fig. 8:08A

of seat rail.   [3] *Square-scroll* and *T-shaped arms* have built-up edges on armtop when they will be stuffed more than ½ inch thick.   [4] *Modern square arms* seldom have built-up edges. Building the top with an edge would prevent neat, firm installation of the cover and its welt (Fig. *a* 1:42) along the outer edge.   [5] *Exposed-wood arms* have built-up edges along rabbets, but at least ½ inch from the exposed wood, when an upholstered surface will stand out more than ½ inch from rabbets or exposed wood (Fig. *a* 1:52). Install built-up edges after webbing and burlapping an arm (Secs. 8:09, 8:10). Many exposed-wood arms of this type are too small to hold a built-up edge, have insufficient space for tacking it; these, after webbing and burlapping, are bridle-built with hard edges (Sec. 7:18): I—Tack understuffing burlap cover to the rabbet surfaces ½ inch from the exposed wood; tack burlap to arm liner, and to back post when arm upholstery is not to finish through arm cavity. II—Stitch hard edges along exposed-wood portions only. III—Build the rest of this type of exposed-wood arm the same as a fully upholstered arm. [6] *Inside arm and wing upholstered together* (Fig. *b* 1:48). If built-up edges will be used, install a single edge for arm and wing (Sec. 9:08) before upholstering arm. [7] *Bordered inside arms* (Figs. *b* 1:42, 1:63) ordinarily do not need built-up edges regardless of stuffing to be used. However, if just below armtop (Fig. *b* 1:42) or armtop border (Fig. 1:63) a loose-stuffing inside arm will puff out abruptly more than ½ inch, install a built-up edge. Edge, stuffing, and muslin casing usually are installed after armtop or armtop border cover (Secs. 14:02, 14:05); webbing and burlapping may be done then, or earlier (Secs. 8:09, 8:10).

Sec. 8:08B   Edge Placement Due to Covering of Arm Face /
Placement of arm built-up edges depends on how arm front will be covered. [1] *When arm front is up to about 2½ inches wide* (Fig. *a* 1:31), inside arm muslin casing and cover usually go around post to finish on the outer side. No built-up edge needed. [2] *When an arm front will be much more than about 3 inches wide,* a separate post panel or facing may cover it (Fig. *e* 1:45). In scooped arms (Fig. *b* 1:46) the appearance of a post panel is made by a border. Also, a pull-around cover may be used for the lower part of an arm front and a button for the top (Fig. *d* 1:48). For all these styles of finishing arm fronts, install built-up edges to project slightly in front of the face of a post to allow panel, border, or button to seem set into the face. When no built-up edge is used, the effect of one may be simulated with felted cotton when installing the cover. [3] *Instead of a post panel, border, or button,* 3-inch and wider arm fronts often are covered by boxing (Figs. *b* 1:31, *c* 1:42). When a built-up edge is used for this style of covering, install it to finish flush with the surface of the arm front.

**SEC. 8:09
WEBBING
INSIDE ARMS**

Sec. 8:09A /   Usually a few vertical strips of webbing 3 or 4 inches apart are enough support for inside arm upholstery. Vertical strips preserve the intended shape of a curved arm, and support all arm upholstery better than longer, front-to-back strips. Placement of webbing depends on how arm upholstery finishes at the back. Stretch arm webbing tight only by hand; most arm liners will not withstand the pressure exerted by a webbing stretcher. Traditional jute strip webbing is the most commonly used for arms; rubber webbing tends to hold inside arm upholstery in better shape. *Tools:* Upholsterer's hammer, shears (Secs. 2:02, 2:04). *Materials:* Tacks, jute or rubber webbing (Secs. 3:03, 3:11, 3:20).

Sec. 8:09B   How Arm Upholstery Finishes at the Back /   [1] *Small and medium size chairs* (Fig. 1:35) seldom have slats or uprights in a back frame, and arm and back upholstery usually finish through arm cavity. It may be more practical to build the inside back before the arms. Set rear strip of vertical arm webbing parallel to but about ½ inch from back post. Double-over the strip, Fig. *a* 8:09B, to give extra support to arm upholstery finishing through cavity. Space other webbing equally between rear strip and front post. [2] *Large chairs* (Figs. 1:42–1:49), *sofas, and other articles* may or may not have back slats, Fig. *b* 8:09B. Regardless, arm upholstery generally finishes through back cavity. Space strips of arm webbing equally between back and front posts. [3] *Many barrel or tub chairs* (Fig. *b* 1:38), *but not all* (Fig. *a* 1:37) have inside arm and back upholsteries joined together, Fig. *c* 8:09B, instead of finishing through a cavity. Space arm webbing equally between front and back posts. Chairs are not designed for this style of upholstery exclusively. Most articles done this way could be upholstered, probably more easily, with inside arms and back finishing through arm cavities.

SEC. 8:09C   VERTICAL PLACEMENT OF ARM WEBBING / [1] *Fully upholstered arms and those treated as such*, except T-shaped and bordered inside arms, [2], [3] below. Webbing extends from inner surface of arm liner up to finish on that of the armboard.

NOTE: When possible with exposed-wood arms, tack webbing at least ¾ inch from the limits of arm upholstery to leave space for tacking other upholstery materials; if ends of webbing will be less than ½ inch from limits of upholstery, tack webbing to under surface of armboard (Sec. 10:06).

[2] *T-shaped arms.* Webbing extends from inner side of underarm strip to that of the arm liner. Tack webbing on underarm strip about ¾ inch below armboard. Do not overturn this end of webbing; usually the lower part of the inside arm is stuffed only with felted padding, and a double thickness of webbing could show through a cover. [3] *Bordered inside arms* (Figs. *b* 1:42, 1:63). Webbing extends from inner surface of arm liner up to finish, usually, on armboard about ¾ inch above the lower edge; if much higher, it probably would interfere with neat installation of armtop cover or border. If webbing will not leave space for neat installation of armtop cover or border, tack it to under surface of armboard (Sec. 10:06).

**SEC. 8:10
BURLAPPING
INSIDE ARMS**

SEC. 8:10A / Place and install burlap according to how inside arm upholstery finishes at the top and back. Basic shape of an armtop (Fig. *a* 8:09B) usually is built with loose stuffing, although compact may be used. *Tools:* Upholsterer's hammer, shears, tape measure (Secs. 2:02, 2:04, 2:16). *Materials:* Tacks, burlap (Secs. 3:03, 3:24).

a

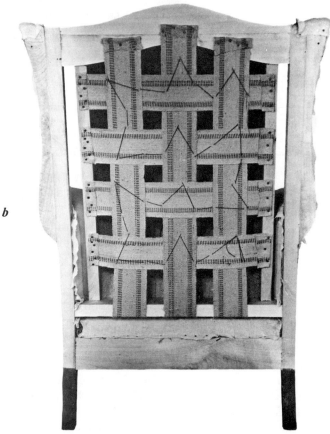

b

Fig. a, b 8:09B

Fig. c 8:09B

SEC. 8:10B   ARMTOP BURLAP / For knife-edge, scroll, and rounded arms, make inside arm burlap large enough to incase understuffing for basic shape of armtop (Secs. 8:11, 8:12). Do not overturn it when tacking on inner side of armboard.

SEC. 8:10C   MEASURE, INSTALL INSIDE ARM BURLAP / [1] *Back of arm finishes through arm cavity.* Measure for burlap from top of inner side of armboard to bottom inner side of arm liner, and from face of front post to 2 inches behind back post. Extra goods at the back allows arm upholstery to finish through arm cavity and be tacked to the back post. Add 2 inches to both measured length and width for general handling. After installing burlap, cut it (Sec. 5:15) from the back edge to corners of the arm cavity and pull flap through (Fig. *a* 8:09B). [2] *Back of arm finishes through back cavity.* Same as [1] above except at back. There, burlap reaches to and is tacked permanently along middle of the back post (Fig. *b* 8:09B), or along vertical arm liner or upright (Fig. *c* 4:14) put in many chairs and sofas designed for thick backs.   [*3*] *Back of arm joining inside back upholstery* (Fig. *c* 8:09B). Same as [*1*] above except at back. There, burlap reaches to and is tacked permanently along middle of back of back post.   [*4*] *T-shaped arm.* Burlap as in [*1*] and [*2*] above, but at top of inside arm tack burlap permanently along inner side of underarm strip, about ¾-inch below armboard when possible.   [*5*] *Exposed-wood arm.* Unless inside arm is exposed-wood at the back, burlap as in [*1*] through [*4*] above according to where upholstery finishes. Along exposed-wood parts tack burlap at least ½ inch from limits of arm upholstery; ¾ inch is better. Install built-up edge, if any (Sec. 8:08).

**SEC. 8:11
PLANNING
ARMTOPS**

SEC. 8:11A /   Basic types of arms are in Fig. 8:02. Except for scroll and rounded arms, which must be understuffed for basic shape, building up an armtop is optional. However, the size of an armtop in relation to the rest of an article, the stature of the person for whom an article is built, and installation of the cover should be considered. If cloth-tuft or loop buttons (Sec. 3:60) will be used, drill small holes in armboard for twines of buttons.

SEC. 8:11B KNIFE-EDGE ARMTOP /   Understuff for durability of cover. Incase armtop loose stuffing with burlap (Sec. 8:10B) to keep it from sagging.

SEC. 8:11C FLAT CURVED, BORDERED ARMTOPS /   These usually are not understuffed when a plain cover will be used on all or part of the inside surface (Fig. *a* 1:37). Due to the curve, a cover would not finish neatly over the armtop. For an example of a bordered armtop, see Fig. *e* 1:48.

SEC. 8:11D PROPORTION /   What are "good" or "pleasing" proportions is a matter of personal taste, but here are some generally accepted features.   [*1*] *Scroll and rounded arms.* Shape of a front post generally sets a good proportionate size for the armtop.   [*2*] *Square-scroll arms.* These are relatively square at the front. If the top is not built up enough it often seems too flat and weak, and may be difficult to finish at the front with a separate post facing. If built up too much for its width, an armtop seems top-heavy and weak.   [*3*] *T-shaped arms.* The armtops usually are rectangular rather than square at the front (Fig. *b* 1:46). The effects of building up an armtop are the same as in [*2*] above.   [*4*] *Modern square and bordered inside arms.* Building up a modern square armtop (Fig. *c* 1:42), or the armtop of a bordered inside arm (Figs. *b* 1:42, 1:63) affects only height of arm.

SEC. 8:11E HEIGHT OF USER / Most short people are more comfortable in chairs with low rather than high arms. But more important than general stature is a person's height between hips and shoulders. People tall in this respect usually are more comfortable when chair arms are moderately high instead of low.

SEC. 8:11F EFFECT ON COVER / [*1*] *Knife-edge, scroll, and rounded arms.* Because these do not have definite breaks between inside arms and tops (Figs. *b* 1:38, *c* 1:45, *a* 1:46), building up the top has no effect on installing a cover. [*2*] *Square-scroll, modern square, and T-shaped arms.* When these armtops are built up appreciably with a soft stuffing, the breaks between top, sides, and front are apt to be rounded instead of fairly sharp. Most modern square (Fig. *c* 1:42) and square-scroll arms (Fig. *b* 1:46) look better when the top edges are fairly sharp. For T-shaped arms (Fig. *a* 1:46) a slightly rounded break often is preferred. The desired final shape of these armtops determines the understuffing for building basic shape (Sec. 8:11G).

SEC. 8:11G STUFFING FOR SQUARE-SCROLL AND T-SHAPED ARMTOPS / Use either loose or compact stuffing (Secs. 3:27–3:44). Compact stuffing generally is easier to use and, for inexperienced upholsterers, more practical. [*1*] *When armtop will be built up appreciably* and be fairly soft, use hair-and-fiber loose stuffing or medium density compact stuffing. Loose stuffing must be stitched to build and hold shape. [*2*] *When sharp breaks* between top, front, and sides are wanted, compact stuffing generally is used. Loose stuffing requires careful stitching to build and hold shape. [*3*] *An especially flat* armtop generally is built up with wood and felted padding (Sec. 3:49). [*4*] *When an armtop is not to be built up* but merely stuffed enough to protect the cover, loose stuffing may be used. But as a rule medium or hard foam rubber or polyfoam, or felted padding, is used for simplicity and more evenly distributed stuffing.

SEC. 8:11H MODERN SQUARE ARM / The cover generally is welted (Sec. 11:08) along the top of the inside and outside arms (Fig. *c* 1:42). Inside welting is machine sewn to inside arm cover. Outside welting may be sewn, but usually is tacked to frame. To do this neatly and firmly along outer edge of armtop, it must have very little stuffing. Most modern square armtops are stuffed with a thin layer of polyfoam, foam rubber, or felted padding. An appreciable armtop build-up is done with wood.

SEC. 8:11I BORDERED INSIDE ARM / The armtop cover is usually a simple pull-around, finishing on inner and outer surfaces some distance down from the top (Figs. *b* 1:42, 1:63). Usually there are fairly sharp breaks between top and other surfaces. For stuffing, see Sec. 8:11G.

**SEC. 8:12
BUILDING
KNIFE-EDGE,
SCROLL, AND
ROUNDED
ARMTOPS**

SEC. 8:12A / Most of these frames are flat and have only a suggestion of shape. For example, in Fig. 8:13E only the top of the front post indicates that the arm is meant to be a scroll type. First understuff (Fig. 8:09B) armtop to build basic shape, then stuff or "overstuff" for resilience, softness, and final shape. Scroll and rounded armtops are understuffed for durability, shape, and softness; knife-edge armtops for durability (Sec. 8:11B). Basic shape usually is about the same as that of a finished armtop, but smaller throughout; compare understuffed and finished armtops, Figs. 8:09B and *b* 1:35. Basic shape should be moderately hard and firm rather than resilient. Understuffing should be short-fiber loose stuffing, such as hair-and-fiber (Sec. 3:29), or hard compact stuffing (Secs. 3:41–3:44). *Tools: For loose stuffing:* Upholsterer's hammer, shears, regulator, tape measure; curved needle for roll edge (Secs. 2:02, 2:04, 2:07, 2:16; 2:06). *For compact stuffing:* Shears, tape measure. *Materials: For loose stuffing:* Tacks, burlap; twine for roll edge (Secs. 3:03, 3:14; 3:08). *For compact stuffing:* Bonding agent (Sec. 3:46).

SEC. 8:12B LOOSE STUFFING / Unless armtop casing was allowed when burlapping an inside arm (Sec. 8:10), measure a strip of burlap long enough to cover armtop understuffing from front to back posts, and wide enough to cover from side to side of armboard. Measure width along top of post that does not have a built-up edge; if there is a built-up edge, measure width along the top of it. [1] *For knife-edge armtops width* of casing should be about 1 inch more than the distance from the inside bottom to the outside top of the armboard. [2] *For all armtop casings* add 2 inches to measured length and 4 to measured width for general handling of goods. [3] *Install* (Sec. 5:02) burlap strip from front to back post. I—For knife-edge arms tack strip near the bottom edge of the inner side of the armboard. II—For scroll (Fig. 8:09B) and rounded arms, tack burlap strip along the inner side of the armboard.

SEC. 8:12C INSTALL UNDERSTUFFING / Install (Secs. 5:11A–C) enough loose stuffing on armboard to build desired basic shape. [1] *Be sure to use enough stuffing* at the front; otherwise the finished armtop is apt to sag just behind the front post or built-up edge. [2] *Basic shape* should be firm and moderately hard for a finished arm to hold shape. [3] *Knife-edge armtops* seldom are built up much more than ½ inch with understuffing. [4] *In all arms*, the basic top should follow, in general, shape of the armboard and of the post above it

(Fig. 8:09B). [*5*] *Build some crown* (Sec. 5:14) into basic shape; it will simplify building final shape of arm.

SEC. 8:12D INCASE UNDERSTUFFING / Draw burlap casing carefully over loose stuffing while pressing the latter toward inner side of armboard. Work casing smooth and tight (Sec. 5:18); knead and squeeze, pound if necessary, armtop into the wanted basic shape. To avoid lumps in cover on outer side of armtop, do not overturn burlap when tacking it. Depending on type of armtop, tack casing first at the middle, then near the front and back, and complete installing from the middle working toward the front and back. [*1*] *Knife-edge arms:* Tack casing along top of armboard close to the edge. [*2*] *Scroll and rounded arms:* Tack casing along outer side of armboard (Fig. 8:09B).

SEC. 8:12E AT THE FRONT / [*1*] *Front post without built-up edge.* Tack burlap casing along top of post from one side of armboard to the other. [*2*] *Front post with built-up edge.* If it is a roll edge or prebuilt edging, sew burlap to it with a running stitch (Fig. 7:24C) from side to side of armboard. If built-up edge is paper, rope, or any material that cannot be stitched, pull burlap casing over it and tack close to bottom of edge; or, overturn casing, pull it fairly tight against understuffing and built-up edge, and tack to post at the armboard.

SEC. 8:12F AT THE BACK / Cut and underturn arm burlap casing to fit snug against post; tack in place. [*1*] *Open-frame wing:* Cut tabs in casing to pull between members of the wing frame, tack to outer side of armboard, Fig. *a* 8:12F. [*2*] *Solid wing:* Cut burlap as necessary to tack it along inner side of wing, *b*, to maintain basic shape of armtop.

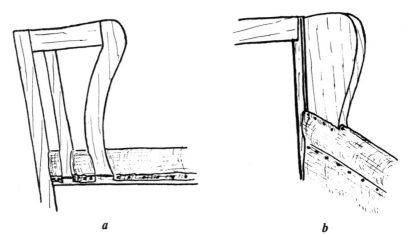

Fig. 8:12F   *a*   *b*

SEC. 8:12G   FINISHING UNDERSTUFFING / Regulate understuffing (Sec. 5:07) to eliminate lumps and hollows, and work it toward the inner side of an armboard if necessary. Do not regulate stuffing away from the outer side of an armtop. If armtop seems weak and flabby after regulating, loosen casing, add stuffing, and re-incase. Do not make understuffing too hard; it should be firm and fairly hard—but not hard as wood.

SEC. 8:12H   COMPACT STUFFING / Rubberized hair understuffing for knife-edge, scroll, and rounded armtops is easy to install and trim to shape. Firm density rubberized hair is preferred for understuffing, but medium density may be used (Sec. 8:12L). Rubberized hair should be as thick as, or slightly thicker than, the maximum planned build-up for an armtop; allow for crown. This simplifies trimming stuffing to shape and reduces waste; two or more layers may be bonded together to build needed thickness.

NOTE: Other compact stuffings are commonly used to understuff knife-edge, scroll, and rounded armtops, but they often are difficult for inexperienced workers to trim to shape. Use the same thickness of these stuffings as rubberized hair; although hard grades are preferred, medium grades can be satisfactory (Sec. 8:12L).

SEC. 8:12I   PREPARE COMPACT UNDERSTUFFING / When understuffing with compact stuffing, a roll edge or prebuilt edging is not needed to build up a surface. Instead, armtop understuffing extends over the top and sides of a front post to its face. Thickness of the stuffing over the top and sides is the desired build-up of the post. *[1] Cut compact stuffing* the size and shape of the top of an armboard from back of front post to front of back post. If a front post is to be built up, understuffing must be long enough to reach the front of the post. *[2] When armtop will be built up* more than 1 inch and the back post slants back appreciably above the armboard, use understuffing long enough to reach the back post throughout; as a rule adding 1 inch to the length of the top of an armboard is enough to allow for slant of back post.

SEC. 8:12J   INSTALL COMPACT UNDERSTUFFING / Fasten (Sec. 3:36) understuffing along top of armboard from front to back. Stuffing often must be shaped at front or back in order to fit snugly. *[1] When front post* will be built up (Sec. 8:12I), cut understuffing to fit smoothly against the back and around top and sides of post. *[2] When back post* slants away from an armboard, shape understuffing to fit smoothly into the corner made by armboard and back post. *[3] When there are wings,* shape understuffing to fit around frame members and through cavities of an open-frame wing (Fig. *a* 8:12F), along inner surface of a solid wing, *b*.   [*4*] *Trim compact understuffing* to wanted basic shape of armtop (Sec. 8:12H); shape by snipping off small pieces, not large chunks. Trim both arms simultaneously, part by part, for best results and to build arms as nearly alike as possible.

SEC. 8:12K MUSLIN CASING / Incasing compact understuffing of proper density or hardness (Sec. 8:12H) is not necessary when it has been trimmed smoothly to basic shape; shape made with compact stuffing need not be any smoother than that made with loose stuffing (Figs. 7:29A, 8:09B). Inexperienced upholsterers may find it easier to trim understuffing to nearly the proper basic shape, then complete shaping by incasing with burlap (Secs. 8:12B–F).

SEC. 8:12L SUBSTITUTE COMPACT STUFFING DENSITY / When compact stuffing of the preferred density for armtop basic shape (Sec. 8:12H) is not available, medium density or hardness may be used. Prepare, install, and trim to basic shape (Secs. 8:12I, J) except: [*1*] *It should project* about ½ inch on each side of armboard (and of the front post if that is to be built up), and ½ inch above the planned maximum height of basic shape.   [*2*] *Incase trimmed* understuffing with burlap (Secs. 8:12B–F) to reduce it to wanted basic shape; this usually makes the understuffing satisfactorily firm.

**SEC. 8:13
BUILDING
SQUARE-
SCROLL,
MODERN
SQUARE,
T-SHAPED, AND
BORDERED
INSIDE ARM
ARMTOPS**

SEC. 8:13A / The frames of most square-scroll (Fig. *b* 1:46), modern square (Fig. *a* 1:42), T-shaped (Fig. *a* 1:46), and bordered inside arms (Figs. *b* 1:42, 1:63) set the shape of an armtop.   [*1*] *Tops of square-scroll and T-shaped arms* usually are built up with understuffing for appearance and comfort, but it may be done with wood for looks only.   [*2*] *Modern square and bordered inside arm armtops* may or may not be built up, since it has little effect on the overall appearance of an article. How arms are built up determines how the cover can be installed. If a modern square armtop is built up more than about ½ inch with stuffing or padding, welt along the top of outside arm (Fig. *a* 1:42) cannot be tacked to the armboard but must be sewn to armtop boxing. To keep from doing this and yet build up the armtop, nail a piece of wood on armboard and then install minimum stuffing or padding. Treat the top of a bordered inside arm (Figs. *b* 1:42, 1:63) as a covered armboard (Sec. 8:07).   [*3*] *Either loose or compact stuffing* is suitable for building basic shape of square-scroll, modern square, and T-shaped arms; sometimes wood is used (Secs. 8:13B, C). Basic shape should be moderately hard, and firm rather than resilient. Understuffing should be short fiber loose stuffing, such as hair-and-fiber (Sec. 3:29); or hard or firm compact stuffing. Tools and materials are the same as in Sec. 8:12A, plus muslin (Sec. 3:48) if using loose stuffing.

SEC. 8:13B   SQUARE-SCROLL ARM   /   To strengthen the front of a square-scroll armtop being built up appreciably with stuffing, and to shape it for a sharper break between top and front, fasten a wooden shaping block to the top of the post, Fig. 8:13B; use wood at least 1-inch thick.   [1] *For loose stuffing* make shaping block large enough to build top to just a little less than planned finished height of armtop.   [2] *For compact stuffing* make shaping block large enough to build top to at least ½ inch less than the planned finished height of armtop.   [3] *At back,* if armboard projects out from the back post, install a shaping block similar to the one at the front.   [4] *It is better* to make a shaping block too low than too high; it can be built to the wanted height with stuffing. If a block is too high and the necessary amount of stuffing to protect the cover is used, the armtop will be higher than planned, perhaps too high to be in good proportion to its width.

Fig. 8:13B

SEC. 8:13C   LOOSE STUFFING: SQUARE-SCROLL AND T-SHAPED ARMS   /   When these armtops will be built up more than about 2 inches and are to be upholstered with loose stuffing, first build up with wood to eliminate a large and possibly weak roll edge or prebuilt edging. Use wood thick enough to allow for a built-up edge not more than 1½ inches high; cut it the shape and size of the armtop, and fasten permanently to armboard.   [1] *Install built-up edges* (Secs. 5:05, 5:06) on armtop along all parts that will be exposed when arm is completely upholstered, Fig. *a* 8:13C. If there are shaping blocks, the top of the built-up edges must be flush with tops of blocks, *b.*   [2] *Stuff armtop* (Secs. 5:11A–C). Be sure to place enough stuffing along all built-up edges; otherwise armtop may pack down and let the relatively hard edges work against and wear out the cover.   [3] *Incase understuffed armtop* with muslin (Secs. 6:02D–F), tacking on sides, front, and back just below top surfaces. Push back stuffing that works over built-up edges; it may cause lumps in the cover.   [4] *Regulate* (Sec. 5:07) stuffing to make a smooth, even surface. Do not work stuffing away from built-up edges.   [5] *If incased stuffing* is weak or has notice-

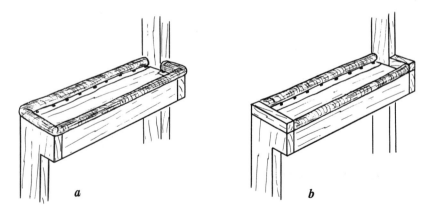

Fig. 8:13C   *a*   *b*

able go-down away from built-up edges, restuff armtop. Square-scroll, modern square, and T-shaped arms, being basically flat, may be forced out of shape under normal usage more than rounded arms. To keep them from packing down away from edges, understuffing should be as high as the top of the built-up edges, and firm enough to maintain that height.

SEC. 8:13D COMPACT STUFFING: SQUARE-SCROLL, MODERN SQUARE, AND T-SHAPED ARM ARMTOPS / When armtop only is to be upholstered with compact stuffing, install a slab (Secs. 5:11F, 5:13) cut to fit it exactly, Fig. *a* 8:13D. If there are shaping blocks (Sec. 8:13B) cut stuffing to fit snugly over them, or bond one slab onto another, *b*.

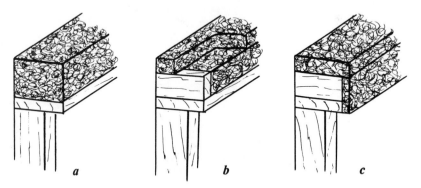

Fig. 8:13D   *a*   *b*   *c*

In square-scroll arms an additional slab of stuffing often is fastened to outer side of armtop, *c*, to make it a little puffier; install it before top slab.

*NOTE: If square-scroll and modern square arms are to be completely upholstered with compact stuffing and armtops are **not** to be built up, stuff them when stuffing inside arms (Sec. 8:14).*

SEC. 8:13E   T-SHAPED ARM   /   Stuff top of T-shaped arm as in Fig. *a* 8:13D, but in better proportion of width to height (Fig. *a* 1:46).

SEC. 8:13F   SQUARE-SCROLL ARM   /   When inside arms and top are upholstered with compact stuffing without shaping blocks, first install inside arm stuffing (Sec. 8:14), then armtop stuffing, Fig. *a* 8:13F. If

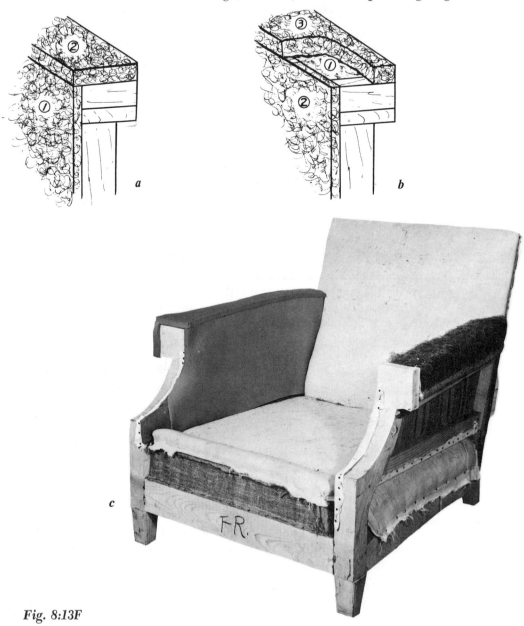

Fig. 8:13F

there are shaping blocks, *b*, first install stuffing cut to fit armtop between blocks; then stuff inside arm, and possibly the outer side of the armtop (Sec. 8:13D); lastly, stuff armtop. This builds an evenly soft, smooth top surface, which is especially important when stuffing with rubberized hair. Built-up square-scroll arms overstuffed with polyfoam or foam rubber often have rubberized hair understuffing, Fig. *c* 8:13F. It should completely cover the armboard and be as high as, or even slightly higher than, the shaping blocks, if any.

SEC. 8:13G FELTED PADDING / For a very hard square-scroll or modern square armtop, stuff with felted padding (Sec. 5:12). To keep lines of top clear and sharp, tear off padding that overhangs sides of armboard. If armtop is to be built up, first fasten a strip of wood of the proper size, shape, and thickness to entire top of arm.

SEC. 8:14 STUFFING FULLY UPHOLSTERED ARMS	**SEC. 8:14A** / For stuffings, see Sec. 8:05. Rounded arms (Fig. *d* 1:45) often are upholstered throughout with loose stuffing due to the cost of using compact stuffing for outside arms. *Tools:* Upholsterer's hammer, shears, tape measure; for loose stuffing, large curved needle, regulator (Secs. 2:02, 2:04, 2:16; 2:06, 2:07). *Materials:* Tacks, stuffing, muslin; for loose stuffing, upholstery twine; for compact stuffing, bonding agent (Secs. 3:03, 3:28–3:47, 3:48; 3:08; 3:06D).

SEC. 8:14B LOOSE STUFFING / According to the type arm and how the front will be covered, install loose stuffing, tacking and stitching to frame and burlap. [*1*] *Back post.* When arm upholstery finishes through arm cavity (Sec. 8:09B), do not tack stuffing to back post. [*2*] *Knife-edge, scroll, and rounded arms.* Cover inside arm with stuffing from outer side of armboard to bottom of liner. [*3*] *Square-scroll, and modern square arms.* Cover inside arm with stuffing up to but not over top edge of the armboard, and down to bottom of liner. [*4*] *T-shaped arm.* Armtop: Install enough stuffing along sides and front of armtop to smooth out irregularities in built-up edges, and to shape arm. Stuff back of armtop only if it will be exposed when article is completely upholstered. Most T-shaped arms finish into back (Fig. *a* 1:46), not away from it. Below armtop: The inside arm is generally stuffed only with felted padding. [*5*] *Exposed-wood arm.* Do not tack or stitch stuffing closer than about 1 inch to limits of arm upholstery. [*6*] *Bordered armtop.* Install stuffing up to but not over top of armboard. [*7*] *Bordered inside arm.* Stuffing extends to planned lower limit of armboard cover (Fig. *b* 1:42) or of inside arm border (Fig. 1:63). For armboard (Sec. 8:07). [*8*] *Front cover.* If a pull-around (Figs. 1:30, 1:42) or a similar boxed cover (Fig. *b* 1:31) is planned, put a thin layer of stuffing over the face of the front post

from top to: I—An inch or so below seat or deck when it has a roll or a hard edge, or a spring edge attached to post. II—The seat rail when a seat has a spring edge not attached to post, which is the case in most loose-cushion spring-edge seats.

NOTE: Regardless of the type cover planned for the face of a front post and the type edge on a seat, the fronts of square-scroll, modern square, and T-shaped arms are usually stuffed only with felted padding.

SEC. 8:14C   SHAPING LOOSE STUFFING / Complete stuffing arm to desired shape and fullness. Shape cannot be accurately known until stuffing is incased, but must be judged while stuffing. "Desired shape" is a matter of taste, but some points should be observed as a general rule. The overall arm from bottom to top usually is fairly straight, Fig. *a* 8:14C, or flares slightly outward, *b*. In straight arms some crown toward seat between top and bottom is needed to keep them from becoming hollow. But in very few articles does an arm flare inward at the top, *c*.

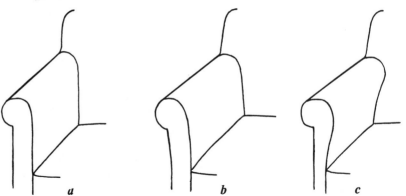

Fig. 8:14C   *a*   *b*   *c*

NOTE: While stuffing to build shape from top to bottom, be careful to preserve shape from front to back—straight or curved.

SEC. 8:14D   AMOUNT OF LOOSE STUFFING / How much stuffing is needed, Fig. 8:14D, varies with the type of arm and its wanted thickness. Install at least enough stuffing to keep tacks and stitches from being felt through muslin casing, and to build shape. [*1*] *Bottom.* Use enough stuffing at the bottom, along arm liner, for seat and arm to meet without a gap. [*2*] *Front post.* If post has a built-up edge, be sure to install enough stuffing along the back of it; otherwise arms will eventually slump or sag, and built-up edge will wear through cover. [*3*] *Pull-around inside arm cover.* For this type cover (Fig. *c* 1:35), place enough stuffing along the inner side and face of front post to

Fig. 8:14D

build a distinct, but rounded instead of sharp, inside corner. [4] *Knife-edge arms.* Use enough stuffing along outer top to build a small simulated roll edge. Without it, the frame soon may work against and wear out the cover. Do not tack this stuffing to outer side of arm-board; it will interfere with good installation of outside arm welt. [5] *Arm cavity.* When arm upholstery finishes through arm cavity, put enough stuffing between rear strip of webbing and post for arm and inside back upholsteries to meet without a gap; it may be altered during and after installation of arm and back muslin casings. [6] *Rounded arms.* These usually have very little overstuffing. If the inside arm and top are stuffed too much, there may be a noticeable break between the top and outside arm unless it also is stuffed (outside arms generally are not stuffed). But if a rounded arm has a built-up edge along the sides and top of the front post, the outside arm must be stuffed, usually when upholstering the outside arm (Chapter 18).

SEC. 8:14E COMPACT STUFFING / Before measuring and installing compact stuffing (Secs. 8:14F–I), inside arms should be lightly uphol-stered with loose stuffing and incased with muslin. This simplifies building shape and crown, and provides a smooth, even surface for bonding compact stuffing. Install loose stuffing (Secs. 8:14B–D) but do not stuff arm fronts. Incase with muslin (Secs. 8:15–8:22) except: [1] *Front:* Tack casing on face of front post near inner edge (Fig.

8:13H) regardless of how front will be covered. [2] *Square-scroll and modern square arms:* Tack casing on armboard near inner top edge.

Sec. 8:14F   Width of Compact Stuffing / Regardless of the type arm, use compact stuffing wide enough to reach from the front edge of a front post, Fig. 8:14F, or from about ½ inch behind the front limits of upholstery in exposed-wood arms, to: [1] *The back post* when arm upholstery finishes through arm cavity. [2] *An inch or so* beyond the surface of an inside back when arm upholstery finishes through a back cavity. Thickness of back must be planned in advance (Secs. 10:00–10:04). [3] *The middle of* the front of a back post when inside arm and back upholsteries join one another (Fig. *c* 8:09B).

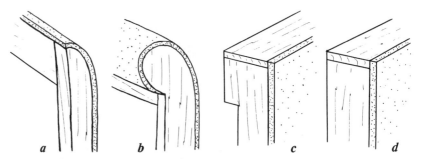

Fig. 8:14F   *a*   *b*   *c*   *d*

Sec. 8:14G   Length of Compact Stuffing / For all arms except T-shaped (Sec. 8:14J), use compact stuffing long enough to reach from inner bottom edge of arm liner to, depending on the type arm, the point of finishing at the top: [1] *Knife-edge arms.* The outer edge of armboard (Fig. *a* 8:14F). [2] *Scroll arms.* The lower outside edge of armboard (*b*). [3] *Bordered armtop.* The inner top edge of armboard (*c*). [4] *Exposed-wood arms.* About ½ inch below the upper limits of arm upholstery. [5] *Square-scroll* and *modern square arms.* The inner top edge of armboard (*c, d*) built up or not, or stuffed with felted padding. [6] *Modern square arms.* Inside and top may be upholstered with a single sheet of compact stuffing instead of two, Fig. 8:14G. A single sheet, *b*, makes a rounded break at the inner top edge. But unless using fairly thick compact stuffing, the seam allowances of the cover usually fill in the rounded portion and give a fairly sharp break. [7] *Bordered inside arm.* Stuffing extends to planned lower limit of armboard cover (Fig. *b* 1:42), or of inside armboard (Fig. 1:63). For armboard (Sec. 8:07).

NOTE: For understuffing tops of arms listed in [1]–[5] above, see Sec. 8:13.

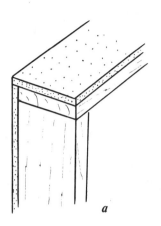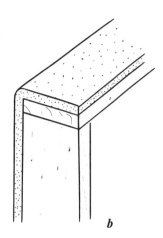

Fig. 8:14G   *a*   *b*

SEC. 8:14H SIZE ALLOWANCES / Add 1 inch to both measured width and length for general handling of compact stuffing, and to allow for some pull-over at front and top edges of front post. For mechanics of installing compact stuffing, Secs. 5:11D, 5:13. Start installation at bottom of arm liner and work toward point of finishing at top. When using tacking tape take care not to pull compact stuffing over those parts, such as the outer side of a knife-edge armboard, on which muslin casing and cover will be tacked. Stuffing on these parts could interfere with good installation of casing and cover.

SEC. 8:14I FOR PULL-AROUND, BOXED COVERS / After upholstering inside arm and top with compact stuffing, install two layers of felted padding (Sec. 5:12) on face of front post (Sec. 8:14B[8]). Tear off padding that overhangs outer side of post; it could interfere with good installation of the cover and make a lumpy edge.

SEC. 8:14J FELTED PADDING / T-shaped inside arms, below armboards, usually are stuffed with two or three layers of felted padding, depending on desired thickness, shape, and crown; some inside arms are quite flat, others are somewhat puffy. Use felted padding wide enough to reach, without stretching, from front edge of front post to the back (Sec. 8:14F); and long enough to reach from the bottom of arm liner to about ¾ inch below armboard. Whether or not padding is used as stuffing on the face of a front post depends on how cover will be installed (Sec. 8:14I). Install one layer of padding at a time. Inside arm padding may be installed separately from that, if any, for front of post; the final layer should cover both. Interlocking of fibers holds the second layer of padding to the one tacked to arm front. Friction between padding, burlap, and muslin casing holds inside arm padding in place.

SEC. 8:14K   INCASE WITH MUSLIN / Muslin casing for arms upholstered with compact stuffing or felted padding is not essential, but is
advisable for inexperienced upholsterers as it gives valuable practice
for covering. Also, an incased article shows clearly where changes or
corrections should be made before or while covering.

**SEC. 8:15
MUSLIN
CASING
FOR FULLY
UPHOLSTERED
ARMS**

SEC. 8:15A / For best results in preparing arm muslin casing,
especially by inexperienced upholsterers, make generous measurements, and plan and mark measurements straight along warp and weft
of goods, not on the bias. Casing for most arms except T-shaped (Sec.
8:15C) is a simple, single sheet of goods. However, use: [*1*] *Boxed
casing* (Sec. 11:06) for square-scroll and modern square arms, Fig.
8:15A, when the front is stuffed or padded.   [*2*] *Single-piece casing*
for a square-scroll arm when the front will be covered by a panel or
border.   *Tools:* Shears, tape measure, sewing machine for boxed casing (Secs. 2:04, 2:15, 2:16).   *Materials:* Muslin; thread for boxed casing (Secs. 3:48; 3:08).

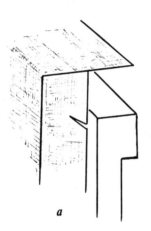
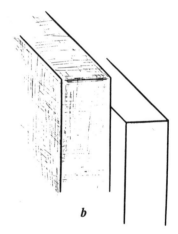

a   *b*

Fig. 8:15A

SEC. 8:15B   MEASURE WIDTH OF CASING / Measure greatest width,
Fig. 8:15B, from front to back of an inside arm depending on how
arm upholstery will finish at front and back.   [*1*] *Front of arm stuffed.*
Finish muslin casing around and on outer side of post.   [*2*] *Front of
arm not stuffed.* Finish casing on inner front edge of post, or, for a
bordered inside arm (Fig. 1:63), at planned inner limit of the border.
[*3*] *Square-scroll, modern square boxed casing.* Inside arm casing extends about 1 inch beyond inner front edge of post. Boxing or arm
front casing for a square-scroll arm and boxing for top and front of a
modern square arm (Fig. 8:15A) should be about 2 inches wider than
armtop.   [*4*] *Exposed-wood arm.* Casing extends to about ½ inch back
from the front limits of inside arm upholstery.   [*5*] *Arm cavity.* When

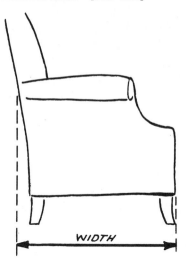

Fig. 8:15B

arm upholstery finishes through arm cavity, measure for muslin casing to a couple of inches beyond the back post; this allows arm upholstery to be pulled through the cavity and tacked to the side of the back post. [6] *Back cavity.* When arm upholstery finishes through back cavity, casings extend only to the back of the post or an inch or so beyond it. [7] *Inside arm and back upholsteries joined.* Arm casing extends an inch or so beyond the front of the back post.

SEC. 8:15C T-SHAPED ARM / Measure width of inside arm casing below armboard (Sec. 8:15B). Measure armtop casing from the bottom of one side of an armboard to that of the other; add 4 inches for general handling of goods.

SEC. 8:15D MEASURE LENGTH OF CASING / Measure greatest length of inside arm muslin casing from outer side of arm liner, under it and up inner surface as follows, depending on the type arm. [1] *Knife-edge arm.* Casing finishes on outer top edge of armboard (Fig. 8:09D). [2] *Scroll arm.* Casing finishes on outer side of underarm strip (Fig. 8:16E). [3] *Rounded arm.* Casing extends over armtop and down to outer bottom edge of seat rail. Casing this long eliminates a definite break between outside arm and armtop, and allows outside arm stuffing, if any, to be incased. [4] *Square-scroll arm.* Casing extends to bottom of outer side of armboard. Arm boxing extends from about 1 inch above top of front post to: I—an inch or so below top of seat or deck when it has a roll edge, hard edge, or spring edge attached to the front post; II—the seat rail when spring-edge is not attached to post. [5] *Modern square arm.* Casing extends to inner top edge of armboard. Top-and-front boxing goes from back post to seat rail as in [4] above. [6] *T-shaped arm.* Inside arm casing extends to top of inner side of underarm strip. Armtop casing extends from front bottom of armboard to that at the back when the back of an armtop will be exposed when upholstery is completed, or to the back post when an armtop finishes into inside back upholstery (Fig. *a* 1:46).   [*7*] *Bordered armtop.* Casing finishes on inner top edge of armboard (Figs. *a* 1:37, *b* 1:48).   [*8*] *Exposed-wood arm.* Casing extends to ½ inch below top limits of inside arm upholstery.   [*9*] *Bordered inside arm.* Casing extends to ½ inch below planned lower limits of armboard cover (Fig. *b* 1:42) or of inside arm border (Fig. 1:63).

SEC. 8:15E MEASURING, PREPARING CASING / To reduce waste, compress loose stuffing slightly with the tape when measuring for casing. Add 4 inches to all measurements for general handling of casing. Sew together inside arm and top, or top and front, casings for square-scroll and modern square arms (Fig. 8:15A). Sew with ½-inch seam allowances, and sew as straight as possible. Seam allowances are on inside of finished casing. The straighter seams are, the sharper will be the breaks along edges of an armtop, and the easier it is to install casing smoothly and neatly. To install casing on curved arms see Secs. 8:16–8:20; straight arms, Secs. 8:21, 8:22.

SEC. 8:16 CURVED ARM MUSLIN CASING	SEC. 8:16A / To establish shape of an inside arm that curves from front to back, tighten casing (Sec. 5:18) mostly in a vertical direction. Slicktack casing (Sec. 5:16) until completely adjusted. Cut (Sec. 5:15) where necessary. *Tools:* Upholsterer's hammer, shears, regulator (Secs. 2:02, 2:04, 2:07). *Materials:* Tacks (Sec. 3:03).

SEC. 8:16B POSITION, SET CURVED ARM CASING / Center casing over stuffing, pull bottom edge under arm liner. Start at middle of arm. Pull casing moderately snug to point of finishing at top and tack it, Point 1, Fig. 8:16B. The order of tacking keeps stuffing in place and sets casing straight.   [*1*] *Scroll arm.* Finish muslin casing on the outer side of underarm strip close to armboard, *a;* this basically shapes entire armtop. Finishing it close to armboard allows inside arm and outside arm covers to be set tight against bottom of armboard, making their junction less noticeable.   [*2*] *Knife-edge arm.* Finish casing on outer side of armboard, *b,* about ¾ inch below top edge to leave space for the cover.   [*3*] *Bordered armtop.* Finish casing about ¾ inch from inner top edge of armboard, *c,* to leave space for the cover.   [*4*] *Exposed-wood arm.* Finish casing when possible ½ inch from limits of inside arm upholstery, *d,* to leave space for the cover.   [*5*] *Tighten and work casing* moderately snug toward bottom of inside arm, and sliptack it to the outer side of the liner directly below the first tack, Point 2. This establishes basic shape or curve of arm.

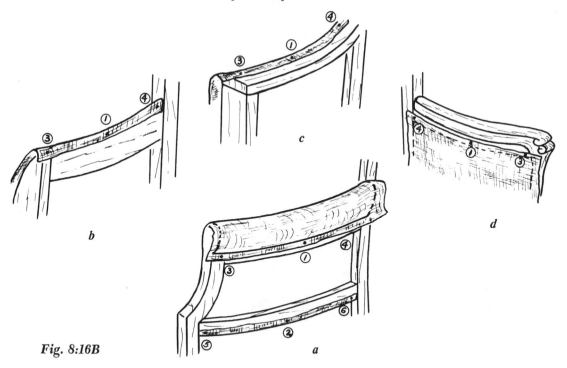

Fig. 8:16B

SEC. 8:16C / Tighten curved arm cover or casing primarily in a vertical direction in order to establish and maintain shape; tighten just enough horizontally to make it smooth and taut. Tighten horizontally gradually from middle toward front and back of a curved arm; basic shape will not be altered unless casing is worked unreasonably tight. While setting casing as in Fig. 8:16B, tighten it enough vertically and horizontally to fit fairly snug, but do not try to build final shape. Midway between seat and top surface of an arm draw casing around the inner edge of the front post. Tighten casing enough to keep it smooth and its grain fairly straight on the inside arm proper; due to crown, the grain may not be perfectly straight. [1] *Front of arm not stuffed or padded.* Finish casing near inner edge of the front of post. [2] *Front of arm stuffed or padded.* Finish casing on outer side of post about ¾ inch from front edge. [3] *Scooped arm front.* Cut or notch casing at several points for it to expand along the scoop, Fig. 8:16C. Due to the scoop, the vertical grain of a casing or cover slants toward outer side of post.

SEC. 8:16D   CURVED ARM WITH WING / One type of curved-arm wing follows the curve of an arm from front to back; the other type is straight from front to back regardless of the arm and usually is a solid base, Fig. 8:16D. There are chairs in which a back curves into arms (Fig. *b* 1:38), and the parts of the back above arms may be called wings;

Fig. 8:16C

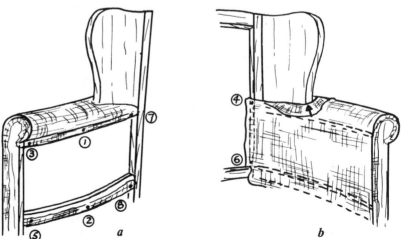

Fig. 8:16D   *a*   *b*

they usually are upholstered as part of a back. Except for fitting it
around wing, set in place muslin casing for a curved arm with wing

the same way as for a plain curved arm.   [*1*] *At Points 1, 2, and 3,* Fig. 8:16D, install casing as in Secs. 8:16B, C.   [*2*] *Tack casing at:* Point 4 on inner side or on back of back post slightly above armboard; Point 5 on outer side of arm liner at front post; Point 6 below Point 4 at top of back liner.   [*3*] *Cut casing* to fit around inner front edge of wing. For best results cut along the same thread of goods from edge to wing. If the first point of tacking comes loose during cutting, after completing the cut simply retack at Point 1.   [*4*] *Draw upper portion* of cut casing over armtop and tack in place: I—If wing follows curve of outer side of armboard, tack casing (Point 7) to outer side of armboard ½ inch behind front of wing; II—if wing is straight and solid base, instead of following the outer curve of the armboard, the bottom of a wing may be set back from it. In this case shape of the armtop usually is carried along the outer side of a wing to the back, and Point 7 of setting the casing is on the outer side of the armboard at the back post; but first install additional stuffing to extend the shape of the armtop to the back.

NOTE: For both I and II, cut casing to fit around outer front edge of wing; as well as allowing casing or cover to fit smoothly, this cut leaves a small tab that later will be tacked to front of wing.

[*5*] *Cut casing* to fit around back and arm liners, Fig. *b* 8:16D, cut from corner of goods to frame. This leaves material on each side of cut for underturning and making the strongest final tacking.   [*6*] *Draw bottom of casing* under arm liner and tack to outer side of it at the back post, Point 8, *a*.   [*7*] *At the front* set casing as in Sec. 8:16C.

**SEC. 8:17
TIGHTENING
CURVED ARM
CASING**

SEC. 8:17A /   Additional loose stuffing, or felted padding if upholstering with compact stuffing, usually is needed to improve shape when tightening casing. When upholstering with loose stuffing, small lumps and hollows usually can be regulated (Sec. 5:07); if not, open casing and alter stuffing. Noticeable hollows and lumps sometimes may be hidden by felted padding installed with the cover, but this is poor upholstering practice. Good final shape seldom can be built by inexperienced upholsterers in a single tightening of casing or cover. If tightened too much or too quickly, the shape may be rough and the goods loose in some places, too tight in others. Avoid pullmarks (Sec. 5:19); they often cause grooves or hollows in the casing, especially in knife-edge and scroll arms, which may show through the cover.

SEC. 8:17B INITIAL TIGHTENING /   Tighten the major portion of a curved arm first, then the front and back. On most arms the grain of a casing or cover works down toward the front bottom; this is due to crown at the middle of an inside arm proper, and to tightening goods around front post. Often this downward slant tendency may be overcome by tightening toward the front top; however, for good appearance it is more important to keep the grain straight at the top than at the bottom of an inside arm. Start tightening at the first point of setting casing or cover on a curved arm in order to preserve its shape. Remove sliptack, work goods smooth and fairly tight from the middle toward the top, resliptack at Point 1 in Figs. 8:16B, D. [*1*] *Knife-edge arm.* Stuffing should extend slightly beyond, but not hang down over, the outer top edge of the frame. Push back enough stuffing, or add some if necessary, to build a small simulated roll edge along outer top edge of armboard, Fig. *a* 8:17B. Padding the sharp edge of a frame protects the cover; but stuffing hanging over edge may interfere with good installation of cover. [*2*] *Scroll arm.* Stuffing extends down to outer bottom of armboard but not under it, *b.* By extending to bottom of armboard, stuffing completes shaping the outer side of an armtop. But stuffing under an armboard may interfere with good installation of cover. [*3*] *Bordered armtop.* Stuffing extends slightly over inner top edge of armboard, *c*, to protect cover. [*4*] *Exposed-wood arm.* I—if arm does not have a built-up edge, *d*, push stuffing back enough, or add some, to make it firm and to build a small edge at least ½ inch from the limits of arm upholstery; II—if arm has a built-up edge, *e*, push back stuffing that overhangs it, as it could cause lumps in the finished arm.

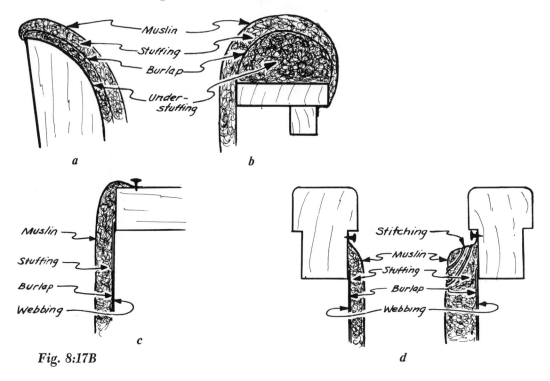

Fig. 8:17B

NOTE: There should not be any stuffing on the part of a rabbet to which the cover will be tacked.

SEC. 8:17C TIGHTEN TOWARD TOP AND FRONT, BACK / Tighten arm casing from middle toward top and front, and tack to same part of frame as the first tack, but an inch or so toward the front. Tighten goods from middle toward top and back; tack as before, but toward back. Throughout the setting of these tacks, keep grain of goods fairly straight, allowing for crown of inner surface.

SEC. 8:17D TIGHTEN DOWNWARD / Repeat operations in Secs. 8:17B, C, at Point 2 on arm liner (Figs. 8:16B, D), tightening goods from middle down. If after tightening around liner there is a gap between an inside arm and the seat or deck, loosen arm casing or cover and add enough stuffing to fill gap.

SEC. 8:17E GENERAL TIGHTENING / Continue tightening casing on a curved arm (Secs. 8:17B–D), working alternately from middle toward front and back, and between top and bottom. When tightening near front post, especially on a scooped arm, goods may be worked directly toward the front. This simplifies building shape into the lower front part of the inside arm proper.

SEC. 8:17F CURVED ARM WITH WING / Except at wing, tighten casing or cover the same way as for a plain arm (Secs. 8:17A–E). [*1*] *Open-frame wing* upholstered independently of arm, Fig. *a* 8:17F. Cut inside arm goods to form tabs or strips that can be drawn between members of wing frame. Tighten goods from middle toward top and back of arm. Tack armtop tabs to same part of armboard as the rest of a casing or cover. [*2*] *Solid-base wing* upholstered independently of arm, *b*. Tighten goods from middle toward top and back of arm.

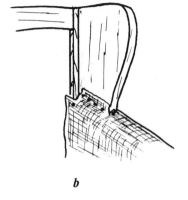

Fig. 8:17F   *a*   *b*

Tack along inner side of wing in a line that preserves the shape of the inner armtop. If wing is straight and set back from the outer side of an armboard (Fig. 8:16D), tighten outer armtop casing toward back, and along outer surface of the wing to preserve shape of armtop toward the back.   [3] *Inside wing joining* inside arm upholstery (Figs. 1:15, *b* 1:48). Tighten arm casing from middle toward top and back. Later, goods are stitched together throughout wing area (Sec. 9:12D).

NOTE: For all types of wings, when tightening casing it usually is necessary to make new cuts or lengthen others to fit around frame.

[4] *The small tab of goods left in front* of a wing when setting casing or cover (Sec. 8:16F), and possibly enlarged while tightening, is now sliptacked to front of wing frame at level of armtop casing or cover. If the tab is tacked too high or too low it will interfere with good installation of inside arm and wing covers.

SEC. 8:17G CHECKING CASING   /   While tightening casing or cover, which may have to be done several times before they are taut enough and the shape smooth and regular, rub arm rather heavily every so often to test for uniform smoothness and softness. Small lumps or hollows in loose stuffing usually are corrected by regulating; but if there are large flaws, remove casing and alter stuffing. Often there is a fairly large hollow or soft area between strips of arm webbing; correct these by adding stuffing to the soft areas, although in severe cases it is better to restuff an arm. Be sure there is enough stuffing at the front of an armtop; if not, it tends to sag or slump after relatively little use.

**SEC. 8:18
COMPLETING
CASING AT
LOWER ARM
FRONT**

SEC. 8:18A   /   Cut casing just behind front post. Cut from bottom edge of goods to lower inside junction of post and arm liner, Fig. *a* 8:18A. Tighten inside arm casing downward and toward front, and complete sliptacking it along outer side of arm liner to the front post, Point 1, *b*. Tighten tab of goods left from cut enough to keep it smooth and its grain or seam straight. Tack to back of post, Point 2, just below arm liner and as far down post as seat or deck upholstery allows. This holds the arm front casing or cover securely in place and lets it be tightened around the post.

SEC. 8:18B   /   Pull bottom of casing or cover around inner front edge of post. Pull on a downward slant to the point of finishing on the outer side (Fig. 8:16C) or on the face, Fig. 8:18B.   [1] *When seat or deck has roll edge, hard edge, or spring edge attached to front post,* underturn bottom of casing or cover to fit smoothly and tightly against corner of seat (Fig. 8:16C).   [2] *When seat or deck has spring edge not attached to post,* underturn bottom edge of goods to fit smoothly

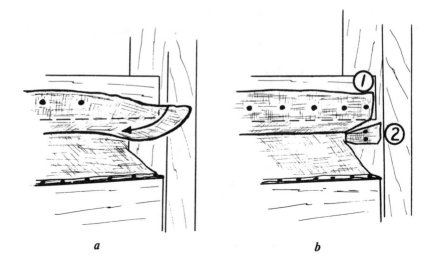

Fig. 8:18A   *a*   *b*

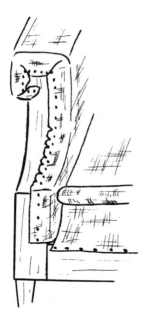

Fig. 8:18B

and tightly against seat rail or casing, Fig. 8:18B.   [3] *Start at middle of front post*, tighten goods toward front and bottom, and sliptack down to bottom.

SEC. 8:18C   ADDITIONAL STUFFING, PADDING / Often stuffing or padding must be added to that already on the face of a front post. [1] *When a panel or border* will cover face of post but there is no built-up edge, place enough stuffing or padding along inner front edge of post and around top to build a small simulated edge projecting about ¼ inch from face.   [2] *When a pull-around casing* is to be used (Fig. 8:16C), stuffing or padding on face of a post should extend evenly and smoothly down to bottom of casing.

SEC. 8:19 COMPLETING CASING AT UPPER ARM FRONT

Sec. 8:19A /   Finishing a casing or cover neatly and smoothly on the upper part of an arm front is not difficult if necessary pleats (Sec. 5:17) and cuts (Sec. 5:15) are made. If a casing is not neat and smooth there may be lumps in a finished armtop at the front, a very noticeable part of a chair or sofa. If a casing is tightened uniformly, depressions in a pleated armtop are due to misplacement of, or insufficient, stuffing. Complete tightening of goods toward front and top of an arm until pleating is necessary. When scooped arm casing finishes on the outer side of a post (Sec. 8:16C), cuts usually must be lengthened or new ones made. After pleating is finished satisfactorily, rub armtop casing lightly toward back to tighten pleats. In addition to other tools and materials for arm upholstery, a small curved needle, upholstery skewers, and upholstery twine may be needed (Secs. 2:06, 2:08, 3:08).

Sec. 8:19B Knife-Edge Arm /   Pleat casing that finishes on front of post as in Fig. *a* 8:19B; one finishing on outer side as in *b*.

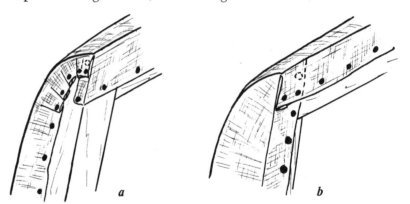

Fig. 8:19B

a   *b*

Sec. 8:19C Scroll Arm Casing Finishing on Post Face /   Pleat as in Sec. 5:17F.

Sec. 8:19D Scroll Arm Casing Finishing on Outer Side of Front Post /   Pleating properly may be difficult. Inexperienced upholsterers should expect to work this several times before producing a neat, strong job (Fig. 8:16C).   [1] *Remove* the front few sliptacks holding armtop casing to underarm strip.   [2] *Tighten* casing from inside arm around scroll toward outer and top edges, drawing it back over them, Fig. *a* 8:19D. The tighter a casing is worked into position here, the easier the rest of the work will be and the smoother and

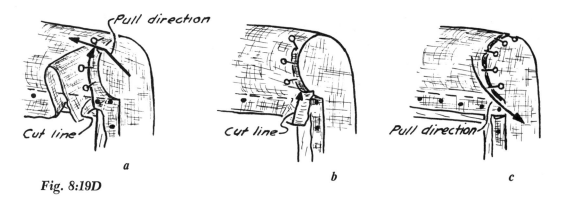

Fig. 8:19D

stronger the finished job. Tack casing at bottom of scroll, and at one or two points along underarm strip. Pin casing in place along outer side of scroll; stuffing often must be altered during this work. After casing is smooth and tight across face of a scroll, cut it along the crease, *a*, to finish about ½ inch from the end of it.   [3] *Draw armtop casing* over front of scroll and cut to finish about ½ inch beyond post, *b*. This eliminates excess goods at the front, which might cause lumps in a finished arm.   [4] *Underturn* front edge of armtop casing, tighten forward and down, *c*. While setting the folded edge along or slightly behind the front edge of a scroll, remove skewers holding face casing, and pin armtop and face casings in place. Tack armtop casing to outer side of post at bottom of scroll. Adjust casings, pushing face casing back under armtop casing, and repin.   [5] *If both casings* are tightened enough and tacked securely, friction will hold them in place along a scroll, especially a small one. But when casings cannot be tightened sufficiently, due to size of a scroll or lack of a worker's skill, blind-stitch (Sec. 13:04) them along the front edge.

SEC. 8:19E   ROUNDED ARM   /   Pleat casing (Sec. 5:17F) except that pleating usually ends at about the level of the outer side of an armboard opposite the point of starting to pleat.

SEC. 8:19F   SQUARE-SCROLL ARM CASING FINISHING ON FRONT OF ARM (FIG 8:18C)   /   Pleat at corners, Fig. 8:19F.

SEC. 8:19G   SQUARE-SCROLL ARM WITH PRE-SEWN CASING   /   [1] *Remove* front few sliptacks holding armtop casing to bottom of armboard. Fold casing back and, if necessary, cut seam between it and face casing; cut to outer top corner of arm, Point 1 in Fig. *a* 8:19G.   [2] *Tighten* face casing downward toward outer side of arm, and tack to bottom of scroll about ¾ inch from front edge, Point 2. Do not tighten casing enough to pull seams away from edges. Trim off excess goods at

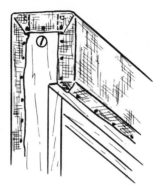

Fig. 8:19F

lower corner of scroll to eliminate unnecessary thicknesses of goods under the covers. [3] *Draw face casing* fairly tight around outer side of armtop, Point 3. Underturn edge of armtop casing, lay fold along edge of scroll and tack to bottom of armboard. [4] *Starting at the top*, push face casing under the fold to tighten it, and pin in place through armtop casing, *b*. Blindstitch (Sec. 13:04) casings together along front edge.

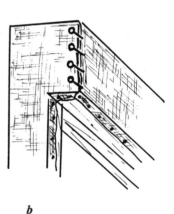

Fig. 8:19G   *a*   *b*

SEC. 8:19H MODERN SQUARE ARM / Pleat on outer side of armboard and front post, Fig. 8:19H.

SEC. 8:19I T-SHAPED ARMTOP / Pleat armtop at corners on underside of armboard, Fig. 8:19I. The inside arm proper usually does not need pleating.

SEC. 8:19J BORDERED ARMTOP / Pleat at corners on top surface of armboard, Fig. 8:19J.

SEC. 8:19K EXPOSED-WOOD ARM / Pleat as in Sec. 5:17D.

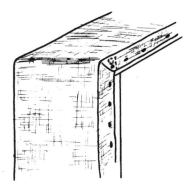

Fig. 8:19H

Fig. 8:19I

Fig. 8:19J

SEC. 8:20 COMPLETING ARM CASING AT BACK OF FULLY UPHOLSTERED ARM	**SEC. 8:20A ARM UPHOLSTERY FINISHING THROUGH INSIDE BACK CAVITY** / Cut casing at arm and back liners to leave a small tab, Fig. 8:20A, to be tacked to inner side of back post to hold bottom of arm casing against the back. Without it, the arm bottom tends to work away from an inside back, forming unsightly wrinkles or a gap between surfaces. *NOTE: When arm upholstery finishes through arm cavity, such a tab, if made, is tacked to the front of a back post under the arm liner.*

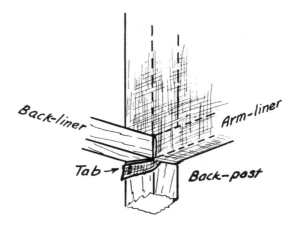

Fig. 8:20A

Tighten arm casing toward back if necessary, and tack permanently along the inner side of the rear of the back post.

SEC. 8:20B   ARM UPHOLSTERY FINISHING THROUGH ARM CAVITY /
Cut inside arm casing straight from the back edge to bottom of arm-board at back post, and from the back edge straight to top of arm liner, Points 1 and 2 in Fig. 8:20B; see Sec. 8:20A for possible holding tab. Draw casing flap through arm cavity, work fairly tight toward outer side of post and sliptack (Fig. 8:16C). Do not tack flap permanently until inside arm and back covers have been installed. Complete tacking of casing along outer side of arm liner. If there is a large gap between arm upholstery and back post, insert enough stuffing or felted padding between arm burlap and casing, or compact stuffing, to re-

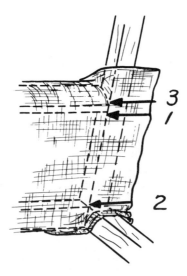

Fig. 8:20B

duce gap to ½ inch at most; this may be done after upholstering the inside back.

SEC. 8:20C   ARM AND INSIDE BACK UPHOLSTERIES JOINED / Tighten arm casing toward back, sliptack along face of back post. Push into arm any stuffing that works out at the back. Trim off excess casing 1 inch beyond sliptacks. Later, inside arm and back casings are stitched together (Sec. 10:24).

SEC. 8:20D   ARMTOP CASING / [1] *Inside wing upholstered independently of arm.* Cut arm casing straight from back edge to upper level of armboard, Point 3 (Fig. 8:20B). Complete installing arm casing through an open-frame wing, along inner surface on a solid-base wing. [2] *Inside arm and wing upholsteries to be joined together.* Trim off excess arm casing 1 inch above bottom of wing. Later, arm and wing casings are stitched together (Sec. 9:12H). [3] *Arm upholstery finishing through arm cavity.* Loosen casing above cut at Point 1 (Fig. 8:20B). Work casing over armtop to fit smoothly and tightly against back post. Cut off excess goods at the back but only after casing has been carefully fitted. In arms of this type, fit and shape the back portion of the top temporarily until the inside arm has been built in muslin. A neater job usually results from finishing armtop casing over inside back casing, Fig. 8:20D. [4] *Arm upholstery finishing through inside back cavity.* Cut arm casing straight from back edge to upper level of armboard, Point 3 (Fig. 8:20B). Work casing over arm-

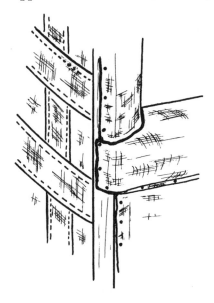

Fig. 8:20D

top to fit smoothly and tightly against back post.   [5] *Outer side of armboard finishing flush or nearly flush with rear of back post.* Outer side of armtop upholstery usually tapers to an end on back of post, Fig. 8:20D. In other arms the relation of the outer side of an armboard to the outer side or to the back of a post sets the method of finishing an armtop at the back. Often it is advisable to finish the armtop temporarily until the inside back is incased by muslin, and then build a smooth, neat finish for the armtop.

SEC. 8:21 STRAIGHT ARM MUSLIN CASING

SEC. 8:21A   /   To establish shape of a straight arm from front to back, tighten (Sec. 5:18) its casing or cover primarily in a horizontal direction; tighten vertically enough to make it smooth and taut. Basic work, tools, and materials are the same as for a curved arm (Sec. 8:16A).

SEC. 8:21B   POSITION, SET STRAIGHT ARM CASING   /   Center casing over stuffing, pull bottom edge under arm liner. The order of setting casing on all straight arms except T-shaped, exposed-wood, and bordered armtops (Secs. 8:21G, H) is shown in Fig. 8:21B. This sequence keeps stuffing in place and sets casing straight. Draw front edge of casing moderately snug to its first point of finishing on front post, Point 1.   [1] *When a panel or a border* will cover post face, Point 1 is at the upper level of the armboard in scroll and rounded arms, but at the bottom level in knife-edge and square-scroll arms.   [2] *When a pull-around or boxed* cover will incase front post, Point 1 is at the lower level of an armboard, or at top of post below scroll.   [3] *From Point 1* draw casing fairly snug straight toward the back. Sliptack on inner side of post, as at Point 2, *a,* or on back of post at the same level if necessary. Tighten casing straight toward back from Point 1; if tightened on the bias it may stretch irregularly.   [4] *While setting casing or cover* at all other points in Fig. 8:21B, tighten toward the front or back and bottom or top enough to keep the grain of the goods fairly straight, but not so much as to try to build final shape.

SEC. 8:21C   SET CASING AT FRONT OF ARM   /   Draw front edge of casing fairly tight around armtop and toward front to the third point of finishing on the post, Point 3 (Fig. 8:21B). Keep grain of goods as straight as possible. Tighten a sewn casing or cover straight over armtop to keep seams straight along inner and/or front edge.   [1] *When a panel or a border* will cover post face, Point 3 is at the bottom of a scroll in scroll and square-scroll arms, midway between top and bottom of armboard in knife-edge arms, at the level of Point 1 in rounded arms.   [2] *When a pull-around or a boxed* cover will incase post

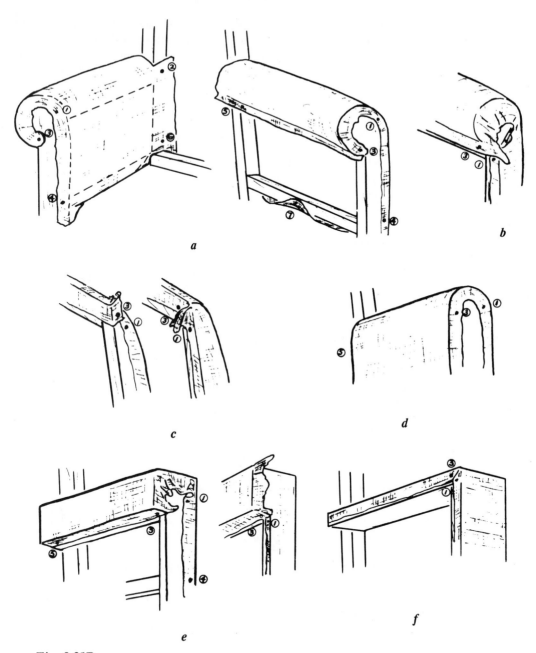

Fig. 8:21B

face, Point 3 is on the post at bottom of scroll in scroll and square-scroll arms, about ¾ inch from the edges of the top corner in knife-edge and modern square arms.   [3] *Draw front edge* of casing fairly tight down and around front post to the fourth point of finishing, Point 4 (Fig. 8:21B). This is on the same surface of the post as Point 1, but slightly above arm liner. If the lower part of an arm front will have a pull-around cover but the top will not (Fig. 1:44), Point 4 is on outer side of post.

SEC. 8:21D   SET CASING AT BACK OF ARM   /   [1] Cut casing straight from back edge to a point that is slightly above Point 2 (Fig. 8:21B). Cut to end of armboard in order for casing to fit around the armtop and against the front of the back post (Fig. *a* 8:21B). When arm and back frames finish at the same level (Fig. 1:20), cut casing to fit around and over the back toprail.   [2] *Draw casing over armtop,* and tack on outer side of back post straight back from Points 3 and 5 (Fig. 8:21B). I—*When the outer side* of a finished armtop projects outward from the back, Point 5 is on armboard or on back of back post. II—*When arm and back* finish at the same level (Fig. *a* 1:20), Point 5 usually is on back of post.   [3] *Draw back edge of casing* over back liner, and tack to inner side of post straight back from Points 4 and 6 (Fig. 8:21B). Draw bottom of casing under middle of arm liner, and tack to outer side, Point 7.   [4] *For many straight arms,* the completion of step [3] above holds stuffing in position and sets a casing or cover for tightening. But additional setting or other work is needed before tightening *scooped arms, arms with wings, T-shaped armtops, bordered armtops, exposed-wood arms, T-shaped inside arms proper,* and *bordered inside arms* (Secs. 8:21E–H).

SEC. 8:21E   SCOOPED ARM   / Notch arm front casing (Sec. 8:16C).

SEC. 8:21F   ARM WITH WING   / Cut and set casing (Sec. 8:16C).

SEC. 8:21G   T-SHAPED ARM ARMTOP   / Set and complete T-shaped arm armtop casing before inside arm proper casing.   [1] *Center* casing over armtop.   [2] *Draw middle* of front edge of casing fairly snug to front of armtop, tack to bottom of armboard, Point 1, Fig. *a* 8:21G.   [3] *When armtop finishes* into a back that will be fully upholstered (Fig. *a* 1:46), draw casing fairly snug toward the back, tack to face of back post, Point 2.   [4] *If rear of armtop* will be exposed when an article is finished, the second point of setting casing usually is at the middle of the bottom of the armboard at the back.   [5] *Draw casing over sides* of armtop at the middle, tack on bottom of armboard, Points 3 and 4.   [6] *Loosen armtop casing* at Point 1, tighten straight forward from middle and retack at Point 1.   [7] *Tighten casing* from middle of armtop forward and toward sides, tack at intervals of about 1 inch on each side of Point 1. Push back loose stuffing or padding that works over built-up edges or under armboard in order to keep lines of armtop free of lumps.   [8] *If rear of armtop* will be exposed when an

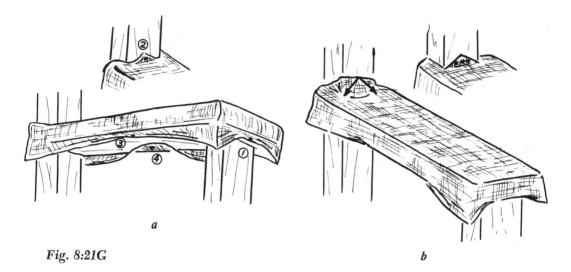

a

Fig. 8:21G   *b*

article is finished, repeat tightening in step [7] above at rear of arm-top.   [9] *When an armtop finishes* into an inside back that will be fully upholstered (Fig. *a* 1:46), then at Point 2 and on each side of it, tack casing to face of back post at the level of the top surface of the arm, Fig. *b* 8:21G. If necessary, cut casing from back edge to junctions of stuffed armtop and edges of back post, arrows, *b*. Tighten tabs straight back and downward, sliptack on bottom of armboard.   [10] *Alternating between front and rear* of armboard, set casing smooth and tight. Then tighten from the middle toward Points 3 and 4, *a*, and retack. Work alternately on each side of armtop, tighten and tack casing toward front and back until pleating at corners is necessary (Fig. 8:19J, Sec. 5:17E).

SEC. 8:21H   BORDERED ARMTOP, EXPOSED-WOOD ARM, T-SHAPED INSIDE ARM PROPER, BORDERED INSIDE ARM /   Center casing on inside arm, draw front edge moderately snug to first point of tacking on front post, Point 1, Fig. 8:21H, close to top except in exposed-wood and bordered inside arms.   [1] *Exposed-wood arms:* When possible, tack casing ¼ to ½ inch away from limits of upholstery in order to leave space for the cover.   [2] *Bordered inside arms:* Tack casing ½ inch away from planned lower limits of armboard cover (Fig. *b* 1:42) or of the inside arm border (Fig. 1:63).   [3] *When a panel or a border* will cover post face, Point 1 is on front of post.   [4] *When a pull-around or a boxed cover* will incase post face, Point 1 is on outer side of post about ¾ inch from front edge.   [5] *Draw casing fairly snug* straight back from Point 1, Fig. 8:21H, tack to inner side of back post, Point 2. Tack midway between Points 1 and 2, tightening casing upward only enough to keep grain fairly straight from front to back; in a bordered armtop,

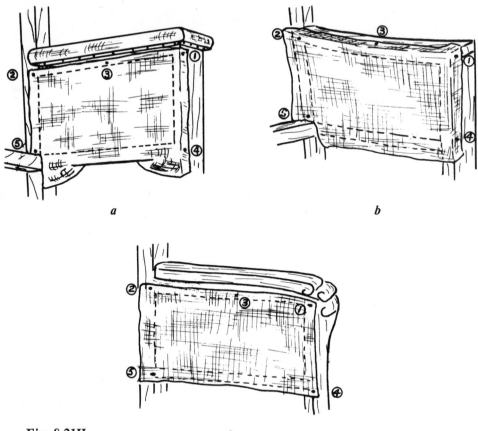

a

b

Fig. 8:21H   *c*

Point 3 is on top of the armboard about ¾ inch from the inner edge. [6] *Draw front of casing* to the fourth tacking point, Point 4, which is on the same surface as Point 1 but slightly above the arm liner. [7] *Draw casing straight back* from Point 4 over inside back liner, tack to inner side of back post, Point 5. [8] *Draw bottom of casing* under middle of arm liner, tack to outer side, Point 6. [9] *The stuffing is now held in place* and the casing ready for tightening to build final shape.

SEC. 8:22
TIGHTENING
STRAIGHT ARM
CASING

SEC. 8:22A / For general notes on tightening arm casing, see Secs. 8:17A, B, G. Most tightening on straight arms is toward the back and front. Tighten a sewn casing primarily toward the back and bottom; tighten toward front and outer side of armtop only enough to fit casing smooth and snug and to hold seams along edges. Tighten single-piece casings, Fig. 8:22A, primarily toward the front and back. When tightening vertically, work casing evenly and regularly in place; if tight-

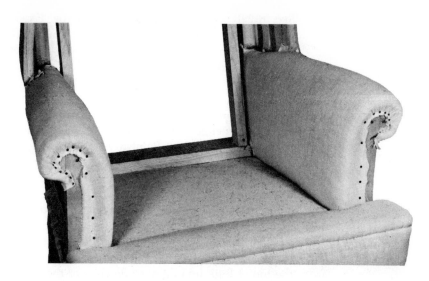

Fig. 8:22A

ened irregularly, the inside arm may be made concave or convex instead of relatively straight. However, straight arms require some crown (Sec. 5:14). Start tightening at the first point of setting straight arm casing (Figs. 8:21B, H). Loosen casing, work it smooth and fairly tight from the middle of an inside arm straight toward the first point of setting it, retack. Tighten casing from middle toward front and bottom, tack at two or three points an inch or so apart down from Point 1.   [*1*] *Casing finishing on face of front post.* If post has a built-up edge, push back stuffing or padding that works over it to prevent lumps in finished surface. If post does not have a built-up edge, place enough stuffing or padding along the inner and top edges to pad them slightly to protect the cover. To give a post panel or a border a "set in" appearance (Fig. *b* 1:46), spread enough stuffing or felted padding along appropriate edges of the front surface to make a simulated built-up edge at least ¼ inch high when compressed by casing. Width and height of a simulated edge is a matter of personal taste.   [*2*] *Casing finishing on outer side of front post.* Push back stuffing or padding that works over the outer edge of a post; it might prevent good installation of the cover.   [*3*] *Exposed-wood arm.* Push back stuffing or padding that works over the top of built-up edges; it might cause lumps in the cover. If an arm does not have built-up edges, push stuffing back, or add enough, to make a small but fairly firm edge ½ inch from limits of arm upholstery. Do not leave any stuffing or padding on the part of a rabbet to which cover will be tacked.   [*4*] *Loosen casing at second point* of setting (Fig. 8:21B), and also at the third point in T-shaped, bordered armtop, and exposed-wood arms (Fig. 8:21H). Tighten casing from middle of arm straight toward back, retack. Tighten toward back and downward from middle, and tack below Point 2 at three or four places about 1 inch apart.

SEC. 8:22B   T-SHAPED, BORDERED ARMTOP, EXPOSED-WOOD ARM, BORDERED INSIDE ARM   /   Tighten casing from middle toward top enough to keep grain straight from front to back, and retack at Point 3 (Fig. 8:21H). Handle stuffing for a bordered arm as in Sec. 8:17B.

SEC. 8:22C   SCROLL, KNIFE-EDGE, ROUNDED, SQUARE-SCROLL, MODERN SQUARE ARMS   /   Loosen casing at Point 3 (Fig. 8:21B), then: [*1*] *Scroll, knife-edge, rounded arms.* Tighten casing around armtop and toward front, retack at Point 3. Handle stuffing as in Sec. 8:17B. Push back loose stuffing or padding that works over the top of a built-up edge; it might cause lumps in the cover.   [*2*] *Square-scroll arms with single-piece casing.* Tighten casing straight around armtop and slightly toward the front, retack at Point 3.   [*3*] *Square-scroll arm with boxed casing, modern square arm.* Tighten casing enough around armtop and toward back to set seam or grain of goods straight along front edge. Retack at Point 3. Push back loose stuffing or padding that works over the top of built-up edges, or down over the outer top edge of an armboard; it could cause lumps in the cover.

SECS 8:22D   SCROLL, KNIFE-EDGE, ROUNDED, SQUARE-SCROLL, MODERN SQUARE ARMS   /   Loosen casing at Point 5 (Fig. 8:21B), or just in front of wing. Tighten casing over armtop and toward back, retack. Do not tack rounded arm casing on outer side of armboard; it could cause a line of depression in the cover. When covering the outside of a rounded arm, tack muslin casing to seat rail.

SEC. 8:22E   SCROLL, KNIFE-EDGE, SQUARE-SCROLL, MODERN SQUARE ARMS   /   Tighten casing straight over armtop midway between Points 3 and 5 (Fig. 8:21B). Tack to underarm strip of scroll arms, to under side of armboard in square-scroll arms, to outer side of armboard in knife-edge and modern square arms. Do not tighten casing enough to destroy shape or necessary crown in an armtop. If tightened too much over an armtop, especially of scroll and knife-edge arms, casing may flatten the top or even cause a depression.

SEC. 8:22F   FINISHING CASING   /   Complete adjusting a straight arm casing horizontally on the inner side from the top down to just above the liner. Tighten from middle downward and toward front and back. Keep grain, and seams of a boxed casing, as straight as possible throughout while allowing for the necessary crown of an inside arm. Tighten casing vertically (Sec. 8:16) but not enough to change the straight front-to-back shape. If tightened too much vertically, especially midway between front and back, it may build a flat or even a slightly depressed shape. Complete casing at front and back (Secs. 8:18–8:20).

**SEC. 8:23
SPRING
ARMTOP**

Sec. 8:23A / Spring armtops are generally only on straight scroll or rounded arms when an especially large overstuffed or puffy arm is wanted, Figs. *a* 26:00 *e* 1:45. Spring arms are exceptionally soft and resilient. But one built with soft compact stuffing and padded with polyester fiber (Sec. 3:49C) will be about as soft and resilient as the spring-built arm, much easier to upholster, and probably more durable.

Sec. 8:23B Frame / Arm frames must be built for spring upholstery. Frame *a* in Fig. 8:23B is for pad upholstery. Frame *b*, built for spring upholstery, has a larger scroll in front, and the armboard is further down from the top of the scroll than in *a*. The greater width of scroll and depth of armboard give springs in armtop space to work and so create the desired softness and resilience of a spring arm. Many straight scroll and rounded arms designed for pad upholstery can be modified for springs by enlarging front post and widening armboard. But since the rest of the article was not designed for spring arms, which usually are much fatter than pad arms, the final result may not be pleasing.

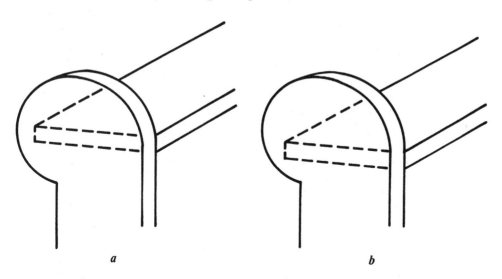

a   *b*

Fig. 8:23B

Sec. 8:23C Go-Down / The major problem in building spring armtops is that of making proper allowance for go-down. Without it, the casing and cover will rip out at front and back after relatively little use (Sec. 5:14C).

Sec. 8:23D Upholstery Methods / Spring armtops may be upholstered by either traditional or modern methods, with loose or com-

pact stuffing. Traditional upholstery usually has one row of 6-inch
back or pillow springs (Sec. 3:15B) and loose stuffing, although many
top quality upholsterers use compact stuffing (Secs. 3:28–3:44). In
modern upholstery a "spring" armtop is built with compact stuffing, or
with rubber webbing (Sec. 3:22) and compact stuffing. For each
method, first web inside arm (Sec. 8:09).   *Tools:* Upholsterer's hammer, webbing stretcher, shears, large curved needle if using springs,
steel tape measure (Secs. 2:02, 2:03, 2:04, 2:06, 2:16).   *Materials:*
Tacks; upholstery twine if using loose stuffing, springs and webbing
for traditional construction; burlap, stuffing (Secs. 3:03, 3:08, 3:11,
3:15, 3:24, 3:28–3:44); rubber webbing (Sec. 3:22).

SEC. 8:23E   TRADITIONAL UPHOLSTERY   /   Traditional armtop spring-

ing consists of a row of coil springs compressed by two or more strips
of webbing.   *[1] Install armtop webbing* (Sec. 5:01D) at back of arm,
Fig. *a* 8:23E. Depending on width of armtop, there should be two or
more strips long enough to reach from the front of the back post to
the front of the front post. Strips should overlap throughout to make a
solid surface for compressing springs.   *[2] Tack webbing to back post*
about ½ inch below the top of front post. Ends of strips should roughly
follow the planned curve of an armtop. Tack strips so that each one
can be pulled straight forward to finish neatly on top surface of front
post, *b;* do not tack at front now.   *[3] Fasten springs* (Sec. 7:09)
along middle of armboard at least 1 inch from each other and the
front and back posts.   *[4] Pull strips of webbing* over springs and the
top, and possibly partway down the sides, of the front post. Pull
webbing tight enough to make a smooth, relatively flat surface from
front to back, *b,* although there must be some crown (Sec. 5:14) at
middle of an armtop. Tack webbing along top and sides of the post
about ½ inch from the front edges. Do not overturn ends of webbing;
cut them off flush with front of post. When stretching webbing from
back to front be careful not to loosen or pull out strips at back.   *[5]*

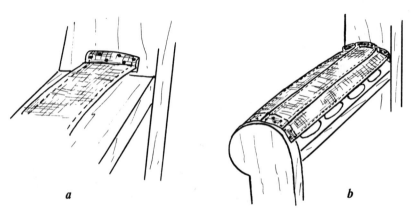

Fig. 8:23E   *a*   *b*

Stitch webbing to top coils of springs (Sec. 7:18). Be sure springs are perfectly upright.

SEC. 8:23F   BURLAP INSIDE ARM AND ARMTOP / (Sec. 8:10.) Stitch burlap to armtop webbing and springs (Sec. 7:18).

SEC. 8:23G   COMPLETE UPHOLSTERING AS FOR STRAIGHT SCROLL OR ROUNDED ARM / (Secs. 8:14–8:22.) [*1*] *Loose stuffing:* Install built-up edge if needed (Sec. 8:08). Tack three or four pieces of upholstery twine along sprung-up armtop from back to front; they should be parallel, evenly spaced between sides of arm, and fairly tight against the burlap spring cover. When stuffing armtop (Secs. 5:11A–C), work a thin layer under twines to hold it in place. [*2*] *Compact stuffing:* Install a fairly thin understuffing on burlap spring cover, incase with muslin, then complete with compact stuffing. Build understuffing thick enough for crown and desired basic shape.

SEC. 8:23H   MODERN UPHOLSTERY: COMPACT STUFFING / Upholstery of many modern spring-type armtops is a block of compact stuffing or stuffings (Sec. 8:23K). Durability of arm and cover depends greatly on firmness of stuffing and its shape. Softness and comfort depend on stuffing, and on the padding (Sec. 3:49) installed with the cover. The block of stuffing usually follows the shape of an armboard from side to side and, overlapping the front post, fills the space between front and back posts, Fig. 8:23H. To protect the cover, the stuffing crowns (Sec. 5:14) between front and back, *a;* usually less crown is needed for compact stuffing than for spring-built armtops,

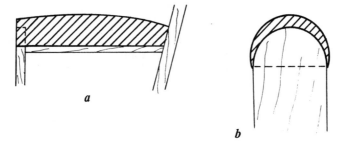

a

b

Fig. 8:23H

since stuffing usually has less go-down. As a rule stuffing over the front post, *b,* tapers to end at about the level of the armboard to keep from making an armtop too wide or thick. This might not matter on the outer side, but on the inside could cause a somewhat unusual shape (Figs. *c* 8:14C, 8:23E). The thicker the stuffing, the less noticeable the top of a post is, both to sight and feel, in a finished arm; however, if stuffing is too thick, it may be difficult to build a smooth surface at the front and cover it neatly. For best results, stuff and incase with muslin temporarily; desirable changes usually are quite apparent and easily made. One or two compact stuffings may be used for spring-type armtops.   [*1*] *One stuffing*. Usually it is firm or medium density. The firmer it is, the stronger the armtop, the less chance of excessive go-down, which could tear out the cover, and the less springy and comfortable an armtop will be. But firmness often can be concealed by installing one or even two layers of highly resilient felted padding (Sec. 3:39B) with the cover.   [*2*] *Two stuffings*. The first or understuffing (Sec. 5:13) is medium or firm density to prevent excessive go-down and build basic shape. The second or overstuffing usually is soft density to build a pillowy feel into an armtop. Overstuffing generally is ½- to 1-inch thick; thinner stock may not give the wanted softness; stock much thicker than 1-inch often is difficult to shape and install smoothly. Make understuffing block small enough to allow overstuffing to build the desired final shape of an armtop, but take care not to make understuffing too small. Usually it is better to make understuffing slightly larger than it apparently should be; the casing and/or cover will as a rule compress overstuffing satisfactorily.   [*3*] *Prepare* compact stuffing (Sec. 3:46).   [*4*] *Install compact stuffing* on armboard (Secs. 5:11D–G). Complete upholstery as a straight scroll or rounded arm (Secs. 8:14–8:22).

SEC. 8:23I   MODERN UPHOLSTERY: RUBBER WEBBING   /   Compensate with stuffing for a rubber webbing surface being flat instead of crowned (Sec. 5:17). This usually is done by making stuffing about 1- to 1½-inches thicker at the middle than at the front and back of an armtop. Except for installing webbing, burlap, and stuffing, a rubber webbing armtop is built essentially the same way as a traditional spring arm (Secs. 8:23E–G). Most rubber webbing armtops are upholstered with compact stuffing only; as a rule loose stuffing is used only as an overstuffing on rubberized hair to build crown. Install rubber webbing (Sec. 3:22F) the same way as webbing for traditional upholstery (Sec. 8:23F), except: [*1*] *Do not overlap* strips of rubber webbing. If necessary, butt them together at the back of an arm, and possibly on the top and sides of the front post. Overlapping tends to weaken installation and may cause lumps in the cover.   [*2*] *Pull rubber webbing* tight only by hand. Pulling enough to take out initial looseness (Sec. 3:22D) usually is sufficient.

SEC. 8:23J   BURLAPPING   /   Burlap inside arm proper the usual way (Sec. 8:10). Burlap the armtop separately to provide for go-down without tearing burlap loose.   [*1*] *Make burlap armtop cover* wide enough to cover webbed armtop from bottom of one side of armboard to that of the other, and at least 3 inches longer than the distance from where it is to be tacked at the front and back ends of arm.   [2] *Draw burlap strip* over armtop from side to side. Tack to sides of armboard at the middle and at 1-inch intervals to points about midway between middle and front and back ends of arm.   [3] *When tacking burlap* in place at front and back, leave at least 1-inch loose or slack material within armtop area. This usually is enough to allow for go-down without tearing the burlap loose.   [4] *Do not stitch* burlap to rubber webbing.

SEC. 8:23K STUFFING / Prepare compact stuffing for inside arm and possibly the outside of a rounded arm, the usual way. It may be installed with armtop stuffing, but usually it is easier to install them separately. Prepare compact stuffing for overstuffing of a scroll or rounded armtop (Secs. 8:14F–H) except: [1] *Shape stuffing* (Sec. 3:46) to build necessary crown at middle of an arm. Depending on thickness of stuffing, crown should be from about 1- to 1½-inches; the thinner the stuffing, the thicker the crown should be.   [2] *Instead of shaping stuffing for crown,* crown may be built with extra thicknesses of felted padding when covering arm. When stuffing with rubberized hair, crown may be built with loose stuffing covered by a layer or two of felted padding.   [3] *Install compact stuffing* the usual way (Secs. 5:11D–G), except that it should be bonded to burlap cover only at the middle and a few inches toward front and back of armtop, and at front and back. At the front, instead of tacking stuffing to frame, fasten it with tacking tape stuck to front surface of stuffing and tacked on front of post.

9

building
wings

SEC. 9:00   Any part of a chair, etc., attached to the front or side of a back above an arm is a wing. One extending the line of an inside back (Figs. *a* 1:09, *b* 1:38) usually is upholstered as part of it (Chapter 10). Wings at an angle to an inside back (Figs. 1:15, *a* 1:48) are upholstered separately from the back but may be upholstered as part of arms. The surface facing or flush with an inside back is the "inside wing." The other major surface, the "outside wing," generally is upholstered just before covering outside arms (Chapter 18). Inside wings are pad upholstery (Chapter 6). To build wings as nearly identical as possible, upholster them step by step together throughout.

SEC. 9:01   Basic types of wing posts and top rails, Fig. 9:01, are subject to many variations in overall shape. For example, the top of a straight-post knife-edge wing may be scooped, flat, or arched, and from front to back it may curve inward, be straight, or curve outward. Most inside wings are upholstered independently of the arms, but some finish

346

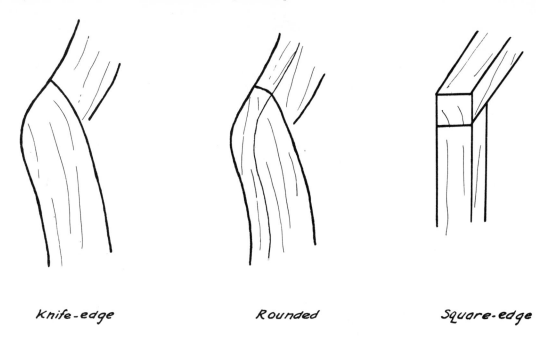

Knife-edge   Rounded   Square-edge

Fig. 9:01

down into arms (Figs. 1:15, *b* 1:48) in which case the inner side of the wing post is flush with that of the armboard.   [*1*] *In knife-edge and rounded wings* the inside wing cover usually finishes on the outer side (Fig. *d* 1:48).   [*2*] *Square-edge wings* generally have a boxed (Fig. 1:15) or a bordered (Fig. *b* 1:48) cover.

SEC. 9:02 **WING FRAMES**	Wings are open-frame and solid-base. Chief differences in upholstering them are due to the frame at the back post. If wing upholstery is done improperly at the back post; the final shape of an inside wing may not be compatible with inside arm and back shapes. [*1*] *Open frame with liner:* Upholstery finishes between wing liner and back post (Fig. 4:00A). Most wing frames are much thinner than the back post; if wing upholstery finishes through back instead of wing cavity, it will be appreciably thicker at the back than at the front, making it wedge-shaped. Also, if wing post and liner are curved (Fig. 4:00A), finishing wing upholstery through the back cavity will destroy intended shape of wing. [*2*] *Open frame without liner:* Finish wing upholstery through back cavity. [*3*] *Solid base wing:* Most of these frames are flat, having simple shaping, if any, at top and front, and usually are straight at the back, Fig. 9:02. Where upholstery finishes at the back depends on relative thickness of the back of a wing and the back post: I—if the back post is slightly wider than rear of wing, *a*, finish wing

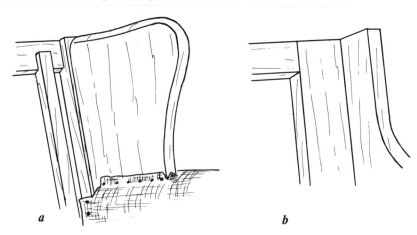

Fig. 9:02   *a*   *b*

upholstery through back cavity; most medium-size and large articles with solid-base wings are upholstered this way; II—if back post is much wider than rear of wing, *b*, to prevent making wing wedge-shaped, step *[1]* above, upholster it after covering inside back (Sec. 9:13); this type wing is more common on small than on medium-size or large articles.

SEC. 9:03 GENERAL WING UPHOLSTERY

Inside wings usually are finished plain. If cloth-tuft or loop buttons (Sec. 3:60) will be used with a solid-base wing, drill small holes for button twines. Channeling and tufting (Chapters 20, 21) seldom show to good advantage on wings.

SEC. 9:04 STUFFING

Base choice of stuffing for an inside wing on its probable use—decoration, or comfort and decoration. As a rule, stuffing for inside arms or back is satisfactory for wings; they usually take so little that getting a cheaper grade is not a worthwhile saving, and more expensive stuffing will not make much difference in comfort. Very small wings (Fig. 1:15) are chiefly decorative, and stuffing is for building and holding shape; a firm stuffing usually is better than a soft one. In medium-size and large articles, wings may be chiefly decorative (Fig. *a* 1:48) or also a comfortable headrest (Figs. *d* 1:48, *a* 1:49). As a rule, inside wings upholstered for comfort should have soft stuffing; however, it should not be too soft, or a wing too weakly stuffed, to build and hold shape. *[1]* *Loose stuffing* (Secs. 3:27–3:39) is suitable for all inside wing upholstery. For roll edges and understuffing (Secs. 5:05, 5:11F, 5:13), a hair-and-fiber mixture usually is better than all-hair and costs less. *[2]* *Compact stuffing* (Secs. 3:41–3:44) is excellent for inside wings, especially those built for comfort.   *[3]* *Felted padding* (Sec. 3:49). Natural cotton is a common stuffing for wings of small articles, and for wings that are chiefly decorative and do not finish much thicker than the frame. Because of cost, synthetic cotton or polyester fiber is used more as overstuffing on compact stuffing than as the only stuffing of a wing.

SEC. 9:05 **THICKNESS OF** **WINGS**	How thick to build wings is a matter of personal taste, but there are some appearance factors to consider. Wings that nearly follow vertical lines of inside arms usually are built for the inner surface to be either slightly behind or directly above the inner surface of an arm (Fig. *a* 1:48). Wings set out from an armtop (Fig. *b* 1:49) usually are built to finish about half as thick as the lower part of the arm front. Wings that finish into armtops (Fig. *b* 1:48) are built to extend the vertical plane of the inside arm.
SEC. 9:06 **WEBBING** **WINGS**	Wings, subjected to very little strain or weight in use, seldom are webbed unless the space between wing post and liner, or back post of an open-frame wing without a liner, is more than 7 or 8 inches wide. Traditional strip webbing (Sec. 3:11) is suitable for any stuffing, rubber webbing (Sec. 3:22) only for compact stuffing. Two strips of webbing, about 2 inches apart over widest part of a frame, usually are enough. As a rule, webbing is parallel with the inner surface of the back post or wing liner, but if a wing is appreciably shaped or curves between top and bottom, either run webbing horizontally or, at the widest part, interlace two horizontal with vertical strips. For webbing an open frame see Sec. 5:01, but stretch it only by hand; most wing frames are too weak to withstand the pressure exerted by a webbing stretcher.
SEC. 9:07 **BURLAPPING** **WINGS**	Burlap covers or fills a wing cavity from wing post to liner, or to the inner side of a back post when a wing does not have a liner, and from wing rail down to armtop. Install burlap smooth and moderately tight (Sec. 5:02), but do not work it tight enough in the wrong direction to destroy planned shape of wing. For wings shaped or curved between top and bottom, major pull on burlap is from back to front. Across the bottom of a wing, pull burlap tight; it can seldom be tacked there. *NOTE: If rubber webbing was installed (Sec. 9:06), tighten burlap to top, front, and back just enough to make it fairly smooth; some slack is needed to allow for go-down of webbing although the natural stretch of burlap is usually enough. The larger a wing, the greater the need for go-down allowance.*
SEC. 9:08 **BUILT-UP** **EDGES**	Whether or not built-up edges (Secs. 5:04, 5:05) are needed for a wing depends on stuffing, the basic shape of wing (Fig. 9:01), and how thick it will be upholstered. [1] *Compact stuffing:* Built-up edges not

needed.   [2] *Knife-edge, rounded wings:* These seldom have built-up edges unless they are to be upholstered with loose stuffing and made appreciably wider and higher than the frame. Most finished wings are welted (Sec. 11:08) along outer surface close to the front and top edges (Fig. *e* 1:48). With a built-up edge along the outer side of the top and front surfaces, welt must be set back from those edges; it can be set back any distance but generally shows to best advantage when set back about ½ inch or less. When a wing will be upholstered with loose stuffing about ½ inch wider and higher than frame, install a built-up edge large enough for the planned width and height along the outer edge of the front and top surfaces, Fig. *a* 9:08, from the rear top edge of the back post to armtop casing.

NOTE: *If width and height of a finished wing are to be much more than about ½ inch larger than the frame, usually it is better to re-style frame with wood before upholstering it.*

[3] *Square-edge wings:* Install a built-up edge large enough to uphol-ster wing with loose stuffing to the planned thickness along top and front edges of the inside surface, *b*, from the front of the back post to the armtop.   [4] *Single-piece cover:* When an inside arm and wing have a single-piece continuous cover (Figs. 1:15, *b* 1:48), install built-up edge, if any, when installing an edge for the inside arm (Sec. 8:08).

Fig. 9:08   *a*   *b*

SEC. 9:09
STUFFING
WINGS

SEC. 9:09A   /   Placement of stuffing depends on where inside wing upholstery will finish and on the style cover. Understuffing may be needed for compact stuffing (Sec. 9:09C). Inside wing stuffing extends: [1] *To inner front edge* of back post when wing upholstery finishes through back cavity.   [2] *To inner back edge* of wing liner when wing upholstery finishes through wing cavity (Fig. 9:12A).   [3] *To armtop casing* when wing upholstery does not finish into arm upholstery (Fig. *b* 1:49).   [4] *Down into inside arm* stuffing when inside wing and arm will have a single-piece cover (Fig. *b* 1:48).   [5] *To outer edges* of the front and top surfaces of wing, and outer and rear edges of a back post when a pull-around cover will be used (Figs. *e* 1:48, 1:49).   [6] *To front and top edges* of inner surface when a boxed (Fig. 1:15) or a bordered (Fig. *b* 1:48) cover will be installed, usually on square-edge wings only.

Sec. 9:09B   Loose Stuffing /   When wing upholstery finishes through wing cavity, place enough stuffing along inner and rear surfaces of liner to help fill gap between it and back post; stuffing can be altered while upholstering inside back. When a wing has a built-up edge, be sure to install enough stuffing behind it; with too little, the finished wing is apt to sag and the built-up edges may show through and wear out the cover. Install loose stuffing (Secs. 5:11A–C).

Sec. 9:09C   Compact Stuffing /   Medium-size and large wings built with compact stuffing usually are first understuffed (Secs. 5:11F, 5:13) and incased with muslin to build basic shape. Although advisable for all wings, this usually is not done on small wings that are fairly flat throughout (Fig. 1:15). The larger a wing and more shape it has, the greater need for understuffing it.   [1] *Understuff lightly* with loose stuffing (Sec. 9:09B); incase with muslin (Secs. 9:10–9:12).   [2] *After shaping* compact stuffing if necessary (Sec. 3:46), install it (Secs. 5:11D–F). Start at lower back corner of wing area to be stuffed; work toward front and top.   [3] *In knife-edge and rounded wings,* do not apply bonding agent to stuffing or wing near top front corner until notching stuffing to fit there smoothly. After bonding stuffing to wing, bond edges of notch together.

Sec. 9:09D   Felted Padding /   If using felted natural or synthetic cotton padding (Sec. 9:04) as wing stuffing, install two or three layers, depending on its thickness when compressed by a cover. Install (Sec. 5:12) over area of wing to be stuffed (Sec. 9:09A). Tear off padding overhanging outer sides, or top and front surfaces when they are not stuffed, as it may interfere with good installation of the cover and cause lumps in it. Build crown (Sec. 5:14) by installing a small extra layer or two of padding over middle area of wing.

**SEC. 9:10
MUSLIN
CASING**

Incasing inside wings with muslin to establish shape is more important for large than for small wings, and when using loose stuffing for any size wing. When measuring for casing, add 3 inches to each greatest measurement for general handling; compress loose stuffing lightly with a tape measure.   [1] *At the back,* when wing upholstery finishes through back cavity, measure greatest width from rear of back post;

when wing upholstery finishes through wing cavity, measure from outer side of liner.   [2] *For a pull-around casing,* used on most knife-edge and rounded wings, measure greatest width from outer front edge of wing post, greatest length from outer top edge of wing rail to bottom of wing.   [3] *For a boxed* or a bordered cover, both common on square-edge wings, measure greatest width from inner front edge of wing post, greatest length from inner edge of wing rail to bottom of wing.

SEC. 9:11 **MUSLIN** **INCASING** **WING**	**SEC. 9:11A** / Sliptack (Sec. 5:16) inside wing casing until it is completely adjusted. Cut (Sec. 5:15) where necessary. *Tools:* Upholsterer's hammer, shears (Secs. 2:02, 2:04). *Materials:* Tacks, muslin (Secs. 3:03, 3:48).

SEC. 9:11B   POSITION, SET WING MUSLIN CASING / Center casing over stuffing. Pull back edge through inside back or wing cavity according to where wing upholstery is to finish. The sequence of setting and tacking wing casing in Fig. 9:11B keeps loose stuffing in place and sets casing straight.   [1] *Pull back edge* of casing moderately snug to first point of finishing at back, Point 1, *a, b,* midway between top and bottom of wing.   [2] *Pull front edge* of casing fairly snug straight from Point 1 to second point of setting it, at front, Point 2, *a, c.* For pull-around casing, tack about ¾ inch from edge of frame to leave space for tacking cover. When casing finishes on front of wing post, tack about ½ inch from inner edge.   [3] *Work casing moderately tight from the middle of wing down toward the front bottom* and tack, Point 3, on same surface as Point 2, *a, c,* but just above armtop. Repeat toward back, Point 4, tacking at same level as Point 3 and on same surface as Point 1, *a, b.*   [4] *Work casing moderately tight from middle of wing upward toward back corner.* When casing finishes through back cavity, *d, e, h,* cut it to finish around back top rail. When casing finishes through wing cavity, *f, i,* cut it to fit under wing rail and up over back post. When a wing rail is appreciably lower than the top of a back post, *g,* cut casing to fit around wing rail. For all these cuts tack casing at Point 5, *a, b,* on the same surface as Point 1. [5] *Work casing moderately tight from middle of wing up toward the front.* Tack at Point 6, *a, c,* straight ahead of Point 5 on same surface as Point 2. Keep grain of casing as straight as possible.   [6] *Work casing moderately tight from middle of wing straight up.* Tack at Point 7, on the same surface as Point 6.

SEC. 9:12 **TIGHTENING** **WING CASING**	**SEC. 9:12A** / Additional loose stuffing, or felted padding for wings built with compact stuffing or padding, usually is needed to improve shape, Fig. 9:12A, when tightening wing casing. When upholstered

Fig. 9:11B

Fig. 9:12A

with loose stuffing, regulating (Sec. 5:07) may correct small lumps and hollows; if not, remove casing where necessary and rework stuffing. Although hollows, and sometimes lumps, may be hidden by padding installed with a cover, this should not be done. Final shape seldom can be built satisfactorily by a single tightening (Sec. 5:18) of a casing. If tightened too much at each point or too quickly, the shape may be rough, and the casing loose in some places, too tight in others. Avoid pullmarks (Sec. 5:19); those in a casing often cause grooves in the cover. Tighten major part of a wing first, then bottom and top. Additional tools and materials needed: Small curved needle, regulator, upholstery skewers, upholstery twine (Secs. 2:06, 2:07, 2:08, 3:08).

SEC. 9:12B STUFFING / Throughout tightening an inside wing casing, set stuffing according to type of wing and where casing finishes. [1] *Knife-edge, rounded wings:* Same as knife-edge arms (Sec. 8:17B). [2] *Square-edge wings:* When casing finishes on front and top surfaces of wing frame, push back stuffing that works over inner edges and build a firm, simulated roll edge at least ¼ inch high; add stuffing or padding as necessary. The simulated roll edge protects cover against sharp edges of a frame. When a border will be used, make the simulated roll edge at least ½ inch wide, and perhaps slightly higher, in order to give the border a "set in" appearance.   [3] *Push back loose stuffing* that works over a roll edge; it could cause lumps in the cover.

Sec. 9:12C   Tighten Major Part of Wing   /   [1] *Start* at Point 2 of setting wing casing (Fig. 9:11C).   [2] *Loosen casing*, tighten from middle straight forward, retack. Tighten forward and down from middle, tack at three or four places about 1 inch apart down wing post from Point 2. In a scooped wing it may be necessary to notch casing (Sec. 8:16C).   [3] *Tighten casing forward* and up from middle, tack at three or four places about 1 inch apart up wing post from Point 2.   [4] *Tighten casing from middle* of wing straight toward back, retack at Point 1.   [5] *Tighten toward back* and bottom, tack at five or six places about 1 inch apart down back post, or wing liner, from Point 1. Repeat this toward top of wing, tightening casing to back and upwards.   [6] *Work alternately* at front and back of wing until top and bottom are approached. Increase cut to top of a back, and make additional cuts, if necessary.

Sec. 9:12D   Tighten Bottom of Wing   /   [1] *Cut off excess* casing about 1 inch below bottom of wing.   [2] *When inside arm and wing are upholstered separately* (Fig. e 1:48), loosen wing casing at bottom, underturn it, draw fold down to fit tight and smooth against armtop. It may be necessary to cut wing casing up from the bottom edge to make a neat fit; but folding to fit is better than cutting. Tack casing in place at bottom of wing post. Tighten casing toward back and down-ward, tack to back post or wing liner close to level of armboard.   [3] *When inside arm and wing upholsteries will be joined smoothly*, per-haps with a single-piece cover (Fig. d 1:48), loosen arm casing and adjust wing and arm stuffings to make a smooth, continuous surface. Underturn upper edge of arm casing and retack it. Underturn bottom edge of wing casing; tighten downward until fold slightly overlaps arm casing. Tack wing casing to bottom of wing post. Tighten casing toward back and downward, tack to back post or wing liner close to level of armboard. Tighten arm and wing casings toward each other, pin together, then sew together with a simple running stitch.   [4] *If wing casing wrinkles* appreciably at front bottom, the arm casing probably was tacked too high on wing post. Loosen and retack arm casing, then adjust and tack wing casing.

Sec. 9:12E   Tighten Top of Wing   /   [1] *Tighten wing casing up-ward* and retack at Point 7 (Fig. 9:11B). Tighten up and forward, tack from Point 7 toward the front at intervals of about 1 inch until pleating (Sec. 5:17) is necessary. However, due to size of wings, stretch of casing, and the outside cover reaching the edges of a wing frame, pleating often is not necessary.   [2] *When a pull-around casing is used*, draw top portion straight over back post (Fig. *e* 9:11C) and down over rear edges. Add stuffing or padding if necessary in order to pad rear corner to protect cover. Tighten casing to back and along outer side of wing rail toward back, tacking about ¾ inch below edges. Pleat at corner.   [3] *When casing finishes on top surface* of a wing, tighten it back over the top of a back post (*h*), and tack.   [4] *When wing rail is appreciably lower* than the top of a back post (*g*), tighten casing over rail and slightly toward rear, and tack in place.

SEC. 9:12F   FINISHING CASING   /   After checking a wing for uniform shape, firmness, and tension of casing, drive tacks permanently. Trim off excess goods ½ inch from tacks.

**SEC. 9:13
WINGS
UPHOLSTERED
AFTER
INSIDE BACK**

SEC. 9:13A   /   The wings of some small articles (Fig. 1:15) are upholstered after the inside back is covered (Sec. 9:02). This type wing may be built with loose or compact stuffing, but often is small enough to be stuffed satisfactorily with felted padding and not require muslin casing. The inside wing cover is installed first.   *Tools:* Upholsterer's hammer, shears (Secs. 2:02, 2:04).   *Materials:* Tacks, cardboard stripping, stuffing or felted padding, muslin if using a stuffing, prepared wing cover (Secs. 3:03, 3:26, 3:27–3:44, 3:48, 3:49; Chapter 15).

SEC. 9:13B   /   This type frame (Figs. 9:08, 1:08) does not have a suitable cavity for inside back upholstery to finish through. The back cover (Chapter 16) is tacked along inner surface of wing close to back post, Fig. 9:13B.   [1] *Place prepared wing cover*, wrong-side-out, on back cover. Center wing cover in place, tighten toward top and bot-

Fig. 9:13B

tom, tack permanently along wing close to back post, Fig. 9:13B, at enough points, usually about 3 inches apart, to hold it securely. If incasing wing, install it on top of the cover the same way. Cover and casing, if any, must be worked smooth, tight, and straight while being tacked.   [2] *Tack cardboard stripping* over wing cover, or casing, from bottom to top. Press edge of stripping firmly against back post, but tack to inner side of wing. Tack along middle of strip at 1-inch intervals. Tacks too close together or too near an edge may split cardboard; tacks too far apart may not hold goods securely. Cardboarding or blind-tacking (back-tacking) a cover holds it firmly in place and finishes it with a smooth, even line.   [3] *Complete wing upholstery* as in Secs. 9:09–9:12 if muslin casing is used. When drawing casing or cover over wing stuffing, press stuffing gently but firmly toward back to keep casing or cover from shifting stuffing and building a hollow along rear of wing. For finishing wing cover, see Chapter 15.

10

building backs

SEC. 10:00A / The inside back may be the most influential part of a chair or wider article. It sets seat depth; one that is too shallow or too deep is uncomfortable (Sec. 10:01B). A back's pitch, slope, or tilt greatly affects comfort; one too straight-up-and-down is generally uncomfortable; when a back has too much tilt, sitters often must strain to sit up straight, and may have difficulty getting out of an article. From the point of appearance, a back that is too tall can make an article seem thin, top-heavy; too low a back can make an article seem squat, bulky; a back too thin for its height and width can make an article seem weak and rickety, while too thick a back can make an article look pudgy. What constitutes good proportions of a back is to great extent a matter of personal taste, but the above points should be kept in mind. Backs usually can be upholstered in more than one style or finish (Fig. 1:35). The surface of a back facing the front of a chair, etc., is the "inside back"; the other is the "outside back." Except for French backs (Sec. 10:05), upholster outside backs after completely covering the seat, arms, wings, inside back, and sides and top of a back (Sec. 18:11). Build plain and buttoned inside backs (Figs. *a* 1:35, *e* 1:48, 1:62) alike until buttoning. For channeling (Figs. *b* 1:35, 1:37), see Chapter 20. For tufting (Figs. *c* 1:35, *c* 1:49, 1:63), see Chapter 21.

SEC. 10:00B   STYLES OF FINISHING / Plan the style of finishing before starting any back upholstery, since some styles require different basic work than others. Most back frames can be upholstered in more than one style. Styles often can be changed after basic work is done but may require much doing over. As to how inside backs may be finished: [*1*] *Most exposed-wood* dining, side chairs, and large articles (Figs. 1:03, *c* 1:28, *a* 1:52) commonly have completely separate inside and outside backs. [*2*] *Small and medium-size chairs* often have inside back upholstery finishing around the sides and over the top into the outside back (Figs. 1:13, *a* 1:09, 1:19, *c* 1:29, *b* 1:36, *b* 1:38, 1:41). This also is common for inside backs of loose-pillow articles (Fig. *b* 1:33, 1:34, *b* 1:46, 1:60). In small and medium-size chairs an inside back cover often finishes over the top into the outside back (Fig. 1:16) but with the sides upholstered separately. [*3*] *Combined inside back and seat covers* are used for some small chairs (Figs. 1:14, 1:17). They present a sometimes difficult problem of getting the seat-back cover on tight enough to hold shape without ripping out. Wrinkles and wear lines often develop along the junction of seat and back. This style must be planned from the start, as seat and back upholstery must finish smoothly into one another. [*4*] *Most large club or lounge type* upholstered articles usually have an inside back finishing into definite sides and a top, which in turn finish into the outside back (Figs. *a, b* 1:42, 1:58). Especially with thick backs, this covering is easier to do and finishes neater and smoother than a pull-around cover, which tends to wrinkle at thick corners. [*5*] *In most articles with fully upholstered arms* an inside back usually butts against arm covers (Figs. 1:30, *b* 1:31, *c* 1:35, 1:41, *b* 1:42, 1:57, 1:63) and against arm and wing covers (Figs. 1:47, *a, c* 1:48). [*6*] *Slimline, modern, Scandinavian, office, and fraternity house* type articles usually have inside back upholstery attached to or used with, but not actually part of, the back frame. In Figs. 1:24, 1:25 back upholstery is a simple padded unit fastened to exposed-wood frames. In Fig. *b* 1:55, back upholstery is thickly padded solid-base units fastened by cover "sleeves" to frames (Fig. 16:15A). In Figs. 1:26, *a* 1:55, back upholstery is upholstery pillows resting against lightly webbed frames (Sec. 10:35). [*7*] *In barrel or tub chairs* (Figs. 1:37, 1:38), the inside back usually curves smoothly, sometimes in almost the same arc, into the arms. Barrel chairs offer a wide variety of styles of finishing, some easier and more practical for inexperienced upholsterers than others:

I—Channel back and plain arms, and channel back and arms (Fig. 1:37) are the easiest styles of finishing; arms and back can be upholstered separately throughout. II—Button treatments (Fig. 1:40) are more difficult than channeling, since back upholstery finishes into arms, and back and arms have a single-piece cover. In Fig. *a* 1:40, the surface can be built as a plain finish, and buttons installed with the cover; or, a buttoned pad may be built in muslin, tacked to a frame, then covered and buttoned. In Fig. *b* 1:40 the simplest upholstery is to build a pad in muslin to fit back and arms, and prepare cover essentially as for an attached-cushion ottoman (Sec. 22:06). III—The tufting style in Fig. 1:39 is no more difficult than other deep tufting, although inside back upholstery should finish into the arms. The cover can be a single piece for arms and back, or it may be pieces joined together at the apparent junctions of back and arms. IV—Plain inside back and arms sewn together at the junctions (Fig. *b* 1:38) is the most difficult style of finishing a barrel back article. Back and arm upholsteries must blend smoothly together throughout, covers must be precision sewn and installed to fit tightly without hollows, bumps, or wrinkles. If all work is not done properly, after relatively little use the cover often splits along junctions of arms and back.

SEC. 10:00C SOLID, PILLOW BACKS / Regardless of size or construction, the basic types of inside backs are: solid, pillowless, or tight (Sec. 10:00D); loose-pillow, usually called "pillow back" (Sec. 10:00E); and attached-pillow (Sec. 10:00F). However, a pillow back usually is a relatively thin solid back supporting a loose or non-attached upholstery pillow or cushion, and an attached-pillow back often is a solid back upholstered to look like a loose-pillow back.

SEC. 10:00D SOLID BACK / Most small and medium-size chairs (Figs. 1:12–1:41), exposed-wood articles (Fig. 1:52), and small love seats (Figs. 1:54, 1:57) have solid backs. They tend to be neater than pillow backs, do not need as much machine sewing and cover goods, and may be used for any shape back. There are of course exceptions, such as Figs. *b* 1:33, 1:34 with pillow backs, and Fig. *a* 1:33, an attached-pillow back. Regardless of size, most wing chairs, especially those with shaped wings (Figs. *b* 1:49, *c* 1:48), have solid backs. As for the large lounge or club type articles, fashions and tastes change.

SEC. 10:00E PILLOW BACK / This may seem the easiest to build, being a relatively thin solid back and a loose upholstery cushion or pillow. But pillows and cushions usually need considerable machine sewing, which home machines often cannot do satisfactorily (Sec. 2:15). Pillow backs usually appear to be more comfortable than the solids; but actual comfort depends on pillow or cushion upholstery

(Sec. 3:61, Chapter 17). Although medium-size chairs (Figs. *b* 1:33, 1:34) often have pillow backs, they are more in large lounge or club type chairs (Fig. 1:46) and three-place and wider sofas (Figs. 1:59, 1:60, 1:66).

SEC. 10:00F   ATTACHED-PILLOW BACK /   This often is used to combine the looks and apparent comfort of a pillow back (Figs. *a* 1:33, *b* 1:40, 1:58, 1:64) with the savings in cover offered by a solid back. Attached-pillow backs are not difficult to build but require most of the machine sewing needed for pillow backs.

**SEC. 10:01
GENERAL
CONSTRUC-
TION**

SEC. 10:01A /   All designs and types of inside backs can be either pad or spring upholstery. Some back frames are suitable for either upholstery, but others are better suited to one than the other (Sec. 10:01D); base your choice on the method which will allow for a comfortable back and seat (Sec. 10:01B). Except that backs usually have softer materials than seats, both surfaces are upholstered much the same way. Basic types of back upholstery are traditional and modern, and each may be done with either traditional or modern materials (Sec. 3:00C). For general pad upholstery, see Chapter 6; for details on pad back upholstery see Secs. 10:05–10:10. All pad back upholstery is under the general heading of "TRADITIONAL UPHOLSTERY —TRADITIONAL MATERIALS," since the only difference between traditional and modern pad upholstery is the stuffing. Spring seat and back upholstery are alike in many respects, but there are important differences. Some methods and materials are used more for one surface than the other; for example, spring-edge work (Sec. 7:15) is more common in seats than in backs. For general spring upholstery, see Chapter 7; details of spring back upholstery start in Sec. 10:11.

SEC. 10:01B   SEAT DEPTH /   The inner surface of a finished back sets seat depth, the distance from front to back of the sitting area. For the average person comfortable seat depth on dining, desk and other small chairs designed for upright sitting is 16 to 20 inches; on articles designed for lounging, from about 21 to 25 inches.

SEC. 10:01C   BACK TILT, PITCH /   Tilt or pitch of an inside back (its slope in relation to the surface of a seat) greatly affects the comfort of a chair, love seat, or sofa. The tilt or pitch built into frames (Sec. 4:00E) is usually satisfactory for small and medium-size articles, and is maintained by building the inner surface of a back parallel to that of the frame. Most large backs are thinner at the top, usually for appearance. Built-in frame pitch can be changed by stuffing in a pad back, by springs and stuffing in a spring back. After incasing a pad back with muslin but before trimming off excess goods, test seat and back for comfort. After all spring work is finished spread a pad about 1-inch thick over the back, sit and test the article; a fluffy blanket or thick comforter is a satisfactory pad for testing.

Sec. 10:01D Pad, Spring Upholstery / Generally, an inside back is pad upholstery if springing it would make the seat too shallow for comfort (Sec. 10:01B); however, rubber webbing (Sec. 3:22) often is used to get the softness of springs without making a seat too shallow. [*1*] *Most small and medium-size chairs* have pad backs (Figs. 1:07–1:41), although the larger ones may be spring built.   [*2*] *The inside back proper of pillow back articles* (Figs. 1:34, *b* 1:46, 1:60) generally is pad (Sec. 10:00E). Springs (Sec. 10:31) or rubber webbing (Sec. 10:33) often are used for an appreciable gain in back softness; be careful not to make a back so soft that it is too weak for comfort.   [*3*] *Solid backs in most large articles* (Figs. 1:42, 1:45, 1:48, 1:49, 1:52, 1:54, 1:63, 1:64) usually are spring upholstery.   [*4*] *Flat backs*, in which the inner surface of a top rail is straight between posts (Fig. 4:00A), are either pad or spring upholstered.   [*5*] *Barrel backs*, in which a top rail curves between posts (Fig. 4:06), usually are pad upholstery. A slightly curved pad barrel back may be finished plain, buttoned, channeled, or tufted. But when curvature is quite pronounced (Fig. 1:37), buttoning, channeling, or tufting usually holds it better into the desired shape. Spring barrel backs often are tufted; it allows the cover to expand and contract, which is necessary for comfort and durability on a flexible, curved surface.

SEC. 10:02 PLANNING PAD BACK THICKNESS

Plan the thickness of a pad back to estimate the amount of loose stuffing or the thickness of compact stuffing needed (Secs. 3:27–3:44). [*1*] *Measure actual* seat depth from the front edge of a seat to the inner surface of the lower rail of an exposed-wood back (Figs. 1:07, 1:28) or to the outer surface of the back liner of a fully upholstered back, Fig. 10:02.   [*2*] *Set desired* seat depth (Sec. 10:01B).   [*3*] *The*

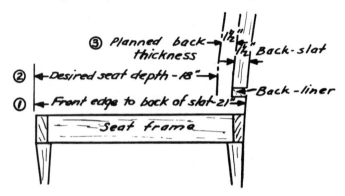

Fig. 10:02

difference between actual and desired seat depths is planned thickness of an inside back. From this subtract an allowance for thickness of frame, in the case of a back to be fully upholstered, to determine the thickness of stuffing.

SEC. 10:03 PLANNING SPRING BACK THICKNESS	**Sec. 10:03A** / Plan spring back thickness essentially the same way for all springing materials. However, differences due to each kind of springing—traditional coil springs, inner-spring units, zigzag springs, rubber webbing—make it more practical to figure planned thickness with each kind of springing rather than here. Basic planning of back thickness for traditional coil springs is given below (Sec. 10:03B); for inner-spring units (Sec. 10:29); zigzag springs (Sec. 10:31); rubber webbing (Sec. 10:33).

Sec. 10:03B   **Traditional Coil Spring Back** / Plan thickness of a traditional spring back to estimate size of pillow springs (Secs. 3:14, 3:17) needed.   [*1*] *Measure maximum seat frame depth*, the distance from the front edge of a seat to the back of the back post or slat at the back liner, Point 1, Fig. 10:03B. Most spring backs are webbed on these surfaces. A back having slats (Fig. 4:00A) usually is webbed on them.   [*2*] *Subtract desired seat depth* (Sec. 10:01B), Point 2, Fig. 10:03B, from maximum seat frame depth to find planned thickness of spring back, Point 3.   [*3*] *Subtract thickness of stuffing*, Point 4, from planned thickness of back to determine tied-down height (Sec. 3:16D) of springs, Point 5. Stuffing approximately 1 or 2 inches thick is used on most spring backs.   [*4*] *Tied-down height of springs* plus about 1 or 2 inches for tie-down equals free height or size of pillow springs

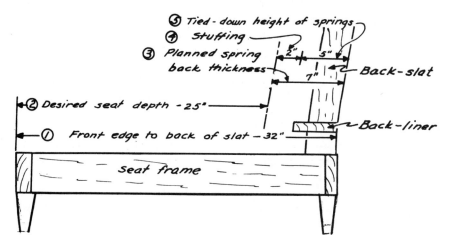

Fig. 10:03B

(Sec. 3:16E) needed for most of a back.   [5] *Lumbar area.* When there are three or more horizontal rows of springs in a solid back, those in the bottom row should be one or two sizes larger than the others to give greater pressure or support in the lumbar region of a sitter's back. This extra support makes an article, especially a chair, more comfortable. Tie lumbar area springs down to the same height as the others; the extra spring compression builds a firmer surface. Properly stuffed, a finished back has equal surface softness throughout, but under sitter-pressure it becomes firmer in the lumbar area. Springing for the lumbar area usually is the mark of superior upholstering.   [6] *Sharp edge breaks.* When planning sharp breaks (Fig. *a* 1:42) between the inner surfaces, sides and top, and using loose stuffing, 6-inch back springs are generally placed along these edges (Fig. *b* 10:11D).   [7] *Pillow backs.* The back proper of a pillow-back article usually has 6-inch springs.   [8] *Top coils* of inside back springs should project ahead of the inner surfaces of back posts or slats in: I—*Small backs* (Fig. *b* 1:31) at least 1 inch. II—*Medium-size backs* (Fig. *a* 1:33) at least 2 inches. III—*Large backs* (Figs. *c* 1:42, 1:57, 1:64) 3 or more inches.   [9] *If springs large enough* for planned thickness are not available, a smaller size may be used satisfactorily by webbing the back on the inner instead of the outer surfaces of a frame. Also, thickness can be increased with stuffing.

SEC. 10:04 **STUFFING**	**SEC. 10:04A** / Inside back stuffing is of major importance. Non-resilient loose stuffing, or one not thoroughly picked and smoothly spread, makes a lumpy and unnecessarily hard back; it becomes harder and less comfortable through use. Compact stuffing in good condition and installed properly can hardly do anything but build a smooth surface. Always use the best stuffing available, and enough to keep the webbing of a pad back, or the springs, from being felt as individual items. [1] *Loose stuffing* is suitable for all inside back upholstery. For roll edges and understuffing (Secs. 5:05, 5:11D, 5:13, 7:01B, 8:12C, D) a hair-and-fiber mixture is better than all-hair and costs less. But for all overstuffing, or an only stuffing, use the finest quality hair. [2] *Polyfoam and foam rubber* are excellent for overstuffing and as the only stuffing in all backs, especially when fairly sharp breaks are wanted between inner, top, and side surfaces (Fig. *a* 1:42). This type back—flat top, square sides—is sprung-up and upholstered differently when it is to be built with compact (Sec. 10:28) instead of loose stuffing. [3] *Soft rubberized hair* is a good, easy-to-handle stuffing for all backs. It is installed the same way as polyfoam and foam rubber and often is the understuffing for those materials. Rubberized hair understuffing need not be incased with muslin. When rubberized hair is the only stuffing or the overstuffing for a back, pad the exposed surfaces (such as the inner surface of a back) with a fairly

thin layer of top quality loose-hair stuffing or felted padding. [4] *Felted padding* is not recommended as a stuffing for any except exposed-wood flat pad backs that are to be upholstered as thinly as possible. The cane panel back of a chair often is changed to an upholstered panel. As a rule, the upholstery is not more than about ½-inch thick in order to keep from making the seat too shallow for comfort (Sec. 10:01B).

SEC. 10:04B SPRING BARREL BACKS / Fairly thick spring barrel backs (Fig. *a* 1:50) usually are upholstered with compact and loose stuffings. Compact understuffing simplifies the building of a smooth basic shape. For the very deep channeling or tufting that gives this type of back maximum comfort and durability, it often is easier to build shape with a top quality loose than a compact stuffing.

TRADITIONAL UPHOLSTERY

SEC. 10:05 FRENCH BACK	**SEC. 10:05A** / In French backs, Figs. 10:05A, 1:28, install the outside back cover first; it cannot be corrected later without removing all other work. The tacking space or rabbet usually is fairly small and must be treated carefully; use the smallest tacks that will hold upholstery materials satisfactorily. Use any good stuffing, preferably a top quality compact. For working convenience, place chair outside-back-down on upholstery trestles. *Tools:* Upholsterer's hammer, shears; large curved needle, regulator if using loose stuffing (Secs. 2:02, 2:04; 2:06, 2:07). *Materials:* Tacks; upholstery twine if using loose stuffing; burlap or canvas, stuffing, felted padding, cover goods (Secs. 3:03; 3:08; 3:24, 3:27–3:44, 3:49).

SEC. 10:05B OUTSIDE BACK COVER / Prepare outside back cover (Chapter 11). Cut two pieces of burlap or canvas the same size as the back cover. There is no space for webbing in a French back; instead, install two thicknesses of burlap or canvas. Canvas makes a firmer and more durable back, but is more difficult to install. Center the outside back cover, wrong side up, on inner surface of back frame. Sliptack (Sec. 5:16) ½ inch from edges of the frame when possible. Keep grain of cover straight throughout setting it; sloppy work now will be difficult to correct later. [1] *Tack first at the middle* of the bottom, Point 1, Fig. 10:05B. [2] *Draw cover fairly tight* from Point 1 straight toward the middle of the top, Point 2; tack. Draw cover fairly tight toward top and sides, sliptack midway between sides and top, Points 3 and 4; repeat at bottom, Points 5 and 6. [3] *Draw cover fairly tight* toward middle of sides, tack at Points 7 and 8. [4] *Tighten cover* (Sec. 5:18) toward the bottom, retack at Point 1. Working a

Fig. 10:05A

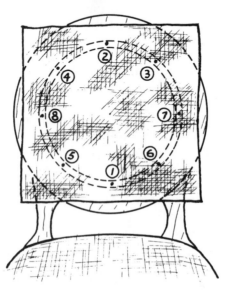

Fig. 10:05B

couple of inches toward one side of Point 1, then to the other, tighten cover toward bottom and sides, sliptacking at intervals of about ½ inch. Repeat this process at the top, tightening cover upward and to sides enough to keep it straight, free of wrinkles, and uniformly tight. Tighten and sliptack cover throughout, working alternately toward top and bottom and to the sides.   [5] *Do not work cover drumhead tight;* some residual stretch is needed so it will not rip out under normal usage. If a cover can be pinched up easily at any point, it is too loose.   [6] *Set chair upright,* examine cover carefully from the outside before driving tacks permanently. After driving tacks, trim off excess cover goods close to tackheads.

SEC. 10:05C   COMPLETE OUTSIDE BACK UPHOLSTERY / Set chair back in place on trestles.   [1] *Spread a layer of padding* over the cover extending to just beyond the cavity edges of the frame without overlapping the tacks. If padding does not completely cover outside back cavity, the finished outside back will be rough and lumpy. If padding overlaps edges of a frame too far, it may prevent good installation of inside back upholstery.   [2] *Using the same method* as for the outside back cover (Sec. 10:05B), install both sheets of burlap or canvas over padding. Tightened and tacked firmly at close enough intervals, the burlap or canvas is sufficient foundation for inside back upholstery.

SEC. 10:05D   INSIDE BACK UPHOLSTERY / [1] *Loose stuffing.* Stuff and complete French back the same as any other pad exposed-wood inside back (Sec. 10:09).   [2] *Compact stuffing.* Cut it the exact shape of but ½ inch smaller all around than the area bounded by the edges of the rabbet on the inside back. This space is needed for tight and permanent tacking of casing and cover along rabbet. Center stuffing in place, and bond or cement it to the burlap or canvas. Incase with muslin and complete the inside back the same as for any other exposed-wood article (Sec. 10:09).

SEC. 10:06 **PARTIALLY** **UPHOLSTERED** **PAD BACK**	To keep a flat pad back (Fig. 1:07) from being built too thick and to eliminate lumps at the edges, install webbing inside the cavity, Fig. *a* 10:06. Tack a strip of webbing to the inner side of the rail or post, *b*, so that it will fold down or across close to the front surface. Pull webbing tight by hand, tack the same way on the inner side of the opposite rail or post, *c*. If webbing is pulled tight enough and the first few tacks in the free end, *c*, are far enough back from the inner edge, it will be pulled sufficiently tight when the remaining tacks, set fairly close to the inner edge, are fully driven.

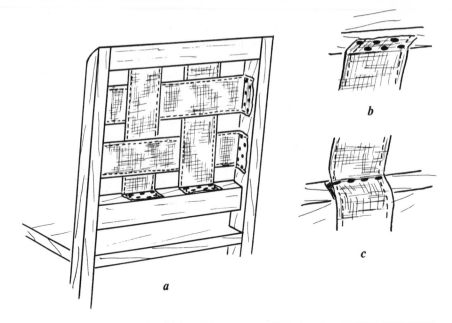

b

c

a

Fig. 10:06

SEC. 10:07 FLAT PAD BACK	This is built much the same as a flat pad seat (Sec. 6:02) and generally is used with that type of furniture. Flat pad backs usually are webbed as in Sec. 10:06. But some are built the same as French backs (Sec. 10:05).
SEC. 10:08 SLIP-BACK	Upholster the same way as a slip-seat (Secs. 6:03, 10:37). However, in addition it often is necessary to install an outside back cover (Sec. 18:11).
SEC. 10:09 EXPOSED-WOOD PAD BACK	This may be upholstered with either loose or compact stuffing; the latter is generally easier to handle, especially for inexperienced upholsterers. [1] *Loose stuffing.* Upholstering an exposed-wood pad back with loose stuffing may be the same as for a roll-edge seat (Sec. 6:04). However, if the rabbet of an open-frame back is too narrow to hold a built-up edge and leave space for tacking of casing and cover satisfactorily, the inside back is bridle-built with a hard edge (Secs. 7:21, 7:26). The hard edge usually has three rows of stitching; the third is the same as the second and is set about the same distance from the second row as the second row is from the first.

NOTE: When bridle-stitching a French back (Sec. 10:05), stitch understuffing with a large curved needle; do not stitch through outside back felted padding.

[2] *Compact stuffing.* Install compact stuffing on exposed-wood pad backs essentially the same as on a pad seat (Secs. 6:04G, H) except

for the points of finishing it. On very small backs (width or height less than about 14 inches), understuffing to build crown seldom is practical; instead, an extra layer or two of felted padding several inches smaller than width and height of the surface can build necessary crown. [3] *Most backs* having exposed-wood posts only (Figs. 1:09, 1:12) are treated as fully upholstered backs.

SEC. 10:10 **WEBBING** **FULLY** **UPHOLSTERED** **PAD BACKS**	**Sec. 10:10A** / Subject to less weight and pressure in use, backs need less webbing than seats. Web pad backs on the inner surfaces of a frame. How inside arms and wings finish at the back must be taken into account. Install webbing (Sec. 5:01), but stretch tight only by hand; most back liners cannot withstand the pressure exerted by a webbing stretcher. Webbing a back cavity that is less than about 6 inches high (Fig. 1:09) is desirable but not necessary. Strips of webbing that follow and maintain shape of a back frame usually provide major support. [1] *Flat backs* (Fig. *a* 10:11D). Vertical and horizontal webbing maintain shape and may provide equal support, step [5] below. [2] *Curved or barrel backs* (Figs. 1:19, *c* 1:29, *b* 1:36, *a* 1:37, 1:38, 1:41). Vertical webbing maintains shape and provides major back support, horizontal webbing gives additional support; do not tighten horizontal webbing enough to change planned shape of back. [3] *Back curving between top and bottom* (Fig. 1:12). Horizontal webbing maintains shape and provides major support, vertical webbing gives additional support; do not tighten vertical webbing enough to change planned shape of back. [4] *Back and seat to have single-piece cover* (Sec. 6:04B). Horizontal webbing sets shape, particularly at junction of seat and back, and provides major support; do not tighten vertical webbing enough to change shape of article, especially at the junction of seat and back. [5] *Sides of back finishing through slatless back cavity* (Sec. 10:12D). Vertical webbing provides major support for sides of upholstery. [6] *Inside wings upholstered as part of back.* Web vertically or horizontally, whichever frame permits and will maintain shape of a wing; wing cavities often are too small to need webbing.

Sec. 10:10B Vertical Webbing / [1] *In armless articles and when arms and wings do not finish through back cavity or finish through back cavity that has slats*, set vertical strips of webbing 1 or 2 inches apart and from posts or slats. [2] *When inside arms and/or wings finish through slatless back cavity*, at the sides of a back, double over lengthwise vertical strips of webbing and set them tight against arm casings; this gives maximum support to back upholstery where it finishes through the cavity. Set other vertical webbing strips at equal intervals along the liner. [3] *Space vertical webbing strips* equally along top rail. Set webbing at sides, [2] above, against the wing

casings finishing through a back cavity, or close to the posts of other backs.

SEC. 10:10C HORIZONTAL WEBBING / Armless articles usually are webbed horizontally at about 2-inch intervals between top rail and liner, or between top rail and the rearmost strip of seat webbing in articles having a single-piece seat and back cover (Sec. 6:04). Other articles usually need only a couple of strips of webbing at equal spacings. [1] *Flat backs.* Interlace horizontal and vertical webbing. [2] *Curved and barrel backs.* Pass all horizontal strips behind all verticals; install them just tight enough to fit snug against vertical webbing without displacing it. [3] *Vertical back webbing extending from seat.*

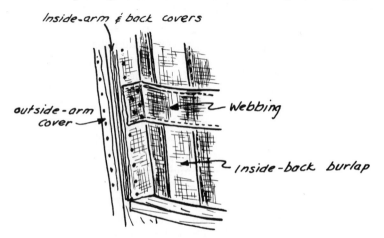

Fig. 10:10C

In flat backs, interlace horizontal webbing with vertical and, if it is to be tacked to faces of back posts, tighten with webbing stretcher. Tighten cautiously; back frames are weaker than seat frames. [4] *In armless articles and when arms and wings do not finish through back cavity or finish through back cavity that has slats* (Fig. *a* 10:11D): Tack horizontal webbing permanently to faces of back posts or slats. [5] *When arms and/or wings finish through slatless pad back cavity:* Sliptack horizontal webbing from arms and wings to sides of back posts. I—Loose stuffing: After burlapping inside back and stitching stuffing in place, loosen horizontal webbing; when upholstering the outside back, tack horizontal strips permanently (Sec. 10:06) to support and maintain lines of back, Fig. 10:10C. II—Compact stuffing: Install horizontal webbing (Sec. 10:06) when upholstering the outside back.

SEC. 10:10D / For burlapping pad backs see Sec. 10:18.

SEC. 10:11
WEBBING
SPRING BACKS

SEC. 10:11A / Webbing of a spring inside back depends on the springs, planned thickness of back (Sec. 10:03), stuffing, how back frame is built, and how inside back, arm, and wing upholsteries finish at the back. Webbing is placed primarily to accommodate springs. [1] *Coil springs.* Most backs having traditional coil springs are webbed on the outer surface (Sec. 10:03); for best results, plan webbing for bottom coils to be on crossings of vertical and horizontal strips (Fig. *a* 10:11D).

NOTE: A back inner-spring unit, [2] below, nearly always can substitute for back coil springs, is usually easier to handle, and needs less work.

[2] *Inner-spring units.* Most backs built with inner-spring units (Sec. 3:63) are webbed on the inner surfaces. For best support, plan webbing so that each edge of a unit that is not on the frame lies along a strip of webbing. Depending on shapes of back and unit, it may be necessary to cut springs out of a unit, or add springs to it, as often happens with T-shaped backs (Sec. 10:11D[2]). Backs less than about 5 inches thick overall seldom have inner-spring units. When finished overall thickness is not more than about 7 inches, placement of webbing depends on the general thickness of a frame; if webbing the inner surface would make a back too thick or require a spring unit to be compressed or tied down, web on outer surfaces.

NOTE: In most cases, recommended clearances of a spring unit from various parts of a frame are the same as for coil springs.

[3] *Stuffing.* Space permitting, coil springs and inner-spring units usually are set nearer the edges of a back frame for loose stuffing than for compact. Either kind of stuffing can be used for all spring backs. But for some styles of finishing and kinds of backs, one stuffing may be easier to work with and generally produce better results than the other.   [4] *Back cavity.* In a back frame with slats (Fig. 4:00A), horizontal webbing usually is tacked to them permanently during basic webbing installation (Sec. 10:11D[1]). In a slatless back cavity horizontal webbing may or may not be tacked permanently to posts during basic installation; it depends on where inside back, arm, and wing upholsteries finish.   [5] *Upholsteries finishing at the back.* When inside back, arms, and wings finish through a slatless back cavity (Fig. 10:11K), horizontal webbing usually is sliptacked during basic installation, and tacked permanently after covering the inside back, arms, and wings.   [6] *Shape of back.* In curved and barrel spring backs, treat horizontal webbing as in similar pad backs (Sec. 10:10A).   [7] *Stretching.* Install webbing (Sec. 5:01), but stretch tight only by hand; most back liners cannot withstand the pressure exerted by a webbing stretcher.

Sec. 10:11B Vertical Webbing / Inside back coil springs usually are set 2 to 5 inches apart; a closer setting might interfere with tying them, a wider setting could make a weak back. Where possible, the entire bottom coil should rest on webbing. Vertical rows of springs next to the back posts or slats help shape the sides of back upholstery; side rows usually parallel the inner sides of posts or slats (Fig. *a* 10:11D). Space the middle vertical row or rows equally between side rows of springs. An excessively fan-shaped back often has one more vertical row of springs in the upper than in the lower part to prevent excessive space between upper springs.

Sec. 10:11C Armless Articles / Space between inner sides of back posts and bottom coils of springs depends on the planned shape of the sides and the stuffing. [*1*] *Loose stuffing:* For tapering sides (Fig. 1:13), set springs about 2 inches from posts; for square and rounded sides (Figs. 1:14, 1:16), set springs almost touching posts. [*2*] *Compact stuffing:* Space between springs and posts should be a little less than the thickness of the stuffing.

Sec. 10:11D Armchairs, Similar Articles / Place side vertical rows of springs according to inside arms at the back, desired shape of back above arms, and stuffing. [*1*] *Armboards flush with inner sides of back posts,* Fig. *a* 10:11D. For loose stuffing, the side springs or sides of an inner-spring unit usually are 2 or 3 inches from the slats, or posts of a slatless back; set springs above arms at the same spacing. For compact stuffing set springs according to thickness of stuffing (Sec. 10:11C). [*2*] *Armboards set in from inner sides of back posts.* Side vertical rows of springs above arms generally are fastened to horizontal webbing and/or the top rail. I—Square sides: For loose stuffing set coil springs almost touching back posts, set the side of a spring unit about ½ inch from outer side of post; for compact stuffing set coil springs or side of spring unit about 2 inches from posts. II—Rounded sides: Regardless of stuffing, set coil springs or side of spring unit about 2 inches from post. III—T-shaped back: In fairly thick T-shaped backs (Fig. 1:42), often a 6-inch back spring is fastened to the face of a back post, Fig. *b* 10:11D, when upholstering with loose stuffing.

Sec. 10:11E Wing Articles / Set side vertical rows of springs or sides of inner-spring unit 2 or 3 inches from back slats (Fig. *a* 10:11D) or from posts of a slatless back cavity. Wings upholstered as part of a spring inside back usually are pad built (Chapter 9).

Sec. 10:11F Horizontal Webbing / Horizontal rows of back springs are located according to the type of seat, desired shape of top

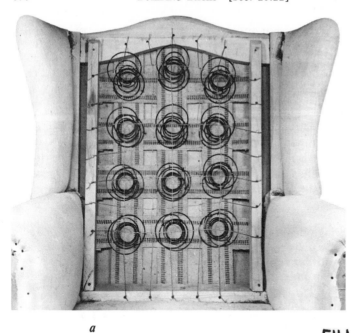

a

FILLER STRIP   TOP RAIL

b

Fig. 10:11D / NOTE: Professional upholsterers often spring-up a seat and inside back before working the arms. This requires special skill and judgment and is not recommended to inexperienced upholsterers.

of back, and stuffing. For inner spring units there are, of course, no horizontal "rows" except top and bottom.

Sec. 10:11G   Seat   /   [*1*] *The middle of the bottom horizontal row* of coil springs, or lower side of an inner-spring unit, generally is about 3 inches above the rear of a solid seat, about 7 inches above the deck of a loose-cushion seat. Springs set lower may lessen comfort of an article by strengthening the bottom of a back below the lumbar area (Sec. 10:03B[*4*]). But when armtops are quite low in relation to the surface of a finished seat, as in many so-called modern designs, the bottom horizontal row of springs often is 1 or 2 inches below armtops regardless of a seat being solid or loose-cushion.

NOTE: Springs can be set for the best lumbar effect only when upholstering an article for a specific person. Many custom upholsterers actually find out what setting of lumbar-area springs is best for a customer. But in most cases this is not practical, and the above settings are acceptably comfortable for most people.

[*2*] *Second and third horizontal rows* of springs (the third row usually in only fairly tall backs, Fig. *a* 10:11D) generally are about midway between the bottom and top rows (Sec. 10:11H).   [*3*] *In fairly thick T-shaped backs,* the middle horizontal row usually is about 2 inches above the top of the armboards (Fig. *b* 10:11D). For inner-spring units there are, of course, no horizontal "rows" except top and bottom.

Sec. 10:11H   Top Horizontal Row   /   Location of the top horizontal row of coil springs or side of an inner-spring unit depends on shape of back and stuffing.   [*1*] *Scroll, rounded, loose-pillow, knife-edge backs* (Figs. *c, e* 1:45, *a* 1:48). I—Loose stuffing: Set top horizontal row of springs parallel to but about 2 inches below bottom of top rail, following the arch or scoop of a rail, if any (Fig. *a* 10:11D); this cannot be done with an inner-spring unit (Sec. 10:29). Set webbing for top row to support the greatest number of springs. II—Compact stuffing: Set coil springs or inner-spring unit as for loose stuffing, above. For most of these backs, it usually is necessary to build basic shape and incase with muslin (Sec. 10:19) before installing compact stuffing.   [*2*] *Flat-top backs* (Fig. *a* 1:42). I—Loose stuffing: Set top row of coil springs parallel to and almost touching the bottom of the filler strip (Fig. *b* 10:11D); the folded strip of webbing on the face of the top rail is to silence, not hold, springs and may be omitted. Setting springs close to filler strip simplifies building shape and strengthens an inside back. If using an inner-spring unit, set the top about ½ inch below top of rail or filler strip. II—Compact stuffing: Spacing of coil springs or spring unit from the above-mentioned points depends on stuffing thickness (Sec. 10:11C).   [3] *Exposed-wood at top and fairly sharp break between inner and top upholstered surfaces.* I—Loose stuffing: Set top row of coil springs or edge of inner-spring unit parallel to but about 1 inch below top rail. II—Compact stuffing: Spacing of coil springs or spring unit from top rail depends on stuffing thickness (Sec. 10:11C).   [4] *Same as* [3] *above but without the sharp break at top.* Regardless of stuffing, set coil springs or inner-spring unit 2 or 3 inches from top rail.

Sec. 10:11I INSTALL WEBBING / Vertical webbing for traditional coil springs usually is tacked to the back or bottom of a back liner and back of a top rail, Fig. 10:11I. Sometimes it is necessary to web on inner surfaces (Sec. 10:03B[9]); take care not to change planned pitch of back (Sec. 10:01A). For inner-spring unit or units, webbing usually

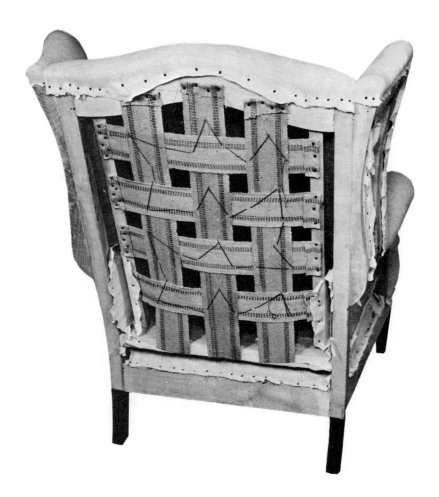

Fig. 10:11I

is tacked on the front surfaces of a back frame. Be careful not to change the planned pitch of a back; in most articles built for this type of springing, the front surface of a back frame usually has adequate pitch.

Sec. 10:11J Horizontal Webbing / Installation of horizontal webbing in a spring back depends on the shape of a back and whether or not a cavity has slats. *[1] Curved or barrel back.* Horizontal webbing usually is installed while upholstering the outside back (Sec. 10:10C). Install webbing tight enough to support springs without altering shape of back. *[2] Flat back.* Interlace horizontal and vertical webbing and for backs with slats, tack horizontal webbing permanently to the backs of slats (Fig. 10:11I). For backs without slats, armless articles, and when inside arms and wings do not finish through back cavity, tack horizontal webbing permanently to backs of posts. But when arms and/or wings finish through a slatless back cavity, sliptack horizontal webbing in place at the appropriate levels; after springing the back, leave ends of horizontal strips free (Fig. 10:11J) until upholstering the outside back.

Fig. 10:11J

NOTE: When vertical webbing is tacked to the front surfaces of a back frame, so is the horizontal.

**SEC. 10:12
EDGE-WIRE
TO SHAPE,
SUPPORT BACK
UPHOLSTERY**

SEC. 10:12A / When instead of butting against arms, an inside back projects over and around them (Figs. *c* 1:42, *a* 1:45), spring edge-wire shapes and strengthens back upholstery at the arms. When a back butts against inside arms finishing through a slatless back cavity (Fig. *c* 1:45), edge-wire or strip webbing shapes and supports sides and holds horizontal spring ties. *Tools:* Upholsterer's hammer, shears, wire bender, tape measure (Secs. 2:02, 2:04, 2:11, 2:16). *Materials:* Tacks, webbing, spring edge-wire (Secs. 3:03, 3:11, 3:19).

SEC. 10:12B PREPARE, INSTALL EDGE-WIRE / Patterns for measuring edge-wire used as in Sec. 10:12A are in Fig. 10:12B. *[1] The measurement from Point 1 to 2 should be vertical to allow adequate distance from Point 3 to 4. Measure accurately, add 9 inches to total for fastening ends of edge-wire. [2] Allowing 4 inches for fastening end of wire, bend it* (Sec. 2:11) *to fit smooth and snug against face of back liner, Point 1. [3] From face of back liner, Point 1, up to arm-top, edge-wire slants toward the back to lie about 1½ inches behind* the tied-down top coils of springs or inner surface of an inner-spring

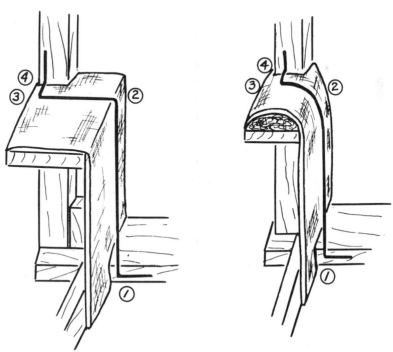

Fig. 10:12B

unit. Hold spring or edge of unit and edge-wire in place, mark wire for bend that goes straight toward the outer side of the armtop, Point 2. Bend and shape wire to clear armtop casing by ½ inch throughout. If wire is closer to casing, it may be difficult to complete upholstering of back and arm.   [4] *At Point* 3, bend wire straight toward the back post to finish about ½ inch from the outer edge, Point 4. Bend wire at back of arm to fit smooth and snug against face of back post.   [5] *Fasten edge-wire* in place to maintain the position for which it was shaped. It should clear the inside arm casing throughout by ½ inch. Fasten ends of wire by folding a small piece of webbing over wire and tacking permanently close to it (Fig. *b* 10:11D).

Sec. 10:12C   Slatless Back Cavity   /   When arms finish through a slatless back cavity, edge-wire extends from the middle of the back liner to the middle of the face of the back post just above armtop casing, Fig. *a* 10:12C; add 9 inches for fastening ends of wire. Shape (Sec. 2:11) and install wire to follow shape of arm but clearing it by ½ inch throughout; fasten ends (Sec. 10:12B). Instead of edge-wire, a doubled-over strip of webbing may be used, Fig. *b* 10:12C. Tack webbing permanently to face of back liner just touching arm casing.

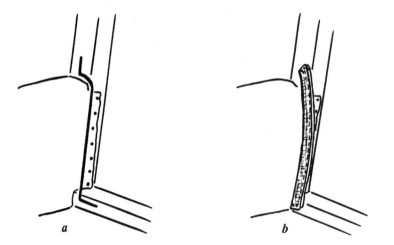

Fig. 10:12C   *a*   *b*

Pull webbing tight by hand, tack to face of back post 2 or 3 inches above armtop. Webbing should fit snug against arm casing but not press into it.

NOTE: When inside arms and/or wing finish through a slatless spring back cavity, edge-wire or webbing used as above would not be strong enough to hold horizontal spring-ties satisfactorily. Back slats should be installed.

**SEC. 10:13
INSTALL BACK
SPRINGS**

Before installing coil springs or inner-spring units, place them on webbing, check all positioning factors for back being upholstered (Sec. 10:11). *[1] Coil springs.* Stitch (Sec. 7:08) springs to webbing (Fig. 10:11J). Staple (Sec. 7:09) springs set on frame. *[2] Inner-spring units.* When back is webbed on the outer surface, stitch (Sec. 7:08) unit to webbing. When back is webbed on the front surface, tack spring unit casing to frame where possible, stitch to webbing elsewhere. If unit is in good condition throughout (no broken ties or rips in casing), it is necessary as a rule to stitch only the coils along the outer edges. After installing spring units, stuff back; no burlap spring cover needed.

**SEC. 10:14
WOODEN SLAT
WEBBING**

Wooden slat webbing allows springs to be set at any point within a back cavity that will produce a necessary thickness (Sec. 10:03). Slat webbing is easy to install in flat backs but often difficult in curved or barrel backs. Slats extend from back liner to top rail. Spring placement is the same as for strip webbing (Sec. 10:11). Staple springs to slat webbing before installing it (Secs. 7:09, 7:10).

**SEC. 10:15
TYING
SPRINGS:
FLAT BACKS**

Sec. 10:15A / Base tied-down height of springs (Sec. 3:16D) on pitch and planned thickness of back (Secs. 10:01A, 10:03). Tools, materials, and mechanics of tying back springs are the same as for seat springs (Secs. 7:11–7:14) for roll or hard edges except: *[1] Use back spring* instead of seat spring twine. *[2] Instead of diagonal ties,* use filler ties (Sec. 10:15E). *[3] Anchor ties* on edge-wire or webbing installed to shape and/or strengthen sides of a back (Sec. 10:12). *[4] For tying spring-edge* backs, see Sec. 10:16.

Sec. 10:15B Vertical Tying / Tie vertical rows of springs first. Start with middle row, tie from back liner to top rail. Return-twine ordinarily is not used at the bottom of a back. *[1] A spring less than about 5 inches* from liner usually is tied first on the second coil from the top when it projects about 2 inches in front of a liner. When projection is less, the first tie may be on the top coil; when projection is more, the first tie may be on the third or even fourth coil from the top. *[2] A spring more than about 5 inches* from liner usually is tied first on the top coil. But if a spring is large or, when tied, will project more than about 3 inches in front of a liner, it may be necessary to tie first on the second coil in order to prevent tilting the top one. *[3] The second tie* always is on the top coil away from the liner. *[4] Tie springs between bottom and top* of a row from top coil to top coil throughout (Fig. *a* 10:11D).

Sec. 10:15C Top of Vertical Rows / How springs at the top of vertical rows are tied depends on planned shape of top of back and stuffing. [1] *Scroll, knife-edge, rounded back tops* (Figs. *c* 1:45, *a* 1:48, *a* 1:49). Regardless of stuffing, tie the upper side of the top spring in a row on any coil, usually the second or third, which tends to keep twine straight from the lower side of the top coil to the point of tacking on the rail (Fig. *a* 10:11D). [2] *Flat-top back* (Fig. *a* 1:42). I—Loose stuffing: Tie spring at the top of a row as in step [1] above, but pull it toward top of back until the upper side of the top coil is level with top of back rail. Correct tilt of top coil by return-twine, Fig. 10:15C. From its anchorage at Point 1, tie return-twine to the upper side of the top coil, Point 2, so as to bring that point down to the approximate level of the top of the other springs. From Point 2,

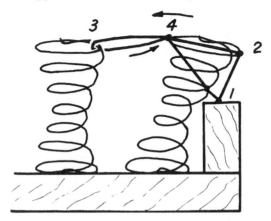

Fig. 10:15C

loop return-twine over upper side of top coil of the next lower spring in the vertical row, Point 3; pull twine toward Point 2 enough to draw Point 2 back about ½ inch from the level of the top of a filler strip or rail. Encompass all twines with a tie on the lower side of the top coil of the top spring in a row, Point 4. When return-twine is completed, the top spring should resist any reasonable effort to push it toward the middle of a back. II—Compact stuffing: Tie top springs in vertical rows as in [1] above. Shape will be built by the stuffing. [3] *Exposed-wood top rail* (Fig. *a* 1:52). Tie top springs in vertical rows as in step [1] above. Use regular return-twine tying as in a seat (Sec. 7:15D) to: I—Hold top coil flat when there is to be a sharp break between inner and top surfaces, and when upholstering with loose stuffing. II—Tilt top coil down toward rail when building a rounded top, or one tapering to the inner surface with any stuffing, or when a sharp break between inner and top surfaces is to be made with compact stuffing.

SEC. 10:15D HORIZONTAL TYING / Tie horizontal rows of springs in a flat back nearly the same way as in vertical rows except for points of anchoring twines. Work from bottom to top. [1] *Armless articles.* Anchor ties on faces of back posts. [2] *Back cavity with slats.* Anchor horizontal ties on faces of slats (Fig. *a* 10:11D). [3] *Back cavity without slats.* Anchor horizontal ties to edge-wire or webbing installed to shape and support the sides of a back where arms finish through back cavity (Sec. 10:12). [4] *Rounded, tapering sides regardless of stuffing; square sides compact stuffing.* Tie vertical rows of springs next to back slats or posts (Sec. 10:15C[1]). When considerable taper at sides is wanted and springs are close to slats or posts, regular return-twine tying as in a roll-edge seat (Sec. 7:14E) may be done. [5] *Square sides loose stuffing.* Tie side springs horizontally (Sec. 10:15C[2]).

Sec. 10:15E Filler Ties, Edge Ties / These help support and shape inside back upholstery; tie with simple overhand knot. [1] *Filler ties.* These are vertical and horizontal ties lying between springs and knotted to horizontal and vertical spring ties (Fig. 10:11D). Filler ties build a mesh to help support back upholstery. They are more important for thinly than thickly stuffed backs and for loose stuffing, but should be used regardless of stuffing and its thickness. [2] *Edge ties.* On large backs spring-built for square sides and flat top, and especially when upholstering with loose stuffing, additional filler ties often encompass a spring area much as spring edge-wire would, Fig. 10:15E.

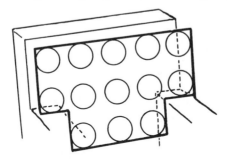

Fig. 10:15E

These ties hold a spring cover smooth and even between springs. Tie on outer edges of top coils; pull twine tight between springs but not enough to shift top coils.

SEC. 10:16
SPRING-EDGE
BACK

When upholstered with loose stuffing, large backs with square sides and flat top (Fig. *a* 1:42) frequently have spring edges (Sec. 5:04). This is not recommended for inexperienced upholsterers, because if springs are not tied exactly the correct way, the finished back is apt to sag between corners; and unless a back is stuffed properly, edges may be hard and uncomfortable. Build a spring-edge back, Fig. 10:16, essen-

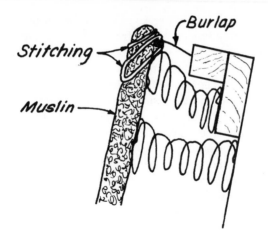

Fig. 10:16

tially as a bridle-built spring-edge seat (Secs. 7:15–7:29) except: [*1*] *Use back* materials throughout. [*2*] *Web and install springs* (Secs. 10:11, 10:13). Below armtops set springs ½ inch from inside arm casing (Fig. 10:15E). [*3*] *Above arms* tie springs (Sec. 10:15) so that the outer edges of the top coils lie ½ inch back from the outer sides of a frame instead of at the outer edges as in a spring-edge seat. [*4*] *Below armtops* tie springs as for a hard-edge seat (Sec. 7:14). [*5*] *Before covering springs with burlap,* check spring action or go-down, make sure that no springs hang up on twines; if they do, change twine anchor positions. [*6*] *For a softer back,* cover understuffing with muslin instead of burlap. [*7*] *Before building* a spring-edge back, study the remainder of this chapter carefully.

SEC. 10:17 TYING SPRINGS: CURVED OR BARREL BACK	**SEC. 10:17A** / Coil springs in curved or barrel backs (Figs. *a* 1:35, *a* 1:37) usually are tied in vertical rows only. The horizontal space between any two springs in a barrel back is less at the tied surface, A, Fig. 10:17A, than at the webbing, B. Horizontal ties would hold springs together and force them to slant instead of go down straight under compression, 2 toward 1. This constant distortion would ruin springs, and the top coils would wear holes in the spring cover and possibly damage the stuffing. Coil springs can be tied horizontally without ill effects, but a simpler and equally satisfactory method is to stuff between vertical rows (Sec. 10:17D); use the finest quality loose hair stuffing. *Tools:* Upholsterer's hammer, shears, large curved needle, tape measure (Secs. 2:02, 2:04, 2:06, 2:16). *Materials:* Tacks, back-spring twine, stitching twine, burlap, quality loose hair stuffing (Secs. 3:03, 3:08, 3:24, 3:29).

SEC. 10:17B TIE VERTICAL ROWS / Tie vertical rows of springs (Secs. 10:15B, C). Tie filler-type ties (Sec. 10:15E) on vertical rows

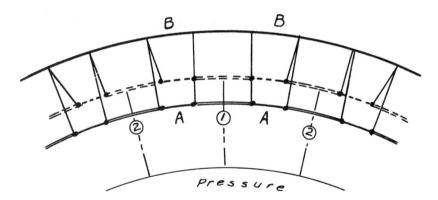

Fig. 10:17A

along outer sides of top coils from liner to top rail. These help shape and support the spring cover and loose stuffing placed between vertical rows (Secs. 10:17C, D).

SEC. 10:17C SPRING COVER / The burlap spring cover must be wide enough to reach from side to side of an inside back (Sec. 10:18) when pushed down loosely to the faces of the liner and top rail between each vertical row of springs. It must be long enough to reach over springs, without compressing them, from the middle of the face of the liner to that of the top rail. Add 2 inches to each measurement for general handling. No additional burlap is required, except for building roll edges and basic shape, if needed (Secs. 10:19–10:21). [1] *Center spring cover* over inside back, push down loosely in place near middle of back. [2] *Tack bottom* of first trough to face of liner. Draw burlap in trough fairly tight toward the top, tack to face of top rail. Working from middle toward sides, push burlap down between vertical rows of springs to form troughs similar to the first, tack to liner and top rail the same way, Fig. 10:17C. At the middle of each vertical row of springs, tack burlap to liner and top rail. Make it tight enough to fit against springs without compressing them. Pleat (Sec. 5:17) excess burlap. [3] *Stitch burlap* (Sec. 7:18) to springs and ties in vertical rows only. Do not extend twine from one row to another.

Fig. 10:17C

[4] Install loose stuffing in troughs. Fill with enough stuffing to push burlap in under top coils of springs. Pack stuffing rather firmly, but not hard.

SEC. 10:17D   STUFF BACKS / *[1] Install loose stuffing* for a spring barrel back (Sec. 10:22). *[2] Install compact stuffing* for spring barrel backs (Sec. 10:28). *[3] For channeling and tufting*, styles recommended for spring barrel backs (Chapters 20 and 21).

SEC. 10:18 **BURLAPPING** **INSIDE BACKS**	**SEC. 10:18A** / In most backs, burlap is tacked to liner and top rail, then along slats or posts. But when a back curves between top and bottom (Figs. 1:12, 1:14), tack burlap first on slats or posts, working from bottom to top, then along liner and top rail. For spring backs, draw burlap snugly over the springs without compressing them. For general mechanics of burlapping, see Sec. 5:02. Pleat (Sec. 5:17) at corners of a spring back where necessary. *Tools:* Upholsterer's hammer, shears, large curved needle, tape measure (Secs. 2:02, 2:04, 2:06, 2:16). *Materials:* Tacks, stitching twine, burlap (Secs. 3:03, 3:08, 3:24).

SEC. 10:18B   PREPARE, INSTALL BURLAP / Save time and materials when upholstering pad rounded or scroll backs by using burlap long enough to build basic shape into the top (Secs. 10:19–10:21). *[1] For most backs.* Burlap reaches from the middle of the face of a liner to that of the top rail. However, when planning a single-piece cover for seat and back (Figs. 1:14, 1:17), inside back burlap generally is an extension of seat burlap (Sec. 6:04B). *[2] Inside arms and wings not finishing through back cavity.* Inside back burlap extends from middle of face of one back post to that of the other (Fig. 8:09B). *[3] Inside arm and/or wings finishing through back cavity with slats.* Burlap extends from middle of face of one slat to that of the other, Fig. *a* 10:18B. Fill gaps between posts and slats with small strips of burlap for arms or wings not finishing through back cavity. *[4] Inside arms and/or wings finishing through slatless back cavity.* Burlap extends around back-supporting edge-wire or burlap (Sec. 10:12) to backs of posts. Stitch burlap (Sec. 7:18) to webbing or edge-wire, *b.* When upholstering outside back, burlap pulled through the back cavity will be tacked to inner sides of posts (Fig. 10:10C). If only arms finish through a back cavity, tack burlap above them to faces of posts; cut burlap to pull under webbing or edge-wire set along an arm, Fig. *b* 10:18B. If only wings finish through a back cavity, tack burlap to faces of posts below wings, and cut it to allow a pull-through at the wings. *[5] Wings upholstered as part of inside back.* Burlap extends to middle of wing posts. *[6] Stitch burlap* (Sec. 7:18) to springs, *a.* When planning

a

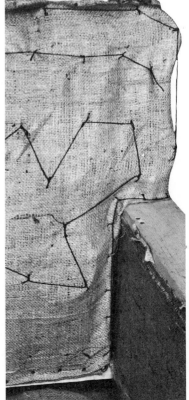

b

Fig. 10:18B

sharp breaks between inner, top, and side surfaces, stitch burlap around outer top coils of springs, *b*, and along spring edge-wire or filler ties, if any.

SEC. 10:19 **BUILDING** **BASIC SHAPE**	Pad and spring inside backs usually are specially "padded" along sides and top to build basic shape for upholstery. As a rule, it is easier and more practical to build basic shape first and develop final shape from it, than to build final shape in one operation. Basic shape also is built to help protect the cover. Build basic shape after burlapping an inside back. Basic shape construction depends chiefly on how a back will be stuffed. [*1*] *Roll edges* (Sec. 5:05) generally are used when upholstering with loose stuffing. But for exposed-wood and thick backs (Sec. 10:20), bridle-built hard edges may be easier. [*2*] *Bridle-built hard edges* (Sec. 7:21) often are used instead of roll edges in exposed-wood and thick backs (Sec. 10:20) and sometimes used as a base for compact stuffing (Sec. 10:28). [*3*] *For a thick back with square sides and flat top*, often it is necessary to stitch loose stuffing to hold shape along sides and top (Sec. 10:25). Do this after incasing back with muslin (Fig. 10:11J). [*4*] *Understuffing*, used most commonly to shape the top of a spring back (Sec. 10:21), is done for loose and compact stuffings. Compact stuffing frequently is the understuffing (Sec. 10:28J).
SEC. 10:20 **EDGES FOR** **BACKS**	Pad backs usually have roll edges; spring backs have roll or bridle-built hard edges. Spring-edge backs (Sec. 10:16) have basic shape and do not need additional work of this type. Whether a roll or a hard edge is used depends on the planned thickness and shape of a back at the top, sides, and bottom and the type of back. For tools, materials, and mechanics of roll edges and prebuilt edging (Secs. 5:05, 5:06). For bridle-built hard edges (Sec. 7:21); usually three rows of stitching are needed, the second and third being the same type. [*1*] *Exposed-wood back treated as fully upholstered* (Fig. *a* 1:52). On exposed-wood edges there must be at least ½ inch space between the basic shape upholstery edge and the frame side of a rabbet for finishing the cover. When a rabbet is too narrow to have this space if a roll edge or prebuilt edging is installed, build a bridle hard edge. It also should be used in exposed-wood backs when they will be more than about 2 inches thick near the exposed wood and there is to be a sharp break between the inner and other surfaces of a back. [*2*] *Back to be upholstered with loose stuffing ½ to 2 inches thick along outer edges of inner surface.* Use roll edges depending on shape to be built. When stuffing will be more than about 2 inches thick, shape edges by stitching after back is incased with muslin (Sec. 10:25). [*3*] *Sharp breaks between inner and top and/or side surfaces of back* (Figs. 1:14, *b* 1:45). Install roll edge on face of top rail or filler strip and/or on faces of

back posts, Fig. 10:20. When a roll edge is built only on a post, *b*, it tapers to an ending, usually at the upper rear edge of a top rail, or at the end of a scroll in a scroll back.   [*4*] *For cover border or panel on back post* (Fig. 1:16), install roll edge along outer edges of the post faces to give the border or panel a "set in" appearance. If a roll edge is not installed, a similar appearance may be achieved with felted padding when covering.   [*5*] *Roll edges on spring barrel backs* should be relatively soft, but not flimsy.

 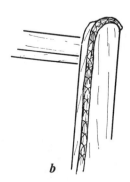

Fig. 10:20   *a*   *b*

SEC. 10:21
UNDER-
STUFFING
BACKS

SEC. 10:21A / Pad and spring backs are understuffed differently. In pad backs, understuffing is chiefly for building basic shape in rounded and scroll tops similar to armtops (Fig. *a*, *b* 8:17B). In spring backs, by filling hollows between springs and roll edges or frame, as at top of back in Fig. 10:18, understuffing builds an even, firm foundation for overstuffing. Except where square sides are wanted (Fig. *a* 1:42), usually only the top of a back is understuffed. For best results with loose stuffing, use a fiber-hair mix (Sec. 3:30) instead of top quality hair. Compact stuffing often understuffs a back with square sides and/or a flat top (Fig. *a* 1:42, Sec. 10:28).   *Tools:* Upholsterer's hammer, shears, large curved needle, regulator, upholstery skewers, tape measure (Secs. 2:02, 2:04, 2:06, 2:07, 2:08, 2:16).   *Materials:* Tacks, stitching twine, burlap, stuffing (Secs. 3:03, 3:08, 3:24, 10:04A).

SEC. 10:21B PAD BACKS / [*1*] *Rounded, scroll tops.* Understuff as similar armtops (Sec. 8:12). [*2*] *Knife-edge, flat tops.* Usually not understuffed.

SEC. 10:21C SPRING BACKS: KNIFE-EDGE, ROUNDED, SCROLL / [*1*] *Understuffing builds back shape* from upper limits of spring area, Fig. 10:21C, to rear top edge of rail in knife-edge and rounded backs, to end of scroll in scroll backs. [*2*] *Length of burlap.* Use burlap 3 inches longer than the planned shape of understuffing from spring area to back of top rail. Measure length by roughly forming planned

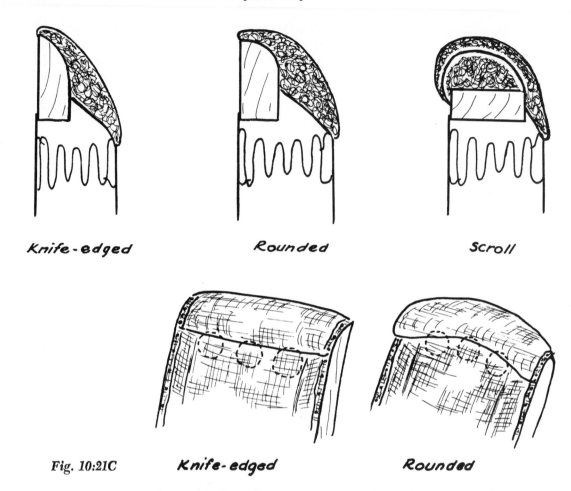

Knife-edged   Rounded   Scroll

Fig. 10:21C   Knife-edged   Rounded

shape of understuffing with a tape measure; allow for roll edges if any.
[3] *Width of stuffing.* Cut burlap flap 3 inches wider than measurement. Understuffing crosses a back: I—Between outer sides of back
posts in wingless articles. II—Between outer sides of wing posts when
inside wings are upholstered as part of back. III—Between wings that
are upholstered independently (Fig. 10:18B). [4] *Wingless knife-
edge, rounded backs; wings upholstered as part of back.* Understuffing
usually tapers smoothly from sides of spring area to those of the back
posts, Fig. 10:21C, or wing posts.   [5] *Scroll backs; inside wings upholstered separately.* Understuffing is about the same thickness throughout, but slightly thicker at the middle of a back to build crown (Sec.
5:14).

SEC. 10:21D BUILD UNDERSTUFFING /   [1] *Center burlap* on inside
back with its upper edge 1 inch above upper limits of spring area.

[2] *Overturn upper edge* of burlap 1 inch, pin in place across back, then stitch to springs, ties, and burlap spring cover (Sec. 7:18). Pull burlap strip fairly tight to sides without compressing springs; tack to frame. [3] *Install loose stuffing* (Secs. 5:11A, B, C) to build desired shape and firmness of understuffing. Stitch down full amount of stuffing to help build a firm shape. Completed understuffing should curve smoothly and regularly from spring area to back of top rail, with the same degree of taper to the sides. It should be moderately hard throughout. Flabby or soft understuffing will not hold shape; if too hard, it makes an uncomfortable shoulder or head rest. When there are built-up edges, be sure to place enough stuffing along them; otherwise a back may sag between built-up edges, allowing them to show through and wear out the cover. [4] *Hold understuffing firmly* in place while drawing casing over it, as a casing tends to force stuffing away from the inner side of a back. Push back stuffing that works over the outer side of a top rail; it could prevent good installation of the cover. [5] *Tack casing* to back of top rail near upper edge. When understuffing does not taper to an end at the side of a back, fold end of casing in under stuffing before tacking at the side along a top rail in order to seal in stuffing. Regulate stuffing (Sec. 5:07) to correct lumps and hollows, and work it toward the rear upper edge of a top rail.

**SEC. 10:22
STUFFING
INSIDE BACKS**

Sec. 10:22A / When upholstering inside backs with loose stuffing take special care to install it (Secs. 5:11A–C) smoothly and with uniform density throughout. Lumps, hollows, and irregular densities make a back uncomfortable. It should be uniformly soft to the touch and uniformly firm under pressure but with a band of extra firmness across the back in the lumbar area (Sec. 10:03B[4]). When upholstering with compact stuffing, for best results first build backs lightly with loose stuffing and incase with muslin; this provides a smooth, shaped base for compact stuffing. *Tools:* Same as Sec. 10:21A. *Materials:* Tacks, stitching twine, stuffing, muslin (Secs. 3:03, 3:08, 3:27–3:44, 3:48).

Sec. 10:22B **Placement of Stuffing** / [1] *Knife-edge, rounded tops.* Stuffing extends to rear upper edge of top rail. [2] *Scroll top.* Stuffing covers scroll down to outer side of top rail or under-rail strip. Do not tack overstuffing along rail or strip; it could prevent good installation of the covers. [3] *Flat top; and when border, boxing to be used* (Secs. 11:05, 11:06). Loose stuffing installed across face of top rail extends to lower side of built-up edges, if any; if no built-up edge, stuffing usually extends to but not over top front edge of rail. For compact stuffing see Sec. 10:28. [4] *Tapered, rounded sides.* Stuffing extends to but not around rear outer edges of back or wing posts. [5]

Square sides; and when panel, border, boxing to be used. If there are built-up edges along back posts, loose stuffing extends to inner sides of edges. If no built-up edges, stuffing extends to but not over outer edges of back posts. For compact stuffing see Sec. 10:28.   [6] *Inside arms, wings not part of back.* Stuffing extends as close as possible to arm and wing casings. I—When casings do not finish through back cavity, tack stuffing to faces of back posts. II—When arms or wings finish through back cavity, fasten stuffing along back slats or to the burlap along side-supporting edge-wire or webbing (Sec. 10:12).   [7] *Inside arms, wings finishing into back.* Stuffing extends to join that of arms and wings throughout.   [8] *Bottom of back away from seat* (Figs. 1:09, 1:19, 1:22). Stuff along bottom of back as at the top and sides.   [9] *Bottom of back against seat.* Extend stuffing down to but not over lower edge of the face of the back liner; tack to liner.   [*10*] *Back finishing into seat* (Figs. 1:14, 1:17). Inside back stuffing joins seat stuffing (Sec. 6:04D).

SEC. 10:22C   AMOUNT OF STUFFING   /   [*1*] *Due to size,* most inside backs need more loose stuffing to build crown (Sec. 5:14) and more crown than other surfaces.   [2] *Built-up edges.* Use ample loose stuffing along inner sides of built-up edges; otherwise they may show through and wear out the cover.   [3] *Arms, wings not part of back.* Use enough stuffing at sides to build back snug and flush against arms and wings. This stuffing can be altered while incasing back with muslin. Also, arms and wings usually can be opened and restuffed to keep a back from being made out of proportion to the rest of an article.   [4] *Bottom of back.* Place enough stuffing at bottom of back finishing against a seat to close any gap between them. But do not stuff back so much as to reduce desired seat depth (Sec. 10:01B).   [5] *Back projects over and around arms.* Be sure to place enough stuffing in these corners of a back. Without it, they will develop unsightly and hard-to-repair sags.   [6] *Top and/or sides of back to be shaped by stitching* (Sec. 10:25). Place a large amount of loose stuffing along these parts. Of course, the actual amount needed depends on the size of a back and thickness at top and/or sides. This stuffing can be altered to fit back and build desired shape while incasing with muslin. [7] *For greatest comfort,* install stuffing firmly enough to hold shape and build a soft surface. Inside back stuffing usually is much softer than that of arms.

**SEC. 10:23
PREPARING
MUSLIN
CASING**

SEC. 10:23A   /   Inside back muslin casings are single-piece and boxed (Fig. 10:23C). Boxed casings (Sec. 11:06) are chiefly for large spring backs (Fig. *a* 1:42) that have flat tops and square sides; single-piece casings are for most other backs. A major advantage of boxed

casing for inexperienced upholsterers is the practice it gives for preparing a boxed cover.   *Tools:* Shears, sewing machine for boxed cover,
tape measure (Secs. 2:04, 2:15, 2:16).   *Materials:* Upholstery thread
for boxed casing, muslin (Secs. 3:09, 3:48).

SEC. 10:23B SINGLE-PIECE CASING / [1] *Width of casing* is the
greatest distance across an inside back, usually at or near the top;
measure along inner surface of curved and barrel-type backs. I—Casing
for rounded and tapering sides usually finishes on backs of posts. II—
When a post panel, border, or boxing will be used, casing finishes on
outer sides of posts.   **[2]** *Length of casing* is the greatest distance
from the back of a liner or bottom rail, except when seat and back
upholsteries are joined together (Sec. 6:04M), to the back of a top rail
in knife-edge, rounded, and scroll tops, but only to the top of a top
rail in flat-top backs or when a border or boxing will be used. When
measuring length, allow for overall shape of a back, Fig. 10:23B.   **[3]**
Casing for exposed-wood backs finishes on rabbets of exposed-wood
parts.   **[4]** *Add at least 3 inches* to measured width and length for
general handling of casing.

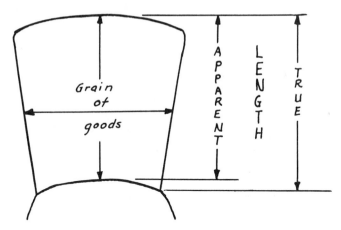

Fig. 10:23B

SEC. 10:23C BOXED CASING / A boxed casing is a sheet of casing
for the inner surface of a back to which is sewn a strip of casing for
the sides and top, Fig. 10:23C. Boxed casings are not essential to neat
upholstery, but simplify work and are recommended for all inside
backs that will be more than about 2 inches thick, from back of frame
to edges of the inner surface, and have square sides and a flat top
(Fig. *a* 1:42).   **[1]** *Measure and block-cut casing* for inner surface of
back, Fig. *a* 10:23C. It should be 3 inches wider than a back frame at
its widest point, and 5 inches longer than the distance from the plane
of the top of a top rail down the inner surface of a back and under the
liner to its rear edge, down to the seat when seat and back upholsteries

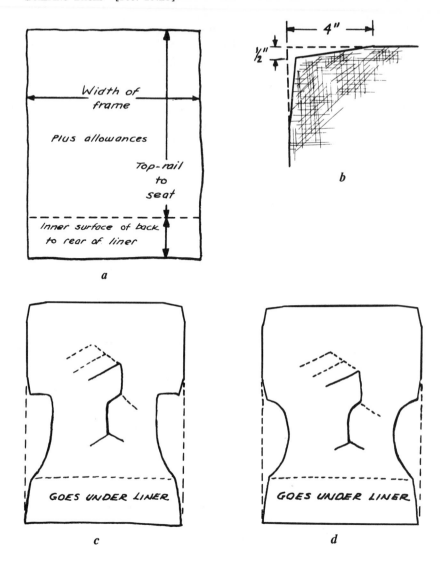

Fig. 10:23C

a

b

c

d

are joined together (Sec. 6:04M). "Block-cut" means to cut goods in a simple rectangle based on width and length. Shape cutting, as for arms, is done later.   [2] *Crown allowance.* In order for boxed casing seams to lie fairly straight along the edges of an inside back and to prevent puckering of casing at the corners, an allowance must be made for crown (Sec. 5:14). Crown of the inner surface of a back has the effect of drawing a casing away from the middle of the top, sides, and bottom. Allow for crown by cutting the corners of an inner-surface casing, *b*. For the average back, the sides of each corner-cut are about 4 inches long from a ½-inch base.   [3] *Plot for arms.* Measure distance from top of top rail down along the front edge of a back post to armtop casing. At this distance from the top corner of the inner surface casing, cut (Sec. 5:15) inward from the edges to follow shape of armtop and junction of inside back and arm, *c, d*. Note that at the seat, the patterns flare out slightly; this is needed to fill junctions of seat, arms, and back.   [4] *Seam allowance*. Cut inner-surface casing to allow for a ½-inch seam for sewing boxing.   [5] *Measure boxing*. Measure width of boxing along top edges of inner-surface casing and down the sides to the position of a back liner. Length of boxing is the planned thickness of a back from the inner surface to faces of posts and rail. Add 3 inches to width and 2 to length to allow for seams and general handling. Backs often are thicker at the bottom than the top, so a boxing may be longer at and below armtops than at the top of a back.

NOTE: For muslin casing, width may be cut the long way of the goods. But for cover, width is measured across the goods, and strips of cover usually are pieced together to make the needed width of boxing.

Sec. 10:23D   Sew Casing   /   Center boxing on inner-surface casing, usually at the middle of the top, and sew together with a ½-inch flat seam, Fig. 10:23D and Sec. 12:02. For very thick backs it may be necessary to sew cover stretchers (Sec. 11:09) to boxing at and below inner sides of armtops.

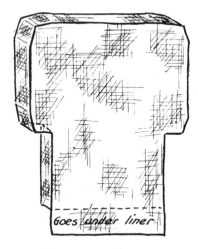

Goes under liner

Fig. 10:23D

SEC. 10:24
INCASING
INSIDE BACK

Sec. 10:24A   /   A small amount of loose stuffing, or felted padding if upholstering with compact stuffing, usually is needed for correcting shape while incasing a back with muslin.   *Tools:* Upholsterer's hammer, shears, small curved needle, regulator for loose stuffing, upholstery skewers (Secs. 2:02, 2:04, 2:06, 2:07, 2:08).   *Materials:* Tacks, upholstery twine, loose stuffing or felted padding (Secs. 3:03, 3:08, 3:28, 3:49).

SEC. 10:24B   POSITION CASING   /   Center casing on inside back, pull bottom edge under liner or lower rail except, of course, when seat and back upholsteries are joined together (Sec. 6:04M). Sequence of tacking and tightening (Sec. 5:18) inside back casing, essentially the same for all backs and methods of upholstering, is shown in Fig. 10:24C. Variations and additional points of finishing a casing are given for specific kinds of backs, arms, and wings. For single-piece casings see Sec. 10:24C; boxed casings, Sec. 10:24D; for back curved between top and bottom, Sec. 10:24E.

SEC. 10:24C   SINGLE-PIECE CASING   /   [1] *Draw casing fairly snug* to first point of finishing at middle of top, Point 1 in Fig. *a, b* 10:24C; sliptack. Draw casing fairly snug under bottom of back, sliptack at middle of back liner or lower rail, Point 2. Tighten casing moderately from middle toward top midway between Point 1 and corners; sliptack at Points 3 and 4. Repeat this toward bottom and corners, Points 5 and 6, which should be on the same grain of goods as Points 3 and 4 to avoid tacking on the bias. Throughout positioning and sliptacking keep grain of casing straight or regularly curving. Complete setting a casing across the top rail and liner or lower rail as on a curved arm (Sec. 8:17) to the point at which it begins to wrinkle at the sides and cutting or pleating (Secs. 5:15, 5:17) is necessary.   [2] *Armless articles.* Following the sequence in *a, b,* tighten casing from middle of back toward sides, sliptack at points about midway between top rail and liner or lower rail, Points 7 and 8. Tighten casing upward from middle toward a side, tack at Point 9, about midway between Point 8 and corner. Repeat toward bottom to tack at Point 10, then on the other side for Points 11 and 12. Tighten casing along sides from middle to top and bottom as along the top rail and liner or lower rail. I—Barrel back: Do not tighten casing enough to change planned shape of back. II—Rounded, tapering sides: Push back stuffing that works over outer rear edges of posts; it could prevent good installation of the cover. III—Built-up edges: Push back stuffing that works over built-up edges; it could cause lumps in the cover. IV—Post panel, border: Place enough loose stuffing or felted padding over the front edge of a post to make a small, simulated built-up edge to protect the cover and give the panel or border a "set-in" appearance; simulated edges may be altered or completely built with felted padding when covering.   [3] *Arm, wing articles.* Cut (Sec. 5:15) back casing to finish through same cavity as arms and wings. Set and tighten back casing above arms when there are no wings at Points 1 through 12, *c, d,* the same way as for armless articles, [2] above. Finishing a back over arms often is the hardest part

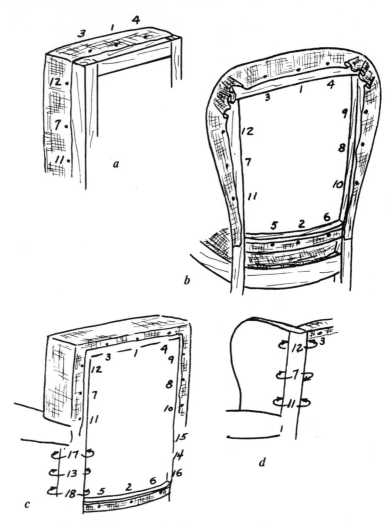

Fig. 10:24C

of incasing an inside back. Arms frequently must be opened at the back and the stuffing altered in order to fit smoothly against a back. When an armtop is rounded, open casing at back; finish back casing over armtop, then replace armtop casing, adding stuffing if necessary so that lines of the arm extend smoothly to the outer edge of a back. To finish back casing around an armtop, pull edge of goods tightly between armtop casing and back stuffing, draw it tight to the point of finishing on the back post to follow shape of armtop. If this is not done, back stuffing will not be sealed in effectively, and there probably will be an appreciable gap between armtop and inside back. In wing articles, finish back casing over wing casings except when wings are upholstered after an inside back is covered (Sec. 10:26). Set and tighten casing below the same way as above arms, except for finishing around armtops, at Points 13 through 18, *c, d:* I—When arm and back casings finish into each other (Fig. 8:09D), loosen arm casing and pin to back casing while setting and tightening the latter; then trim both casings along junction of arm and back, allowing a ½-inch seam for each; underturn edges of casings, repin them tight and smooth in place, sew together with an overhand or whip stitch. II—Regardless of how back casing finishes at the sides, when the bottom of a back fits flush against a seat, cut a small tab to go under each arm liner (Fig. 8:20A); pulled tight and tacked to faces or outer sides of back posts, tabs hold bottom of back casing in place. [4] *Tighten and adjust back casing* until desired shape, thickness (Sec. 10:01B), and firmness are built. Work from middle of top, bottom, and sides to corners in order to make as symmetrical a shape as possible. Alter stuffing (Sec. 10:22) as necessary. From time to time, rub casing all over lightly with the flat of your hand to locate lumps or hollows. Small flaws usually can be regulated (Sec. 5:07), but when flaws are large, wide, or deep, open casing and rework stuffing. Pleat (Sec. 5:17) at corners.

Sec. 10:24D   Boxed Casing /   (Fig. 10:11J). Install single-piece and boxed inside back casings essentially the same way (Sec. 10:24C). Differences are due to a boxed casing having been made to fit a back, particularly at the arms; it must be installed to fit properly.   [1] *Work casing over inside back,* centering it carefully to fit at arms and top. Do not displace stuffing.   [2] *Align top corners* of casing and frame; sliptack.   [3] *Align corners of casing at arms and frame,* cutting to fit it around back posts; sliptack to outer sides of posts.   [4] *Push back casing in place* over armtops and between inner surfaces of arms and back.   [5] *Midway between top corners of back* draw casing to where it is to finish on filler strip or top rail; sliptack.   [6] *Midway between top corners and armtops,* draw casing to where it is to finish on posts; sliptack.   [7] *Tighten casing moderately* from the middle of the inner surface down to the bottom; sliptack to back of liner or lower rail. Do not pull casing down over arms or away from top of back.   [8] *Boxed inside back casing is now set* and shape of back established.   [9] *After boxed back casing is initially set,* follow basic system of tightening a back casing (Sec. 10:24C). However, complete setting the sides above arms before the lower sides, and tighten upper sides completely before tightening the lower sides. Keep casing seams smooth and regular throughout. When a back is to be shaped by stitching (Sec. 10:25), there must be enough loose stuffing along the top and sides to keep stitching from making a depression. Make a rough estimate of the stuffing needed by squeezing a back into the desired shape along the top and sides; when squeezed fairly flat they should be firm and moderately hard. Stitched, these surfaces should project about ½ inch beyond the planes of a frame. By exerting a small amount of pressure outward against the cover, these projections help prevent sagging of the top and sides of a finished back.

SEC. 10:24E   BACK CURVED BETWEEN TOP AND BOTTOM / (Fig. 1:12). Except that setting and tightening are done primarily along the sides from the point of greatest curve toward top and bottom, and then along top and bottom, install inside back casing as in Sec. 10:24C. When tightening toward top and bottom, do not work casing tight enough to change planned shape of back.

SEC. 10:24F   CHECKING, FINISHING BACK / Before considering a back casing finished, check carefully for uniform softness, shape, tightness of casing, and general comfort.   [1] *Except where sharp breaks* are planned between surfaces, backs usually seem to flow smoothly from one part into another.   [2] *Try to pinch up casing* at the middle of an inner surface; if it can be done easily without pressing into the stuffing, the casing is too loose to hold shape satisfactorily.   [3] *Pleats* should be as tight and nearly as smooth as the rest of a casing.   [4] *Try it!* Put an upholstery cushion or folded soft blanket on the deck of a loose-cushion article, and SIT! Squirm around! Is the back comfortable?   [5] *Except for back stitching*, if any (Sec. 10:25), the comfort, shape, and appearance of an inside back are now, Fig. 10:24F, basically what they will be when it is covered. Minor changes in shape, but not in comfort, usually can be made with felted padding while covering it. However, too much of this can make a back hard and uncomfortable; reworking stuffing and casing is the better solution. After a back checks out satisfactorily, drive tacks permanently at all points except on casing that finishes through a slatless back cavity. This must be loosened for installing inside arm and back covers, and then is tacked permanently. Trim off excess casing 1 inch from fully driven tacks except along exposed-wood edges; there trim off about ¼ inch from tacks.

**SEC. 10:25
STITCHING
FLAT TOP,
SQUARE SIDES**

SEC. 10:25A / (Fig. 10:11J). Having enough stuffing on the top and sides is essential to building a durable shape. With too little, a finished back will sag between top corners, and pull in between top and arms, conditions remedied only by reupholstering a back. When stitching holds a top surface down to less than ½ inch above the level of the top of a filler strip or top rail, or pulls a side surface in to project less than ½ inch beyond the outer side of a back post, rip out stitching in that general area, open casing, and restuff. After stitching, often it is necessary to regulate (Sec. 5:07) stuffing at the edges of the inner surface in order to build sharp breaks between it and the top and/or sides.

Fig. 10:24F

Tools: Large double-pointed straight needle, regulator (Secs. 2:06, 2:07). *Materials:* Upholstery twine (Sec. 3:08).

SEC. 10:25B STITCHING, SHAPING / While making each stitch, squeeze stuffed surface to desired shape. Do not squeeze too hard on the top and side surfaces, or they probably will be rough with "hills and valleys" instead of smooth. Also be careful not to press too hard on the inner surface; it also may become rough and uncomfortable. [1] *Jab long point* of needle into top or side surface, as in Fig. *a* 10:25B, at a point about one-third the distance from the frame to the inner surface or planned edge of a back. Aim needle to emerge on inner surface at a point that is the same distance from the planned edge as its point of entry is from the edge. [2] *Draw needle through back* until short point is about halfway between inner and top or side surfaces; then jab needle back to complete stitch, directing it to emerge about halfway between initial entry point and planned edge,

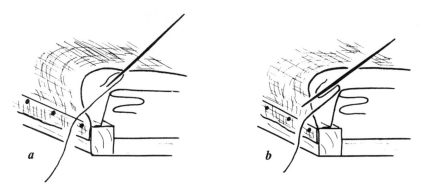

Fig. 10:25B

a   *b*

b. [3] *Tie first stitch* with a slipknot (Sec. 5:03). While pulling twine tight, squeeze surfaces to wanted shape; stitching is to hold shape, not create it.   [4] *In all other stitches* loop twine twice around needle as it emerges from top or side surface to complete a stitch (Fig. 5:05H).   [5] *After completing the last stitch* tie free end of twine around the preceding stitch.

SEC. 10:26 INSIDE BACK WITH SOLID-BASE WINGS NOT FINISHING THROUGH BACK CAVITY	This type of back-wing upholstery is fairly common for small wing chairs (Fig. 1:15). Usually the inside back is completely upholstered before wings (Sec. 9:13). Upholster inside back essentially as any other small back of similar shape, except at sides. There the burlap and muslin casing usually are tacked along back posts close to wings. The cover usually is tacked on wings close to back posts.

SEC. 10:27 INCASING KEYHOLE BACK	(Fig. 1:10.) Install muslin casings (Sec. 10:24) for top, sides, and bottom separately. Miter corners together, trimming casing to allow a ½-inch seam from outer to inner corners. Tack casing strips along inner edges of outside back, underfold, and pin together along planned miter lines. After adjusting casing and stuffing for shape and firmness, blind-stitch (Sec. 13:04) casings together along miter lines, and complete tacking to inner corners.

SEC. 10:28 COMPACT STUFFING	**SEC. 10:28A /** Compact stuffings (Secs. 3:40–3:43) are commonly used for all inside backs except loose-cushion and spring barrel. Most upholsterers feel it is wasted in loose-pillow backs where comfort depends chiefly on the pillow. As for spring barrel backs (Sec. 10:17), many upholsterers believe that loose stuffing allows greater freedom of spring movement, resulting in greater comfort and a more durable job; however, excellent barrel backs are built with compact stuffing. In some ways compact stuffing simplifies upholstering, while in oth-

ers it may not. But in all cases—and this is particularly important for inside backs—compact stuffing is a great help in building smooth, regularly shaped, and comfortable surfaces. For all backs, planning is generally the same for compact as for loose stuffing (Secs. 10:00–10:04). The major difference between compact and loose stuffing work is in building crown (Sec. 5:14). [1] *Pad backs.* Build crown by understuffing with loose stuffing, or by placing loose stuffing over compact when incasing with muslin, or by installing extra felted padding with the cover. [2] *Most spring backs.* Understuffing with loose stuffing is almost essential; with a combination of springs and understuffing, crown is easily built. [3] *Fairly thick spring backs with square sides, flat top* (Fig. *a* 1:42). Compact stuffing is often understuffing for top and sides, and to build crown.

Sec. 10:28B / Secs. 10:00–10:27 deal primarily with loose stuffing but also have "how to" for compact stuffing upholstery. Here in Sec. 10:28 the how to for compact stuffing work is isolated and given as "the same as for loose stuffing, Sec. . . ." or "the same as for loose stuffing, except. . . ." For flat pad and spring backs, Secs. 10:28E–K; curved or barrel backs, Sec. 10:28L.

Sec. 10:28C Casings / All except very small backs (Figs. 1:07, 1:09, 1:10, 1:12) should have two muslin casings. First, incasing of loose understuffing used to build basic shape and crown and provide in spring backs a smooth foundation for compact stuffing. The second casing, for overstuffing, is not as necessary for compact as for loose stuffing, since compact builds a solid surface. But incasing compact stuffing is an excellent opportunity to correct and improve shape. For very small inside backs, as listed above, required crown is so small that it can be built satisfactorily with felted padding when covering. In most small exposed-wood backs (Figs. 1:07, 1:12) there is not enough space for worthwhile understuffing and incasing before installing compact stuffing.

Sec. 10:28D Exposed-Wood Backs / In order to fit smoothly and leave enough space for tacking casing and cover, prepare compact stuffing to parallel, from a distance of ½ inch, the line of the inner edge of the rabbet or marked limits of upholstery.

Sec. 10:28E Flat Pad, Spring Backs: Pad Backs / [1] *French back* (Sec. 10:05). Prepare compact stuffing the proper size and shape (Sec. 10:28D), and bond to the burlap or canvas over the outside back padding. Build crown (Sec. 10:28A). [2] *Flat, slip, exposed-wood pad backs.* Upholster with compact stuffing (Secs. 10:07–10:09), except: I—No hard or other built-up edges; compact stuffing provides them. II—For exposed-wood backs, prepare stuffing (Sec. 10:28D), bond to solid back or burlap cover. [*3*] *Fully upholstered pad backs.* Web for compact stuffing (Secs. 10:10, 10:12).

SEC. 10:28F SPRING BACKS / [*1*] *Web* for compact stuffing (Secs. 10:10, 10:12). [*2*] *Position coil springs* for compact as for loose stuffing (Secs. 10:13, 10:14) except when building a fairly thick back with square sides and flat top (Fig. *a* 1:42). Instead of setting springs close to outer edges of sides and top of frame, set them back. The amount of set-back usually is the thickness of the compact stuffing. For placement of inner-spring units for compact stuffing (Secs. 10:19, 10:30). [*3*] *Tie springs* for flat backs for compact stuffing as in Sec. 10:15 except that for a fairly thick back with square sides and flat top, tie springs as for knife-edge, rounded, and scroll backs (Sec. 10:15C). For spring-edge back construction (Sec. 10:16).

SEC. 10:28G PAD AND SPRING BACKS / [*1*] *Burlap* pad and spring backs for compact stuffing (Sec. 10:18). [*2*] *Building basic* along the edges of a back, usually done for loose stuffing (Secs. 10:19, 10:20), is not as a rule done for compact stuffing. [*3*] *Border or panel on back post.* When a cover will have a border or panel (Sec. 10:20), the "set-in" appearance generally is made by projecting compact stuffing beyond the outer sides of posts; how far is up to the upholsterer. However, projection of less than ¼ inch is not sufficiently noticeable and more than about ¾ inch may seem too puffy. [*4*] *Understuffing to build shape* in pad backs (Sec. 10:21B) and in spring backs to fill between spring area and the rest of a back (Secs. 10:21C, D), is done the same way for compact as for loose stuffing.

SEC. 10:28H FLAT SPRING-BACK UNDERSTUFFING / Except when upholstering with inner-spring units (Secs. 10:29, 10:30), understuff spring backs and incase with muslin to provide a smooth, regular, shaped foundation for compact stuffing. Understuff and incase with muslin (Secs. 10:22–10:25), except: [*1*] *Thickness.* Build understuffing just thick enough to fill hollows between spring area and frame and between spring coils and ties. The only purpose of this understuffing is to build a smooth shape. The purpose of compact stuffing is to build comfort; the thicker it is, the greater the comfort. But the thicker the understuffing is, the thinner the compact stuffing must be. [*2*] *Knife-edge, rounded, scroll tops.* Extend understuffing and casing to points listed in Sec. 10:22B. [*3*] *All other back tops, sides.* Finish understuffing and casing on front surfaces of frame near the inner edges. [*4*] *Thick back with square sides, flat top* (Fig. *a* 1:42). Understuffing may be stitched to hold shape (Sec. 10:25). But many experienced upholsterers understuff the sides and/or top with compact stuffing (Sec. 10:28I).

SEC. 10:28I FLAT BACK COMPACT STUFFING INSTALLATION / With few differences, extend compact stuffing for flat inside backs to the same points and treat in the same manner as loose stuffing (Sec. 10:22). [*1*] *Fastening.* All compact stuffings may be bonded (Sec. 5:11) to frame and understuffing casing. But rubberized hair commonly is tacked to a frame and stitched elsewhere. [*2*] *Taper.* When compact stuffing for an inside back is to finish at the outer edges of a frame, as at the top and sides of a knife-edge back, at the top of a rounded back, and just below the top on the outside surface, as in a scroll back, taper stuffing on the underside, as indicated by dash-lines in Fig. *a* 10:28I. Tapering the underside keeps the inner surface of stuffing smooth. Amount and steepness of taper depend on the shape to be made. Taper usually can be easily changed by trimming off or bonding on pieces of stuffing. When stuffing is not more than about ½ inch thick, tapering may not be necessary; instead, a casing or cover may be used to hold stuffing to shape. [*3*] *Fairly thin inside back.*

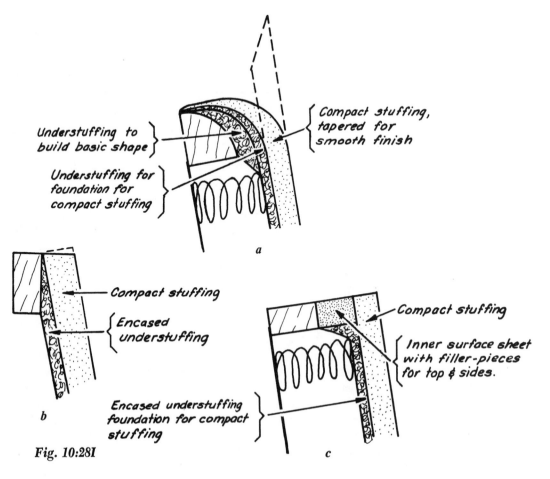

Understuffing to build basic shape

Understuffing for foundation for compact stuffing

Compact stuffing, tapered for smooth finish

a

Compact stuffing

Encased understuffing

b

Encased understuffing foundation for compact stuffing

Compact stuffing

Inner surface sheet with filler-pieces for top & sides.

c

Fig. 10:28I

When building with compact stuffing not more than 1-inch thick, and there will be sharp breaks between inner and other surfaces (Fig. 1:14), stuffing generally is a single sheet extending to the outer edges, Fig. *b* 10:28I. Depending on shape built by understuffing, it may be necessary to trim edges of the inner surface stuffing to make desired sharp breaks. [4] *Compact stuffing more than 1-inch thick.* When there are to be sharp breaks between inner and other surfaces (Fig. *a* 1:42), instead of using a single sheet of stuffing and bending it to form the sides and top, often it is easier to use a single sheet for the inner surface and filler strips for sides and top, as in Fig. *c* 10:28I. Prepare stuffing large enough for the complete inner surface; install carefully in proper position. For best results filler strips must exactly fit spaces between the frame and undersurface of the main stuffing, neither pushing up nor pulling it down at the edges. It is advisable, especially when an understuffing slopes appreciably from the front of a frame, to trim the filler strips for a smooth, tight fit against the frame and the understuffing.

Sec. 10:28J   Flat Back with Compact Understuffing / Instead of loose stuffing, flat inside backs often are understuffed with compact stuffing. It is an easier way to build smooth, regular shape and a more comfortable back but may cost more. Rubberized hair is a popular understuffing because, when more than about 1 inch thick, it can be installed with good results directly on a burlap webbing or spring cover (Sec. 10:18). A small amount of loose stuffing usually is needed to build basic shape at the top and sides of some backs, and to build crown (Sec. 10:28A). Rubberized hair also may be the main or overstuffing, although polyfoam and foam rubber are more common. [1] *Roll, bridle hard edges; back stitching.* Not for compact stuffing. [2] *Back tops.* Tops of some backs are understuffed to build basic shape (Sec. 10:21), usually with loose stuffing, but compact may be used. Trim compact stuffing carefully to fit space and build shape; incasing with burlap not necessary. [3] *Knife-edge, rounded, scroll tops; tapered, rounded sides.* Extend compact stuffing to points listed in Sec. 10:22B. Taper stuffing to its points of finishing (Sec. 10:28I). [4] *Most sides, tops without tapered understuffing.* Overstuffing usually extends to outer edges of front surfaces of frame. To allow for this, understuffing should not come nearer the point of finishing the overstuffing than the thickness of the overstuffing. [5] *Crown built after installation of understuffing.* Instead of loose stuffing or felted padding, crown (Sec. 10:28A) may be made by installing a shaped thin layer of compact stuffing; this seldom is worth the extra work. [6] *Incasing compact understuffing.* This is seldom necessary, even when building crown with loose stuffing. It may be done to correct shape; but as a rule it is easier and better to correct shape by trimming, adding to, or changing compact understuffing.   [7] *Install compact overstuffing* (Sec. 10:28I).

SEC. 10:28K   MUSLIN CASING   /   Incase compact stuffed inside backs with muslin (Secs. 10:23, 10:24).

SEC. 10:28L   CURVED, BARREL-TYPE PAD, SPRING BACKS   /   All types and sizes of curved or barrel backs commonly are upholstered with compact stuffing. Usually they are slightly firmer than flat backs and are built with a single layer of stuffing instead of more conventional under- and overstuffing. The slight loss of softness and comfort generally is more than made up for by the "hugging" effect of many curved or barrel shapes. As a rule the only loose stuffing needed is to build basic shape (Secs. 10:19–10:21) and, in spring backs, to keep coils and ties from cutting into a compact stuffing. The little required crown generally is made with felted padding when installing the cover. Any compact stuffing is satisfactory; many upholsterers prefer rubberized hair (Sec. 3:43) because of its easy installation.   [1] *Placement of compact stuffing*. Extend stuffing to parts of back listed in Sec. 10:22. To simplify cutting compact stuffing to shape, first make a full-size paper pattern, like the outline in Fig. 10:28L.   [2] *Spring backs*. Install enough loose stuffing over spring area to build a smooth pad just thick enough to keep coils and ties from cutting into compact stuffing.   [3] *Set stuffing in place*. If polyfoam or rubberized hair (Sec. 5:11J), tack it along top and bottom of back frame. A practical tacking sequence is in Fig. 10:28L. Work from middle of back or point of deepest curve, Point 1, alternately to sides. When tacking, press stuffing straight back to the frame; do not tighten or stretch toward sides or compress toward the middle.   [4] *Rubberized hair*. About midway between top and bottom on a line with the tacking points when possible, like the Xs in Fig. 10:28L, stitch rubberized hair to

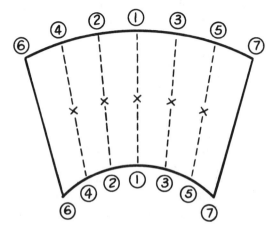

Fig. 10:28L

the webbing of a pad back or to top coils of a spring back to help hold it in place and keep it from pushing out at the middle. Stitch (Sec. 7:08) except that only one stitch per point is needed. Stitches should come up in the stuffing just far enough, as a rule ½ inch, to hold without tearing out. [5] *Channeling, tufting.* See Chapters 20 and 21 for further preparation of stuffing. [6] *Shallow buttoned, plain* (Figs. 1:32, *a* 1:38). Incase with muslin (Secs. 10:23, 10:24).

SEC. 10:29 **INNER-SPRING** **UNIT BACK** **UPHOLSTERY**	**SEC. 10:29A** / Excellent medium-size and large flat, square-type backs (Figs. *a* 1:42, 1:64) are built with inner-spring units (Sec. 3:63, Fig. 10:29C) instead of coil springs. Upholstery is simplified throughout, especially when using compact stuffing. Except for installing webbing and the spring unit, back upholstery is much the same as if done with individual coil springs. In most backs the spring unit sets within a cavity (Fig. 10:29C); but for small articles and frames built for other springing, unit usually is on the inner surface of the frame and webbing.

SEC. 10:29B **WEBBING** / Medium-size and large flat, square-type backs upholstered with inner-spring units usually are webbed on the outer surfaces of a frame (Figs. *b* 10:11D, 10:11J) if pitch or slope (Sec. 10:01C) of the outer surface is satisfactory for the inner surface of a finished back. But if pitches of inner and outer surfaces are different, make necessary adjustment by installing back webbing parallel to desired pitch of the inner surface, Fig. 10:29B. Place vertical strips of webbing parallel to outer surfaces of back slats when they are the same thickness from top to bottom; when they are not, install webbing parallel to inner surfaces of slats. Install webbing (Secs. 10:10, 10:11).

NOTE: For some small articles, and especially when installing a spring unit on a frame built for traditional coil springing, webbing often is on the inner surfaces of a frame, so that a wider and taller unit can be used than could be placed within a cavity.

SEC. 10:29C **INNER-SPRING UNIT** / The size unit for a back depends on how it will be installed and the stuffing. Inner-spring units are the same shape as, but smaller than, the planned final shape of an inside back. For a T-shaped back, stitch extra incased springs to a unit to fill space above arms, Fig. 10:29C; stitch casings, not coils, of extra springs and unit, and stitch only the inner surface. [1] *Unit set within cavity, loose stuffing.* Unit should be large enough to fill cavity without touching frame or slats. [2] *Unit set within cavity, compact stuffing.* Size of unit depends on thickness of stuffing. Units usually are just large enough to fill cavity without touching frame or slats, and compact stuffing about ¼ inch thicker than the distance from the outer

Fig. 10:29B

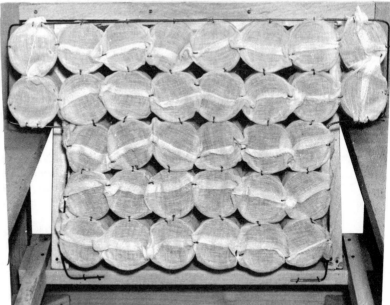

Fig. 10:29C

surfaces of a unit to those of the frame is used. But if there is less than about 1 inch between the outer surfaces of unit and frame, it may be advisable to use a smaller unit and thicker stuffing; this, however, may make a weak, wobbly back instead of one that is soft but holds shape.

The problem of too little space between outer surfaces of unit and frame usually occurs only when attempting to force the use of materials that are basically wrong for a particular job.   [3] *Unit set within cavity, fastening.* Stitch springs to webbing (Sec. 7:08). In T-shaped backs, tack casing of extra springs to frame.   [4] *Unit set on inner surfaces of webbed back, zigzag springs* (Sec. 10:32). Top and side surfaces of unit usually are at least 1 inch from corresponding surfaces of frame regardless of stuffing to be used. This allows for 1¼ inch compact stuffing, usually the minimum practical thickness. Regarding thicker stuffing, see [2] above. Tack casing to frame where possible; stitch elsewhere (Sec. 7:08) to webbing or zigzag springs.

Sec. 10:29D   Completing Inside Back /   [1] *Regardless of stuffing to be used,* reinforce the inner surface edges of a spring unit with edge-wire (Sec. 3:19, Fig. 10:29C). The back will hold shape better and be less apt to sag or break from abuse.   [2] *When upholstering with loose stuffing throughout,* after installing edge-wire, stuff and incase back (Secs. 10:22–10:25).   [3] *When upholstering with compact stuffing,* after installing edge-wire, understuff with loose stuffing and incase with muslin (Sec. 10:21); then install compact stuffing (Sec. 10:28). Make understuffing just thick and firm enough to hold casing to a smooth, regularly shaped base for compact stuffing.

SEC. 10:30 FACTORY SPRINGING

Sec. 10:30A /   Factory spring bars, back-spring units and similar items (Sec. 3:20) usually are not available new to home upholsterers. [1] *Salvaging for use in a different article* is not advisable (Sec. 7:31). [2] *Most factory spring materials are made for a particular* size and shape back to be upholstered a certain way, and may not be satisfactory if a back is made wider and/or higher, or flat, or curved. A back generally can be made thicker, and possibly softer, by installing thicker stuffing than was in it originally. But this may make an uncomfortable seat depth (Sec. 10:01B).   [3] *Reusing factory spring materials by duplicating* the original installation should, if all other upholstery is duplicated, restore original shape and comfort. But this is quite difficult to do, especially if original ties or other means of holding springs to shape are broken or have stretched appreciably. Also, upholstered surfaces generally become more comfortable with use, usually due to upholstery packing and reshaping—and restored surfaces are different and seem uncomfortable.

Sec. 10:30B   Rewebbing /   When reupholstering with factory back-spring units (Fig. *b, c* 3:20C), replace webbing that is broken or badly stretched. Mark frame clearly for placement of each strip. Without removing ties or other means used to hold spring unit to frame, remove old webbing, install new strips, and stitch springs to webbing (Secs. 10:13, 7:08).

NOTE: This method of replacing webbing is for installations in which webbing strips cross at the bottom coil of each spring (Fig. a 10:11D). If original webbing was not installed this way, for best results place new webbing for strips to cross at each spring where possible.

SEC. 10:30C TYING SPRINGS / Common factory coil spring bars are shown in Fig. 3:20B. When retying, they should as a rule be tied at the same points as was done originally. But when upholstering with loose stuffing, it may be advisable to add two or three vertical and horizontal rows of tying to make a better mesh support for the stuffing. Although the original tying plan should as a rule be duplicated: *[1]* *Free coil bar springs* (Fig. *a, b* 3:20B). Tie the same way for the type of back built with traditional coil springs (Secs. 10:15–10:17). *[2]* *Wired coil bars* (*c, d, e*). These usually are tied from side to side at enough points to hold them in place; two or three horizontal ties equally spaced between top and bottom are common. Vertically, short ties from the bottom end of the wire and uppermost point of the top spring coil to frame are all that are used; wires uniting springs are sufficient vertical "tying." *[3]* *Wire spring-back units* (Fig. *b, c* 3:20C). Most of these are tied or otherwise fastened from the edge or border wire to the frame at enough points to hold them securely. Three or four ties equally spaced between corners along sides, top, and bottom of a frame cavity are fairly common; more than four ties per edge seldom are necessary.

SEC. 10:30D COMPLETING INSIDE BACKS / After tying factory back springing materials, upholster back with loose or compact stuffing (Secs. 10:18–10:28).

**SEC. 10:31
ZIGZAG
SPRINGS**

SEC. 10:31A / (Sec. 3:21). These are common in small and medium-size solid inside backs (Figs. 1:24, *b* 1:31) and, with inner-spring units (Sec. 10:32), in fairly thick flat backs (Figs. *a* 1:42, 1:65). Zigzags simplify building resilient, well-shaped, fairly thin, comfortable backs. Use loose or compact stuffing (Sec. 3:27), and except for installing zigzags, work the same as if upholstering with traditional coil springs.

SEC. 10:31B INSTALLATION / In most solid backs, zigzag springs are installed vertically from the inner surface of a back liner to that of the top rail, Fig. 10:31B. As a rule two, at most three, horizontal ties are enough to assure vertical stability of springs; more ties tend

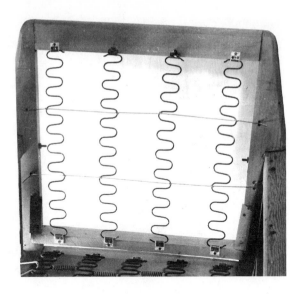

Fig. 10:31B

to make a back somewhat stiff and reduce individual action of the springs. But for very thin backs built with loose stuffing, it is advisable to use a few more horizontal ties, and perhaps one or two more strands of spring, to provide a fine enough mesh to hold stuffing satisfactorily. After spring-up is completed, burlap inside back and upholster as for a similar back built with loose or compact stuffing (Secs. 10:18–10:28).

SEC. 10:32 ZIGZAGS AND INNER-SPRING UNITS	**Sec. 10:32A** / Excellent medium size and large flat, square-type backs (Figs. *a* 1:42, 1:64) often are upholstered with inner-spring units (Fig. 10:29C) mounted on zigzag springs. Except for zigzag springs instead of strip webbing, upholster as in Sec. 10:29. Zigzag spring construction has two major advantages. First, it has more go-down and resilience than webbing; the finished back has more comfort-giving action. Second, the natural crown of zigzags (Sec. 3:21K) is transfered to the inner surface of a spring unit and simplifies building a smooth shape.

Sec. 10:32B Installation / Place zigzag springs for installation the same way as vertical strips of webbing; compare Figs. 10:29B and 10:32B. To complete the spring-up job in Fig. 10:32B, tie springs horizontally as in Fig. 10:31B. When installing inner-spring unit, stitch bottom coils to loops and bars of zigzags; hog rings may be used instead of stitching. |
| **SEC. 10:33 RUBBER WEBBING** | **Sec. 10:33A** / (Sec. 3:22). Most kinds and sizes of open-frame inside backs can be upholstered satisfactorily with rubber webbing. It frequently is in plain and shallow-buttoned backs of all sizes and |

Fig. 10:32B

shapes that have minimum crown (Figs. 1:13, *a* 1:20, *a* 1:35, 1:44), small and medium-size backs that are fairly well crowned (Figs. *b* 1:29, 1:30), and channeled and tufted backs (Figs. *b*, *c* 1:35, *a* 1:37). [*1*] *Rubber webbing simplifies* building comfortable thin inside backs of the type popular in much open-frame loose-cushion and slimline furniture (Secs. 10:35, 10:36).   [*2*] *Rubber webbing is a fast way* to upholster fairly thick, flat backs (Sec. 10:33G).   [*3*] *Backs usually pad built on traditional strip webbing* (Sec. 10:10) have more resilience and can be more comfortable if built with rubber webbing. But there are certain requirements for good installation of rubber webbing that can make it impractical for some backs (Sec. 10:33F). Rubber webbing is not recommended for French backs (Sec. 10:05).   [*4*] *Backs usually spring-built* may be more, equally, or less comfortable if built with rubber webbing, depending on webbing installation and stuffing (Sec. 10:33E).   [*5*] *Spring-edge backs* (Sec. 10:16) cannot be built or even closely simulated with rubber webbing. But the general appearance of a spring-edge back, and to a great extent its comfort can be closely imitated by the stuffing of a rubber webbing back (Sec. 10:33D).   [*6*] *Due to the nature of rubber webbing*, special handling of the burlap "spring cover" and stuffing are needed (Sec. 7:33B).   [*7*] *Use only compact stuffing* with rubber webbing. Thickness of stuffing determines number and placement of webbing strips; the thicker the stuffing, the further apart webbing strips can be (Sec. 3:22E[*1*], [*8*]).   [*8*] *If there will be lumbar area* rubber webbing (Sec. 10:03B[*4*]), it may not be possible to finish back and arm upholsteries through a back cavity (Sec. 10:33C), an important point to consider when arms are to be fully upholstered.   [*9*] *Whether a rubber webbing installation* should be primarily vertical or horizontal depends on shape and size of an inside back (Sec. 10:33B). The number of strips needed depends on thickness of stuffing, [7] above.

SEC. 10:33B DIRECTION OF WEBBING / Rubber webbing may be primarily vertical (Fig. 10:33C) or horizontal (Fig. 7:33C). [*1*] *Curved or barrel-type backs* (Figs. *b* 1:36, *b* 1:37). Web vertically to build desired shape (Sec. 10:10A); horizontal webbing (Sec. 10:10C) is limited to one or two strips for lumbar support (Sec. 10:33C). [*2*] *Flat backs high rather than wide.* Web primarily, if not exclusively (Fig. 7:33C), horizontally; being shorter than vertical strips would be, horizontal strips tend to make a stronger foundation with better support for back upholstery. [*3*] *Flat backs wide rather than high* (Fig. 10:33C). Web vertically with one or two horizontal strips for lumbar support (Sec. 10:33C); the shorter vertical strips tend to make a stronger foundation with better support for back upholstery than the longer, horizontal strips would. This is more important when building love seats, sofas, and other articles that usually have backs much wider than in chairs.

SEC. 10:33C LUMBAR WEBBING / Comfort due to lumbar area webbing (Sec. 10:03B[*4*]) usually is more noticeable in thin than in thickly stuffed backs. Lumbar strips should be installed when stuffing is up to 2 inches thick and is highly desirable when stuffing is 2 to 3 inches thick. For thicker backs, lumbar strips are recommended when stuffing is very soft. Where there are back slats or uprights (Fig. 4:00A), fasten lumbar webbing on inner surfaces; inside back and arm upholsteries can finish through the back cavity. When there are no back slats or uprights, fasten lumbar webbing to inner surfaces of posts, Fig. 10:33C; back and arm upholsteries cannot finish through

Fig. 10:33C

back cavity.   [*1*] *Placement of lumbar strips* is a matter of the upholsterer's judgment. In Fig. 10:33C, one strip at the armtops was considered adequate for a loose-cushion, low-arm chair. For a solid seat, it probably would have been about 2 inches lower. For best results, sit in the article and feel at what height a lumbar strip is most comfortable; this generally is at the waist or an inch or so below. If a seat will be loose-cushion, place an upholstery cushion or fold of blanket about 3 inches thick on it before testing.   [*2*] *One lumbar strip* usually is enough. For very high backs or for backs built especially for very long-bodied people, two strips set close together may be used. [*3*] *Lumbar strips usually are not interlaced,* but pass behind all vertical strips in order to build a more uniform surface throughout the lumbar area.   [*4*] *When using only horizontal webbing* (Fig. 7:33C), the lumbar strip may be a different grade of rubber webbing, one with less natural stretch than used for the rest of a back (Sec. 3:22C); or it may be the same as the other webbing, but given about 12½% instead of the usual 10% initial stretch (Sec. 3:22D); or it may be broader—for example, 2-inch webbing where the rest is ¾- or 1⅛-inch.

SEC. 10:33D SPRING-EDGE /   A rubber webbing "spring-edge" back could be made by building up corners with blocks of wood as for a flexible-edge seat (Sec. 7:33C), but probably would not be comfortable. However, a back closely approaching in comfort and looks a typical spring-edge back (Fig. *a* 1:42) can be built with rubber webbing and compact stuffing 3 or more inches thick. Shape it (Sec. 10:28) for sharp breaks between inner, top, and side surfaces; install a boxed, preferably welted, cover (Secs. 16:10, 16:11).

SEC. 10:33E INSTALL WEBBING, STUFFING /   Comfort, durability, and appearance of a rubber webbing inside back depend on webbing, installation, and stuffing.   [*1*] *Use only back webbing* (Sec. 3:22C) for inside backs except possibly for lumbar support (Sec. 10:33C). Substituting seat for back webbing is not recommended, as the greater stretch of back webbing makes a more comfortable back.   [*2*] *Give webbing full factory recommended initial stretch* (Sec. 3:22D). With less stretch, a surface may be weak and have too much go-down to hold stuffing properly; with too much initial stretch, a surface may be too hard for comfort. Also, if webbing is widely spaced as well as given too much initial stretch, in relatively short time a back may develop depressions between strips of webbing.   [*3*] *Stuffing and webbing should complement each other.* That is, the thicker and firmer the stuffing, the further apart strips of webbing can be; and the thinner and softer the stuffing, the closer together webbing strips must be. For very thinly stuffed backs, use the finest available stuffing to try to prevent transfer of the general outline of the webbing strips to the finished inner surface of a back.   [4] *For stuffing more than about 3½ inches thick,* frequently backs are first understuffed with rubberized hair, then overstuffed with a soft polyfoam or foam rubber (Sec. 10:28), giving the back surface softness for initial comfort and a firm base for good body support.

Sec. 10:33F   Webbing Within a Cavity   /   It is not advisable to install rubber webbing within a cavity, as is done when upholstering some small backs with traditional webbing (Sec. 10:06). In order to fasten rubber webbing securely without excessive tacking, it would be necessary to nail small blocks of wood to hold it; most small frames could not withstand this.

Sec. 10:33G   Fast Upholstering   /   A fast way to upholster fairly thick, flat inside backs is shown in Fig. 7:33C. Install rubber webbing (Sec. 10:33C), and over it a sheet of compact stuffing; then padding and cover (Chapter 16). However, the job is not as easy as it may first appear.   [1] *Stuffing for top of back and wings* is a separate piece bonded to inside back stuffing because it extends at the sides to stuff the wings.   [2] *Inside back stuffing* is set directly on webbing. This eliminates the work of setting the burlap "spring cover" (Sec. 7:33B)— and eliminates the protection it gives stuffing.   [3] *The most difficult* part of this upholstering is preparing the cover. It must be cut and sewn to fit smoothly across the top and down the junction of inside back and wing surfaces.   [4] *This overall method* of upholstering inside backs is not recommended for quality custom work, but may be quite satisfactory when upholstering within a very limited budget.

Sec. 10:33H   Completing Upholstering   /   Except for webbing and stuffing (Secs. 10:33A–F), upholster rubber webbing inside backs the same way as those built with traditional materials and compact stuffing (Secs. 10:18–10:28). Inner-spring unit upholstery (Sec. 10:29) may be done with rubber webbing, but seldom is; the extra resilience of rubber webbing would not be noticeable.

MODERN BACK UPHOLSTERY

SEC. 10:34 METHODS, MATERIALS MORE THAN BASIC DESIGN	The popularity of much so-called "modern back upholstery" often is due more to materials and methods of upholstering than to basic design. Examples of nearly all modern shapes or designs can be found in furniture built in the 1890s and earlier; but either they could not be made comfortable with the materials then available, or it was too complicated and costly. For example, back upholstery of the famous Morris chair was a thick, hard, hair-filled pad resting on wooden bars

in an adjustable frame; comfort was due to shape of the pad and tilt of the back frame. The modern version has a soft back cushion and rests on, preferably, rubber webbing (Sec. 10:35). Other modern materials (Sec. 3:00E) and improved traditionals enable upholsterers to build, at reasonable cost, comfortable slimline and slipframe backs (Secs. 10:36, 10:37).

SEC. 10:35 OPEN-FRAME LOOSE-CUSHION BACKS

These are easy to upholster with modern materials (Sec. 3:00C) and should be comfortable. Comfort depends more on the pitch of a back (Sec. 10:01E) and how it supports a sitter than on general softness. A soft cushion and rubber webbing are common upholstery. The lack of crown in a rubber webbing "spring" base allows a cushion to lie flatter against the back frame and usually prevents excessive gaps between cushion and top and side rails. Also, rubber webbing is smooth and causes less wear on a cushion cover than metal springs, wires, or bars. Install rubber webbing for open-frame loose-cushion backs (Secs. 10:33A–E). To reduce wear on a cushion cover or to allow use of a thinner than ordinary back cushion (Chapter 17), set strips of webbing closer together than usual (Sec. 3:22E[*1*]); the farther apart they are, the thicker or firmer a cushion must be to keep webbing strips from being readily felt on the inner surface. Since the comfort of this type back depends chiefly on the support it gives a sitter, lumbar webbing (Sec. 10:33C) is important. Rubber webbing for this type back usually finishes on the inner surfaces of a frame as on the top surface of a seat frame (Sec. 7:34D).

SEC. 10:36 SLIMLINE BACK UPHOLSTERY

Sec. 10:36A / Upholstered backs less than about 2½ inches thick often are called "slimline," and from time to time are regarded as "modern." But for years thin backs have been common in dining and side chairs (Figs. 1:07, 1:12, 1:13), French backs (Fig. 1:28), and some period pieces. Most backs were small, pad-built, and usually not very comfortable. But with modern materials such as zigzag springs, rubber webbing, and compact stuffings (Secs. 3:21, 3:22, 3:41–3:44), slimline backs can be comfortable and fairly large (Fig. 1:41). Most back frames designed for slimline upholstery have basic shape planned for good body support. It involves pitch of a back (Sec. 10:01C), width, height, and curvature between sides and/or top and bottom. These factors are carefully combined in good quality frames, and as a rule, a comfortable slimline back results from following its basic shape as closely as good upholstering permits.

NOTE: The French back cited above as an example of slimline upholstery should be upholstered only the traditional way (Sec.

10:05); most such frames are not adequate for zigzag springs of rubber webbing, and the extra go-down of rubber webbing would stretch the outside back cover excessively.

SEC. 10:36B ZIGZAG SPRINGS / Whether these should be used for a back depends on their necessary span and the desired thickness of slimline upholstery. [*1*] *Span.* When strips of springs will have a span or reach of more than about 16 inches, zigzags usually are practical, depending on planned thickness of upholstery. But if span is much less than 16 inches, zigzags with their natural crown (Sec. 3:21K) may make it difficult to build a satisfactorily thin and flat surface. [*2*] *Thickness.* If upholstery (springs and stuffing) will be more than about 1½ inches thick at the middle of a back, zigzags will usually build a smooth, comfortable surface. But if back upholstery will be much thinner, then building a smooth surface over zigzags may require stuffing that is too firm for comfort, one strong and stiff enough to bridge gaps between springs without leaving depressions. Sometimes stuffing less than 1-inch thick can be used; strips of zigzags may be set closer together than normal, or there may be excessive cross-ties or connectors, to build a "tight mesh" foundation to support stuffing and build a smooth surface. But this tends to make a hard and unyielding instead of resilient inside back. Install zigzag springs for slimline backs (Sec. 10:31), except that they should have less-than-normal crown (Sec. 3:21K) to simplify building a flat, thin surface. Most such backs are upholstered with compact stuffing (Secs. 10:36D, E); loose stuffing may be used.

SEC. 10:36C RUBBER WEBBING / This is satisfactory for slimline upholstery in any back. It builds a flat surface and the thinnest comfortable back. But unless allowance is made for lack of crown (Sec. 5:14), the cover may tear out. Install rubber webbing (Sec. 10:33) for slimline backs except that strips may be set closer together than usual to allow for using very thin stuffing. The thinner the stuffing, the closer the strips must be to build a smooth surface; when stuffing is less than about ¾-inch thick, strips of webbing should almost butt together. This makes a surface harder than normal, but the thinner a surface is, the firmer it usually must be in order to hold shape. Use any compact stuffing for rubber webbing (Secs. 7:33, 10:28, 10:36D, F). When stuffing will be less than about 1½ inches thick, rubberized hair usually is preferred.

SEC. 10:36D STUFFING / Most slimline backs are upholstered with compact stuffing (Secs. 3:41–3:44), as it allows a fairly soft smooth surface to be built with a thinner layer than would be needed for loose stuffing. Compact stuffing also eliminates need of built-up edges. With zigzag springs, a small amount of loose stuffing often is used to fill depressions between strips of springs (Sec. 10:36E). The minimum thickness of stuffing for slimline backs is that which builds a surface through which springs or webbing cannot be felt as individual items. If they can be, eventually they will make wear and soil lines in the cover. The maximum thickness is whatever looks best. Thinner stuffing generally is more satisfactory with rubber webbing, but with it, stuffing must be thick enough or sufficiently crowned (Sec. 5:14) to protect the cover.

SEC. 10:36E STUFFING ZIGZAG SPRINGS / Burlap the sprung-up back (Sec. 10:18). [*1*] *Compact stuffing.* For best results install enough loose stuffing (Secs. 5:11A–C) between springs and cross-ties or connectors to fill depressions and build a very thin smooth surface overall; incase understuffing with muslin (Secs. 10:23, 10:24). Prepare compact stuffing the proper size and shape (Sec. 10:28), fasten to casing and frame (Secs. 3:45–3:47, 5:11G–J). [*2*] *Loose stuffing.* Install roll edges where necessary (Sec. 10:20). Install loose stuffing as above, then build a smooth surface of desired thickness. For slimline upholstery, "felt" loose stuffing in small handfuls. The more thorough the felting is (the better the handfuls of stuffing are shredded and worked into one another), the stronger the stuffing will be without becoming hard. The stronger the stuffing is, the thinner it can be and still build a satisfactory smooth surface.

SEC. 10:36F STUFFING RUBBER WEBBING / Burlapping (Sec. 10:18) is not essential for compact stuffing, but helps minimize wear between webbing and stuffing. Prepare compact stuffing the proper size and shape for a back (Sec. 10:28), fasten (Secs. 3:45–3:47, 5:11G–J) to burlap and frame at several points. Bonding stuffing to burlap helps reduce wear, but since stuffing must be able to move slightly when a back is used, do not bond burlap to webbing. Bond, or preferably tack, stuffing along the top rail, side rails, and liner to lock stuffing (which usually is oversize) in place and keep it from shifting. Do not fasten stuffing to a frame where it will prevent arm or wing upholstery finishing through a back cavity if that is planned (Sec. 10:11K). Build crown (Sec. 7:33B) and incase back with muslin (Secs. 10:23, 10:24); the more oversize the stuffing is, the more advisable it is to incase.

NOTE: Because rubber webbing has go-down but no crown, inexperienced upholsterers should incase a back, and test by sitting and leaning hard against it; tearing a casing due to too little crown is better than tearing the cover.

**SEC. 10:37
SLIPFRAME
BACK
UPHOLSTERY**

SEC. 10:37A / Slipseats (Sec. 6:03) have long been common for dining and other small chairs (Figs. 1:02, 1:12), but slipframe upholstery for larger chairs was not popular until compact stuffings were developed (Secs. 3:41–3:44). The major demand for slipframe upholstery came when, because of generally simple and clean-cut lines, many buyers wanted open-frame furniture (Figs. 1:24, 1:25, 1:55) for regular home use. Because they were simple and less costly to build, repair, and re-cover than traditional upholstered furniture, slipframe articles were demanded for offices, hotels, clubs, etc. Upholster slipframe backs with modern or traditional materials (Sec. 3:00E). To save time and work, especially when upholstery will be fairly thick (Sec. 10:37C, Figs. 1:24, 1:25) most modern slipbacks are built with modern materials, mainly compact stuffing. Slipbacks are solid-base or open-frame (Sec. 4:00C); solid-base is easier to upholster and need not be less comfortable. The smaller a back and thinner its upholstery, the more likely it is solid-base; backs larger than in Fig. 1:24 usually are open-frame. Most traditionally built slipbacks are pad upholstery (Sec. 6:00A). Unless back upholstery is to be more than 4 inches thick, there is not enough space for satisfactory go-down of coil springs (Secs. 3:15–3:16) or an inner-spring unit (Sec. 10:29). But zigzag springs and rubber webbing (Secs. 3:21, 3:22) are often used. Whether working with modern or traditional materials, except for differences in softness of upholstery and installation of the cover, upholster a slipback essentially as a slipseat. For upholstering with modern materials, see Secs. 10:37C–E; traditional, Secs. 10:37F–O. It is not essential, but inexperienced upholsterers should incase a slipback with muslin (Secs. 10:23, 10:24).

SEC. 10:37B SHAPE / Much of the attractiveness of a slipback depends on its edges and the shape from the inner surface to the side, top, and bottom surfaces. Shape is most important when there are square edges (sharp breaks from the inner surface) and/or a back is isolated (Fig. 1:24). Shape is less critical when edges are rounded and/or butt against arms and/or seat. Shaping edges is simple when upholstering with compact stuffing; with loose stuffing, built-up edges or edge stitching (Secs. 5:05, 10:25) usually is required. The shape of edge built generally is based on the type of cover. [1] *Boxed cover* (Sec. 11:06, Figs. 1:24, 1:25). Build sharp breaks between inner and all other surfaces. A pull-around cover may be used instead, but it complicates building of sharp breaks, and all corners must be expertly pleated (Sec. 5:17) or they will not hold shape well and a cover may work loose. [2] *Pull-around cover.* Generally used when an inner surface curves or rounds into the other. Degree of curve is optional; some upholsterers like a gradual, puffy, pillowy shape from inner surface to top and sides, while others prefer fairly sharp curves at the sides and a more gradual one at the top. The curve at the bottom usually is fairly sharp, and curve from the inner to side surfaces generally is sharper when back and arms butt against each other.

Sec. 10:37C   Modern Upholstery   /   The inner surface of modern slipbacks usually is basically flat (Figs. 1:24, 1:25) with only enough crown to hold a cover smooth. [*1*] *Solid-base.* To upholster with compact stuffing only, prepare and install a sheet or slab the proper thickness and shape (Secs. 3:45–3:47, 10:37B). Stuffing often is about ¼-inch larger all around than the base in order to exert extra pressure against the cover throughout and so build a more durable shape. Or the stuffing may be the same size as a base, and padding (Sec. 13:10) used to create extra pressure. Instead of relying solely on stuffing for comfort, an inner-spring unit may be tacked to the base and upholstered as in Sec. 10:29. But unless the finished surface will be more than about 4 inches thick, it may be too weak to prevent "bottoming" against a solid base. [*2*] *Open-frame, traditional webbing.* Web an open-frame the traditional way (Secs. 10:10, 10:11), upholster with compact stuffing, or with an inner-spring unit and compact stuffing, [*1*] above. Due to the "give" of webbing, this slipback usually is more comfortable than a solid-base; also, inner-spring unit construction generally is satisfactory when upholstery is at least 3½ inches thick. [*3*] *Open-frame, rubber webbing.* Install rubber webbing (Secs. 3:22, 10:10, 10:11); prepare, install compact stuffing, [*1*] above. Inner-spring unit upholstery (Sec. 10:29) can be done with rubber webbing, but seldom is; rubber webbing's extra resilience would not be sufficiently noticeable. [*4*] *Open-frame, zigzag springs.* This type upholstery, with or without an inner-spring unit, can make an exceptionally resilient slipback. A problem may be zigzags' natural crown (Sec. 3:21K). It may not be too much for the flatness usually wanted in modern slipbacks if zigzags are installed with minimum crown, especially in a small clubchair or larger back. But for smaller backs (Figs. 1:24, 1:25), or if zigzags cannot be installed with minimum crown, crown may be reduced with compact stuffing or an inner-spring unit and compact stuffing (Secs. 10:37D, E).

Sec. 10:37D   Zigzag Springs, Compact Stuffing   /   Install zigzags, burlap, understuff, incase with muslin (Secs. 3:21, 10:31, 10:18, 10:36E). Prepare compact stuffing (Sec. 10:37C[*1*]), and place on incased spring surface parallel to inner surfaces of frame. Compact stuffing usually is stiff enough to lie fairly flat on a spring surface, Fig. 10:37D; if not, place a yardstick with a flat side on the spring surface, and the stuffing on the yardstick. Prepare a filler wedge for each outer edge of the slipback; filler wedges should be thick enough

FILLER WEDGE

BURLAPPED ZIGZAG SPRING

Fig. 10:37D

at the outer edges for the stuffing to drop slightly below the high point of the spring surface. The larger the slipback, the greater the drop should be; it usually ranges from ¾ inch for occasional chair backs (Fig. 1:24) to about 1½ inches for small clubchair and larger backs. The smoother and more evenly shaped filler wedges are, the better; however, uniform thickness along outer edges is more important.

SEC. 10:37E ZIGZAG SPRINGS AND INNER-SPRING UNIT / Install, burlap zigzags (Secs. 3:21, 10:31). Install inner-spring unit (Secs. 10:36E, 10:32B). Prepare compact stuffing (Sec. 10:37C[*1*]), install with filler strips (Sec. 10:28I[*4*]). Filler strips should go completely around a slipframe, just as filler wedges do (Sec. 10:37E), and be just high enough to hold stuffing to the desired crown. With stuffing more than about 1-inch thick, usually there is no need to fill in space, near the edges, between stuffing and spring unit. But with thinner stuffing, and when space between stuffing and spring unit is more than about 1 inch, fill it with scrap stuffing in order to build a uniformly strong and smooth surface.

SEC. 10:37F TRADITIONAL UPHOLSTERY / The major difference between modern and traditional upholstering of a modern slipback is the stuffing. With compact stuffing (Secs. 10:37C–E), edges are cut or built to shape (Sec. 10:37B). With loose stuffing, roll edges or stitched edging (Secs. 5:05, 7:21, 10:25) are needed for sharp breaks from the inner surface to sides, bottom, and/or top. Also, rubber webbing is not recommended for loose stuffing upholstery.

SEC. 10:37G SOLID BASE, PAD UPHOLSTERY, SHARP BREAKS FROM INNER SURFACE / First decide whether to build sharp breaks for shape (Sec. 10:37B) with roll edges or by edge stitching (Secs. 5:05, 10:25). For loose stuffing not more than about 2 inches thick, roll edges are satisfactory (Sec. 10:37H); for thicker stuffing, stitching usually is better (Sec. 10:37I). For initial softness, smooth shape, and to protect the cover, double-stuffing and muslin casing is recommended (Sec. 10:37J), especially for inexperienced upholsterers. Some backs have fairly sharp breaks from the inner to the side and/or bottom surfaces, but a rounded shape at the top (Sec. 10:37K): build each shape the usual way, join them together smoothly where they meet (Sec. 10:37L).

SEC. 10:37H   ROLL EDGE UPHOLSTERY / Install roll edges (Secs. 5:05, 5:06), stuff (Secs. 5:11A–C) slipframe to desired thickness. Compressed by burlap or muslin casing (Sec. 10:37K), stuffing should build a fairly firm smooth surface crowning slightly above the built-up edges, Fig. 10:37H. If stuffing is not high enough or is too weak, the built-up edges will stand out, making an uncomfortable surface and tending to wear through the cover.

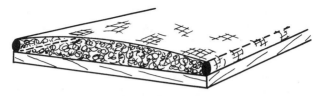

Fig. 10:37H

SEC. 10:37I   STITCHED EDGE UPHOLSTERY / Upholster essentially as a bridle hard edge (Secs. 7:21, 7:22) or as a stitched flat-top back (Sec. 10:25), except that in pad upholstery there are no springs, and edge stitching is done only along edges. The bridle hard-edge is suitable for any ordinary thickness and is recommended when there are to be very sharp, almost square breaks from inner surface to sides, top, and/or bottom; but in use, the hard-edge generally is easier to feel and less comfortable than back-stitching. The latter is not recommended if a slipback is to be stuffed more than about 3 inches thick, unless it is spring-built (Sec. 10:37O). For best results with either type edge, understuff the slipback, overstuff, and incase with muslin (Sec. 10:37J).   [1] *Regardless of edge construction,* stuff surface (Secs. 5:11A–C) to desired thickness, incase with burlap (Sec. 7:21C), as in Fig. *a* 10:37I. Tack burlap to sides of slipframe, not on bottom or outer surfaces.

NOTE: If edges will be back-stitched and the back will not be double-stuffed (Sec. 10:37K), incase with muslin, not burlap.

[2] *Bridle hard-edge.* This stitching (Secs. 7:21, 7:22) tends to pull the inner surface down slightly below the top of the hard-edge (Fig. 7:22A) as in Fig. *b* 10:37I. To fill the depression, thicker overstuffing (Sec. 10:37J) is needed to build final shape—and the greater the initial softness and resilience of the surface tend to be. But do not make the understuffing edge too hard in order to have an excessive depression; it will require excessive overstuffing, and the excessively hard edge will probably still be noticeable.   [3] *Flat-top back stitching.* Because

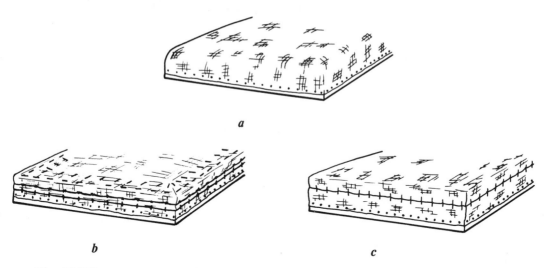

a

b   *c*

Fig. 10:37I

stitching (Sec. 10:25) goes from the "sides" only partway to the inner
surface (Fig. 10:25B) as in Fig. *c* 10:37I, along the edges a surface is
softer and weaker than one having hard-edge construction, [2] above;
also, there should be no pull-down of the inner surface and less overstuffing needed (Sec. 10:37J) to build final shape. Backs often are
stuffed somewhat fuller than they would be for hard-edge upholstery,
and they are shaped by flat-top stitching without overstuffing. The
weakness of a flat-top stitched back makes it less shape-holding than
the hard-edge type. With pad upholstery, backs need more frequent
patting or pushing to restore shape. But for a spring back (Sec.
10:37O), the weakness of flat-top stitching gives greater go-down and
fight-back or return, making it a more comfortable back with good
shape-holding property.

SEC. 10:37J DOUBLE-STUFFING, MUSLIN CASING / Double-stuff a
slipback as the top of a full back (Sec. 10:21), except that it is for all,
not just part, of a back. Understuffing (Secs. 10:37H, I) usually is incased with burlap, which is less pliable than muslin. But for a spring-
built back with flat-top stitching (Sec. 10:37I), muslin generally is
used. All overstuffing should be incased with muslin. [1] *Overstuffing.* Anchoring loose stuffing overstuffing usually is not done as an
understuffing casing is rough enough to hold it in place. Install overstuffing by felting it; build a smooth, even surface. Stuff "sides" (top,
bottom, side surfaces) that have built-up, bridle hard, or flat-top
stitched edges; stuff just enough to fill and smooth out hollows and
irregularities due to stitching. Stuffing should extend to but not over

crests of built-up edges.   [2] *Muslin casing*. Incasing simplifies covering by establishing definite shape of a slipback and provides valuable
experience for covering. Incase with muslin (Secs. 5:15–5:19); regulate
(Sec. 5:07) as necessary. When an inner surface has "square sides"
(Fig. 1:24), casing usually is tacked to the outer surfaces of frame
near the back edges. When "sides" are rounded, draw casing over
outer front edges of frame and tack on outer surfaces close to the
front edges. Push back stuffing that works over frame edges with
casing; it may prevent good installation of the cover.

SEC. 10:37K   SOLID-BASE, PAD UPHOLSTERY, ROUNDED BREAKS FROM INNER SURFACE

/   For rounded "sides" on a slipback, install a fairly
small built-up edge (Secs. 5:05, 5:06) along edges of frame to build
shape and help hold stuffing in place. If the outer edge of a rounded
side is to be fairly thick and full (Fig. *c* 1:09), the built-up edge
usually is about 1 or 1½ inches high; for a fairly thin surface, the edge
usually is about ½ to 1 inch high. After installing edges, complete upholstering (Sec. 10:37J).

*NOTE: Some slipbacks have both sharp breaks from an inner sur-
face (Sec. 10:37G) and rounded "sides," usually the top. For best
results, first build junctions of the different shapes into a smooth
basic surface with understuffing, then overstuff, and incase with muslin. Take special care in pleating (Sec. 5:17) casing at junctions of
different shapes; careless pleating may make sharp-breaking surfaces
rounded, and rounded surfaces sharp-breaking.*

SEC. 10:37L   SOLID-BASE, INNER-SPRING UNIT

/   The spring unit
(Sec. 3:63) should be at least 2 inches smaller in length and width than
a slipframe to allow for at least a 1-inch thick stuffing along the sides,
top, and bottom. With thinner stuffing, they are apt to be weak and
not hold shape well. With stuffing more than about 2 inches thick
along the "sides," a surface is likely to be too hard along the edges and
so defeat the purpose of a spring unit.   [1] *Install spring unit*. Center
inner-spring unit on back; tack casing along edges at 1-inch intervals.
[2] *Rounded "side."* For a rounded side, tie top coils of spring unit
down to build basic shape, Fig. 10:37L. To the outer edge of each
appropriate top coil, tie a short length of upholstery twine (Sec. 3:08);
press coil to desired slope, anchor twine with a single tack (Sec.
7:14B). This usually is done only if a rounded edge is to be fairly thin.
Install a roll edge (Secs. 5:05, 5:06) not more than ¾-inch high (Sec.
10:37H).   [3] *Stuffing*. Use the finest quality, most resilient loose
stuffing available (Sec. 3:27); the better the stuffing, the more effective
the action of a spring unit. Stuff (Secs. 5:11A–C) slipback to desired
thickness along side, top, bottom, and inner surfaces; incase with
muslin (Sec. 10:37J). The more resilient the stuffing, the higher it must

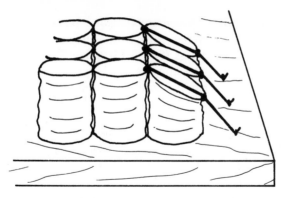

Fig. 10:37L

be piled (Fig. 8:14B) to build desired thickness when compressed by casing. But if excessive stuffing is used, a surface will be hard and firm instead of resilient. When there will be fairly sharp breaks from an inner surface (Fig. 1:24), "sides" usually are stitched (Sec. 10:37I). Shape rounded "sides" (Sec. 10:37K).

SEC. 10:37M OPEN-FRAME, TRADITIONAL WEBBING, PAD OR INNER-SPRING UNIT UPHOLSTERY / This type slipback is upholstered as in Secs. 10:37G–L except that the frame is webbed and burlapped before stuffing or springing it, and the stuffing and/or spring unit usually is stitched instead of, or as well as, being tacked.   [1] *Install traditional strip webbing* (Secs. 3:11, 5:01, 6:03), but tighten only by hand; slip-frames often are too weak to withstand pressure exerted by a webbing stretcher.   [2] *Install burlap* (Secs. 3:24, 5:02, 6:03). Where roll edges (Sec. 5:05) will be made, save time and materials by allowing burlap for them when cutting it for a frame; do not overturn burlap allowed for roll edges.   [3] *Install stuffing* (Secs. 5:11A–C) if not using an inner-spring unit.   [4] *Install inner-spring unit*. Stitch spring unit in place along its edges when possible. For a large slipback, especially one that curves, also stitch unit to webbing at a few points near the middle of a back. Stitch (Sec. 7:08), except that just one stitch per coil along edges of unit is needed and only two stitches per coil near the middle of a back.

SEC. 10:37N OPEN-FRAME, ZIGZAG SPRINGS, LOOSE STUFFING, INNER-SPRING UNIT / Except for springing with zigzags (Sec. 3:21) and need of a burlap spring cover foundation for loose stuffing (Sec. 10:37M[2]), upholster this type slipback as in Secs. 10:37G–L. If an inner-spring unit (Sec. 3:63) is to be used (Sec. 10:37D[4]), stitch in place after burlapping zigzags (Sec. 10:37M[4]). Where possible, each stitch should enclose a unit coil and part of a zigzag; but along its outer edges, often a unit can be stitched only to burlap, or possibly to a spring connector or tie.

SEC. 10:37O   TRADITIONAL COIL SPRING, LOOSE STUFFING / Slip-backs upholstered with loose stuffing seldom are built with tradi-tional coil springs (Sec. 3:15) unless they should have a spring-edge (Sec. 5:04). The appearance, but not the resilience or comfort, of a spring-edge can be closely imitated by other construction, such as the stitched edge (Sec. 10:37I). Traditional coil spring upholstery with roll, hard or stitched, or spring edges may be done on solid-base or open-frame slipbacks. Roll edges generally are used where the inner surface is to have rounded "sides"; some backs have roll and hard edges (Sec. 10:37K). Hard or stitched edges (Sec. 10:37I) usually are made where there are sharp breaks from an inner to the other surfaces (Fig. 1:24). Spring edges are used when there are to be sharp or small sharply rounded breaks from an inner to the other surfaces, and there is to be maximum resilience or spring-action along edges. Spring-edge upholstery offers the greatest variety in covering a slipback. Most have a simple boxed (Sec. 11:06) cover (Figs. 1:25, *a* 1:42) but some have a pullover cover or a banded (Sec. 11:04) cover (seat, Fig. 1:58). Shape of a spring-edge surface depends greatly on the edge-wire and its anchorage to a frame (Secs. 7:15, 7:16). Since edge-wire cannot be anchored satisfactorily to a slipframe, all "sides" must be spring-built. Except that twine, springs, and edge-wire if any, suitable for back up-holstery are used (Secs. 3:08, 3:15–3:19), upholster coil spring, loose stuffing slipbacks essentially as roll, hard, and spring-edge seats and backs.   [*1*] *Install webbing* (Secs. 3:11, 5:01, 6:03, 10:11).   [*2*] *Plan coil springs* according to desired thickness of slipback and type edge to be built (Secs. 3:15–3:17, 10:11).   [*3*] *Install springs* (Secs. 7:08, 7:09).   [*4*] *Tie springs* according to edge to be built (Secs. 7:11, 7:12, 10:15, 10:16). However, slipframe springs usually are tied to the same height throughout, as a satisfactory pitch of back (Sec. 10:01C) is built into the main frame. Spring-edge springs for a back usually are not shaped (Sec. 7:07D); they are soft enough to be held in position and shaped by ties.   [*5*] *Spring edge only.* Install edge-wire (Sec. 7:16) around spring area.   [*6*] *All backs.* Install burlap spring cover (Sec. 5:02) snugly but without compressing springs; allow burlap for roll edges, if any (Sec. 10:37M[2]). Tack burlap along inner surfaces of a slipback close to outer edges. Stitch burlap to springs (Sec. 7:18). [*7*] *Roll, hard, stitched edges.* Build basic shape where necessary. Stuff, incase with muslin, stitch edges to shape where necessary (Secs. 10:19–10:25).   [*8*] *Spring-edge.* Complete (Sec. 10:16) except that all spring edges of a slipback are treated as being "exposed when uphol-stery is finished"; there is no point at which the inner surface of a slipback can be anchored to the main frame to hold upholstery se-curely in place.

11

measuring, plotting, and cutting covers

SEC. 11:00 GENERAL NOTES ON COVER GOODS	SEC. 11:00A / Reduce cover costs by carefully measuring and plotting (Sec. 11:24) each part of an article to get the most cuts or pieces from the least yardage. If measurements are accurate and recommended allowances are made, making extra allowances is not necessary or, in many cases, desirable. For example, a consistent ½-inch seam allowance always places stitching where it belongs; but if the allowance is sometimes more than ½ inch, it will be extremely difficult to do smooth, even stitching. Fabrics, plastics, leathers, and various types of each, seldom react the same way to the work of installing a cover. Some goods fit readily to a surface; others, stiff and unyielding, must be worked carefully into place for a smooth job. Some goods do not rip or tear easily, others give way under the slightest pull. Most suitable cover goods will hold the shape of a surface, but some stretch and sag after installation. And there are fabrics that ravel despite the most careful handling. A smooth, top quality job results only when the qualities of a goods are taken into account, and it is worked, not forced,

into position. As a rule very little handling is needed, even by inexperienced upholsterers, to get the "feel" of a cover and be able to work it satisfactorily.

SEC. 11:00B   /   Width and design of a cover goods can greatly affect the yardage needed. Unless using a plain or solid goods, or one with small figures or stripes, it is best to make a full size paper pattern of the design for plotting a cover. The larger the design, figures, or stripes, the more important a pattern is. Cover stretchers and decking (Secs. 11:09, 11:10) can greatly reduce the amount of goods needed.

SEC. 11:00C   /   Measure and plot fabric and plastic cover goods the same way.   [*1*] *Plastics* generally are handled and installed the same way as fabrics of similar weight (Sec. 3:53).   [*2*] *Heavy and nonporous plastics* are often handled much the same way as leather (Chapter 19).   [*3*] *For channeled, tufted surfaces* (Chapters 20, 21).

SEC. 11:01
QUALITIES,
NAMES

SEC. 11:01A   TOP END   /   Upholstery fabrics and some plastics usually have a "top" end. For consistent color and design (Fig. 1:58), and to protect some fabrics, most covers are installed with the top end lying or pointing to the top of a vertical surface, to the back of a horizontal surface—to the top of arms, wings, and backs, to the rear of seats and seat cushions. When the top end of a cover lies to the side of a surface—as to a side instead of the top of a back—it is "railroaded" (Sec. 11:01B).   [*1*] *Patterned, figured goods.* Designs usually point to the top end. They may be so noticeable (Figs. 1:13, *a* 1:42, 1:58) that if railroaded the surface would look unbalanced or (Fig. 1:58) absurd. Designs in which the top end is less apparent usually are railroaded satisfactorily. Some of these are small figures in a dense pattern (Fig. 1:22); close-set repeats of identical simple figures (Fig. *a* 1:45); designs in which major figures could point just as well in two or three directions.   [*2*] *Flat, plain, striped fabrics; some plastics.* The apparent color of some goods is the same whether viewed from top or bottom. But due to weave of a fabric, and texture or simulated weave of a plastic, there may be different apparent tints or shades of color when viewed from top and bottom. It is important that the top ends of such goods be placed consistently throughout an article.   [*3*] *Pile fabrics.* The pile leans from the top toward the bottom end of the goods. This affects a goods' apparent color and durability. If consistently rubbed the "wrong way" or upward, pile threads may bend and eventually break off; the longer or deeper a pile, the greater these effects are. The shorter and denser the pile, the sturdier a fabric is and, as a rule, the less change in apparent color. Today there are many pile fabrics that hold color well, are sturdy, have good wear resistance, and can be railroaded satisfactorily. Find the top end of a pile fabric by stroking it softly; it is more noticeable with a long, deep pile than a short, dense one. Stroke toward the bottom, the cloth feels soft; stroke toward the top, bristly. If grain cannot be felt, lay goods on a table or work bench, set a small coin on the goods, hit the table or bench fairly hard several times; the coin moves toward the bottom of the goods.

SEC. 11:01B RAILROAD / Unless pieced together (Sec. 11:02), a cover goods may be too narrow to set top-to-top with a vertical surface or top-to-rear with a horizontal surface, and piecing may not be desirable. In this case a cover is "railroaded" (Sec. 11:01A). Whether a cover is railroaded with its top end to right or left makes little difference as long as it is consistent; that is, the goods lies to the same end or side of both inside and outside surfaces of an article, such as inside and outside backs of a sofa. As a rule, long or deep pile fabrics are not railroaded, but short, dense pile goods commonly are.

SEC. 11:02 PIECING TOGETHER

This means the joining of goods with a flat seam (Sec. 12:02) instead of welt, or a French seam. Piecing is advisable only when and where it will not be very noticeable and should be planned when measuring an article for cover. [1] *Piecing is fairly common* for the outside back of love seats and wider articles. [2] *A straight seam* along the edge of a stripe may make piecing nearly unnoticeable. [3] *Patterned and figured goods* usually piece together well if the designs are aligned. [4] *Piecing of pile goods* usually is quite noticeable, especially if the grains do not lie in the same direction; pile fabrics may be steamed after piecing to make it less noticeable, but should not be ironed. [5] *Plain, hard-surfaced textiles; most plastics; leather, and leather substitutes* show piecing very clearly. [6] *Piecing is least noticeable* when treated as a style of finishing; if the left inside arm cover is pieced near the back, duplicate it on the right arm. [7] *Seats, inside backs* are subject to greatest notice and wear; avoid piecing.

SEC. 11:03

The names of most cuts of cover are obvious—seat, inside arms, outside back, etc. (Secs. 11:13–11:23). In addition there are cuts that may be used with or on seats, arms, etc. (Secs. 11:04–11:08).

SEC. 11:04 BANDING

Banding is a strip of goods, with or without welt (Sec. 11:08), *hand stitched* in place; it is used most in spring edge seats (Figs. 1:18, b 1:45).

SEC. 11:05 **BORDER**	A border is a strip of goods, with or without welt (Sec. 11:08), *tacked* on one or both sides to a frame. Borders are common in seats (Fig. *a* 1:45), used frequently in arms and backs (Fig. *a* 1:37) and occasionally in wings (Fig. *b* 1:48).
SEC. 11:06 **BOXING**	Boxing is a strip of goods, with or without welt (Sec. 11:08), *machine sewn* to a cover; it is common on seats, arms, and back and upholstery cushions (Figs. 1:09, *a* 1:42).
SEC. 11:07 **PANEL, FACING**	A panel or facing is a strip of cover, with or without welt (Sec. 11:08) usually tacked to a shaped piece of wood or ⅛-inch or thicker chip-board, which later is nailed to a frame. Panels are common on the sides of armless seats and backs (Fig. 1:16), and arm fronts (Fig. *e* 1:45), although these frequently are boxed (Fig. *b* 1:31) or bordered (Fig. *b* 1:46). Base the choice of a panel, border, or boxing on the desired appearance of an article and on the shape of the surface to be covered. Scooped arms, as in Fig. *b* 1:46, often have a combination panel and border.
SEC. 11:08 **WELT,** **WELTING,** **CORDING,** **PIPING**	SEC. 11:08A / The most widely used decorative item in upholstering, welt is a strip of cover sewn around a filler cord. There is single-welt, Fig. *b* 11:08A, and French or double-welt, *c*. "Welt" commonly means single-welt; the other is usually specified as double-welt. With one exception, [3] below, welt and double-welt cannot be substituted satisfactorily for each other. [1] *Welt* generally is used wherever covers or parts of covers are machine sewn, hand stitched, or tacked together. In Fig. *a* 1:42, welt is sewn to the inside back and arm covers and boxings, seat cushion casing, and banding at the front of the seat;

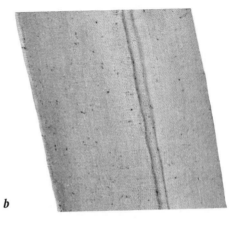

Fig. a, b 11:08A   *a*   *b*

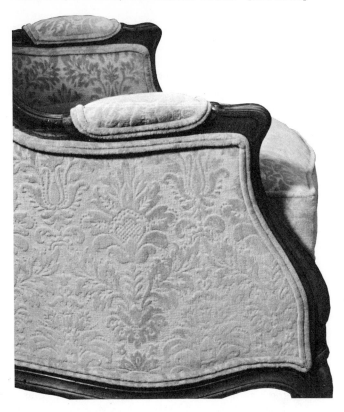

Fig. c 11:08A

welted seat banding is hand stitched to the seat spring edge; welt is tacked along the top and front edges of the outside arms. Welt is optional; its basic purpose is to decorate, and it is not essential for construction. But for appearance, welt is generally considered as almost essential, since it enhances seams, stitching, and tacking lines. Welt also makes blind-stitching less noticeable; compare Fig. *a* and *b* 11:08A. There are of course times when joining covers smoothly without welt may be more attractive and practical, such as inside arm and back covers in some types of barrel chairs (Fig. *b* 1:38).   [2] *Double-welt*, used instead of gimp (Sec. 3:59) is glued along edges of exposed-wood surfaces such as inside arms and outside arms and armrests, Fig. *c* 11:08A. Due to its construction, double-welt cannot usually be sewn, stitched, or tacked satisfactorily. Preparing double-welt is not difficult—for experienced sewers. Machine sewing is the practical way, but it can be stitched satisfactorily by hand (Sec. 12:08). A special foot is needed for machine sewing. The double-piping attachments for some home machines usually will handle very thin light-weight goods (Sec. 3:53B). But for heavier goods an industrial foot is needed; few can be used on home machines without extensive modification. In most cases it is better to have an upholstery shop sew your double-welt. [3] *Welt instead of double-welt* may be used on exposed-wood surfaces (Fig. 13:07E).

SEC. 11:08B / Most welt and double-welt are made of the cover goods and planned with it (Sec. 11:08C). But both weltings often are used for decoration in their own right, such as striped welt with a plain cover (Fig. *b* 1:31), dark welting with a light cover, light welting with dark, different shades or tints of welting and cover, and so forth. Using goods other than the cover for welting may be done from necessity—not enough cover goods.

SEC. 11:08C PLANNING WELTING / Although cover for welting may come from pieces left over when fitting larger cuts on a plot (Sec. 11:24), always measure the amount needed just as accurately as the rest of a cover. [1] *For best results in most cases,* cut welting covers on the bias (Sec. 11:25); leftover pieces usually are too small for practical bias cuts. [2] *Cover for single-welt* may be cut with (Fig. 11:24B) or across a fabric instead of on the bias. The welt will be more difficult to install around sharp bends or turns but will use far less goods than bias welt, an important point when upholstering within a limited budget. [3] *With striped goods* and welting cover cut with or across a fabric, not on the bias, the welt stripes can lie with or across the cover stripes. This of course presents a problem when welting around a corner. Cutting welt on the bias eliminates problems of matching stripes in the welt to those in a cover (Figs. *b* 1:46, *a* 1:48). [4] *Cut and use the longest* possible lengths of welting cover. The less piecing together, the easier the work and smoother a finished job will be.

SEC. 11:08D WELTING COVERS / [1] *Welt.* For welt filler or cord (Sec. 3:58) up to 5/16-inch diameter, make the cover 1½ inches wide. This provides a ½-inch seam allowance along the length of a welt and simplifies sewing and installation. For larger filler, measure its circumference and add 1⅙ inches for seam allowance. Bias-cut welt cover is easier to handle than nonbias. [2] *Double-welt.* For welt fillers or cords (Sec. 3:58) up to 5/16-inch diameter, make the cover 2 inches wide. For thicker filler measure its circumference, multiply by 2, add ¾ inch for seam allowance. Double-welt cover nearly always is bias-cut, especially when it must curve much, as across the top of the back in Fig. *a* 1:28. But for fairly straight installation, as along the sides of the back in Fig. *a* 1:28, a nonbias cut may be satisfactory. [3] *Self-welt for cushions, pillows.* When sewing heavy goods with a light machine, it is advisable to include welt cover in a cushion or pillow boxing (Sec. 11:06). This is "self-welting," and eliminates one thickness of goods to be sewn (Sec. 17:08). It is not as neat as conventional welting and is not recommended if a machine can sew four thicknesses of a cover goods. Allow ¾ inch extra goods on each edge that is to be self-welted when using filler cord up to ⁵⁄₁₆-inch diameter.

SEC. 11:09 **COVER** **STRETCHERS**	These are pieces of muslin, denim, or other relatively inexpensive but strong goods sewn to a cover to extend it from just beyond the junction of upholstered surfaces, such as an inside arm and seat. Well-planned cover stretchers are not seen in a finished article. They are highly recommended to reduce cover costs, especially for a cover that ravels or tears easily.
SEC. 11:10 **DECKING**	Decking (Sec. 3:56) is goods other than the cover used in the part of a loose cushion seat that ordinarily is not seen (Fig. 13:17D). It offers a worthwhile saving in cover cost.
SEC. 11:11 **MEASURING** **COVER**	When measuring a surface incased by muslin, hold the tape measure snug against it but not tight enough to change its shape. For surfaces not incased, draw the tape measure fairly tight against the stuffing, compressing it to the approximate final shape and size. Use any consistent system of measuring. *Width* of a surface generally is measured first as it, not length, is the key to the number of cuts contained in a piece of goods. Measure maximum width and length of a surface. Plot each piece of cover first as a rectangle. Small cuts or pieces often can be fitted between larger ones when plotting (Sec. 11:24) for the least yardage needed.
SEC. 11:12 **CODING** **COVER**	Keep each cut or piece of cover plainly marked from time of measuring to its actual installation. Pin marks to goods or chalk-mark on the wrong side. Marks usually are in the following code:

A	Inside arm, armrest, armboard.
B	Inside back.
BX	Boxing, border, or banding with additional code marks to specify use in seat, arms, etc.
C	Cushion, pillow cover.
OA	Outside arm.
OB	Outside back.
OW	Outside wing.
P	Panel or facing, or post pieces, with additional code marks to specify use in seat, arm, or back.
S	Seat.
SK	Skirt or flounce.
W	Inside wing.
WT	Welting.

2   Placed before a code mark, this specifies the number of identical cuts needed; "2 OW" means "2 outside wing cuts this size and shape."

SEC. 11:13 SEATS

SEC. 11:13A SEAT COVERS / The seat cover proper incases the major part of a seat. It completely incases a seat in some articles (Fig. 1:19); in others it is extended to the bottom by banding, border, boxing, or panels, depending on the type seat and seat edge (Fig. *e* 1:45), and arms and back. The top end of a seat cover (Sec. 11:01) usually points to the back. Measure greatest width from side to side, length from back to front; add 3 inches to each measurement for handling goods. [*1*] *Exposed-wood pad seats* (Fig. 1:01). Measure greatest width and length between outer edges of rabbets (Fig. 13:07B), or between scratch lines. [*2*] *Slipseats* (Fig. 1:02) finish on bottom surface about 1 inch from the edges of a frame. Measure greatest width and length from bottom edges over the top surface. [*3*] *Solid seats.* Pull-over covers finish on the bottom of seat rails, on the rabbets of exposed-wood seats. Pull-over covers are common on fully exposed seats (Fig. *b* 1:09), on the front of armless articles (Fig. 1:16), and on the front of an armchair having a roll edge or a hard edge seat (Fig. *a* 1:20). Pull-over covers are not practical on spring-edge solid seats; with nothing to hold a cover along the top of the spring-edge, it shifts around in use, wrinkles, and soils easily. Cover stretchers may be used (Sec. 11:13B). [*4*] *Loose-cushion seats* usually have fully upholstered arms and backs finishing against the seat, and hard or spring edges. Decking (Sec. 11:10) extends from the back of the hard or spring edge to the back rail and across a seat from side rail to side rail. Cover stretchers may be used (Sec. 11:13B). Measure width of the seat cover between its points of finishing at the sides; measure length from the back of a hard or spring edge to where a cover will finish on the frame, or seat edge, or be joined to boxing or banding (Secs. 11:13C, F). [*5*] *How seats may be covered satisfactorily* largely depends on the muslin casings. Seats stuffed without a break down to the bottom of the rails can take only a pull-over or, if the top edges are fairly sharp, a boxed cover. Seats stuffed down only to the tops of rails can, depending on the top edges, take a pull-over, or boxed cover, or one having banding, borders, or panels.

SEC. 11:13B COVER STRETCHERS / When fully upholstered arms and/or backs finish against a seat, stretchers (Sec. 11:09) extend a cover for the top of a seat from about 1 inch beyond its junction with arms and/or back to the frame, Fig. 11:13B; cover stretchers at the arms start about 1 inch behind the front posts. The use of cover stretchers often makes a T-shaped seat cover; but plot it first as a

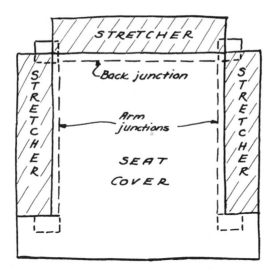

Fig. 11:13B

rectangle based on *greatest width,* generally measured across the front edge, and *greatest length,* generally measured at the middle of a seat. Goods saved by cover stretchers may be used for small cuts, such as panels or nonbias welt cover (Sec. 11:08); fit these in while plotting cover (Sec. 11:24).

NOTE: Here the use of cover stretchers is given in terms of seats primarily. Stretchers may be used wherever adjacent surfaces are close enough together to conceal stretchers, such as along the sides of a back in a wingchair (Fig. b 1:48).

SEC. 11:13C BOXING / Boxing (Sec. 11:06) is used on armless (Fig. 1:13) and on fully exposed (Fig. *a* 1:09) solid seats when there are sharp breaks between the top and other surfaces. These seats usually have roll or hard edges that hold boxing neatly in place; spring edges cannot do this. Boxing seldom is on seats having fully upholstered arms; there seldom is space for it to show well. A disadvantage of seat boxing is that the customary welt between it and the cover readily becomes soiled and worn. When a back is fully upholstered, seat boxing ends on the back of the posts. Measure *width* of seat boxing along seat rails; add 2 inches per cut for handling. Measure *length* from the edge of the top surface of a seat to the bottom of the rail or rabbet unless a border (Sec. 11:13D) will be used; add 2 inches for seam allowance and general handling. Measure seat cover proper from just below the edges of the top surface; add ½ inch seam allowance wherever boxing will be sewn to it.

SEC. 11:13D BORDER / Borders (Sec. 11:05, Fig. *b* 1:29) are used on any seat except, as a rule, exposed-wood. As well as often improving appearance by eliminating a solid expanse of seat cover, borders add to the life of a pull-over or banded (Sec. 11:04) cover by letting it be tacked near the top of a seat rail instead of on the bottom; this decreases the amount of cover that puffs out when a seat is used. [*1*] *When a back is fully upholstered,* finish seat border on backs of posts. [*2*] *When inside arm covers* finish on outer sides of arm posts (Fig. 1:30), seat borders usually finish there; this also applies to setback arms (Fig. 1:34). [*3*] *When the front of a fully upholstered arm* will have a panel, border, or boxing (Fig. *b* 1:31), finish seat border on face of post. [*4*] *Seat borders usually are tacked* near the top of a rail but may be placed somewhat below as a matter of personal taste. [*5*] *Measure width of seat border* along the outer surfaces of a rail; add 2 inches per cut for handling. Measure length from where the top of a border is to finish at or near the top of a rail down to the bottom, or to the top of the border below it (sometimes there are two borders, one directly below the other); add 2 inches for handling. [*6*] *Measure seat cover* from about 1 inch below the planned top of border; add 1½ inches wherever there will be a border.

SEC. 11:13E PANEL / Panels (Sec. 11:07) for seats are usually put only on the sides of armless articles (Fig. 1:16); they serve the same purpose as, and may be replaced by, borders (Sec. 11:13D). Side panel covers usually lie in the same direction as a seat cover proper; take into account the shape of a panel and how it will be set on a seat (Fig. 11:13E) when measuring width and length. For side panels, *width* generally is measured from top to bottom, *length* from back to front, actual measurement depending on size and shape of panel; add 2 inches to each greatest measurement for handling. Measure seat cover proper from ½ inch inside the area to be covered by panel; add 1 inch per panel for handling of cover.

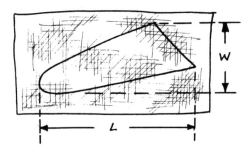

Fig. 11:13E

SEC. 11:13F BANDING / Banding (Sec. 11:04) generally is used only for spring-edge seats (Figs. 1:18, *c* 1:45). As well as shaping a spring-edge and eliminating a solid expanse of cover from top to bottom of the front and/or sides, banding adds to the life and looks of a seat cover by decreasing the amount of puff-out when a seat is used. Install banding only when muslin casing is stitched to the spring edge-wire (Fig. 7:29A); banding extends from the top of the edge-wire down to where it will finish on the rail. Banding often finishes on the bottom of a rail, but this can give quite a bit of puff-out in large seats. Banding encompasses the spring-edge portion of a seat. [1] *When spring-edge is not attached to front posts,* banding extends to inner back edges of posts; cover stretchers (Sec. 11:13B) extend it to seat rail. [2] *When spring-edge is attached to front posts,* banding usually finishes on posts about 1 inch from inner edges. [3] *On armless articles,* banding generally finishes on the outer sides of the back posts. [4] *Measure* width of seat banding along rails; add 2 inches per cut for handling. Measure length from spring edge-wire down to where banding will finish on rail; add 2 inches for stitching and handling. [5] *Measure seat cover proper* from just below spring edge-wire; add 2 inches for stitching and handling wherever there is banding.

**SEC. 11:14
ARM COVERS—
PARTIALLY
UPHOLSTERED
ARMS**

Sec. 11:14A Armrest Pad Covers / Armrest pad (Fig. *c* 1:28) covers often are fitted into cuts planned for larger surfaces, such as seats. The top end of armrest pad covers usually lies in the same direction as the seat cover. Measure width from side to side over pad from the outer edge of one rabbet to that of the other; measure length similarly from back to front. Add 2 inches to each measurement for handling.

Sec. 11:14B Partially Upholstered Arm / [1] *A single piece to cover both inside and outside arms* may be used for this general type of partially upholstered arm (Fig. 1:22). Finish top and bottom ends of cover on the underside of the lower arm rail; the top end of the cover usually lies to the top of the inside arm. Measure width from where cover will finish on front post to the outer back edge of the back post; measure length to encompass thickest part of arm. Add 3 inches to each measurement for handling goods. As a rule, much small pleating (Sec. 5:17) is needed at the front. [2] *Another treatment for partially upholstered arms* is one cover for inside, another for outside surfaces. I—The inside arm cover goes from the bottom of the lower arm rail over the armtop to the outer side of the armboard tacking strip; this is the cover's length; measure width as in [1] above; add 3 inches to each measurement for handling. II—The outside cover goes from where it will finish on the front post to the outer back edge of the back post; this is width. Measure length from the bottom of the lower arm rail to the top of the tacking strip on the armboard. Add 3 inches to each measurement.

SEC. 11:14C COVERED ARMBOARDS / [*1*] *Covers may encompass an armboard* (Fig. *d* 1:29), or finish on the underside ½ inch from outer edges; use the latter method for wide or peculiarly shaped armboards. At the back, covers generally finish on the back of the back post. Measure greatest width around armboard from its points of finishing. Measure greatest length from the underside of the front of armboard over it to the point of finishing at the back. Add 2 inches to each measurement for handling. [*2*] *Armboard covers for bordered inside arms* usually finish on the side of an armboard somewhat below the top (Fig. *b* 1:42) or near the upper edge (Fig. 1:63), strictly a matter of design. At the back, an armboard cover may finish on the back of a back post (Figs. *b* 1:42, 1:63), or on the side. For small or short arms (Fig. *b* 1:42), measure greatest width over armboard from where cover will finish on sides; measure greatest length from where cover will finish at the front over the arm to the point of finishing at the back; add 2 inches to each measurement. Cover for long arms often is rail-roaded (Sec. 11:01B) to avoid piecing it. For railroading, measure armboard cover as above, but treat width as length, and length as width.

SEC. 11:15 **ARM COVERS—** **FULLY** **UPHOLSTERED** **ARMS**	**SEC. 11:15A** / The top end of inside and outside arm covers generally lies toward the armtop in fully upholstered arms. Measure width from back to front, length from top to bottom. Due to the shape of most backs, measure greatest width of inside and outside arms between lines perpendicular to the floor passing through the foremost and rearmost points (Fig. 8:15B); total measurement depends on where covers finish on arm, seat, and back. Arm covers include borders, boxing, panels, stretchers, and post pieces.

SEC. 11:15B INSIDE ARMS / In fully upholstered arms and others treated as such (Fig. *a* 1:52), add stretchers (Sec. 11:09) to bottom and back of inside arm covers (Fig. 11:15B). [*1*] *Stretcher extends inside arm cover down* from a point 2 inches below the junction of seat and inside arm to the seat rail; the bottom of an arm liner generally is

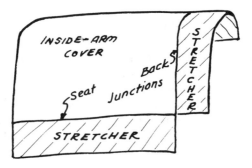

Fig. 11:15B

about 1 inch below arm and seat junction. [2] *Except when inside arm and back covers are joined or pieced together* (Fig. *b* 1:38), stretcher extends arm cover from 1 inch behind arm and back junction to where arm cover finishes on a back post. [3] *Except when a post piece is included in the cover* (Sec. 11:15C), inside arm cover stretchers run the full way of the bottom and back of a cover. They should be 2 inches wider than the distance from the edges of a cover to the points of tacking on seat rail and back post.

SEC. 11:15C POST PIECE / Since inside arm cover goods usually end just below an arm liner (Sec. 11:15B), when front of seat is not attached to a front post, there is a gap between inside arm and seat rail covers. Fill this by a post piece (Fig. *a* 5:16). If a post panel (Sec. 11:15G) is flush with the inner side of a post (Fig. *e* 1:45), the post piece usually is a scrap of goods. When a post panel is not flush with the inner side of a post, the post piece may be sewn to the front bottom part of an inside arm cover; but for a neater job, include post piece in the inside arm cover, Fig. 11:15C; cover goods behind a post piece may be used for nonbias welt and other small cuts. Measure width of a post piece from the back of a post to where it finishes at the front; measure length down from the bottom of an inside arm cover to 2 inches below the top of the seat rail. For post pieces not part of inside arm cover, add 3 inches to both measurements for handling.

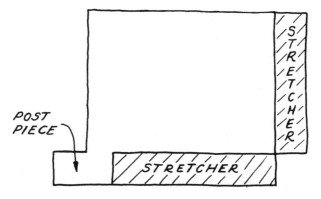

Fig. 11:15C

SEC. 11:15D WIDTH OF INSIDE ARM COVER / Measure from back to point of finishing at front (Secs. 11:15A, B). If front edge of seat is not attached to front post, a post piece is needed (Sec. 11:15C). For all covers listed below except [5] (*boxed*), to greatest measured width add 1½ inches for handling goods. [1] *Pull-around arm covers* (Fig. 1:30) finish on outer side of front post. [2] *When post panel or border will be used* (Figs. *c* 1:45, *b* 1:46), finish arm cover in area to be covered by panel or border. [3] *For exposed-wood inside arm* (Fig. *a* 1:52), cover extends to edges of rabbets. [4] *Inside arm covers bordered at front* (Sec. 11:05, Fig. 1:63) usually finish the same distance back from the front edge as the top of the cover is down from the armboard cover.   [5] *For boxed arm front* (Sec. 11:06, Figs. *b* 1:31, *a* 1:42, *c* 1:45), extend inside arm cover to inner front edge of the stuffed surface. Add ½ inch to greatest measured width for seam allowance.

SEC. 11:15E   LENGTH OF INSIDE ARM COVER / Measure length from point of finishing at the armtop to the bottom (Sec. 11:15B). If front edge of seat is not attached to the front post, a post piece is needed (Sec. 11:15C). For all covers listed below except [6] (*boxed*), add 1½ inches to greatest measured length for handling of goods.   [1] *Pull-around arm covers* finish on outer side of armboard: I—About 1 inch below top edge of a knife-edge arm (Fig. *a* 1:20). II—On outer side of underarm strip close to armboard in scroll and square-scroll arms (Figs. *b* 1:31, *b* 1:46).   [2] *In rounded arms* (Fig. *d* 1:45), inside and outside covers usually are one length of goods going up the inside and down the outside. Whether top end of goods lies up on inside or on outside is a matter of choice except possibly for pile fabrics (Sec. 11:01A[3]).   [3] *For bordered armtop* (Fig. *a* 1:37), finish inside arm cover on top of armboard in area to be covered by border.   [4] *When arm finishes into wing*, the inside arm cover usually extends to top of wing (Fig. 1:15). To save goods, wing and arm covers may be pieced or welted together; this also applies to outside arm and wing covers. [5] *The inside arm cover of a bordered-type or a bordered inside arm* (Figs. *b* 1:42, 1:63) extends to bottom of armboard cover or border. [6] *For boxed armtop* (Fig. *a* 1:42), inside arm cover extends to inner top edge of arm. Add ½ inch to greatest measured length for seam allowance.

SEC. 11:15F   T-SHAPED ARM / Width of the top of a T-shaped arm (Fig. *a* 1:46) usually is measured over it from the inner to the outer sides of the underarm strip or strips; length is measured from the point of finishing at the back to the front of the front post. Add 3 inches to each measurement for handling of goods. The rest of the arm, measured as any other, finishes at the top on the underarm strip.

SEC. 11:15G   PANEL / Arm-front panels (Sec. 11:07) generally are used only on straight posts (Fig. *e* 1:45). Most scooped arms (Figs. *b* 1:46, *a, e* 1:48) have a border or boxing (Secs. 11:05, 11:06) instead of panel. Goods for any of these post face covers generally lie in the same direction as the inside arm cover; therefore the shape of a panel or armfront and how the cover will lie must be considered, Fig. 11:15G. Width of cover usually is measured between inside and outside arms,

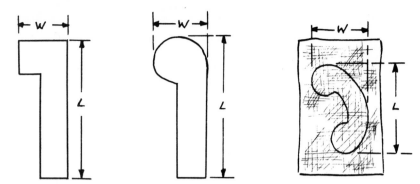

Fig. 11:15G

length from top to bottom. Add 2 inches to each measurement for handling.

Sec. 11:15H   Armtop Border /   An armtop border (Sec. 11:05) may be an extension of a border on the armfront (Fig. *b* 1:48), or it may be limited to the armtop and perhaps the backtop (Fig. *a* 1:37). [*1*] *Measure* a border extending from armfront (Sec. 11:15G).   [*2*] *For armtop border of straight arm,* measure width between inside and outside arms, length from back to front. Add 2 inches to each greatest measurement for handling.   [*3*] *When arm- and backtops have a continuous border* (Fig. *a* 1:37), a single-piece border usually looks better than one that is pieced; be sure to use maximum measurements (Sec. 11:15I). Overall width is the greatest distance across the article from the outside of one arm to that of the other, Fig. 11:15H; length is the greatest distance from the outside back to a straight line between the front of the armtops. Add at least 4 inches to each measurement for handling of goods. This oversize cover has much surplus in which other cuts may be fitted when plotting goods; but this should not be attempted while making initial measurement of the

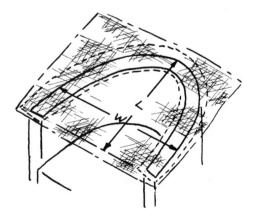

Fig. 11:15H

goods needed. It is advisable to make a full size paper template or pattern of this type border for plotting and cutting (Sec. 11:15I).

SEC. 11:15I MAKING TEMPLATES FOR BORDERS / When making a template for a continuous arm- and backtop border (Sec. 11:15H), in-experienced upholsterers should make very generous allowances for fitting cover onto an article. Unless it lies in place naturally, without being stretched or squeezed to fit, there are apt to be ridges in the finished job. [*1*] *Set a sheet of fairly heavy paper* on the article. It must follow all contours of the border area; as well as reaching all edges, the template must be pressed down into any scoops in arm and/or back. [*2*] *Hold a stick of chalk* or soft pencil vertically; move it snugly along all sides of the border area to outline them on the underside of the template sheet. [*3*] *Remove template sheet*, blend irregularities of marking into a neat, smooth outline of the border area. If there are major irregularities, repeat [*2*] above. [*4*] *Transfer outline* from underside to the top side of the template sheet by making pinholes in it every inch along the outline, or by holding the paper against a light and tracing the outline. [*5*] *Make a second or cutting outline* 2 inches larger on all edges than the first outline; 2 inches outside all outside-surface lines, 2 inches inside all inside-surface lines. [*6*] *Cut template* along cutting lines. Handle it as little as possible in order to keep it in true shape.

SEC. 11:15J ARMFRONT, ARMTOP BOXING / For boxing (Sec. 11:06) on scooped arms see Sec. 11:15G. [*1*] *Scroll arms* (Fig. *b* 1:31) often are boxed in front when fairly sharp breaks are wanted between inner, outer, and front surfaces, and the front is relatively flat. [*2*] *Measure* greatest width between inside and outside arms, greatest length from top to bottom of armfront. Add 2 inches to each measurement for seam allowance and general handling. [*3*] *Shape of armfront* affects setting of cover goods; usually the weft or horizontal line of boxing goods parallels the floor. [*4*] *When boxing and a panel are used,* boxing generally is a narrow strip extending from the front edge of the inside arm cover to under the panel throughout the arm cover. [*5*] *Armtop and front boxing* is common on modern-type articles (Figs. 1:15, *a* 1:42). Measure the same way as armfront boxing (Secs. 11:15D, E) except that length is from the back of the back post to the bottom of the front rail.

SEC. 11:15K OUTSIDE ARMS / Measure greatest width and length (Sec. 11:15A); add 3 inches to each for handling. [*1*] *Width.* Outside arm covers finish on the back of the back post. At the front, covers usually finish along the outer front edge of a post except: I—When a post panel or substitute is used, the cover finishes on the area to be covered by the panel, border, or boxing (Fig. *b* 1:46). II—In an exposed-wood arm, the cover finishes at the edges of the rabbet. [2] *Length.* At the top, an outside arm cover finishes along the top edge of an armboard or rabbet in all arms except scroll (Fig. *b* 1:31), rounded (Sec. 11:15E[2]), square-scroll (Fig. *b* 1:46), and T-shaped (Sec. 11:15F). In square and square-scroll arms, outside arm covers finish on underarm strip close to the armboard. At the bottom, outside arm covers finish on the bottom of the seat rail or on the rabbet of an exposed-wood arm (Fig. 1:52).

SEC. 11:16 **WING COVERS**	**SEC. 11:16A /** The top end of cover goods usually lies to the top of inside and outside wings. Width is from back to front, length from top to bottom.

SEC. 11:16B INSIDE WING / The top of an inside wing cover generally finishes at the back on the outside back frame unless wing boxing (Fig. 1:15) or border (Fig. *b* 1:48) is used, or the top of a wing is below the top of a back (Fig. *e* 1:48). Measure greatest width from back of back post to where cover finishes at the front; greatest length from topmost part of wing down to the armtop. Add 4 inches to each measurement for handling. [1] *Pull-over inside wing covers* (Fig. *d* 1:48) finish on outer side of wing frame. [2] *In bordered wings* (Fig. *b* 1:48), finish inside cover on the front and top surfaces of wing frame. Measure border (Sec. 11:15I). [3] *In boxed wings* (Fig. 1:15) inside cover extends ½ inch above and in front of the inner top and front edges of wing. Measure boxing (Sec. 11:15J).

SEC. 11:16C OUTSIDE WING / Outside wing covers finish on the back of a back post, along top and front edges of a wing frame, and along the armboard except when arm and wing are to be covered by a single piece of goods. Measure greatest width and length accordingly; add 2 inches to width, 3 to length for stitching and handling.

SEC. 11:17 **BACK COVERS**	**SEC. 11:17A /** The top end of cover goods generally lies to the top of inside and outside backs, unless railroading is necessary (Sec. 11:01B). Measure width from side to side, length from top to bottom. Be sure to measure true length (Fig. 10:23B) for back covers.

SEC. 11:17B PARTLY UPHOLSTERED INSIDE BACK COVERS / [1] *Exposed-wood backs* (Figs. 1:03, 1:28). Measure greatest width and length between outer edges of rabbets. Add 3 inches to each measurement for handling. [2] *Slipbacks* (Sec. 11:13A[2]).

Sec. 11:17C Fully Upholstered Inside Back Covers / When seat and fully upholstered arms and/or wings finish against an inside back (Fig. *e* 1:48), stretchers (Sec. 11:09) extend covers from 1 inch behind junctions of these surfaces (Fig. 11:17C) to points of finishing on the frame.

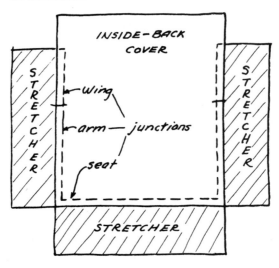

Fig. 11:17C

Sec. 11:17D Width of Inside Back Cover / Measure width between points of finishing at the sides. Add 3 inches to greatest measured width for handling goods except for [4] and [5]: [1] *A pull-around cover* (Figs. 1:09, 1:34, *b* 1:38) finishes on outside back frame. [2] *For paneled backs* (Figs. 1:16, 1:18, *c* 1:45), measure greatest width from about the middle of the outer side of one post to that of the other. [3] *For exposed-wood backs* (Figs. 1:07, *b* 1:28), measure greatest width between outer edges of side rabbets. [4] *For boxed backs* (Figs. 1:14, *a* 1:42), measure greatest width to just beyond the top of the side edges of the inner surface. Add 1 inch for seam allowances. [5] *For joined arm and back covers* (Fig. *b* 1:38), when measuring width, be sure that the back cover extends at least 1 inch beyond the points of joining arm covers.

Sec. 11:17E Length of Inside Back Cover / Measure length from the point of finishing at the top to the point of adding a stretcher (Sec. 11:17C) or to the bottom of the lower rail of a partially upholstered back (Figs. 1:09, 1:18). Add 3 inches to greatest measured length for handling goods except for [3] and [4]: [1] *Pull-over covers* (Figs. 1:09, 1:62) finish on outer side of top rail. [2] *Exposed-wood backs* (Figs. 1:07, *b* 1:28, *a* 1:52); measure greatest length from top edge of the upper rabbet to bottom edge of the lower rabbet or to the point of attaching a cover stretcher. [3] *For boxed covers* (Figs.

b 1:31, *a* 1:42), measure greatest length from just above the top edge of the inner surface. Add ½ inch seam allowance. [4] *In bordered backs* (Fig. *a* 1:37), finish the inside cover on top of the back rail in the area to be covered by a border. Add 2 inches for handling.

SEC. 11:17F BOXING / Many large backs are thicker at the bottom than at the top. This makes back boxing or border (Sec. 11:17H) wider at the arms than at the top. Below armtops, cover often is saved by cutting the goods about 2 inches long and adding a stretcher (Sec. 11:09), preferably a color similar to that of the cover, to reach the points of finishing at the back. Width of boxing may be measured from back to front or from top to bottom; it depends on where the boxing goes and on how the upholsterer wants the cover to lie. [1] *When only the sides are boxed,* boxing usually is set with the weft or horizontal line of a cover parallel to the floor (Fig. 1:14), or with its pattern following that of the inside back cover (Fig. *a* 1:45). I—If weft is to parallel the floor, measure greatest width of boxing between lines perpendicular to the floor passing through the rearmost point at the top and foremost point at the bottom. II—If boxing is to follow the direction of the inside cover pattern, measure greatest width from the edge of the inner surface to the back of the post. In both cases, add 2 inches to greatest measured width for seam allowance and general handling. Also, measure greatest length from the top to the lowest point of finishing in armless articles, to inner side of armboard in other articles; add 1½ inches for seam allowance and handling. [2] *When top and sides are boxed or boxed and bordered,* the top end of the cover goods generally lies to the outside back. Measure greatest width across top of back and down sides to arms, where boxing may finish under the outside arm cover (Fig. *a* 1:42) or at the inner side of an armboard (Fig. *c* 1:42). Add 3 inches for seam allowance and general handling plus 1 inch per cut of boxing for piecing widths of plain goods; for patterned or floral covers, plan widths for the figures to fit together. Measure greatest length of boxing from the outer edge of the inner surface to the outside back frame, or to the point of finishing on the sides of the posts or top of the filler strip when a boxed and bordered cover will be used. Add 2 inches for seam allowance and handling.

SEC. 11:17G PANELS / Back panel covers generally lie in the direction of the inside back cover (Fig. 1:16). Shape of panel and the way its cover will lie must be taken into account (Sec. 11:15G). Measure greatest width between inside and outside backs, greatest length from top to bottom. Add 1 inch to each measurement for handling goods.

Sec. 11:17H   Border / [1] *Borders often replace panels* on the sides of backs (Sec. 11:17G). [2] *For borders on top and sides of flat backs* (Fig. *c* 1:42), the top end of the border cover goods usually lies to the outside back. Measure the same way as for boxing (Sec. 11:17F) except that length is from the point of finishing on the filler strip or posts to the back of the frame. [3] *For top border on barrel back* (Fig. *a* 1:37), see Sec. 11:15I.

Sec. 11:17I   Banding / Banding is used only on spring-edge backs (Fig. 1:50). Measure the same way as for back boxing (Sec. 11:17F).

Sec. 11:17J   Outside Back Covers / Except when back panels are used (Fig. 1:16), outside back covers finish along the extreme edges of a frame and on the bottom of the seat rail, or rabbets of an exposed-wood back, or lower rail of a partially upholstered back. Add 2 inches to both greatest measurements for handling and stitching. When panels are used, the sides of an outside back cover finish on the outer sides of the posts except when covering with leather, leather substitutes, silk, most plastics—any goods in which small nailholes cannot be eliminated by rubbing threads back in place (in this case the cover finishes the same way as any other outside back).

SEC. 11:18 CUSHION CASINGS

Sec. 11:18A / Most upholstery seat cushions are boxed (Sec. 11:06, Figs. *a* 1:35, *c* 1:49). The top end of goods for both top and bottom cushion covers usually lies to the back of a seat. Seat cushions usually butt against the inside back (Sec. 11:19B *Note*). [1] *Cover costs may be reduced* by using decking, denim, or some other inexpensive but durable goods instead of cover for the bottom of a cushion; use a strip of cover goods about 4 inches long for the front portion of the bottom cover. This type cushion is not reversible. [2] *Boxing and cushion covers* usually are the same goods, and as a rule the top end of the boxing goods lies to the top cushion cover. But this is only a matter of general practice, and a novel treatment may be made by using different goods or design for boxing.

Sec. 11:18B   Cushion Covers / Measure greatest width of a seat, generally across the front edge. When measuring greatest length, allow for the back corners of a seat; in many flat-back articles, a seat is deeper or longer at the sides than at the middle. A cushion should fit snugly into all parts of a seat. Add 1 inch to each measurement for sewing cushion together. For down-filled cushions (Sec. 3:62), add an extra ¾ inch to compensate for puffiness of the filling.

Sec. 11:18C   Cushion Boxing / Boxing for most cushions must be pieced (Sec. 11:02); usually this is done at the sides and back. The two ways of making boxed cushions are: [1] *Traditional.* Boxing is solid throughout and is hand stitched in part to the bottom cover after the casing is filled (Sec. 17:06A). [2] *Modern.* Boxing at the back has a zippered opening for filling the casing (Sec. 17:06B). There is no hand stitching. A modern cushion needs slightly more boxing material than the traditional but as a rule not enough to greatly affect cover cost.

SEC. 11:18D WIDTHS / Width of boxing installed the usual way (Sec. 11:18A[2]) is the circumference of a cushion. [1] *Traditional construction.* Measure along outlines of a seat or along edges of a seat cover. To total measured width of boxing, add 1 inch for joining the ends when assembling the casing plus 1 inch per cut of boxing for piecing together. The basic piecing allowance is for plain goods; for patterned or floral goods plan width for the figures to fit together. [2] *Modern construction.* Measure width and make the same allowances for modern as for traditional boxing, but add 3 more inches for covering the ends of the zipper (Sec. 17:06C).

SEC. 11:18E LENGTHS / Length of boxing installed the usual way is the distance between top and bottom cushion covers. Usually this is based on accepted standards of desirable cushion thickness rather than on actual measurement. Cushion thickness is, of course, a matter of personal taste, and thicknesses other than the so-called standards are perfectly acceptable. Lengths given below contain ½-inch seam allowances top and bottom and are for all cushion boxing except the zipper portion of a modern casing (Sec. 17:06C); for zipper boxing, add 1 inch. [1] *For all cushion fillings except down* (Secs. 3:61–3:73), boxing generally is 4¼ to 4½ inches long. Self-welted boxing (Sec. 11:08G[3]) for these fillings usually is about 5½ inches long. [2] *Down-filled cushions* (Sec. 17:03B) generally have 3½-inch long boxing, as they tend to puff up considerably at the edges and be thicker than the length of boxing suggests. Self-welted boxing for down cushions is usually about 4½ inches long.

| SEC. 11:19 PILLOW CASINGS | SEC. 11:19A / Upholstery back pillows often are not boxed (Sec. 11:06, Fig. 1:34) but as a rule are more satisfactory when boxed on bottom and sides (Fig. *b* 1:46). Boxed pillows are traditional and modern in construction (Secs. 11:18C, D, E); for modern construction the extra lengths and widths for a zipper, at the bottom, are the same as for modern cushion casing. Measure pillow width from side to side of a back at its widest part, length from top to bottom. Pillows generally require more cover goods than inexperienced upholsterers expect. The allowances given below are minimums. To avoid making a |

back pillow too small for comfort and good appearance, whenever possible add 2 or 3 inches to minimum cover allowances.

Sec. 11:19B Boxed Pillows / For front and back covers, measure greatest width of an inside back between the breaks from inner to side surfaces. Measure greatest length from the break between inner and top surfaces down to the top of a solid seat or planned top of a seat cushion. Estimate the top of a seat cushion by adding the length of its boxing (Sec. 11:18E) to the top of the decking. Add at least 4 inches to each measurement to allow for sewing, general handling of goods, and puff-out of a finished pillow.

NOTE: Instead of a back pillow resting on top of a seat cushion, some upholsterers prefer the pillow to rest on the seat deck and the seat cushion to butt against it; modification of cushion and pillow lengths for this is obvious.

Thickness of a boxed pillow is due primarily to width or length of boxing. Thickness of a back pillow is optional but usually is 4 to 6 inches at sides and bottom; make boxing 1 inch wider or longer than planned thickness for ½-inch seam allowances at cover. [*1*] *When top end of boxing lies to the top of a pillow,* width of boxing determines thickness of pillow. [*2*] *When top end of boxing lies to the back cover,* length of boxing determines thickness of pillow. [*3*] *Whether to set top end of boxing* as in [*1*] or [*2*] is a matter of choice. [*4*] *Boxing usually extends* down around pillow covers from one top corner to the other. Add 1 inch per cut for piecing plus 1 inch for joining at the bottom. The piecing allowance is for plain goods; for patterned or floral goods, plan cuts of boxing for the figures to fit together. [*5*] *Instead of going partway around a pillow* ([*4*] above), boxing may go completely around it. However, boxing across the top may allow the front cover to sag and wrinkle.

Sec. 11:19C Unboxed Pillows / Thickness of unboxed pillows (Fig. 1:34) is due to width and length of front and back covers; measure the same way as for boxed pillow covers (Sec. 11:19B). Add at least 3 inches to each measurement for puff-out, sewing, and general handling. Then add to each cover one-half of the desired thickness of the pillow at the side and bottom edges. For example, for a pillow to be approximately 4-inches thick at the sides, in addition to allowances for puff-out, etc., add 2 inches to width and length of each cover for desired thickness.

**SEC. 11:20
SKIRTS,
FLOUNCES**

Sec. 11:20A / The top end of cover goods in a skirt or flounce (Secs. 18:03–18:08) usually lies toward the seat rails (Fig. *a* 1:35). Measure width along seat rails, length from rails to floor. There are two important factors to consider when planning length of a skirt or how high to set the top of it on a seat; how low it can be set is determined by a seat frame (Figs. 1:18, 1:45, 1:57). First, the longer a skirt is, the better it hangs and usually looks, especially at pleats; the shorter a skirt, the more it appears to flare out at pleats (Fig. c 1:42). Second, a skirt and the rest of the visible part of a seat (the front, in articles having fully upholstered arms) should be planned as they are seen—as a unit. Many experienced upholsterers believe that a unit looks best when it has only two or three parts. In Figs. b 1:20, and a 1:29, there are two parts: pull-over seat cover and skirt. In Figs. b 1:29 and a 1:31, there are three parts: pull-over seat cover, border, and skirt. In Figs. b 1:31 and a 1:35, there are three parts: cushion, pull-over seat cover, and skirt. With more than three parts, a unit may appear crowded or busy, as Fig. 1:34 compared to Fig. b 1:35; but this is a matter of personal taste. Fabric flange and box-pleated skirts, and those made with delicate plastic goods, should be lined with sateen or muslin; lining is especially important for satin or any textile that ravels easily. Measure lining the same way as a skirt or flounce; however, it can be done accurately only after a skirt is planned.

Sec. 11:20B   Width   /   Always measure width of a skirt on the seat frame at the planned height of the top of the skirt.   [1] *Traditional flange skirt* (Secs. 18:04, 18:05). Measure width of goods completely around a seat; add 12 to 16 inches for each pleat. Pleats, generally 3 to 4 inches deep, are at each corner. Love seat and wider articles often have one or more additional pleats in front (Figs. 1:57, 1:63).   [2] *Modern flange skirt* (Secs. 18:04, 18:06). Measure width of goods for each panel between the pertinent corners of a seat; add 4 inches for turn-back of ends. Each corner has a corner piece, usually 8 inches wide, for a simulated pleat. In love seat and wider articles (Figs. 1:57, 1:63), one or more simulated pleats, with regulation corner piece, often are in front; for these, measure width of each front skirt panel, add 4 inches for turn-back.   [3] *Box-pleated skirt* (Sec. 18:07). For all box-pleated skirts, add at least 4 inches per cut of goods for piecing (Sec. 11:02) within a pleat plus 8 inches for finishing ends of skirt. Width of goods needed for a box-pleated skirt is based on the circumference of a seat plus allowances for the desired fullness of pleats: I—When all inside and outside pleats touch (Fig. a 1:35), width of goods needed is 3 times the circumference; this is the fullest skirt and is especially advisable for small pleats. II—When inside pleats touch but between outside pleats there is a space of one-third the width of a pleat (Fig. c 1:29), width of goods is 2½ times the circumference. Touching inside pleats give fullness to a skirt. A space between outside pleats may improve the appearance of a skirt. III—When there is a space of one-third the width of a pleat between inside and outside pleats, width of goods needed is 2 times the circumference. This type skirt lacks fullness and generally should be avoided. [*4*] *Gathered or shirred skirt* (Sec. 18:08). Width of goods needed is 2 times the circumference of a seat plus 4 inches for finishing ends of skirt; add 1 inch per cut of goods for piecing. Less cover goods may be used; the minimum should be 1½ times the circumference plus allowances.

SEC. 11:20C LENGTH / Measure length of skirt goods from the point of finishing at the top (Sec. 11:20A) on the front of a seat down to a point that will be about ¾ inch above the floor; if leg glides or castors have not been installed, allow for them when measuring length. To the basic height or length of a skirt: [*1*] *All skirts.* Add ½-inch seam allowance at the top. [*2*] *Traditional flange, box-pleated, gathered or shirred skirts.* Add 2 or 3 inches for hem at the bottom; the deeper a hem, the better pleats and gathers hold shape. [*3*] *Modern flange skirt.* Add ½ inch seam allowance at the bottom.

SEC. 11:21
WELTING

Measure the amount of welting (Sec. 11:08) needed for each part of an article—seat, outside arms, cushion, etc. [*1*] *Single-welt.* Add 2 inches for each part of an article for finishing ends of welt; add 1 or 2 inches to each cut that probably will have to be pieced to another. Often, much of the cover for nonbias welt can be taken from goods left over from larger cuts; do not "guess" this, do it in the plotting (Sec. 11:24). [*2*] *Double- or French welt.* Add 2 or 3 inches to each part of an article for general handling. As a rule, double-welt cannot be pieced or joined at the ends satisfactorily except by gluing (Sec. 12:08B). Cover for double-welt usually is cut on the bias (Sec. 11:08A) and is not taken from goods left over from larger cuts.

SEC. 11:22
RUCHE,
RUCHING

Ruche is an extra trim often put on backs of small or medium size chairs (Fig. *a* 1:35). From a decoration standpoint, it may be treated the same ways as welt (Sec. 11:08B). Ruche generally is pleated, ruffled, or gathered, and the width of goods needed usually is 3 times the length over which it is to go; in Fig. *a* 1:35 it goes along the outer edges of the outside back from armtop to armtop, in Fig. *b* 1:36 it extends to the bottom of a seat. Add 6 inches for general handling plus 2 inches per cut for piecing. Length of ruching usually is twice its exposed height above the point of tacking to a frame plus 1 inch for sewing and tacking.

SEC. 11:23
BUTTON
COVERS

These usually come from scraps of goods trimmed off during installation of the larger cuts or pieces. But when many buttons, especially large ones, will be used, measure goods for them. For any buttons other than round, cover goods should lie in the same direction as the surface on which they are to go. Measure greatest width and length of a button, add about 2 inches for general handling.

**SEC. 11:24
PLOTTING
COVER**

SEC. 11:24A PAPER PLOT / After measuring and adding allowances for all cuts of cover goods, make a paper plot or diagram of all pieces needed. Plots are made to find the *least yardage needed of a specific cover goods.* This mainly involves width of goods and arranging cuts for a cover design to show to best advantage throughout an article.

SEC. 11:24B COVER DESIGNS / Plain covers and most striped and patterned goods having small, close-set figures generally are plotted according only to width, Fig. 11:24B. Minor balancing, such as that to set the top of a figure in a border to the welt, is done while sewing or installing covers; as a rule the "handling" allowance is enough for this. For greatest accuracy, draw the paper plot to full size, and mark on it the dimensions of each cut (Sec. 11:12). Work upward from the bottom end of the goods. Plot cuts in order of decreasing width as much as possible, but place side by side those pieces whose combined widths equal or nearly equal the width of the goods. Often, several paper plots must be made before finding the minimum yardage needed. Use the final paper plot for actual plotting of the goods prior to cutting.

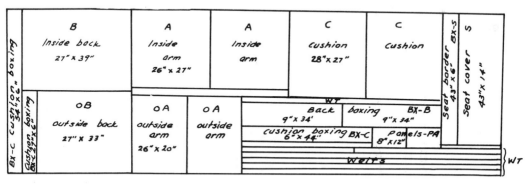

Fig. 11:24B

SEC. 11:24C PATTERNED COVERS / Patterned covers usually are placed with a dominant figure at the approximate middle of the larger surfaces, Fig. 11:24C, especially the seat front, seat proper, cushion, inside arms, inside back or back pillow, and outside back. These cuts, generally plotted first, are plotted outward from a dominant figure; that is, a cut 24 inches wide would be plotted 12 inches

a

b

Fig. 11:24C

to left and to right from the center of a dominant figure. To reduce waste, outside arms, Fig. *b* 11:24C, and wings often have a figure other than the dominant one centered. Goods between large cuts are used for nonbias welt and other pieces too small to contain all or most of a dominant figure.

SEC. 11:24D SCENIC GOODS / Plan scenic goods to present an entire picture rather than place the dominant figure in the middle of a surface. Often, there are several pictures or scenes, but one usually dominates, Fig. 11:24D. Note how these scenes are utilized (Fig. 1:58) on seat cushions and inside back, the most prominent parts of an article.

Fig. 11:24D

SEC. 11:24E DESIGN REPEATS / When plotting patterned or scenic covers, the distance between repeats of a design, Fig. 11:24E, must be taken into account if a dominant figure is to be centered properly throughout. In most goods made in the United States of America, the distance between repeats is 27 inches, which makes it easy for ex-

Fig. 11:24E

perienced upholsterers to figure yardage for a job (Sec. 11:24F). But others should measure actual repeat distance and the center of the dominant figure on a sample of the goods and, as the first step in plotting, mark the paper plot outline for repeats and dominant figures. Then arrange cuts for minimum scrap or waste. The visible bottom of the inside arms and back of a loose-cushion seat is the level of the top of the cushion. Make a full size paper template for each large cut when using goods that need extra care for centering. Mark templates for the center of dominant figures and for pattern repeats.

Sec. 11:24F   Yardage for Repeats / When purchasing goods with distinctive figures or patterns that will be centered on various surfaces, the number of pattern repeats as well as total yardage needed must be considered. If, for example, 14½ yards are needed and 20 repeats are planned, then the total yardage must be increased to 15 (20 repeats × 27 inches between repeats = 540 inches, or 15 yards). When you cannot supervise the cutting of yardage from stock, it is advisable to order one more pattern repeat than you need; this may give you some waste, but will prevent you from not getting enough goods. For example, 20 repeats are needed; if 20 are ordered and for some reason cutting starts in the middle of the dominant figure instead of midway between such figures, you may get 19 full pattern repeats and 2 half patterns. By ordering 21 repeats you will get 20 full patterns. Experienced upholsterers often count the number of pattern repeats needed and base necessary yardage on this. But for this method to be reasonably accurate, the upholsterer must know how the goods will handle, how figures must be placed to show to best advantage, and what effect width of the goods will have on the yardage needed.

**SEC. 11:25
BIAS-PLOTTING**

Woven goods have more stretch and are far more flexible when worked on the bias than along warp or weft, Fig. 11:25. When welt (Sec. 11:08) cover is cut on the bias it is easier to shape the welting around a surface and it tends to be smoother. The thicker or wider a welting, the greater the benefit of bias-cutting the cover, especially for double-welt. The main disadvantage of bias-cutting welt, and why it often is not done, is the amount of cover waste. The economy of fitting welt cover into goods (Fig. 11:24B) cannot be done with bias-cutting, and goods left after bias-cutting, Fig. 11:25, usually are not large enough for anything except buttons and small panels. Another drawback to bias-cutting welt cover is that the shorter the length of goods, the shorter the cuts of welt cover and the more piecing needed; but the longer the goods, the more waste. To plot for bias-cutting welting cover: [1] *Measure length of goods* available for bias-cutting,

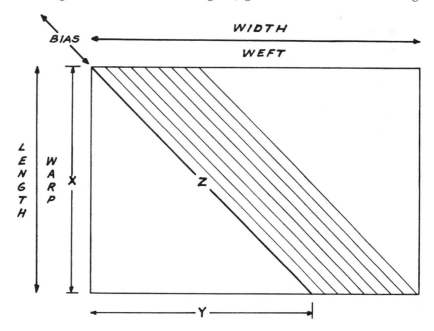

Fig. 11:25

X in Fig. 11:25. [2] *From lower corner of goods* mark off Y, a distance equal to the length. [3] *From the end* of Y, draw line Z to the upper corner of the goods. This is the base for all bias-cutting for that piece of goods. Plot all bias-cuts parallel to it. [4] *Measure width of welting cover* (Sec. 11:08) perpendicular to the bias base line, Z. Do not measure actual width along top or bottom lines. [5] *When a yard of goods* (line X in Fig. 11:15) is allowed for bias-cut welting, the longest cuts are slightly less than 51 inches. Cuts within the area formed by lines X, Y, and Z, and the other similar area, will be progressively shorter. For this reason, bias-cutting welt may be highly impractical when a cover is 36-inches wide or narrower.

SEC. 11:26 **PLOTTING** **GOODS**	Start at bottom end of yardage and transfer the final paper plot by actual measurements to the goods. Measurements should be exact to a quarter-inch, laid out with a yardstick or other straight edge, and marked lightly with chalk on the right side of the goods. Keep chalk pencil-point sharp; draw thin, light lines. Due to the way fabrics are rolled at the mill, as a rule the selvages (sides) must be worked lightly toward the bottom end to straighten the weft threads. Chalk, label (Sec. 11:12), and check all pieces for accuracy against the paper plot before cutting.
SEC. 11:27 **CUTTING**	Cut along the middle of each chalk line (Sec. 11:26), but follow the warp and weft of textiles. Often this makes width-cuts somewhat curved, but they will straighten later. As each piece of cover is cut, label it with a pinned paper tag or with chalk on the wrong side. Be sure to indicate clearly which is the top end of each piece of cover; a chalked arrow usually is satisfactory.
SEC. 11:28 **HANDLING** **CUT FABRICS**	Handle cut fabrics as little as possible, particularly those that ravel, tear, or soil easily. When practical, leave all pieces on the cutting table until needed. When storing cut textiles, fold the edges in toward the center before removing from the cutting table. To prevent raveling of loosely woven goods, machine sew it about ¼-inch from all edges.

12

sewing covers

SEC. 12:00 MACHINE SEWING	Except for cushion and pillow casings, welting, and skirts, there is little machine sewing in upholstering. Blind-stitching (Sec. 13:04) is hand work. Aside from French seams and quilting (Secs. 12:04, 12:05) all machine sewing is much alike. A cording or zipper foot (Sec. 2:15), preferably a righthand one, is nearly essential for sewing welt (Fig. *a* 11:08A), and commonly is used for all sewing except double-welt (*c*) when the latter is done with a double-welting foot. Dressmaking double-piping foots for many home sewing machines usually are satisfactory for double-welt with lightweight goods (Sec. 3:58B) but not for heavier materials. Double-welt foots are available for most industrial sewing machines; some can be adapted to home machines. If only a small amount of double-welt is needed, it may be practical to sew it by hand (Sec. 12:08); for large amounts, having it sewn by an upholstery shop probably is better.

SEC. 12:01
SEAMS

Seam allowances, the space between edge of goods and stitching, generally are ½ inch throughout. This provides ample goods for blind-stitching or blind-tacking. Also, having exact ½-inch seam allowances throughout simplifies sewing that must be done with the wrong side of a goods up, and precision work when two or more thicknesses of cover must be aligned and sewn to a definite size. [1] *Double, even triple, sewing* of seams on loosely woven fabrics is advisable. However, goods so loose as to need this are seldom satisfactory for upholstery; after installation they stretch and sag, causing wrinkles that soil and wear easily. [2] *Except when stitching is to be removed,* as in some parts of a cushion casing: I—Sew all fabrics with short stitches. II—Sew plastics, leather, leather substitutes, and other nonwoven goods with long stitches; short stitches have a cutting and weakening effect. [3] *Goods are commonly pinned together* but seldom basted as covers are usually fitted together on an article just before sewing.

SEC. 12:02
FLAT SEAM

The flat seam, Fig. 12:02, is chiefly for general *piecing of textiles* (Sec. 11:02); for joining covers that are not welted, such as the inside arms and back in Fig. *b* 1:38; and for mock-tufting (Sec. 21:11). Place goods right-side-to-right-side, align edges of seam allowances, and sew ½ inch from them. After sewing (except mock-tufting), spread seam allowances in opposite directions to avoid an excessive lump on a side of the stitching.

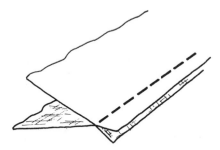

Fig. 12:02

SEC. 12:03
TOP-SEWN
SEAM

This is chiefly for *piecing plastics, leather, leather substitutes, and other nonwoven goods.* Leather, however, usually is skived and joined (Sec. 19:06) instead of sewn. Top-sewn seams sometimes are done for decoration since they are more noticeable than regular flat seams (Sec. 12:02). To make a top-sewn seam, first make a conventional flat seam, (Fig. 12:02). Then, keeping seam allowances together, spread covers in opposite directions, Fig. 12:03, and sew through the three thicknesses. The foldover of goods should be snug against the flat seam stitching. Stitching to complete a top-sewn seam should be about ¼ inch from the foldover of goods.

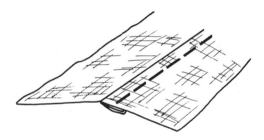

Fig. 12:03

SEC. 12:04
FRENCH SEAM

The French seam is chiefly for decorating textiles. Place goods right-side-to-right-side as for a flat seam (Sec. 12:02), but sew them together ⅜ inch from edges of seam allowances. Fold covers over wrong-side-to-wrong-side, and sew through all four thicknesses, Fig. 12:04, ¼ inch from foldover.

Fig. 12:04

SEC. 12:05
QUILTING

SEC. 12:05A QUILTING / Quilting is ornamental sewing to outline and emphasize parts of a pattern (Fig. 12:05B) or to create a geometric pattern (Fig. 1:34). Quilting adds thickness and depth to a cover and, overall, makes an article appear more luxurious. Light- and medium-weight goods (Sec. 3:53B) usually quilt best; most heavy goods are too thick and stiff for quilting to be sufficiently noticeable. All or only part of an article may have a quilted cover; sometimes quilting inside covers and leaving the others plain is more attractive than quilting all covers. Prequilted fabrics and plastics with simulated quilting are available at most upholstery shops, often with matching plain goods. Quilting is not recommended for plastics, leather, and other nonwoven goods; the amount of stitching could have a serious cutting effect. [1] *Quilting* usually is done with a regular presser foot. [2] *Set machine for long stitches* in order to avoid making excessively deep grooves in quilting. [3] *Quilting material* (Sec. 3:57) should be at least 2 inches wider and longer than goods to be quilted. [4] *Center goods*, right-side-up, on quilting material.

SEC. 12:05B FIGURE QUILTING / In figure quilting, Fig. 12:05B, decide which parts of a pattern or design you want to emphasize, and

Fig. 12:05B

sew along the outlines. Lines of quilt stitching often cross. There is no rule of thumb, but generally there are no more than about 2 inches between lines of stitching. If they are too far apart, the finished cover may not have the puffy effect that makes quilting so noticeable. If lines are too close together throughout, the finished cover tends to look and feel hard instead of soft.

SEC. 12:05C GEOMETRIC QUILTING / This, usually done only with plain goods, can have an infinite variety of designs. The common diamond- or cross-quilt pattern is shown in Fig. 1:34; any other geometric design is quilted essentially the same way. [*1*] *Chalkmark or press a straight line* across a large portion of goods; quilt along this line. [*2*] *Set quilting guide attachment* to the desired space between quilting lines. A length of stiff wire rigidly attached to the sewing head and shaped to touch the goods at the desired distance between quilting lines, Fig. 12:05C, is a good substitute for a guide attachment. Keep guide along the previous quilt while sewing. [*3*] *For a geometric pattern more intricate than diamond- or cross-quilt*, draw the pattern and a repeat in each direction on paper, and measure the distance from one quilt line to the next. Set guide attachment accordingly for sewing each successive quilt line.

SEC. 12:06
WELTING

In order to make welting (Sec. 11:08) for a job more uniform, sew at one time all lengths that probably will be needed. Welt is sewn to cover goods or tacked to a frame. French or double-welt (Sec. 12:08) is glued in place (Sec. 18:17).

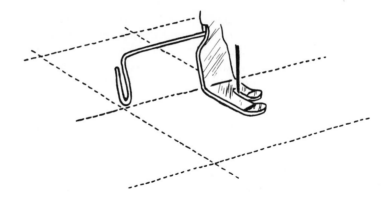

Fig. 12:05C

SEC. 12:07
SEWING WELT

Sec. 12:07A Sewing Welt / Fold welt cover right-side-out around filler or cord (Sec. 3:58), and align edges. Sew with cording or zipper foot close to cord, but not tight against it. [1] *When welt is sewn to a cover,* that stitching should fit between the welt cord and original welt stitching in order to hide the latter. [2] *When welt is tacked,* cardboard stripping (Sec. 3:26) takes up slack between welt cord and stitching. [3] *Piece together welt covers* (Sec. 12:07C) only as needed in sewing.

Sec. 12:07B Sewing Welt to Cover / Place welt on right side of cover goods and align edges of seam allowances, Fig. *a* 12:07B. Sew tightly against, but not through, the welt cord. To turn a corner with welt: [1] *Sew welt to cover* to a point ½ inch from a corner, *a.* [2] *Make three diagonal cuts* in the welt seam allowance from the edge nearly to the stitching to let it "expand" smoothly for turning the corner. [3] *Sew welt to cover up to the corner,* which should be ½

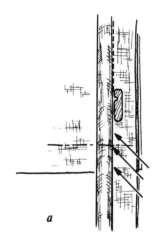

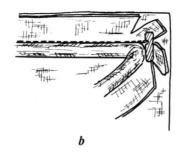

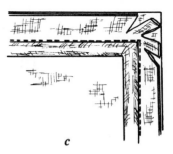

a

b

c

Fig. 12:07B

inch from the adjacent side, *b*. Leave needle down to hold the goods. [4] *Bend welt around corner* and back toward itself, pivoting goods around the needle. Hold welt in place, and sew about ¼ inch along the new side.   [5] *Align edges* of welt seam allowances and of the new side of the cover, *c*, and continue sewing the usual way.

NOTE: Unless welt is sewn tight around a corner, the corner will not hold shape. Often corners must be resewn.

SEC. 12:07C PIECING WELT / To sew welt ends together, smooth the covers snugly in place at the junction, Fig. 12:07C, and sew them together with a flat seam (Sec. 12:02). Cut off excess goods ½ inch from stitching, and fold remainders back from each other to lie flat. Cut welt cord for its ends to butt together at the joint. Fold cover back over welt cord, and complete regular welt stitching. With very loosely woven goods, sew tight against welt cord at the joint.

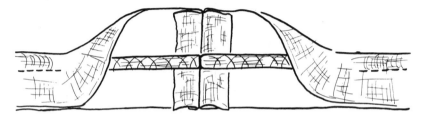

Fig. 12:07C

SEC. 12:08
DOUBLE-,
FRENCH WELT

SEC. 12:08A METHODS OF PREPARATION / There are two common methods (Secs. 12:08C, D) of preparing French or double-welt (Sec. 11:08); each requires a special sewing machine foot, Fig. 12:08A. If the type foot you want is not manufactured for your machine, possibly it can be made from another attachment, or an industrial foot may be adapted to your machine. If only a small amount of double-welt is needed, hand sewing may be used for the second stitching in the first method; but usually it is more practical to have an upholstery shop

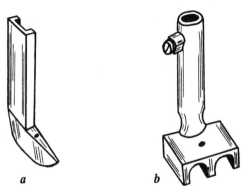

Fig. 12:08A   *a*   *b*

sew it. Strips of welt cover are the same size for both methods of preparing double-welt. Strips of double-welt cover cannot be pieced, nor can the ends of strips be joined together satisfactorily, the same way as welt (Sec. 12:07); the extra layers of goods would make objectionable lumps in the finished job, and fairly thick or heavy goods could prevent satisfactory sewing. Instead of sewing ends of double-welt strips together, glue them (Sec. 18:17). For easiest and neatest work, cut each strip of welt cover just long enough for a particular installation, or for the combined lengths of two or more specific installations; add 3 inches to the total length for general handling.

SEC. 12:08B SPECIAL SEWING FOOT / The special sewing foot in Fig. *a* 12:08A is a design used by many custom upholsterers. It may be made from any attachment that, at the needle hole, is at least ¼-inch high. Grind the lower part of the shank and foot to a thickness of about ¹⁄₁₆ inch; grind to keep the needle midway between the sides. The thinner the foot, the less it tends to push aside the welt cords while sewing; but it must be wide enough to keep the goods clear of the needle. The foot should be about ¼-inch high throughout to give it the strength needed to press the goods down tight against the feed and to keep goods clear of the needle. After grinding to shape and size, polish the foot to remove burrs that could snag cover goods.

SEC. 12:08C DOUBLE-WELTING, METHOD ONE / This method has two sewing operations, and needs a regular cording or zipper sewing machine foot and a special foot (Sec. 12:08B). Hand stitching may be used instead of the second machine sewing. This method of preparing double-welt can be used with any size welt cord and any cover goods and almost guarantees a tight, durable double-welt. It also allows for easier hand stitching if that must replace the second machine sewing. [1] *Set first welt cord* in place on the wrong side of the cover strip near its left edge.   [2] *Fold goods on the left* over welt cord and sew to cover strip, dashed line in Fig. *a* 12:08C. Hold goods to fit snug around welt cord while sewing, but do not pinch or crush cord; if that happens, the finished welting will be rough and lumpy. Sew with a ¼-inch seam allowance. Sew the entire strip of welting.   [3] *Replace*

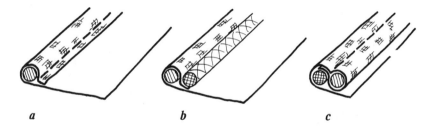

Fig. 12:08C   *a*   *b*   *c*

cording foot with special foot (Sec. 12:08B).   [*4*] *Set second length of welt cord* in place on wrong side of cover strip and just touching the cover of the first cord. Usually the second cord will be on top of the seam allowance for the first stitching, *b*. Or due to the size of cord and nature of the cover goods, the seam allowance may tend to go between a covered welt and the second cord. The important thing is that throughout the welting, the seam allowance goods is either under the second cord or between it and the cover of the first cord.   [*5*] *Fold covered welt* to the right and over the second cord to lie on the wrong side of the cover strip, *c*. Center the sewing foot between welt cords, and sew the strip from end to end, dashed line in *c*. Be sure to set and hold the cover just right throughout this sewing, or one welting will be thicker than the other. Sew a couple of inches of double-welt, and examine it carefully. It usually is quite obvious whether the cover of the second cord should be looser or tighter.   [*6*] *Trim off excess goods* ⅛ inch from stitching.

NOTE: Hand stitching can replace machine work in [5] above. Stitch to bring the cover down toward the "bottom" of the welting, c.

SEC. 12:08D   DOUBLE-WELTING, METHOD TWO   /   This method has only one sewing operation, done with a double-welting foot (Fig. *b* 12:08A). Single sewing and less handling of goods are the advantages of this method. But often it is difficult to make a double-welting foot work properly with welt cord larger than about ³⁄₁₆-inch diameter and fairly thick cover goods; also, unless special care is taken while sewing, a layer of goods may not be stitched securely, which in time may pull out and let the welting come apart.   [*1*] *Set both lengths of welt cord* or single length of double-welt cord on wrong side of cover strip near the left edge.   [*2*] *Fold left edge of cover* over cords to about the middle of the inner cord, Fig. *a* 12:08D. Cords should lie against each other throughout the strip, but do not squeeze or press them tightly together. The edge of the cover should lie along the middle of the inner cord.   [*3*] *Turn folded cover and cords* over carefully toward the right to lie on the wrong side of the cover strip, *b*. Be sure cover and cords are evenly in place throughout.

NOTE: Instead of folding cover and cords over into place on the wrong side of the goods, the cover to the right of the cords may be

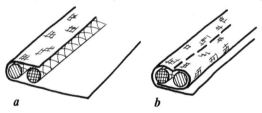

Fig. 12:08D   *a*   *b*

drawn over the cords and cover; then turn the complete unit over to lie as in **b.**

[4] *Center wrapped welting* in place under the double-welting foot and sew, dashed line in *b*. Be sure to hold cover and cords in place throughout sewing; otherwise, one welt may be thicker than the other. Also, and worse, the side of the goods first folded in place, *a*, may work out of position and not be stitched; in time the cover will pull loose and the welting come apart. After sewing a couple of inches of welting, examine it carefully. Usually it is obvious how the cover should be adjusted to make the welts uniform and if the inside edge is sewn securely.   [5] *Trim off excess goods* ⅛ inch from stitching.

13

covering
seats

**SEC. 13:00
TYPE OF
COVER**

The type of seat, pad or spring, and its muslin casing need not always determine its type of cover. A small roll edge spring seat (Fig. *b* 7:19C) may have a plain or a welted pull-over cover (Fig. *b* 1:09) or a bordered or a boxed cover (Fig. 1:13). A large spring edge seat (Fig. 7:29A) may have a banded or a pull-over cover (Fig. *a, c* 1:42). [1] *Upholster plain and buttoned* surfaces alike until installing outside covers (Chapter 18). Seat panels, gimp and other trim, antique nails, fringe, dust cover, ruching, and skirts usually are installed then too. [2] *When a skirt, or fringe* around the bottom of a seat, is to be installed, pad down the sides of seat rails only to the planned top of skirt or fringe. Padding lower than this may cause pullmarks (Fig. 5:15A) in the rail cover.

**SEC. 13:01
WELTING**

There are two kinds of welting (Sec. 11:08). Double-welt, treated like gimp in many respects, usually is installed as such (Sec. 18:17). Welt generally is installed as part of or with seat, arm, back and other

464

covers; pertinent handling of welt is in those chapters. Much of the durability and neatness of tacked welt depends on how it starts and ends and turns a corner on the same surface (Sec. 13:02).

**SEC. 13:02
TACKING
WELT**

SEC. 13:02A STARTING, ENDING WELT / [1] *To start or end welt on or against a surface,* as at the top of a leg (Fig. 1:07), cut it off ½ inch beyond the point of starting or ending. Peel welt cover back, cut off welt cord at the point of starting or ending. Smooth cover out over end of cord and fold back under the welt at a slant toward edges of the seam allowance, Fig. *a* 13:02A. **[2]** *To end welt under welt or against a welt end, b,* cut it off ½ inch beyond the point of ending. Peel welt cover back and cut cord to butt firmly against the other welt. Smooth cover straight forward over end of cord and under the other welt. If this makes too much of a lump: I—Hammer the lump at the seam allowance of the second welt several times to flatten the layers of cover; drive a fairly large tack to hold goods flat. Or, II—End first welt the usual way. To keep welts firmly against each other, stitch together at the seams.

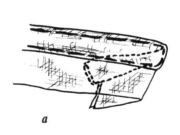

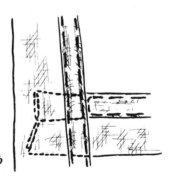

a

b

Fig. 13:02A

SEC. 13:02B CORNER WELTING ON SAME SURFACE / [1] *When welt turns inward around a corner,* Fig. *a* 13:02B, cut the seam allowance in from the edges almost to the stitching at enough points for it to "expand" smoothly. **[2]** *When welt turns outward around a corner, b,* pleat (Sec. 5:17) at the curve or corner. For heavy or thick goods, to avoid making a lump at the corner pleat cut out part of the

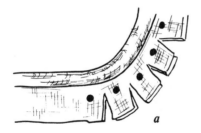

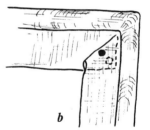

Fig. 13:02B   *a*   *b*

seam allowance. But, if it can be done satisfactorily, it is better to reduce a lump by hammering it after pleating.

SEC. 13:03 **BLIND-, BACK-** **TACKING**	For general information on blind- or back-tacking and for blind-tacking a plain cover, see Sec. 9:13D. To blind-tack a welted cover, or a cover to welt, or cardboarding a welt, Fig. 13:03, set edge of cardboard strip tight against, but not overlapping, the welt cord through the cover. If cardboard is not tight against welt cord, a welt will be loose and flabby. If cardboard overlaps cord, it usually cannot be tacked tightly and permanently.

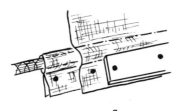 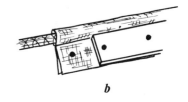

b

Fig. 13:03   *a*

SEC. 13:04 **BLIND-** **STITCHING**	**SEC. 13:04A** / Blind-stitch when it is impossible or highly impractical to blind-tack. Well done blind-stitching holds covers smooth and tight (Fig. *a* 11:08A); it is less noticeable when done to or through welt (*b*). Methods of blind-stitching are traditional (Secs. 13:04B, C) and production or factory (Secs. 13:04D–G). Traditional can be used for all jobs—stitching from cover directly into cover, from cover into welt, and from cover through welt into another cover. Factory blind-stitching actually is a tacking operation and can be done only where covers finish on a frame; it is not used with goods that can be damaged by being hammered, such as pile fabrics, glazed materials, thin and hard-surfaced goods, etc. For traditional blind-stitching: *Tools:* Shears, small curved needle, upholstery skewers (Secs. 2:04, 2:06, 2:08). *Materials:* Stitching twine (Sec. 3:08).

SEC. 13:04B PREPARATION FOR TRADITIONAL BLIND-STITCHING / Pin covers in place with edges underturned ½ inch. With more underturn, the goods may wrinkle and develop small lumps that will readily collect dirt if the goods is a thin material. With less underturn, blind-stitching may pull out, especially when a goods ravels easily. Due to the stretch of most upholstery cover goods and variations in the shape of most upholstery surfaces, the point of stitching on a fold often shifts during work; this seldom matters as long as a cover is stitched smooth and tight. Do not stitch a cover until it is sliptacked (Sec. 5:16) and/or pinned in place on all sides; stitching could draw a cover away from a loose side, causing wrinkles and crooked grain at

both sides. When stitching opposite sides of a cover, as in an outside
back, stitch along each side just a few inches at a time; this tends to
keep a cover straight and smooth throughout. On arched surfaces,
stitch from the middle toward each side or end just a few inches at a
time. [1] *Length of stitches.* Except for turning a sharp corner or
curve on the same surface, where shorter stitches are needed to pull a
cover into position, make ½-inch stitches. This is short enough to hold
goods securely, long enough to let it spread evenly. Half-inch stitches
are less noticeable than shorter ones. [2] *Direction of stitching.*
Blind-stitch from top to bottom, from front to back of a surface. Slack
that may develop in a cover can be taken out by resliptacking or
pinning at the bottom or back of a surface, and in most cases twine
can be ended on the frame. [3] *For stitching:* I—Cover to cover, set
folded edge to the point of stitching (Fig. *a* 11:08A). II—Cover to or
through welt, set folded edge to finish between cardboard strip and
welt cord, or between welt stitching and cord of noncardboarded welt
(Fig. *b* 11:08A).

SEC. 13:04C TRADITIONAL BLIND-STITCHING / Fig. 13:04C. [1]
Knot end of twine. Bury it by stitching from just below the fold on
the underturned side of goods, aiming needle to the crest of the fold.

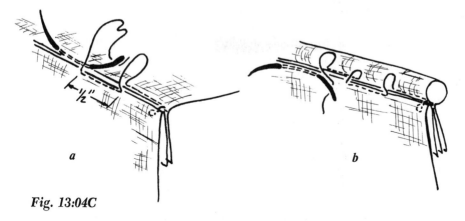

a   *b*

Fig. 13:04C

Make the burying stitch opposite the planned direction of stitching to
draw goods over it. [2] *Stitch into each cover at the exact point* at
which twine emerges from the other cover, and aim needle to come
out ½ inch from the point of entry. Simplify aligning stitches by drawing the slack twine from one cover straight over the other. Unless
stitches are aligned, wrinkles or even small tears may result when the
twine is pulled tight. [3] *Blind-stitch through welt* into the other
cover when welt is not cardboarded, or when it is cardboarded and
goes around a sharp corner. This is done to hold covers and welt snug

against each other.   [4] *Tighten twine* while stitching only enough to remove slack and prevent knotting. But after every three or four complete stitches, tighten twine with a smooth, even pull, and lightly rub the cover into place. Tightening at intervals allows a cover to stretch or compress smoothly between stitches.   [5] *End blind-stitching* on a frame by leading twine to a point that will be covered; set a small tack, loop twine tightly around it twice, and drive tack in full. When twine cannot be tacked, end it by blind-stitching backward for about 2 inches, then pulling twine quite tight and cutting it off close to goods; rub goods lightly and the twine end will back out of sight.

SEC. 13:04D   PRODUCTION, FACTORY BLIND-STITCHING / Production or factory blind-stitching is a method of tacking a cover with special materials. It is easily distinguished from traditional blind-stitching. In Fig. 13:04D, the outside wing cover is traditionally blind-stitched to welt at top and front; note how the edge of the cover fits into the bottom of the welt. The outside back cover also was traditionally stitched across the top, but down the side was factory blind-stitched. Due to the mechanics of this work, the edge of a cover cannot fit into the bottom of welt; instead, it presses against the side and usually leaves a gap along the top surface of the cover. The rougher or nubbier the goods, the less noticeable the gap; in most cases it is not objectionable and may be considered as a style of finishing. Production blind-stitching is used chiefly in factories but for certain jobs is often used by top quality custom upholsterers. For appearance, most custom upholsterers and manufacturers of better quality furniture use welt with production blind-stitching. Except for installing welt, the work is the same with or without welt. Production blind-stitching generally is limited to outside back covers. It can be done along curved as well as straight lines but is more difficult. A common method of production blind-stitching uses metal tape in which tacks are imbedded (Sec. 13:04F); another uses thin strips of wood (Sec. 13:04G). Neither method is difficult if preparatory work is done properly.

SEC. 13:04E   PREPARATION / Production blind-stitching is easier, and there is less chance of spoiling a job if the following points are observed.   [1] *When tacking* other covers on a surface where production blind-stitching will be done, tack at least ¾ inch from the edge to prevent trying to drive a blind-stitching tack through another tack. [2] *Do not pad* where production blind-stitching is to be tacked; padding can prevent tight, permanent tacking of the strip.   [3] *Tack welt only* at enough points to hold it in place. If welt is pulled fairly tight, tacking every 3 or 4 inches usually is enough. Also, space welt tacks at different distances than tacks of the blind-stitching strip.   [4]

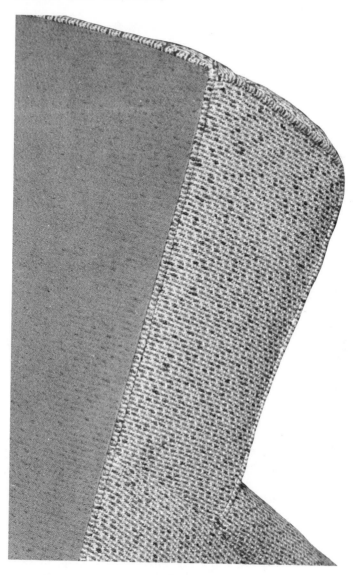

Fig. 13:04D

Do not cardboard welt; it will merely push the cover higher along the sides of the welt. The blind-stitching strip holds welt in place almost as well as cardboard stripping.

SEC. 13:04F   BLIND-STITCHING TAPE   /   In a common type of production blind-stitching metal tape, Fig. *a* 13:04F, tacks are held by a strip of fiber incased by tightly crimped metal. Similar materials are all-metal, metal and plastic, plastic, etc. Production blind-stitching metal tape and similar materials usually are available in a variety of tack sizes and spacings; use the smallest size tack that will hold the

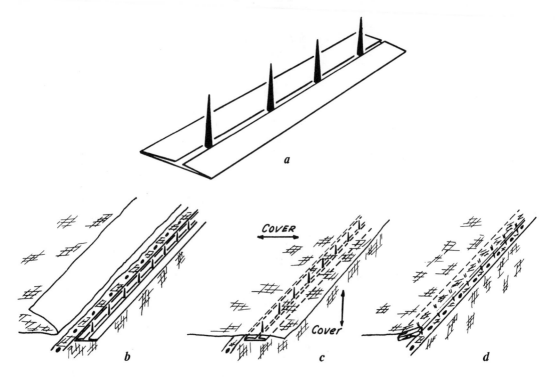

Fig. 13:04F

cover goods satisfactorily (Sec. 3:03D). To minimize damaging goods, use a mallet instead of a hammer, and hold cardboard over the goods while driving tacks. This method of production blind-stitching should not be used with pile fabrics, glazed chintz, or any thin hard-surfaced textile, leather, or plastic; there is danger of the metal strip cutting through these as a result of the hammering.   [1] *Set cover in place,* work it tight and ready for permanent tacking. An outside back cover, for example, usually is blind-tacked or traditionally blind-stitched across the top, then tightened (Sec. 5:18) toward bottom and sides. [2] *Place strip of blind-stitching tape,* tacks pointing up, along the edge of the surface, *b.* Work cover out evenly over the tacks, press down firmly onto the tape, *c.*   [3] *Loosen enough goods* at the bottom of a surface for it to be lifted, along the sides, high enough for the tape to be turned over and tacked, *d,* along the edge of a frame or against the side of a welt.   [4] *Hammer tape lightly* at enough points to hold it securely in place, then drive tacks permanently.   [5] *Re-tack cover* at bottom of surface.

NOTE: To show work more clearly, welt was omitted in Fig. 13: 04F. Except for positioning a strip when turning it over, work is the same whether or not a surface is welted.

Sec. 13:04G   Blind-Stitching Wood Strips / A strip of ¹⁄₁₆ inch plywood, or stiff chipboard, at least ¾ inch wide often is used for production blind-stitching. Use this method only with fabrics loosely enough woven for threads to be pushed aside so that nailing through it will not show. The work is the same as in Sec. 13:04F except: [*1*] *After adjusting cover* to bottom and sides, place the strip of wood or chipboard along the edge of the surface being covered, Fig. *a* 13:04G.

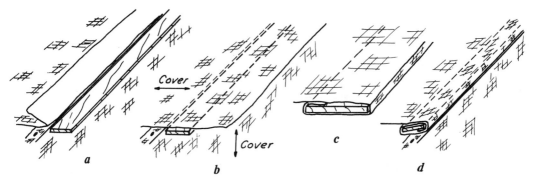

Fig. 13:04G

[2] *Spread cover out evenly over strip,* and cut off surplus beyond the outer edge of the strip, *b;* the cover after cutting should extend beyond the outer edge of the strip a distance equal to the width of the strip plus ¼ to ½ inch.   [3] *Turn cover goods back tightly under strip, c,* and work the edge between the strip and the cover to hold goods around the strip while completing installation.   [4] *After turning strip over and in under the main cover, d,* press it in place along the edge of the surface or inner side of welt, and nail down with finishing or headless nails; 1 to 1¼ inch No. 18 panel nails usually are satisfactory. Nail at 4 or 5 inch intervals when possible and spread threads of goods apart for nailing; drive nail down flush with the top of a strip, then rub the goods a few times to work threads back in place. If this does not work, pick threads back in place with the point of a sharp pin.

SEC. 13:05 COVERING AROUND A LEG TOP

Sec. 13:05A / This method of installing a cover is not essential if it is properly tightened and tacked around the top of a leg. But this method is strongly recommended for top quality upholstery, especially on small armless articles that do not have skirts, because it holds a cover firmly in place. *Tools:* Upholsterer's hammer, shears, small curved needle (Secs. 2:02, 2:04, 2:06). *Materials:* Tacks, upholstery twine, cardboard stripping, scrap of cover goods (Secs. 3:03, 3:08, 3:26).

SEC. 13:05B INSTALLING COVER / [1] *Fold scrap of cover goods* tightly around a small strip of cardboard; tack to frame so as to carry the line of the bottom of a seat around top of leg, Fig. *a* 13:05B. [2] *Tighten seat cover* (Sec. 5:18) along rail to leg, cut goods at a slant from the outer side of leg and rail junction to a point just short of the junction, *b;* underturn cover around leg top to extend the line of the bottom of the rail, *c.* [3] *When cover ends or will be pleated around leg,* tack it to the rail just above the cardboard on the side that will be covered later, *c.* Tack cover in place along bottom of rail to leg. Blind-stitch (Sec. 13:04) cover along top of leg to covering of the cardboard.

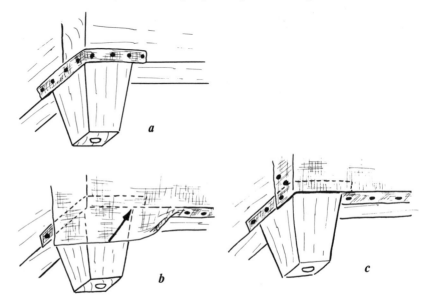

Fig. 13:05B

When pleating (Sec. 5:17) at a leg, blind-stitch seat cover from the top of the pleat down to bottom of rail, then to the covered cardboard (Fig. *a* 11:08A). [4] *When unpleated cover* goes around or across a leg top, cut goods to underturn on both sides of leg. Tack goods in place on both sides, then blind-stitch to covered cardboard. [5] *If a skirt or flounce* will be installed, do not use covered cardboard; the skirt will be cardboarded and hold the cover in place around the leg top. Cut cover, [2] above, and draw it tightly around the leg. Blind-stitching pleats above a skirt is optional.

**SEC. 13:06
WELTING
BOTTOM OF
SEAT**

SEC. 13:06A / For extra decoration in small armless articles, the bottom of a seat often is welted (Fig. 1:13). For tools and materials, Sec. 13:05; a wood rasp is needed for work in Sec. 13:06C.

SEC. 13:06B   /   Tack cover in place along the bottom of a seat rail and close to the sides of the legs. Sliptack (Sec. 5:16) welt in place along bottom of rail and close to sides of legs. The middle of the welt cord should lie along the front edge of a rail. If welt does not project beyond the front edge, it may not be sufficiently noticeable; if it projects too far, it will be weak and tend to sag after installation.   [*1*] *When welt is properly placed* and is smooth and tight from side to side, loosen it and the cover near each leg.   [*2*] *Cut cover and welt* at a slant from the outer side of leg and rail junction to a point just short of the junction (Fig. *b* 13:05B); cut welt from the raw edge to but not through the stitching.   [*3*] *Twist welt cover* so that its seam edges lie toward the top of the seat. Draw welt tightly around top of leg so as to carry the line of welting smoothly around the corner from the bottom of one rail to that of the other.   [*4*] *Cardboard* (Sec. 13:03) welt in place around corner.   [*5*] *Retack loosened cover and welt* in place to the side of the leg. Underturn cover and draw it tight around welted corner, then work it in place against the welt and blind-stitch it to welt (Sec. 13:04C).   [*6*] *Cardboard welt* along bottom of rail.

SEC. 13:06C   /   With the method of welting the bottom of a seat in Sec. 13:06B, welt going around a corner tends to project slightly, which may be objectionable. To prevent it, make a shallow groove along the top of a leg where welt will go; this may be done with a wood rasp. Test depth of groove often by pressing welt firmly into it. Welt around the top of a leg should neither protrude above nor sink below welt on the rails.

SEC. 13:07 COVERING EXPOSED-WOOD SEATS

SEC. 13:07A   /   Covers on exposed-wood seats and other surfaces are finished without or with welt. The traditional way is without welt; a cover is tacked, trimmed, and its edges covered by gimp (Fig. 18:16D). In the modern method, welt is cardboarded along the tacking strip or limits of upholstery and the cover blind-stitched to it (Fig. 13:07C). Both methods are used on period and modern articles. The mechanics of both methods are much alike, especially for the more popular general types of exposed-wood articles (Figs. 1:07, *b, c* 1:28, *b* 1:52). The method of finishing along exposed-wood parts does not affect installation of the general seat, arm, back, etc., covers. The chief problem in covering an exposed-wood surface is at exposed posts; this also applies to covers that are welted only at such posts.

SEC. 13:07B WITHOUT WELT   /   Before covering along exposed-wood posts, tighten and adjust the cover throughout the rest of a seat or other surface. Unless a cover fits tightly over the surface and against each post, it will not stay smooth and may not seal in the padding. Often a cover must be loosened at one or more points and the surface built up with padding in order to eliminate wrinkles and to set the grain of a goods evenly at that part of the surface. [1] *When a post has an upholstery edge or block*, Fig. 13:07B, tack cover on it close to exposed-wood portion of post. [2] *When a post does not have an upholstery edge or block*, cut cover to allow an underturn of ½ inch. Tighten cover toward post and downward; poke excess cover goods down between post and padding.

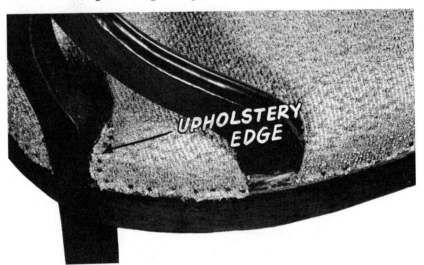

Fig. 13:07B

SEC. 13:07C   WITH WELT   / Covers on exposed-wood surfaces are often welted, Fig. 13:07C; double-welt is installed as an outside cover trim (Sec. 18:17). Before installing the cover, cardboard welt along the edges of the seat or other surface being covered. Set welt tight against the rabbet or other marked limits of upholstery. [1] *When a post has an upholstery edge or block* (Fig. 13:07B), tack welt on it tight against the exposed-wood post; usually it is necessary to cut welt seam allowance at the corners of a post (Fig. 13:02). [2] *If post does not have upholstery edge or block*, set welt tightly in place around post from

Fig. 13:07C

one regular tacking surface to the other. At each of these two points cut welt seam allowance to but not through the welt stitching. Twist welt cover around for the seam allowance to go down along the post; cardboard welt in place.

SEC. 13:07D **INSTALLING COVER** / Install seat or other cover the usual way for a particular surface, but work it smooth and tight and pin it in place before blind-stitching. When cover is adjusted satisfactorily throughout, start blind-stitching from the middle of a side toward corners or posts. Take a few stitches at a time; work alternately on opposite sides of a surface. Unless work is done gradually and equally along each side, a cover is apt to wrinkle. Often it is necessary to loosen a cover near corners or posts and build up the surface with padding in order to prevent wrinkles and to set the grain of a goods evenly at that part of a seat or other surface. [1] *For welted seat cover,* Fig. 13:07D, cardboard welt along rail close to the post (Sec. 13:03). [2] *For a plain cover,* tack a covered strip of cardboard (Sec. 13:05) on rail close to the post. Cut cover to allow an underturn of ½ inch; one much larger may wrinkle at the edges and, especially in thin goods, cause dirt-collecting lumps in the cover. [3] *Padding*

Fig. 13:07D

should extend to welt cord, or to sides of the post when a covered cardboard is used. [4] *Complete adjusting cover* along rail, then blind-stitch it (Sec. 13:04) to welt or covered cardboard.

SEC. 13:07E PARTIALLY COVERED POST / For a partially covered post (Fig. *d* 1:29), cut a cover about 3 inches larger than needed to reach from the inner side of a post to the bottom of the rail and to incase the uncovered area along seat and rail. Pad that area up to and around the post. Cut and underturn cover to fit neatly around post. Tack cover in place around post and to the bottom of the rail. Pin seat covers together while completing adjustment; then blind-stitch them.

SEC. 13:08 **INSTALLING** **BORDERS**	SEC. 13:08A / If border is to be welted, sew it to top end of border goods (Secs. 12:06, 12:07). For a plain seat cover with exposed-wood posts (Sec. 13:11), make border welt long enough to finish along post and on the bottom of a seat rail. When a seat cover is welted for exposed-wood posts (Sec. 13:12), welt usually is long enough to finish on bottom of seat. Border welt usually ends against seat welt (Sec. 13:01). For tools and materials, Sec. 13:05.

SEC. 13:08B PREPARATION, INSTALLATION / [1] *Chalkmark installed cover* for placement of top of border, Point 1 in Fig. 13:08B. The border line should be the same distance from the edge of a frame throughout. To keep a border line from showing in the finished job, set it as a guide for the stitches or for the seam ends of a welted border. [2] *Set the middle of a welted border* to the middle of the front rail, tack in place through the seam allowances of border and welt, Point 2. Tighten border to each side of the center, tack at enough points, 3 or 4 inches apart, to hold it in position. [3] *Tack border in place* throughout seat, then cardboard it (Sec. 13:03), Point 3. I— When border ends against an exposed-wood post, rip it from the welt back far enough for it to finish against the post. If the seat cover is welted, cardboard it along the rail to finish against the post. End border welt against seat welt (Sec. 13:01). If seat cover is plain, finish the border welt down the rail (Sec. 13:02), cardboarding it against the post. II—When a border ends under another cover, as at a back that is to be fully upholstered, finish welt and border around the corner of that surface. Do not end welt (Sec. 13:01) until installing the other cover. [4] *After cardboarding top end of border*, spread a layer of felted padding (Sec. 3:49) over the cardboard flush against the cover and along the frame down to the bottom edge, Point 4. While tightening (Sec. 5:18) border, usually enough padding works over the edge of a frame to protect the cover. Pad the entire area to be covered by a border before drawing it over the padding. Start at

Fig. 13:08B

the corners. While drawing border carefully over the padding, press padding lightly but firmly toward the welt. This overcomes the tendency of a cover to force padding away from a welt or other cardboarded edge. Set border in place throughout seat. [5] *Starting at middle of the front rail* and working alternately to either side around a seat, tack border in place, Point 5, keeping grain of goods straight. Cover around legs (Sec. 13:05) and along exposed-wood posts (Sec. 13:07).

SEC. 13:08C BORDER SUBSTITUTING FOR PANEL / Borders often are used instead of panels in seats and arms (Secs. 11:13D, E). Chalkmark the panel area and install the top end of border essentially as in Sec. 13:08B[*1*]–[*3*]. Cardboard welt along other limits of panel area, then complete installation of border (Sec. 13:08B[*4*], [*5*]) but blind-stitch it (Sec. 13:04) to the welt.

SEC. 13:09 COVERING FLAT PAD SEATS

(Fig. 1:01.) Spread a layer of felted padding (Sec. 3:49) on seat, extending to ½ inch from the marked limits of upholstery or sides of rabbets. Padding beyond these points may interfere with good installation of the cover. Install cover (Sec. 6:02F). Tack close to the marked limits or sides of rabbets. Trim off excess goods just beyond fully driven tacks (Fig. 13:07B).

SEC. 13:10 **COVERING** **SLIPSEATS**	Spread a layer of felted padding (Sec. 3:49) over slipseat down to but not below bottom edges of frame. Padding on the bottom may interfere with installing the seat in a chair. Install cover (Sec. 6:03); finish it, regardless of the thickness of a slipseat, on bottom of frame 1 inch from the edges. Trim off excess goods close to tacks. On thick slipseats covered by a loosely woven fabric, it is advisable to blind-stitch the pleats (Sec. 13:04).

ROLL AND HARD EDGE SEATS

SEC. 13:11 **PLAIN** **PULL-OVER** **COVER**	SEC. 13:11A PLAIN PULL-OVER COVER / For examples of plain pull-over covers for roll and hard edge seats either fully exposed or with a fully upholstered back, see Figs. 1:03, 1:21, *a* 1:29, *c* 1:51. Pull-over covers also are installed on modern, fully exposed-seat articles (Figs. *b* 1:09, 1:19); however, welted cover (Sec. 13:12) usually has a more tailored or professional look. When a back is to be fully upholstered, sew a stretcher to the back of the seat cover (Secs. 11:09, 12:02). *Tools:* Upholsterer's hammer, shears, small curved needle, regulator, sewing machine (Secs. 2:02, 2:04, 2:06, 2:07, 2:15). *Materials:* Tacks, stitching twine, upholstery thread, felted padding (Secs. 3:03, 3:08, 3:09, 3:49). SEC. 13:11B PADDING / Spread a layer of felted padding over seat. [1] *Exposed-wood seat.* Padding extends to ½ inch from the marked limits of upholstery or ends of rabbets and to ½ inch from exposed portions of posts having upholstery edges (Sec. 13:07B). Padding beyond these points may interfere with installing the cover. [2] *Fully upholstered seat.* Padding extends down to but not below bottom edges of rails. While tightening a cover, enough padding usually works over the bottom edges to protect it. Sometimes an additional layer or two of padding, preferably placed under the initial one, is needed to build crown (Sec. 5:14) and give shape to a surface below roll or hard edges. [3] *Fully upholstered back.* Padding extends to an inch or so behind junction of seat and inside back. SEC. 13:11C COVERING / Install cover and work it fairly tight, essentially as in Secs. 6:02F–H, until cutting for posts and/or legs becomes necessary. Keep grain of goods straight or regularly curved throughout. [1] *Exposed-wood seat* (Fig. 13:07B). On seat rails, tack cover close to marked limits of upholstery or ends of rabbets. On posts having upholstery edges, tack close to exposed-wood part of post. [2] *Fully upholstered seat.* Tack on bottom of seat rails ½ inch from outer edges where possible. [3] *Fully upholstered back.* Tack seat cover on same part of rails as the muslin casing. [4] *Cover around*

legs and along exposed-wood posts (Secs. 13:05, 13:07). [5] *When back is fully upholstered,* cut (Sec. 5:15) seat cover to fit around back posts, leaving small tabs sticking up against the front and outer sides of the back, Fig. 13:11C. These simplify setting the inside back cover without gaps between it and the seat cover. At the bottom, cover around legs, and finish cover on the back of the back posts about ¾ inch from outer edges.

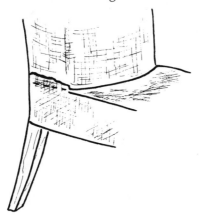

Fig. 13:11C

<table>
<tr><td>

SEC. 13:12
WELTED
PULL-OVER
COVER

</td><td>

Sec. 13:12A / For examples of welted pull-over covers for roll and hard edge fully exposed seats, see Figs. *b* 1:09, 1:19. In addition to tools and materials in Sec. 13:11, upholstery skewers, cardboard stripping, welt cord, chalk, and a fairly large sheet of paper are needed (Secs. 2:08, 3:26, 3:58).

</td></tr>
</table>

Sec. 13:12B Prepare Cover / Make a paper template or pattern, and prepare welted pull-over cover. [1] *Pin sheet of paper* on muslin incased seat; cut it to fit snug against the sides of all posts at the top surface of the seat. [2] *Mark the exact middle* of the bottom edges of front and back seat rails on template. Remove it carefully. [3] *Mark cover from template.* Because the template was cut to fit flush against the sides of the posts, the post cuts are too large. When marking the cover, extend by ½ inch the edges of the cuts to which welt will be sewn, Fig. 13:12B; this is needed for sewing on welt with a ½-inch seam allowance. Cut at right angles from this edge to the edge of the goods. Trim off excess goods to make a cut about ½-inch narrower than that needed to fit around the post. Mark the middle of the front and back of the cover from the template. [4] *Sew welt to cover* (Secs. 12:06, 12:07). I—When cover will finish around three sides of a post, sew welt to cover on the middle side only. II—When cover finishes along two sides of a post, sew welt to cover at the corner and to about ½ inch from the corner on each side.

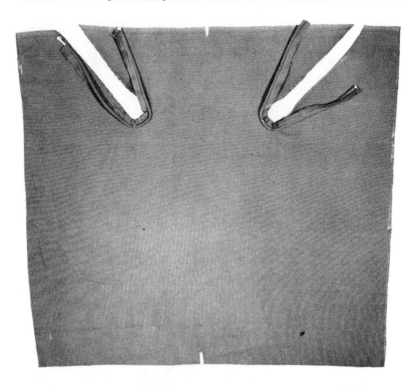

Fig. 13:12B

Sec. 13:12C Padding, Covering / Install felted padding and cover (Sec. 13:11), aligning the centering marks on the cover with the middle of the front and back seat rails. Poke welt and cover seam allowances down between padding and post; this prevents dirt-collecting lumps in the cover and seals in padding. Pull welt fairly tight along the post; tack to sides and bottom of the seat rail. Complete as in Sec. 13:07.

**SEC. 13:13
BORDERED OR
PANELED
COVER**

Sec. 13:13A / For examples of bordered or paneled covers on roll and hard edge seats having either a fully exposed seat or a fully upholstered back, see Figs. *c* 1:09, 1:16. Borders (Sec. 11:05) may be installed on all exposed rails of a seat and may be set at any height. Panels, which may be replaced by borders, usually are installed only on side rails and are set along the bottom edges of rails. In addition to tools and materials in Sec. 13:11, chalk, tape measure, cardboard stripping, and welt cord are needed for a bordered cover (Secs. 2:16, 3:26, 3:58). Panels are treated as part of the outside cover (Chapter 18).

Sec. 13:13B / Install plain or welted pull-over cover (Secs. 13:11, 13:12). Cover welt should be long enough to finish on the bottom of the rails when a border is planned.   [1] *Bordered seat.* Finish seat cover on sides of exposed seat rails ¾ inch below where the top of the border will go in order to leave space for tacking the border. [2] *Paneled seat*. Finish seat cover on the bottom of the front rail, on the outer sides of side rails, Fig. 13:13B, about ½ inch inside area to be covered by panel. [3] *Place enough felted padding* just above the limits of a border or panel to build a rounded, tapering surface extending smoothly into the main surface of a seat. Size of this simulated roll edge is optional, but usually is large enough to give border or panel welt a "set in" appearance (Fig. 1:16). [4] *Install border* (Sec. 13:08). Usually a seat panel or border substituting for it is installed after the dust cover (Chapter 18).

Fig. 13:13B

SEC. 13:14	SEC. 13:14A / For examples of boxed covers on roll and hard edge
BOXED COVER	

SEC. 13:14A / For examples of boxed covers on roll and hard edge seats with either fully exposed seat or fully upholstered back, see Figs. *a* 1:09, *c* 1:29. In most small articles, boxing extends from top to bottom of a seat. However, it may go from the top down to any desired point on the side of a rail, and a border may then be used to carry the cover down to the bottom of a seat. In addition to tools and materials in Sec. 13:11, upholstery skewers, cardboard stripping, welt cord, and a fairly large sheet of paper are needed (Secs. 2:08, 3:26, 3:58).

SEC. 13:14B PREPARATION / Make a paper template or pattern

(Sec. 13:12) of the top of a seat and prepare cover. [*1*] *Pin paper smoothly to seat.* At the exposed sides, cut template off smoothly ½ inch outside the sharp break at the edges in order to leave a ½-inch seam allowance for welt and boxing. [*2*] *Sew welt to cover* (Secs. 12:06, 12:07). I—When seat is fully exposed (Fig. *a* 1:09), sew welt completely around cover, ending it at the middle of the back. At the post cuts, piece on (Sec. 13:01) additional strips of welt to reach the point of finishing boxing on the seat rail. II—When a back will be fully upholstered (Fig. *c* 1:29), sew welt around cover to back posts, adding enough to finish on the back of the posts. [*3*] *Center boxing* at the middle of the front edge of the cover. Sew along the welted cover to the post cuts for a fully exposed seat, or to the ends of the welts when a back will be fully upholstered.

Sec. 13:14C Padding, Covering / Install felted padding and boxed cover (Secs. 13:11, 13:12). Turn seam allowances of boxing, welt, and cover down along the sides of a seat to eliminate small lumps on the top surface, where they are more noticeable and readily collect dirt. When tightening the cover, keep welt at the same height above the bottom of seat rails throughout. When a back will be fully upholstered, seat boxing usually is sliptacked at the back until the inside back cover is installed; then boxing is loosened and finished over the inside back cover.

SEC. 13:15 SINGLE-PIECE COVER FOR SEAT, INSIDE BACK

Sec. 13:15A / For examples of armless articles having roll or hard edges and a single-piece cover for seat and inside back, see Figs. 1:14, 1:17. Sides of seat and back usually have boxing (Sec. 11:06), which may be in one or two pieces. A single-piece cover can be quite attractive but may lack durability. The more go-down in seat and back, the more strain there may be on the cover and the faster it will wear out. Because of the effects of seat and back go-down, a single-piece cover is not recommended for articles with spring seats and/or backs. In addition to tools and materials in Sec. 13:11, upholstery skewers, cardboard stripping, welt cord, and a large sheet of paper or, better, fairly stiff cardboard for boxing templates are needed (Secs. 2:08, 3:26, 3:58).

Sec. 13:15B Prepare Boxing / Make templates or patterns and prepare boxing for sides of seat and back; work must be accurate for a cover to fit smoothly. [*1*] *The upper edge of a seat template and inner edge of a back template* should extend to the line at which welt is to be sewn, usually at the break from the sides into the main surfaces of seat and back. [*2*] *Seat boxing template ends,* at front, at the break between side and front of seat, Fig. 13:15B. [*3*] *Back boxing template ends,* at top, at the break between side and top of back. [*4*]

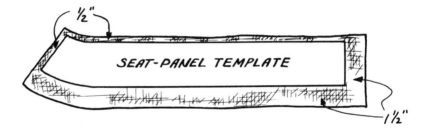

Fig. 13:15B

If separate seat and back boxing templates are made, they must fit together perfectly at their junction, usually a line from the junction of the main seat and back surfaces to that of the bottom of a seat and outer surface of the back. Two-piece may need less cover goods than single-piece boxing, since two fairly long pieces (one for each side of an article) may demand more yardage than four short pieces; but unless using a plain, nonpatterned goods, it may be difficult to fit small cuts together attractively.   [5] *Mark and cut boxings* from template or templates. At upper and inner edges, add ½ inch for seam allowances for sewing welt and cover. For two-piece boxing, add ½ inch to each for seam allowances where they are to be joined. At front of seat boxing and at top of back boxing, add 1½ inches for general handling—do not cut the ends of these strips for the shape of the front of a seat and top of a back. At bottom and back of boxings, add 1½ inches for handling. Mark boxings for breaks at the front of a seat and top of a back.   [6] *If separate boxings for seat and back* are cut, piece them with a flat seam (Sec. 12:02).

SEC. 13:15C PREPARE COVER / [1] *Spread and pin* single-piece cover goods in place on seat and inside back. It must reach the points of finishing on the bottom of the front rail and back of the top rail. [2] *Pin boxings in place.* Chalkmark cover along edges of the boxings from the front of the seat to the top of the back, Fig. 13:15C. Make three or four register marks (one at the junction of seat and back) on boxings and cover so that they can be aligned when sewing them together. Register marks on the cover should be on the same thread of the goods at both boxings; unless the grain of a cover is straight across the seat and back, the goods will not stretch evenly.   [3] *Mark cover and boxings* for the start of the breaks at the front of a seat and top of a back, Point 1.   [4] *Remove cover;* on it blend into smooth lines the chalkmarks made along the edges of the boxings.   [5] *Cut cover 1* inch outside these lines. This compensates for the ½-inch seam allowance on the boxing and adds ½ inch for the cover seam.   [6] *Sew welt to cover,* and then sew boxing to welt and cover (Secs. 12:06, 12:07); be sure to keep cover and boxing register marks aligned. Usually it is advisable to sew from the register mark at the junction of seat and

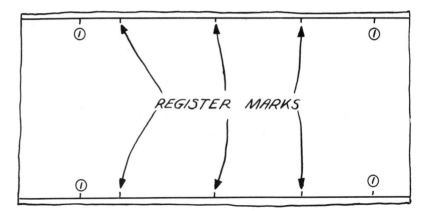

Fig. 13:15C

back. Do not sew boxings, welt, and cover together beyond break marks at front of a seat and top of back. There must, of course, be enough welt to extend from the breaks to the bottom of the seat rail and back of the top rail.

SEC. 13:15D PADDING, COVERING / [*1*] *Pad seat and inside back* with, preferably, a continuous layer of felted padding reaching to the bottom and back edges of the frame. [*2*] *Pad sides* enough to make them perpendicular to the frame and to build a sharp break between the main and side surfaces. [*3*] *Install cover* the same way as muslin casing (Sec. 6:04I), but finish it on the back and bottom of the rails. Turn seam allowances of cover, boxing, and welt down over the sides of seat and back to eliminate small lumps in the main cover. Cover around legs (Sec. 13:05). Keep boxing smooth and straight throughout, and set welt evenly. [*4*] *Pin boxing, welt, and cover* into position at the corners of the front of the seat and top of the back. Blind-stitch them (Sec. 13:04).

**SEC. 13:16
ROLL AND
HARD EDGE
SEATS, FULLY
UPHOLSTERED
ARMS**

SEC. 13:16A / In articles with fully upholstered arms, solid and loose-cushion roll and hard edge seats may have either a pull-over (Figs. *a* 1:20, *b* 1:31) or a bordered cover (Figs. 1:30, 1:34). In addition to the tools and materials in Sec. 13:11A, a large curved needle and cardboard stripping are needed (Sec. 3:26).

SEC. 13:16B SOLID SEAT / Spread a layer of felted padding on seat. [*1*] *Padding extends an inch or so* beyond junctions of seat, inside arms, and back. [*2*] *Pull-over cover.* Padding extends to but not below the bottom of the front rail. When tightening cover, enough padding usually works over the bottom edge to protect it. [*3*] *Bordered cover.* Padding extends down the front rail to the planned top of the border. [4] *On front rail.* Padding extends to outer edges of front posts when a pull-around inside arm cover will be used. For a paneled, bordered, or boxed arm cover, front seat rail padding extends to the planned inner limits of the post panel or border, to ½ inch or so beyond the inner edges of the posts for boxed arm covers. An additional layer or two of padding may be needed on the front rail to build shape and crown (Sec. 5:14); place it under the initial layer of padding.

Sec. 13:16C Cover / Sew stretchers to sides and back of seat cover (Sec. 11:13B). Install solid seat cover essentially the same as muslin casing on a bridle-built hard edge seat (Secs. 7:26C, D), depending in part on the planned inside arm covers. [1] *Pull-over seat cover.* Finish on bottom of front rail; cover around legs (Sec. 13:05). [2] *Bordered seat cover.* Finish about ¾ inch below planned top of border. [3] *Pull-around inside arm cover.* Finish seat cover on outer side of front post about ¾ inch behind front edge. Cut seat cover to leave a small tab sticking up on the front and outer side of the post, Fig. 13:16C, to simplify setting the inside arm cover so as to avoid a sag between it and the seat cover. Tack tabs to post to hold cover in place above leg. [4] *Paneled, bordered, boxed inside arm covers.*

Fig. 13:16C

Finish seat cover on front of post about ¾ inch beyond the planned inner limits of panel or border, about ¾ inch beyond the inner front edge for a boxed arm cover. Cut cover to leave small tabs, [3] above. [5] *T-shaped seat.* These usually are bordered near top of seat rail to avoid making high pleats in a seat cover. Finish cover on rail and outer sides of front posts. Cut covers to leave small tabs, [3] above.

Sec. 13:16D Border / Install seat border now (Sec. 13:08), but leave it loose at the ends, or install after inside arm covers. Because of welt, seat borders usually finish over inside arm covers (Fig. 1:30). Finish border on the same surfaces of the front posts as the seat cover.

SEC. 13:16E   LOOSE-CUSHION SEAT   /   Sew decking (Sec. 11:13A[4]) to seat cover, Figs. 13:16E, 13:17D. Install decking and seat cover at the inner limits of a hard edge the same way as muslin casing (Sec. 7:27).

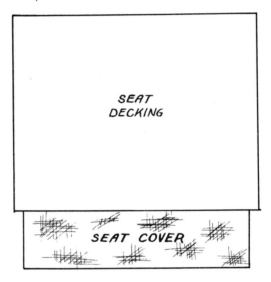

Fig. 13:16E

SEC. 13:16F   PADDING, COVERING   /   [1] *Spread a layer of felted padding on the deck.* Set it flush against the stitched side of the decking and extend to an inch or so beyond the junctions of seat, inside arms, and back. While drawing the decking in place, press padding lightly but firmly toward the cover seam to keep it from being displaced.   [2] *Install decking* the same as muslin casing.   [3] *Spread a layer of felted padding over the front of the seat* from the decking seam over the front edge down to where the cover will finish (Secs. 13:16B–D). While drawing cover in place, press padding lightly but firmly against the decking seam to keep padding from shifting.

SPRING EDGE SEATS

SEC. 13:17 SOLID, LOOSE-CUSHION SEATS

SEC. 13:17A   /   Almost without exception spring edge seats have fully upholstered backs and arms; there are, of course, armless spring edge seats (Fig. 1:18). Solid and loose-cushion spring edge seats usually have banded (Sec. 11:04) covers (Fig. *a* 1:45) or banded and bordered covers (Fig. *c* 1:45). Pull-over covers (Fig. *c* 1:42) are seldom as satisfactory as the other types for spring edge seats. In addition to the tools and materials in Sec. 13:11A, a large curved needle and cardboard stripping are needed (Sec. 3:26).

SEC. 13:17B SOLID SEAT / Sew stretchers to sides and back of seat cover (Sec. 11:13B) when inside arms and back are fully upholstered, to back of seat cover only in an armless article (Fig. 1:18) or when arms are not fully upholstered. Sew stretchers to banding of a T-shaped seat, Fig. 13:17B; sew welt to banding (Secs. 12:06, 12:07).

Fig. 13:17B

SEC. 13:17C PADDING / Spread a layer of felted padding over seat. [*1*] *Arms and/or back fully upholstered.* Padding extends to an inch or so beyond junctions of seat, arms, back. [*2*] *Banded spring edge.* Padding extends over seat down to but not below the top of the spring edge-wire. [*3*] *Pull-over seat cover.* Padding extends down to points of finishing the cover. An additional layer or two of padding, preferably placed under the initial one, may be needed to build shape and crown (Sec. 5:14) in the area below the top of a seat.

SEC. 13:17D SEAT COVER / Install seat cover the same as muslin casing (Sec. 7:28). If banding will be used, stitch cover to seat along the top of the spring edge-wire, Fig. 13:17D. A pull-over cover is, of course, tacked on the exposed portions of a seat. When only the inside back is fully upholstered (Fig. 1:18), cut cover there as in Sec. 13:11C[5].

SEC. 13:17E BANDING / Install cover banding essentially the same as muslin banding (Secs. 7:29D–G). Pin in place through seam allowances, not through banding proper. Stitch through seams with 1-inch running stitches just below the sewing in a welted banding. Spread a layer of felted padding over area to be covered by banding. [*1*] *Top.* Place padding flush against sewing of welted banding. [*2*] *Banding or pull-over cover only.* Padding extends down to but not below bottom edge of seat rail. While tightening goods, usually enough padding works over the bottom edges to protect it. An additional layer or two of padding, preferably placed under the initial one, may be needed to shape cover and build crown (Sec. 5:14). [*3*] *Banding, or cover, and border.* Padding extends down to planned top of border. [*4*] *Com-*

Fig. 13:17D

plete installing of cover banding the same as muslin banding. While drawing it in place, press padding lightly but firmly toward the banding welt in order to keep the cover from displacing the padding and leaving a hollow line across the seat.

Sec. 13:17F / Finish only banded or pull-over covers around legs (Sec. 13:05).

Sec. 13:17G Border / Install border (Sec. 13:08) now on T-shaped seats, Fig. 13:17G, and when the inside arm cover is not a pull-around.   [1] *A seat border extends* to about ¾ inch beyond the inner

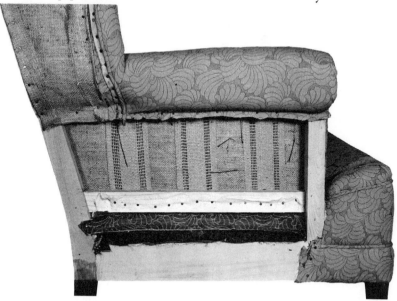

Fig. 13:17G

limits of a front post panel or border, or beyond the inner edge of a post when the arm front is to be boxed.   [2] *Because of the border welt,* if a pull-around inside arm cover will be used, the seat border usually is left free at the ends until after the arms are covered, or the border may be completely installed after covering inside arms.

SEC. 13:17H   LOOSE-CUSHION SEAT   /   Install decking and seat cover as for a hard edge loose-cushion seat (Sec. 13:16). Sew welt to banding; sew stretchers to banding of a T-shaped seat. Complete on exposed sides (Secs. 13:17C–G).

**SEC. 13:18
ARMS NOT
FULLY
UPHOLSTERED**

Spring edge seats having arms but exposed sides are seldom made. Usually only the front of the seat is spring edge construction. With a continuous spring edge for front and sides, the seat would tend to wobble and soon lose shape. Therefore the front usually is spring edge, the sides hard edge. Cover the front as a spring edge seat (Sec. 13:17). Cover exposed sides the same as a hard edge seat front (Sec. 13:16). Finish seat banding at the sides snug against the arms.

14

covering
inside
arms

SEC. 14:00 **INSTALLATION**	Install inside arm covers almost exactly the same as muslin casings. Buttons, fringe, panels, borders, gimp, antique nails, and other trim usually are installed with the outside cover (Chapter 18).
SEC. 14:01 **ARMREST**	**Sec. 14:01A** / Aside from office furniture, padded armrests are chiefly on so-called traditional styles of chairs (Fig. 1:28). The traditional way of finishing the cover is with gimp (Fig. *c* 1:28); other popular finishings are welt (Fig. 1:22) and double-welt (Fig. *c* 11:08A). Welt finish should be undertaken somewhat cautiously by inexperienced upholsterers; if there is less than ½ inch of good tacking space on the rabbet or within the marked limits of upholstery, installing welt neatly and securely may be quite difficult. Install armrest covers the same way whether they are to be finished with gimp or double-welt, both of which are treated as part of the outside cover (Chapter 18). For welt finishing, install welt, then the cover. *Tools:* Upholsterer's hammer, shears, regulator; for gimp, double-welt, a sharp knife or razor

blade; for welt, small curved needle, upholstery skewers (Secs. 2:02, 2:04, 2:07; 2:06, 2:08). *Materials:* Tacks, felted padding; for welt, stitching twine, cardboard stripping (Secs. 3:03, 3:49; 3:08, 3:26).

Sec. 14:01B Gimp, Double-Welt Finish / Spread a layer of felted padding over muslin incased armrest, ending ½ inch from the marked limits of upholstery or sides of rabbets (Fig. 8:06D). Padding beyond these points may prevent good installation of the cover. Install cover the same as muslin casing (Sec. 8:06). Tack close to marked limits of upholstery or sides of rabbets. Trim off excess goods with a sharp knife or razor blade just within the marked limits or away from the sides of rabbets (Fig. 13:07B). Install gimp, double-welt (Secs. 18:16, 18:17).

Sec. 14:01C Welt Finish / Prepare welt at least 1 inch longer than the circumference of the marked limits of upholstery or sides of rabbets of an armrest. Tack welt along the marked limits or sides of rabbets at just enough points to hold it in place. Butt welt ends together at the middle of the back of the pad (Sec. 13:02); take a few stitches in welt covers, near seams, to hold ends securely together. Cardboard welt (Sec. 13:03). Spread a layer of padding over muslined armrest extending to but not beyond the welt stitching. Install armrest cover the same as muslin casing (Sec. 8:06) except: [*1*] *Underturn edges of cover;* pin them in place along the seam of the welt. [*2*] *After tightening and adjusting,* blind-stitch cover to welt (Sec. 13:04).

SEC. 14:02 COVERED ARMBOARD

Sec. 14:02A / The popularity of covered armboards (Fig. *d* 1:29) fluctuates. When reupholstering or re-covering, often it is more practical to cover badly damaged or discolored armboards than to refinish them. For best results, stuff armboard, and incase with muslin (Sec. 8:07). Install cover the same way whether an armboard is plain wood or stuffed and incased. *Tools:* Upholsterer's hammer, shears, regulator (Secs. 2:02, 2:04, 2:07). *Materials:* Tacks, felted padding (Secs. 3:03, 3:49).

Sec. 14:02B Padding / Spread a layer of felted padding over armboard from the outer back edge of the back post to the front of the armboard, and down to the bottom edges. Tear off excess padding even with bottom edges; padding beyond edges may prevent good installation of the cover.

Sec. 14:02C Covering / [*1*] *Center cover* on arm. [*2*] *Draw both side edges moderately tight under armboard,* about halfway between front and back. Sliptack cover ½ inch from edges, Points 1 and

2, in Fig. *a* 14:02C.   [*3*] *Draw cover moderately tight straight toward the front,* sliptack on bottom of armboard, Point 3.   [*4*] *Draw cover moderately tight straight back* from the middle of the outer side of armboard. Depending on the thickness of a back and width of an arm cover, it may be necessary to cut the cover now to fit at the back, *b.* Cut (Sec. 5:15) cautiously. The small tabs at the top, inner side, and bottom and the large tab on the outer side will prevent gaps between arm and inside back covers. Tack arm cover on the outside back midway between top and bottom of armboard, Point 4, *a.*   [*5*] *Starting at middle of armboard* and working alternately toward front and back, set cover smooth and tight. Keep grain of goods as straight as possible throughout. After adjusting cover to front, pleat it (Sec. 5:17) snugly around armfront; blind-stitch pleats (Sec. 13:04) if using a loosely woven fabric.   [*6*] *At the back,* tack inner tab to inner side of armboard ½ inch behind the inner surface of the back, *b,* when possible. When tacking the outer tab, often several layers of padding must be placed under it to build a smooth, even surface from arm to outside back. Do not underturn the ends of this tab when tacking; the extra thicknesses may prevent good installation of the cover.   [*7*] *After tacking permanently* along armboard from front post to back, trim off excess goods. Later, finish the underside with a dust cover. Some upholsterers finish the underside by blind-stitching a piece of cover goods across it from side to side and front to back.

EXPOSED-WOOD INSIDE ARMS

SEC. 14:03 GENERAL TREATMENT

Covers of exposed-wood inside arms (Fig. *a* 1:52) usually finish at the wood edges the same as the seat—with gimp, double-welt, or welt (Sec. 13:07). At the bottom, a stretcher usually is added (Sec. 11:13B), and the arm cover tacked in place on top of the seat cover on the outer side of the rail. In most exposed-wood inside arm articles, the arm and back covers are joined together with welt (Fig. *a* 1:52), but some are stitched together without welt (Fig. *b* 1:38). Whether these covers are joined with or without welt, there are two methods of doing it. The preferred way is to machine sew covers together and install them as a unit (Sec. 14:04). Inexperienced upholsterers usually do a better job by installing the covers separately, and then blind-stitching them (Sec. 14:05).

SEC. 14:04 JOINING INSIDE ARM AND BACK COVERS

SEC. 14:04A MACHINE SEWING / Sewing inside arm and back covers together, with or without welt, and installing them as a single cover (Sec. 14:03) can produce the best job. For welt, the sewing machine must be able to handle four thicknesses of cover goods. Inside arm and back covers usually are joined along a straight line down

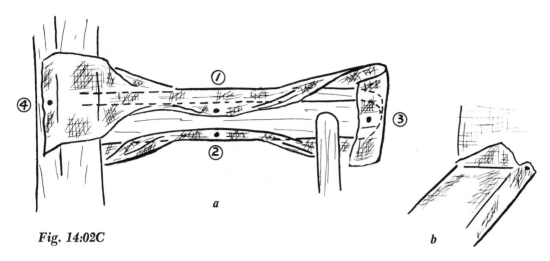

a

b

Fig. 14:02C

the middle of the inner surface of the back post. To plot this line, set a No. 6 tack (Sec. 3:03) firmly in place at the middle of the post surface at the top of the upholstery area and at the top of the seat.

Sec. 14:04B Prepare Covers / Mark inside back and arm covers for joining. Because the back cover is easier to work with, it is usually marked first and used as a pattern for marking arm covers. [*1*] *Set inside back cover in place,* centering it for design and making sure it reaches all points of finishing (Sec. 16:06). Work cover smooth and just tight enough to prevent wrinkling; sliptack in place along top of frame and on seat rail. Pin cover in place to muslin casing down along the sides. Do not work cover as tight as it would be for final installation. [*2*] *Mark back cover and frame clearly* at top and bottom for registration or replacement after sewing. [*3*] *At top of upholstery area and just above seat,* loosen cover enough so that when it is under-turned, it will just clear junction marking tacks (Sec. 14:04A). [*4*] *Lay a flexible steel tape measure* snugly in place from tack to tack, and draw a smooth chalk line between them. These are the basic junction lines for inside back and arm covers and are used for plotting junction lines on the arm covers. [*5*] *Remove inside back cover.* Fold it wrong-side-to-wrong-side and align junction lines. If necessary, stick pins through the covers to see how well the junctions actually do align. The closer they are to being identical, the better the finished job. If there are large differences between lines, an error probably was made in marking them, and it should be done over. But as a rule, there are very slight differences, which can be ignored. Often there are small wobbles in the lines, due to marking on a soft surface; compromise these into smooth, regular lines. [*6*] *Pin sides of cover together,* [*5*] above, and cut off excess goods ½ inch outside the junction line. [*7*]

Set inside arm covers in place, centering them for design and making certain they reach all points of finishing (Sec. 14:08). Work covers smooth and tight, [1] above. [8] *Use registration marks,* [2] above, to replace inside back cover exactly as it was. [9] *Keep edges of inside back cover smoothly in place* and draw a chalk line on each arm cover along edge of back cover. These are *NOT* junction lines for arm covers but are used for plotting those lines. [10] *At top of each planned junction,* mark back and arm covers for registration. Experienced upholsterers often do this by holding the covers smoothly together an inch or so above the top of the upholstery area and cutting them. [11] *Remove* inside back cover. [12] *Mark each arm cover* at the point where the line made in [9] above crosses the marked limits of upholstery or sides of the rabbet. [13] *Remove arm covers.* Set them together wrong-side-to-wrong-side with chalk lines aligned and in registration at the top. Check and adjust as necessary, [5] above. [14] *Pin arm covers* securely together and draw a smooth chalk line ½ inch outside the final line made in [13] above. This line represents the junction of arm and back covers. Trim off excess goods ½ inch outside the junction line to leave a ½-inch seam allowance for sewing the covers.

Sec. 14:04C Sewing Covers / [1] *If arm and back covers are not to be welted,* align and sew them together ½ inch from edges of seam allowances. Sew from top to bottom. [2] *If covers are to be welted,* prepare enough welt (Sec. 11:08) to reach from top to bottom of the arm covers. Align arm cover, welt, and back cover, and sew together. For best results, sew on the welt cord side of the welt stitching but not through the cord.

Sec. 14:04D Install Cover / Although the sewn arms-back cover is installed as a unit, the covers finish at the same points as they would if installed separately. Finish exposed-wood areas (Sec. 13:07). Pad and install inside arm and back covers (Secs. 14:08, 16:06). [1] *When padding,* if possible use one continuous layer instead of fitting pieces of padding together. With piecing there always is a chance of making a line of thicker or harder padding. If piecing is necessary, do it along planned junctions of back and arm covers. [2] *Start installing covers* by centering the inside back cover. Work from there, alternately on each side, toward the front of the arms. [3] *At the back posts,* cut covers apart along the junctions up from the bottom just far enough to be able to work them smooth and tight down the post area and around it. The top of the split between covers should, of course, be below the top of the seat. Tack covers to the sides of the back posts, trim off excess goods.

SEC. 14:05
BLIND-
STITCHING
COVERS

Sec. 14:05A / For blind-stitching inside arm and back covers together with or without welt (Sec. 14:03), first prepare covers (Secs. 14:04A, B). [1] *If welt will not be used,* install covers immediately after preparation (Sec. 14:05B). Weltless installation is not recommended, because no matter how expertly blind-stitching is done, it will be quite noticeable. Welt makes any blind-stitching look better; compare Fig. *a* and *b* 11:08A. [2] *Welt usually is machine sewn* to arm covers and blind-stitched to the back cover, because the side of welt at the back of an arm usually is more noticeable than the other side, and the machine-sewn side of a welt generally is smoother and neater than the blind-stitched side. Prepare enough welt (Sec. 11:08) to reach from top to bottom of the inside arm covers at the back. Align edges of cover and welt, and sew them together.

Sec. 14:05B Installing Covers / Install inside arm covers, then the back cover, and blind-stitch together. [1] *Finish covers* along exposed-wood portions (Sec. 13:07). [2] *Pad and install* inside arm and back covers (Secs. 14:04D, 14:08, 16:06). [3] *When tightening and adjusting covers,* be sure to develop equally smooth and thick surfaces along both sides of arm and back junctions. Otherwise covers will not be smooth and neat after being stitched together. [4] *If covers are not welted,* underturn them for folded edges to meet, without any overlap, along the planned junctions. They must form smooth, regular lines from top to bottom; they should be as alike as possible on both sides of the back. Pin covers in place. Blind-stitch from top to bottom, working alternately a few inches on one side, then the other. [5] *If covers are welted,* underturn edges of the inside back cover for the fold to fit snugly, without any overlap, against the welt stitching. Pin and blind-stitch, [4] above.

FULLY UPHOLSTERED ARMS

SEC. 14:06
POST PIECE

To install a separate post piece (Sec. 11:15C), spread a layer of felted padding over that part of the front post from just behind the back edge to the site of the planned post panel or border. If panel or border will be set back from the inner edge of the post, build up that area with padding to make a smooth, simulated roll edge (Sec. 5:05); it should be the same size as the roll edge above the post piece. Center post piece cover around post; tack to back of post. [1] *When a post panel or border is flush with the inner side of a post* (Fig. *e* 1:45), the post piece at the front finishes under the seat cover (Fig. *a* 5:16). [2] *When post piece is part of an inside arm cover,* treat it as such. In this case, a post piece generally finishes over seat banding or a pull-over cover (Fig. *c* 1:35) but under a welted border.

SEC. 14:07
PREPARING
COVERS FOR
FULLY
UPHOLSTERED
ARMS

SEC. 14:07A / The arms of most upholstered articles seldom are identical, especially when built with loose stuffing. But usually they are enough alike that corrections in size and shape are minor and can be made with felted padding. But if differences between arms are quite noticeable, rebuild one to match the other. Most inside arm covers are a single sheet of goods and are worked to desired shape during installation. But boxed arms (Figs. b 1:31, a 1:42) must be sewn to shape before installation; this requires special marking and handling (Secs. 14:07C, D). *Tools:* Shears, upholstery skewers, sewing machine, chalk (Secs. 2:04, 2:08, 2:15, 2:16). *Materials:* Upholstery thread, cover stretchers; welt cord for boxed arms (Secs. 3:09, 3:55, 3:58).

SEC. 14:07B ALL INSIDE ARMS / Sew cover stretchers to back and bottom of inside arm covers (Sec. 11:15B). When using a sewn post piece (Sec. 14:06), first sew it to the cover stretcher, then sew them to the cover. When post piece is part of the cover, cut out excess goods behind the post piece, and complete the cover with a stretcher.

SEC. 14:07C BOXED INSIDE ARMS / Because boxing is sewn to an inside arm cover before installation, the final shape of an arm and fit of the cover are fairly well established before the cover is installed. Only minor corrections can be made with felted padding during installation. The more accurately cover and boxing are sewn together to fit an arm, the easier installation is and the better the cover will look and last. The accuracy of cover-boxing sewing depends on marking the inside arm cover. [1] *Set inside arm cover smoothly in place;* center it for design and to reach all points of finishing. [2] *Pin or sliptack cover* at enough points to hold it in place, but do not attempt to work cover as tight as it should be for final installation. [3] *Make a series of chalkmarks* to outline the front and top of an arm: I—When front post is perpendicular to the seat rail throughout (Fig. b 1:31): i. All arms, chalkmark along break from inner to front surface; ii. Modern square arms (Fig. a 1:42), chalkmark along break from inner to top surface; iii. Scroll and square-scroll arms with solid boxing (Fig. b 1:31), chalkmark cover behind the boxing line at the start of the scroll on the inner surface. II—For boxed scoop and other arms that are not perpendicular to seat rail throughout: i. All arms, chalkmark cover for location of welt, marking along breaks between the front and other surfaces; ii. Scroll and square-scroll arms with solid boxing (Fig. 1:34), chalkmark the cover behind the boxing line at the start of the scroll on the inner surface. [4] *Remove cover,* and draw straight lines along chalkmarks; slight irregularities may be compromised into straight lines; reshape arm stuffing and remark cover if there are large errors. [5] *Trim off excess goods* ½ inch outside chalk lines to leave proper seam allowance for sewing boxing.

Sec. 14:07D Sewing Boxed Arm Covers / [*1*] *Sew welt to cover* (Secs. 12:06, 12:07). Extend each end of welt 1½ inches beyond the cover for handling: I—Modern square arms: Make welt long enough to reach from the point of finishing on the bottom of the front rail to the back of the back post. II—Scroll and square-scroll arms having solid boxing: Welt encompasses arm front and finishes on the bottom of the seat rails. III—Scroll and square-scroll arms having a bordered or paneled boxing: Welt reaches from the bottom of the front rail, at the inner side of the post, to the top end of the arm cover. But when an arm cover ends under a panel (Fig. *e* 1:45), welt ends at the bottom of the arm cover. [*2*] *Sew boxing to welted cover:* I—Modern square, and scroll and square-scroll arms with bordered or paneled boxing: Sew boxing to welt throughout length of welt. II—Scroll and square-scroll arms with solid boxing: Sew boxing to welt from the bottom of the inside arm welt to the chalkmark on the cover that indicates the start of the scroll; boxing must be long enough to finish on top of the scroll. III—Double-scroll arm (Fig. *a* 1:49): Sew boxing in place along the least curving portion of the inside arm cover.

SEC. 14:08
PLAIN
COVERS
ON MOST
ARMS

Sec. 14:08A / For scroll, Figs. 14:08A, *a* 1:41, knife-edge (Fig. *b* 1:38), rounded (Fig. *d* 1:45), square-scroll (Fig. *b* 1:46), modern square (Fig. *c* 1:42), bordered armtop (Fig. 1:43), and exposed-wood arms (Fig. *a* 1:52). *Tools:* Upholsterer's hammer, shears, small curved needle, regulator (Secs. 2:02, 2:04, 2:06, 2:07). *Materials:* Tacks, stitching twine, felted padding (Secs. 3:03, 3:08, 3:49).

Sec. 14:08B Padding / Install a layer of felted padding. [*1*] *Scroll, square-scroll arms:* Padding goes over armtop down to, but not on, underarm strip. [*2*] *Knife-edge, modern square arms:* Padding goes to, but not over, outer top edge of armboard. [*3*] *Rounded arm:* Padding extends over armtop to a few inches below outer side of armboard. [*4*] *Bordered armtop:* Padding extends over inner top edge of armboard to the planned site of the border. Use enough padding on the top to build a small, simulated roll edge (Sec. 5:05) extending smoothly over into the inside arm. Size of the roll is optional; usually it is high enough so that when the border is installed, its welt will not rise appreciably above the inside arm cover. [*5*] *Exposed-wood arm:* Padding ends ½ inch from the marked limits of upholstery or side of the rabbet. [*6*] *At bottom:* Pad to just below the junction of seat and inside arm. [*7*] *At back:* Pad to just behind junction of arm and inside back. At the outer side of an armtop, padding extends to the outer back edge of the back post when an arm cover is to finish on the back of the post. [*8*] *At front for a pull-around cover:* Pad to but not over the outer front edge of the post; pad enough to build a fairly well-rounded surface (Fig. *c* 1:35). [*9*] *At front for a panel or*

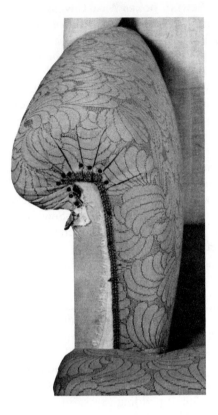

Fig. 14:08A

border: Pad over the front edge of the post to the planned site of the panel or border. Pad enough to build a smooth, simulated roll edge (Sec. 5:05) high enough to give the panel or border a "set in" appearance.

SEC. 14:08C · COVERING / Install inside arm cover the same as the muslin casing (Secs. 8:16–8:22), except: [*1*] *All arms:* Tack bottom of cover on seat rail, not arm liner.   [*2*] *All arms:* At front bottom, finish arm cover over seat cover or post piece so as not to leave a gap between covers.   [*3*] *In articles other than wing chairs, modern club-chairs, and similar items with a back boxing or border extending under the outside arm cover* (Fig. *a, c* 1:42): Finish armtop cover around and on back of back post. Extra padding may be needed to build a smooth, even surface between the end of an arm and the back of a post. Do not underturn goods tacked to the back of a post; the extra thicknesses may prevent good installation of the outside back cover. [*4*] *Scroll arm:* When a button covers the goods finishing on a post face (Fig. *d* 1:48), pleating may not be desirable. Adjust cover throughout arm, then make small gathers on a twine, Fig. 14:08C, in the goods

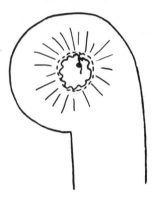

Fig. 14:08C

near the center of the scroll. Distribute gathers evenly, pull twine tight, and knot it (Sec. 5:03). Tack twine to post.   [5] *Square-scroll arms:* Tack armtop cover to underarm strip and outer side of the front post at that level. When installing heavy or nubby goods, blind-stitch (Sec. 13:04) the pleats (Sec. 5:17). For a boxed cover, pin boxing to the outer side of the scroll while making final adjustments. Set and pin welt in place along the front edge of a scroll; tack it to the front post at the level of the underarm strip. Blind-stitch boxing and welt. Set and pin cover; blind-stitch to welt.

SEC. 14:09 **BOXED** **COVERS**	**Sec. 14:09A** / Except for fitting and finishing at the front of a scroll, install boxed covers essentially as in Sec. 14:08. [1] *Set welts smooth and even* on all parts of an arm. To prevent lumps in the arm-top, where they show most and collect soil most readily, place seam allowances of boxing, welt, and cover along the post face of scroll and square-scroll arms, the inside arm proper of modern square arms. [2] *Below the bottom of an inside arm cover* (Fig. *b* 1:31), blind-tack (Sec. 13:03) welted boxing to seat rail where possible. If necessary, open the seat cover, banding, or border, and remove padding that extends into the area to be cardboarded, as tacking through padding often makes pullmarks (Sec. 5:19). When blind-tacking cannot be done, blind-stitch seat cover to welt at that area after completing the arm. Pin these covers in place while installing the arm cover. [3] *Finish boxing at the bottom of a post* the same as covering around a legtop (Sec. 13:05).

Sec. 14:09B   Bordered, Paneled Boxing / Finish boxing on post face within area to be covered by border or panel. With heavy or nubby goods, blind-stitch pleats on a square-scroll arm. Lay cover seam allowance along armfront to prevent lumps in the inside arm cover, where they would be more noticeable.

Sec. 14:09C   Modern Square Arm / Padding extends to but not over outer front edges of post and outer top edges of armboard. Use enough padding to build a smooth, even surface. At the back, cut boxing to finish smoothly on each side of the back post.

SEC. 14:09D   SOLID BOXING: SCROLL, SQUARE-SCROLL ARMS   /   Padding extends to but not over outer front edges of post. Lay cover seam allowance along the inside arm proper and back over the scroll so that the boxing can finish under the cover along the scroll.   [*1*] *Install cover* essentially as a pull-around muslin casing on a scroll arm or a boxed casing on a square-scroll arm (Secs. 8:19–8:22); keep welt lying smooth and even along the breaks of a scroll.   [*2*] *When finishing arm cover around a scroll,* tighten boxing up and back over it, and pin in place under the arm cover. Tighten cover over boxing along scroll; tack to frame at bottom of scroll. Pin boxing to welt, and then blind-stitch.   [*3*] *Cardboard rest of welt* down the front outer edge of the post; end it at top of leg (Sec. 13:01).

| SEC. 14:10 COVERING T-SHAPED ARM | SEC. 14:10A   /   Complete armtop before starting inside arm proper. Inside arm cover may or may not be welted along the top. In addition to the tools and materials in Sec. 14:08A, cardboard stripping is needed (Sec. 3:26). |

SEC. 14:10B   ARMTOP   /   [*1*] *Spread a layer of padding* over armtop down to but not on the underarm strip.   [*2*] *Install armtop cover* the same as muslin casing (Secs. 8:21G, H, 8:22), but tack to the underarm strip and to the front post close to the armboard.

SEC. 14:10C   INSIDE ARM COVER   /   [*1*] *Center inside arm cover* on arm with the top edge, wrong side toward the seat, all along the underarm strip; be sure it reaches all points of finishing (Sec. 14:08). Sliptack cover at middle, front, and back of underarm strip.   [*2*] *Lay goods in place down over inside arm.* Due to the slant in many arms, if the vertical grain of a cover is to be perpendicular to the floor, as it should be, Fig. 14:10C, a cover cannot be tacked across the top on its horizontal grain. When an arm slopes down toward the back, tack the back of a cover further from the top edge than at the front. Before blind-stitching or marking a cover for welts, if any, be sure it will hang down straight when installed.   [*3*] *When blind-tacking* (Sec. 13:03) an inside arm cover, start at the middle, and tighten toward front and back.   [*4*] *Install padding, complete covering inside arm* (Sec. 14:08). While drawing cover down into place, press padding firmly but lightly against the underside of the armboard to prevent displacement of padding, which could leave a hollow at the top of an inside arm.

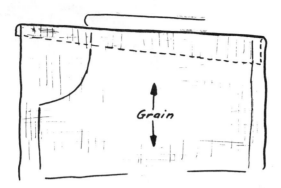

Fig. 14:10C

Sec. 14:11A Arm Finishing into Inside Back / (Fig. *b* 1:38). *Tools:* Upholsterer's hammer, shears, regulator, upholstery skewers, sewing machine, chalk (Secs. 2:02, 2:04, 2:07, 2:08, 2:15, 2:16). *Materials:* Tacks, upholstery thread, felted padding (Secs. 3:03, 3:09, 3:49).

Sec. 14:11B Prepare Arm, Back Covers, Welt / [1] *Set and pin inside arm and back covers,* with stretchers (Sec. 11:13), smoothly in place and reaching to all points of finishing (Secs. 14:05, 14:07, 14:08). Arm covers often must be notched at the back, Fig. 14:11B, in order to fit smoothly. [2] *Chalkmark arm and back covers* along stitching of muslin casing; lines on the arm covers should be identical. If necessary, compromise or adjust lines until they are identical (Sec. 14:04B), and fit the lines of the inside back cover accordingly. [3] *Make at least two register marks* behind the corrected lines in each cover, or make small cuts close to the lines, for fitting the covers together properly while joining them. Unless covers are matched accurately while being sewn, they will not finish smoothly on an article. [4] *Remove covers.* Cut off excess goods ½ inch outside chalk lines for seam allowances. [5] *Prepare enough welt* (Secs. 11:08, 12:06) to reach from the bottom of the covers to the point of finishing on the outer side of the armboard. [6] *Sew welt* to one cover, then sew on the other cover. When sewing the second cover, stitch close against, but not into, the welt cord in order to keep the finished welt from wobbling.

Sec. 14:11C Covering / Working from the middle of a back to the front of the arms, install inside back cover (Sec. 16:06) and arm covers (Sec. 14:08).

Fig. 14:11B

**SEC. 14:12
SINGLE COVER
FOR INSIDE
ARM AND
WING**

These may be bordered (Fig. *b* 1:48) or boxed (Fig. 1:15).   [*1*] *Bordered cover.* After adding cover stretchers (Sec. 14:07B), install cover along the level of the arms as a bordered armtop and front post cover (Sec. 14:08); above armtop, install as an inside wing (Sec. 15:03).   [*2*] *Boxed cover.* Prepare cover (Sec. 14:07) with boxing long enough to finish on the back of the back post. Install it along the level of the arm as a modern square boxed arm cover (Sec. 14:09). Above armtop, install cover as a boxed inside wing (Sec. 15:04).

**SEC. 14:13
"SLIPARM"
COVERS**

Articles with so-called modern slipbacks frequently have similar "sliparms" (Sec. 16:15).

15

covering inside wings

SEC. 15:00	The basic upholstery of an inside wing determines whether it is covered as a separate item (Figs. *a* 1:48, *b* 1:49), or as part of an arm or back, in which case a single-piece cover generally is installed. When using a single-piece cover for inside arm and wing (Figs. 1:15, *b* 1:48), where they join, cover the wing as part of the arm (Sec. 14:12), and above that as a wing. Cover wings that finish into an inside back (Figs. 1:09, *b* 1:38) as part of the back (Secs. 16:03, 16:05–16:13). Install border, buttons, fringe, etc., with outside covers (Chapter 18).
SEC. 15:01 PLAIN PULL-AROUND WING COVER	**SEC. 15:01A** / (Figs. *e* 1:48, *a*, *b* 1:49). *Tools:* Upholsterer's hammer, shears (Secs. 2:02, 2:04). *Materials:* Tacks, felted padding (Secs. 3:03, 3:49).
	SEC. 15:01B PADDING / Spread a layer of padding smoothly over inside wing and back post area to be covered. [1] At *back*. Padding

extends 1 inch beyond junction of inside back and wing when they finish through a cavity.   [2] *At top and front.* Tear off padding that overhangs outer edges of frame; it could prevent good installation of the outside cover.   [3] *At bottom.* Padding extends about 1 inch beyond wing and arm junction when wing is upholstered as a separate unit. When it is treated as an extension of an arm (Figs. 1:15, *b* 1:48), blend wing and arm padding smoothly together.

SEC. 15:01C   COVERING   /   Install pull-around wing cover the same as muslin casing (Secs. 9:11, 9:12).   [1] *Cut cover* (Sec. 5:15) enough for it to be pulled tight and smooth against the frame.   [2] *Underturn cover* when tacking it above arm.   [3] *At the top,* cut to leave a small tab extending a few inches along the back, Fig. 15:01C. When the top of a wing is below the top of a back post, cut to leave a tab along the back post casing.   [4] *Do not underturn* cover goods tacked on the outer side of a back post; the extra thicknesses could prevent good installation of the outside covers.   [5] *Plain wing covers often wrinkle* at the front bottom, usually due to faulty cutting along the bottom of a cover around the wing post. To correct, loosen cover and make enough small cuts up from the bottom edge to let the cover "expand." When tightening at the outer side of a wing, the cover is pulled on the bias, allowing it to stretch around the bottom of the front of a wing.

**SEC. 15:02
WELTED PULL-
AROUND WING
COVER**

SEC. 15:02A   /   (Fig. *a, d* 1:48). *Tools:* Upholsterer's hammer, shears, small curved needle, regulator, sewing machine, chalk (Secs. 2:02, 2:04, 2:06, 2:07, 2:15, 2:16). *Materials:* Tacks, upholstery twine, upholstery thread, felted padding, welt cord (Secs. 3:03, 3:08, 3:09, 3:49, 3:58).

SEC. 15:02B   PREPARE COVER   /   [1] *Center cover on muslin-incased inside wing,* and draw back edge through the same cavity as the muslin. Sliptack at Points 1, 2, 7 (Fig. *a, b, c* 9:11C). Be sure that the cover reaches around wing to all points of finishing and that the grain is straight. The cover should be fairly tight. Press it lightly into the junction of the arm and bottom of wing.   [2] *Chalkmark cover* from behind the junction of the inside back and wing to the outside bottom of the wing.   [3] *Remove cover.* If necessary, blend chalkmarks into a regular, smooth line. Often, due to the shape of an arm and slants of wing and back, the line may be fairly straight across a cover—or it may be at an appreciable angle. Lines on both wing covers should be identical; check by pinning (Sec. 14:05B[13]).   [4] *Cut off excess* cover ½ inch below the corrected line.   [5] *Prepare welt* for the width of the wing cover as measured along the chalk line, and sew to cover (Secs. 12:06, 12:07). Allow 1½ inches of welt at each end for handling.

Fig. 15:01C

SEC. 15:02C PADDING, COVERING / [*1*] *Install padding* (Sec. 15:-01B). [*2*] *Replace cover* (Sec. 15:02B). Fit welt and cover seams into junction of arm and wing, pull welt tight in place, and tack to outer side of frame at front and back. It should lie snug against the arm throughout and appear to be joined to the arm cover. Wrinkles in a welted wing cover usually may be eliminated by altering the amount or placement of padding along the bottom. [*3*] *Sliptack cover in place.* Start at the bottom; alternating between front and back, tighten and sliptack cover upward and toward the back and front. After working to a point 3 or 4 inches above the bottom, loosen welt, tighten, and retack it. Usually it is necessary to retighten and retack the cover upward from the bottom. After working about halfway up a wing, tighten cover straight toward the middle of the top.   [4] *Complete installing of cover* (Sec. 15:01). Blind-stitch (Sec. 13:04) arm cover to wing welt from just behind junction of wing and back to the end of the wing cover at the front.   [5] *With puffy wings and arms* and a welt set deeply between them (Fig. *a* 1:49), blind-stitching arm to welt may not be necessary.

SEC. 15:03 **BORDERED** **WING COVER**	(Fig. *b* 1:48.) In addition to tools and materials in Sec. 15:02A, cardboard stripping is needed (Sec. 3:26). Install a bordered wing cover as in Sec. 15:01 except for the following. [1] *Padding* extends to planned inner limits of wing border. Use enough padding to build a small yet smooth simulated roll edge (Sec. 5:05) from the front and top into the inner surface wing; size is optional, but usually it is large enough to give the border a "set in" appearance. [2] *Tack wing cover on the front and top surfaces* of the frame ½ inch within the planned area of the border. Push back padding that works into the planned border area; it could cause pullmarks in the cover (Sec. 5:19). [3] *Install border* (Sec. 13:08) after the inside back cover (Chapter 16).

SEC. 15:04 **BOXED WING** **COVER**	Sec. 15:04A / (Fig. 1:15). Tools and materials are the same as in Sec. 15:02A except curved needle and cardboard stripping are not needed. Sec. 15:04B Prepare Cover, Welt, Boxing / [1] *Center cover on muslin-incased wing,* and draw the rear edge through the same cavity as the muslin. Pin cover smooth and tight in place; be sure it reaches all points of finishing at top, bottom, front, and back. [2] *Chalkmark cover* along inner front and top edges of wing. [3] *Remove cover.* Blend chalkmarks into regular, smooth lines. They should be an accurate profile of the wing from the front bottom to the top back. Lines on both wing covers should be identical; check by pinning (Sec. 14:04B[13]). If there are minor differences, the lines usually are made the same and compensating adjustments made in the wings with padding. If there are major differences, but the wings are basically in good shape and proportions, rebuild one to match the other. Cut off excess cover ½ inch outside the adjusted chalk lines to leave the necessary seam allowance. [4] *Prepare welt,* and sew to wing cover by aligning seam allowances (Secs. 12:06, 12:07). Sew boxing to welted cover; sew between welt stitching and welt cord, but do not sew into cord. Be sure welt and boxing are long enough to finish on the back of the back post.

SEC. 15:04C PADDING / Pad inside wing (Sec. 15:01B). On front and top surfaces an additional layer or two of padding usually is needed to build them to the level of the stuffing at the inner edges of the frame. Otherwise, instead of being neat and squared, the boxing may slope across the top and front surfaces. Tear off padding that overhangs the outer edges; it could prevent good installation of the outside cover.

SEC. 15:04D COVERING / Replace boxed cover on wing. In order for the welt to lie smooth and straight along the inner edges of a wing, set and tighten a boxed cover from the top front corner to the back and to the bottom as in Fig. 15:04D. *[1] Draw cover straight across wing corner;* tack midway between sides of corner, Point 1. *[2] Draw cover straight toward back;* tack just in front of back post, Point 2. *[3] Draw cover fairly snug straight down from front corner,* keeping welt along the inner front edge; tack midway between top and bottom, Point 3. *[4] Draw cover fairly snug straight toward back from* Point 3, tack to same surface as muslin casing, Point 4. *[5] Draw cover fairly snug straight back from* Point 3, tack at bottom of wing, Point 5. *[6] Draw cover straight back from* Point 5, tack at back of wing, Point 6.

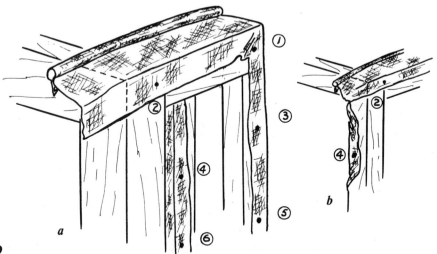

Fig. 15:04D

SEC. 15:04E COMPLETING COVER / Tighten and adjust cover, working from the top front corner toward the back and toward the bottom. Before cutting (Sec. 5:15) at the back, rip boxing and welt from cover. Cut cover to fit at the back (Secs. 9:12, 15:01C). Sliptack wing boxing to the back of the back post until installing the inside back cover. Finish inside back cover under wing boxing. Tack boxing in place; blind-stitch (Sec. 13:04) inside back cover to wing boxing.

16

covering
inside
backs

Sᴇᴄ. 16:00A / For the most part, inside back covers are installed the same as muslin casing except that they usually overlap or fit snug against all other inside covers finishing at the back other than wing border or boxing. The main difference between casing and cover is where the cover finishes at the seat and rear of inside arms and wings; here the inside back cover usually is tacked on top of the others to help the surfaces fit smooth and tight against each other. Plain and buttoned backs are covered alike. Buttons, gimp, and other trim are installed when covering the outside surfaces (Chapter 18). Covering traditional types of inside backs is in Secs. 16:01–16:13. For modern open-frame loose-cushion backs, see Sec. 16:14; for modern slipframe backs, Sec. 16:15.

Sᴇᴄ. 16:00B / The inside back is the most noticeable part of an article. Give it the greatest care throughout, starting with planning the cover, chiefly placement of the dominant figure or design. With some

508

covers good placement is quite limited (Fig. *a, b* 1:28). In a large design, usually one figure, because of size and/or color, is outstanding (Figs. *c* 1:29, 1:30, *a* 1:35); this is usually set midway between the sides of a back but noticeably nearer the top than the seat (Figs. *c* 1:29, 1:30) or the seat cushion (Fig. *a* 1:35). The smaller the figures, the less important such placement becomes. With very regular, close-repeat designs (Fig. *a* 1:42), the top of a row of figures usually is set to or just below the top of an inside back. Inside back and wing covers often are fitted together (Figs. *d* 1:48, *b* 1:49). Special care should also be taken for installing an inside back cover. Where it goes around posts or rails, it must be cut (Sec. 5:15) to fit snug and tight without binding due to cuts that are too short or looseness due to cuts that are too long. Poorly installed inside back covers develop wrinkles in fairly short time; the continual downward rubbing on a back soon makes wrinkles into lines of soil and wear.

SEC. 16:01 **THIN PAD** **BACKS**	**SEC. 16:01A** / So-called thin or flat pad and similar exposed-wood inside backs (Figs. 1:07, 1:12, 1:28) may be finished along exposed-wood edges with gimp, double-welt (Fig. 11:08C), or welt (Fig. 13:07C). *Tools:* Upholsterer's hammer, shears, regulator (Secs. 2:02, 2:04, 2:07). *Materials:* Tacks, felted padding; cardboard stripping for welt (Secs. 3:03, 3:49; 3:26).

SEC. 16:01B INSTALL COVER / (Sec. 13:09). [1] *Inside back curving between top and bottom* (Fig. 1:12); set and tighten cover (Sec. 10:24E). [2] *Oval back* (Fig. *c* 1:28); set and tighten cover (Sec. 10:05). [3] *For gimp or double-welt*, see Secs. 18:15, 18:16. [4] *For welt finish*, see Secs. 13:07C, D.

SEC. 16:02 **SLIPBACKS**	Cover a traditional slipback the same as a slipseat (Sec. 13:10).

SEC. 16:03 **BACK** **FINISHING** **AWAY FROM** **SEAT**	**SEC. 16:03A SOLID BACK** / Fully upholstered dining and side chair backs (Fig. 1:09) often finish away from the seat and are independent units. They may or may not be permanently fastened to the posts. For plain or buttoned backs (Figs. 1:09, 1:19, Sec. 16:03B). For a channeled back (Chapter 20). *Tools:* Upholsterer's hammer, shears, regulator (Secs. 2:02, 2:04, 2:07). *Materials:* Tacks, felted padding (Secs. 3:03, 3:49).

SEC. 16:03B PADDING, COVERING / [1] *Spread a layer of padding* over the inside back reaching to the outer back edges of frame. [2] *Tear off padding* overhanging outer edges, as it could prevent good

installation of the covers.   [*3*] *Install cover* the same as muslin casing (Sec. 10:24).

SEC. 16:04 **KEYHOLE** **BACK**	**SEC. 16:04A /** Keyhole inside backs have either a plain (Fig. 1:10) or a welted cover; the plain usually is more durable. Across the corners between breaks to the sides the cover may be machine sewn or blind-stitched; machine sewing is neater but more difficult. *Tools:* Upholsterer's hammer, shears, small curved needle, regulator, skewers, chalk; sewing machine for sewn cover (Secs. 2:02, 2:04, 2:06, 2:07, 2:08, 2:16; 2:15). *Materials:* Tacks, upholstery twine, felted padding; upholstery thread for machine sewing; welt cord for welted cover (Secs. 3:03, 3:08, 3:49; 3:09; 3:58).

SEC. 16:04B PLAIN COVER, UNSEWN /   Pad inside back (Sec. 16:-03B). Install cover the same as muslin casing (Sec. 10:27).

SEC. 16:04C PLAIN COVER, SEWN /   Pin separate strips of cover smoothly in place on muslin-incased inside back, finishing them on the outside back. Each strip must overlap adjacent strips by at least 1 inch throughout.   [*1*] *Chalkmark each strip* at each corner of the inside back from the inner rear edge of the frame to the outer one; draw this line so that it **appears** to be straight when strips are on inside back. [*2*] *Make two register marks on each strip* at each corner so that they can be aligned for sewing and to set the limits of sewing. Make one register mark at the break from the front to the outer surface, the other at the break to the inner surface.   [*3*] *Remove cover strips,* blend chalkmark into smooth, regular lines if necessary, and cut off excess goods ½ inch outside lines.   [*4*] *Sew cover strips together* along corner lines between register marks; sew with flat ½-inch seam (Sec. 12:05).   [*5*] *Install sewn cover* (Sec. 16:04B), keeping seams straight across corners. Blind-stitch (Sec. 13:04) from ends of sewing to outside back.   [*6*] *If cover wrinkles along seams,* usually it is necessary to rip out seams part way, reset cover, and blind-stitch it. Building this type surface with additional padding to try to remove wrinkles seldom is satisfactory.

SEC. 16:04D WELTED COVER /   Prepare enough welt (Sec. 12:06) to encompass each corner of the inside back and finish on the backs of the rails.   [*1*] *Cover strips may be installed* as in Sec. 16:04B, and welts set in place while tightening covers at the corners; when covers are adjusted, blind-stitch them through welts.   [*2*] *Welts may be installed* by sewing them to cover strips as in Sec. 16:04C, then blind-stitching covers through welts after tightening cover strips throughout.

BACK FINISHING AGAINST SEAT OR DECK

SEC. 16:05
COVER
STRETCHERS

In fully upholstered and exposed-wood backs that finish against a seat or deck (Figs. 1:30, *b* 1:31, *b* 1:52), tack inside back cover or stretcher on top of seat cover on the seat rail (Fig. 16:05). Cover stretchers (Sec. 11:17C) usually are a worthwhile saving in cover goods.   [1] *Inside back finishing flush against seat or deck.* Sew cover stretcher across bottom of inside back cover. Set top of stretcher at least 1 inch below where back and seat or deck touch one another.   [2] *Inside arms and wings flush against back but upholstered separately.* Sew cover

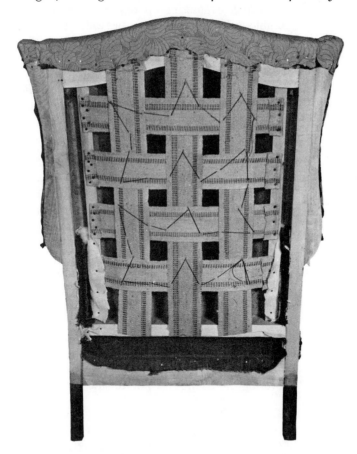

Fig. 16:05

stretchers up sides of back cover from bottom to within a few inches of the top.   [3] *Armchairs, davenports without wings.* Determine which part of back cover will be at the level of the armtops; sew stretchers from bottom of back cover up to those points.

**SEC. 16:06
EXPOSED-
WOOD INSIDE
BACK**

SEC. 16:06A / (Fig. *a* 1:52). This type back cover is a combination of the basic pad cover (Sec. 16:01) and the plain pull-around (Sec. 16:07). Add cover stretcher (Sec. 16:05). Pad as required for each method or place of finishing cover. *Tools:* Upholsterer's hammer, shears, regulator; sewing machine for welted cover (Secs. 2:02, 2:04, 2:07; 2:15). *Materials:* Tacks, upholstery thread, felted padding; welt cord for welted cover (Secs. 3:03, 3:09, 3:49; 3:58).

SEC. 16:06B PADDING, COVERING / [*1*] *At the bottom,* finish back cover the usual way (Sec. 16:05). Pad bottom of inside back enough to shape it against the seat or deck cover. Often an additional layer or two of padding is needed; place them under the main layer of padding. [*2*] *Along exposed-wood edges,* cover may be finished with gimp, double-welt (Fig. 11:08C), or welt (Fig. 13:07C). Install gimp or double-welt as part of outside covers (Secs. 18:15, 18:16); for finishing with welt (Sec. 13:07C). [*3*] *In most articles of this design* (Fig. *a* 1:52), inside back and arm covers are installed as a unit (Secs. 14:03– 14:05). [*4*] *If inside back and arm covers finish through cavities at their junctions,* install back cover the same as muslin casing except that on the outer surface, it is tacked on top of the arm covers. Additional padding may be needed to shape the sides of the back to fit tight against the rear ends of the arms, [*1*] above.

**SEC. 16:07
PLAIN COVER**

SEC. 16:07A / Plain inside back covers (Figs. 1:13, 1:30, *e* 1:45, *b* 1:46), generally the easiest to install, are suitable for most kinds of upholstered articles. Add cover stretchers (Sec. 16:05). Tools and materials are as in Sec. 16:06A except for welt cord.

SEC. 16:07B PADDING / [*1*] *Spread a layer of padding* over the inside back to about 1 inch behind the junctions of the back and other stuffed surfaces. Extend padding to but not over the rear outer edges of the frame; padding overhanging edges can prevent good installation of the cover. [*2*] *If muslin casing does not finish on the backs of the back posts,* an additional layer or two of padding may be needed to shape the outer sides of a back. Set these layers under the large one covering the back from side to side and top to bottom.

SEC. 16:07C COVERING / Install cover the same as muslin casing (Sec. 10:24) except for tacking the bottom on the seat rail (Fig. 16:05). [*1*] *Draw back cover tight* into junctions with other surfaces; underturn it as it emerges. [*2*] *When cover finishes into junction* of the back and another stuffed surface, such as an armtop, usually the back cover must be cut at several points along the junction; cuts ½- to 1-inch long are generally sufficient. The effect of the cuts is that the cover is tightened on the bias, allowing the maximum stretch that is needed here. Many plastic goods do not have a bias; but the short cuts allow for greater than normal stretch.   [3] *For boxed or bordered wings,* finish inside back cover over back posts in area to be covered by wing goods. Do not underturn inside back cover; the extra thicknesses of goods could prevent good installation of the other covers.

SEC. 16:08 **PANELED,** **BORDERED** **INSIDE BACKS**	(Figs. 1:16, *c* 1:45.) Install cover as in Sec. 16:07 except that padding extends around the back posts to the area to be covered by panel or border. [1] *Place enough padding along sides of posts* to build a small, simulated roll edge (Sec. 5:05). Size is optional; usually it is just large enough to give a panel or border a "set in" appearance. [2] *Finish inside back cover on sides of posts* 1 inch within area to be covered by panel or border (Fig. 13:13B). [3] *Panels and borders* generally are installed with the outside covers (Chapter 18).
SEC. 16:09 **WELTED** **INSIDE BACK** **COVER**	(Fig. *d* 1:29.) Prepare cover as for a welted pull-over seat cover (Sec. 13:12). Prepare and install back cover (Sec. 16:07). Blind-stitch (Sec. 13:04) arm cover to welt.
SEC. 16:10 **FULLY BOXED** **COVER**	**SEC. 16:10A** / Boxing may finish under outside arm cover (Fig. *a* 1:42) or around armtop (Fig. *c* 1:42). In addition to the tools and materials in Sec. 16:06A, upholstery skewers and chalk are needed (Secs. 2:08, 2:16). **SEC. 16:10B PREPARE COVER** / Prepare cover essentially the same as boxed muslin casing (Secs. 10:23, 10:24). [1] *Pin inside back cover proper* smooth and tight in place on muslin-incased back, extending it to all points of finishing; add stretchers (Sec. 16:05). [2] *Chalk-mark cover* accurately along breaks between the inner and other surfaces throughout back. [3] *Remove cover, blend chalkmarks* into smooth, regular lines that should be identical on right and left sides of back; check them by pinning (Sec. 14:04B[13]). Slight differences may be compromised or adjusted into identical lines, and the shape of the back may be corrected with padding when covering it. If differences between sides of a back are large and the cover is marked accurately, probably one side of the back is wider, thicker, or higher than the other; open casing and alter stuffing to build sides more nearly alike. [4] *When boxing ends under outside arm cover* (Fig. *a* 1:42), cut the inside back cover ½ inch outside the corrected back lines along the top and down the sides to the armtops. Below armtops, cut off excess goods about 1½ inches outside the lines. Sew cover

stretchers along this area. [5] *When boxing finishes around arms* (Fig. *c* 1:42), cut inside back cover ½ inch outside the corrected back lines. [6] *At each top corner and over arms,* cut for crown allowance (Sec. 10:23C[2]).

SEC. 16:10C   COMPLETING COVER   /   [1] *Prepare, sew welt* (Secs. 12:06, 12:07) around cover: I—When boxing ends under outside arm cover, welt extends to the corners of a back at the outer sides of the armtops; add 3 or 4 inches of welt for finishing it. II—When boxing finishes around armtop, boxing extends to an inch or so below the level of the seat or deck. [2] *Sew boxing to cover all along welt.* Often strips of cover must be pieced together for inside back boxing (Sec. 12:02); piece along the exact top corners or below the armtops; turn seam ends in opposite directions to minimize lumps in the finished back. Add cover stretchers where practical.

SEC. 16:10D   PADDING   /   Spread a layer of padding over the inside back to about 1 inch behind the junctions of the back and other surfaces. [1] *When only boxing is used,* extend padding to, but not over, rear edges of frame. [2] *When a border will be used* (Fig. *c* 1:42), extend padding to planned inner limits of border. [3] *Additional padding* may be needed at boxed corners to make them firm and prevent wrinkles.

SEC. 16:10E   COVERING   /   Install cover essentially the same as muslin casing (Sec. 10:24). [1] *Lay seam allowances* of boxing, welt, and cover along top and side surfaces. If set under the inside back cover proper, they may cause lumps that are more noticeable and collect dirt more readily than on the top and side surfaces. [2] *When boxing ends under outside arm cover,* cut cover stretchers straight in from the back edge and, if necessary, into the cover at enough points to finish the back cover smoothly along arms. [3] *Install border,* if any (Sec. 13:08); center and piece it the same as boxing.

SEC. 16:11
PARTLY BOXED
COVER

SEC. 16:11A   /   Inside back covers often have a plain or pull-over top (Sec. 16:07) and boxed (Sec. 16:10) sides (Figs. 1:17, *b* 1:45). Add cover stretchers where practical (Sec. 16:05). Tools and materials (Sec. 16:10A).

SEC. 16:11B   PREPARE COVER   /   [1] *Pin inside back cover* snugly in place, extending to all points of finishing at top and bottom. [2] *Pin pleats* (Sec. 5:17) into cover along sides of the top corners. [3] *Chalkmark cover along breaks* between inner and side surfaces. Due to the curve of most backs, chalkmarks should be corrected and made into smooth lines before removing cover for sewing. [4] *Pin boxings* snugly in place, chalkmark for curves at the top corners. [5] *Remove boxings and cover* without disturbing pleats. [6] *Sew pleats into cover* along chalk lines; cut off excess goods ½ inch outside chalk lines. [7] *Prepare, sew welt* (Secs. 12:06, 12:07) to cover along the chalk lines, starting at the top of the cover. When practical, there should be enough welt to reach from the top end of the inside back cover to the bottom of the outside back as measured along the posts. [8] *Cut off excess boxing* ½ inch outside chalk lines; sew to welted portions of inside back cover.

SEC. 16:11C PADDING, COVERING / [1] *Pad* as in pertinent parts of Secs. 16:07, 16:10. [2] *Install boxed cover* essentially as a plain cover (Sec. 16:07). [3] *Lay seam allowances* of boxing, welt, and cover along the sides of a back in order to avoid lumps in the inside back cover proper, where they would be more noticeable. [4] *Tighten cover* from the top toward the bottom more than from the middle toward top and bottom. When tightening toward the sides, keep welt straight and even along the breaks between the inner and side surfaces. [5] *Additional padding* may be needed at the top corners to strengthen pleats and at the corners above the arms to prevent the cover from wrinkling.

SEC. 16:12 BANDED COVER

SEC. 16:12A / Banded inside back covers are for spring edge backs (Sec. 10:16). In addition to tools and materials in Sec. 16:10A, a small curved needle and upholstery twine are needed (Secs. 2:06, 3:08).

SEC. 16:12B PREPARE COVER / Add stretcher to bottom of cover (Sec. 16:05). Pin cover tightly and smoothly in place on the muslin-incased inside back, making sure it reaches all points of finishing. [1] *Above arms,* or points at which they contact an inside back, the cover extends an inch or so beyond the spring edge-wire. [2] *From the points of contact between armtops and back down to the seat or deck,* treat the back cover throughout the same as a fully boxed back cover finishing under outside arm covers (Sec. 16:10).

SEC. 16:12C PADDING, COVERING / [1] *Spread a layer of padding* over the inside back (Sec. 16:07) but extending over the exposed portions only to the spring edge-wire. [2] *Install cover* the same as muslin casing, pinning and then sewing it in place along the edge-wire the same as on a spring edge seat (Sec. 13:17). Finish it through the back the same way seat banding finishes under the arms and on the seat rail.

**SEC. 16:13
SOLID-BASE
WING, NO
FRAME CAVITY**

(Fig. 1:15, Sec. 9:13.) Install inside back cover the same as muslin casing and a plain cover (Sec. 16:07) except: [*1*] *At sides,* extend padding only to wing frames. [*2*] *Tack inside back cover along sides of wing frames* close to back posts at intervals close enough just to hold it securely until blind-tacking the wing covers in place.

MISCELLANEOUS BACKS

**SEC. 16:14
OPEN-FRAME
LOOSE-
CUSHION
BACK**

SEC. 16:14A / Side and top rails of open-frame loose-cushion backs are usually but not necessarily covered. It is optional if the wood is attractive, the webbing neatly installed, and the rails are **not** built up (Sec. 7:34D); otherwise rails should be covered. But even when covering is not necessary, it commonly is done to make a smoother surface and to reduce wear of the cushion cover. *Tools:* Upholsterer's hammer, shears, small curved needle; sewing machine if welt used (Secs. 2:02, 2:04, 2:06; 2:15). *Materials:* Tacks, felted padding; cardboard stripping, upholstery thread, welt cord if welt used (Secs. 3:03, 3:09, 3:49; 3:26, 3:58).

SEC. 16:14B COVERING / Only the top and outer surfaces of seat rails for open-frame loose-cushion upholstery need be covered (Fig. *b, c* 7:34D). In backs, all side and top rail surfaces usually are covered, Fig. 16:14B. Whether the front surface is only lightly padded, *a,* or has a roll edge (Sec. 5:05), cover the same way. [*1*] *Install top end of cover* around strips of webbing the same as on a seat (Sec. 7:34F). [*2*] *After installing the top end,* draw cover over the front surface,

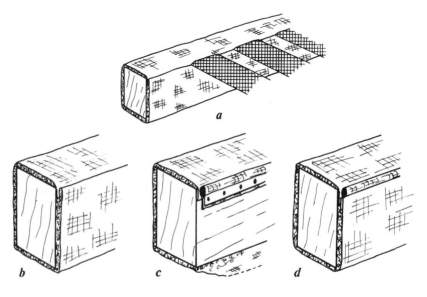

Fig. 16:14B   *b*   *c*   *d*

a

down the outer and under the bottom surfaces, then up the inner surface to finish at the front edge, *a*. At the front edge, finish the free or bottom end of the cover by: I—Simple blind-stitching (Sec. 13:04). Underturn end of cover, and through the fold, blind-stitch it to the top end of the cover along the rail, *b* (Fig. *a* 11:08A). Before stitching, decide how to finish the cover behind the strips of webbing, where there is no cover to stitch to. The folded edge may be tacked to the rail close to the webbing. Or a piece of cardboard stripping wrapped tightly with cover goods may be tacked to butt against the webbing, and the fold blind-stitched to it near the webbing. II— Welting. Prepare, install, and cardboard welt (Secs. 12:06, 13:01– 13:03) along the inner surface of a rail at the front edge, Fig. *c* 16:14B; welt stitching should be just below the edge. Install welt the length of each rail; it should butt snugly, not necessarily hard, against the webbing. Underturn bottom edge of cover the usual way, and blind-stitch to welt, *d*.

SEC. 16:14C CUSHIONS / Back cushions for open-frame upholstery usually are boxed (Chapter 17). Most cushions are "reversible" for sake of appearance; however, webbing may make permanent lines across a cushion cover. Any filling (Secs. 3:61–3:73) may be used; but to keep a back cushion fairly flat throughout, foam rubber, polyfoam, and rubberized hair are used most.

**SEC. 16:15
MODERN
SLIPBACK
COVERS**

SEC. 16:15A / Most so-called modern slipbacks (Sec. 10:37) have what is essentially a two-piece cover: one for the inner surface and sides, the other for the outside back, Fig. *a* 16:15A. Frequently these articles have similar or matching slipframe arms. Upholstering is essentially the same for arms and back, except that as a rule arms are installed straight up-and-down and the back at a slant or tilt, and that although the back occasionally is spring edge (Sec. 16:15E) the arms almost never are. In addition to the tools and materials in Sec. 16:14A, upholstery twine is needed (Sec. 3:08).

SEC. 16:15B / When the "sides" of a modern slipback are appreciably rounded, the inner surface cover usually is a simple pull-around cover finishing on the rear surface of the slipframe. A pull-around cover also may be used for a spring edge back; it would be similar to the seat cover in Fig. 1:65. With a pull-around cover, special care must be taken in pleating the corners (Sec. 5:17); if a cover is weak or too stretchy, it is advisable to blind-stitch the pleats (Sec. 13:04).

SEC. 16:15C / When there are sharp breaks from the inner to other surfaces (Fig. 1:24), a boxed (Sec. 11:06) cover generally is used. It

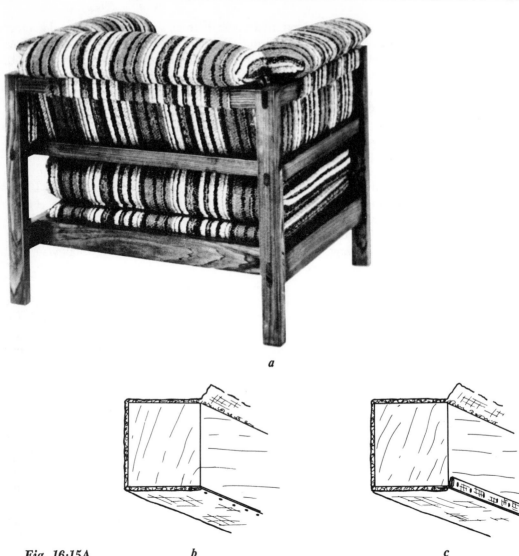

a

Fig. 16:15A   *b*   *c*

is made, with or without welt, the same as the top surface and boxing of a typical square-edge upholstery cushion (Chapter 17), except that the boxing is "long" enough to finish on the rear of the slipframe. Make the boxed cover to fit the muslin-incased slipback snugly.

Sec. 16:15D / When there are two basic kinds of "sides"—rounded at the top and with sharp breaks at the sides, as in Fig. *a* 1:45—as a rule, the sharp-breaking sides are boxed and a pull-around cover is used for the rounded portions. Careful fitting, pleating at the corners, and possible blind-stitching along corners is recommended (Sec. 16:15B).

Sec. 16:15E / When a spring edge back has a bordered (Sec. 11:-04) cover, such as the seat in Fig. 1:58, a single piece of cover is used for the inner surface; pull it over the spring edge and stitch along the edge-wire the same as on a spring edge seat (Sec. 13:17). Borders, with or without welt, are stitched along the edge-wire and tacked on the rear surface of a slipframe.

Sec. 16:15F Padding / Regardless of the type cover used, padding should extend only to the outer edges of a slipframe. Padding placed around the edges can prevent good installation of the outside back cover. When installing the inside back cover, enough padding will work over the rear edges to protect it.

Sec. 16:15G Outside Cover / See Sec. 18:19.

17

cushions
and
pillows

SEC. 17:00 **GENERAL** **INFORMATION**	Upholstery cushions and pillows should fit snugly into an article, and their covers should harmonize with the design, pattern, or stripes on the seat and inside back covers. The word "cushion" generally is used with seat, and "pillow" with back. Construction of a cushion or pillow depends on the cover goods, the filling, and how it will be installed. Newly made cushions and pillows tend to be puffy when properly filled but usually pack soon to the right size. The following generally are needed for cushion and pillow upholstery: *Tools:* Shears, small curved needle, upholstery skewers, cushion closing equalizer, cushion hard-irons, sewing machine, chalk (Secs. 2:02, 2:06, 2:08, 2:13–2:16). *Materials:* Stitching twine, upholstery thread, soft welt cord (Secs. 3:08, 3:09, 3:58). Other items are listed with the work-steps involved.
SEC. 17:01 **BUILDING**	Build cushions and pillows after covering seat, inside arms, wings, and back so that the casings can be planned and cut for an exact and attractive fit (Sec. 17:02). Build them before covering the outside sur-

faces to simplify changing, if necessary, the padding of the inside arms and back for a cushion or pillow to fit smoothly.

SEC. 17:02 **PLANNING**	Harmony of design is another reason for doing cushions and pillows after covering seat and inside surfaces. The major planning of where a cover's dominant figures or design will go on cushions and pillows (Figs. *d* 1:48, 1:58, 1:60) is done when planning a cover (Sec. 11:23). If pieces allowed for cushion and pillow covers are large enough, they can usually be shifted somewhat from the original plan so as to fit them to the installed seat and inside back covers. This is often necessary with striped goods (Figs. *b* 1:46, 1:55, 1:57). If stripes at the front of a seat or cushion, and at the back or pillow, are not fairly well aligned, the effect may displease many people. If the intended pieces of cushion or pillow cover are not large enough for necessary shifting, and if more cover goods is not available, perhaps pieces planned for the outside back or arms may be used. If they are satisfactory for the cushion or pillow but cannot be replaced by the cushion or pillow pieces, it may be practical to use a different cover goods for the outside surfaces. For example, if a figured or patterned cover has a distinctive overall background color, for replacement use a plain, solid-color goods the same color as, or one harmonizing with, the distinctive background color.

SEC. 17:03 **GENERAL** **CONSTRUC-** **TION**	**Sec. 17:03A** / The filling of a cushion or pillow determines its type—down-filled, foam rubber, inner-spring, etc. Any type can be used for an article, but sometimes one may be considered better or more appropriate than others; a relatively thin down-filled cushion without boxing often seems more in keeping with an Italian Renaissance chair than a conventional 3½-inch or thicker boxed inner-spring one. Before selecting a filling, find out what must be done because of it, the cover goods for the casing, and how the filling will be installed. For detailed information on fillings, see Secs. 3:61–3:73. Work-steps for cushion and pillow casings, tickings, filling casings, etc., are in Secs. 17:04–17:18; those for pillows only are in Secs. 17:16–17:18. For loose-cushion upholstery, see Sec. 17:20. In Secs. 17:03B, C, cushions and pillows, despite important differences, are treated as if they were the same.

Sec. 17:03B Ticking / [1] *Down fillings* must be in down-proof ticking (Sec. 3:62B). [2] *Hair filling*, other than rubberized hair, should be in hair-proof ticking (Sec. 3:64). [3] *Kapok* should be in a good quality muslin ticking. [4] *Synthetic cotton* or polyester fiber (Sec. 3:70) can be placed directly into a casing, but inexperienced upholsterers usually do better by using a muslin ticking.

Sec. 17:03C Padding / [1] *Do not use padding* with a down-filled cushion or pillow. [2] *Use padding* with a plain inner-spring unit and any hair filling. A regular or traditional inner-spring unit filling should have about ½ pound of top quality loose hair stuffing spread on the top and bottom surfaces before being padded to provide a smoother foundation for the padding. Hair filling is padded to eliminate its scratchy noise. [3] *Padding may or may not be needed* for foam rubber or polyfoam units or units having those materials on their outer surfaces. I—Some pile fabrics (Sec. 3:53B[3]) need padding to keep pile threads from being pulled out by foam rubber or polyfoam; if in doubt regarding the need for padding, use it. II—Some plastics and fabric coatings may be "allergic" to foam rubber or polyfoam (Sec. 3:53B[4]); padding is advisable. III—For a puffier cushion or pillow and greater initial softness, wrap foam rubber and polyfoam units with a layer or two of synthetic cotton; natural cotton tends to make a cushion feel harder instead of softer. IV—Some early makes of foam rubber units had core holes an inch or so in diameter in top and bottom surfaces to make them soft; wrap this type unit with one or more layers of padding to prevent core holes showing in the casing. V—Some poorer grades of foam rubber and polyfoam deteriorate on the surface into powdery granules, which may be fine enough to work through a casing; wrap these units with padding.

Sec. 17:03D Casing Goods / A cushion or pillow casing made of plastic, leather, leather substitute, or other air-tight goods must be able to "breathe." Unless air can move freely in and out, a casing will not hold shape well and may split along the seams. Breathing is provided by breather vents or by coarse fabric in a casing. Breather vents are wire mesh set in fairly large eyelets or grommets. The larger the vents and the more of them, the less chance of a cushion or pillow making loud wheezing noises. Most home upholsterers should have breather vents installed by an upholstery shop. [1] *Boxed seat cushion.* Install breather vents along rear and both side boxings. [2] *Boxed back cushion, pillow.* Install vents in bottom boxing and in side boxings at least 4 inches below armtops. [3] *Unboxed seat cushion.* Install vents in bottom near the back. [4] *Unboxed back pillow.* Install vents in rear cover near bottom. [5] *Instead of breather vents,* fairly coarse fabric such as denim or any other strong goods may be used for part of the casing. This usually is less expensive than breather vents and gives greater assurance of making a quiet cushion or pillow; however, some upholsterers feel it makes a weaker casing. I—For seat cushions, use regular cover goods for the front 4 inches of the bottom cover; use breather fabric for the rest of that cover. II—For boxed back cushions or pillows, use breather fabric for boxing across the bottom and up the sides to points at least 4 inches below armtops.

**SEC. 17:04
SEAT CUSHION
CASINGS**

SEC. 17:04A PREPARATION / Cut top and bottom covers the approximate shape of a deck but at least 2 inches wider and longer for general handling. Cover shapes in Fig. 17:04A are for a T-shaped seat. For many upholsterers, the easiest way to prepare covers is to first make a paper pattern. Press a large-enough sheet of fairly pliable paper down in place gently but firmly along the edges of the seat, deck, and all other parts. Mark the outline with chalk, crayon, soft lead pencil, etc., as in Secs. 17:04B, C. Do not use newspaper unless ink is thoroughly dry.

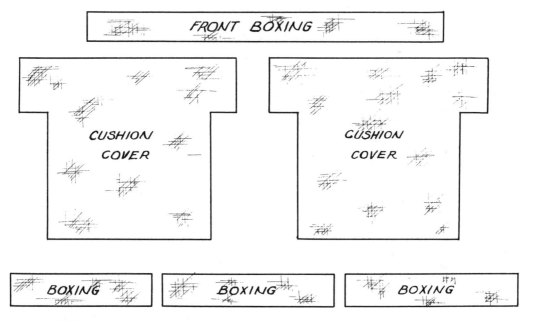

Fig. 17:04A

SEC. 17:04B MARKING / Mark one cover piece **top** on the wrong side. Place it smoothly right-side-up on the seat deck. Press it lightly but snugly against all places where deck, arms, and back meet. Hold a stick of chalk vertically, and mark along these junctions carefully with a series of short dashes. To mark the front edges of a seat: *[1] Place a sheet of heavy cardboard* or a large book on top of cover at front of seat. *[2] Hold cover up smoothly* against cardboard or book. Hold the side of the stick of chalk against the edge of the seat and mark wrong side of cover with a series of short dashes. *[3] Remove cover,* and pin through chalkmarks to transfer them to the right side of goods; chalkmark along pins.

SEC. 17:04C DIFFERING RIGHT AND LEFT SEAT OUTLINES / Blend chalkmarks into smooth, regular lines. They should be identical on right and left halves of a cover, but usually are slightly different due to an arm and/or a side of the back being slightly thicker than the other. [1] *When right and left seat outlines differ slightly*, they usually are made the same by adjusting a little on each side. This allows the finished cushion to fit a seat smoothly enough, no matter whether the top or bottom cover is upward. [2] *When right and left seat outlines are considerably different*, the cover may not have been marked accurately, or there actually are great differences in thickness or shape of arms and/or sides of a back. Often this can be remedied somewhat by loosening arm or back cover on the thin side, and adding padding at and to a couple of inches above the deck. But if considerable difference in left and right outlines persists, the cushion will fit the seat smoothly only when one cover is upward.

SEC. 17:05
CUT CUSHION
COVERS

Sec. 17:05A / After completing chalk outlines in the top cover (Sec. 17:04), cut off excess goods (Secs. 17:05B, C). These cut-offs are for plastics, leather, leather substitutes, and most fabrics. For loosely woven or stretchy goods, it is advisable to cut cushion and pillow covers slightly smaller than a seat or back normally require. There is no rule of thumb for this allowance for loose weave or abnormal stretch, although allowances of from ½- to 1-inch are common. The looser the weave or the more stretch and the larger a cushion or pillow, the greater the allowance should be. Sometimes the only practical solution is to make a cushion or pillow—and after a couple of months, take it apart and remake it.

Sec. 17:05B / The planned filling determines how much excess cover goods to cut off. [1] *Down-filling*. Cut off excess goods ¾ inch outside chalked outlines. [2] *All other fillings, including spring-down*. Cut off excess goods ½ inch outside chalked outline.

Sec. 17:05C / When a seat is straight across the front, cut cushion cover at corners (Sec. 10:23B) to allow for crown. Make similar but smaller cuts on sides of tabs in T-shaped cushions (Fig. 17:04A). Without these cuts the finished corners are likely to be acute or pointed instead of square or slightly rounded.

Sec. 17:05D / Use the trimmed top cover as an exact pattern for cutting the bottom one. Be sure to set covers wrong-side-to-wrong-side before outlining or cutting the bottom cover.

SEC. 17:06
CUSHION
BOXING

Sec. 17:06A Traditional Casings / Boxing for traditional cushions and pillows is machine sewn first completely around the top or front cover, then partly around the bottom or back cover. When sewing to the bottom or back cover, leave a space for inserting the filling (Sec. 17:07F). After filling, blind-stitch boxing to cover. For this type casing, the same size boxing is used throughout (Sec. 11:18C).

SEC. 17:06B MODERN CASING / In so-called modern cushions and pillows (Sec. 3:00C), instead of leaving a space when sewing boxing to the bottom or back cover, sew a zipper in the boxing (Fig. 17:06B).

Fig. 17:06B

The zipper opening should be about 1 inch longer than the space left for filling traditional casings (Sec. 17:07D); location is the same except that the zipper is midway between casing covers. Top quality upholsterers use zippers partly to save time but mainly because machine sewing usually looks better than hand stitching. Zippered boxing is prepared differently than traditional (Sec. 17:06C).

NOTE: Furniture buyers may be told that boxing is zippered so that the filling can easily be removed and the casing cleaned. Don't try it! Filling is extremely difficult to remove and replace, and the cleaned casing will not match the uncleaned parts of an article.

SEC. 17:06C BOXING FOR ZIPPERED CASINGS / Zippered cushion and pillow casings have two types of boxing. [1] *Regular boxing* encompasses the covers except where the zipper goes. In custom upholstering regular boxing usually is about 3 inches wider (Sec. 11:18C, D, E) than is actually needed in order to cover the ends of the zipper boxing, Fig. 17:06C. The length of regular boxing for a zippered casing is the same as for traditional casing. [2] *Zipper boxing replaces the space left for filling* traditional casing (Sec. 17:07F). However, zipper boxing usually is about 2 inches wider than the space left in traditional work and 1 inch longer than the regular boxing for the casing.

SEC. 17:06D ZIPPER / Dress and suit zippers usually are not satisfactory for cushions and pillows. As a rule they are too weak, and it is difficult to get them in the necessary lengths. Most zippers used by

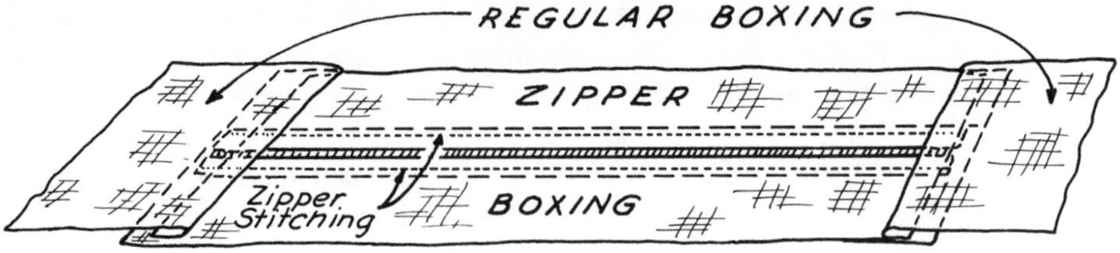

Fig. 17:06C

upholstery shops are made up for the job. Zipper material comes in a roll of one row of teeth. Two lengths are cut and assembled with a slide fastener, then sewn to the boxing. Unless a sewing machine can handle three or four thicknesses of cover goods, usually it is advisable to have cushions and pillows made by an upholstery shop.

Sec. 17:06E   Prepare Zipper Boxing /   [*1*] *Cut zipper boxing* midway between top and bottom (Sec. 11:18C).   [*2*] *Install zipper* (Sec. 17:06D), sewing one length to the upper side of the bottom strip of boxing, the other to the lower side of the upper strip.   [*3*] *Close zipper*. The completed zipper boxing probably is a little longer than the regular boxing. Center the zipper line between top and bottom of the regular boxing; trim to the same length as the regular boxing. [*4*] *Sew boxing* to covers (Secs. 17:07A, F).

SEC. 17:07 SEWING CUSHION CASINGS

Sec. 17:07A /   In most seat cushions, welt is sewn first to covers, then to boxing, the generally preferred and neater method. But sometimes it is more practical to use self-welted boxing (Sec. 17:08).   [*1*] *Sew welt around each cover* (Secs. 12:06, 12:07) to about 2 inches from each side of the planned joining point, usually at the middle of a back but sometimes on a side. Join welt ends.   [*2*] *If using fringe instead of welt*, sew it to the right side of the cover the same as welt. Join the ends of fringe with a short overlap, preferably at a back corner.

Sec. 17:07B   Traditional Casing /   Sew boxing to welted or fringed top cover. Center boxing at the middle of the front edge of the cover, and sew first to one side, then to the other. When piecing (Secs. 11:02, 12:02) boxing, fold seam allowances of both strips toward the front of a seat casing, top of a back casing to simplify filling it. Join ends of boxing with a flat seam, preferably at the middle of the back.

Sec. 17:07C /   Set boxing to welted or fringed bottom cover. Unless boxing and covers are exactly aligned at the corners, the finished cushion probably will wrinkle badly there.   [*1*] *Follow a thread* of fabric boxing at each front corner from top to bottom. For plastic, leather, and other nonwoven goods, locate the exact corner at the top cover, and at this point fold boxing back on itself wrong-side-to-wrong-side. Align bottom edges; if boxing was cut straight, the upper corner is now transferred to the bottom edge.   [*2*] *Locate exact corner of bottom cover,* pin to boxing corner.   [*3*] *Pin boxing and bottom cover* together at enough points along the front to prevent slippage or misalignment of the casing parts.   [*4*] *Often there is excess cover or boxing between corners.* A small excess usually is eliminated by slightly stretching or compressing the goods. A large excess indicates that top and bottom corners are not aligned or that top and bottom covers are not identical in shape and/or size; rip out the large one, rewelt or refringe it.

SEC. 17:07D / Sew boxing and bottom cover together. First sew along front from corner to corner. Then align each front corner with the next adjacent corner (Sec. 17:07C), and sew from the front to that corner. Continue aligning corners and sewing to them. How far around bottom cover to sew boxing depends on the cushion filling and how it will be put in a casing.   [*1*] *Down, kapok:* Sew boxing to bottom cover along each side and far enough across the back to leave a space about 10 inches wide.   [*2*] *Inner-spring, foam rubber, polyfoam, spring-down units to be inserted by irons* (Sec. 2:14) *or a machine:* Sew boxing to bottom cover along sides to points about 5 inches from back corners.   [*3*] *Inner-spring, foam rubber, polyfoam, spring-down units to be inserted by hand only, and for hair, natural cotton, synthetic cotton fillings:* Sew boxing to bottom cover to points about 2 inches behind front corners of a plain cushion, 1 inch behind front tabs of T-shaped and similar cushions.

SEC. 17:07E PROTECTIVE SEWING / If a casing is a loose weave, run a line of long-stitch sewing, to prevent raveling, in all parts of boxing not sewn to a cover. Sew about ¼ inch from the edge. Cushion casing is now ready for filling (Secs. 17:12, 17:13).

SEC. 17:07F MODERN CASING / For cushions and pillows with zippered boxing (Secs. 17:06C, E), sew boxing and covers together the same as for traditional casings, above, except where the regular overlaps zippered boxing (Figs. 17:06B, C).   [*1*] *Pin zipper boxing in place* along the back of a welted or fringed top cover of a seat cushion, and around the back corners if necessary, to leave the necessary insertion opening (Sec. 17:07D).   [*2*] *Sew regular boxing* to top cover (Sec. 17:07B) except where it meets the pinned zipper boxing. Note, in Figs. 17:06B, C, that regular boxing finishes on top of zipper boxing and that regular boxing is ended by folding it back under itself. [*3*] *Unpin zipper boxing*, and align top edges of regular and zipper boxings with those of the welt or cover. Smooth boxings in place; with goods wrong-side-up for sewing, regular boxing is on top of the welt or cover, and zipper boxing is on top of the regular. [*4*] *Sew boxings, welt, and cover together* to a point about ½ inch beyond the start of the zipper boxing. [*5*] *Underturn end of regular boxing* about ¼ to ½ inch, and complete sewing boxings in place. [*6*] *Pin and sew boxings* to bottom cover, [*1*] through [*5*] above.

**SEC. 17:08
SELF-WELTED
BOXING**

Sec. 17:08A / In self-welted boxing, as in Fig. 17:08A, welt, usually a separate item, is made by folding the top and bottom edges of boxing around welt cord and sewing it (Sec. 12:06). Self-welted boxing is advisable only for a striped cover goods or if a sewing machine cannot handle four thicknesses of cover. A self-welted boxing cushion or pillow is not as neat, due to two rows of stitching showing on the boxing, as those welted the usual way, but it allows for perfect alignment of stripes in boxing and cover at the front and back. If self-welting must be done because of the sewing machine, it is advisable to have the casing made by an upholstery shop; the charge usually is small and the extra neatness of the casing well worth it. For self-welted boxing add to the planned length of regular boxing (Sec. 11:18E) ½ inch at top and bottom for welt cord up to $5/16$-inch diameter (Sec. 11:08C[*1*]). Width of boxing depends on the cover (Sec. 17:08B).

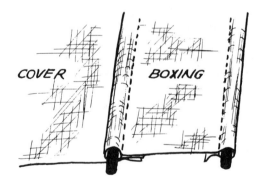

COVER   BOXING

Fig. 17:08A

Sec. 17:08B Traditional Casing / To self-welt boxing for a traditionally made casing, first fold the edge of a boxing right-side-out around the welt cord for a ½-inch seam allowance (Fig. 17:08A). Sew close to cord, but not tight against it, to leave space for another stitching, between the first and the cord. Piece strips of boxing as necessary (Sec. 17:07A[*1*]). Prepare enough boxing for entire casing. [*1*] *Nonstriped goods.* Prepare enough boxing to encompass casing with an overlap of about 2 inches at the joining point. For seat cushions, this usually is at the middle of the back of a casing; for back cushions and pillows, at the middle of the bottom. [2] *Striped goods.* For a seat cushion, prepare two strips of boxing: one to be centered across the front, the other across the back of a casing; allow a 2-inch overlap for joining boxings at the middle of each side. For a back pillow or cushion, prepare enough boxing to encompass the casing with a 2-inch overlap at the joining point, usually at the middle of the bottom. Center boxing at the middle of the top end of the casing.

SEC. 17:08C SEWING / Center self-welted boxing, right-side-up, on the right side of the front of the top cover (Fig. 17:08A) of a seat cushion, at the top of the front cover of a back cushion or pillow. Align edges of cover and welt seam allowance. Sew between first welt stitching and welt cord, but not through cord. Turn corners (Sec. 13:02B); join ends (Sec. 17:07A[1]). [1] *Nonstriped goods.* Start at righthand side or back of cover, sew to joining point. [2] *Striped goods seat cushion.* Sew from the middle of the front edge of the cover to the point of joining at a side; then sew from the middle to the other point of joining. Sew other boxing the same way from middle of back edge to joining points. Join boxings; be sure joint is straight. [3] *Striped goods back pillow, cushion.* Sew first to one side, then the other from middle of top to joining point, usually at the middle of bottom. [4] *Sew self-welted boxing* to bottom cover of seat cushion, back cover of back cushion or pillow, essentially the same as above. Corners of cover and boxing must be aligned but cannot be pinned together. Where possible, mark exact corner of boxing with a large pin or upholstery skewer (Sec. 2:08), and set it to the exact pivot point of the corner of the bottom or back cover. Sew boxing and cover to the points in Sec. 17:07D.

SEC. 17:08D MODERN CASING / Prepare and install self-welted boxing on modern cushion and pillow casings almost the same as on traditional. Prepare two strips of boxing. One is regular boxing; the other may be zipper boxing only (Secs. 17:06C, E) or a combination of zipper and regular boxings, depending on width of opening needed for inserting a filling. [1] *Self-welt regular and zipper boxings* (Sec. 17:08B) but only after placement (Sec. 17:08E) of boxings on cover has been determined. [2] *Where regular boxing finishes over zipper boxing* (Figs. 17:06B, C), align edges of boxings. Smooth boxings into place, with zipper boxing next to welt cord, and sew them together to about ¼ inch beyond start of zipper boxing; then underturn ¼ to ½ inch of the end of the regular boxing, and complete sewing.

SEC. 17:08E PLACEMENT / Pin zipper boxing in place along the back of the top cover of a seat cushion, the bottom of the front cover of a back cushion or pillow, and around the back or side corners if necessary, to set insertion opening in place (Sec. 17:07D).   [*1*] *Non-striped goods.* Prepare enough regular boxing to encompass cover with 1½ inches overlap at each end of the zipper boxing.   [*2*] *Striped goods seat cushion.* Prepare two strips of boxing. One, centered along front of cover, usually is regular boxing. The other, centered along back of cover, usually is a combination of regular and zipper boxings (Secs. 17:06C, E); regular boxing extends from 1½ inches inside ends of zipper boxing to where front and back boxings will join, usually at the middle of each side. Allow a 2-inch overlap for joining boxings.   [*3*] *Striped goods back pillow, cushion.* Prepare enough boxing to encompass cover with an overlap of 1½ inches at each end of zipper boxing. Center boxing at the middle of the top end of cover.

NOTE: When aligning stripes in boxing, it is more important to get a perfect fit where they are pieced or joined than where regular boxing overlaps zipper boxing. Normally, overlaps will not be seen but joinings may be quite noticeable.

SEC. 17:09 TICKINGS

SEC. 17:09A   /   Particles of down and other fillings may be fine enough to work through fabrics and through stitchings of casings made of plastics, leather, glazed weaves, and other so-called airtight goods. To prevent this, certain fillings should be in tickings (Sec. 17:03B). Handle down-proof ticking (Sec. 3:62B) carefully and avoid making tight creases in it; these could break the coating and allow filling to work out.

SEC. 17:09B   DOWN-PROOF TICKINGS   /   Down-proof tickings for upholstery cushions and pillows should have boxing between top and bottom, or front and back, covers. Tickings should be at least 1 inch larger overall than a casing; if a ticking is not larger, the down cannot completely fill and shape a casing. When sewing, set goods coated-side-to-coated-side; sew with short stitches and a ½-inch seam allowance. If ticking seams are not tight, down may work through them and eventually through the casing.   [*1*] *For small cushions* a plain ticking is satisfactory (Sec. 17:09C).   [*2*] *For large cushions and most back pillows* use a partitioned ticking (Sec. 17:09D).   [*3*] *For spring-down cushions* use a partitioned ticking pad (Sec. 17:09E).

SEC. 17:09C   PLAIN TICKING   /   Sew boxing and covers together, leaving an 8 or 9 inch space between them to insert filling. Do not pull ticking inside out (Sec. 17:09B) after sewing; seam allowances are needed outside for sewing a ticking closed after filling it.

SEC. 17:09D   REGULAR PARTITIONED TICKING   /   Cut covers, boxing, and partitions. Partitions are usually 6 to 9 inches apart and go from side to side, Fig. 17:09D. At their ends, partitions are the same height as boxing; they increase smoothly in height until, about 5 inches from the ends, they are twice the height of boxing. Add 1 inch in height throughout all partitions, and to length, for seam allowances. Sew boxings, covers, and partitions together any convenient way. [*1*] *Mark both covers* for locations of partitions. [*2*] *Sew boxing* completely around one cover; sew ends of boxing together. [*3*] *Sew partitions* to boxing and cover, *a*. [*4*] *Sew other cover* to partitions, *b*, then to boxing along a side and both ends of ticking. Leave one side open for filling ticking. [*5*] *After filling* (Sec. 17:09G), sew ticking closed. The ticking seam allowances being on the outside is all right.

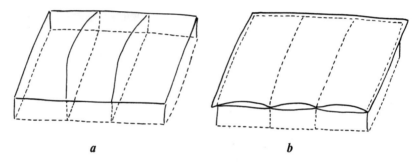

Fig. 17:09D   *a*   *b*

SEC. 17:09E PARTITIONED TICKING PAD / The pad needed to keep down-filling in place around an inner-spring unit (Sec. 3:63C) must be large enough to cover it loosely top and bottom and fold over to encompass the front, back, and sides, Fig. *a* 17:09E. An easy-to-make

Fig. a 17:09E

pad, consisting of two partitioned tickings joined by boxing, is diagrammed in *b*. Prepare and fill each ticking as in Sec. 17:09D except that instead of boxing, sew the top and bottom covers together, Fig. *a* 17:09E. Each ticking is the same shape as the top of a seat or front of a back cushion casing but 2½ inches larger all around—front, back, each side—to allow for foldover and seams.

Boxing — *Partitioned Tickings* — *Boxing*

Fig. b 17:09E

SEC. 17:09F / The completed tickings are 3 inches apart vertically (Fig. b 17:09E); the spring unit goes between them, [3] below. [1] *Cut enough muslin boxing* to encompass tickings—sides, front, back. It should be 5 inches high to allow for thicknesses of both tickings, the space between for the spring unit, plus ½ inch top and bottom for seam allowances. [2] *Starting at a back corner,* sew muslin boxing completely around upper ticking. Sew boxing the same way to lower ticking except that it is not sewn across the back until after inserting the spring unit. [3] *Starting and ending at the back,* wrap two layers of felted padding around inner-spring unit. Work padding from top and bottom in place along sides of unit. Compress wrapped unit enough by hand to insert it between the tickings. [4] *Sew muslin boxing* shut across back to lower ticking.

SEC. 17:09G STUFF TICKING / If ticking is partitioned, fill partitions evenly. As a rule, less down is needed than inexperienced upholsterers expect, since it is quite puffy; if too much is used, a cushion or pillow will be solid and hard instead of resilient. When apparently enough down has been inserted, pin ticking closed and beat it with both fists to help distribute filling evenly. A cushion or pillow that is filled with enough top quality down does not flatten appreciably from use.

NOTE: A convenient way to fill a down-proof ticking is to tie it over the bag connection of a vacuum cleaner and blow in the down. Be sure to tie ticking tightly to the vacuum cleaner. If it becomes loose, down will be blown around freely; it is quite difficult to pick up.

SEC. 17:10
KAPOK

Prepare and fill a muslin casing for a kapok cushion or pillow the same as for a down-filled one (Sec. 17:09). Partitioned tickings usually are for back pillows only.

**SEC. 17:11
INNER-SPRING
UNIT**

Sec. 17:11A / Simplify stuffing an inner-spring cushion by hand (Sec. 17:13) by using a muslin casing similar to a down-proof ticking (Sec. 17:09C). It should be at least 1 inch larger overall than the cushion casing. Sew boxing completely around one ticking cover; sew ends of boxing together. Sew the front edge of the other ticking cover from corner to corner to boxing.

Sec. 17:11B Fill Ticking / Spread three layers of top quality felted padding from back to front in boxed ticking; they should be long enough to reach, without excessive stretching, up over the spring unit at the front and back to join padding at the back of a ticking. [1] *T-shaped and similar cushions:* Pack wads of padding or kapok firmly into front tabs. [2] *Spread a moderately thick layer of top quality hair stuffing* (Secs. 5:11A–C) over area to be covered by spring unit; put more toward the center of the area to build necessary crown. [3] *Set spring unit in place* on hair. Center unit between sides of ticking but 1 or 2 inches nearer the front than the back. [4] *Spread hair* over top of unit, [2] above. [5] *Draw padding back over spring unit* a layer at a time. Fold each layer neatly in place with the other padding along the sides and back of the ticking. Additional padding may be needed along sides and back to fill them out evenly with the front; fold extra padding into rolls of the proper size, and fit them in place.

Sec. 17:11C Close Ticking / Draw ticking cover over padding, disturbing it as little as possible, and pin in place along sides and back of boxing. Padding and spring unit must be compressed in order for the cover to reach boxing at all points. Push straight down gently but firmly with an open hand, and draw cover and boxing together and pin them for a few inches; then move the hand compressing padding and spring unit, and pin along for a few more inches. When ticking is pinned shut all around, sew it with a simple overhand whip stitch.

**SEC. 17:12
NATURAL,
SYNTHETIC
COTTON**

Sec. 17:12A / Cotton cushion and pillow fillings consist of a cotton core wrapped with three layers of cotton. Cotton filling can be put directly into a casing, but inexperienced upholsterers usually get better results by first putting it in a ticking when a casing will be stuffed by hand (Sec. 17:13). Prepare ticking (Sec. 17:11). [1] *T-shaped and similar casings.* Pack wads of cotton firmly into front or other tabs. [2] *Prepare cotton core.* This is several layers of felted cotton that, except for tabs of T-shaped and similar casings, are the size and shape of the top cover of a seat cushion, front cover of a back cushion or pillow casing. How many layers to use depends on desired thickness and firmness of the cushion or pillow and thickness of cotton. As a rule, a stack of core layers about five times the height of a casing boxing will compress to a satisfactory thickness. To test, push straight down with an open hand on the middle of the top layer; the stack should feel fairly firm when pressed down to about the height of the boxing. Do not hold cotton down for an appreciable length of time—just long enough to feel if more or less is needed.

NOTE: Instead of a cotton core, either foam rubber, polyfoam, or rubberized hair may be used (Sec. 17:12B).

[3] *Spread three layers of felted cotton in ticking from back to front.* They should be long enough to reach, without excessive stretching, up over the cotton core at the front and back to join the layers of padding at the back. [4] *Place core on padding in ticking,* centered between front, back, and sides. [5] *Complete installation* of padding (Sec. 17:11B[5]); close ticking (Sec. 17:11C).

SEC. 17:12B / Due to cost and because it may be too soft for real comfort, synthetic cotton cushions and pillows often have a core of foam rubber, polyfoam, or rubberized hair (Secs. 17:18B, H).

SEC. 17:13
LOOSE,
RUBBERIZED
HAIR

SEC. 17:13A / Hair cushions and pillows are used more for benches than chairs and sofas, although they are somewhat common in so-called modern loose-cushion upholstery (Sec. 17:23). Hair units generally are quite firm, have moderate resilience, and are relatively flat. Thickness and crown are optional. [1] *Loose hair filling* usually is made into a pad (Sec. 17:13B). It may be incased by a ticking (Sec. 17:11) except that no loose hair is needed to pad the surface. Or a hair pad may be placed directly in a casing (Sec. 17:14). [2] *Rubberized hair* should be incased by a ticking (Sec. 17:11) by inexperienced upholsterers when stuffing a casing by hand only. [3] *Hair filling* of either type usually is about 1 inch smaller in length, width, and height than the casing.

SEC. 17:13B HAIR PAD / In addition to other tools and materials, a double-pointed straight needle and stitching twine are needed (Secs. 2:06, 3:08). [1] *Prepare a plain* hair-proof ticking (Secs. 3:64, 17:09C) the proper size and shape (Sec. 17:13A), but leave an end open for filling it. [2] *Fill ticking,* Fig. 17:13B. Install loose hair by felting it (Sec. 5:11B), build up small sections at a time, alternating between sides of ticking and working toward the middle; fill from closed to open end. Build a rather firm pad of the same density throughout. Usually the middle of a pad has a noticeable amount of crown (Sec.

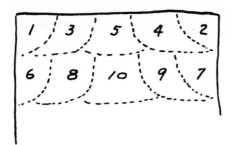

Fig. 17:13B

5:14). How much filling is needed depends on its quality and resilience and how firm a pad is meant to be. Test by pressing it down with open hands to the wanted thickness. The pad should be quite firm; if weak or flimsy it will not hold shape. When ticking is filled, stitch it shut.   [3] *Stitch pad* (Sec. 6:05G) in a regular pattern to pull filling down to the planned height and to hold it in shape throughout. Usually these "buttoning" points are 5 to 6 inches apart in parallel rows; enclose a small wad of padding with each loop of twine.   [4] *Shape and strengthen sides of pad* by stitching (Sec. 10:25); make stitches showing on sides parallel to top and bottom of boxing. Usually there are two rows of stitching, one slanting toward the top, the other toward the bottom cover. Locate stitching points by drawing four parallel lines equally spaced between and from top and bottom of boxing; stitch along the two middle lines.

SEC. 17:13C IMPERIAL STITCH / To strengthen the upper and lower edges of a pad more than about 4 inches thick at the boxing, it may be necessary to Imperial stitch them, Fig. 17:13C.   [1] *On the top cover* draw a line parallel to the boxing and located the same distance from the boxing as the seam is from the uppermost line drawn for shaping the sides (Sec. 17:13B[4].   [2] *Draw a similar line* on the bottom cover.   [3] *Stitch between cover and boxing lines.* Jab a straight needle through the pad from one line to the other, pull clear and stitch back 1½ inches to the right, and pull clear; shift 1½ inches

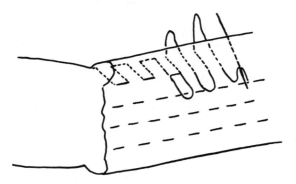

Fig. 17:13C

to right and start next stitch. Stitch completely around pad, shaping the edge by hand while stitching. Usually it is necessary to adjust the shape in places when stitching is completed; tighten or loosen twine accordingly stitch by stitch around a pad. Tie start and finish ends of twine together.

SEC. 17:14 **STUFF CASING**	**SEC. 17:14A STUFF BY HAND ONLY** / A casing stuffed by hand only need not in any way be inferior to one stuffed by hand-irons (Sec. 2:14) or a machine. How it is done depends on the filling and its preparation. After being stuffed, traditional casings are blind-stitched closed (Secs. 17:14B, C); with modern casings (Sec. 17:06), pull zipper. Regardless of filling and method of stuffing a casing, additional padding usually is needed in tabs of T-shaped and similar casings. [1] *Down, kapok filled tickings:* Insert directly in casing; they usually can be compressed easily by hand to fit through a small opening. [2] *Inner-spring unit in ticking:* Insert directly in casing; additional padding may be needed along sides and back. [3] *Inner-spring unit without ticking:* Insert with padding and hair into casing the same as filling ticking (Sec. 17:11). The disadvantage to this method, especially for inexperienced upholsterers, is the damage that may be done a casing by the greater amount of pinning usually needed. [4] *Foam rubber, polyfoam units:* Usually inserted directly in casing. As a rule they are 1 to 2 inches longer, wider, and thicker than a casing, and no padding is needed except for tabs of T-shaped and similar casings (Sec. 17:11B[1]). For extra softness and puffiness, wrap a layer or two of felted polyester padding (Sec. 3:49) around unit before insertion; if natural cotton is used, the cushion or pillow will be made slightly harder.

NOTE: Use padding if casing is velvet or any other pile fabric or a plastic and there is a possibility that it will react to foam rubber or polyfoam (Sec. 3:53B[3]).

[5] *Spring-down unit:* Insert directly in casing.   [6] *Natural, synthetic cotton in ticking:* Insert directly in casing.   [7] *Natural, synthetic cotton without ticking:* Insert in casing the same as filling ticking (Sec. 17:11); for disadvantage see [3] above.   [8] *Hair filling in ticking:* Insert directly in casing.   [9] *Hair filling without ticking:* To suppress scratchy noise that hair filling usually makes and to keep hair from working out of a casing, wrap a unit with at least two layers of top quality felted padding. Synthetic makes a softer article than natural cotton padding. Except that no additional hair is needed, install padding and hair unit in casing (Sec. 17:11B); for disadvantage see [3] above.

SEC. 17:14B CLOSING: DOWN, KAPOK CUSHIONS, PILLOWS / Stretch bottom cover and boxing with cushion-closing equalizer (Sec. 2:13). Pin boxing and cover together at enough points to prevent slippage. Blind-stitch shut (Sec. 13:04).

Sec. 17:14C Closing: Inner-spring, Foam Rubber, Polyfoam, Spring-Down, Cotton, Hair Cushions, Pillows

/ [1] *Draw cover over filling*, usually padded, disturbing it as little as possible. Pin cover to boxing, Fig. 17:14C, throughout casing. [2] *Loosen a side of the casing*, check corners of cover and boxing for alignment. If they are not properly aligned, loosen entire cover and boxing, and repin. [3] *When loosened side*, above, is properly set, stretch it with cushion-closing equalizer (Sec. 2:13). Repin cover and boxing at enough points to prevent slippage. Blind-stitch (Sec. 13:04) cover and boxing together from the front to a couple of inches from the back corner. [4] *Repeat* [3] *above* on other side of casing. Use twine long enough to go around the back corner and across back to the other corner. [5] *Place cushion or pillow on flat surface*, rub top and bottom covers with a slapping action from the front edge toward the back of a seat cushion, from top edge toward bottom of a back pillow cushion or pillow, to work filling toward the front or top where it is most needed. [6] *Beat cushion or pillow hard with both fists* to pack padding and locate any hollow areas. Fill these by loosening casing at the back or bottom then folding a large-enough wad of padding around the fingertips or end of a yardstick and pushing it into place. [7] *Additional padding* may be needed along the back or bottom in front corners, and in tabs of T-shaped and similar casings. Corners especially should be smooth, firm, and moderately hard. Depending

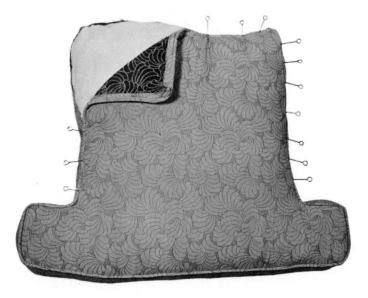

Fig. 17:14C

upon the casing goods, padding may be regulated (Sec. 5:07) into corners; but because padding will pack into hard lumps, regulate carefully. Do not attempt to regulate a spring-down filling. [8] *Align back corners* of boxing and cover. Stretch with cushion-closing equalizer, pin at enough points to prevent slippage, and blind-stitch shut. Complete blind-stitching of first side, [3] above, to corner and into other stitching.

SEC. 17:15 **STUFF BY** **HAND-IRONS,** **MACHINE**	The mechanics of filling a casing by hand-irons or machine are in Sec. 2:14. Here are the preparatory and follow-up work-steps. *NOTE: A ticking may be necessary to contain a filling, such as down, but not for inserting a filling in a casing by hand-irons or a machine.* [1] *Down, kapok cushions, pillows:* Usually insert by hand (Sec. 17:14A). [2] *Inner-spring unit:* Arrange felted padding, hair, spring unit in hand-irons or machine (Sec. 17:11). [3] *Foam rubber, poly-foam unit:* Place directly in hand-irons or machine without padding, unless it is wanted for special purpose (Sec. 17:14A[4]). [4] *Spring-down unit:* Place directly in hard-irons or machine without padding. [5] *Hair units:* Place at least two layers of felted padding (Sec. 17:14A[8]) in hand-irons or machine. [6] *Natural, synthetic cotton unit:* Place directly in hand-irons or machine without padding. [7] *T-shaped or similar casing:* Before filling, stuff tabs of casing with felted cotton or kapok. They should be firm, smooth, and moderately hard. [8] *Insert filling* in casing (Sec. 2:14). [9] *Align back corners* of cover and boxing; stretch with cushion-closing equalizer (Sec. 2:13). Pin boxing and cover together at enough points to prevent slippage. Blind-stitch (Sec. 13:04) boxing to cover; complete as in Sec. 17:14C[5]–[7].
SEC. 17:16 **PILLOWS**	Back pillows usually are more difficult than seat cushions to build for a neat, smooth fit into a chair or other article. To avoid waste of cover goods due to cutting a casing too small, inexperienced upholsterers should build and stuff the ticking (Secs. 17:09–17:13) before starting the pillow casing. Whether a back pillow rests on the deck or on top of a seat cushion is for the upholsterer to decide; it usually extends an inch or so above the top of the back.
SEC. 17:17 **DOWN, KAPOK** **BACK PILLOWS**	SEC. 17:17A / These usually are not boxed across the top; instead, front and back covers are sewn together from corner to corner. Boxing may be omitted on sides and bottom (Fig. 1:34), but pillows usually seem neater when boxed (Figs. 1:43, *b* 1:46, *a* 1:55). Secs. 17:17B–F are for preparing and filling tickings; except for dimensions and that

the seams usually are welted or fringed (Sec. 17:07), ticking and casing are about the same. A ticking usually is several inches wider and longer than seems necessary. It must be at least 1 inch larger overall than the casing to allow the filling to fill the casing without restraint; however, ticking larger than this does not spoil the looks or comfort of a pillow. [1] *After completing a ticking,* set it in place on an article and note carefully how it fits; if it is too narrow or short, additional pieces of ticking may be sewn to the original and filled. [2] *When ticking is satisfactory,* cut a paper pattern from the front cover, and on it mark all dimensions, locations of cuts, pleats, etc. Mark pattern accurately; it will be the guide for cutting the pillow casing.

Sec. 17:17B Prepare Ticking / Cut front and back pillow ticking covers the approximate shape of an inside back. [1] *Boxed pillow:* Ticking covers are at least 3 inches wider than the greatest distance between breaks from the inner to the side surfaces of a back and are 3 inches longer than the greatest length between top of seat cushion and break from the inner to top surface of a back. [2] *Plain pillow:* Ticking covers are at least 7 inches wider than the greatest distance between breaks from the inner to the side surfaces of a back, plus allowance for pillow thickness (Sec. 11:19), and are 7 inches longer than the greatest length between top of seat cushion and break from the inner to top surface of a back, plus allowance for pillow thickness.

Sec. 17:17C / Mark one ticking cover "front" on the wrong side. [1] *Place it smoothly* right-side-up on inside back. Press it lightly against all junctions of back, wings, arms, and seat cushion. [2] *Hold a stick of chalk vertically* and make a series of short dashes along junctions. Also mark cover along upper portions of a back and along breaks from inner to top and side surfaces. [3] *Remove cover and blend chalkmarks* into smooth, regular lines that should be the same on right and left halves of the cover. Differences usually are small enough to compromise or adjust into identical lines. Large differences in outline nearly always are due to inaccurate marking. [4] *Boxed pillow:* Cut ticking cover parallel to, but at least 1 inch outside, the sides and bottom of the corrected inside back outline, Fig. *a* 17:17C, and 1½ to 2½ inches above the top line; this includes ½-inch seam allowances. [5] *Plain pillow:* Mark pillow thickness-allowance outline outside and parallel to the corrected inside back outline, *b.* Cut ticking cover parallel to, but 3 to 3½ inches outside, the pillow thickness outline.

Sec. 17:17D / Cut ticking boxing for sides and bottom of back pillow and also for top if it is to be boxed. Boxing should be at least 2 inches wider than the planned thickness of a pillow at its edges.

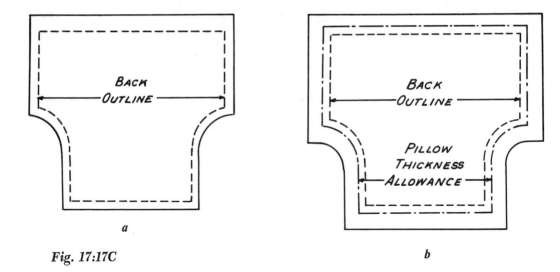

Fig. 17:17C   *b*

[1] *Top boxed:* A pillow boxed across the top may be thicker at the bottom than the top, thickness gradually increasing from top to bottom. Unless there is an appreciable difference between top and bottom thickness, adjusting ticking boxing is not necessary. [2] *Top plain:* From any desirable point, usually 3 or 4 inches below top corners of a back pillow, taper boxing toward the middle of the side, Fig. *a* 17:17D; leave a 1-inch wide tab at the top for sewing boxing to covers. Shape of taper is optional.

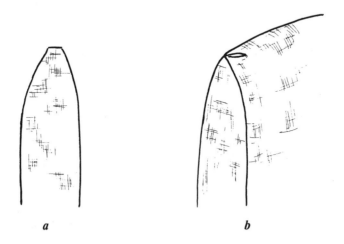

Fig. 17:17D   *a*   *b*

SEC. 17:17E   SEW, FILL PILLOW TICKING / (Secs. 17:09A–D, G, 17:10). [1] *Top boxed:* Assemble, sew, and fill. [2] *Top plain:* Before sewing ticking, pleat (Sec. 5:17) front and back covers at top corners to take up excess goods when stitched to the tapered top of the boxing (Fig. *b* 17:17D). To form pleats, fold goods right-side-to-right-side over itself, align edges, and sew from edges toward fold, Fig. 17:17E. The angles of sewing and of the seam in relation to the fold shape the finished pleat. The pleat line from the inner surface of a cover to the corner or edge should be square or rounded (Fig. *b* 17:17D), not pointed or acute. Especially when using down-proof ticking, inexperienced upholsterers should experiment with a scrap of muslin first. Cut off excess goods ½ inch beyond pleat line. Assemble, sew, and fill ticking.   [3] *Plain pillow:* Pleat, [2] above, all corners of front and back ticking covers that are to be stitched together without boxing. Assemble, sew, and fill ticking with or without partitions. Partitions are cut and installed as for a boxed ticking except that they taper to about 1-inch widths at the ends for stitching to the sides of the front and back covers. However, most plain pillow tickings are not partitioned.

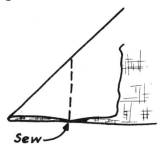

Fig. 17:17E   Sew

Sec. 17:17F Casing / Set completed ticking in article, and prepare paper pattern for front cover of casing (Sec. 17:17A). [1] *Cut pattern* with ½-inch seam allowances throughout cover; cut front and back casing covers. [2] *Cut boxing* for planned width or thickness of a pillow at its edges plus ½-inch seam allowances front and back. If the top of a pillow will be thinner than the bottom or if the top is not boxed, adjust side boxings accordingly. Self-welted boxing may be used (Sec. 17:08).

Sec. 17:17G / Assemble and sew casing essentially the same as a ticking except that there are no partitions. Sew welt or fringe to covers (Sec. 17:07) when boxed, to front cover only where not boxed. [1] *Boxed pillow, top boxed:* Sew boxing to front cover, encompassing it and joining ends at, preferably, the middle of the bottom. Center striped goods at the top (Sec. 17:08A). Sew back cover to boxing, leaving a 12- to 14-inch gap or space at the bottom for inserting the down- or kapok-filled ticking. [2] *Boxed pillow, top plain:* Starting at top corners, sew boxing to front cover for 5 or 6 inches; then sew front and back covers together completely across top. Finish sewing boxing to front cover; join ends at, preferably, the middle of the bottom. Starting at top corners, sew back cover to boxing, leaving the necessary space at or near the bottom to insert filling.   [3] *Plain pillow:* Sew covers together, leaving a space at or near the bottom to insert filling.   [4] *Fill casing, and close* (Sec. 17:14).

SEC. 17:18
PILLOW
CONSTRUC-
TION

Sec. 17:18A / Back pillows and cushions may rest on the deck or on top of a seat cushion. Measure length or height from the deck or top of a seat cushion to an inch or more above the top of a back. Back pillows and cushions usually are as wide as, or slightly wider than, the inside back. Some kinds of back pillows and cushions are more likely than others to be boxed across the top.

Sec. 17:18B Down, Kapok Pillows / These are essentially the same as down and kapok seat cushions. They may or may not be boxed across the top. Follow construction of a down or kapok seat cushion (Secs. 17:09, 17:10), treating the top of a pillow as the front of a seat cushion.

Sec. 17:18C Inner-Spring Pillow / The inner-spring back pillow, often called back cushion, is essentially the same as an inner-spring seat cushion. Almost without exception, inner-spring pillows are boxed across the top. Build as a boxed seat cushion (Secs. 17:14, 17:15), treating the top of the pillow as the front of a seat cushion.

Sec. 17:18D Foam Rubber, Polyfoam Pillows / These may or may not be boxed across the top. Before building casing, prepare a foam rubber or polyfoam unit the desired shape of a pillow but at least 1 inch longer, wider, and thicker throughout.   [1] *Boxed portions:* For all boxed parts, make the sides of a unit straight and square to the top and bottom surfaces.   [2] *Plain portions:* Shape these surfaces (such as the top, sides, and bottom of an unboxed pillow) by first building a unit with all sides straight and square to the top and bottom surfaces. Then cut a V-shaped trough of the necessary width and depth to make the desired slope or taper from front and back surfaces to the edges of a pillow. Bond sides of trough together (Sec. 3:46).   [3] *Prepare and make casing* (Sec. 17:17) using the shaped unit as a pattern for it. However, pillow casing should be at least 1 inch less in length, width, and thickness than the unit. Also, be sure to leave casing a ½-inch seam allowance throughout. Self-welted boxing may be used (Sec. 17:08). Sew casing (Sec. 17:07), fill, and close (Sec. 17:14).

Sec. 17:18E Natural, Synthetic Cotton Pillows / Natural cotton filled pillows generally are not practical as, after relatively little use, the cotton tends to pack into hard lumps and then break into almost a powder. But synthetic cotton, such as polyester fiber, is an excellent although costly pillow filling. However, its high degree of softness, which makes it so comfortable for many people, may make it very uncomfortable for others.

Sec. 17:18F / Natural or synthetic cotton may be the only filling (Sec. 17:12) for a pillow. But more often there is a core of foam rubber, polyfoam, or compact rubberized hair in order to have a firmer basic shape. The core often is 4 or 5 inches narrower and shorter than the planned size of a pillow and only 2 or 3 inches thick. Carefully wrap loose layers of felted natural or synthetic cotton padding around core to build a unit the desired shape of a pillow but 3 or 4 inches longer, wider, and thicker throughout. The larger size is needed for the filling to help shape a pillow, hold it in shape, and prevent excessive wrinkling of a casing. But if a unit is too much larger than a casing, the filling may become harder than wanted. For this reason it is advisable to make a muslin ticking, fill it, and test it for comfort, firmness, and resilience before filling the casing. According to how the casing will be made—boxed top, sides, bottom; boxed sides, bottom; no boxing—prepare muslin ticking (Sec. 17:17) except: [*1*] *Sew second cover to first,* or to boxing if any, only along top of ticking. [*2*] *Place filling in ticking and close it* (Sec. 17:11C) except that the covers are stitched together if there is no boxing. Before closing ticking permanently, test the upper portions of a flare-type pillow (Fig. 17:17C) for consistent density, softness, and resilience of the filling. [*3*] *Construct casing* (Sec. 17:18D[3]).

Sec. 17:18G Spring-Down Pillow / This is usually boxed top, sides, and bottom. Prepare boxed casing (Secs. 17:05–17:07), and partitioned down-proof ticking pad (Secs. 17:09E, F, G). Insert unit in casing (Secs. 17:14, 17:15).

Sec. 17:18H Loose, Rubberized Hair Pillows / Loose-hair back pillows seldom are made, except for loose-cushion upholstery (Sec. 17:20), because of their hardness, noise, and tendency to pack toward the bottom even when stitched (Sec. 17:13). When there is appreciable packing, hold pillow upside-down and beat it with open hands to shift filling back in place. Compact rubberized hair may be used the same way as a foam rubber or polyfoam unit (Sec. 17:18D), except that plain portions, if any, are shaped by trimming the front and back surfaces for the wanted taper; it may also be used as a core for cotton pillows (Secs. 17:12B, 17:18F) when a soft surface but firm pillow is wanted. Whether or not a hair filling is in a plain ticking (Secs. 17:09B, C), it should be wrapped with felted padding to eliminate its natural scratchy sound. Hair pillows may or may not be boxed top, sides, and bottom; prepare casing accordingly. Insert hair filling in casing (Secs. 17:14, 17:15).

SEC. 17:19 **BUILDING AN** **INNER-SPRING** **UNIT**	**SEC. 17:19A** / Ordinarily, building an inner-spring unit (Sec. 3:63) is not a worthwhile economy. But for an unusually shaped article, it may be necessary as well as practical. Springs in good condition (no distortion, no kinks) may be salvaged from a used unit that is less than about 6 years old; older springs often have lost some resilience. *Tools:* Shears, small curved needle, sewing machine, spring compressor (Secs. 2:04, 2:06, 2:15, 17:19C). *Materials:* Upholstery twine and thread, cushion springs, burlap or muslin (Secs. 3:08, 3:09, 3:15, 3:24, 3:48).

SEC. 17:19B / Sew a strip of spring pockets large enough to hold each spring to the desired height; this usually is about 3½ inches and requires goods about 14 inches wide. Make pockets large enough to hold springs snugly but not so tight that coils press sideways against the goods. Fold goods lengthwise, and sew across for each pocket. Sew all pockets for a row of springs; then leave enough space for the next row to fold back along the preceding row.

SEC. 17:19C / Insert springs in pockets with a cushion spring compressor, Fig. 17:19C, or similarly grooved smooth piece of wood. Hold spring in pocket while removing compressor. After inserting a row of springs, sew pockets shut. Turn springs over inside pockets to press against the closing seam. When all rows are completed, fold them back and forth into the wanted shape of a unit. Stitch top and bottom surfaces (Fig. 3:63B, Sec. 7:18B).

SEC. 17:20 **LOOSE-** **CUSHION** **UPHOLSTERY**	**SEC. 17:20A** / Loose-cushion upholstery (similar to Figs. 1:24–1:26) is practical, easy to do, and can be very comfortable. It is common for home and office as well as garden and patio furniture. Loose-cushion upholstery consists of, and its comfort depends on, the frame, cushion support, and cushions.

SEC. 17:20B FRAME / Most loose-cushion upholstery frames have satisfactory seat slope and back pitch (Sec. 4:00E); adjustable backs are common. Both seat and back usually are open-frame (Sec. 4:01B); for the sake of comfort, a solid-base seat or back would require an exceptionally thick cushion. However, some people prefer a very firm seat and back, and insist cushions be built that way. A wood frame may or may not be covered (Sec. 16:14).

SEC. 17:20C CUSHION SUPPORT / Cushion support in both seat

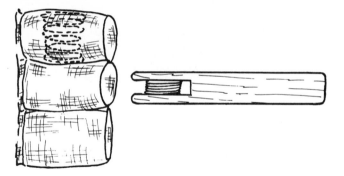

Fig. 17:19C

and back frames can be jute or rubber webbing, plain or spring-held metal strips, elastic ropes, or any other so-called flat spring. Zigzag springs (Sec. 3:21) seldom are used due to their natural crown and possible effect on a cushion casing. The more springy a cushion support is, the more comfortable a seat and back are for most people. However, support generally is somewhat firm; with too much go-down, especially in a seat, an article can be difficult and uncomfortable to get out of. When a frame permits, install jute and rubber strip webbing (Secs. 3:11, 3:22) from side to side and front to back in seats (Sec. 5:01) and bottom to top in backs (Sec. 10:10).

SEC. 17:20D CUSHIONS / Since cushion support is not padded and since for appearance the cushions generally are fairly thin, they are usually somewhat firm basically. Any cushion or pillow filling can be used (Secs. 3:61–3:73), but the most common are foam rubber and polyfoam (Sec. 17:20E). A more complicated filling is rubberized hair compact stuffing incased by foam rubber or polyfoam. For a softer surface, a filling may be wrapped with one or more layers of polyester fiber, with natural cotton for a harder surface (Sec. 3:49); one or the other may be highly advisable (Sec. 17:03C). Seat and back cushions usually are completely boxed; prepare casing, insert filling, close casing (Secs. 17:03–17:08, 17:14, 17:15).

SEC. 17:20E CUSHION FILLINGS / [1] *Foam rubber, polyfoam.* Prepare cushion unit (Sec. 17:14A[4]). It usually is medium to firm density, flat rather than crowned (Sec. 5:14), and often laminated (Secs. 3:67, 3:68). [2] *Incased rubberized hair.* Prepare a laminated rubberized hair compact stuffing foam rubber/polyfoam unit to size (Sec. 17:14A[4]). Size of rubberized hair core, Fig. 17:20E, depends on the foam rubber or polyfoam incasing it. Incasing stock usually is from about ½- to ¾-inch thick, soft to medium density or firmness; rubberized hair core usually is firm. When assembling a unit, make strong bonds (Sec. 3:46) between top and bottom layers of foam rubber or polyfoam and the filler strips between layers; it is this bonding, rather

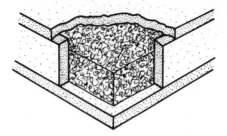

Fig. 17:20E

than that between incasing stock and rubberized hair, that holds a unit together.

**SEC. 17:21
LOOSE-
CUSHION
UPHOLSTERY
TREATMENT**

Sec. 17:21A / Much work and cover goods are saved by preparing and permanently installing a loose cushion, as on the inside back in Fig. 1:32. To save cover goods, the back surface of the cushion or pillow casing usually has strips of cover about 3 inches wide at the sides from top to bottom, the rest being denim or decking, Fig. *a* 17:21A. Similarly, the sides of the inside back (Fig. 1:32) would be cover goods and the rest denim or decking.

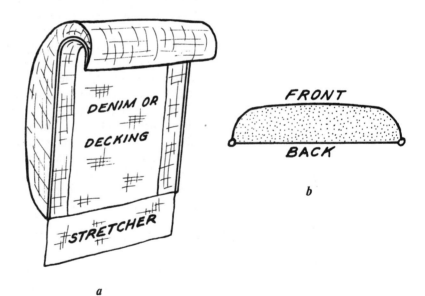

Fig. 17:21A

Sec. 17:21B Filling / Any cushion filling (Sec. 3:61) can be used, but foam rubber or polyfoam wrapped with two or three layers of synthetic cotton usually is best. An inner-spring unit would require excessive padding at the top and sides to build and hold smooth shape. Do not use down-filling if a cushion or pillow will be buttoned or tufted.

SEC. 17:21C CUSHION, PILLOW CONSTRUCTION / The casing (Fig. 1:32) usually is not boxed; it would be extremely difficult to produce a wrinkle-free boxing on a flexible, curved surface such as the top of a back. Prepare casing essentially as an unboxed pillow (Sec. 17:16) except that the back surface is planned to be flat (Fig. *b* 17:21A), with all the shaping of the casing allowed in the front cover or surface. The casing extends from about 2 inches beyond the tacking point at the top to 1 inch below the top of a loose cushion seat deck, 1½ inches below the edge of a solid seat; add a stretcher at the bottom (*a*), to reach the tacking points on the seat or other frame. The most difficult part of preparing the casing is planning and sewing pleats (Sec. 5:17) for a curved or pull-over area (Fig. 1:32); for best results set a thick-enough pad of cotton or blanket in place and make a muslin pleat pattern. When filling the casing (Secs. 17:14, 17:15), allow for taper to the edges at the top, bottom, and sides; tapered areas should be smooth and firm, not weak. Stitching the casing shut across the top is not necessary. For planned buttoning or tufting points, Secs. 21:03, 21:04; for buttons, Sec. 18:01.

18

outside

covers

SEC. 18:00 GENERAL FACTS	Outside covers for all parts of an article are installed essentially the same way. Differences are due to the points of finishing and, in some places, the type of cover goods. Most outside covers are set and tightened from top to bottom, from the middle to the sides of a surface. Blind-stitching (Sec. 13:04) usually is done only when blind-tacking (Sec. 9:13D) is impractical or would be unsatisfactory. Items included with outside covers—buttons, panels, ruching, skirts, fringe, etc.—should be prepared in advance. For the average article: *Tools:* Upholsterer's hammer, shears, small curved needle, regulator, upholstery skewers, sewing machine, tape measure, chalk (Secs. 2:02, 2:04, 2:06, 2:07, 2:08, 2:15, 2:16). *Materials:* Tacks, stitching twine, upholstery thread, burlap, cardboard stripping, felted padding, welt cord (Secs. 3:03, 3:08, 3:09, 3:24, 3:26, 3:49, 3:58).
SEC. 18:01 BUTTONS	**SEC. 18:01A PREPARATION** / Ordinary upholstery buttons (Sec. 3:60) can be covered satisfactorily only by a button machine. The

548

covering charge at most upholstery shops is quite reasonable. Large buttons usually are covered the same as post panels (Sec. 18:02). Shape button base to fit the surface it goes on, such as an inside back, to help prevent wrinkles in that surface.   [1] *Stitched button.* When button will be stitched in place, Fig. 18:01A, drill two small holes near the middle of the base for tie twines; insert them before covering button.   [2] *Nailed button.* When button will be nailed in place (Fig. 3:59E), drill a hole for the nail (a 1-inch nail usually is large enough) in the middle of the base; the hole should be the same size as or slightly smaller than the shank of the nail. Before covering button, set it in place and drive the nail ¼ inch into the frame to establish a clean nailing point; remove button base; cover it. Depending on cover goods, large buttons may be installed with headless panel brads in the same manner as a panel (Sec. 18:02).

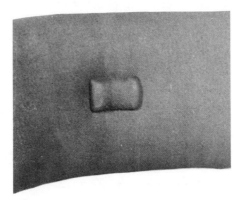

Fig. 18:01A

SEC. 18:01B   **INSTALLATION** / A 10- or 12-inch double-pointed straight needle (Sec. 2:06) is needed for nearly all twine-held button installations. The thicker a surface, the more the needle simplifies work. Install twine-held buttons before any outside cover. Install cloth-tuft, loop, and other twine-held buttons essentially as in Sec. 6:05G. Thread both ends of twine in needle before setting cloth-tuft or loop buttons. Cloth-tuft buttons should naturally lie flat against a surface. To make loop buttons lie flat and snug, work the eye of a loop into the twine hole in a cover. Except for extremely deep buttoning or tufting (Chapter 21), anchor or fasten twines of buttons: [1] *Solid-base surface.* Tack button twines to frame.   [2] *Open frame surface other than sag seat.* Tie button twines to burlap spring cover, or to burlap and/or webbing of a pad surface.   [3] *Sag seat.* See Sec. 6:05.

NOTE: *For extremely thick surfaces, especially spring built, there are two common methods of anchoring button twines (Secs. 18:01C, D).*

Sec. 18:01C Thick Surface, Method 1 / Tie button twines to webbing of coil spring surfaces or, if zigzags (Sec. 3:21) are used, to the springs. For pad surfaces, tie twines to the *auxiliary* webbing, which is similar to that of a sag seat (Sec. 6:05G). This method is fast, but with coil spring surfaces there is a chance that, due to the extra flexing of button twines as a surface goes down and rebounds in use, twines may break in relatively short time.

Sec. 18:01D Thick Surface, Method 2 / This method of fastening twine-held buttons in extremely thick, coil-spring surfaces places less strain on twines (Sec. 18:01C) and is the easiest way to repair broken button twines in finished articles. Install twine first in large buttons (Sec. 18:01A). Cloth-tuft and loop buttons may be threaded with twine in the last step. [1] *Insert long end* of double-pointed straight needle in surface at planned site of button. [2] *Push needle through stuffed surface* until it emerges from burlap spring cover, Fig. *a* 18:01D. Push needle straight through stuffing, not at a slant.

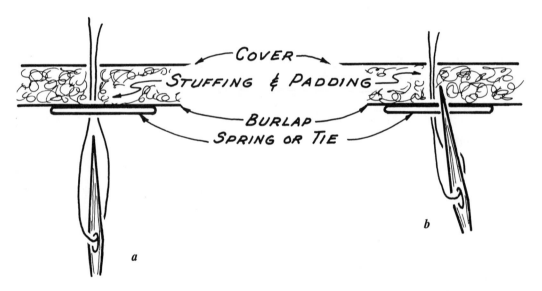

Fig. 18:01D

[3] *Pull needle clear of burlap,* and start return stitch with short end of needle, *b*. If the top coil of a spring, or a spring tie, is ½ inch or less from the entering stitch, the return stitch should encompass it. If a coil or tie is not convenient, start the return stitch ½ inch from the entering stitch, and place a small wad of padding for the button twines to pass around. Button twines are passed around a spring coil or tie, or wad of padding, to keep them from sawing into the burlap spring cover and stuffing. [4] *Direct needle on return stitch* to

emerge as near as possible to the start of the entering stitch. [5] *Thread button* on one of the twines and work it in place against the cover. Press it firmly to the amount of depression wanted for a button; pull button twines tight at the cover, and hold them firmly together. [6] *Press button* far enough into the surface to make twines slack enough for tying them together with a regular overhand knot. Work knot into twine hole in the cover, and ease button into place.

Sᴇᴄ. 18:01E   Tᴀᴄᴋᴇᴅ, Nᴀɪʟᴇᴅ Bᴜᴛᴛᴏɴs / These usually are installed after an article is completely upholstered. Protect button cover by padding the top of it with cardboard while hammering it.

SEC. 18:02 COVERING PANELS, LARGE BUTTONS

Sᴇᴄ. 18:02A / The method of covering a panel depends on the cover goods. Most large buttons are covered the same as textile-covered panels except that buttons are usually not welted. [1] *Cut goods large enough* to cover a panel (Secs. 11:15G, 11:17G). Whether a panel lies with the grain of a cover or at an angle depends on the position it will have when installed. [2] *Spread a thin layer of padding* on the face of a panel or button base. It should extend to but not around the back edges, where it could interfere with good installation of a panel or button.

Sᴇᴄ. 18:02B   Mᴏsᴛ Tᴇxᴛɪʟᴇs / Wrap cover around the front of a panel or button base; tack on the back. Cut and pleat (Secs. 5:15, 5:17) for it to fit tight and smooth, Fig. 18:02B. When cover cannot be tacked, as on a pressed-fiber button base, cross-stitch or glue in place. Welting a panel is optional, but most look better welted, *b*. Prepare welt (Sec. 12:06), and fasten to panel; tack to wood panels, and blind-stitch (Sec. 13:04) to cover of other panels. [1] *Panel not extending to bottom of post or seat rail* (Fig. *c* 1:45). Use enough welt to encompass panel from the bottom of its inner side and to reach to the bottom of the seat rail, *b*. Notch welt seam allowance just above bottom of panel. At that point, twist welt around to finish on a different surface of the post. [2] *Panel extending to bottom of post or seat rail* (Fig. *e* 1:45) *or to butt against another panel* (Fig. 1:18). Finish welt flush with end of panel on both sides.

Sᴇᴄ. 18:02C   Pʟᴀsᴛɪᴄs, Sɪʟᴋ, Gʟᴀᴢᴇᴅ Fᴀʙʀɪᴄs, Lᴇᴀᴛʜᴇʀ, Sɪᴍɪʟᴀʀ Cᴏᴠᴇʀs / Because these and other hard surfaced nonporous goods cannot be nailed through without permanent damage, panels are only partly covered by them before installation. Drive a 1-inch nail through the scroll or top area of a panel. Position it on the frame; drive nail in ¼ inch to establish a clear nailing point. Remove panel carefully, and drive nail into it fully. Tack a small piece of leather or sturdy plastic over nailhead. Cut and install cover on panel; leave about 1½ inches of

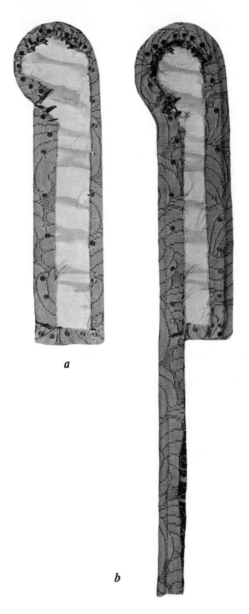

a

b

Fig. 18:02B

excess goods on the scroll or outer side of a panel. [*1*] *Cover panel*
(Secs. 18:02A, B) but only along the inner side, the bottom near the
inner side, and around the top to the end of the scroll, or to the outer
top corner of a panel not having a scroll. [*2*] *Prepare enough welt*
(Sec. 12:06) to encompass panel from its inner bottom edge up around
the top and down to the bottom of the seat rail at that post. [*3*]
Install welt along panel from the inner bottom corner and up around

the top to the end of the scroll, or to the outer top corner of a panel not having a scroll.   [4] *Notch welt seam allowance,* and cut cover at the end of a scroll, or at the outer top corner of a panel not having a scroll, so they can finish on the adjacent surfaces of the post when installed.

SEC. 18:03
SKIRTS,
FLOUNCES

There are three types of upholstery skirts or flounces (Sec. 11:20). The traditional flange (Fig. *b* 1:31) and modern flange (Fig. 18:06A) are formal types. The box pleat (Fig. *a* 1:35) is neither formal nor informal. The gathered or shirred skirt (Fig. 18:08) is chiefly for bedroom, sunroom, informal sitting room chairs, and other furniture. However, choice of a skirt for a particular article is a matter of personal taste. Nor does a particular type of article necessarily require one type of skirt. For example, the small armchairs in Fig. *a, b* 1:35 have identical frames. The real differences in upholstery, aside from covers, are the inside backs and skirts. The channel back chair could have had a box pleated instead of flange skirt, and the effect of the pleats with the lines of the channels might be interesting. For the plain back chair, a more consistent repeat of pattern, such as below the dominant flower on the back, could have been made with a flange skirt. Either of these chairs could have had a shirred or gathered skirt (Fig. 18:08).   [1] *Skirts are primarily decorative* and can greatly alter the appearance of an article (Fig. 1:20). Skirts also are used for practical reasons, such as adding mass to the bottom of a chair to make it look less top-heavy, or to draw attention away from the upper part of an article, or to make a davenport look broader or lower. And skirts are used simply to hide marred or unattractive legs.   [2] *Skirts usually are the same goods* as the rest of a cover. This is primarily tradition. Distinguishing trim effects may be made by using different goods for a skirt. A solid color skirt with a pattern cover . . . a figured skirt with a solid color cover . . . dark skirt with light cover . . . striped skirt with a solid cover— possibilities are limited only by an upholsterer's imagination and materials available. The modern flange skirt (Sec. 18:06) is doubly useful in offering a saving of cover goods and a variety of novel covering treatments.   [3] *Textile skirts should in most cases be lined.* It adds fullness and helps a skirt hold shape. Lining also aids appearance by eliminating stitching that would be near the bottom of a skirt if the goods was merely turned up and hemmed to prevent raveling. Common lining materials are muslin and sateen.   [4] *Leather and most plastic skirts* usually are not lined. They do not ravel and, as a rule, are stiff enough for a satisfactory appearance of fullness. But if using a very light, delicate plastic goods, lining probably will make a better looking skirt.   [5] *Install skirts* after the dust cover.

**SEC. 18:04
FLANGE
SKIRTS**

Sec. 18:04A / Flange skirts are classed as traditional (Figs. *a* 1:29, *b* 1:35, *c* 1:42) and modern (Fig. 18:06A); differences are in construction rather than appearance. Both kinds should have a neat, tailored look, and to get it, flange skirts must be planned, made, and installed with more care than the other types of skirts. For example, corner pleats must be at the corners, and center pleats must be at the center of a seat, not an inch or so away. Lining a flange skirt is particularly important because of the fullness it gives and its help in holding the shape of a skirt. However, lining can harm instead of improve appearance. With a thin, loosely woven lightweight cover, lining in a traditional flange skirt (Sec. 18:05) tends to puff out a skirt near the corners instead of letting it hang down fairly straight. Such puffout usually can be prevented, or greatly lessened, by using a modern flange skirt (Sec. 18:06). In addition to other tools for outside covers (Sec. 18:00), a steam iron and an ironing board or pad are needed.

Sec. 18:04B Construction Differences / Traditional and modern flange skirts are nearly identical in looks, but there are two major differences in construction. A traditional flange skirt is essentially a single strip of cover encompassing a seat, whereas a modern flange consists of separate strips, or skirt panels, Fig. *b* 18:04B, for front,

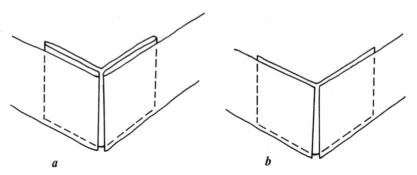

Fig. 18:04B   *a*   *b*

sides, and back. Traditional flange skirt pleats are made by folding the goods back over itself, *a*, whereas a modern flange has simulated pleats, made by finishing the ends of skirt panels over pleat pieces, *b*. With fewer layers of goods in a modern flange skirt's simulated pleats, there is less chance of undesirable puffout (Sec. 18:04A), and sewing may be done with a lighter machine than would be needed for traditional flange pleats. Since a modern flange skirt consists of separate panels, piecing of goods is seldom necessary; also, goods may be saved by using large enough scraps of cover for pleat pieces. Novel skirt treatments can be made by using a goods other than the regular cover or skirt for pleat pieces.

SEC. 18:05
TRADITIONAL
FLANGE SKIRT

SEC. 18:05A PLANNING / Because of its importance, plan the lining first. The bottom of a skirt should be ¾ inch above the floor covering so it can hang freely and stay clean. Inexperienced upholsterers often think that planning the bottom of a skirt is not necessary, because the top can be set as high as need be on a seat frame. But thickness of seat rails determines just how high a skirt can be tacked. Also, when the front of a seat and other outside covers were installed, before the skirt, it was over a layer of padding that should come down to the intended height of the top of a skirt. If a skirt is tacked above this point, padding may keep the tacks from holding securely. [*1*] *At the bottom of a skirt,* 1 to 1½ inches of goods usually is turned up for hem and seam allowance for sewing the lining. This is not required for leather and similar covers (Sec. 18:03). [*2*] *Lining usually extends* from top of hem to top of skirt. Cut lining ½ inch longer for seam allowance than the distance from the edge of the bottom of a skirt, when turned up, to the top of a skirt. [*3*] *Place lining* on the right surface of the skirt goods. Align edges of lining and bottom of skirt; sew together with a ½-inch flat seat (Sec. 12:02). [*4*] *Turn up goods* the necessary amount throughout a skirt, taking care to turn up the same amount at all points. Steam-press the hem area. Sew lining to wrong side of skirt ½ inch below the planned top edge.

SEC. 18:05B PREPARE, INSTALL SKIRT / Measure and cut goods for an entire traditional flange skirt (Sec. 11:20). [*1*] *Mark accurately the location of each pleat;* when piecing is necessary, do it inside a pleat, Fig. *a* 18:05B. [*2*] *Sew across pleats* ¼ inch below top of skirt. [*3*] *Prepare enough welt* to encompass skirt, and sew to top of skirt (Secs. 12:06, 12:07); join welt ends at middle of back. [*4*] *Mark seat rail covers* for the top of a skirt so that it will clear the floor by the proper amount (Sec. 18:05A). [*5*] *Set article upside-down.* [*6*] *Fit completely assembled skirt* over legs onto seat frame. Center pleats at corners, *b*. [*7*] *Tack skirt* at enough points to hold it in place; then cardboard it (Sec. 13:03).

SEC. 18:06
MODERN
FLANGE SKIRT

SEC. 18:06A PLANNING / (Sec. 18:04B, Figs. 18:06A, *a* 1:41). Sizes of skirt panels are based on their finished measurements plus various allowances (Sec. 18:06B). Panel lining is narrower than a panel's width. Pleat pieces and linings are the same size and shape. Prepare skirt panels and pleat pieces the same way (Secs. 18:06B–D) regardless of how skirt will be installed: [*1*] *Sew welt*, pleat pieces, and skirt panels together into a unit to encompass a seat; install (Sec. 18:06E); or [*2*] *Tack* welt, pleat pieces, and skirt panels separately on seat frame (Sec. 18:06F).

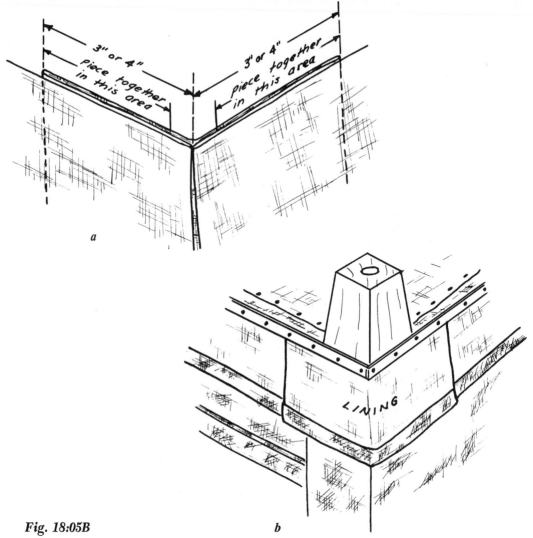

3" or 4" piece together in this area

3" or 4" piece together in this area

LINING

a

b

Fig. 18:05B

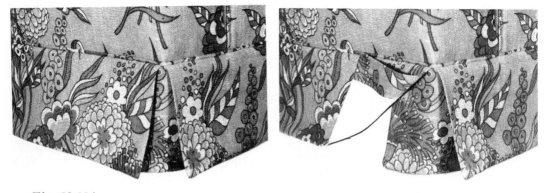

Fig. 18:06A   *a*   *b*

Sec. 18:06B Plan Modern Flange Skirt / Measure front, sides, and back of seat for width and height of skirt panels, and add allowances. Measure where the top of a skirt will be.   [1] *Width of skirt panel* usually is the distance from the outer edge of one corner to that of an adjacent corner. If there will be a center pleat, measure width from the outer edge of a corner to the middle of a seat rail. To measured width add 4 inches to allow for a 2-inch turnback at each end of a panel, Fig. 18:06B; this is an allowance of 1½ inches of cover to show if a pleat flaps open plus ½ inch seam allowance for sewing lining. In Fig. 18:06B: if measured width is 17 inches, 2-inch turnback at each end makes total width 21 inches.   [2] *Height of skirt panel* is the distance from the proposed bottom of a skirt (Sec. 18:05A) to the top. To measured height add 1 inch; this is a ½-inch seam allowance for sewing lining to the bottom of a skirt plus the same allowance for finishing a skirt at the top and installing it.   [3] *Width of panel lining* is 4 inches less than the measured width of a panel plus 1 inch for seam allowances, or a net of 3 inches less than measured width. As a rule, ½ inch more width is allowed for general handling of a lining and possible adjustment.   [4] *Height of panel lining* is the same as that of the panel with allowances.

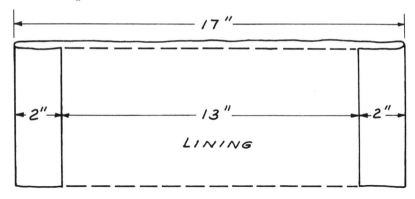

Fig. 18:06B

Sec. 18:06C Sewing Modern Flange Skirt / Sew skirt panel goods and lining together.   [1] *Center skirt panel strip in place,* right side out, on seat rail; pin at enough points to hold it securely. Pin all panels in place at this time to make sure that each is in its proper place and so that the overall appearance of skirt and seat covers can be judged and possibly adjusted. With patterned or figured goods, it may be that a skirt panel planned for one place will look better in another. Sometimes front and back panels may be exchanged, but usually a back panel is too narrow to use on the front. Often a panel must be shifted to right or left to fit its stripes, pattern, or figures into those of the seat cover (as at the left in Fig. *a* 18:06A). A shift up to 1 inch usually can be made without complicating the sewing of panel and lining; but if greater shifting is necessary, as a rule it is better to cut a new panel or abandon trying to fit panel and seat cover designs together.

NOTE: When using a solid color cover or one with figures so small and close together that there is no need to fit skirt and seat cover designs together, experienced upholsterers often do not pin skirt panels to a seat; instead, they work by width measurements (Sec. 18:06B) and the gap, [2] below, for hanging a modern flange skirt.

[2] *Mark the planned right and left ends of each panel* where they will be turned back, Fig. *d* 18:06C, with fine chalklines. These usually are about ⅛ inch from the corners and from the center line of a seat when there is a center pleat. Skirts usually hang better with gaps of about ¼ inch between panels. Spaces between the chalklines and ends

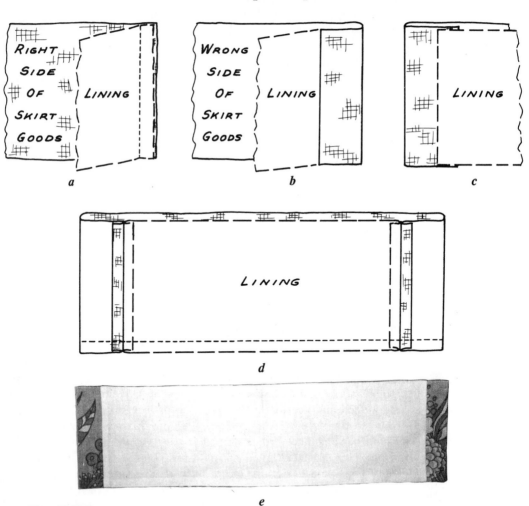

Fig. 18:06C

of a panel should be equal. But if a panel is shifted, [*1*] above, space will be greater at one end. To simplify sewing panel and lining with equal turnbacks, *e*, trim long end to the same length as the short end. Instead of nearly butting panels together, they may be set appreciably apart at corners and center pleat; they should, of course, be the same distance apart at all pleats.   [*3*] *Remove a skirt panel.* Place lining on right side of panel goods, aligning it with the edges of the top, bottom, and end of a turnback, *a*. Sew lining and panel together ½ inch from the end. Spread seam allowances apart, and steam-press them flat.   [*4*] *Turn panel over,* right-side-down, on the ironing board or pressing pad. Fold seam end back on the turnback chalkline, [*2*] above, and draw lining smoothly in place over the wrong side of the goods, *b*. Align top and bottom edges of panel, turnback, and lining. Steam-press first along the fold and then the rest of the lining and panel.   [*5*] *Turn back unsewn end of panel* on chalkline, [*2*] above, and steam-press fold.   [*6*] *Lay free end of lining in place* on unsewn turnback; steam-press them smooth. Mark lining top to bottom 1 inch from the edge of the turnback goods toward the end of the panel; cut lining along this line, *c*. This 1-inch markoff on the lining provides for ½-inch seam allowances on panel and lining for sewing them together. [*7*] *Place lining on right surface of panel,* with edges of the free end of lining and unsewn turnback aligned top, bottom, and ends *a*. Sew together ½ inch from end. Spread seam allowances apart; steam-press them flat.   [*8*] *Align bottom edges* of panel, turnbacks, and lining; be sure ends are turned back exactly on the pressed folds. Sew across bottom of panel, end to end, with a ½-inch seam allowance, *d*.   [*9*] *Turn lined panel inside-out.* Work goods down into bottom corners to make them square or slightly blunt or rounded, *e;* they should not be acute, pointed, or V-shaped.   [*10*] *Steam-press completed panel* on back or lining side. Pressing along edges gives a skirt a sharp, tailored look. The panel is now ready for installation.

Sec. 18:06D   Prepare Pleat Pieces / Cover and lining for modern flange skirt pleat pieces (Sec. 18:04B) usually are 8 inches wide and the same overall height of the skirt panels (Sec. 18:06B).   [*1*] *Place lining on right side of cover goods,* and align all edges.   [*2*] *Sew,* with ½-inch seam allowance, lining and cover together on sides and bottom.   [*3*] *Steam-press pleat piece* smooth and flat.   [*4*] *Turn lined pleat piece inside-out,* and work goods down into bottom corners (Sec. 18:06C[*9*]).   [*5*] *Steam-press the completed pleat piece* (Sec. 18:06C[*10*]).

Sec. 18:06E   Method 1: Install Modern Flange Skirt / Sew skirt panels and pleat pieces to welt to make a single unit skirt encompassing a seat. Install as a traditional flange skirt (Sec. 18:05B).

Sewing usually starts with an end of the welt set to the middle of the back or a side panel so that when welt ends are joined (Sec. 12:07), there will be the least number of thicknesses of goods to sew. The back and sides of a modern flange skirt seldom have a center pleat. Panels of most modern flange skirts are ¼ inch apart at the pleats (Sec. 18:06C[2]) and are sewn that way. If panels are further apart, plan the space between them for half of it to be on each side of a corner, or on each side of the center line for a center pleat. [1] *Prepare enough welt* (Sec. 12:06) to encompass seat at planned height of top of skirt. [2] *Set the back or a side panel* in place, lining surface up, on welt. Set end of welt to middle of panel. Align edges of welt and panel seam allowances. [3] *Sew panel to welt* the usual way, to a point about ½ inch from where the pleat piece will be placed, Fig. *a* 18:06E.

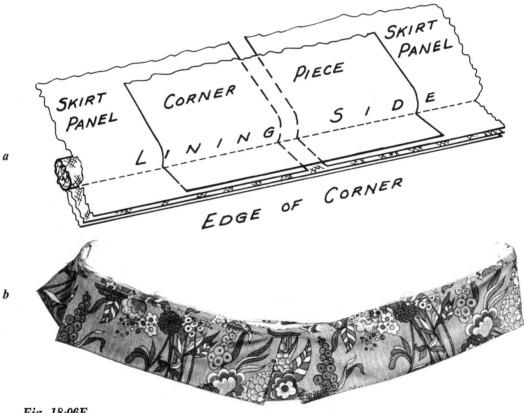

Fig. 18:06E

[4] *Stop machine with needle down* to hold goods, and set pleat piece in place. Align all seam allowance edges, and sew to a point about ½ inch from where the next panel will start. [5] *Stop machine with needle down,* set panel in place under pleat piece, align all seam al-

lowance edges, and sew as in [3] above. [6] *Repeat steps [3], [4], and [5] above*, sewing panels and pleat pieces to welt until reaching the starting point, [2] above. Join welt ends (Sec. 12:07C), and complete sewing (Fig. *b* 18:06E). [7] *Install skirt* (Sec. 18:05B).

NOTE: If the top of a skirt is not welted, work as above except for there being no welt; when sewing, be sure to leave ½-inch seam allowance for installing skirt. However, when there is no welt, custom upholsterers often butt all panels together to make a simple, unbroken line across the top of a skirt.

SEC. 18:06F   METHOD 2: INSTALL MODERN FLANGE SKIRT / Tack welt, skirt panels, and pleat pieces to seat frame, and cardboard them (Sec. 13:03). The disadvantage of Method 1 (Sec. 18:06E) for some upholsterers is the amount of precision machine sewing needed. The disadvantage of Method 2 is the amount of tacking. [1] *Prepare enough welt* (Sec. 12:06) to encompass seat at planned height of top of skirt. [2] *Tack welt in place* at planned height of top of skirt completely around seat, starting and ending at the middle of the back. Tack only at enough points, usually 5 or 6 inches apart, to hold welt firmly in place while installing skirt panels. [3] *Place article upside-down* to prevent having to pin panels up out of the way while working; pinning could damage the seat and other outside covers. [4] *Set skirt panels in place*, lining-side-out and the edges of the top of the panels aligned with those of the welt seam allowance. Panel ends usually do not quite meet (Sec. 18:06E). Tack panels at enough points, usually 5 or 6 inches apart, to hold them securely for cardboarding. Panel tacks usually are midway between welt tacks. [5] *Set pleat pieces in place*, [4] *above*, except that regardless of space between panels, pleat pieces are centered for corners and for the center line of a seat for center pleats, if any. Pleat pieces usually are tacked only at each end. [6] *Cardboard* (Sec. 13:03) panels and pleat pieces to welt.

NOTE: If top of skirt is not welted, chalkmark the planned height of the top completely around the seat. Draw a parallel line exactly ½ inch from the height line. Work as in [3] through [6] above except that the top edges of the skirt panels are set along the second or lower chalkline.

SEC. 18:07
BOX PLEATED
SKIRTS

SEC. 18:07A   COMMON TYPES / (Figs. *b* 1:29, *a* 1:35). Three common types of box pleats (Fig. 18:07A) are: *a*—inside and outside pleats meeting without a gap; *b*—inside pleats meet, but between outside pleats there is a gap or space equal to one-third the width of an outside pleat; *c*—gaps or spaces between inside and outside pleats equal to one-third the width of the pleats. [1] *Plan box pleated skirts* for consistent finishing of the pleats at the corners of a seat. In Fig. *a* 1:35,

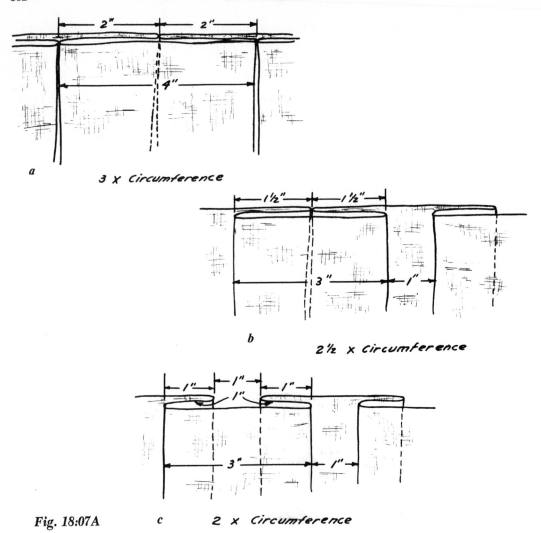

Fig. 18:07A   c   2 x Circumference

outside pleats meet at the corners of the seat; had there been gaps between outside pleats, they would have been centered at the corners. In Fig. *a* 1:31, an outside pleat is centered around a corner. Centering a pleat or gap at the corners is desirable. But when it is not practical, as in Fig. *b* 1:29, set pleats the same distance from the front corners. [2] *Textile box pleated skirts should be lined* (Sec. 18:03). If a skirt will not be lined, turn up goods to make a fold at the bottom ¾ inch above the floor covering (Sec. 18:05A). This hem, at the bottom of a skirt, should be at least 1-inch deep. More depth is advisable; the deeper a hem is, the better a skirt holds pleats. Hemstitch with thread matching the dominant or background color of the goods.

Sec. 18:07B Prepare Box Pleated Skirt / To start making pleats, underturn 1 to 2 inches of goods at the end of a skirt, and sew across it ¼ inch from the top end, Fig. *a* 18:07B. Any method of forming and sewing pleats is satisfactory as long as widths and gaps, if any, are consistent throughout. Piece goods within a pleat. Prepare enough welt to encompass a seat at the planned height of the top of a skirt, and sew to the top end (Secs. 12:06, 12:07). Start welt by folding back ½ inch of goods, wrong-side-to-wrong-side, and by setting the end of the welt cord just behind the fold, *b*. Set this end of the welt to the starting end of the skirt.

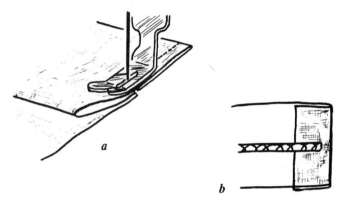

Fig. 18:07B

Sec. 18:07C Install Box Pleated Skirt / Except that it is not sewn together at the ends, install a box pleated skirt in the same manner as a traditional flange skirt (Sec. 18:05B). Center it for pleats to finish consistently at each front corner (Sec. 18:07A). Start and end skirt near middle of back. [*1*] *Complete installing skirt* around seat to the starting point, 1, in Fig. *a* 18:07C. End cardboard stripping just short of the starting end of the welt. [*2*] *Cut off finishing end of skirt*, 2 *a*, for it to reach 2 or 3 inches beyond the joint. Peel back welt cover and cut cord to butt against the starting end of welt. Cardboard welt up to the joint, and then tack the ending of the welt cover and skirt on a slight slant toward the bottom of the seat rail, *b*.

SEC. 18:08 **GATHERED,** **SHIRRED** **SKIRT**	Gathered or shirred skirts should be lined or hemmed (Secs. 18:03, 18:07A). For height of skirt (Sec. 18:05A). [*1*] *Gathers or ruffles may be any size* but usually are ¼- to ½-inch deep. They are readily formed by hand; accordian-fold goods into gathers or ruffles. [*2*] *Stitch through the middle* of the formed gathers or ruffles with stitching twine or heavy sewing thread ¼ inch below top end of goods, Fig. 18:08. [*3*] *Distribute goods evenly* along twine or thread; then prepare to sew to welt (Secs. 12:06, 12:07, 18:07B). [*4*] *Install skirt* (Sec. 18:07C).

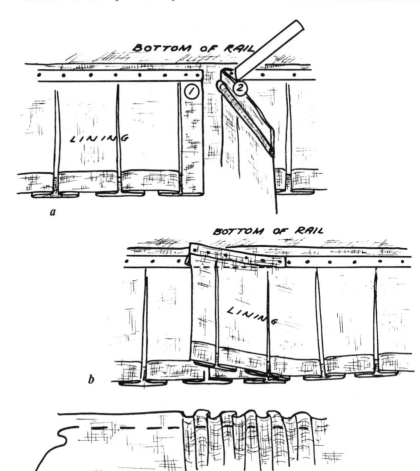

Fig. 18:07C

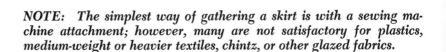

Fig. 18:08

NOTE: The simplest way of gathering a skirt is with a sewing machine attachment; however, many are not satisfactory for plastics, medium-weight or heavier textiles, chintz, or other glazed fabrics.

SEC. 18:09 FRINGE

SEC. 18:09A EDGING OR BRUSH-FRINGE / (Figs. *d* 1:45, *b* 1:48). Edging or brush-fringe can be used instead of welt on boxed cushions and when sewing banding to a cover, such as the inside back in Fig. *d* 1:45. When edging or brush-fringe is used on outside surfaces, as in Fig. *b* 1:48, tack it in place the same as welt. For best results, after tacking edging or brush-fringe at enough points to hold it in place, cardboard welt over it, or welt the cover to be installed and blind-tack it over the fringe or edging.

SEC. 18:09B HANGING FRINGE / (Fig. 1:18). Install after dust cover. Hand-stitch it to the cover with short, neat stitches, which usually can be concealed in the heading of a fringe. The nearer stitches are to the top of a heading, the tighter the fringe holds to the cover and the longer the finished job will keep its good appearance.

SEC. 18:10 RUCHING

(Fig. *b* 1:36.) Ruche or ruching should jut up or out from a surface, such as an outside back (Figs. *b* 1:36, *a* 1:35). Because it easily can be bent out of shape or "broken," it should not be used where it is apt to be handled or pressed down. [*1*] *Prepare ruching* the same as a box pleated skirt (Sec. 18:07) with inside and outside pleats butting throughout. Before pleating, fold goods over right-side-out. For best results, reinforce ruching with a strip of crinoline, cambric, or light buckram inserted between the two sides before pleating. [*2*] *Install ruching* while installing the outside cover. Center ruching at the middle of an area, such as the top of an outside back. Place stitching just below or away from the outer edge of a rail or frame. Tack ruching at enough points to hold it in place; while tacking, tighten it only enough to lie flat. [*3*] *At corners,* it usually is necessary to squeeze the bottom of ruching together so that it may turn a corner without stretching the top of the pleats. [*4*] *Ruching usually is ended* by ripping out the seam 1 inch, folding the edge of the side in between the goods, and then tacking it in place the regular way. [*5*] *Tack welt* over ruching; then install outside cover.

SEC. 18:11 OUTSIDE COVERS

Sec. 18:11A Installation / All outside covers are installed essentially the same way. Burlap (Sec. 5:02) all cavities except the bottom of a seat. When there is enough space on a frame, tack burlap to it, Fig. 18:11A. But in many scroll, square-scroll, and T-shaped arms, there is too little space on the underarm strip for separately tacking burlap and cover (Sec. 18:13C). In addition to providing a base or foundation for building shape and crown in an outside surface, burlapping protects a cover by cushioning it against impacts. Inferior upholstery often has a sheet of heavy cardboard in place of burlap. It may protect a cover slightly; but the cardboard usually is too stiff to give under an impact on the cover, with the result that the cover is either bruised or badly dented. In the poorest grade of upholstery, an outside cover has no support behind it; these covers are weak and tend to sag. A layer of padding goes over the burlap and frame. It gives additional protection to a cover and builds the slight crown (Sec. 5:14) necessary and desirable in most large surfaces. The cover is then installed.

Sec. 18:11B Stuffing / When an outside surface is more than very slightly curved, as in barrel backs and some arms (Fig. 1:37), the cavity may be stuffed before burlapping in order to shape a surface.

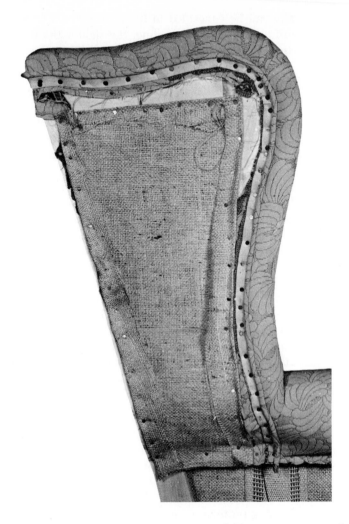

Fig. 18:11A

Stuff with scrap padding, hair-and-fiber, moss, or palm fiber (Sec. 5:08).

SEC. 18:11C INSTALLATION SEQUENCE / Outside covers usually are installed in the following sequence: [1] *Wings first,* since the bottom of an outside wing cover usually finishes under the top of an outside arm cover;   [2] *Arms second,* because at the back they usually finish under the outside back cover;   [3] *Back third,* since it generally finishes on top of the ends of inside back-outside wing and arm covers; [4] *Dust cover fourth,* because it usually finishes on top of the bottom ends of seat, outside arm, and back covers.

SEC. 18:12
OUTSIDE
WINGS

When a wing cavity is large and curves appreciably, stuffing it before burlapping is advisable (Sec. 18:11B).   [*1*] *Burlap* (Sec. 5:02) outside wing cavity (Fig. 18:11A).   [*2*] *Welted outside wing.* Install welt from the top of the back of a back post down to the underarm strip (Fig. 18:11A).   [*3*] *If top or front of wing is straight* (Fig. 1:15), blind-tack welt and cover along that area; it cannot, of course, be done along more than one edge of a surface without special production stripping (Sec. 13:04).   [*4*] *Cardboard welt* throughout an outside wing except where cover can be blind-tacked.   [*5*] *Spread a layer of padding* over wing area extending to welt cord, to but not beyond the outer rear edge of the back post, and down to but not below the underarm strip. [*6*] *Center outside wing cover* in place, and install smoothly. Cut (Sec. 5:15) for scoops where necessary.   [*7*] *Tack cover* along back of back post and on underarm strip.   [*8*] *Pin cover* in place along welted portions until cover is completely adjusted; then blind-stitch to welt, Fig. 18:12.

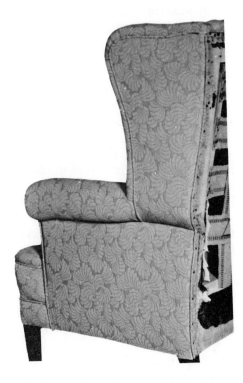

Fig. 18:12

SEC. 18:13
OUTSIDE ARMS

SEC. 18:13A FINISH / How cover finishes at the front and top of an outside arm depends on the goods and the method of covering the armfront. When an outside arm curves appreciably, stuffing before burlapping is advisable (Sec. 18:11B). *For a bordered armtop* (Fig. *a* 1:37), first install armtop border (Sec. 13:08), finishing it on the outer sides of the armboard.

Sec. 18:13B Welting / Install outside arm welt. [1] *For knife-edge* (Fig. *a* 1:20) *and similar non-scroll arms having a pull-around inside arm cover, bordered armtops* (Fig. *a* 1:37), *and modern square arms* (Fig. *a* 1:42), welt goes along top edge of armboard from the back of a back post to the outer top corner of the front post and from there down along the outer edge of the post to end at the top of the leg. However, in barrel chairs of this type (Fig. *b* 1:37), welt usually is installed completely around the outside arms and back at the same time. [2] *For scroll arms having a pull-around cover* (Fig. *c* 1:35), install outside arm welt along the outer front edge of the front post from bottom of scroll to top of leg.

Sec. 18:13C Burlapping / Most arms other than scroll, square-scroll, and T-shaped have enough frame for tacking burlap separately along the outer side of an armboard. But on scroll, square-scroll, and T-shaped arms burlap usually must be blind-tacked with the cover to the underarm strip. In this case, first set cover in position, wrong-side-out and upside-down, with its top end along the lower edge of the underarm strip. Place burlap on top of cover, and cardboard them both in place. Press edge of cardboard up tight against the underside of the arm, and tack at enough points, usually about ¾-inch apart, to hold them securely; while tacking, work cover reasonably tight toward front and back. Then install the rest of the burlap over the cavity. For all arms, tack burlap to the outer sides of the front and back posts and seat rail regardless of how the top end is installed.

Sec. 18:13D Positioning Cover / [1] *Allow for slope of arm* (Sec. 14:10C) when installing outside arm cover. [2] *Top end of cover.* Blind-tack top end of cover in place when the shape of an armboard permits it. Blind-tacking generally gives a stronger, smoother job than blind-stitching. When positioning cover across the top for blind-tacking, be sure to tighten it properly from middle to front and back in order to take out slack.

Sec. 18:13E Pad Outside Arm / Spread a layer of padding over the outside arm area depending on where a cover will finish. [1] *Exposed-wood surfaces:* Padding extends to ½ inch from the marked limits of upholstery or outer ends of rabbets. [2] *Bottom:* If a skirt is not to be installed, padding extends down to the lower edge of the seat rail. If there will be a skirt, padding extends down to planned top of skirt. [3] *Back:* Padding usually extends to outer rear edge of back post. [4] *Front:* When a front post already is welted, padding extends to but not beyond the welt cord; the outside cover will be blind-stitched to the welt. If a front post is not welted, placement of padding at the front depends on the method of covering the armfront (Sec. 18:13F). [5] *Do not extend padding* beyond or over the limits given above; it could prevent good installation of the covers.

Sec. 18:13F   Covering Armfronts / When an armfront is covered by a border (Fig. *b* 1:46) or has a panel that is covered by most kinds of textiles (Sec. 18:02B), an outside arm cover usually finishes on the face of a front post and down it to the bottom of the border or panel. [1] *Border.* A border usually extends down to the top of a leg. Install outside arm cover, finishing it on the face of the post. Place enough padding along the outer edges of the post-face to give the border, when installed, a "set in" appearance. Post-face borders are installed essentially the same as any other border (Sec. 13:08). Usually a piece of fairly stiff, thick cardboard is shaped to resemble the top of a panel that would fit into the top of the border area. Cover it with the top end of the border, and install as an ordinary panel (Sec. 18:13G). Blind-tack the rest of a border down along the inner side of the border area to the bottom of it. Cardboard welt to outer side of border area; blind-stitch border to it. Finish border around leg top (Sec. 13:05). [2] *Full-length panel* (Fig. *e* 1:45). Finish outside arm cover on face of post throughout. [3] *Short panel* (Fig. 1:43). Finish outside arm cover on front of post down to bottom of panel area. At that point, cut cover to finish along the front outer edge of the post. After installing panel, tack end of panel welt on the outer side of the post. Cardboard welt; then blind-stitch outside arm cover to it (Fig. 18:12).

Sec. 18:13G   Installing Panels / The kind of cover goods determines how a panel should be installed. For best results, shape a panel to fit smoothly and snugly into its area. Panels that do not fit well have poor appearance and usually can be dislodged easily. Sometimes it is more practical, due to the necessary shaping of a panel and/or the kind of cover, to use a border instead of a panel. [1] *Most textiles.* Install panels by driving three or four smooth, headless 1-inch finishing nails through the cover into the panel and post. Minimize cover damage by first spreading threads apart at point of nailing. Nail along the sides of a panel or through a heavy part of the cover design. After nailing, with a sharp pin pluck cover out near the nail, and rub threads lightly back in place. [2] *Plastic, silk, leather, glazed textiles, etc.* These and other hard-surfaced goods cannot be nailed through without permanent damage. After covering a panel (Sec. 18:02C), set it in place with a nail embedded in the back. Turn cover back carefully from the lower part of a panel, Fig. *a* 18:13G, fold padding aside, and nail panel to post at two or three points. Draw cover back around panel, and work it smooth and tight in under the bottom of the panel. Bend panel welt aside at the notch (Sec. 18:02C), and finish panel cover on the adjacent side of the post. Cut and twist panel welt around, tack, and cardboard it over the panel cover along the edge of the post. Blind-stitch outside cover to panel welt, *b*.

SEC. 18:13H ROUNDED ARM / (Fig. *d* 1:45). Complete upholstering the outside arm the same as the inside arm. Burlap arm cavity, and place enough layers of padding to build it the same thickness as the inside arm. Complete incasing arm with muslin, and then cover.

**SEC. 18:14
OUTSIDE
BACKS**

SEC. 18:14A FINISHING AT SIDES / The major difference between covering outside backs and arms (Fig. *b* 11:24C) is the finishing of back covers at the sides. Outside back covers usually are blind-stitched from top to bottom on both sides unless special production tacking strips are used (Sec. 13:04). When the line of the top of an outside back cover is flat from side to side, the cover, with or without welt, usually is blind-tacked. But when the top is either arched or scooped: [1] *Cardboard welt* along outer top edge of back, and blind-stitch cover to it (Fig. *b* 11:24C). This method is preferred by many custom upholsterers, as it preserves the line of a back. [2] *If an inside back cover or its boxing or border finishes far enough down* the outside back, draw a chalkline straight across it from side to side at the highest point; blind-tack the outside cover along the line. Welt may be used with this method but generally is not, as it draws too much attention to the conflict of lines between top of back and top of back cover. [3] *Blind-stitch the top of the outside back cover* to the inside back cover or its boxing or border along the outer top edge of a back. This is structurally poor and usually not attractive.

SEC. 18:14B / Stuff back cavity if advisable (Sec. 18:11B). Install burlap and padding the usual way.

SEC. 18:14C WELTING / Most outside back covers are welted top and sides (Fig. *b* 11:24C). Two common exceptions are scroll backs (Fig. *c* 1:45), in which the top of the outside cover fits tight against the bottom of the scroll (Fig. *b* 18:13G); and armless backs (Fig. 1:16) and others having full-length post panels, boxing, or borders on the sides. These exceptions generally are welted along the sides and may be, but usually are not, welted across the top. Aside from these exceptions, welt should be used on a back where a cover cannot be blind-tacked at top or sides.

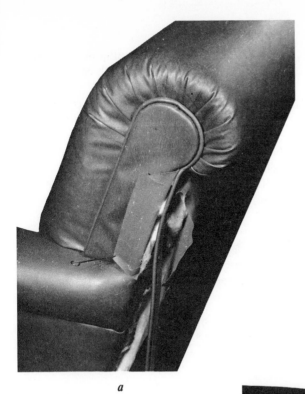

a

b

Fig. 18:13G

571

SEC. 18:14D PULL-AROUND COVER / Install a pull-around outside back cover the same as a pull-around seat or inside back cover.

SEC. 18:14E KEYHOLE BACK / A keyhole back outside cover (Fig. 13:07B) requires special handling. It may be a single piece of goods (Sec. 18:14F), or separate strips of goods (Sec. 18:14G), or strips machine sewn together before installation (Sec. 18:14H). Because the cover must be blind-stitched in so many places, the outside back should be welted along all outer and inner edges. Before installing a back cover, install welt, and cardboard it except where the cover will be blind-tacked, Fig. 18:14E.

Fig. 18:14E

SEC. 18:14F SINGLE PIECE COVER FOR KEYHOLE BACK / This is the simplest keyhole outside back cover. [1] *Blind-tack cover* across top of back (Fig. 18:14E), working it smooth and tight. [2] *Spread a layer of padding* on the outside back extending to, but not beyond, welt cords. To avoid making an outside back too puffy, a half instead of full thickness of padding may be used. While drawing cover in place to the bottom edge of the lower back rail, press padding lightly but firmly against the top welt to prevent its shifting and leaving a hollow across the top. [3] *Work cover smooth and tight* against welt along the bottom of the lower rail; pin in place. [4] *Mark cover carefully* ½ inch below welt along bottom of the upper rail, and cut. Cut to ½ inch from the inner sides of the keyhole; then cut diagonally into each corner.   [5] *Work cover smooth and tight* against welt on the bottom of the upper rail; blind-stitch from corner to corner.   [6] *Cut and install cover* down the outer sides of the back, then the inner sides, and then along both the upper and lower edges of the lower rail.

SEC. 18:14G STRIP COVERS FOR KEYHOLE BACK / Separate strips

are used for the top, sides, and bottom of the outside back. This method is chiefly for saving cover goods for a back that is quite large overall and has a large keyhole or hollow.   [1] *Cut strips of cover* for top, bottom, and sides of outside back. Each strip should be 1¼ inches wider than the area it must span from outer edge to inner edge and should be 1½ inches longer than the distance along the outer edge. [2] *Blind-tack each strip* along the outer edge of the frame. Butt them together at the corners.   [3] *Install padding* (Sec. 18:14F[2]), holding it in place to prevent hollows while drawing cover strips into position. [4] *Work cover strips smooth and tight* along inner edges of the rails; trim off excess goods ½ inch beyond welt. Underturn edges, work cover strips back in place, and pin along welts. Work close to each inside corner. Cut off excess goods ½ inch above the surfaces from the inner to the outer corners; underturn edges smoothly, and fit strips neatly together at and along each corner and diagonal between corners.   [5] *Blind-stitch strips* along inner welts first; then together along diagonals between inner and outer corners. Often restitching is necessary, especially near the inner corners, to make a cover smooth and tight. The more carefully strips are worked and pinned first, as a rule the less restitching is needed.

SEC. 18:14H MACHINE-SEWN COVER FOR KEYHOLE BACK / Ma-

chine-sewn strips are used to save cover goods (Sec. 18:14G) or to allow precise fitting of stripes or other parts of a cover design at the corners of a keyhole back. It also can be a neater cover than one blind-stitched diagonally.   [1] *Make an accurate paper pattern* of each planned strip of outside back cover; patterns for the sides should be identical.   [2] *Position patterns on cover goods* according to how stripes or other parts of a design are to fit together. Mark each corner diagonal accurately; cut cover strips to leave a ½-inch seam allowance at each diagonal. Cut each strip with a 1¼-inch allowance in width (Sec. 18:14G[1]).   [3] *Machine sew strips* together wrong-side-to-wrong-side with a flat seam along corner diagonals.   [4] *Install assembled cover* essentially the same as a single piece cover (Sec. 18:14F) except that the bottom of the top strip is worked in place on its welt first instead of working the complete cover down along the bottom of the lower rail.

Sec. 18:14I French Back / Install outside back cover (Fig. 10:-05A) while upholstering the inside back.

**SEC. 18:15
DUST COVER**

Except for skirt, gimp, and other trim, a dust cover usually is the last piece of "cover" installed. Any fabric may be used (Sec. 3:74), but dust covers usually are black or a dark-color crinoline, cambric, or continuous filament goods. A light color might be quite noticeable. Non-porous goods are not recommended, as a dust cover should allow a seat to "breathe" silently in use. Install dust cover, shiny-side-out, on the bottom of a seat, underturning edges and tacking it over all other covers. The shiny side attracts less dirt and dust than the dull side.

**SEC. 18:16
TRIMS**

Sec. 18:16A Gimp / Usually less gimp is wasted and there is less chance of not having enough for a job, by not cutting it until reaching the end of a strip or surface being gimped. It should be glued. If only nailed or tacked, the edges will curl up, trap dust and dirt, and tear easily. Spread enough glue on the back of gimp to coat it evenly and noticeably from side to side but not enough to work through and perhaps discolor it. Depending on how fast the glue sets, coat only about a foot of gimp or less at a time. Press glued gimp firmly in place, and sliptack at enough points to hold it securely while glue dries. From time to time while drying, press gimp lightly against the other surface. When glue is thoroughly dry, remove tacks carefully.

Sec. 18:16B Installation / Start and end a length of gimp by underturning about ½ inch, gluing the underside and sliptacking in place. For best appearance, the start or end should butt against another surface, such as the end of a rabbet, another length of gimp, etc. When a stuffed surface rises rather abruptly from a rabbet, first tack along the rabbet a strip of sturdy cardboard that is slightly narrower than the gimp. This holds down the upholstery and allows gimp to lie flat. Glue gimp to cardboard.

Sec. 18:16C Curves, Corners / [1] *Around curves,* Fig. *a* 18:-16C, lay gimp in place, forming and compressing or squeezing it to fit neatly. Do not stretch gimp to fit; later it may shrink or pull back. [2] *At right-angle corners, b, c,* install gimp along one side of a rabbet until it butts against the other or until it reaches the marked limits of upholstery for the other side of a corner. Fold gimp back over itself. "Quarter" it by drawing two lines across gimp, the first line as far from the corner as the width of the gimp, the second line halfway between the first and the corner, *b*. Draw a third line midway between edges of gimp. Tack gimp permanently in the middle of the appropriate "quar-

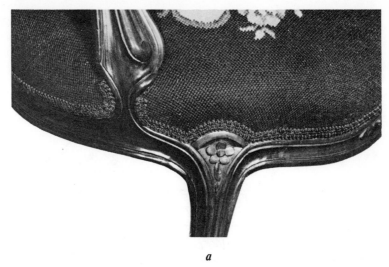

a

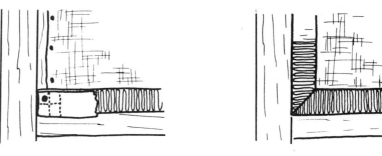

Fig. 18:16C   *b*   *c*

ter" or square, and set new length of gimp along the adjacent side of the corner, *c*.

**SEC. 18:17
DOUBLE-WELT**

Sec. 18:17A General Installation / The mechanics of gluing double-welt (Sec. 11:08) are the same as for gimp (Sec. 18:16A), but the rest of installation is different. When double-welt cover is cut on the bias, as it should be, usually it is flexible enough to be worked smoothly along most curves, and even into right-angle corners as at the upper right in Fig. *c* 11:08A. But at the lower right corner, the bend-back is so acute that cutting and joining welt (Sec. 18:17B) usually is more practical and produces a better job. Some upholsterers prefer to cut and join at right-angle corners, as on the inside back of Fig. *a* 1:28. Join the ends of double-welt by gluing the covers together. (Sec. 18:17B). Plan installation of welt for joints to be at relatively un-noticeable places, such as near the back of the inner side of an armrest

(Fig. *c* 11:08A). If there must be two or more joints on a surface, plan them for places where, while noticeable, they will not be objectionable; in Fig. *a* 1:28, welt joints are at the corners of the inside back and of the seat.

Sec. 18:17B Joints /   Whether making a straight or a corner joint with double-welt, Fig. 18:17B, the methods are essentially the same.

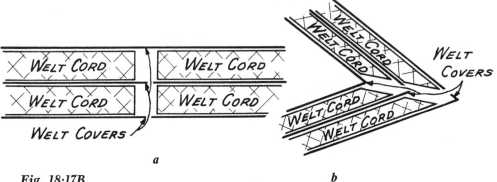

Fig. 18:17B   *b*

a

[1] *Bring ends of welts* smoothly into position, and cut them to fit tightly together; cut neatly through covers and welt cords. It is important for the covers to fit as tightly as possible against each other without overlapping. If they do not meet, the finished joint may be weak and flat. If they overlap, there may be a lump in the finished joint. [2] *Slide the cover of each welt end* back far enough so that ⅟16 inch or less can be cut off each welt cord. Some of each cord must be cut off for the covers to be glued together without forming a lump. But if too much is cut off, there will be a flat spot in the joint.   [3] *Install welt smoothly in place* the usual way, with ends aligned and covers brought neatly together. This is not difficult with a relatively straight joint, *a*. But in a corner joint, *b*, sometimes a little extra stretching or trimming of a cover is needed to fit them together smoothly. Smoothness is more noticeable in a relatively straight than in a corner joint. [4] *Coat ends of covers with glue* and, with a sharp pin or needle, work them into each other. Joints should be smooth, without gaps between covers or lumps due to too much cover goods being forced together. Use enough glue to hold covers securely but not enough to stain or otherwise make a joint more noticeable.

Sec. 18:17C Starting, Ending Against Another Surface /   To start or end double-welt against another surface, such as a post, or the end of a rabbet: [1] *Bring welt smoothly into position.* Cut it off about ⅟16 inch beyond where it would just butt firmly against the other surface. Cut neatly through cover and cords.   [2] *Slide cover back* far enough so that ⅛ inch can be cut off each welt cord. This ends the cords 1⁄16 inch from the other surface, leaving space for the cover ends to be worked into place. With very thick or heavy goods, it may be necessary to trim a little more than ⅛ inch off cords; with thin or very light goods, possibly a little less than ⅛ inch.   [3] *Coat ends of cover with glue* and, with a sharp pin or needle, work them together over ends of welt cords. As much as possible, preserve the overall shape of the double-welt. The finished ending should be smooth, without gaps or lumps.

SEC. 18:18 ANTIQUE, TRIM NAILS	Place these at any desired intervals, but keep the same spacing throughout. When driving fancy-head nails, reduce the chance of marring them by holding a piece of cardboard on the head while hammering it. For the most attractive results when using antique or trim nails on a cover that finishes on a rabbet or along marked limits of upholstery, gimp it (Sec. 18:16) before installing nails.

SEC. 18:19 MODERN SLIPBACK OUTSIDE BACK

SEC. 18:19A   GENERAL FACTS /   Modern slipframe outside back and arm covers are installed, with or without welt, essentially as in Secs. 18:14A–C. To keep the outside back from being too puffy, only half a thickness of padding may be used. If the top and sides of an outside back are welted, the bottom usually is; blind-tack welt and cover across the top; cardboard welt along sides and bottom, and blind-stitch cover to welts. How a slipback will be installed in an article may affect preparation of the outside back cover. If a covered slipback is simply set in place and fastened, there is no special preparation of the back cover. In many articles, the crossbar on which the upper part of a slipback rests is covered (Fig. 16:15A).

SEC. 18:19B   CROSSBAR COVER /   The crossbar cover may be any width but (Fig. *a* 16:15A) usually is at least wide enough to conceal the screws or other means of fastening a slipback; add 1 inch to measured width to allow for ½-inch hems on each side. The cover should be long enough to wrap around the top, back, and bottom surfaces of the crossbar; add at least 2 inches for general handling.   [1] *Along sides only,* underturn goods and sew ½-inch hems.   [2] *Pin outside back cover* temporarily in place on slipback; work goods smooth and fairly tight. Set slipback in place on article, and draw a thin chalkline across the back cover where it touches the inner top edge of a crossbar.   [3] *Set prepared crossbar cover in place* on top surface of bar, and mark the outside back cover for the sides of the crossbar cover. [4] *Remove outside back cover* from slipback. Place crossbar cover on it, right-side-to-right-side, with the top end upside-down, and sew together with a ½-inch seam. To allow for a possible shift in positioning the outside back cover when permanently installing it, sew the crossbar cover about ½ inch below the chalkline.   [5] *Install outside back cover* permanently on slipback.

NOTE: Instead of removing the outside back cover and sewing the crossbar cover to it, some upholsterers prepare crossbar cover, permanently install outside back cover on slipback, set it in place and mark for placement of crossbar cover, remove slipback, and handstitch crossbar cover in place. Be careful not to stitch through padding under the outside back cover.

SEC. 18:19C SLIPBACK INSTALLATION / There are two common ways to complete installation of a slipback.   *Method 1:* Screw or otherwise permanently install slipback on article; be sure crossbar cover is not pinched in by screws or other fasteners. Pad crossbar (Sec. 5:12); padding should not extend beyond the edges of the side hems; padding should encompass a bar from the inner front edge of the top to about ½ inch from the front edge of the bottom. Wrap crossbar cover around bar; work it smooth and tight. Carefully underturn the bottom end of the cover to fold about ⅟₁₆ inch from the front edge of the bottom, and tack (Fig. *b* 16:15A). For best appearance, tack with trim or antique nails. But since this tacking is seldom seen, regular upholstery tacks are generally used.   *Method 2:* Cover a length of cardboard stripping (Sec. 13:05B), and tack along the bottom of the inner surface of the crossbar (Fig. *c* 16:15A). The covered cardboard should be 1 inch longer than the width of the hemmed crossbar cover to allow for possible stretch when installing the cover. The covered edge of the cardboard should be flush with the bottom of the crossbar. Pad crossbar, and work cover in place, but underturn bottom end to fold along front bottom edge of crossbar. Blind-stitch fold to covered cardboard strip.

19

notes on leather and heavy plastics

SEC. 19:00A GENERAL FACTS / Leather, leather substitutes, and heavy plastics are handled the same way in most phases of upholstery. To avoid repetition, all are grouped under the word "leather" in this chapter. Differences between them are specified in pertinent sections. Covering with leather is not particularly difficult, but inexperienced upholsterers should not attempt it, especially with genuine leather, until somewhat practiced in handling fairly heavy textiles and plastics. Leather has some stretch but seldom fits itself to surfaces as most textiles and light plastics do. Handled properly, leather pleats (Sec. 5:17) neatly and stays smooth. Few articles originally upholstered for a textile or light- to medium-weight plastic cover can be re-covered satisfactorily with leather unless the stuffing is altered (Sec. 19:01). Leather substitutes and plastic cover goods are sold in yardage and plotted the usual way (Sec. 11:24). Genuine leather is sold by hides and yardage (Sec. 19:06).

579

Sec. 19:00B   Machine Sewing / Machine sewing of leather ordinarily requires a special leather needle made for that make and model machine. Leather substitutes and heavy plastics usually can be machine-sewn satisfactorily with regular needles. Keep all sewing and hand-stitching needles sharp and smooth. Sew with long stitches; short stitches have a cutting effect. Hand-stitch with 3-square point needles (Sec. 2:06); keep blades sharp so that needles will cut rather than tear through leather.

SEC. 19:01 **STUFFING**	Use top quality, highly resilient stuffing (Secs. 3:28–3:44) for leather upholstery. For best results, stuffed surfaces should be quite firm. Soft surfaces do not hold leather covers in place, especially on armtops and other parts subject to much use; inadequately stuffed, they tend to sag in fairly short time.
SEC. 19:02 **REGULATING**	Leather and other solid- or hard-surfaced covers cannot be regulated (Sec. 5:07) without permanent damage. Develop shape fully, fill all hollows, and smooth away lumps before completing a covering job.
SEC. 19:03 **BREATHING**	Quiet and generally better seat cushions result when the bottom cover, except for a 4-inch strip across the front, is fabric (Sec. 17:03D). Otherwise there should be at least three breather vents in the back and each side boxing of the average cushion.
SEC. 19:04 **WELT**	Cut welt covers (Secs. 11:08) in strips as long as possible to minimize piecing. Except in a fabric-backed plastic, there is no possible bias-cutting. Double-welt seldom is practical.
SEC. 19:05 **GIMP**	Cut gimp (Sec. 3:59) strips where possible for the full length of an edge or surface.
SEC. 19:06 **GENUINE** **LEATHER**	Sec. 19:06A Hide, Yardage / Genuine upholstery leather is commonly sold by the whole or half hide and as yardage and is available in a variety of embossed grains and natural and decorator colors. [1] *Yardage leather* comes in various widths and lengths. It is the most expensive way, in gross cost, to buy leather, but there is no waste due to shape of hide or skin flaws. Yardage is the easiest leather to plot (Sec. 11:24) since it is treated the same as fabric or plastic yardage. [2] *Hide leathers* have waste due to shape and skin flaws. These factors are taken into account when a hide is marked as containing so many square feet of cover. But this is only an estimate, as the actual amount of useful leather depends on sizes and shapes of cuts needed. Plot all needed pieces before marking a hide (Secs. 19:06B, C).

Sec. 19:06B Plotting Covers / Measure each needed cut of cover accurately (Chapter 11); add seam allowances. Although covers should be plotted first as rectangles, some, such as the inside of a flaring back, will have considerable waste if plotted and cut that way. For economy, plot such pieces and cut them strictly according to measured size and shape; be cautious, a misjudgment can make this an expensive economy. Cut completed paper plots into full-size patterns or templates with seam and other allowances. Fit them together on a hide according to usage (Sec. 19:06C). Allow a minimum of excess goods for general handling. Wastage, which may run as high as 25% of a hide, often is due almost entirely to poor arrangement of cuts. However, hides frequently have holes or other flaws causing wastage. Use cover stretchers (Sec. 11:09).

Sec. 19:06C Plotting Hide Leather / From the middle of a whole or half hide, cut those pieces of cover that are subject to the most use and wear: armtops, inside back, and seat or top cushion covers.

**SEC. 19:07
PLIABILITY**

Work leather in a warm, fairly humid room to keep it pliable. Pliability of inferior grades of leather often is increased by dampening the *wrong* side from time to time with clean water. This usually is not necessary when using top-grain leather.

**SEC. 19:08
PIECING**

To piece together leather covers, welt, boxing strips, etc., skive the end or edge of each piece to be joined. Skive the wrong side to taper, from about ½ inch from the edge, to a sharp edge at the end, Fig. *a* 19:08A.

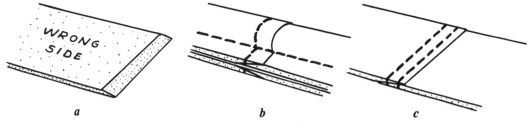

a   *b*   *c*

Fig. 19:08

To skive, hold leather right-side-down on a smooth board or marble slab, and slice toward the end with a sharp knife; start close to the end, and gradually work back to the start of the taper. Hone blade often to keep it sharp. If skived properly, the end will be smooth and not have bits of leather sticking out. [1] *Welt.* Sew leather welt the usual way (Sec. 12:06). To piece strips of welt together, fit the skived end of one inside the other, *b.* [2] *Boxing.* Fit strips of leather boxing together, one skived end overlapping the other, *c,* and sew across joint a short distance back from each end.

20

channeling

SEC. 20:00	SEC. 20:00A METHODS / Inside backs are the surfaces most often

SEC. 20:00
GENERAL
FACTS

SEC. 20:00A METHODS / Inside backs are the surfaces most often channeled, fluted, or piped. Before channeling, study the upholstering of plain surfaces, as channeling does not change the parts of a frame on which muslin casings and covers finish. Methods of channeling are: [1] *Muslin casing and cover*, generally best for open-frame surfaces. [2] *Cover only*, generally best for channeling on a solid base (Fig. 1:23). [3] *Channeled pad*, the quickest and, in some ways, simplest method; but on spring built surfaces channeled pads may not be as comfortable or as durable as channeling in muslin casing and cover.

NOTE: Channeling and tufting (Chapter 21) often are combined (Fig. b 1:36).

SEC. 20:00B UPHOLSTERY MATERIALS / Channels are built with loose stuffing, felted padding, and compact stuffing. [1] *With loose stuffing* (Secs. 3:28–3:38), it is easier to make variations in shape and firmness of channels, factors affecting looks and comfort of a finished

583

job. But more careful work is required throughout to build smooth, consistent shapes with loose stuffing than with felted padding or compact stuffing. [2] *Felted padding* (Sec. 3:49) provides for fast, easy building of consistently shaped channels. But padding channels generally are not as resilient and durable as those made with loose or compact stuffings. When channeling is primarily for decoration, not use, padding channels may be the most practical. [3] *Compact stuffing* (Secs. 3:41–3:44) for channels may offer fast, easy building of desired shape. But it is not always as easy for inexperienced upholsterers to build shape and crown with compact as with loose stuffing. Nor is it as easy to change shape or firmness throughout a channel with compact stuffing.

SEC. 20:01 CHANNELING WITH LOOSE STUFFING	Upholster plain and channeled surfaces alike through webbing, burlapping, and basic shape, if any, as along the top of a back (Sec. 10:21). Roll edges (Sec. 5:05) seldom are used with channels except on scroll surfaces that are to be finished with borders or post panels (Secs. 11:05, 11:07). For channeled pad upholstery, see Sec. 20:12.
SEC. 20:02 STUFFING	For best results with loose stuffing, use top quality curled hair. It builds a surface soft enough for comfort and resilient enough to maintain shape.
SEC. 20:03 CHANNELS	Number and placement of channels on a surface is optional. Many small channels often creates a heightening and narrowing effect; a few wide channels may make an article seem broader and lower than it is. Horizontal channels (Fig. 1:23) generally are less comfortable than the vertical and usually have a broadening effect. [1] *For the average chair,* channels 3 to 5 inches wide at the crevices about midway between top and bottom are comfortable and show to good advantage. Narrower channels often seem crowded together. Channels much wider than about 5 inches may appear flat instead of fairly well rounded. [2] *Crevices between channels* should be on relatively firm foundations in order to hold channels in shape. Unless using a channeled pad, for best results on surfaces built with coil springs, zigzags, or rubber webbing, crevices should lie along springs or webbing. Crevices are sewn to the base of channeled pads. [3] *Placement and width* of channels are less important than uniform size and width. For comfort and durability, stuff all channels of a surface to the same density or firmness.
SEC. 20:04 BASIC CHANNELS	There are two types of channels on most surfaces: *End channels,* such as those at the sides of the back of an armless chair or above arms in wingless chairs (Fig. *b* 1:35), and *closed channels,* which are between

channels or which finish entirely against another surface (Fig. *a* 1:37). End channels are the same width as the closed on a surface, but the cover usually finishes on the outer side or back of a frame instead of the front surface. Unless allowance is made for this during planning and upholstering, end channels may be noticeably wider than the others.

SEC. 20:05 PLANNING VERTICAL CHANNELS	**SEC. 20:05A** / Before marking a surface for channels, decide on the number of channels and whether a channel or a crevice will lie along the middle (Sec. 20:03). With an even number of channels, a crevice lies along the middle of a surface; with an odd number, the middle of a channel lies along it. Widths of the top and bottom of a surface divided by the number of channels gives approximate widths of the tops and bottoms of the channels. *Tools:* Tape measure; chalk, crayon, or quick-drying paint (Sec. 2:16).

SEC. 20:05B   SIZE, SHAPE OF VERTICAL CHANNELS / [1] *Mark exact middle* of the top and bottom of surface being channeled; connect points with a straight line. [2] *Mark top and bottom* of surface for location of each crevice as based on planned channel width (Sec. 20:05A); work from middle line toward sides. When a crevice lies along the middle of a surface, the middle line establishes it. When a channel lies along the middle line or straddles it, its crevices are equally spaced from the middle line. I—Closed channels: Distances between all crevices at the same level should be identical. II—End channels: The space between the end or edge of a surface and the crevice on the other side of the proposed channel should be about ½ inch less than the space between closed channel crevices at the same levels. [3] *Draw lines connecting corresponding top and bottom* crevice marks. When the sides of a surface are relatively straight, Fig. *a* 20:05B, straight lines usually connect top and bottom points. When the overall shape of a surface changes between top and bottom, as at the armtops in many barrel backs, curved lines connect top and bottom crevice points. Plot these carefully, point by point, before making

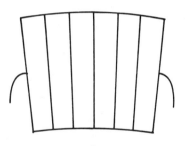 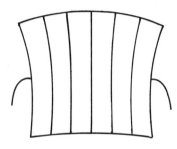

Fig. 20:05B   *a*   *b*

permanent marks. At any level between top and bottom, all crevice lines should be the same distance apart. However, channeling is flexible, and the patterns of crevices and widths can be arranged to suit the upholsterer.

**SEC. 20:06
MUSLIN
CASING FOR
VERTICAL
CHANNELS**

SEC. 20:06A / The amount of muslin casing needed depends on planned shape and thickness of channels. Often they are about 2 inches thick throughout midway between crevices, and curve slightly from the middle to fairly sharp breaks into the crevices, Fig. *a* 20:06A. To increase slope of a surface, channels may be appreciably thicker although narrower at the bottom than the top, *b;* to decrease slope, they may be thinner at the bottom than the top, *c.* For best results, build the middle and adjacent channels temporarily with skewers, stuffing, and muslin to determine the shape and fullness that seem best on a particular surface.

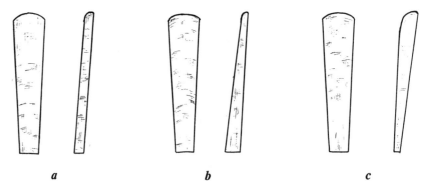

Fig. 20:06A   *a*   *b*   *c*

NOTE: Four inches is a fairly common channel width midway between top and bottom of a surface. When channels will have the same fullness throughout, a, *many upholsterers simply add 1½ to 2 inches to width to allow for fullness.*

Most inexperienced upholsterers get better results by building channels temporarily and then measuring the width of casing needed, especially when channels flare, *b.* *Tools:* Upholsterer's hammer, shears, large curved needle, regulator, upholstery skewers, sewing machine, chalk (Secs. 2:02, 2:04, 2:06, 2:07, 2:08, 2:15, 2:16). *Materials:* Tacks, upholstery twine, upholstery thread, muslin casing, large sheet of paper (Secs. 3:03, 3:08, 3:09, 3:48).

SEC. 20:06B CHANNEL PATTERNS / Prepare full-size paper patterns for channel muslin casings; save them for the cover. When all channels will be the same shape and fullness, a pattern based on the middle one is enough; but when channel shape and/or fullness changes, patterns for the middle one and for all those to one side are needed (on the assumption that both sides from the middle are to be identical). [*1*] *Measure distance between top and bottom* of a channel, and plot it full-size on paper, as at Point 1 in Fig. 20:06B; this line represents the middle of a channel. [*2*] *Form planned shape of top of channel* with a tape measure, and plot half this measurement on each side of the center line at the top, Point 2. Shape and plot casing width of bottom of channel the same way, Point 3. When shape and/or fullness of a channel will not be the same throughout, plot casing widths at several other points; the more points, the easier it is to make a smooth, consistently shaped pattern. [*3*] *Connect width marks* with lines to form the sides of a channel casing, Point 4. They should curve smoothly and be identical; minor differences usually are adjusted to satisfactory lines, but major differences can indicate inaccuracies in measuring and/or plotting, and should be reworked. Draw dash lines parallel to and ½ inch outside the finished width lines to provide ½-inch seam allowances. Extend width lines, Point 4 solid and dash, far enough for casing to finish on frame. Cut pattern along dash lines to make a template for cutting and sewing the casing and cover. [*5*] *For end channels* add enough width to the appropriate side of a casing or cover to finish on the outer side or on the back of a surface.

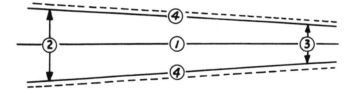

Fig. 20:06B

SEC. 20:06C CUTTING, SEWING CASING / Chalkmark and cut a muslin casing for each channel from the pattern or patterns. Sew them together the entire length with a flat, ½-inch seam (Sec. 12:02). Simplify installation by marking each channel casing at the bottom where it will meet the lower inner edge of the surface being channeled.

SEC. 20:07 BUILDING CHANNELS

SEC. 20:07A / Start with a channel at or next to the middle (Sec. 20:05B) of a surface. [*1*] *Center prepared casing* on surface with the bottom mark set to the lower inner edge of the frame. [*2*] *Tack casing*, at seam stitching, to the face of the bottom of the surface on the appropriate crevice line; draw casing tight toward top of crevice line and tack to the front surface, Fig. 20:07A. [*3*] *Cut a length of upholstery twine* to reach from bottom to top of channel plus 4 or 5 inches for handling. Tack it permanently at the bottom next to where casing is tacked. Stitch casing to burlap from bottom to top with a running stitch close to the seam stitching; pull twine tight and tack permanently at top.

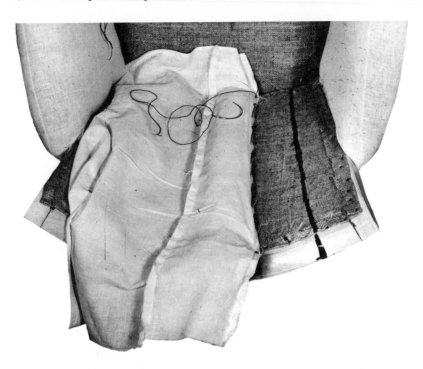

Fig. 20:07A

SEC. 20:07B **STUFF CHANNELS** / [1] *Install loose stuffing* (Secs. 5:11A–C) along marked channel. Use enough to make it quite firm; with too little stuffing, a channel will not hold shape. Stuffing should extend 3 or 4 inches beyond the top for it to crown above the top edge. At the bottom, stuffing should extend to the seat or deck of a chair or sofa or, in other articles, to an inch or so beyond the bottom edge. Use the same amount of stuffing for all closed channels of equal height, width, and fullness. [2] *Press stuffing* lightly but firmly toward the stitched down side of a channel while drawing the casing over it. Tack and stitch casing along the appropriate crevice line, as in Fig. 20:07A, tightening casing toward the top while stitching it. Build all closed channels this way. Do not finish them at top and bottom (Sec. 20:07D) until all channels are built.

SEC. 20:07C **END CHANNELS** / These usually need slightly more stuffing than the closed channels. [1] *In scroll surfaces having border or post panel* (Fig. *c* 1:45), casing finishes on outer sides of posts. [2] *When a pull-around cover* will be used, if an end channel is to puff out over another surface, such as an armtop, the muslin casing usually finishes on the back of a post. [3] *If an end channel has very little puff-out* at the sides (Fig. *b* 1:35), the casing usually finishes on the outer side of a post.

SEC. 20:07D   CLOSING CHANNELS / Close or finish top and bottom ends of channels essentially the same way. Pack in enough loose stuffing to build firm, smooth shapes for ends of channels as they wrap around the bottom and top edges of a surface or frame.   [1] *Bottom ends* usually project just far enough to fit flush against an adjacent surface, such as the seat or deck of a chair or sofa. Build bottom ends fairly flat in order to prevent gaps between adjacent surfaces.   [2] *Top ends* usually project 1 or more inches from the edge of a surface or frame. They should have appreciable crown (Sec. 5:14), the shape of which is optional.   [3] *When closing channels* at top and bottom, rip out seam stitching in order to finish casing smoothly. How much to rip out depends on the particular job; but generally it is necessary to rip casing seams to the outer back edge of a frame or surface. All seams can be ripped out the same amount, but it is better to rip out each one when starting work on it.   [4] *Draw casing snugly in place* over end of channel and edge of frame; tack it an inch or so beyond the edge, Fig. 20:07D. Sliptack first on seam stitching line at each crevice, then at the midpoint between crevices. Work channel end into the wanted shape; tack casing permanently at crevices and midpoint.

Fig. 20:07D

[5] *Pleat channel ends* (Sec. 5:17) to build a durable firm shape. For best appearance, pleat near crevices rather than at the middle of a channel. With the sides tightened and tacked permanently, make one or two small pleats from the sides toward the middle; then pleat balance of casing toward crevices. To prevent gaps between casings, finish the side pleat of a channel over the adjacent channel casing.

**SEC. 20:08
COVERING
VERTICAL
CHANNELS**

SEC. 20:08A / First plot channel covers according to length and planned use of a cover design or pattern. Then cut covers to shape from paper patterns (Sec. 20:06B). Channel covers usually are longer than casings (Sec. 20:08B). Use cover stretchers (Sec. 11:09). The method of planning channel covers in Sec. 20:08D is especially important for: [1] *Patterned goods,* to keep the dominant part of a design consistently placed; if it is a real or suggested vertical figure, it usually shows the best advantage if it runs up the middle of channels.

[2] *Fabrics,* to avoid uneven stretch, which generally comes from working them on the bias instead of more or less straight along warp and weft.   *Tools:* Upholsterer's hammer, shears, regulator, sewing machine, chalk (Secs. 2:02, 2:04, 2:07, 2:15, 2:16).   *Materials:* Tacks, back-spring twine, upholstery thread, felted padding (Secs. 3:03, 3:08, 3:09, 3:49).

SEC. 20:08B   COVER SIZE   /   Channel covers usually are longer than casings because of finishing on the seat rail, not on the lower back rail or on the back of an arm rail. Measure combined lengths of cover and stretcher from top of seat rail up over the surface being upholstered to where cover will finish at the top (Chapter 11). Add 2 inches to both top and bottom for general handling. Cover stretchers usually start about 1 inch below the bottom front edge of a back rail, inner edge of an arm rail; add ½ inch to length of cover for sewing stretcher.

SEC. 20:08C   PLAIN, DENSELY PATTERNED GOODS   /   Plot channel covers the same way for plain or nonpatterned goods and *a)* those densely patterned with fairly small and closely grouped regular figures, and *b)* those having large and similar overall figures, such as the leaves in Fig. 11:24E, which are close together or even overlap.   [1] *Mark cover* with a vertical line representing the middle of the channel, the dash line in Fig. *a* 20:08C. Length of this line equals the measured length plus various allowances (Sec. 20:08B).   [2] *On the vertical line,* make a short horizontal mark 1 inch above where the stretcher will start. This represents the lower front edge of an inside back or an arm rail.   [3] *Mark paper pattern* (Sec. 20:06) midway between sides at top and bottom.   [4] *Align top and bottom center marks* on pattern with the vertical center line on the cover. Set bottom of pattern to the short line representing the lower front edge of a back or inner edge of an

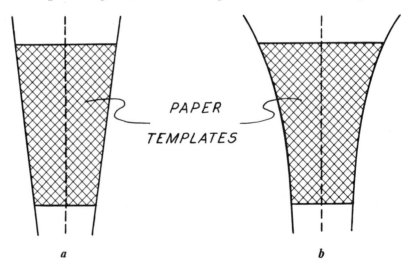

PAPER

TEMPLATES

Fig. 20:08C   *a*   *b*

arm rail, [2] above.   [5] *Mark cover along outer edges of pattern*, solid lines in Fig. *a* 20:08C, extending lines to full length of channel. If channel sides are straight, extensions should be straight; if sides curve or flare, *b*, project extensions to follow that curve. When the sides have appreciable curve or flare, inexperienced upholsterers usually do a better job, and have less chance of spoiling or wasting cover goods, by building a temporary channel with muslin and using it as an exact pattern for the cover.

Sec. 20:08D Lightly Patterned, Dominant-Figure Goods / Usually there is a noticeable, real or imaginary, vertical line in goods having a somewhat open or scattered design or a scenic (Fig. 11:24D). Except for placement of the dominant parts of a design, plot these goods for channels the same as plain covers (Sec. 20:08C).   [1] *Select the real or imaginary vertical* of a design that is to lie along the middle of a channel; mark it clearly on cover goods. With some designs the overall effect may be more attractive if the vertical is to the right or left of the middle of a channel.   [2] *Decide which part of a dominant vertical* will go near the top of a channel. Where the top-figure lies is a matter of choice. Some upholsterers set all top-figures the same distance down from the top edge of a surface; others set them all the same distance up from the bottom. Covers usually offer several attractive ways of setting figures.   [3] *From the top-figure* as marked on the cover, measure the distance down to the lower front edge of a back, inner edge of an arm, rail. Mark this point of the vertical center line. From here on proceed as for a plain cover (Sec. 20:08C[3]–[5]).

Sec. 20:08E Prepare Cover /   [1] *Cut channel covers* as marked on goods. Sew them together the same as muslin casings (Sec. 20:06B[3]).   [2] *Sew stretchers*, if any, across bottom.   [3] *Turn sewn cover wrong-side-up.* At each seam spread goods apart and lay a piece of back-spring twine tight against the stitching. Twine should be 3 or 4 inches longer than cover and stretcher combined. Sew covers together close to but not tight against twine. The twine is to hold covers tight into the crevices between channels; but unless it is loose enough for the covers to move somewhat freely, twine may bind them and cause wrinkles.   [4] *Mark each channel cover at the bottom* where it is to be set to the level of the lower edge of the back or arm rail.

SEC. 20:09 INSTALLING COVER ON MUSLIN CHANNELS

Sec. 20:09A /   Except for where they finish at top and bottom and for sliding along crevice twines (Sec. 20:08E), channel covers are treated much the same as muslin casings. Spread a separate layer of padding over each channel. It should extend an inch or so beyond junctions of channels and adjacent surfaces, and to the outer rear edge of a frame when a pull-around cover is used on end channels (Figs. *b* 1:36, *b* 1:37). [*1*] *At top of knife-edge and rounded backs*, extend padding to rear edge of top rail. [*2*] *In scroll backs and arms*, extend padding to but not below top of underrail strip. [*3*] *At crevices*, extend padding smoothly to stitching.

SEC. 20:09B   INSTALL COVER   /   [*1*] *Place cover on padded surface*, with bottom marks on cover set to the lower edge of the rail. Work cover seams carefully into crevices and down to the stitching (Sec. 20:07B). [*2*] *Draw stretcher*, if any, and bottom of cover under the back or arm liner, and sliptack to seat rail at enough points to hold it securely. While tacking, draw cover fairly snug toward seat rail but not tight enough to displace it along the lower edge of the back or arm rail or liner. [*3*] *Tack sewn-in crevice twines* (Sec. 20:08C) permanently to seat rail opposite the crevice of each channel. [*4*] Tighten (Sec. 5:18) covers moderately snugly toward top. Keep grain of goods straight, and sliptack at the middle of each channel. As necessary, rip out an inch or so of the channel cover seams, and tack twines temporarily to the back of a frame about ¾ inch below the top edge. Work each channel cover smooth and tight vertically and into crevices; sliptack at enough points to hold covers securely. While tightening toward the top, be careful not to loosen or displace bottom ends of cover. [*5*] *Tighten covers toward bottom* the same as toward the top. Cut cover stretcher or bottom ends of cover to fit around tacked crevice twines.

SEC. 20:09C   CLOSING CHANNELS   /   After tightening and adjusting covers fairly well throughout, loosen a crevice twine at or next to the middle of the top and pull it as tightly as possible downward over the top of a frame. Rip out as much seam between channel covers as is necessary for them to fit smoothly over the top and into the crevices. While pulling twines tight, smooth the cover upward and over the top. Tack twines permanently about ¾ inch below top edge of frame. Treat all channels the same way, working from the middle alternately toward the sides of a surface. [*1*] *At the top*, close ends of channel covers the same as muslin casings (Sec. 20:07D). Due to stretch of cover goods and shape of channel ends, wrinkles often develop at the top along crevices. Eliminate them by altering the padding. [*2*] *At the bottom*, extra padding usually is wadded into the channels to build the ends flush against a seat or deck.

SEC. 20:09D   END CHANNELS   /   Finish these along the back of a frame as a pull-around inside back cover (Sec. 16:07), or on outer sides of posts as a paneled or bordered plain inside back cover (Sec. 16:08). Below armtops, finish end channels at the sides as any inside back cover.

SEC. 20:10 CHANNELING WITH COVER ONLY ON OPEN-FRAME SURFACE

SEC. 20:10A OPEN-FRAME SURFACE / This section deals with vertical channeling with a cover only on an open-frame surface; for solid-base work, see Sec. 20:11. The disadvantage of channeling with cover only is that it must be installed properly from the start; it cannot, without considerable extra work, be loosened and adjusted after other work has been done. [*1*] *Prepare surface for channels* (Sec. 20:05). [*2*] *Prepare channel covers,* and assemble cover for installation without twines or twine stitching (Secs. 20:06, 20:08). [*3*] *Build channels* with loose stuffing and padding or with padding-only. Stuffing and padding (Sec. 20:10B) generally produce more resilient, durable, and better shape-holding channels. Using padding-only is easier and faster (Sec. 20:10C).

SEC. 20:10B LOOSE STUFFING AND PADDING / Build channels (Sec. 20:07), but cover stuffing with a layer of padding (Sec. 20:09A). Then draw cover over padding, and stitch to burlap. Adjust cover tightly and evenly from middle to top and bottom before or during stitching, as later it cannot be adjusted without ripping out stitching. While drawing channel covers in place, hold stuffing and padding in shape and against the stitched-down side of a channel. While setting and stitching-down the side of a stuffed channel, take care not to displace stuffing-padding. Finish top and bottom ends of channels (Secs. 20:09C, D).

SEC. 20:10C PADDING-ONLY / The amount of padding needed depends on the width, length, desired fullness and firmness of channels. For a back or arm channel about 4 inches wide between crevices and having 5 inches of cover between seams, top quality upholstery felted padding about 14 inches wide and 5 inches longer than a channel usually makes a moderately soft but satisfactory channel; use about 1½ times this amount for seat channels. Fold padding for each channel loosely into a smooth roll; place it the same way as loose stuffing, and build channels (Sec. 20:07). For best results, inexperienced upholsterers should build one or two test channels to get the shape they want and to find out how much padding actually is needed.

NOTE: For padding-only channels, install cover as in Sec. 20:10B.

SEC. 20:11 CHANNELING WITH COVER ONLY ON SOLID-BASE SURFACE

SEC. 20:11A / Channeling on a solid base is done with cover goods only. Work each channel "finally" smooth and tight while installing it; later it cannot be adjusted for placement or to remove wrinkles except by untacking and redoing the job. For more resilient, durable, and better shape-holding channels, upholster with loose stuffing and padding. But for primarily decorative channels, padding-only is usually satisfactory. *Tools:* Upholsterer's hammer, shears, regulator, sewing machine, chalk, yardstick (Secs. 2:02, 2:04, 2:07, 2:15, 2:16). *Materials:* Tacks, upholstery thread, cardboard stripping, loose stuffing and/or felted padding (Secs. 3:03, 3:09, 3:26, 3:28–3:38, 3:49).

SEC. 20:11B PREPARATION / [1] *Plan channel* placements and widths (Sec. 20:05). Mark crevice lines; then draw a line parallel to each crevice line ½ inch from it in the direction of working, Fig. 20:11B. These are quide lines for tacking seam edges of the sewn cover so that the sides of channels will lie neat and straight along crevice lines. [2] *Prepare channel covers,* and assemble cover for installation without twines or twine stitching (Secs. 20:06, 20:08). [3] *Place appropriate cover seam* along a middle crevice line, with the bottom cover mark set to the lower front edge of a frame or base, and the edge of the seam along the guide line. Tack cover permanently along middle of seam allowance at enough points, usually 3 or 4 inches apart, to hold it securely; work from bottom toward top, and tighten goods for final adjustment while tacking. [4] *Cardboard cover* (Sec. 9:13D) from bottom to top, with the edge of the stripping set along the seam stitching; if the edge is on either side of the stitching, channels will not be satisfactory.

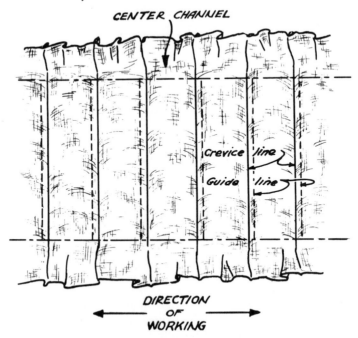

CENTER CHANNEL

Crevice line

Guide line

DIRECTION OF WORKING

Fig. 20:11B

SEC. 20:11C LOOSE STUFFING AND PADDING / Set desired amount of loose stuffing in place close to the cardboarded side of a channel and extending to but not beyond the seam line for the free side of a channel. Tack stuffing (Secs. 5:11A–C). Spread a layer of padding over stuffing from the cardboarded to the free side of a channel. Stuffing and padding must not extend beyond the seam line of a base; they can prevent good installation of the cover. Complete covering of the side of the channel, and start the next one (Secs. 20:11B[3], [4]); often it is necessary to hold edges of a seam allowance to a guide line with the point of a regulator while tacking and cardboarding the cover seam of a stuffed channel. Cover tops and bottoms of channels, and end channels (Secs. 20:09C, D).

SEC. 20:11D PADDING-ONLY / Prepare padding-only stuffing (Sec. 20:10C). Set a roll of padding on the base close to cardboarded side of a channel. While drawing cover over padding, press padding firmly but lightly toward the tacked side to keep it from being displaced. Complete covering as in Sec. 20:11C.

**SEC. 20:12
CHANNELED
PAD**

SEC. 20:12A PAD CHANNELING / This term means building channels on a base of burlap or other material and tacking the pad of channels to a frame. It usually is done for an open frame; it is easier to channel direct on a solid base (Sec. 20:11). Pad channeling is fast and may enable inexperienced upholsterers to do a smooth job more easily. But since a channeled pad is tacked to a frame and not attached to support upholstery, such as webbing or a burlap cover (Sec. 5:02), it is not held there although it may fit snugly in place. Pad channeling usually is on a somewhat unyielding surface, such as a firm inside pad back (Sec. 20:12B). On a surface that has much go-down, such as most spring surfaces, a channeled pad is likely to tear loose from the frame. Channels are usually stuffed with padding only.   *Tools:* Upholsterer's hammer, shears, sewing machine, chalk, flat stuffing rod (Secs. 2:02, 2:04, 2:15, 2:16, 20:12F).   *Materials:* Tacks, upholstery thread, burlap or other pad-base material, upholstery padding, large sheet of paper (Secs. 3:03, 3:09, 3:24, 3:49).

SEC. 20:12B TWO PREPARATION METHODS / Pad channeling may be done on a surface that has been properly webbed and burlapped. A better method is to build a plain surface with a light layer of loose stuffing, incase with muslin, then install channeled pad. The stuffed surface usually is about 1-inch thick, and tapers to a smooth but firm junction with the inner edges of a frame. There are two ways to prepare a channel pad.   [1] *The traditional* method (Sec. 20:12C) is to machine sew channel covers to a sheet of base material. The advantages are: Three instead of four thicknesses of goods to sew, and the base, a solid sheet of goods, is stronger and easier to install without uneven or irregular stretching. The disadvantage is that the sewn cover-and-base can be a hard-to-handle bundle in a sewing machine.

[2] *The modern* method is to cut cover and base material into strips for each channel, and sew them together (Secs. 20:12D, E). The major advantage is there is no bunching of goods in the sewing machine. Disadvantages are that a pad may be appreciably weaker than the solid base along crevices, and there are 4 thicknesses of goods to sew.

SEC. 20:12C TRADITIONAL PAD CHANNELING / [1] *Cut burlap* or other base material the shape of the surface to be channeled. It should be 2 inches wider than the surface, and for an inside back or arm, should be long enough to reach from the finishing point at the top down to the seat rail plus 4 inches for handling. [2] *Sliptack base material* in place along the inner surface of a frame. Tack at enough points, usually 1 or 2 inches apart, to hold base smooth and tight. On it mark channel crevice lines (Sec. 20:05) and the lower front edge of a surface. Remove base. [3] *Prepare and sew channel cover strips* (Secs. 20:08A–E[2]). However, for pad channeling more than any other method, there is a tendency to base fullness of channels on their width; for a 4-inch wide channel, an additional 1½ to 2 inches of cover commonly is allowed for fullness plus ½ inch on each side for seaming. Note that Sec. 20:08E[3], [4] does not now apply to pad channeling. [4] *Sew cover to marked base* along crevice lines. Be sure to set bottom marks of channel covers to bottom marks on base. Sew close to seam stitching of the covers. Do not sew outer sides of end channels. [5] *If channels are to go over the top of a surface* (Fig. *b* 1:35), install crevice twines (Sec. 20:08E[3], [4]). Start and sew them in place 1 or 2 inches below top of base. [6] *Stuff; install channel pad* (Sec. 20:12F).

SEC. 20:12D MODERN PAD CHANNELING / Use strips of goods for base as well as channel covers. Sew them together—two strips of base and two of cover at the same time—to form pad casing. [1] *Sliptack uncut base material* to frame and mark for channel crevice (Sec. 20:12C[2]); do not remove or cut at this time. [2] *Prepare base paper patterns* from marked base. The more accurate these are, the easier the work and the neater the finished job will be. If all channels are the same width and shape throughout, a master pattern is enough. But when channels are not identical, make a pattern for each. However, patterns for corresponding channels on each side of the middle should be the same. Remove base goods. [3] *Midway between sides at top and bottom,* mark each pattern for centering. Place pattern on base goods, with centering marks set to the same thread of the material to prevent, as much as possible, working the base goods on the bias. Mark sides of base strip ½ inch from sides of pattern to leave necessary seam allowance. [4] *Plan and cut,* but do not sew, channel covers (Secs. 20:08A–E).

Sec. 20:12E   Sew Pad Casing / Sew two strips of base and two of cover together at the same time, Fig. 20:12E, to make channel pad casing. *[1] Assemble base and cover strips* with sides aligned, *a;* a base strip on the bottom, two cover strips right-side-to-right-side, and then a base strip on top. Sew the first channel, an end channel, on one side only, usually the righthand side. In actual work, cover strips extend beyond base strips at top and bottom and are sewn together.

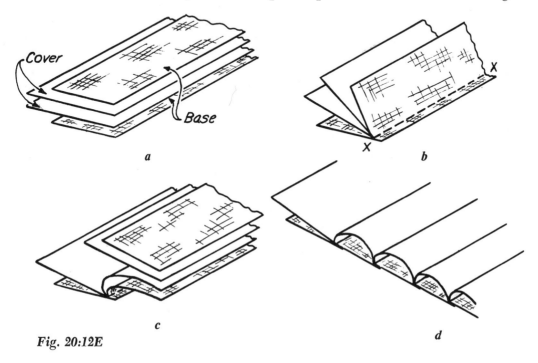

Fig. 20:12E

[2] *Sew the four strips together* ½ inch from the edges, Line X-X, *b*. [3] *Draw the two top strips*—base and cover—to the right over the seams, and align their free edges. Then place and align another cover strip right-side-to-right-side with the first cover strip, and another base strip on top, *c*. Sew the four strips together ½ inch from the edges, Line X-X, *b*. Continue placing and sewing strips of cover and base until all closed channels and the inner sides of the end channels are sewn. The finished casing has a pieced-together base with channel covers sewn into it, *d*. It is most important to use strong thread and do a good sewing job; if the stitching breaks or loosens and the channels come apart, there will be a very difficult repair job. [4] *For channels going over top of surface,* see Sec. 20:12C[5]. [5] *Stuff; install channel pad* (Sec. 20:12F).

Sec. 20:12F   Stuff, Install Channel Pad / Stuff closed channels with rolls of felted padding (Sec. 20:10C). Insert rolls in casing with a flat stuffing rod. This homemade tool is a strip of muslin, about 2 inches wide and at least 6 inches longer than the channels to be stuffed, glued or tacked to the end of a yardstick or similar smooth length of wood; use tacks too small to protrude on either side of wood. [1] *Place roll of padding* on the yardstick close to the fastened cloth; draw cloth strip over it. Push that end of the stuffing rod through channel casing. Slide rod around to work padding into wanted position. [2] *Pull cloth strip* out of the stuffed channel and then the rod.   [3] *Set stuffed channel pad* in place on the front or inner surface of the frame, work it smooth and tight, and tack permanently; before tacking permanently, underturn burlap base so two thicknesses can be tacked for maximum strength. Then stuff end channels with rolls of padding, and complete other channels top and bottom (Sec. 20:09).

SEC. 20:13 HORIZONTAL CHANNELING

Sec. 20:13A /   Horizontal channels usually are satisfactory only on flat surfaces such as a straight arm, flat back, or seat (Fig. 1:23).   [1] *Horizontal channels* make a vertical surface seem wider and lower than it is, perhaps even squatty.   [2] *Stuffing of horizontal channels* on a vertical surface tends to pack down toward the lower sides, making them bottom-heavy instead of smoothly rounded.   [3] *Channel width* (distance between crevices) is the same from side to side or end to end.   [4] *Top and bottom channels* on a surface often are slightly wider than the others.

Sec. 20:13B Construction /   Construction of horizontal channels is basically the same as for verticals (Secs. 20:00–20:12) except: [1] *Right and left ends* of horizontal channels finish on the same surfaces as top and bottom ends of vertical jobs.   [2] *Top and bottom horizontal channels* finish on the same surfaces as top and bottom ends of vertical channels.   [3] *When using horizontal channels on inside arms and backs,* channel crevices of arms and back should meet at the same levels. Due to the flare of arms away from a back, it may be necessary to change the width of arm channels slightly.

SEC. 20:14 CHANNELING WITH COMPACT STUFFING

Sec. 20:14A /   Channeling with compact stuffing (Secs. 3:41–3:44) usually is difficult for inexperienced upholsterers. But the superior softness and durability, especially for an inside back, are well worth the effort. Difficulties are in the handling of stuffing more than the methods of upholstering. Minimize difficulties by using the stuffing easiest to handle.   [1] *Compare handling qualities* of polyfoam, foam rubber, and rubberized hair. Since a satisfactory job can be done with any of them, cost and availability may be reasonable determining factors.   [2] *Compact stuffing 1 to 2 inches thick* is adequate for most channels that are more than about 2 inches wide at their narrowest points. Use thinner stock for thinner and/or very flat channels. [3] *Channeling with compact stuffing* is done on pad and spring surfaces; the methods are the same. With the same size and shape of relatively thick channels and stuffing, pad and spring surfaces have about the same initial softness. [4] *Web, spring-up if a spring surface, and burlap* the same as for a plain surface. Stuff lightly with a loose stuffing, build necessary crown (Sec. 5:14), and incase with muslin the regular way for that particular surface.

SEC. 20:14B PLAN CHANNELS / Plan and mark channel crevice lines on muslin casing (Sec. 20:05). Plan fullness and shape of channels (Sec. 20:06). Prepare a paper pattern for each channel the same as for channel muslin casing, except: [1] *At the sides*, cut patterns along connecting lines, as in Point 4 of Fig. 20:06B. [2] *At the top*, make patterns long enough to reach the point of finishing compact stuffing at the top. Compact stuffing extends to the same points as loose stuffing. [3] *At the bottom*, cut patterns long enough for stuffing to reach at least 1 inch below the top of an adjacent surface; for example, 1 inch below the top of a seat or deck that finishes against an inside arm or back. If a surface being channeled does not finish against another one, treat the bottom of it the same as the top.

SEC. 20:14C PREPARE COMPACT STUFFING / Cut each channel stuffing from its pattern. To strengthen the middle of a channel made of 1-inch or thinner stock, cut a strip of stuffing the full length of a channel and a half-inch or so wide; cement it along the middle of the back of the channel stuffing. Or use scraps of stuffing to build a strengthening strip.

SEC. 20:14D INSTALL COMPACT STUFFING / Cement channel stuffing strips in place. The back of each strip should lie smoothly against the muslin surface, and the sides must lie along the middle of the marked crevice lines. Only for excessively curved surfaces may it be necessary to trim the back of a channel strip in order for it to lie flat against the muslin; on ordinary surfaces stuffing will fit satisfactorily. [1] *If a strengthening strip* is used (Sec. 20:14C), glue stuffing for installation along the back of the strip and inward for about ½ inch along the sides. [2] *Trim back of strip* at the top if necessary to make it fit neatly around and over a frame. [3] *Simplify installing* strips of rubberized hair by stitching them in place along the sides. The stuffing must, of course, be glued to the muslin. Stitching shapes and holds stuffing in place while glue dries. [4] *Keep outer sides of strips* of compact stuffing absolutely free of cement or bonding agent.

SEC. 20:14E   COMPLETE CHANNELING / For best results, incase compact stuffing surface with muslin. Prepare and install casing (Secs. 20:08, 20:09) except that no padding is used. New paper patterns are needed for the casing. Then prepare cover and install it, with padding (Secs. 20:08, 20:09).

NOTE: Polyfoam and foam rubber channels are often covered without first incasing with muslin. This may be done with rubberized hair, too; but to eliminate possible scratching action, rubberized hair should be incased with muslin.

21

tufting

SEC. 21:00 GENERAL FACTS	**Sec. 21:00A Difficult Style** / Tufting or deep buttoning (Figs. c 1:35, a 1:36, c 1:49, d 1:51) is the most difficult style of upholstery. [1] *Unless buttons* are spaced consistently and according to the overall shape of a surface, it may seem or be lopsided. [2] *If stuffing* is placed incorrectly or the wrong amount used, a finished surface is apt to be lumpy instead of smooth between buttons. [3] *If a casing or cover* is installed carelessly, surfaces between buttons will be irregular in size, shape, and density or firmness. [4] *Attractive, durable tufting* usually is the result of trial and correction; tufting should be done first in muslin casing.

NOTE: Tufting and channeling (Chapter 20) often are combined (Fig. b 1:36, Sec. 21:04F).

Sec. 21:00B Common Methods / Before tufting, study the upholstering of a plain surface. The parts of a frame on which muslin casing and cover finish are the same when tufting. Common methods of tufting are: [*1*] *Tufting by individual pockets*, usually done when using a loose stuffing.   [*2*] *Tufting a completely stuffed surface*, built with either a loose or a compact stuffing; many custom upholsterers prefer this method.

SEC. 21:01 **PLAIN,** **TUFTED** **SURFACES** **MUCH ALIKE**	Upholster plain and tufted surfaces the same way through webbing, burlap, and basic shape, if any, as along the top of an inside back (Sec. 10:21). Roll edges (Sec. 5:05) seldom are used with tufting except when upholstering, with loose stuffing, scroll surfaces having post panels or borders; then fronts of arms and sides of backs (Fig. *c* 1:45) have roll edges.
SEC. 21:02 **STUFFING**	[*1*] *Loose stuffings* (Secs. 3:28–3:38). Use only the best quality curled hair. Less resilient stuffings build an unnecessarily hard surface and cannot support casing and cover properly. [*2*] *Compact stuffings* (Secs. 3:41–3:44). Polyfoam and foam rubber are excellent for tufting, especially for inexperienced workers; use soft or medium compression stock. Rubberized hair's stiffness makes it an easier tufting stuffing for flat and slightly rounded surfaces (Fig. *c* 1:35) than those having appreciable curve (Fig. *b* 1:50); use medium stock. [*3*] *Thickness*. Stuffing usually is 1½ to 2 inches thick. However, this is optional. The principal guide to thickness is how soft or firm a tufted surface should be. As a rule, the thicker it is, the softer, and the thinner it is, the firmer, although firm–thick and soft–thin surfaces are built.
SEC. 21:03 **NUMBER,** **PLACEMENT** **OF TUFTING** **POINTS**	Generally, the space between tufting points is in relation to size and thickness of a surface. Large surfaces, such as an inside back, usually are 1½- to 2-inches thick between burlap or other base and cover, and tufting points are 4 to 6 inches apart. In smaller and thinner surfaces, tufting points usually are closer together. Tufting patterns are flexible and should be based on a specific article and its desired appearance, not on any set space between tufting points. For spring barrel backs, plan tufting points to lie in vertical rows on springs or on burlap between springs, not some points on springs and others on burlap.
SEC. 21:04 **PLAN TUFTING** **POINTS**	**SEC. 21:04A** / Plan tufting points carefully, taking into account the overall shape of a surface. Before marking it, decide on the number of horizontal and vertical rows of tufting points and the approximate shaft of the tufts or buns between them. They usually are diamond-shaped (Fig. *c* 1:35); height and width of diamonds are optional. *Tools:* Tape measure, chalk or quick-drying paint. **SEC. 21:04B PLOT TUFTING POINTS** / Connect the exact middle of the top and bottom of a surface by a straight line, Fig. 21:04B. Unless

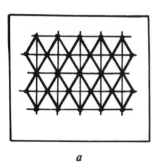 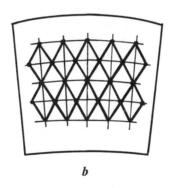 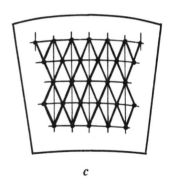

a   b   c

Fig. 21:04B

the middle tuft and tufting points are set accurately, the finished job may appear lopsided. At the desired height of the lowest row of tufting points above the bottom of a surface, draw a horizontal line; often it is 1 to 3 inches higher above the bottom edge than the distance between that line and the one to be drawn above it. On moderately large surfaces, the second horizontal line generally is from 4 to 6 inches above the first. Draw horizontal lines spaced the same distance throughout a surface. The top line usually is set below the top edge of a surface slightly less than the bottom horizontal line is set above the bottom edge. [1] *Flat surfaces.* Horizontal lines usually parallel the bottom edge, *a*. [2] *Barrel-type or curved surfaces.* Horizontal lines generally drop gradually from the mid-point of a surface to the sides, *b*. Droppage is different for each line. The bottom line usually almost parallels the bottom edge. The top line, which actually is parallel to the top edge of a surface, usually has the most downward curve toward the sides. Other horizontal lines curve proportionately. [3] *Approximately rectangular surfaces, a, b.* The bottom horizontal line generally has one less tufting point than the second row; the third row has one less than the second and fourth rows, etc. [4] *Nonrectangular surfaces.* If the same size tufts or buns are built throughout, there are more tufting points on the wider than on the narrower portion, *c*.

SEC. 21:04C LOCATE TUFTING POINTS / Locations of tufting points on horizontal lines determine width and shape of tufts or buns. When width equals the space between horizontal lines, the tufts are square-diamond. Fat-diamond tufts come from making the width greater, thin-diamond tufts from making the width less, than the space between horizontal lines. [1] *Flat rectangular surfaces* (Fig. *a* 21:04B). Tufts or buns usually are the same width throughout. [2] *Flared or barrel-type surfaces.* Tufts either get wider from bottom to top (*b*), or there may be more tufts (*c*). [3] *Locate tufting points on* *bottom horizontal line.* The first tufting point (Fig. 21:04B) usually is at the crossing of the bottom horizontal and middle vertical lines in order to keep a button or tufting point from being too close for good appearance to the corners of a surface. Mark the other tufting points, based on planned width, along the bottom horizontal line; work from middle toward sides. As a rule, the space between the last tufting point and the side of a surface is about the same as the space between adjacent tufting points on that line. [4] *Mark middle tufting points* on alternate horizontal lines—third, fifth, etc. [5] *Locate tufting points on the highest horizontal line that has been marked for a middle tufting point.* With the bottom horizontal line as #1 and counting upward, the highest marked line is odd-numbered. [6] *Same number of tufting points* on corresponding horizontal lines (*a, b*). Carefully measure width of surface along the highest horizontal line that has been marked for a mid-point. Divide measured width by 1 plus the number of tufting points marked on the bottom horizontal line; the result is the width between tufting points along the highest marked horizontal line. On flared and most barrel-type surfaces, widths between tufting points are greater at the top than the bottom. [7] *Same size tufts* throughout a surface (*a, c*). In theory, on the highest horizontal line that has been marked for a middle tufting point, locate the other tufting points the same distance apart as those on the bottom horizontal line. But in actual work, tufting points on the highest marked line usually are closer together than those on the bottom line in order to avoid setting tufting points at the ends of the highest line too near the sides of a surface. For best appearance, a tufting point should not, as a rule, be nearer the side of a surface than half the space between adjacent tufting points on the same line.

SEC. 21:04D ESTABLISH BASIC SHAPE OF TUFTS, PLEAT LINES / Connect corresponding tufting points on the bottom and highest marked horizontal lines; extend connecting lines to top and bottom edges of surface (Fig. 21:04B). Mark tufting points on alternate horizontal lines—third, fifth, etc. [1] *Same number of tufting points* at top and bottom of a nonrectangular surface (*b*). Connecting points are further apart at top than bottom and should be proportionately apart throughout surface. [2] *Same size tufts* throughout surface (*a, c*). On a rectangular flat surface, connecting lines are straight and parallel from top to bottom. On a nonrectangular surface (*c*), connecting lines are straight and usually converge slightly from bottom to top due to the top spacing between tufting points being slightly less than that at the bottom (Sec. 21:04C[7]). [3] *Mark tufting points on even-numbered* horizontal lines—second, fourth, etc., from bottom of surface. Tufting points on these lines are exactly halfway between the vertical connecting lines. Tufting points between a vertical line and the side of a surface should be the same distance from the nearest tufting point as between adjacent tufting points on the same horizontal line. [*4*] *Connect tufting points by diagonal lines* to establish basic shapes of tufts or buns and pleat lines of casing and cover. Throughout a tufted area, pleat (Sec. 5:17) only along diagonal lines. Between a tufted area and the edges of a surface, generally pleating is done only from the edges straight to the nearest tufting points.

Sec. 21:04E   Alternate Placement of Tufting Points / If a tuft or bun, instead of a tufting point, is to be set at the middle of the bottom horizontal line, measure half the width of the tuft to each side of the middle line. Mark these points, and from them mark the remaining tuft widths to right and left. Then proceed as in Secs. 21:04B[3]–21:04D.

NOTE: If there are seven or more horizontal rows of tufting points, plotting them may be started on the lowest even-numbered instead of bottom line; with this change from odd- to even-numbered lines continue as specified above, projecting to the bottom horizontal line as necessary.

Sec. 21:04F   Tufting and Channeling / Combination tufting and channeling often is done on inside backs and other relatively large surfaces (Figs. *b* 1:36, *c* 1:49, *a* 1:50). Mark tufting points; then channel crevices from selected tufting points. [*1*] *Draw middle vertical and horizontal lines for the lowest row of tufting points on a surface* (Sec. 21:04B). Height of this line above a seat or deck is optional; usually it is 2 to 3 inches more above a seat, or top of a cushion, than the distance between the first and second horizontal lines of tufting points. If the first horizontal line is too low, channels do not show to good advantage. [*2*] *Mark tufting points along lowest horizontal line* (Secs. 21:04B–E). Mark channel crevices (Secs. 20:03–20:05) from lowest tufting points to bottom edge of surface, Fig. 21:04F. [*3*] *Mark tufting points* throughout remainder of surface (Secs. 21:04B–D).

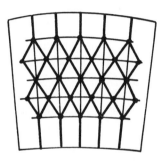   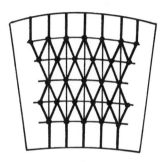

Fig. 21:04F   *a*   *b*

Mark channel crevices from top row of tufting points to top edge of surface. Any number of channels may be built. But when the top of a surface is appreciably wider than the bottom, the best appearance generally comes from having one more channel at the top than at the bottom (*b*). End channels (Sec. 20:04) are often slightly wider than closed channels at the top of a tufted and channeled surface (Fig. *c* 1:35).

SEC. 21:05 **BUTTONS**	When cloth tuft or loop buttons (Sec. 3:60) will be used on a solid base, at each tufting point drill a small hole for button twines.

SEC. 21:06 **MUSLIN** **CASING**	Finish muslin casing on the same parts of a frame whether upholstery is plain or tufted. [*1*] *When measuring width and length* of a surface, form the approximate shape of tufts or buns between tufting points with a steel tape measure. Because tufting is often a trial and correction process for inexperienced workers, it is advisable to build a few complete tufts to determine shape. This also gives a fairly exact amount of goods needed per tuft before cutting casing or cover for an entire surface. [*2*] *Transfer measurements* taken from the sample tufts onto a large sheet of paper. Mark all tufting points, and channel crevices if any; work from the center line of a pattern toward the sides. Plot tufting points and crevice lines accurately; otherwise a tufted surface is apt to be irregular, and the casing cut for it may be too small. [*3*] *Transfer completed paper pattern* to goods by cutting small holes in the paper at the tufting points and marking through them with chalk. Save pattern for layout of the cover; note on it any changes made in tufting measurements while building surface in muslin.

SEC. 21:07 **TUFTING BY** **INDIVIDUAL** **POCKETS**	**Sec. 21:07A** / When using tack buttons (Sec. 3:60), tack muslin casing at tufting points; tack slightly away from the center of a tufting point to leave space for the tack button. When using cloth tuft or loop buttons, stitch casing in place exactly at tufting points. *Tools:* Upholsterer's hammer, shears, long straight and small curved needles, regulator, upholstery skewers (Secs. 2:02, 2:04, 2:06, 2:07, 2:08). *Materials:* Tacks, upholstery twine, stuffing, padding, prepared casing (Secs. 3:03, 3:09, 3:28–3:38, 3:49, 21:06); back-spring twine (Sec. 3:08) for tufting-channeling. **Sec. 21:07B Fasten Casing** / Center casing in place on surface. Fasten the lowest horizontal line of tufting points marked on casing to those marked on surface; then fasten the second horizontal line of tufting points. Stitch casing in place at the two bottom lines of tufting points (Sec. 6:05G). [*1*] *Tie twines against regular webbing and*

burlap in a pad open-frame surface.   [2] *Tie twines against burlap spring cover* of a spring surface.   [3] *If using cloth tuft or loop buttons on a solid base,* stitch through holes (Sec. 21:05), and tack twines to back of base.

Sec. 21:07C Build Tufts /   [1] *Stuff the pockets,* or half-tufts, formed by casing and base (Sec. 21:07B). Stuff the lower row of tufts, or top ends of channels if any, from the lower side of a surface; stuff the lower part of the upper row from the upper side. Insert stuffing carefully, a small wad at a time: fill farthermost point first. The importance of building stuffing to the same density throughout all parts of a tuft cannot be overemphasized. Unless stuffing is packed firmly and uniformly, a finished tuft will not hold shape; if stuffing is too weak at the center, a casing and cover are apt to sag and wrinkle; if stuffing is too weak along pleating lines (Sec. 21:04D), they will not exert enough outward pressure to hold pleats neatly. Tufted surfaces need not and should not be uncomfortably hard. More stuffing usually is in seats, inside backs, and armtops than in other surfaces.   [2] *Pleat excess goods between tufting points,* Fig. 21:07C, by poking it smoothly in place with the blunt end of a regulator. Note that the exposed fold of a pleat points downward. This is especially important for a cover, as it reduces the number of dust-catching edges.   [3]

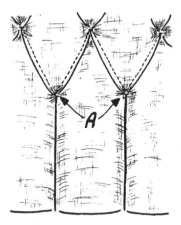

Fig. 21:07C

After stuffing lower halves of upper tuft pockets and upper halves of lower ones, fasten the third horizontal row of tufting points. Stuff the upper halves of the row of tuft pockets immediately below; then stuff the lower halves of the row being started. Pleat casing between tufting points. Continue building lower and upper half-pockets until reaching the top of a surface or the point at which channeling starts.   [4] *Build tufts along bottom, top, and sides* of a surface essentially the same as the other tufts. Casing usually is tacked to the back of a frame unless, particularly in the case of scroll backs and arms, the sides will be finished with post panels or borders; then casing is tacked to the outer sides of a frame.

Sec. 21:07D Channels / To form channels, first fasten a length of back-spring twine to the tufting point at the end of each channel crevice, as at Point A in Fig. 21:07C. Draw casing tight from tufting point to edge of frame, and tack to the usual part of a frame for that particular surface. Pull twine tight along crevice line, and tack at the same point as the casing. Stuff channels to the same density as tufts. Complete channels (Sec. 20:07); cut casing at crevice lines as necessary for smooth pleating at the top and bottom ends.

Sec. 21:07E Regulating / Regulate stuffing where necessary (Sec. 5:07), but do not weaken it along the pleats.

**SEC. 21:08
TUFTING
COMPLETELY
STUFFED
SURFACES**

Sec. 21:08A / Tufting completely stuffed surfaces may be done with tack buttons on a solid base, but results generally are better if cloth tuft or loop buttons are used. Stuffing may be either loose or compact; with the latter, for best results first build a surface with loose stuffing, muslin, and compact stuffing the same as when upholstering a plain surface. For tools and materials, Sec. 21:07A.

Sec. 21:08B Loose Stuffing / [1] *Plan tufting, and prepare* casing (Secs. 21:04–21:06). [2] *Install tufting twines.* For the average surface, tufting twines (upholstery twine) should be about 36 inches long. At each tufting point, draw equal lengths of twine through the surface or base from the back; there should be a ¼-inch space between lengths. Install similar, but 4-inch longer, twine for tufting points at the ends of channel crevices, if any (Sec. 21:07D); a single twine tied to the base may be used instead of double twine. [3] *Install loose stuffing* (Secs. 5:11A–C) over entire surface, building an even, smooth layer of the desired thickness. While spreading stuffing, pull tufting twines through it perpendicular to the base at each tufting point. Do not let stuffing lodge between pairs of twines. [4] *Spread casing* smoothly over the stuffed surface, aligning the marked tufting points with tufting twines. Thread tufting and channeling twines, if any, through tufting points of casing; thread twines ¼- to ½-inch apart.

Sec. 21:08C Build Tufts, Channels / Start at the tufting point at the middle of a surface, Fig. 21:08C. Loop one of a pair of tufting twines around the other, and pull ends tight enough apart to hold casing snugly against stuffing. Working in all directions outward from the middle, set casing the same way throughout a surface. In the same manner, but just by pulling twine ends further apart, tighten casing

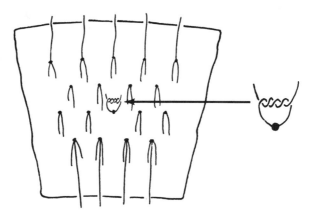

Fig. 21:08C

gradually throughout a surface until it touches the base at all tufting points. If tightened into place too quickly at any point, it may displace stuffing and cause irregular tufts. As each tufting point is finally adjusted to satisfaction, lock tufting twines in place with a square knot; cut off excess twine. Pleat between tufting points (Sec. 21:07C[2]). Complete tufts along edges of a surface and build channels, if any (Secs. 21:07C, D). When channeling, separate the stuffing along crevice lines in order that the casing and back-spring twine can be set tightly against the base.

SEC. 21:08D COMPACT STUFFING / [1] *Install compact stuffing* the same as for a plain surface, and mark for tufting points (Sec. 21:04). **[2]** *Cut or tear a hole* an inch or so in diameter through stuffing at each tufting point; otherwise stuffing may exert too much pressure against the sides of a tuft or bun and not enough against the middle. **[3]** *Prepare muslin casing* (Sec. 21:06). **[4]** *Install tufting* and channeling twines, if any (Sec. 21:08B). Do not enclose stuffing between pairs of twines. **[5]** *Install casing* (Secs. 21:08B[4], C). For channels, cut stuffing about three-quarters through along crevice lines from tufting point to end of surface. Draw casing and back-spring twines as tight as possible along crevice lines.

SEC. 21:08E TUFTING FOR TACK BUTTONS / [1] *When tufting for tack buttons,* tufting twines (Sec. 21:08B) may be tacked to a solid base before installing any stuffing. Mark tufting points (Sec. 21:04), and tack a tufting twine permanently slightly away from the middle of each point; tack channel twines the same way. Then complete tufting with loose or compact stuffing (Secs. 21:08B–D). **[2]** *An alternate method* to the above is to stuff a surface and then tuft by tacking the muslin casing at each tufting point. If channeling, tack a twine to the solid base at each channel crevice tufting point. This method often is easier for inexperienced upholsterers using compact stuffing; cement or bond stuffing directly to a solid base. If this tuft-tacking method is used with loose stuffing, spread it away from each tufting point before tacking casing; considerable regulating (Sec. 5:07) usually is needed to build neat, uniform tufts or buns that will hold casing properly.

SEC. 21:09 **COVERING,** **COVER** **TUFTING**	**SEC. 21:09A** / Tufting may be done with cover goods only. Everything is done as in the preceding sections of this chapter, except that: [*1*] *Cover replaces* muslin casing; [2] *Before installing* cover, pad as in Sec. 21:09B.

NOTE: Although tufting commonly is done with a cover only, it takes a fair amount of skill or specialized training to do a good job; most inexperienced upholsterers will do much better by first building in muslin and then covering.

Tools and materials, except muslin, are the same as in Sec. 21:07A.

SEC. 21:09B TUFTING /   [*1*] *Prepare cover* from corrected paper pattern (Sec. 21:06).   [2] *Pad surface.* Spread a layer of padding over a tufted surface the same as on a similar plain surface. At each tufting point, carefully tear out enough padding to make a neat hole 1 to 2 inches in diameter. This steepens the sides of a tufting point and allows a button to be set tighter against the base, Fig. 21:09B. Tear padding neatly apart along channel crevice lines, if any.   [3] *Install cover.* Set cover in place, aligning its marked tufting points with those of the surface. Press cover firmly but smoothly into tufting points.

Fig. 21:09B

Start with the tufting point at the middle of a surface; working outward in all directions, stitch or tack buttons in place (Sec. 18:01). Tighten them gradually throughout a surface, pleating (Sec. 21:07C) between tufting points. Often, to compensate for a minor error in a muslin tufting, it is necessary to shift a cover tufting point slightly or to set some buttons looser than others.

NOTE: For tack buttons, this work must be more accurate, as shape cannot be adjusted by setting some buttons looser than others.

[4] *Finish cover tufts* along the edges of a surface the same as muslin casing.

SEC. 21:09C CHANNELS / When channels are relatively flat over the edge of a surface (Fig. *c* 1:35), pull their covers tight along crevices, and complete as in Sec. 20:07D. If channels puff up considerably over the edges of a surface, Fig. 21:09C: [1] *For each crevice,* cut a piece of upholstery twine 8 inches longer than the distance from the tufting point to the point of finishing the cover on the frame. Tie an end (Sec. 5:03) of the channel twine securely around the tufting twine, or tack close to tufting point on a solid base.   [2] *Mark parts of cover* that lie along exact bottoms of channel crevices, *a;* fold cover back over tufting points.   [3] *Stitch covers.* Fold cover goods right-side-to-right-side along marked crevice lines and around channel twine. Stitch covers together from tufting point to a point of the cover that will be about 2 inches beyond the inner edge of a frame. Sew with short, even stitches, *b,* about ¼ inch from channel twine. This space will be needed for pleating or gathering cover along the twine.   [4] *Set channel covers in place,* and install (Sec. 20:09), treating the upholstery twine the same as the back-spring twines described in that section.   [5]

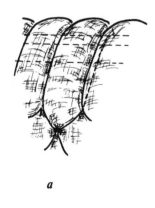

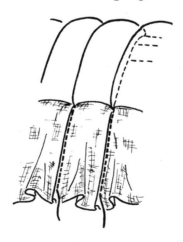

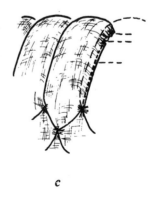

a

c

Fig. 21:09C   *b*

Distribute cover evenly. Due to the shape of a channel, more cover is needed at the crowned area than along the crevices. With the regulator, distribute or gather excess cover evenly and neatly along upholstery twine in the crevice, *c.* [*6*] *After setting and adjusting channel covers*, at each one rip out stitching, [*3*] above, to the back edge of a frame. There cut a small hole in each cover; draw twine through it. Tack twines permanently in place; complete closing channels.

NOTE: **If cover markings are absolutely accurate, channel twines may be machine sewn in place before installing a cover.**

SEC. 21:10 **PIECING**	Piecing together a cover for tufting may prevent having to buy a much greater amount of goods than will be used. Piecing also is done to set a particular part of a design, such as a flower or other definite figure, on the middle of a tuft or bun. When piecing, keep the grains of the covers running in the same direction; otherwise the finished surface may have a mottled or patchwork appearance. [*1*] *Treat each two pieces* to be joined as a separate unit. Mark both pieces from the corrected paper pattern; then trim each one ½ inch beyond the pleating line. Sew covers together (Sec. 12:02) right-side-to-right-side. [*2*] *When only a small piece is to be added*, as at the corner of a surface, they need not be sewn together. Install them together, threading the twines through the tufting points of each piece. Underturn the outer piece for making the pleat between tufting points.
SEC. 21:11 **MOCK** **TUFTING**	**Sec. 21:11A** / In mock tufting, all tufting points and "pleats" between them (Fig. 1:56) are sewn into the cover, which as a rule is completely assembled before installation; usually, but not necessarily, the cover is boxed (Sec. 11:06). In most cases the tufting pattern is square, but it may be diamond-shaped or rectangular. Mock tufting is done on a solid-base or on a webbed open-frame; generally, it is fairly thick pad upholstery with compact stuffing, preferably polyfoam, installed with minimum crown (Sec. 5:14). Tufting points, held by twines, usually are about 1 inch deep and may or may not be buttoned (Secs. 21:11D, E). Plan tufting points (Sec. 21:04); prepare cover the same way regardless of base or buttoning. *Tools:* Shears, double-pointed straight needle at least 8 inches long, sewing machine, tape measure, chalk; plus upholsterer's hammer, sharp skewer or ice pick, ⅛ inch drill for a solid base (Secs. 2:04, 2:06, 2:15, 2:16; 2:02, 2:08). *Materials:* Upholstery twine, compact stuffing, padding (preferably synthetic cotton), welt cord and buttons (optional), cover goods; plus tacks, bonding agent for a solid base (Secs. 3:03, 3:40–3:43, 3:49, 3:58, 3:68; 3:03, 3:06). **Sec. 21:11B** **Prepare Cover** / Pleats in mock tufting usually are

½-inch flat seats (Sec. 12:02); therefore the width and length of cover needed for each square is 1 inch more than the width and length of the square; plan diamond mock tufting patterns the same way, but on the diagonal.   [1] *Measure the area* to be mock tufted, plan the number of tufting patterns, and determine the total amount of goods for the tufted surface cover; add enough for finishing a cover on the frame if it is not to be boxed.   [2] Chalkmark, on the wrong side of the goods, a straight line for each fold or turnback of cover for a square or diamond pattern, Fig. *a, b* 21:11B. The distance between lines is the width or length of cover needed for each tufting pattern.   [3] *Fold cover back*, right-side-to-right-side, along a chalked line and sew ½ inch from the folded edge for the entire length or width of the cover goods (Fig. 12:02); do not cut goods along fold. Fold back and sew all goods in one direction; then fold back and sew goods in the cross direction, which usually is more difficult than the first sewing.   [4] *Boxed cover.* Prepare boxing and welt, if any, and sew to top cover (Sec. 13:14). When arms and inside back are fully upholstered (Fig. 1:56), regular boxing usually extends to about 2 inches behind arm fronts; beyond that, boxing usually is a 1 inch- to 2 inch-high strip of cover at the top, and the rest is filled in with a cover stretcher (Sec. 11:09) or, especially if the top cover is welted, the boxing is decking material.

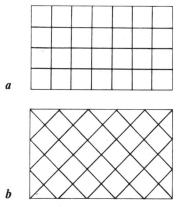

a

b

Fig. 21:11B

SEC. 21:11C SOLID BASE UPHOLSTERY / This is essentially thick slipseat upholstery (Sec. 6:03).   [1] *Prepare solid base* the size and shape to fit the frame cavity, making allowance for thickness of cover and padding if the unit will be completely covered.   [2] *Mark solid base* for each tufting point. Measure from point to point according to the distance and direction between points and from the edges of the base; or fit the cover tightly and carefully on the base, and jab the point of a sharp skewer or ice pick through each tufting point and into the base. Through each marked tufting point drill a ⅛-inch-diameter hole. [3] *Install stuffing,* usually from 4 inches to 6 inches thick. For best results, understuff with a layer of firm compact stuffing 1 inch thinner than the planned total thickness; overstuff with a 1 inch thick layer of medium to soft polyfoam or foam rubber, as in Fig. 21:11D. Stuffing should be ½ inch larger all around than the base. Fasten stuffing to base; laminate thin to thicker stuffing (Secs. 3:46, 5:11).

Sec. 21:11D   Install Padding, Cover / Pad with synthetic cotton for maximum puffiness and initial softness. [1] *Spread one or two layers* of padding over the stuffing extending down the sides to, but not under, the bottom edge of the base. If piecing stuffing, do as much as possible on the first layer in order to leave a smoother top surface. [2] *Starting at a convenient* side or end of the base, set in place the first row of corresponding tufting points or flat seams. Cut tufting twine about 8 inches longer than the distance from bottom of base to top of padding; thread about 3 inches through needle. Jab long end of needle up through the hole in the base and through the cover at the proper tufting point, Fig. 21:11D. [3] *No buttons.* Stitch through cover only between the seam and fold. Hold free end of twine under the base, and pull needle clear of cover and twine; draw free end of twine down over the cover fold and tie, with a couple of half-hitches, to the twine emerging from the padding. Pull twine under the base moderately tight; tack temporarily to base. [4] *Buttons.* Jab needle

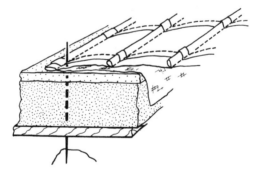

Fig. 21:11D

through cover close to the middle of the tufting point, stitch through button tuft or loop, and jab short end of needle back through cover so as to center button in tufting point; pull free end of twine clear of needle, ties as in [3] above, and tighten and temporarily tack twine under base. [5] *Stitch the first row* of tufting points from side to side or end to end, then stitch the next parallel row, and so on. [6] *After stitching all tufting points,* pull twines under base tight enough to hold all tufting points to the same depth. Before tacking a twine permanently (Sec. 7:14B), set a small wad of padding between it and the edge of the hole in the base.   [7] *Complete installing* the boxed or plain cover the usual way.

Sec. 21:11E   Open-Frame Upholstery   /   Tufting points on open-frame work usually are buttoned; with less work it produces a better looking job (evenly spaced tufting points with more uniform shape and depth) than unbuttoned work, unless the unbuttoned hold-down twines show in the tufting points.   [1] *Web frame* on top surface of seat (Sec. 5:01), on inner surface of back. Jute webbing (Sec. 3:11) is used in most cases; rubber webbing (Sec. 3:22) provides a little spring action.   [2] *Burlap webbing* (Secs. 5:02, 7:33B) is not essential for compact stuffing but reduces frictional wear between webbing and stuffing.   [3] *Prepare compact stuffing* (Sec. 21:11C) large enough to extend ½ inch beyond outer edges of base. Fasten to frame and burlap (Sec. 5:11).   [4] *Install padding* (Sec. 21:11D) and plain or boxed cover the usual way, tightening and adjusting it for all points of finishing.   [5] *Install a button* at each tufting point (Sec. 18:01B).

22

stools, ottomans, and benches

SEC. 22:00 **GENERAL** **FACTS**	Upholster stools, ottomans, and benches essentially the same as pad and spring seats (Chapters 6 and 7). For appearance and ease of work, round stools and benches (Fig. *a, b, c* 1:51) usually are solid seat, while ottomans are more often attached cushion (Fig. *f, h* 1:51) than solid seat (Fig. *d* 1:51). An open lid stool (Fig. *e* 1:51) seldom is a comfortable seat unless the top is well padded; its chief use is as a footstool and container for sewing, magazines, etc. Regular stools and benches usually are upholstered as individual items. Ottomans and open lid stools nearly always are upholstered with and have the same style of finishing as a companion chair (Figs. *c* 1:49, *d* 1:51). Any style of finishing—plain, buttoned, channeled, tufted, with or without skirts —can be used for most stools, ottomans, and benches. Stools and otto-mans not built to go with a chair often are finished in a combination of styles, such as the top plain and the sides channeled.

616

SEC. 22:01 GENERAL CONSTRUCTION	Most stool, ottoman, and bench frames, whether solid-base or open-frame (Sec. 4:01B), can be pad or spring upholstered with either loose or compact stuffing (Sec. 3:27). [*1*] *Size.* Small articles, especially when solid-base, usually are pad upholstery; work can be done with loose stuffing, but compact is far more practical. Large stools and ottomans, and most benches, traditionally are spring upholstered; but excellent results are had with jute or rubber webbing (Secs. 3:11, 3:22) and fairly thick compact stuffing. [*2*] *Springs.* Open-frame stools, etc., are spring built with upholstery coil springs, zigzags, rubber webbing, and inner-spring units (Secs. 3:16, 3:21, 3:22, 3:63); back springs (Sec. 3:17) are too weak for satisfactory seats. For solid-base articles, use hard springs (Sec. 3:16G). [*3*] *Edges.* Since all edges of a stool, etc., are visible, irregularities in height and general shape are quite noticeable. Experienced upholsterers can build regularly shaped seat edges (Sec. 22:02) with loose stuffing, but as a rule, use compact stuffing for faster, easier work. The exception to this is a spring edge.
SEC. 22:02 SEAT EDGES	Stools, ottomans, and benches may not require seat edges (Sec. 5:04). [*1*] *Roll edges* or prebuilt edging (Sec. 3:25) are used most with loose stuffing in pad and spring upholstery. Many designs of stools have legs rising above the top of a frame. Roll edges large enough to finish level with the tops of the legs are commonly used; they should butt firmly against the sides of the leg tops. [*2*] *Spring edges* are generally only in fairly large solid-seat ottomans (Fig. *d* 1:51). [*3*] *Hard edges* seldom are used for stools, etc.; if springs rise enough above a frame to warrant a hard edge, the article will be more comfortable if built with a spring edge. Attached- or loose-cushion articles (Fig. *f, h* 1:51) seldom have spring surfaces rising enough above a frame to require hard edges. [*4*] *No special edge* is needed when building with an inner-spring unit or with compact stuffing. However, if compact stuffing will be installed on a loose stuffing base or understuffing (Secs. 3:45F, 5:13), the understuffing may or may not have roll edges; it depends on thickness of understuffing at the edges of a frame. [*5*] *Whatever edge is used*, it encompasses the top of a stool, etc.
SEC. 22:03 HEIGHT	Build stools, etc., to any comfortable seat height (Sec. 3:16B). But an ottoman built with a chair (Fig. *d* 1:51) usually gives more comfort, as a foot or leg rest, if its top surface is 1 to 3 inches below the top of the chair seat or cushion.
SEC. 22:04 WEB, BURLAP	Web vertically and burlap the sides of an open-frame article throughout the area to be upholstered the same as any outside surface (Sec. 18:11).

**SEC. 22:05
PAD PLAIN
AND
BUTTONED
SOLID-SEAT
STOOLS,
OTTOMANS,
BENCHES**

SEC. 22:05A / Until covering, the upholstering of plain and buttoned pad built solid-seat stools, etc., is essentially the same as for similar seats (Chapter 6). The major difference is that the stool, etc., is built the same on all sides. For basic information on pull-around, bordered, and boxed covers (Secs. 13:11, 13:13, 13:14); for buttons and dust cover (Secs. 18:01, 18:15).

SEC. 22:05B COVERING / [1] *Straight seams ordinarily* are used for piecing (Secs. 12:02, 12:03) borders and boxings. However, they encompass stools, etc., and may puff out appreciably in use. Allow for this when preparing cover by sewing a small amount of curve into piecing seams; experiment with muslin first. If only about a half inch of puff-out is planned and the cover goods has normal stretch, sewing curve into piecing seams seldom is necessary. [2] *When tacking* a cover, border, or boxing along the bottom of a round surface, sliptack and tighten it (Secs. 5:16, 5:18) first at opposite points, then halfway between them, and so on, Fig. 22:05B. This tends to spread a cover evenly, making pleats smaller (Sec. 5:17) or, if a cover has adequate stretch, eliminating them (Fig. *a* 1:51).

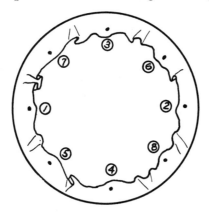

Fig. 22:05B

SEC. 22:05C BORDER / Plan borders for piecing at opposite corners, or at opposite points of a round article, and ending on one of them. Start installing a border at the corner or point opposite where it will end; work alternately along sides from start to ending point. Completely install border around article to ending point. [1] *Finish first end,* as Point 1 in Fig. 22:05C, around corner. [2] *Rip cover and welt* apart back to corner. Peel welt cover back and cut cord to end at the point of the corner. Tack welt cover in place on a downward slant around corner. [3] *Finish second end* of border much the same as the first. Rip border and welt apart; cut welt cord to butt neatly against the first end of the cord. Underturn welt cover on a downward slant; tack in place. Complete regular installation of border to corner.

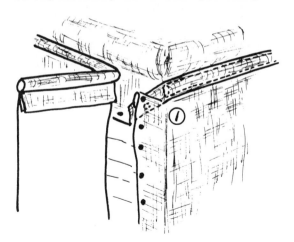

Fig. 22:05C

[4] *Cut off excess border* goods ½ inch beyond corner, underturn the remainder at the corner, and blind-stitch (Sec. 13:04) down corner. Start blind-stitching about 1 inch behind corner on the first side, and stitch the bottoms of the welts at the corner. Complete stitching in a neat, straight line down the corner of an article. [5] *Leather, leather substitutes, plastics, glazed fabrics, most hard-surfaced textiles.* Instead of installing a border on a stool, etc., as above, first machine sew it completely together; measurements and fitting of goods must be accurate for both appearance and durability. Install border as a traditional flange skirt (Sec. 18:05).

SEC. 22:05D BOXING / Prepare boxed covers for stools, etc., the same way as top cover and boxing of a cushion (Sec. 17:06), but fold boxing seam-ends at joining points in opposite directions. Center boxed cover inside-out on top of an article, and work boxing down over the sides to where it will finish. Complete and tack the usual way for that style of upholstering.

**SEC. 22:06
SPRING PLAIN
AND
BUTTONED
SOLID-SEAT
STOOLS,
OTTOMANS,
BENCHES**

SEC. 22:06A / Up to covering, upholster plain and buttoned spring solid-base stools, etc., basically the same way as similar spring seats (Chapter 7). Differences are that stools, etc., are built the same way on all sides, and they may be upholstered with a cushion inner-spring unit instead of coil or zigzag springs or rubber webbing, or with an inner-spring unit and zigzags, coil springs, or rubber webbing.

SEC. 22:06B COIL, ZIGZAG SPRINGS / Determine size and number of hard upholstery coil springs or lengths of zigzags needed (Secs. 3:16, 3:21). Coil springs usually are tied (Secs. 7:11–7:16) and zigzags installed (Sec. 7:32) with slightly more crown (Sec. 5:14) in solid-seat stools, etc., than in similar chair seats. Without extra crown, the finished surface might have too little go-down for comfort.

SEC. 22:06C RUBBER WEBBING / Prepare and install rubber webbing (Sec. 3:22) the usual way for a seat (Sec. 7:33). Rubber webbing being a "flat" spring, crown must be built with stuffing or upholstery padding to safeguard a cover against being ripped or torn out in normal seat use.

SEC. 22:06D INNER-SPRING UNITS / Cushion inner-spring units (Sec. 3:63) are used, except for spring edge work, but they may cost more than a stool, etc., is worth. Use a firm unit, or a finished seat surface may be too weak for comfort. [*1*] *Stuffing.* Depending on the stuffing (Sec. 3:27), the sides of an inner-spring unit should be at least ½ inch from the outer sides of a stool, etc.; ½-inch clearance is enough for loose stuffing, and for compact stuffing at least ¼-inch thick. With thicker stuffing, clearance between spring unit and outer sides of a frame should be about ¼-inch less than thickness of the stuffing. [*2*] *Size of units.* It may be necessary to join two or more units to get the required size and shape. Springs incased by muslin or burlap and tied by twine or hog-rings are easy to take apart and join, top and bottom, to other incased inner springs. Factory wired units are more difficult to rebuild. [*3*] *Mounting units.* Mount inner-spring units on jute webbing or on zigzag springs the same, mechanically, as in backs (Secs. 10:29C, 10:32C). Spring units can be mounted on coil springs and rubber webbing; but most professional upholsterers feel that the slight extra comfort does not justify the extra work.

SEC. 22:06E NO SPRINGS / A fairly thick block of compact stuffing (Secs. 3:41–3:44) may be used instead of springs or a spring unit. For frame cavities more than about 14 inches in any direction, a stool, etc., is more comfortable as a seat if built with rubber instead of jute webbing. Stuffing should extend at least to all outer surfaces of the frame; if stuffing is more than about 2 inches thick, it should extend ½-inch beyond the outer surfaces in order to build firmer sides.

SEC. 22:06F EDGES / Built-up edges usually are in stools, etc., upholstered with loose stuffing (Sec. 22:02). With compact stuffing, build or trim edges of stuffing to make desired shape (Sec. 3:46). [*1*] *Roll edge.* Web stools, etc.; install springs, burlap, roll edge for loose stuffing, stuff, incase with muslin (Secs. 7:03–7:05, 7:07–7:14, 7:18–7:20); cover (Sec. 22:05). [*2*] *Spring edge.* Web article, install springs, burlap, bridle-build the spring edge, incase with muslin (Secs. 7:01B, 7:03–7:05, 7:07–7:13, 7:15, 7:16, 7:18, 7:23, 7:28). I—Install a pull-around or a bordered cover (Sec. 22:05). II—Install banding (Secs.

11:04, 13:17), but join ends at a corner of a stool, etc., the same way as a border (Sec. 22:05) except that banding is hand-stitched in place throughout.   [3] *When stuffed surface is more than about 2½* inches thick, instead of a roll or a spring edge, the top and edges may be stuffed and stitched the same as an inside back with square sides and top (Sec. 10:25). This is similar to a hard edge but softer. After long use, the edges tend to pack down, but usually can be patted back into shape.

**SEC. 22:07
ATTACHED-
CUSHION
OTTOMAN**

SEC. 22:07A / A partial or complete cover for the sides of the base of an attached-cushion ottoman (Fig. *f, h* 1:51) is sewn to the bottom of a cushion, Fig. 22:07A. Make cushion, install on base, and cover sides of base.   [1] *Cushion filling* (Secs. 3:61–3:73). Plain inner-spring units, foam rubber, and polyfoam are the most common ottoman cushion fillings. A down-filled cushion can be exceptionally comfortable but is costly and does not hold shape as well as other fillings.

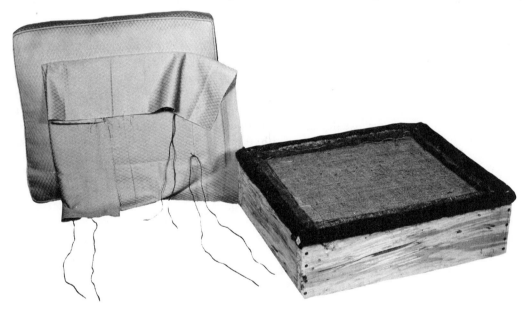

Fig. 22:07A

The main problem with an attached-cushion ottoman is too much gap between cushion and base around the edges. Usually it is prevented by building a base with the center of its top surface flat or even lower than the outer edges, thus giving the crown of the bottom of the cushion somewhere to go. A ½- to 1-inch gap between cushion and base is normal.   [2] *Base.* Most attached-cushion ottoman bases are pad upholstery, adequate for a normally thick, properly filled cushion. Bases also are pad with rubber webbing and are spring built. If an ottoman will be used chiefly for a foot or leg rest, pad upholstery is satisfactory. But if it will be used mainly as a seat, then rubber webbing or spring construction is preferable.

SEC. 22:07B REGULAR PAD BASE / Web, burlap, and install roll edge or prebuilt edging (Secs. 5:01, 5:02, 5:05, 5:06). Throughout the middle of the burlap and about 5 inches from the sides of a frame, install a layer of loose stuffing (Secs. 5:11A, B, C). It should be 1 to 2 inches thick, normally compressed, for a down-filled cushion but only about 1-inch thick for other fillings. The center stuffing keeps an installed cushion from sagging at the middle. Use firm rather than highly resilient stuffing (Sec. 3:27).

SEC. 22:07C RUBBER WEBBING PAD BASE / Prepare and install rubber webbing (Secs. 3:22, 7:33). Leave enough slack in the burlap (Sec. 5:02) to keep it from ripping out in normal use. Install built-up edge (Secs. 5:05, 5:06).

SEC. 22:07D SPRING BASE / Either upholstery coil or zigzag springs may be used (Secs. 3:16, 3:21). Coil springs are the more diffi-cut to install; they must be tied to rise enough above the top of a frame to allow satisfactory go-down without damaging spring ties, but they must not rise so high as to require an unusually large roll edge. Zigzag springs usually are installed on the top surface of a frame (Fig. *d* 3:21C) or below it with drop clips (Sec. 3:21D). For down-filled cushions, tie coil springs or install zigzags with a little more crown than usual. [*1*] *Coil springs*. Install webbing, springs, burlap, roll edge or prebuilt edging, and loose stuffing (Secs. 3:16, 7:01B, 7:04, 7:05, 7:07–7:14, 7:18, 22:07B). [*2*] *Zigzag springs*. Install springs, burlap, roll edge or prebuilt edging, and loose stuffing (Secs. 3:21, 7:18, 5:05, 5:06, 22:07B).

SEC. 22:07E PREPARE CUSHION / Build attached cushion essen-tially as in Secs. 17:00–17:14. [*1*] *Base cover*. Before sewing cushion casing, measure and cut cover for the base. A pull-around cover finishes on the bottom of a base. A bordered cover finishes about ¾-inch below the planned upper limits of the border. Add about 3 inches to greatest measured width and length of a base cover for handling and seams. [*2*] *Sew base, cushion covers*. Center bottom cushion cover on base cover, right-side-to-right-side. Sew together about 4 inches from the edges of the cushion cover (Fig. 22:07A). [*3*] *Com-plete* the cushion casing. [*4*] *Fill, close cushion casing*. When the filling is an inner-spring, polyfoam, or foam rubber unit, no hair is needed on the bottom surface, and a single layer of padding is sufficient.   [5] *Corner-twines.* At each corner where cushion bottom and base cover are sewn together, stitch through, and knot a length of upholstery twine (Fig. 22:07A). Make it long enough for both ends to reach from the burlap spring or webbing cover to the bottom of the base.

NOTE: To save cover goods, the bottom cushion and base covers are often made of strips pieced diagonally at each corner. Also, the area within where the covers are sewn together, [2] above, is muslin or any other strong fabric instead of cover goods; this is highly recommended when the cover is leather, leather substitute, plastic, glazed fabric, or any other air-tight goods.

SEC. 22:07F INSTALL CUSHION / Center cushion on the base. Thread corner twines through the burlap cover at the exact points of contact of the sewn corners and the base.   [1] *Pad base.* Tie twines tight against underside of webbing and/or burlap. Twines should be about ½-inch apart at the knot.   [2] *Spring base.* Tie twines tight against underside of burlap spring cover. Twines should be at least ½-inch apart at the knot and should, when possible, enclose a top spring coil or loop or bar of zigzag springs.   [3] *Padding.* Spread a layer of padding over the base from the stitching of cushion and base covers to the usual places on the sides of a frame for finishing a pull-around or a bordered cover. Cover base (Sec. 22:05).

SEC. 22:08 LOOSE-CUSHION OTTOMAN	Upholster the base and cushion of a loose-cushion ottoman separately throughout. Build the cushion as for a loose-cushion seat. Except that all sides are upholstered the same way, build the base the same as a loose-cushion seat—cover goods over the top edges inward to the decking. [1] *Upholster base* (Secs. 22:07B, C, or D), but do not stuff center or build extra crown with springs except for a down-filled cushion; see Sec. 22:07A[1]. [2] *Stuff and incase* top of base with muslin (Sec. 7:27), upholstering the center of the top surface first. Deck casing should be large enough to be stitched about 4 inches from all sides of base. Be sure to place enough stuffing along the inner sides of the built-up edges; with too little, they may show through and wear out the cover. [3] *Cover base* (Secs. 13:16E, F). Either a pull-around or a bordered cover may be used (Sec. 22:05). [4] *Build cushion* (Secs. 17:00–17:14).
SEC. 22:09 OPEN-LID STOOL	SEC. 22:09A / Upholster the top of an open-lid stool (Fig. *e* 1:51) with loose or compact stuffing (Secs. 3:27–3:44) or with an innerspring unit (Sec. 3:63) and stuffing. The thicker and firmer the stuffing is, the more comfortable the stool is as a seat. Two-inch thick polyfoam, foam rubber, or rubberized hair usually is satisfactory; if it is

much more than 3½-inches thick, there is danger that the sides will bulge and sag in relatively short time. Upholster lid and base separately, and hinge them together; the inside of a stool or base usually is lined.

SEC. 22:09B UPHOLSTER LID / If cover is leather, leather substitute, plastic, or other airtight goods, first drill several ¼-inch breather holes in the lid base. [*1*] *Loose stuffing.* Install roll edge or prebuilt edging, stuff, and incase with muslin the same as a slipseat (Sec. 6:03). [*2*] *Compact stuffing.* Install stuffing, build crown (Sec. 5:15) with loose stuffing or padding, and incase with muslin as a slipseat (Sec. 6:03). [*3*] *Inner-spring unit.* The unit should be 1 to 2 inches smaller overall than the lid. I—Center unit on lid and tack along edges of the casing; staple springs (Sec. 7:09) of an uncased unit along outer edges of coils. II—Spread about ¼ pound of best quality hair stuffing over top of unit to build crown and a smooth surface. III—Spread one or two layers of padding over stuffing and spring unit and down the sides to the top edges of a lid; place enough padding along the sides of the unit to build them, when incased with muslin, about ½ inch beyond the sides of the lid. IV—Incase with muslin as for a slipseat (Sec. 6:03). [*4*] *Cover.* Install a pull-around or a boxed cover (Sec. 22:05), finishing on bottom of lid about ¾ inch from the edges. Do not tack where hinge screws will go. [*5*] *Lid lining.* Line bottom of lid with sateen or other suitable goods. Blind-tack (Sec. 13:03) lining along front edge of lid; blind-stitch (Sec. 13:04) to cover along sides and back. Although not usually done, the bottom of a lid may be padded before lining it; use a quarter thickness of padding.

SEC. 22:09C UPHOLSTER BASE / First cover tops of sides, then install base lining, and then cover the outside. [*1*] *Tops of sides.* Cut strips of cover large enough to incase the tops of the sides of a base and extend ¾-inch below the inner and outer edges. Pad top surfaces with a very thin layer of padding; a quarter thickness usually is adequate. Padding should reach to but not over the top edges, where it could prevent good installation of the outside cover and inside lining. Tack cover strips in place on outer and inner surfaces of sides ½-inch below top edges. At corners, miter strips of cover, and blind-stitch them together (Sec. 13:04). [*2*] *Line base* (Sec. 22:09D). [*3*] *Cover outside.* Install a border (Sec. 22:05) with welt set along the outer top edge of the base or box. The border or cover finishes on the bottom of a base.

SEC. 22:09D LINE BASE / [*1*] *Cut heavy cardboard liners* for the bottom and sides of a base. How they are installed—bottom first and then the sides, or sides first—is optional. They should fit tightly into a base but must not buckle out. [2] *Cover liners.* Spread a quarter layer of padding on the "front" surface of a liner extending to but not over the edges. Wrap lining cover around liner, glue it to the back side. It is advisable to stitch between opposite sides to hold lining in place while glue dries. [3] *Install liners.* Coat the back surface of a liner with glue liberally and set in place in the base. To prevent accidently smearing glue on an adjacent liner, do not spread glue closer than ¼ inch from the edges of a liner. Use clamps or other means to press liners firmly in place while glue dries.

SEC. 22:10 CHANNEL TOP FOR ROUND STOOL, OTTOMAN

SEC. 22:10A / See Chapter 20 for basic channeling. Sunburst channels radiating from the middle of a top usually are attractive and practical for round ottomans and large stools, which often are five or more feet in diameter. The sides usually are plain, but this is optional (Secs. 22:16–22:19). [1] *Top surface* may be open-frame or solid-base (Sec. 4:01); open-frame usually is easier to upholster and more comfortable. [2] *Open-frame articles* may be pad or spring upholstery (Secs. 22:11, 22:12). Spring is preferable for all sizes of ottomans and stools; pad upholstery is not recommended when a top cavity is more than about 16 inches in diameter. Open-frame springing may be with upholstery coil springs or with rubber webbing (Secs. 3:16, 3:22); rubber webbing is not recommended when the top cavity is more than about 36 inches in diameter. [3] *Solid-base top surfaces* usually are pad upholstery (Sec. 22:12). Coil springs can be used; but because of the problems in selecting, placing, and tying them (Sec. 22:11B), coil spring work should not be tried by inexperienced upholsterers. [4] *Stuffing* (Secs. 3:27–3:44). For pad upholstery, the top surface is usually understuffed, with firm rather than resilient loose stuffing, to build necessary crown (Sec. 5:14). For channels, compact stuffing usually provides the simpler way to build uniform shape and density, since a block is made for each channel before any are installed (Secs. 22:13E–I). [5] *Due to difficulties* in building uniform shape and in general handling of materials, square, rectangular, and oval top surfaces seldom are channeled.

SEC. 22:10B   PLOT SUNBURST CHANNELS / Sunburst designs usually have an even number of channels, Fig. 20:10B. The more channels there are, the narrower they are and the more difficult to make neat and uniform. The fewer the channels, the wider they are and generally flatter both at the start and after relatively little use; channel flatness is greatest and most noticeable at the edges of a surface. A good general rule is that channels should be from about 9 to 12 inches wide at the outer edges, except that there should be at least eight channels regardless of width. Measure circumference along outer top edges of a frame, and divide by the desired width of channels at the outer edges

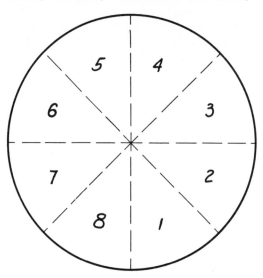

Fig. 22:10B

to figure the number of channels; often several changes in desired width must be made before getting one satisfactory for all channels. Mark outer top edges of frame for each channel crevice.

SEC. 22:10C CHANNEL SURFACE CROWN / The wider a top surface is, the greater its crown (Sec. 5:14) must be. Build crown primarily with springs in a coil spring job, with understuffing in rubber webbing and traditional pad upholstery. Crown usually rises smoothly and regularly from the outer edges to the middle of a surface, and usually ranges from about 1½ inches above the outer edges of a 16-inch wide top to about 4 inches for a 48-inch one.

SEC. 22:10D CHANNEL SHAPE / The overall shape of a channel between crevices is most noticeable at the outer edge of a surface and should be planned for desirable appearance, comfort, and durability; for mechanical reasons they should crown midway between crevices. [*1*] *Appearance.* Variety in channel shape is based chiefly on the relation of width to thickness, Fig. 22:10D. If a particular thickness is wanted, then width primarily controls overall shape, as in *a, b, c;* if a certain width is wanted, then thickness controls shape, as in *a, d, e.* Basic overall shape is modified by the sides of a channel, where curvature can range from relatively flat, *f,* to nearly vertical with a sharp break toward a somewhat flat center, *h;* the wider a channel is in relation to its thickness, the greater the possible variety of curvature at the sides.   [*2*] *Comfort.* Channels fairly thick in relation to width, *b, e,* usually are more comfortable than others, due chiefly to the greater amount of stuffing.   [*3*] *Durability.* Generally, the thicker a channel is in relation to its width, the better it holds shape and the less wear

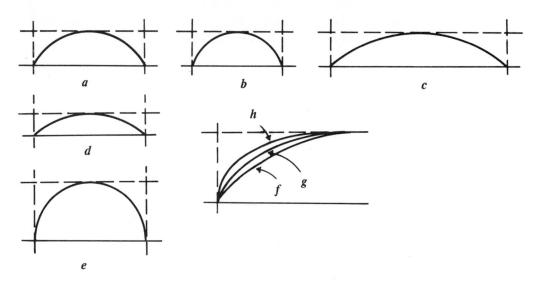

Fig. 22:10D

there is on a cover where it passes over the outer top edges. Relatively thin channels, *c, d,* have little space for go-down and fight-back under normal use; if the shape is continued over the outer edges of a frame, it gives little protection to a cover. A highly resilient stuffing may not be strong enough to build a durable surface unless packed so tight that it loses resiliency. A low resilience stuffing builds a strong but not very springy surface. A good hair or a medium density compact stuffing is usually satisfactory for sunburst channeling.

**SEC. 22:11
CHANNEL TOP:
OPEN-FRAME**

SEC. 22:11A / These may be spring or pad upholstery (Secs. 22:-10A[2], 22:10C).

SEC. 22:11B COIL SPRINGS / In some cases it may be advisable to use two or more sizes of springs, depending on width and crown. [1] *Webbing.* Install strip webbing as for an armless, backless round spring seat (Secs. 3:11, 7:05), depending on condition of frame and size springs to be used, [2] below. Cross a front-to-back and a side-to-side strip exactly at the center of the webbing area for maximum support of the center spring, if any, and to provide the strongest hold-down for the button or other means used to hold the center of the channeled surface. Set other strips of webbing no more than 2 inches apart; ½ inch apart is better. [2] *Springing.* Regardless of stuffing to be used, select and tie springs for a roll edge (Sec. 5:05). Based on planned crown, which sets heights at which springs are tied between the outer edge and the middle of a round surface (Sec. 22:10C), figure the size upholstery spring to use (Sec. 3:16). For cavities more than about 16 inches in diameter, two or more sizes of springs may be needed in order to build a uniformly firm surface. For example, if one size spring is used throughout a surface that is to crown 4 inches, springs near the middle will be tied down or compressed much less than those near the edges, making the surface soft or weak at the middle or unnecessarily hard along the edges. Install springs for roll edges (Secs. 7:07, 7:08, 7:11–7:14). [*3*] *Burlapping.* Burlap spring surface the usual way (Sec. 7:18). [*4*] *Understuff.* Understuff with loose stuffing and incase with muslin (Sec. 7:19), except: I—No built-up edge is needed. II—Incase with burlap instead of muslin to build a tougher surface. III—Use at least enough loose stuffing to build a smooth surface over spring coils and ties. Other than that, base the thickness of understuffing on planned shape and thickness of channels (Sec. 22:10D). If they will be less than about 2 inches thick at the most and will be fairly flat (*c, d* Fig. 22:10D), understuffing should be 2 to 3 inches thick. Thicker channels, or those thicker in relation to width (*a, b*), usually can be built satisfactorily with 1 to 2 inches of understuffing. IV—Finish understuffing casing 1 inch from the outer edges to leave space for built-up edges, if any, or for fastening other stuffing. [*5*] *Install channel pad* (Sec. 22:13K).

SEC. 22:11C RUBBER WEBBING / Plan, prepare, and install rubber webbing (Sec. 3:22) on top surface of frame; burlap, and build basic crown (Sec. 22:10C). [*1*] *Webbing.* Arrange rubber webbing the same as traditional webbing in armless, backless seats (Fig. 6:02A) except that back-to-front and side-to-side strips should leave a 1-inch square space at the middle for passage of twines used to hold the middle of a channel surface in place (Sec. 22:14B). The closer together the other strips of webbing are, the firmer and more durable the finished surface will be. [*2*] *Burlapping, understuffing.* Install burlap "spring cover," and build crown with compact stuffing and incase with muslin or burlap (Secs. 7:33B, 22:11B[4]) except that stuffing and casing should taper smoothly down onto frame about ½ inch from the outer edges, Fig. 22:11C. No roll edges. [*3*] *Test understuffing.*

Fig. 22:11C

After incasing understuffing, test to see if there is sufficient crown to compensate for rubber webbing being a "flat" spring. Spread a pad of soft blankets about 2 inches thick on understuffing. For best results, two fairly heavy people should sit near the middle and bounce around some. If the spring cover and/or casing rip out, the spring cover did not have enough slack, and there was not enough crown for the casing.

If a satisfactory basic shape has too much crown, it can be remedied when building a channel pad.   *[4] Install channel pad* (Sec. 22:13K).

SEC. 22:11D JUTE STRIP WEBBING / Pad upholstering with jute strip webbing (Sec. 3:11) is the same as with rubber webbing (Sec. 22:11C) except that, since jute webbing has so much less go-down, it is not necessary to leave as much slack in the burlap "spring cover;" and, from a mechanical standpoint, it is not necessary to build as much crown when understuffing for basic shape. But for comfort build as much crown or even slightly more for jute webbing than for rubber webbing.

SEC. 22:12 **CHANNEL TOP:** **SOLID-BASE**	**SEC. 22:12A** / These usually are pad upholstered (Secs. 22:-10A[3], 22:10C). First drill ¼-inch-diameter breather holes about 6 inches apart throughout a solid-base surface. At the exact center, drill a hole for passage of twines used to hold the middle of a channeled surface (Sec. 22:14B).

SEC. 22:12B LOOSE STUFFING / Build basic crowned shape (Sec. 22:10C) with firm rather than highly resilient loose stuffing (Secs. 3:27–3:38). Understuff (Sec. 22:11C) except that there is no webbing or burlap. Test for potential comfort; more crown or overall thicker stuffing may increase comfort.

SEC. 22:12C COMPACT STUFFING / Build basic crowned shape (Sec. 22:11C) with medium to firm compact stuffing (Secs. 3:41–3:47), tapering to the frame at the outer edges (Sec. 22:11C). Incasing with muslin is not necessary but is recommended for inexperienced upholsterers to correct irregularities in shape of the understuffing and to gain valuable experience in handling covers.

SEC. 22:13 **SUNBURST** **CHANNEL PAD**	**SEC. 22:13A** / Build sunburst channeled pads for round ottomans and stools essentially as in Sec. 20:12; however, there are important differences in materials and work. For best results build a pad in muslin, install, and cover it. Pad channeling is done with either compact or loose stuffing (Secs. 3:27–3:44). *[1] Compact stuffing* is easier to use when pads are to be the same thickness throughout (Sec. 22:13D). *[2] Loose stuffing* generally is preferred when a pad will be thicker or thinner at the center than the outer edges to increase or decrease crown (Sec. 22:13E).

SEC. 22:13B PREPARE CASING BOTTOM / Prepare the bottom of a sunburst channel pad as in Sec. 20:12B, except: *[1] Muslin generally*

is used, being easier than burlap to machine sew. [2] *The bottom of a pad* should be at least 4 inches wider throughout than the top surface of the article as measured over the understuffing. [3] *Sliptack the bottom* in place along the sides about 1 inch below the top edge. [4] *Mark crevice lines* on muslin bottom and on outer top edge of frame; for best results, mark with ink, paint, heavy black pencil, or marking pen. [5] *On the sides,* set a tack firmly at each crevice ½-inch below the top edge. Run a twine between each of the opposite crevice tacks, pull tight against the pad bottom, and tie; be accurate, as this work affects the symmetry of a finished channeled pad. Where all twines cross should be the exact center of a surface; often some twines must be shifted to make them cross at a common point. When all crevice twines lie satisfactorily, check each from outer edge to center with a yardstick to make certain it is straight throughout. After making all adjustments, mark the center of the surface on the channel pad bottom, and draw a fine line from outer edge to center along each twine. Remove twines and tacks; prepare muslin casing (Secs. 22:12C–G).

SEC. 22:13C PREPARE CHANNEL CASINGS / Each channel has its own muslin casing machine-sewn to the muslin bottom. Unless following a pattern made by an experienced upholsterer, build a temporary channel, and use its casing as an exact pattern for all others. For best results, build two adjacent temporary channels; it simplifies the building of regular shape throughout and the judging of the general appearance of the finished job. [1] *Prepare a full-size paper pattern* for a channel casing (Sec. 20:06B); it will be triangular. [2] *Rough cut a channel casing.* It should be a rectangle 4 inches wider than the widest part of the paper pattern and 6 inches longer. Mark an end of the rectangle for the point of a channel (at the middle of the surface) ½ inch from the end and centered between the sides. Stitch the marked point of the channel to the marked center of the bottom casing (Sec. 22:13B). If building two test channels, prepare and install a second casing the same way as the first. [3] *Sliptack the free end* of the channel casing near the outer top edge of a surface at the two marked crevice points of a channel. Tack the same distance from the edge on each crevice line to keep the goods centered and to prevent uneven stretch due to installing a casing on the bias (Sec. 11:25). Before tacking, pull casing tight enough toward the outer edges of a frame to lie snugly against the bottom muslin. [4] *Temporarily stuff* the test channel or channels to the desired shape (Secs. 22:12D, E), remove casing or casings, and trim to the size and shape needed for all channel casings.

SEC. 22:13D TEMPORARY CHANNELS: COMPACT STUFFING / First prepare stuffing the approximate shape of a channel; then work the casing to complete it.   [*1*] *Prepare a length* of compact stuffing the same shape as the marked channel (Sec. 22:10B) from the center of the surface to at least 1 inch beyond the outer edge.   [*2*] *Trim or build* the sides and top surface of the channel stuffing to the approximate shape of a channel as formed by the paper pattern made for the casing (Sec. 22:13C). To allow for final shaping of stuffing and for necessary compressing by the casing in order to make the finished surface strong enough to hold shape, the stuffing should be at least ½-inch thicker throughout than the channel as formed by the paper pattern.   [*3*] *Loosen free end* of channel casing.   [*4*] *Set the roughly shaped* wedge of compact stuffing firmly in place on the muslin bottom (Sec. 22:13C) aligned with marked crevices; pin stuffing in place if necessary.   [*5*] *Draw channel casing back in place* over stuffing and sliptack at original point. As a rule, a different part of the casing will be tacked now than originally due to the space taken by the stuffing. [*6*] *Build channel to wanted shape* by trial and correction by pressing and trimming off or adding to the stuffing. Working from the center of a surface toward the outer edges, form wanted shape and pin channel casing to the muslin bottom along marked crevice lines; work a few inches at a time alternately along each crevice line. "Satisfactory" shape should not be based on appearance only. When shape looks right, feel if it is uniformly firm throughout; hard and soft spots should be eliminated in order that the finished job keep its good looks.

NOTE: Build channels only to the outer top edge of a surface, where stuffing and casing should overhang; this part is shaped when installing a pad.

[*7*] *When temporary channels are satisfactory to eye and touch,* work casing tight and as free of wrinkles as possible; pleating (Sec. 5:17) may be necessary. Be careful not to alter shape or density of channel. Pin casing to muslin bottom along crevice lines at intervals of about ½ inch. Assemble and sew channel pad casing (Secs. 22:13F, G).

SEC. 22:13E   TEMPORARY CHANNELS: LOOSE STUFFING / First make the approximate shape of a channel with casing. Then stuff casing, and develop final shape by reworking casing.   [*1*] *At points 2 or 3 inches apart,* pin channel casing (Sec. 22:13C) to muslin bottom along crevice lines. Since casing and bottom goods are pinned on the bias, they tend to stretch unevenly; the less of this, the easier it is to build a smooth, regular shape.   [*2*] *Start stuffing* at the inner end of a cased channel. Insert stuffing carefully, a small wad at a time; work them together to make a felted pad of stuffing. Usually a casing must be unpinned at and near where stuffing is being worked in place to allow necessary slack in the goods for building shape. At the start of stuffing, it may be necessary to loosen nearly all of a casing to allow for building shape at the innermost part. This depends on how thick a channel is to be at its point—the thicker, the more stuffing and casing will be needed.   [3] *Complete stuffing and shaping* a channel, [2] above, working a few inches at a time alternately along crevices lines and the middle. Be sure that shape is built with the channel casing, not the muslin bottom; it should lie flat along the surface of the under-stuffing. Also, every few inches check to make sure that the wanted shape is being built: I—Uniformly thick; or, II—Thicker or thinner at the center than the outer edge for increased or decreased crown at the center.   [4] *When the proper shape is built,* feel if channel is uni-formly firm throughout; eliminate hard and soft spots in order that the finished job keep its good looks. This often can be done by regulating (Sec. 5:07); but with sunburst channels, it usually is necessary to add or remove stuffing because of the flaring shape.   [5] *Finish temporary channel* (Sec. 22:13D[7]).

NOTE: Build channel only to the outer top edge of a surface; the rest is built when installing a channel pad.

SEC. 22:13F   ASSEMBLE CHANNEL PAD CASING   /   [1] *Mark temporary channel casing* (Secs. 22:13D, E) along crevice lines from center of surface to outer edges. The finer a line and more accurate it is, the smoother and more regular will be the shape of the finished channels.   [2] *Cut off excess channel casing* ½ inch outside marked crevice lines.   [3] *Make a series of register marks* along one edge of the casing and the muslin bottom; ½-inch dashes are enough, as long as there is a useful length on each surface. Where there is no pleating, marks can be 3 or 4 inches apart. Where there is pleating, marks should be about ½-inch apart; to avoid confusing marks, make them alternately long and short or different colors.   [4] *Remove casing and stuffing.* I—Use shaped compact stuffing as the pattern for stuffing channels. II—Weigh loose stuffing; this is the simplest way to plan how much stuffing is needed for all channels.   [5] *Check and correct temporary channel casing.* Fold channel casing in half lengthwise with the register-marked surface up. Sides of a casing should align perfectly, but seldom do; however, differences should be less than ½ inch. Also, the edge should be exactly ½ inch from the marked crevice line throughout; if there is more space, cut edge accordingly; if there is less, mark those places on the casing so that corrections can be made when cutting the final casings. But if there is much more or less than ½ inch between marked crevices and cut edge, rebuild temporary channel with a new casing.   [6] *Using the corrected temporary channel casing,* [5] above, for an exact pattern, cut casing for each channel.

For best results, the thread pattern (warp and weft threads) should be the same in all casings to make the effect of bias (Sec. 11:25) more uniform.

NOTE: *Do not use the pattern casing in the channel pad; it also is the pattern for cover channels.*

[7] *Align each cut channel casing* perfectly with the pattern casing, and duplicate the register marks. They are needed for sewing pleats, if any, and for sewing casings together and to the muslin bottom of a channel pad. [8] *On muslin bottom of pad*, duplicate at each crevice line the register marks made in [3] above.

SEC. 22:13G   SEW CHANNEL PAD CASING   / The casings and muslin bottom of a channel pad can be sewn together by hand, but machine sewing is preferable; either way, there are two methods. First, sew channel casings together into a unit, and then sew to muslin bottom; this method requires twice the sewing but may be easier for inexperienced machine sewers and provides good practice for sewing the cover. In the second method, pin casings to muslin bottom, then sew. [1] *Sew pleats*, if any, into each channel casing. Set register marks in the same positions on each casing; pin pleats in place. Pin all pleats on all casings before sewing any. Adjust as necessary to make the shape or pocket formed by pleats the same in all casings; usually there are minor differences in pleats, but it does not matter as long as resultant shapes are the same. Sew pleated areas along crevice lines, which if not marked on a casing should be ½ inch from the edge. Pleats on right and left sides of a casing should be identical. [2] *Align two channel casings,* with the register-marked side of one uppermost and on top of the unmarked side of the other, and pin together. This work must be accurate for a finished job to have regular shape throughout. I—If casings are first to be sewn together and then to the muslin bottom, sew them together completely along the pinned side ½ inch from the edge. II—If casings and muslin bottom are to be sewn together in one operation, see [5] below. [3] *Continue sewing channel casings together,* [2] above, until all are joined on both sides. As a rule, they will not come together perfectly at the center. When channel points are less than about 1 inch apart, correction is usually made with stuffing when filling channels, or with padding when covering them, or by both means; also, a button (Sec. 22:15) may cover minor irregularities. But when channel points are more than about 1 inch apart, it is advisable to rip out and resew those that are too far out of place. [4] *Align a sewn channel* with a marked crevice line on the muslin bottom. For best results, casing stitching should lie directly along the crevice line; this simplifies sewing casings and bottom together in a straight line from center to outer edge and brings register marks on casing and bottom close together. Pin casings and muslin bottom together; then sew along casing stitching from the center to the outer edge. Part of this sewing usually is ripped out when installing a channel pad (Secs. 22:13J, K), but it is simpler to sew and rip than to do additional sewing later. Continue pinning and sewing until all casings are sewn to the bottom. Depending on the total thickness of the goods, when sewing the last few casings in place, it may be easier to stitch by hand within a few inches of the center.   [5] *If casings and muslin bottom are to be sewn in one operation,* align pinned casings, [2] above, along a marked crevice line on the muslin bottom, pin together, and then sew along the pinned side ½ inch from the edges of the casings. For best results, pin goods together and sew as in [4] above except that the line of pinning instead of the stitching of the casings is laid along the marked crevice line. For probable corrections at the center, see [3] above; correcting major irregularities is more difficult when casings are sewn directly to the muslin bottom.

SEC. 22:13H   STUFF CHANNEL PAD: COMPACT STUFFING   /   [1] *Prepare stuffing* for each channel the exact size and shape of the final wedge made for the temporary channel (Sec. 22:13D).   [2] *If there is enough work space,* insert all stuffings a little at a time. First bunch the completed channel casing toward the center, and insert stuffings, working them to the point ends of the channels; be careful not to break off stuffing. Then draw casing over the stuffings a few inches, and work it smooth and tight. Stuff a few inches of one channel, then the next, and so on until all are fully stuffed. Check channels often while working to make sure that they are smooth and uniformly shaped, and that there are no hard or soft spots.   [3] *If there is not enough work space to stuff channels simultaneously,* [2] above, stuff them individually. Insert stuffing in channel, and work it into the pointed end; do not break off stuffing. "Working" stuffing is a combination of pressing down on the top and edges and pushing it toward the closed end of the casing, while at the same time pulling the casing and muslin bottom toward the outer end of the stuffing. The first several channels are easy to stuff, the last few fairly difficult.

SEC. 22:13I   STUFF CHANNEL PAD: LOOSE STUFFING   /   [1] *Weigh enough loose stuffing,* based on the temporary channel (Sec. 22:13F[4]), for each remaining channel.   [2] *Stuff each channel* a few inches at a time, checking frequently to make sure they are being built to the same shape and density. Simplify stuffing by using the same number of handfuls for each channel each time around; handfuls will vary in amount of stuffing, and such variations can become important if they are large enough. Keep allotted stuffing for each channel separate.

[*3*] *Stuff all channels* to the outer end. Ends will be reworked while installing a channel pad; but stuffing them fully now makes it easier to plan and develop their shape of the ends.   [*4*] *Check channels carefully* for uniform density, shape, and smoothness. If this is done often while stuffing them, usually the little final adjustment needed can be done by regulating (Sec. 5:07).

SEC. 22:13J INSTALL CHANNELED PAD / [*1*] *Set pad in place* with its crevices to the marked crevice points on the sides of the frame, and with the center of the pad exactly on the center of the built-up base. Sliptack bottom muslin of pad to top of frame about 1 inch from the outer edges. Space along edges is important when a pad is built with loose stuffing.   [*2*] *Check pad placement carefully.* For best results, measure from the outer edge of a frame to the center of a pad along each crevice; reposition pad accordingly.   [*3*] *Check sliptacked pad for appearance.* Examine the article critically from several yards away. Does the crown seem too high, too low, too flat, or satisfactory? To alter crown, it may be necessary to restuff the base. However, crown often can be built, after removing a pad, by installing stuffing on top of a base; if done with loose stuffing, it is advisable to incase with muslin the same way as original base casing. Altering overall crown when covering channels seldom is satisfactory, as the extra padding may change shapes of channels; also, padding is not as strong as stuffing, and tends to pack down.   [*4*] *Check sliptacked pad for go-down.* People often flop down on large ottomans, making that the best test. If the muslin bottom of a pad tears loose, the built-up base does not have enough crown for the go-down. Correct by installing stronger coil springs, by increasing initial stretch of rubber webbing, or by building crown higher with understuffing; the last is the simplest correction and usually is satisfactory. If lack of crown is not corrected, the cover is apt to rip out in short time.   [*5*] *Permanently tack* muslin bottom of channeled pad; cut off excess goods close to tackheads.

SEC. 22:13K CHANNEL ENDS / Stuff and complete outer ends of channels essentially the same way as closing top ends of channels on an inside back (Sec. 20:07D). Channel ends usually project at least 1 inch beyond the sides of an article in order to build some puff-out over the top edges, and usually finish about ½ inch below the top edges; however, puff-out and point of finishing are entirely optional.

**SEC. 22:14
COVERING
SUNBURST
CHANNELS**

SEC. 22:14A / Cut channel covers, machine sew them together, usually with hold-down twines, install much the same way as a channeled pad.   [*1*] *Cut channel covers.* These usually are prepared and cut from a pattern the same as muslin casings (Sec. 22:13F[5], [6]).

But if more or less than the normal amount of padding will be used (Sec. 22:14B), it may be necessary to make a new pattern for the covers (Sec. 22:14C). [2] *Sew channel covers* (Sec. 22:13G). As for pleating at the pointed end of a channel, such work done in a muslin casing may be satisfactory for the cover. But due to changes in shape that often result when stuffing channels, as a rule it is better to pin pleats into one channel cover and to use it as a pattern for the others. [3] *Hold-down twines.* Cut pieces of back-spring twine (Sec. 3:08) 12 inches longer than the distance from the outer edge of a crevice to that of the opposite one. These are hold-down twines to help anchor a cover at the center of the surface and to draw cover seams down into crevices. Sew hold-down twines into cover (Sec. 20:08).

SEC. 22:14B PAD, INSTALL COVER / Use the most resilient padding available. [1] *Prepare separate padding for each channel.* Without being stretched or compressed, padding should reach from the center of a channel surface to a few inches beyond the outer edge, and to the bottom of both crevices. Starting about 1 inch above the bottom of a crevice, taper padding to about half its thickness at the bottom to help seat cover seams in a crevice. Unless crown or shape of channels is to be changed, a single layer of padding throughout generally is ample. I—To increase crown, place a partial layer of padding under the main one. It usually extends from the center to the outer edge, and from the crest of a channel about halfway to the bottom of the crevices, tapering toward the crevices according to the wanted finished shape. II— To decrease crown, place partial layers of padding along each side of a channel. Placement between crest and crevice, and taper of padding toward crest and crevice, depend on the shape to be built. III— If crown or shape of channels is changed in any way, a new pattern for the channel covers should be made (Sec. 22:14C). [2] *Place channel cover.* Set assembled channel cover in place on padding, with the center of the cover directly above the center of the channeled surface and cover seams lying along crevices. Do not displace stuffing. [3] *Anchor twine.* Cut a length of back spring twine (Sec. 3:08) to anchor the center of a channel cover and to shape it. Twine should be at least 8 inches longer than twice the thickness of the center of a channeled surface as measured from the top of a surface to the bottom of the burlap spring cover, webbing cover, or solid base. With a long straight needle (Sec. 2:06), thread one end of the twine at a time down from the top of the center through the burlap cover or hole in a solid base. Anchor twine must encompass all hold-down twines (Sec. 22:14A). Insert needle close to the points of any two opposite channels. The closer anchor twines are to the hold-downs without touching them, the better; however, in an open-frame surface, anchor twines should be ½ inch apart coming through the burlap cover or webbing. Pull anchor twines tight enough to hold the center of a cover down into the center of a surface, and tie or tack temporarily. While and after working channel seams into crevices, it may be necessary or desirable to tighten or loosen the center.   [4] *Work covers in place.* Work on opposite channels and crevices at the same time, tightening covers in place (Sec. 5:18) along channel and into crevices; pull hold-down twines tight enough to hold covers in place. Work around a surface alternately on opposite channels until all covers are satisfactorily smooth and tight throughout. Often it is necessary to alter some padding; it usually should be done on all channels in order to build uniform shape. Except that final shaping is done with padding instead of stuffing, close outer ends of channels the same way and at the same points as muslin casings (Sec. 22:13K). Drive hold-down twine tacks permanently.   [5] *Adjust center.* Adjust the center of a channeled surface to the desired depth. This is a matter of "what looks good to the upholsterer," although the size button at the center, if one will be used (Sec. 22:16A), should be considered. As a rule, the smaller the button, the less the center is pulled down with anchor twines. When it is pulled down sufficiently, set anchor twine on an open frame by tying a slipknot (Sec. 5:03), placing a small wad of padding between twines (Fig. 6:05G), and pulling knot tight. For a solid base, force a wad of padding into the hole in it, and tack at one or two points; pull anchor twines over padding, and tack an inch from the hole.

SEC. 22:14C   ALTERING SHAPE OF CHANNELS WITH PADDING /   If the shape of stuffed channels is to be altered when padding them (Secs. 22:14A, B), it may be advisable to make a new pattern for the covers. To find out: [1] *Using the completed muslin pattern,* cut and sew together three muslin channel "covers"; sew hold-down twines (Sec. 22:14A) in crevices of the middle cover.   [2] *Pad any three adjacent channels* to the desired shape, and install partial muslin cover (Sec. 22:14B). Only the middle cover can be installed the regular way and held down in crevices by twines. Work the other two "covers" smooth and tight into the wanted shape throughout; pin in place near bottom of crevices. Make every effort to finish the middle or test channel exactly as the cover would be.

NOTE: It would be better to use cover goods for test covering, as muslin probably has different stretch and handling characteristics. But due to cost, muslin generally is used.

[3] *When the test "cover" is smooth and tight,* examine it critically, especially the crevices. They should be straight from the outer edge to the center of a surface and far enough below the crests of channels to show that the surface is channeled, not flat. There should be enough crown between crevices, and from the outer edge to the center, to hold

the "cover" smooth and tight. Due to the original stuffed shape being changed, a test cover seldom fits properly. But usually it is obvious where changes must be made to develop a new pattern. Where the bottom of a crevice is too high, and the surface seems flat, as a rule the channel cover should be made wider. When a cover fits too loosely, as a rule it should be made narrower, or padding added. Other adjustments can usually be found by forcing or poking the cover along crevices so as to tighten it, remove wrinkles, increase or decrease crown, and so forth. [4] *Estimate changes* that should be made in the original pattern and, without removing the test covers, repeat steps [1]–[3] above. [5] *Between the two sets of test covers* it is usually easy to arrive at a pattern that will be satisfactory for the real cover. It may be necessary to alter shape again with padding when installing the cover. But this is fairly common even when the original pattern and stuffed shape are used.

SEC. 22:15 **FINISH** **SUNBURST** **CHANNEL** **STOOL,** **OTTOMAN**	[1] *Top.* As a rule the center of a sunburst channel surface is fairly irregular in shape. Cover it with a button (Sec. 18:01) large enough to conceal the irregularities. Channel filling usually is worked back from the ends so that a button can be firmly and smoothly seated. Work channel filling back by pinching and kneading it or, cover permitting, by regulating (Sec. 5:07). [2] *Sides* can be channeled, tufted, or buttoned, but usually are plain. With channeling, tufting, or buttoning (Secs. 22:17–22:19), there is the problem of the sides harmonizing with the outer ends of the channels. Plain sides (Sec. 22:16) attract less attention, thus allowing the top channeling to show better. Any skirt (Secs. 18:03–18:08) can be used. [3] *Dust cover* (Sec. 18:15).
SEC. 22:16 **ROUND STOOL,** **OTTOMAN** **SIDES**	**SEC. 22:16A PLAIN SIDES /** A plain-finish cover for the sides of a round stool or ottoman (Fig. *b* 1:51) is similar to a seat border (Sec. 13:08) in that it extends from the cover at the top down the sides to finish on the bottom surface. A sides cover usually is welted (Sec. 11:08) at the top; welt may be sewn to the cover before installation, or it may be installed separately and the cover tacked or blind-stitched to it. A sides cover usually consists of panels or pieces; it may be completely sewn together before installation or partly sewn and completed by hand-stitching during installation. Open-frame sides usually are burlapped and padded the same as any outside surface (Sec. 18:11); if a cavity is more than about 14 inches high, vertical webbing is advisable.

SEC. 22:16B   PREPARE COVER / A sides cover for most round stools and ottomans consists of two or more panels or pieces. This is a must when the outside circumference of an article is greater than the width

of a cover goods, unless it is to be railroaded (Sec. 11:01B). The use of panels also avoids having only one seam, for joining the ends, which would make that part appear to be the "back" side. Number and width of panels is optional. When a top surface is sunburst channels, side panels usually are wide enough for their seams to follow crevice lines of channel ends.   [1] *Measure circumference* of article at its widest part, usually just above the bottom of the top cover where it finishes on the sides; pull tape snug against but not biting into the cover. If cover goods is thick or heavy (Sec. 3:52B), and the top of a sides cover will be welted, before measuring circumference, wrap two layers of cover goods tightly around that part of the article to allow for thickness of welt. This seldom is done if a cover has more than normal stretch.   [2] *Measure length* of a sides cover from where it is to finish at the top to 1 inch in from the bottom edge. Add 1½ inches for handling.   [3] *Width of panels.* Divide the measured circumference by the planned number of panels to determine width of each panel; add 1 inch to allow ½-inch seams for piecing together (Sec. 12:02) on each side.

NOTE: If the top of an article has channels finishing on the sides, the width of side panels usually is the distance between selected channel crevices; add 1 inch for seam allowances.

SEC. 22:16C SEW COVER / Sew cover panels together from top to bottom with straight flat seams (Sec. 12:02).   [1] *Closed sides cover.* Sew all panels together to make a closed sides cover when it is to be installed by tacking or stitching around the top of the sides and by drawing it down over the padding (Sec. 22:16F). This method usually results in a neater job.   [2] *Open sides cover.* Sew all except the first and last panels together when a sides cover will be installed along the top and bottom; then close by blind-stitching (Sec. 22:16E). This may be easier than using a completely sewn cover, above, but unless it is tightened carefully from side to side during installation, the panels that are blind-stitched together may be wider or narrower than the others. Also, blind-stitched seams usually are quite noticeable in relation to machine-sewn.

SEC. 22:16D WELT / The top of a sides cover usually is welted (Sec. 11:08).   [1] *Prepare enough welt* to encompass article where the top of the sides cover will go plus 2 inches for joining ends. Welt may be sewn to the top of a sides cover (Secs. 12:06, 12:07) and the welted cover installed as a unit; or, welt may be installed first, then the cover (Sec. 22:16E). The first method usually is neater; the second may be easier for inexperienced upholsterers.   [2] *Mark sides of article* for placement of welt. This is usually ½-inch below the level at which the top of the welt is to lie; edges of the welt seam are placed along the marked line.

SEC. 22:16E INSTALL SIDES COVER / [1] *Separate welt and cover.* Sliptack welt in place completely around article on the marked line (Sec. 22:16D); tack 3 or 4 inches apart. Keep welt smooth and level throughout, loosening and retacking as necessary. Drive tacks permanently, and join welt ends (Sec. 13:02A); it is advisable to stitch very thick, heavy welt covers together with fine thread at the butt-joints. There are two ways to install a sides cover: I—Cardboard welt; blind-stitch sides cover to it (Secs. 13:03, 13:04). The appearance of this installation depends on how neat and accurate the stitching is. A major hazard is that while adjusting the cover during stitching, it may be stretched too much for a neat finish at the end. With a closed cover (Sec. 22:16C), only stitching to the welt is required. With an open cover, the open ends are blind-stitched after being worked in place over the padding. II—Blind-tack sides cover to welt (Sec. 13:03). With the cover inside-out and the top end pointing down, align its top edge with the bottom edge of the welt seam. Work cover smoothly in place around welt; tack at points 4 or 5 inches apart. Set cardboard stripping in place on cover, pressing firmly against the lower part of the welt cord but not on top of it; tack at 1-inch intervals. For open and closed covers, see I above. [2] *Welted cover.* Set seam edges of welt, pointing down, along marked welt line (Sec. 22:16D). Sliptack in place through cover and welt seams, and then tack permanently; blind-tack welted cover, [1] above. [3] *Draw sides cover up over top of article* and out of the way. Prepare sides for covering (Sec. 22:16A); for very small articles, a half thickness of padding often is enough. Padding should fit tightly against the top end of a sides cover, welted or not, and extend down to the bottom edge but not around it, as it could interfere with good installation of the cover.

SEC. 22:16F FINISH SIDES COVERING / Wrap a layer of strong paper around sides of article, with an overlap of 4 or 5 inches. It should extend to the top of a cardboarded sides cover, welted or not, and to 3 or 4 inches below the bottom edge. Work paper tight enough to flatten padding as much as possible without crushing it; work paper with a smooth, sliding motion, and do not pinch padding or squeeze it together along the sides. When padding is satisfactorily flattened: [1] *Closed cover.* Work it down in place on the sides over the paper. Work it smooth and tight, especially along the top, welted or not. Pull paper out a few inches, pat cover smooth and tight in place, pull out a few more inches of paper, adjust cover, and so on. When paper is removed, work sides cover over the bottom edges, tighten, and tack (Sec. 22:05B). [2] *Open cover.* Draw cover carefully down in place over the paper, underturn goods for half-inch seams where cover ends are to be blind-stitched, and pin carefully together at 1-inch intervals; do not pin into paper. Blind-stitch (Sec. 13:04) from top to bottom. Remove paper; finish on bottom, [1] above.

SEC. 22:17 BUTTONED SIDES	Install a plain-finish sides cover (Sec. 22:16). Plan and install buttons (Sec. 18:01).

SEC. 22:18 CHANNELED SIDES	Channeled sides of an article usually are built with felted padding and the cover only. Solid-base sides need no special preparation other than drilling breather holes when the cover is leather, leather substitute, plastic, or other air-tight goods. For general channeling, see Chapter 20. [1] *Mark planned channel crevices* on sides of article. [2] *Welt.* Cardboard welt around top of area to be channeled. [3] *Channeling.* Build channel pad (Sec. 20:12) except that the outer sides of the end-channels are sewn shut. Pin stuffed pad in place around article, blind-stitch end-channels together, pleat and blind-stitch top end of pad to welt, and close bottom ends of channels (Sec. 20:07D).

SEC. 22:19 TUFTED SIDES	When tufting (Chapter 21) the sides of an article, tuft in vertical rows and work around it. Vertical rows must be the same width throughout. Make a paper pattern on which all tufting points and possible channel lines are clearly marked. Before installing the cover, cardboard welt around the top of the area to be covered. Install cover the same as muslin casing. To join the ends of casing, and to join the ends of cover, underturn the finishing end along a zigzag vertical pleating line. Pleat and blind-stitch cover to welt at the top. Complete cover at bottom (Sec. 20:07D).

23

love

seats

and

sofas

SEC. 23:00 **GENERAL** **FACTS**	Except for some differences in seat and inside back construction, up-holster love seat and wider articles the same as similar chairs with pad or spring surfaces and traditional or modern (Sec. 3:00C) materials and methods. Large articles often are easier to upholster than small ones, and minor flaws in shape usually are less noticeable. Planning the cover for an article and the article for a cover is one of the most important steps in wide article upholstering. As well as spoiling the looks, faulty planning can cause considerable waste of cover goods. Most love seats have two-cushion seats and similar backs (Fig. 1:58), and most larger articles have three or more seat cushions and back pil-lows or sections (Fig. 1:59), chiefly because of cover goods. Unless it can be railroaded satisfactorily (Sec. 11:01), the width of cushions and sections is based on the width of cover goods. [1] *If goods is not as wide* as planned cushions or sections, it must be pieced together. [2] *If goods is appreciably wider* than planned cushions or sections, prob-ably quite a bit of material will be wasted.

SEATS

SEC. 23:01 **TRADITIONAL** **PAD** **UPHOLSTERY**	Few love seats and larger articles have pad seats, although there is no structural reason for not building them. Except that it is wider, upholster the seat the same as a similar chair (Chapter 6) except that the webbing should be tacked also on top of the cross-brace or -braces as in Sec. 23:02.

SEC. 23:02 **TRADITIONAL** **SPRING** **UPHOLSTERY**	[1] *Build love seat and larger articles with traditional coil springs* (Secs. 3:15–3:19) essentially the same way as similar solid and loose-cushion seats (Chapter 7). [2] *When webbing the bottom of a seat frame* (Fig. 7:05A), after installing all strips, double over a strip of webbing and tack over the other strips on the cross-brace or -braces (Fig. 4:02) from back to front. This supports the middle of a wide seat and prevents tacks cutting through stretched side-to-side webbing. A double thickness of burlap may be used instead of webbing. [3] *Install seat springs* the regular way. Do not fasten spring-ties to cross-brace.

SEC. 23:03 **MODERN** **SPRING** **UPHOLSTERY**	For use of zigzag springs, see Sec. 3:21; rubber webbing, Sec. 3:22.

SEC. 23:04 **COVER**	SEC. 23:04A / If using decking (Sec. 3:56) for a love seat or wider loose-cushion deck cover, insert a strip of cover 4 or 5 inches wide running from back to front at each planned junction of the cushions. Use decking for the rest of a seat cover the usual way. SEC. 23:04B CUSHIONS / As a rule, seat cushions in love seat and wider articles meet at the crevices between back sections or back pillows (Figs. 1:58, 1:60). Two or three cushions of approximate or equal widths are common with buttoned or tufted inside backs (Figs. 1:62, 1:63); with three cushions, the middle one may be wider or narrower than the others. A single cushion may be used with a solid back (Fig. 1:54) or with a loose-cushion or split back (Fig. 1:56).

INSIDE BACKS

SEC. 23:05 **TWO TYPES**	SEC. 23:05A / Love seat and wider article inside backs are solid or split (Figs. *b* 1:52, 1:58). Most back frames have double cross-braces

(Fig. 4:02) and can be upholstered either way; but it must be planned from the start (Sec. 23:05B). When there is a single cross-brace the back must be solid.

Sec. 23:05B / Whether to build a solid or a split inside back, frame permitting, is optional. About as many love seats have one as the other (Figs. *b* 1:52, 1:58). But because individual back pillows let each sitter adjust a back to personal comfort and because overall upholstering is easier and faster, many love seats and the majority of wider articles have solid backs with loose cushions or pillows (Figs. 1:59–1:61); backs usually are simple, thin, pad upholstery, although rubber webbing often is used (Sec. 3:22). As a rule, buttoned and tufted inside backs are solid (Figs. 1:62, 1:63) spring upholstery. Most inside backs are relatively thick spring upholstery.

Sec. 23:05C / See Chapter 10 for upholstering pad and spring inside backs with traditional and modern materials and methods. Except that it is wider, upholster a solid back the same as a chair with similar sides and top. In split backs, the tops of all sections and the outer sides of sections next to the arms are upholstered as the corresponding parts of a similar chair; where sections butt against one another, the sides usually are straight up and down.

SEC. 23:06
SOLID BACK:
THIN PAD
UPHOLSTERY

This back is chiefly a holder for loose cushions or pillows. [1] *Inner surfaces of cross-braces* usually are flush with those of the rest of a back frame in order to keep the center part from sagging or hollowing toward the outside back. [2] *Webbing*. Traditional jute webbing is used most. Rubber webbing often is used when an unusually springy back is wanted; the thinner the back cushions or pillows are, the more noticeable the spring effect. Install either webbing the usual way for a pad inside back, but do not tack to cross-braces. After installing all regular strips, lay a strip of webbing or double thickness of burlap over the cross-braces and webbing, and tack horizontal strips permanently. Horizontal or support strips must be tacked to cross-braces to make an inside back uniformly firm from side to side and to keep a section from being pushed excessively toward the outside. The extra vertical strip keeps support webbing from being cut or worn by tackheads. [3] *Stuffing*. The inside back usually is stuffed just enough to build a smooth, dependable surface; use any good, resilient stuffing with jute webbing, only a compact stuffing with rubber webbing. A surface that is not "dependable" tends to pack and sag in relatively short time, especially when it spans a fairly wide area.

SEC. 23:07 **SOLID BACK:** **THICK PAD** **UPHOLSTERY**	This often is in slimline furniture. Upholster the same way as thin pad backs (Sec. 23:06) except for stuffing. Thickness of stuffing depends on the planned appearance and firmness of a back and on the stuffing to be used. Most of these backs are built with firm compact stuffing; good quality loose stuffing is just as satisfactory but more difficult to install. Usually this type back is built firm, since the article's comfort is due more to the pitch of a back in relation to the seat than to softness.
SEC. 23:08 **SOLID BACK:** **SPRING** **UPHOLSTERY**	These are upholstered as a single unit whether using traditional or modern materials and methods. *[1] Traditional upholstery.* Web inside back and spring it the usual way, Fig. 23:08. Note that vertical ties are between all vertical rows of springs regardless of cross-braces and that spring-ties are not tacked to cross-braces (which would cause a depression along the braces). Tack horizontal strips of webbing to the outer surfaces of the cross-braces to provide uniform support for inside back upholstery and to keep webbing from pushing against the outside back upholstery. Protect horizontal webbing by laying a strip of webbing or double thickness of burlap over it before tacking. *[2] Modern upholstery.* With zigzag springs (Sec. 3:21), use cross-ties or connectors to build a continuous spring surface from side to side.

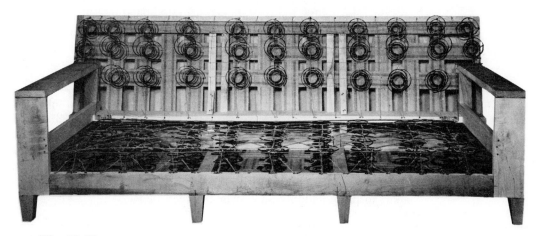

Fig. 23:08

SEC. 23:09	**SEC. 23:09A SOLID BACK COVER** / For methods of covering inside backs, see Chapter 16. To prevent railroading (Sec. 11:01) a solid inside back cover, piece goods together with or without welt at one or more points in a back. If there will not be back cushions or pillows, a welted cover often looks better than a plain one; however, inside back

welt is subject to maximum wear and accumulation of soil. If there will be back cushions or pillows, piecing seams usually are not welted. [*1*] *Piecing cover.at one point.* Set seam to lie along exact middle of back.   [*2*] *Piecing at more than one point.* Set seams so that the middle panel or panels is 1 to 2 inches wider than the side panels as measured just below the armtops. If a middle panel is too narrow, it has a squeezed appearance.

NOTE: Inside back covers of loose-cushion love seats and wider articles are not, as a rule, made with cover goods for the show parts and decking elsewhere, as is common in seats; back cushions and pillows usually pull away from a back so much that decking or other material would show and spoil the article's appearance.

SEC. 23:09B   BACK CUSHIONS, PILLOWS / For construction, see Chapter 17. Back cushions or pillows are the most noticeable part of love seat or wider articles; plan them carefully.   [*1*] *Two cushions or pillows.* When there are two cushions or pillows, they should be the same shape, height, thickness, and width and meet at the exact middle of an inside back.   [*2*] *More than two cushions or pillows.* When there are three or more back cushions or pillows, they usually meet exactly at the points where an inside back cover is pieced together or seamed (Sec. 23:09A). If a cover is not pieced, cushions at the arms are the same width, but the others are 1 to 2 inches wider, as measured just below the armtops, to prevent them having a squeezed appearance. However, when arm and back tops are at the same height (Fig. 1:64), all back cushions or pillows usually are the same width.

**SEC. 23:10
SPLIT INSIDE
BACK**

Whether using traditional or modern materials and methods, upholster each section of a split inside back as a separate unit, Fig. 23:10, but build them simultaneously step-by-step to simplify duplicating shape and comfort.   [*1*] *Plan widths of back sections* the same as back cushions or pillows (Sec. 23:09B).   [*2*] *Build back sections* to finish so tightly against each other (Fig. 1:58) that it is necessary to force them apart to place padding and cover between them.

**SEC. 23:11
SPLIT INSIDE
BACK COVER,
CUSHIONS**

SEC. 23:11A / For methods of covering inside backs, see Chapter 16.   [*1*] *Corners.* When preparing a boxed casing or cover, point-off top corners at the junctions of the sections of a back as well as the other corners (Sec. 10:23C).   [*2*] *Boxing.* Save cover goods on boxings between inside back sections with stretchers, Fig. 23:11A. About 2 inches below the top corner of a boxing and 2 inches from the front edge, first sew a stretcher to fill out boxing to its normal size. Sew an additional stretcher from top corner to bottom that is large enough to extend boxing to the back of the cross-braces.   [*3*] *Install covers.* Set

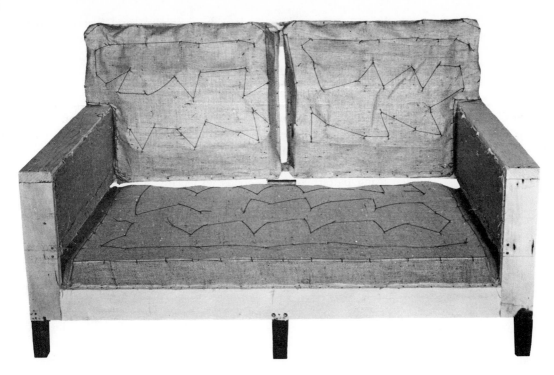

Fig. 23:10

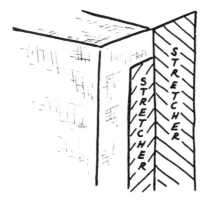

Fig. 23:11A

all inside back section covers in place at the same time. To keep them centered along junctions of the sections while tightening and adjusting them, pin them together along welts.

Sec. 23:11B Cushions / Usually a seat cushion is made for each section of an inside back and meets at the exact junctions of the back sections. However, some split-back articles have two back sections and a single wide seat cushion or four back sections and two wide seat cushions.

OUTSIDE BACKS

SEC. 23:12   For the mechanics of upholstering outside backs, see Chapter 18. When an inside back cover is welted at the middle, the outside back cover usually is, too. On other articles, an outside back cover is generally pieced near but at equal distances from the sides. However, when using patterned cover goods, especially scenics, tying patterns or figures together is more important than the location of seams in relation to an outside back. Certain covers may, of course, be railroaded (Sec. 11:01).

24

re-covering

Articles can often be considerably changed or restyled simply by re-covering them. A pull-over seat cover, Fig. *a* 1:29, can be changed to a bordered, *b*, or a boxed one, *c*. Similar changes may be made on inside arms and backs. Trims such as ruching, Fig. *b* 1:36, and fringe can be added or deleted. Skirts can be added, removed, or the type changed. Re-covering should be given as much thought and planning as when upholstering an article from the raw frame, because the overall effect may not be entirely satisfactory unless frame changes are made. For example, the chair in Fig. *a* 24:00 was to be re-covered and a skirt added to hide badly scratched legs. Since the back was quite low, the skirt could make the chair look too bottom-heavy or dumpy. To prevent this, the back was made higher—an easy job of frame restyling (Chapter 26). The finished chair, *b*, easily passes for an entirely new one.

649

a   *b*

Fig. 24:00

**SEC. 24:01
REMOVE
COVER**

SEC. 24:01A / Avoid tearing cover pieces, as they may be *rough* guides for plotting and cutting the new ones. Identify each piece of cover with a code mark (Sec. 11:12) and an arrow pointing to the top end (Sec. 11:01). While removing a cover, study each piece to see exactly how it was installed. The order of removing a cover is the reverse of installing it. [*1*] *Completely remove* skirt and dust cover. [*2*] *Untack* (Sec. 2:05) all covers finishing on bottom of seat rails or frame. Be careful not to loosen webbing, if any. [*3*] *Complete the removal* of outside covers, the padding and burlap under them, and panels, if any. Outside wings usually cannot be removed until after the outside arms. [*4*] *The order of removing inside covers* is apparent once their points of finishing are seen. Do not untack a muslin casing that finishes directly on the frame; if it finishes on a cover, untack carefully to avoid ripping or tearing it. When a cover is completely free, peel it off a stuffed surface, taking care not to displace the cotton padding under it.

SEC. 24:01B OLD COVER PIECES / Save each old cover piece as a guide for plotting (Chapter 11), cutting, and installing the new one. But do not use the old pieces as templates for the new. During installing they were stretched and trimmed and are now too small for convenient handling. But when no change in size or shape of an article has been made, plotting the new cover often is simplified by spreading the old cuts out on it. For the actual size of the cuts, the article should of course be measured (Chapter 11).

SEC. 24:02 **OLD PADDING**	Removal of the padding under the inside covers depends on whether or not an article was incased in muslin. If incased, usually it is advisable to remove the padding, as the more layers of cotton there are on a stuffed surface, the harder it is; but when removing cotton, save any wads set to fill hollows in the stuffing if they can be replaced smoothly. When an article not incased in muslin is to be re-covered without incasing it, the padding usually should be left in place; not only has it been compressed by the cover to correct minor irregularities in the stuffing, but it acts as a casing.
SEC. 24:03 **MUSLIN** **CASING**	If an article was not incased in muslin, it should be. Incasing sets the shapes of the parts more definitely and gives excellent practice for installing a new cover. For tufted articles, incasing in muslin may bring a considerable saving in cover costs.

25

repairing
furniture

SEC. 25:00 **GENERAL** **FACTS**	Most repairs that will restore an upholstered article to serviceable condition are readily made, often without tearing it down to the frame throughout. There are two kinds of repairs—frame and general upholstery. Frame repair in this book is limited to wooden frames.

FRAME REPAIRS

SEC. 25:01	Wooden frame repairs involving a broken joint and causing a general loosening of a frame are made with wood or metal plates. It is seldom advisable to replace part of a frame with a new piece.
SEC. 25:02 **WOOD** **REPAIRS**	Sec. 25:02A / Use clean, sound semihard wood (Sec. 4:03) or plywood; per inch of thickness plywood is stronger than solid wood, so thinner stock may be used. The necessary thickness of repairing stock

depends on the article and the type of repair. [1] *Cut and shape repairing* pieces to fit exactly, or a repair seldom lasts. For best results make a paper or cardboard template of the repairing piece needed. [2] *Fit a repairing piece* in place and mark it clearly for its exact setting before installing it. If a piece must be curved or otherwise specially shaped, cutting should be done with a band saw.

SEC. 25:02B GLUE REPAIRING PIECES / Most repairs should be double-doweled (Sec. 4:04), but to save time and work, they generally are screwed; drill lead-holes for screws. Use nails only to set and hold a repairing piece in place while glue is drying. Most repairing pieces and all repaired joints should be corner-blocked (Sec. 4:05). Hold a frame together and/or hold repairing pieces to it under pressure with cabinetmaker's or C-clamps, Fig. *a* 25:02B, while glue dries; or use a strong hemp rope twisted tightly in place with a short stick, *b*. Before applying clamps or rope to exposed-wood surfaces, pad them with a thick wad of cotton padding or several thicknesses of heavy fabric.

 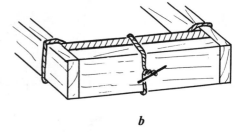

a   *b*

Fig. 25:02B

SEC. 25:02C STRENGTHEN WITH MUSLIN / To strengthen nonexposed-wood joints or repairing pieces that are only glued together (instead of doweled or screwed), glue a piece of muslin over or around the joint. Saturate muslin with glue, stretch it tight in place, and slip-tack (Sec. 5:16). As glue dries, the muslin shrinks and applies permanent pressure to the repair.

**SEC. 25:03
METAL
REPAIRS**

For frame repairs with metal plates or straps, first glue and clamp the joint (Sec. 25:02B). Set metal piece in place; mark carefully where screws are to go. Drill a pilot hole for each screw; drive screws in tight. Often one or both surfaces of a corner joint must be built square before installing a corner plate or brace, Fig. 25:03. Metal repair pieces are as satisfactory as wood, but due to the shape of a frame or part, often they cannot be used satisfactorily. Position them so as not to prevent tacking that may be necessary.

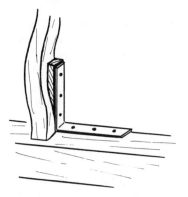

Fig. 25:03

SEC. 25:04
SEAT REPAIR

SEC. 25:04A / A common type of seat frame break, Fig. 25:04A, is at the bottom of each front post; it is often due in great part to the joints being tongue-and-groove instead of double-doweled (Sec. 4:04).

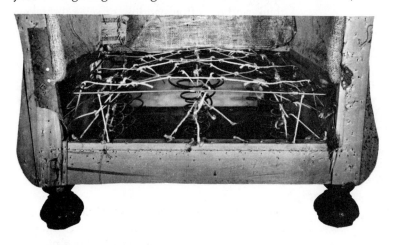

Fig. 25:04A

The entire seat frame was loose. Proper repair required new corner-blocks (Sec. 4:05) throughout the seat; had the frame been tight, corner plate repairs on the front of the arm post and seat rail would have been satisfactory, although the front corner-blocks should be replaced. When only angle-iron repairs are to be made on the front or upper surface of a seat frame, tearing down the entire article is not necessary. For repairing with wood, Sec. 25:02; metal, Sec. 25:03.

SEC. 25:04B WOOD REPAIR / To repair the type of damage in Fig. 25:04A with wood, make a repairing piece to fit snugly on the inner surface of the front rail between the adjacent posts or side rails, Fig. 25:04B, and flush with the top and bottom of the front rail. Use 1¼ inch to 1½ inch thick solid stock, or ½ inch to ¾ inch thick plywood.

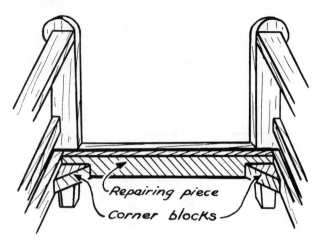

Fig. 25:04B

Repairing piece
Corner blocks

SEC. 25:04C   METAL REPAIR   / To repair the type of damage in Fig. 25:04A with metal, plan the kind of metal plate or brace to use and its location for the least interference with seat and arm upholstery. In Fig. 25:04C, a flat corner plate was placed to go below the tacking line of the front border and within the area that would be covered by the post panel (Fig. *e* 1:45). A corner brace on top of the seat rail would have interfered with seat and arm upholstering. A corner brace on the inner sides of the seat rail and post would have interfered with corner-blocking the seat.

Fig. 25:04C

| SEC. 25:05 ARM REPAIR | Most arm breaks are at the back post. Depending on the shape of an arm, often the simplest repair is an angle-iron set along the inner sides of an armboard and back post. Corner-blocking the underside of an armboard at a post is satisfactory when inside arm and back upholsteries will not finish through an arm cavity; use large corner-blocks. |

**SEC. 25:05
ARM REPAIR**

When arm upholstery will finish through the arm cavity, corner-block with care; if too large, it will interfere with upholstering both the inside arm and back. When an armboard is broken at the front post, an angle-iron may be installed on the inner surfaces or on the bottom of the armboard and back of the post. Or the joint may be corner-blocked on the bottom of the armboard; use a large corner-block.

SEC. 25:06 **WING REPAIR**	[1] *Open frame.* The front bottom of an open-frame wing usually may be repaired with a metal corner-brace set on top of the armboard and back of the wing post. A break at the top front corner also may be repaired by a corner-brace, but often it is better to splint the joint with ¼ inch to ½ inch thick plywood; shape it to fit the outer surface and taper from the corner to the frame, Fig. *a* 25:06; bind with muslin (Sec. 25:02C). Install a similar piece on the other wing so they will have the same basic shape and size. A break at the back top corner of a wing often is repaired by an angle-iron on the inner surfaces of the wing and back rails; it may be necessary to chisel out part of the back post for the iron to fit properly, *b;* after installing the iron, fill the corner with wood. [2] *Solid base.* The best repair for solid-base wings usually is a metal corner-brace set on the inner surfaces of wing and back post. If necessary, cut and chisel a groove in the back post, as in *b,* to set the brace flush on both surfaces. If the inside back cover is to finish along the inner side of a wing close to the back post (Fig. 9:13B), it may be better to put the corner-brace on the outer surfaces.

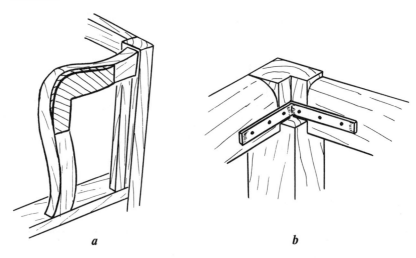

Fig. 25:06   *a*   *b*

SEC. 25:07 **BACK** **REPAIR**	A broken or loose joint at a back post and top rail is readily repaired in most flat backs except scroll by an angle-iron set along the outside surfaces. Or, install a piece of ¼ inch to ½ inch plywood the exact

shape of the back edge of the top rail and posts and extending 2 or 3 inches down the posts; taper as desired at the sides to prevent a depression in the finished outside back. For barrel and scroll backs, often an angle-iron can be set along the inner side of the post and bottom of the top rail. Corner-blocks may be used freely when inside back upholstery does not finish through the back cavity to the top rail. When upholstery finishes through the back cavity at the top, use corner-blocks cautiously, as they could interfere with upholstering.

SEC. 25:08 **LEG REPAIR**	To replace doweled legs that have broken off, drill the remainder of the dowel out of the seat and leg. Repair with a dowel the same diameter as that of the holes. If the exact size of doweling is not available, use one slightly thinner and, after coating it and the holes with glue, wrap a layer of thin cloth around the ends and sides of the dowel; force or hammer it into the holes. In all cases, be sure to use grooved doweling; it lets air and excess glue escape instead of splitting a leg or frame.
SEC. 25:09 **UNEVEN LEGS**	When there are differences in leg lengths, set the article on a surface known to be flat. Build the surface under the short leg or legs with wood until the article holds steady. If the legs have no trim at the bottom, the long legs may be cut off by an amount equal to the thickness of wood under the short legs; be careful not to make a seat too low for comfort (Sec. 3:16B). If cutting off will spoil the looks of the legs, it may be that differences in lengths can be corrected by installing small glides on long legs and large ones on short legs.

UPHOLSTERY REPAIRS

SEC. 25:10 **SEAT** **UPHOLSTERY** **REPAIRS**	Repair of seat upholstery is often more complicated than it first appears; it may be best to take the seat completely apart, particularly if it was built with factory spring bars or units (Sec. 3:20) and related materials. Repairing seat upholstery can greatly affect the comfort of a chair or larger article. Usually there will be a noticeable difference between the softness and go-down of the broken and the repaired seat. Repair often makes a pad seat more comfortable simply by making it more uniform in shape and support. But spring seats frequently have a false softness or go-down due to a break in the upholstery. When it is repaired the seat regains its original firmness—and there may be complaints that it is now too hard for comfort. [1] *A traditional pad seat* that was webbed the usual way (Sec. 5:01) or a modern seat built with *rubber webbing* (Sec. 7:33) requires complete rebuilding if the webbing is broken. This also should be done if *zigzag springs* (Sec. 3:21)

are broken, distorted, or fairly irregular in shape or resilience; replacing just a few is false economy and poor upholstery. [2] *In most traditional spring seats,* webbing usually can be replaced without much tearing down (Sec. 25:12). However, this may be only a partial remedy for a sagging spring seat. If it is used much after one or more strips of webbing break, springs often are deformed and must be replaced for a satisfactory repair job. This work may be done from the bottom of a seat unless the deformed springs are tied (Secs. 7:14–7:16) on any coil other than the top one. If they are, or if spring ties and/or edge-wire are broken, tear the seat down to the springs for necessary repairs.

NOTE: *Often it is better to rebuild small exposed-wood seats, especially antiques, with zigzag springs than to replace coil springs (Sec. 25:11F).*

<table>
<tr><td>

SEC. 25:11
REPAIRING
TRADITIONAL
SPRING SEATS

</td><td>

SEC. 25:11A / [1] *Remove dust cover* (Sec. 2:05); cut stitches holding bottom coils of springs to webbing (Fig. *a* 7:05A). [2] *Remove bottom ends* of seat, outside arm, and back covers as much as is necessary to free the ends of the webbing. Handle covers gently and disturb padding as little as possible, or replacing covers may be quite difficult. [3] *Remove all webbing* and examine burlap spring cover (Sec. 7:18); stitch shut holes in it, being careful not to displace stuffing. [4] *To replace a deformed spring,* cut it off to leave a complete coil against the burlap spring cover. Shape the top end of an OBE spring (Sec. 7:07). Set the top of the new spring against the coil left from the old one; seize them tightly (Sec. 7:16C) with upholstery twine completely around both coils.

</td></tr>
</table>

SEC. 25:11B REPAIR SEAT RAILS / [1] *If seat rails are split* or badly splintered, install bracing strips along inner sides, or use metal repair pieces (Sec. 25:05). If using bracing strips, the new webbing (Sec. 25:11C) may be tacked to them or to the original rails. [2] *If seat rails are only splintered* but otherwise sound, the new webbing may be tacked on the outer sides (Fig. *b* 7:05A); bracing strips are not needed. This method is generally better for repairing the spring-edge part of a seat.

SEC. 25:11C REWEB SEAT / [1] *Tie springs* (Sec. 7:11) front-to-back and side-to-side on bottom coils only. Anchor ties on inner sides of the brace strips or rails an inch from the bottom. If this is impractical, cut or gouge a small groove and hole in the bottom of a rail for each spring-tie to be tacked; holes should be just deep enough for the webbing to finish flat over them. Tie springs to finish as flush as possible with the bottoms of the seat rails. Tie all springs, except those in a spring edge, in a vertical position (Sec. 7:07); tie spring edge-springs with the bottom coil ¼ inch from the inner side of the seat rail. [2] *Web seat* the usual way (Sec. 7:05). If after webbing, the bottom spring coils can easily be shifted about, stitch them to the webbing. Use a curved needle (Sec. 2:06), and stitch as tightly as possible against a coil. It may be necessary to take eight or more stitches for each spring; the tighter they are held in place, the more durable the repair job.

SEC. 25:11D COMPLETING SEAT REPAIR / After webbing and, if necessary, stitching springs, re-install covers and dust cover. Work (Sec. 5:18) covers carefully back in place, pushing them down the sides rather than pulling them from the bottom. Work covers far enough over the bottom edges of the rails to keep the original break-mark of a cover (where it bent around an edge) from showing on the side; it might seem to be a line of dirt. It may be advisable to install a skirt or flounce (Sec. 18:03); it need not be the same pattern or goods as the cover.

SEC. 25:11E SPRING EDGE-WIRE REPAIR / The only satisfactory method of repairing broken spring edge-wire, instead of replacing it, is to install (Sec. 7:16) a new wire along the appropriate side *and around both corners* for 3 or 4 inches. Splinting a break by seizing a short length of edge-wire along it is not a durable repair.

SEC. 25:11F CHANGE SPRINGING / Often, especially with antiques, a seat has been webbed so many times that the bottoms of the rails are almost more tack holes than solid wood (Fig. 4:17). Bracing strips (Sec. 25:04) could have been installed and the seat webbed and spring upholstered the traditional way. But with such a small seat (about the size of Fig. 1:07), four bracing strips and corner-blocks could make the seat cavity too small for a satisfactory number and size of coil springs. Therefore it was decided to use zigzag springs (Sec. 3:21) and completely rebuild the seat. A bracing strip was set along the back rail to strengthen it and give extra support to the left back leg and the split in the side rail.

NOTE: Repairing antiques with modern materials instead of the traditional is frowned on by many purists, but top quality custom upholsterers generally agree that it is best to use materials that will do a job best.

SEC. 25:12 **BACK** **UPHOLSTERY**	More than any other surface, the inside back of a chair or wider article shows unevenness of looks and comfort due to upholstery in need of repair. Repairs often can be done without reupholstering a back,

but results usually are better if it is reupholstered. Much repair work can be done from the outside back; but some articles, such as the French back (Sec. 10:05), must usually be taken completely apart in order to make satisfactory repairs. [1] *In a traditional pad back,* replace broken webbing by installing new strips (Sec. 10:06). [2] *For traditional spring backs,* repairs are essentially the same as for spring seats (Sec. 25:11). [3] *For zigzag spring, rubber webbing, and factory spring bar or unit* backs (Secs. 3:20–3:22), as a rule the most practical repair is to tear down as far as necessary, and reupholster from that point. If possible, especially if an article seems more than about seven years old, all zigzag springs and rubber webbing should be replaced.

SEC. 25:13 **ARM** **UPHOLSTERY**	As a rule, only the webbing can be replaced (as in Sec. 10:06) without tearing down an inside arm.

SEC. 25:14 **TWINE-HELD** **BUTTONS**	Twines for decorative buttons (not for tufting or deep-button work) seem to break more often in thickly upholstered, spring inside backs than in other surfaces. Most broken twines can be replaced without removing the outside back cover provided it is not a tight weave such as silk or chintz, or a hard-surfaced goods such as leather, plastics, or glazed fabrics. [1] *Replace a broken button twine* as in Sec. 18:01D except that the needle is pushed through at the front until the point emerges from the outside back cover. [2] *Pull needle* just far enough through outside back cover to make the return stitch. As a rule, it is necessary to pull the buried end of the needle only about ½ inch clear of the stuffing before starting the return stitch. [3] *Complete the return stitch,* tie twines to hold button to desired depth or setting, and cut off excess twine. Push knot through the hole in the cover made originally by the button loop or twines. [4] *On outside back,* work threads of cover together to close the needle hole.

26

restyling furniture

SEC. 26:00
GENERAL
FACTS

Restyling upholstered furniture, especially modernizing out-of-date articles, Fig. 26:00, need not be difficult since it so often consists of simplifying the shape and slenderizing it. *The main tool needed is the ability to visualize the wanted appearance of an article.* Many of the restyling suggestions in this chapter may be applied to more than one part of an article. [1] *Restyling simply by reupholstering* an article often is very effective: thick upholstery replaced by thinner, a tufted or channeled surface instead of a plain one, a modern for an obviously out-of-date cover. The more completely upholstered an article is, usually the easier it is to modernize it by reupholstering. Exposed-wood articles (Figs. 1:28, 1:52) can be changed by reupholstering them in a different style, such as tufted instead of plain inside backs, but this is more "face-lifting" than true restyling. [2] *Restyling by altering a frame* is the most effective and extensive method. It also enables indus-trious upholsterers to have excellent quality furniture at a fraction of

Fig. 26:00   *a*   *b*

its normal cost. The mechanics of frame restyling are essentially those of repairing (Chapter 25).

SEAT RESTYLING

SEC. 26:01 DEEPENING SEATS

SEC. 26:01A / Generally seats are deepened (greater distance from front to back) when an inside back is changed from pad to spring upholstery. It also often is done simply to make an article more comfortable (Sec. 10:01). Deepening usually requires changes in the arms and front legs, but these are relatively easy.

SEC. 26:01B INCREASE SEAT DEPTH TWO INCHES OR LESS / The simplest way to deepen a seat is to fasten a strip of solid wood to the front rail, Fig. 26:01B. [1] *The restyling piece* is the same height as the seat rail and extends to the outer edges of the posts; its thickness is the wanted increase of seat depth but usually no more than about 2 inches to avoid making an article too heavy. [2] *Shape of the restyling piece* is optional. A seat that curves across the front may be restyled as straight or a straight one made curved. Ends may be sharp-breaking for a modern article, or they may be rounded. [3] *Deepening a seat this way makes it* T-shaped. If not that originally, the resulting front tabs may be too small for good proportion. If the seat

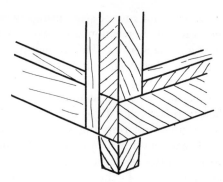

Fig. 26:01B

originally was T-shaped, the additional rail thickness may make the front tabs too large. To maintain the original lines or shape of the front, fasten an additional "front post," the same thickness of the seat-deepening piece, to the face of the original post, Fig. 26:01B. [4] *Move the legs* to the front edge of the seat deepening piece, or cut off old legs and install new; or install skirt on finished seat.

Sec. 26:01C Increase Seat Depth More Than Two Inches / Cut the restyling piece (Sec. 26:01B) as wide as the planned increase of depth, and install with its bottom surface flush with the lower edge of the front rail, Point 1 in Fig. 26:01C. Change arms from set-back to scooped for maximum support of the restyling piece. Cut arm scoop pieces on the lower sides, Point 2, to finish at the level of the bottom of the arm liner. Install an auxiliary front rail, Point 3; generally its top surface is level with the top of the seat rail.

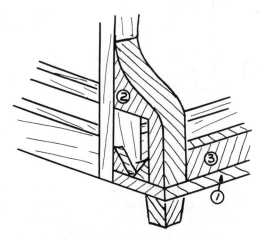

Fig. 26:01C

Sec. 26:01D After Deepening Seat Frame / Springs must usually be repositioned or new ones installed, depending on the type seat and how it was deepened. [1] *Roll and hard edge seats deepened as* *in Sec. 26:01B.* Set front row of seat springs with bottom coils almost touching the seat rail. Reposition other springs for even distribution between front and back rows. Tie springs the usual way.   [2] *Roll and hard edge seats deepened as in Sec. 26:01C.* If seat depth was not increased enough to set springs in front of the original rail, set them forward until bottom coils almost touch the original front rail; spring up seat. Then web (stretch it tight only by hand) and burlap the gap between the original and restyling seat rails. Use additional stuffing on a roll edge seat; build a deeper edge in a hard edge seat. If the space between the original and restyling front rails is wide enough to hold springs, staple them to the seat-deepening piece, Point 1 in Fig. 26:01C, and build seat the usual way.   [3] *Spring edge seat.* Staple No. 1-H or larger coil springs (Secs. 3:15, 3:16) to the front rail or rails the same way as those for tabs of a T-shaped seat (Fig. 7:15A). If the space between original and restyling front rails (Sec. 26:01C) is wide enough, staple springs to the seat-deepening piece and build seat the usual way.

**SEC. 26:02
LOWERING
SEAT RAILS**

Often articles are "out-of-date" because their legs are 2 or 3 inches higher than those of so-called modern pieces; yet the seat is at a comfortable height. The simplest way to modernize may be by installing a flange skirt (Sec. 18:03). If this is not desirable, then lower the seat rails; this does not mean lowering the top of a seat.   [1] *Fasten strips of solid wood* to bottoms of seat rails after webbing seat, Fig. 26:02.

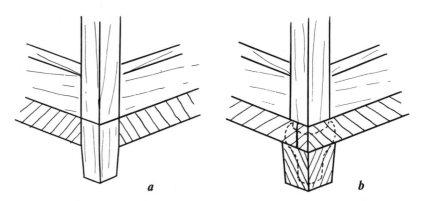

Fig. 26:02   *a*   *b*

Notch lowering strips to fit around webbing ends. Lowering strips should run straight and make tight, smooth corners.   [2] *When legs extend the line of the corner of a seat frame* down to the bottom of the lowering strips, Fig. *a* 26:02, no additional work is needed.   [3] *If legs taper inward and away* from the bottom of the lowering strips, then they will have a set-back appearance and new ones should be installed. Saw them off at the bottom of the original rails, or remove them. Use lowering strips long enough to make a corner, corner-block them when installed, and install new legs, *b*.

SEC. 26:03 **HEIGHTENING** **SEATS**	Usually seats are heightened more for comfort (Sec. 3:16) than for any other reason. Instead of using larger springs, which could build wobble into a seat, bridle-build the seat (Secs. 7:21, 7:23), or install thicker compact stuffing. If the original seat or deck was upholstered with loose stuffing and is in good condition, bridle-build, or use compact stuffing on top of it. For a loose-cushion seat, build the stitched edge to slant upward toward the front without projecting appreciably beyond the front rail.

ARM RESTYLING

SEC. 26:04 **IMPORTANCE** **OF ARM** **RESTYLING**	The general appearance of an article is usually changed most by restyling or altering the arms, which as a rule can be done in several ways. Add rather than cut off wood. When cutting a frame, plan cuts to weaken it as little as possible. Shaping tabs or ears may be removed without weakening a frame.
SEC. 26:05 **SET-BACK TO** **FULL ARM**	This is done when a T-shaped seat is to be changed to a regular one. Restyling consists of installing a new front post and armboard, Fig. 26:05. [*1*] *Prepare new front post*, Point 1. It usually is the same width

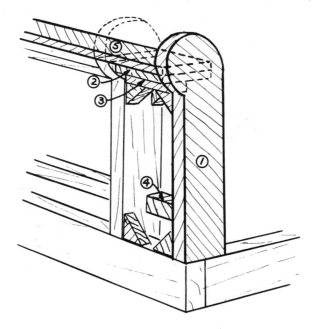

Fig. 26:05

as the original post. Unless armtop is to be restyled, shape new post at the top from the original one.   [2] *Cut top of original post* off flush with top of armboard.   [3] *Install new front post,* Point 1, on seat rails. Between original and new posts install an auxiliary armboard, Point 2, underarm strip, Point 3, and liner, Point 4.   [4] *Install a brace strip,* Point 5 (¾ inch solid wood, ¼ inch to ½ inch plywood), along middle of original and auxiliary armboards from the front of the back post to: I—Scroll, rounded arms: Back of the new front post; brace-strip should clear sides of armboards by at least ½ inch. II—Square scroll and other flat-top arms: Front edge of new front post; brace strip should be exact shape of armtop.   [5] *Strengthen* with corner-blocks or metal corner braces (Secs. 25:02, 25:03) at enough points to build a solid arm.

SEC. 26:06
SET-BACK TO
SCOOPED ARM

This may be done by a single piece of wood shaped to finish smoothly against front post and seat rail or rails (Fig. 26:01C) or by several pieces laminated together. Install an auxiliary arm liner, or cut the scoop pieces to serve as arm liners.

SEC. 26:07
SCOOPED TO
FULL ARM

This is done as much for comfort as for appearance, especially in lounge chairs.   [1] *Cut top of front post* off flush with top of armboard, Fig. 26:07.   [2] *Cut a right-angle notch* across face of front post at the bottom of the scooped area, Point 1, for seating the restyling post.   [3] *Shape, if necessary, and install* restyling post. It should be 1 inch to 1¼ inches semihard solid wood or ¾ inch to 1 inch plywood as wide as the original front post and long enough to finish against the underside of the new armboard unless building a scroll arm. The top of a scroll arm would finish against the front end of the new armboard and above it.   [4] *Shape and install a new armboard* on top of the

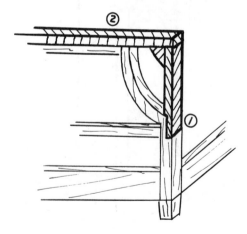

Fig. 26:07

original one. Essentially it is the same as the brace strip (Sec. 26:05[4]).

SEC. 26:08 SCROLL TO MODERN SQUARE, SQUARE SCROLL, T-SHAPED ARMS

None of these changes will weaken the arm of a frame made with standard construction. However, care must be taken that additions or shaping pieces are installed properly and build a sturdy armtop.   [1] *Scroll to modern square.* Cut top of front post off flush with top of armboard, Fig. *a* 26:08. Cut or build outer side of armboard to go straight back from the front post or to taper in a straight line to the outer side of the back post. If the arm is to be made higher, then instead of reshaping the original armboard, fasten a new one of the planned shape (but at least 1 inch thick) on top of the original one.

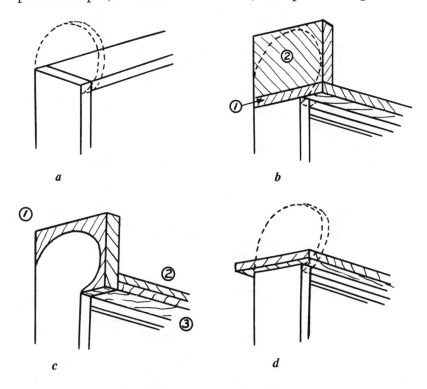

Fig. 26:08   *a*   *b*   *c*   *d*

[2] *Scroll to square scroll.* The first of the following methods of converting scroll to square scroll arms is simpler, the second is better. I—Cut top of front post off flush with top of armboard, *b*. Reshape original armboard, [1] above, and use as underarm strip for restyled arm. Install a new armboard, Point 1 in *b*, on top of the original one; it should extend from the front of the front post to the back of the back post, depending on the desired shape of the arm at the back. The

width and shape of the new armboard is the planned width and shape of the square scroll arm; use solid stock at least 1 inch or ¾ inch plywood. Install a shaping block or blocks, Point 2 in *b,* to shape the front end of the arm (Sec. 8:13); reinforce with corner-block or metal brace. II—Install a shaping piece cut to fit tightly around the scroll, Point 1 in *c.* Install a new armboard, Point 2 in *c,* of the planned shape on top of the original one between front and back posts; it must be flush with the inner surface of the front post and outer side of the shaping piece. Install a new armboard filler strip, Point 3 in *c,* to build the bottom of the new armboard flush with the bottom corner of the shaping piece. The original underarm strip is used in upholstering the restyled arm.   [3] *Scroll to T-shaped.* Cut top of front post off flush with top of armboard, *d.* Reshape original armboard, [1] above; it serves as underarm strip for the restyled arm. Install a new armboard of the planned width, thickness, and length on the original one. When restyling an arm to T-shaped, be careful not to make the seat too narrow (Sec. 8:03).

SEC. 26:09 HEIGHTENING ARMS	Generally an arm frame is made higher only when restyling one that originally was spring built (Sec. 8:23). Install a new armboard of the needed thickness on the old one. If increasing arm height by more than 2 inches, in order to prevent excessive weight build in a new armboard with 1 inch to 1½ inches solid stock. Cut a notch in the back post to seat the new armboard at the wanted height. Between the original and new armboards, install a brace block of the necessary thickness about midway between front and back posts. Build up the front post or cut off the top of the front post to fit under the new armboard.

SEC. 26:10 WIDENING ARMS	This generally is done to add mass to an article, modernize it when wider arms are fashionable, or give the effect of lowering the back. Restyling posts, armboards, and rails should be best quality stock, the same thickness as the original parts, and installed the strongest possible way. [1] *If arm is to be widened only a small amount,* install an auxiliary front post and an armboard, the latter tapering to end at the outer back edge of the back post, Fig. *a* 26:10. To shape the bottom of the outside arm, install an auxiliary seat rail tapering to finish at either the outer front or back of the back post; the latter builds a more consistent arm shape but sets the back leg away from the bottom of the outside arm. [2] *If arm is to be widened considerably, b,* an auxiliary back post will be required in addition to the other restyling pieces, above.

a   *b*

Fig. 26:10

SEC. 26:11 GENERAL FRONT TO BACK SHAPE OF ARMS	Straight and curved arms often may be altered by installing a new armboard on top of the original. Change the arm liner to parallel the inner surface of the new armboard. This restyling should be approached cautiously, because it may require changing the shape of the sides of a seat. Also, changing a curved to a straight arm may make the seat too narrow for comfort (Sec. 8:03).
SEC. 26:12 FILLING IN OPEN-FRAME EXPOSED-WOOD ARMS	Articles with open-frame exposed-wood arms (Fig. 1:21) may be converted into fully upholstered chairs or sofas. Install a front post and an armboard of the wanted widths and shapes; use 1¼ inches to 1½ inches solid stock, ¾ inch to 1 inch plywood. For best results, set the new front post against the top and bottom of the original arm; cut off the latter where necessary so the new post will be vertical. Install an arm liner parallel to the inner side of the armboard and 1 to 2 inches below the top surface of the seat at the arms.

WING RESTYLING

SEC. 26:13 SHAPE, REMOVAL	Wing frame restyling generally is limited to building additional scoop into the upper and front surfaces or to filling in scoop to make them relatively flat. Install strips of wood to build the wanted shape. Small

wing "tabs" attached to the outer sides of back posts often are re-moved to restyle a back.

BACK RESTYLING

SEC. 26:14 **SPRING BACKS**	[1] *Traditional coil spring backs.* When these are restyled and built higher or wider, additional springs may be needed at top and sides. According to the increase of height or width, staple these springs at the ends or between the ends of the rows of springs in the rest of a back. [2] *Modern spring backs.* Unless the back frame cavity is enlarged, which requires longer strips of zigzag springs or rubber webbing, upholster for increased height or width with stuffing.
SEC. 26:15 **HEIGHTENING** **BACKS**	Fasten a new top rail securely to the original one and the posts. The restyling rail, usually solid stock, should be as thick as the posts in order to extend them smoothly; it must be flush with the rear and outer surfaces of the posts.
SEC. 26:16 **LOWERING** **BACKS**	This usually is done to add mass to an article. [1] *Prepare a new top rail* of the necessary size and shape to fit into the restyled back frame as neatly as the original one. [2] *Cut the back posts off* at a point that will hold the new top rail to the wanted height. [3] *Install new top rail;* corner-block and brace it.
SEC. 26:17 **WIDENING** **BACKS**	Usually done only for appearance, widening a back affects just the overall width of an article, not the width of the seat; increasing seat width would be an extensive remaking of the entire frame. Most back widening is done by installing auxiliary back posts on the outer sides of the original ones (Fig. *b* 26:10). Install auxiliary side seat rails in order to build a consistent shape from top to bottom of the outside arm.
SEC. 26:18 **THICKENING** **BACKS**	This is done more for spring than for pad backs, and to give the springs more action. As a rule, the only frame restyling is to build forward the original back liner or else to install a deeper one (Sec. 10:03).
SEC. 26:19 **SQUARING** **BACKS**	Scooped and arched backs are usually made square by adding auxiliary back posts and a top rail. If the original top rail is highly arched, its top surface may be cut off or leveled slightly to make a wider base to help support the new top rail; be careful not to cut off so much as to weaken the entire back.

SEC. 26:20	Articles with open-frame exposed-wood backs (as in Fig. 1:21) may be
FILLING IN	converted into fully upholstered chairs or sofas, with or without re-
OPEN-FRAME	styling the top and/or the sides (Secs. 26:14–26:19). For the lower part
EXPOSED-	of the inside back, install a back liner (Sec. 4:15) 1 or 2 inches below
WOOD	the top level of the seat at the back. The original liner or lower back
BACKS	rail generally is not removed, as this might weaken the frame.

SEC. 26:21	Applications of many of the foregoing restyling operations are shown
APPLICATION	in Fig. 26:21. They were used in the actual remodeling of the chair in
OF	Fig. *a* 26:00.
OPERATIONS	

Fig. 26:21

index

As done throughout Upholstering for Everyone, references in the Index are given by "section numbers," see page xiv. References given in the Index usually contain additional reference section numbers covering specific uses of the upholstery materials or applications of the work-steps listed in the Index.